AF361314

HINDUTVA AND VIOLENCE

*Frontispiece:* Prison Portrait of Vinayak Damodar Savarkar, London (c. 1910/1911).
*Photo credit:* © The British Library Board (L/PJ/6/1069 6A).

# Hindutva and Violence

## V. D. Savarkar and the Politics of History

VINAYAK CHATURVEDI

First published by Permanent Black D-28 Oxford Apts, 11 IP Extension, Delhi 110092 INDIA, for the territory of SOUTH ASIA. First SUNY Press edition 2022. Not for sale in South Asia.

Published by State University of New York Press, Albany

Cover design by Anuradha Roy



For information, contact State University of New York Press, Albany, NY
www.sunypress.edu

Library of Congress Cataloging-in-Publication Data
Names: Chaturvedi, Vinayak, author
Title: Hindutva and violence : V. D. Savarkar and the politics of history
Description: Albany : State University of New York Press, [2022] |
  Includes bibliographical references and index.
Identifiers: ISBN 9781438488776 (hardcover : alk. paper) | ISBN
  9781438488783 (e-book)
Further information is available at the Library of Congress.

10 9 8 7 6 5 4 3 2 1

*for my parents*

YOGESHWAR AND KUSUM CHATURVEDI

# Contents

# Images

# Acknowledgements

HAVE BEEN THINKING about Vinayak Damodar Savarkar for far too long. The consequence is that I have probably discussed something about Savarkar and his interpretations of Hindutva over interactions with many people over the past couple of decades – friends, family, colleagues, and students. This is a humbling reflection, making it difficult to properly acknowledge all my interlocutors. But it also signals something more sobering: the ubiquity of Hindutva has ensured that everyone in India will have Savarkar's ideas in mind for the foreseeable future. For Savarkar, Hindutva was never meant to be understood as bounded by national borders; his ambition was always planetary. Anyone with an interest in South Asia also knows that neither Hindutva nor Savarkar can be ignored today, no matter where they live. The challenge for all of us now is navigating the intellectual and political terrain to think with and against his ideas.

I have been fortunate in the number of individuals who have supported and helped me over this process of thinking and writing. The person who has read and edited nearly everything that I have written over the past twenty years is Robert Moeller: friend, colleague, and editor. I am grateful that he has patiently commented on multiple drafts of this book and helped me improve its argument, language, and style. The formation of my ideas has benefited from discussions with Prathama Banerjee, Partha Chatterjee, Geoff Eley, Ashok Hegde, Aishwary Kumar, Kama Maclean, Romi Mahajan, Rajit Mazumder, Hans Medick, Neeti Nair, Ken Pomeranz, Mahesh Rangarajan, Sanjay Ruparelia, Ajay Skaria, and David Washbrook. I appreciate the time taken by Ashish Koul, Chris Moffat, and Anand Taneja for providing detailed written comments on parts of my work. At the University of California, Irvine, I have been fortunate to have had wonderful colleagues in the Department of History. I owe special thanks to Douglas Haynes, David Igler, Winston James, Mark LeVine, Susan Morrissey,

Alka Patel, Kavita Philip, James Robertson, and Heidi Tinsman. I am saddened that my late mentors and friends Chris Bayly (1945–2015) and Krishna Tewari (1937–2017) did not see this book in print. Both would have read the text carefully and provided critical comments, as they always did with kindness.

I am grateful to Upendra Parchure for sharing the life-story of his father Dr Dattatrey Sadashiv Parchure with me in 2001. My interview with him was formative in helping shape the direction of my research. I appreciate Deepa Bhatnagar and the late Eric Hobsbawm for taking time to answer my detailed questions. Mukul Kumar and Juned Shaikh generously helped me locate sources in Irvine and Seattle, respectively. Pranshu Prakash kindly shared his translation of the preface of Savarkar's *Mazzini Charitra*.

I have been fortunate to have had the support and guidance of Rukun Advani in the process of writing this book. His wonderful editorial skills have improved the language and style of the text. His ethics and patience are extraordinary. It has been an honour to have had him edit and publish this book.

I have had the privilege of presenting my research at a number of universities, research centres, conferences, and workshops over two decades. I have learned a great deal about my own interpretations from conversations with colleagues in North America, Europe, and Asia – for which I am grateful. Much to my regret, to individually thank all the participants and organisers for their generosity is impossible: the list is overwhelming. I hope they will forgive me.

The research for this book has been made possible in part by a British Academy Visiting Fellowship at Oxford University, a Shorenstein Fellowship at Stanford University's Walter H. Shorenstein Asia-Pacific Research Center, a National Endowment for the Humanities Summer Stipend (FT-54058-06), and grants from UC Irvine's Center for Asian Studies and the School of Humanities. I appreciate the generosity of the librarians, archivists, and staff at the British Library (London), Maharashtra State Archives (Mumbai), Nehru Memorial Museum and Library (New Delhi), Centre of South Asian Studies Library and Archive (Cambridge), Hoover Institution Library & Archives (Stanford), and Langson Library (Irvine).

This is an academic book, but the topic of Savarkar is also now part of a family history. It begins with my grandmother Virbati Chaturvedi, who reluctantly agreed to name me Vinayak (after Savarkar), and my aunt Uma Chaturvedi, who encouraged me to investigate the story years later. I am fortunate to have an extended family in the US, UK, Australia, and India that has followed and encouraged my research with great interest. Rajiv Chaturvedi, Rajneesh Chaturvedi, and Urmila Chaturvedi are always eager to discuss my work with humour and critical insights, for which I am grateful. My *compadre* Rafael Navarro's conversations and friendship over the past four decades provide meaning to me in ways that he may not be aware of. Hemlata Parekh, my mother-in-law, has been a great source of guidance and support, including providing assistance when I found myself confronted with challenging Marathi texts. My sister Vinita Chaturvedi has encouraged me in all my intellectual ventures, while also providing important advice along the way.

Arjun Chaturvedi knows more about Savarkar than anyone should know at his age, but he is prepared to interpret the realities of what Hindutva offers to the world. His humour, intelligence, kindness, and sweetness are sources of great inspiration in more ways than he knows. Bina Parekh has had to think about Savarkar's ideas almost as long as I have. This book would not have been completed without her insights, understanding, and encouragement at every step – every day.

My parents Yogeshwar and Kusum Chaturvedi have encouraged and nurtured my interest in this project, and everything else in life. It was my father who first recommended that I read the work of intellectuals who were responsible for conceptualising Hindutva. For him, it was only then that a rigorous critique of Savarkar would be possible. My parents have given me many gifts, but their gifts of history and language have allowed me to interpret the world in ways that would otherwise not be possible. My words here can only be a small gesture of my appreciation for their love and patience. This book is dedicated to them.

Parts of the Introduction were published as "From Peasant Pasts to Hindutva Futures?: Some Reflections on History, Politics, and Methodology," *South Asia*, 34, 3 (2011), 402–20. Portions of Parts I, III, and IV appeared in "Rethinking Knowledge with Action: V.D. Savarkar, the Bhagavad Gita, and Histories of Warfare," *Modern Intellectual*

*History*, 7, 2 (2010), 417–35. Sections of the Introduction and Part III were published as "A Revolutionary's Biography: The Case of V.D. Savarkar," *Postcolonial Studies*, 16, 2 (2013), 124–39. Sections of Part IV were published as "Violence as Civility: V.D. Savarkar and the Mahatma's Assassination," *South Asia History & Culture*, 11, 3 (2020), 239–53. An earlier version of the Coda appeared as "Vinayak & Me: *Hindutva* and the Politics of Naming," *Social History*, 28, 2 (2003), 155–73.

Three of the photographs (Images 2, 3, and 4) included in this book were taken by Narayan Vinayak Virkar (c. 1924). Image 2 was published in *Samagra Savarkar Vanmaya*, vol. 7 (Poona: Maharashtra Prantik Hindusabha, 1965). It also appears in *Samagra Savarkar Vanmaya*, vols 8, 9, and 10, and in *Savarkar Samagra*, vol. 1 (New Delhi: Prabhat Prakashan, 2000). Images 2 and 3 are included in Christopher Pinney, "The Tiger's Nature, but Not the Tiger: Bal Gangadhar Tilak as Mohandas Karamchand Gandhi's Counter-Guru," *Public Culture*, 23, 2 (2011), 395–416. Image 4 was previously published in Kirti Phadtare Pandey, "The Other Savarkar," *The Quint* (March 16, 2021). Chris Pinney was kind enough to provide me high resolution copies of the images and the contact details of Virkar's family in Mumbai. As Virkar and his son have now passed away, I attempted to contact other family members, but without success. Formal acknowledgement of sources for the photographs used in the book is as follows:

*Frontispiece:* Prison Portrait of Vinayak Damodar Savarkar, London (c. 1910/1911). *Photo credit:* © The British Library Board (L/PJ/6/1069 6A).

*Photo 1, fly leaf of Part 1:* Prison Portrait of Vinayak Damodar Savarkar, London (c. 1910/1911). *Photo credit:* © The British Library Board (L/PJ/6/1069 6A).

*Photo 2, fly leaf of Part II:* Vinayak Damodar Savarkar photographed by Narayan Vinayak Virkar (c. 1924). *Photo credit:* This image was previously published in Christopher Pinney, "The Tiger's Nature, but Not the Tiger: Bal Gangadhar Tilak as Mohandas Karamchand Gandhi's Counter-Guru," *Public Culture*, 23, 2 (2011), 395–416.

*Photo 3, fly leaf of Part III:* Vinayak Damodar Savarkar photographed by Narayan Vinayak Virkar (c. 1924). *Photo credit:* This image was previously published in *Samagra Savarkar Vanmaya*, vol. 7 (Poona: Maharashtra Prantik Hindusabha, 1965).

*Photo 4, fly leaf of Part IV: Left to Right:* Vinayak Damodar Savarkar, Narayan Damodar Savarkar, and Ganesh Damodar Savarkar photographed by Narayan Vinayak Virkar (c. 1920s–1930s). *Photo credit:* This image was previously published in Kirti Phadtare Pandey, "The Other Savarkar," *The Quint,* March 16, 2021. https://www.thequint.com/news/india/facts-about-rss-co-founder-ganesh-babarao-savarkar-veer-vd-brother#read-more (accessed January 1, 2022).

*Photo 5, fly leaf of Conclusion:* Suspects in Mahatma Gandhi Assassination Trial (May 27, 1948). *Left to Right: Back row:* V.D. Savarkar and Dr Dattatrey Parchure; *Front row:* Nathuram Godse, Narayan Apte, Vishnu Karkare; *Middle row:* Madan Lal Pahwa, Gopal Godse. Shankar Kistayya and Digamber Badge are obscured and not shown in this image. *Photo credit:* Bettmann Archive via Getty Images.

*Map in Part II:* "India," by An Indian Nationalist, *The Indian War of Independence of 1857* (1909).

# Abbreviations

| | |
|---|---|
| APAC | Asia, Pacific & Africa Collections |
| BL | British Library, London |
| CID | Criminal Intelligence Department |
| *CWMG* | *The Collected Works of Mahatma Gandhi* |
| GOI | Government of India |
| EPP | Proscribed Publications in European Languages |
| HD Pol | Home Department Political |
| HD Spec | Home Department Special |
| IOR | Indian Office Records |
| L/P&J | Public and Judicial Department |
| L/P&S | Political and Secret Department |
| MSA | Maharashtra State Archives, Mumbai |
| Mss.Eur | European Manuscripts |
| NMML | Nehru Memorial Museum and Library, New Delhi |
| OBP | Old Bailey Proceedings Online |
| *RCI* | *Report of the Commission of Inquiry into Conspiracy to Murder Mahatma Gandhi* |

# Introduction

Hindutva is not a word but a history
**Vinayak Damodar Savarkar, *Essentials of Hindutva***

. . . *even the dead* will not be safe from the enemy if he wins
**Walter Benjamin, "Theses on the Philosophy of History"**

Vinayak Damodar Savarkar is a difficult figure. As an intellectual founder of Hindu nationalism, he has emerged as *the* most controversial Indian political thinker of the twentieth century. His arguments for Hindutva transformed political debate by rethinking the concepts "Hindu" and "Hindusthan." He is remembered as an anti-imperialist who simultaneously longed for the resurrection of the lost Hindu Empire of centuries past. He is celebrated and condemned for his roles as a nationalist, a revolutionary, a political prisoner, and president of the Akhil Bharatiya Hindu Mahasabha. He gained notoriety for his programme to "Hinduise Politics and Militarise Hindudom" while also arguing for permanent war against Christians and Muslims. He was never forgotten – and for many, never forgiven – for his associations with the murderers of M.K. Gandhi – the Mahatma. The consequence: Savarkar is declared a martyr by some and condemned as *the* enemy by others.

The historical significance of Savarkar's life is acknowledged and accepted by those familiar with modern South Asian history. Less is known about the corpus of his work. His prolific writings have certainly not received the attention of those of his contemporaries or interlocutors.[1] Moreover, there is a lack of awareness of how much Savarkar actually wrote in his lifetime. The fact that his interpretations, conceptualisations, and ideas were at the epicentre of key debates that shaped the landscape of Indian political thought in the twentieth century

---

[1] In recent years, there has been a growing interest in analysing Savarkar's writings. See, for example, Agrawal, "Surat, Savarkar and Draupadi"; Bakhle, "Country First?"; Bakhle, "Savarkar (1883–1966), Sedition and Surveillance"; Bakhle, "Putting Global Intellectual History in Its Place"; Copland, "Crucibles of Hindutva?"; Heredia, "Gandhi's Hinduism and Savarkar's Hindutva"; Krishan, "Discourses on Modernity"; Kumar, "History and Gender in Savarkar's Nationalist Writings"; Menon, "Between Bodies and Borders"; Nandy, "A Disowned Father of the Nation in India"; Pincince, "On the Verge of Hindutva"; Pincince, "V.D. Savarkar and *The Indian War of Independence*"; Sanadhya, "V.D. Savarkar and the Impossibility of Hindutva"; Sharma, "History as Revenge and Retaliation"; Visana, "Savarkar before Hindutva"; Wolf, "Vinayak Damodar Savarkar's 'Strategic Agnosticism'."

is generally overlooked or simply ignored. There is no agreement about how his work should be represented or remembered given his polarising status within India. As a result, the reception of Savarkar's ideas remains penumbral.

Yet my own initial interest in Savarkar had little to do with academic or public debates. Instead, I was motivated for personal reasons. This is not an assertion typically made at the start of a book in academe – on the contrary. I was named Vinayak after Savarkar by one of his disciples, Dr Dattatrey Parchure – who happened to be my pediatrician. Dr Parchure was known as the "second Savarkar" in central India during the 1930s and 1940s, but what brought him international notoriety was the fact that he supplied the automatic handgun that was used to kill Gandhi.[2] Rather than ignore, hide, or obscure this part of the story, I begin my book with this autobiographical framing: after all, it was the discovery of the origins of my name that started my interest in reading Savarkar's writings. But, more important, it had to do with the realisation that the supporters of Savarkar's arguments about the concepts "Hindu," "Hindutva," and "Hindusthan" wanted to create a Hindu India through diverse cultural and political practices – including the naming of children. The "second Savarkar" was planting seeds with the hope of creating a new generation of Savarkars in post-colonial India. My own life-story was entangled with the politics of Hindu nationalism.

I suppose if I had never learned the origins of my name I would have written a very different book – in its form, presentation, and style. There would be no autobiographical context, and Savarkar would not have been on my mind for such a long time. But I imagine there still would have been an intellectual and political imperative to write about Savarkar. Let me explain.

As I was completing research for my book *Peasant Pasts* (2007), it became apparent that Hindutva was no longer a marginalised idea, as it had been for most of the post-colonial period in Indian history. The state of Gujarat experienced devastating communal violence in 2002, in which nearly 2000 individuals were killed.[3] Approximately 150,000 people were displaced from their homes, and, of those, 100,000 forced

---

[2] *GOI, RCI*, pt I, vol. III, 265.
[3] Chaturvedi, *Peasant Pasts*.

to live in relief camps. Most of the victims were Muslims. In assessing the aftermath of these events in Gujarat, many scholars, activists, and intellectuals argued that not only had the eruption of violence marked an end to the Gandhian ethos of non-violence that had come to define Gujarat in the twentieth century, but that the violence of Hindutva had now replaced the non-violence of Gandhi.

While the histories of Hindu–Muslim conflict and their impact on nationalism remained outside the focus of *Peasant Pasts*, my argument about violence was very different from what was being reported in Gujarat after 2002. In fact, I had examined the history of violence and conflict in the making of nationalism in agrarian Gujarat, especially in an area identified as Gandhi's heartland. I had argued that violence was a feature of everyday life in Gujarat in the nineteenth and twentieth century – a fact that Gandhi himself readily acknowledged in his writings and speeches. Yet I ended *Peasant Pasts* by arguing that, for individuals living on the margins of colonial society, there remained the possibility of being part of the post-colonial nation on their own dynamic terms, even as I recognised the social and economic conditions of the historical actors who had been marginalised from the promises of the nationalist movement in Gujarat. I was not alone in making such an assessment. In fact, it was part of the *zeitgeist* of linking the end of formal empire with the promise of radical transformation within Indian society in the new nation-state. As scholars have argued, nations in post-colonial Asia and Africa exemplified the endless possibilities by subaltern groups of redefining how they want to be governed.[4]

This was, of course, only part of the story. There was also a "dark side" within post-colonial nations in which the poor, marginalised, and subordinated sometimes resorted to violence, often genocidal in nature – at times in collaboration with the state, in other instances independent of it – in order to stake a claim within the nation. The transition from being a colonial subject to a national citizen was fraught and conflictual, especially when considering that many victims of colonial societies became the perpetrators of genocidal violence in post-colonial states.[5] What I did not take into account in *Peasant Pasts*

---

[4] Chatterjee, *The Politics of the Governed.*
[5] Mamdani, *When Victims Become Killers.*

was that some of the individuals and groups I discussed had already turned towards Hindu nationalism, or that others were going to make history as killers in the name of Hindutva.

In the aftermath of the Gujarat violence, an entire historiography developed seeking to explain the confluence of economic, social, political, and cultural factors responsible for the emergence of Hindutva in the region, and its implications for the rest of India. It appeared that Savarkar's ideas always loomed large in writings on the events of Gujarat, even if his name was not always mentioned. This was not a surprise. After all, he was the seminal figure who had theorised the concept of Hindutva. While his ideas largely remained on the margins of political culture for most of the twentieth century, it was evident that threads of his thought were now central to political debate in India. It is at this point that I returned to Savarkar's writings, especially considering his multiple strategies for promoting, circulating, and disseminating the principles of Hindutva. To be clear: my point is not to suggest that reading Savarkar's texts provides an easy explanation for the violence in Gujarat or elsewhere. That is not my purpose here. Rather, it is to point out that the contemporary debates about Gujarat provided an intellectual context in which I started considering how the complex story of Savarkar's ideas became increasingly powerful in the making of political thought in the twentieth and early-twenty-first century. In many ways, the idea for writing this book began here. That I was named after Savarkar as part of an effort to spread Hindutva certainly adds another dimension to interpreting the lasting influence of my namesake – a fact that stays with me every day.

## II

I begin this book with a simple observation: Vinayak Damodar Savarkar struggled with defining Hindutva. The publication of *Essentials of Hindutva* in 1923 marked an important conjuncture in the development of the conceptual history of "Hindutva."[6]

Savarkar was not the first to use the concept: it was already a part

---

[6] The Box provides a brief discussion of the various titles and editions of Savarkar's most cited work.

## NOTE ON THE TITLES AND EDITIONS OF
## SAVARKAR'S *HINDUTVA*

There appears to be no agreement about the title of this book – part of the issue is due to the publishing history of the text. On the title page of the 1923 first edition, the information listed is: "*Hindutva* by 'A Maratha,' May 1923." But on page 1, the title shows as *Essentials of Hindutva*, which, however, is not the title of the chapter because this edition of the book has no chapter titles. What complicates matters is that there is an edition of the book in the British Library in London with the title *Hinduism*, but the rest of the book is identical to the 1923 edition of *Hindutva*. In addition, the title page has the exact same font, but reads "*Hinduism* by 'A Maratha,' May 1923." The title *Hinduism* appears to be an error: I have not seen other copies of the 1923 edition, or any other edition, with this title.

Indra Prakash, the general secretary of the Central Hindu Yuvak Sabha, published an edition of the book in New Delhi in 1938. *Hindutva* is the title on the dust jacket and title page. Instead of listing "A Maratha" as the author, as in the 1923 edition, he is identified as "Swatantrya-vir Br. Vinayakrao Damodar Savarkar." After the title page, copyright information is provided (followed by an image of Savarkar) which lists the title of the book as *Hindutva*. On the next recto, an epigraph is included in Sanskrit with the English translation, but the title above the epigraph is "Who is a Hindu?" A foreword is included in this edition, in which Bhai Parmanand states, "I have been asked to write a foreword to Vir Savarkar's 'Hindutva.'" Note that Parmanand did not refer to the book as either *Essentials of Hindutva* or *Who is a Hindu?*

By the fourth edition of the book, published in 1949, the dust jacket retains the title *Hindutva*, but the title page now lists it as *Who is a Hindu?*, with V.D. Savarkar given as the author. In addition, quotes from the text are now printed on the title page (this is an expansion of the epigraph found in the 1938 edition). *Hindutva* appears on the dust jacket of the sixth edition published in 1989, but the title page gives the title *Hindutva: Who is a Hindu?* Page 1 of the book lists the title as *Essentials of Hindutva*, as in the original 1923 edition, but it now also includes chapter titles and subheadings throughout the text. To further complicate matters, the running heads, i.e. the headers on top of each page, are *Hindutva* on the verso and *Essentials of Hindutva* on the recto.

The same jacket title, title page, and running heads are found in the 2003 edition. The 2007 edition of the *Selected Works of Veer Savarkar, volume 4*, simply lists the title of the book as *Essentials of Hindutva*. An official website of Savarkar's work provides an online edition of the book and also identifies the text as *Essentials of Hindutva* (www. savarkar.org, accessed November 9, 2019).

The Marathi and Hindi translations of the book follow a similar pattern: the dust jackets of the books give the title *Hindutva*, and the first page of both books includes a translation of *Essentials of Hindutva* as the subtitle. In the Marathi, the translation is *Hindutvaci Mulabhuta tattve*; in Hindi it is *Hindutva ke pramukhatam abhilakshan*.

There are other editions and translations of the book that were not considered in this context; those editions may have further modifications. In the secondary literature on Savarkar, scholars have used all three titles in their analyses of the text: *Hindutva*, *Essentials of Hindutva*, and *Who is a Hindu?* For the purposes of this book, I have chosen *Essentials of Hindutva* as it avoids some of the confusion of differentiating between *Hindutva*, the text, and all the other uses and meanings of Hindutva as a concept. *Who is a Hindu?* is a later addition that served more as a subtitle of *Hindutva* in subsequent editions of the work. More important, from my perspective *Essentials of Hindutva* captures the meaning of Savarkar's ideas more succinctly and critically – a point that will be further discussed in this book.

of Bengali vocabulary in the nineteenth century. Chandranath Basu is identified as the individual who invented or conceptualised "Hindutva" – a term he discussed in his book *Hindutva* (1892).[7] However, Savarkar was undoubtedly responsible for the proliferation of the concept in the twentieth century. He explained that Hindutva should not be confused with its "cognate," Hinduism.[8] For Savarkar, Hinduism was a "code" or a "theory" founded on what he called a "spiritual or religious dogma or system."[9] He explains: "Hinduism is only a derivative, a fraction, a part of Hindutva."[10] And he continues: "Had not linguistic

[7] Basu, *Hindutva*.

[8] Savarkar, *Essentials of Hindutva*, 3. All citations are for the 1923 edition of *Essentials of Hindutva*, unless otherwise specified.

[9] Ibid., 4.

[10] Ibid., 3.

usage stood in our way then 'Hinduness' would have been a better word than Hinduism as a near parallel to Hindutva."[11]

But Hinduness is not Hindutva; it only serves as an approximation. To further complicate matters, Savarkar posited that Hindutva was indefinable: "The ideas and ideals, the systems and societies, the thoughts and sentiments[,] which have centred round this name are so varied and rich, so powerful and so subtle, so elusive and yet so varied that the term Hindutva defies all attempts at analysis."[12] The argument is that Hindutva is conceptually defiant. If Hindutva were only the name of an ideology, a theory, a religion, or a movement, it may have been possible to define the term. But it was in fact indefinable because Hindutva was ontological: "Hindutva embraces all the departments of thought and activity of the whole Being of our Hindu race."[13]

Perhaps Savarkar's greatest innovation was to link Hindutva with Being. For him, Hindutva was not *the* ontological Being; rather, in his view Hindutva may best be described as the entity by which Being could be understood. Hindutva was an entity that had priority over other entities. Hindutva – in its anthropomorphic form, as described by Savarkar – not only touched Being, it also embraced all that constitutes Being. Despite this, there is in Savarkar's conceptualisation a distinction between Hindutva and Being – they are not synonymous. Hindutva and Being are posited as having an intimate relationship which is completed in what may be called Hindutva's "embrace of belonging" to Being.[14] It is his characterisation of this embrace that brings together what may otherwise appear impossible: that is, for Savarkar Hindutva is a crucial aspect *of* Being. But Hindutva is not all that constitutes Being, it is only a part of Being.[15] Clearly, there is a conceptual tension, or what seems a philosophical difficulty, that Savarkar introduces in his discussion of Hindutva. According to him,

[11] Ibid., 4.

[12] Ibid., 3.

[13] Ibid., 4.

[14] I have borrowed the useful conceptualisation of an "embrace of belonging" from Aggleton, "The Crystallization of the Impossible," 282–3.

[15] I have found Jacques Derrida's formulation of a "particular regional ontology" and "particular type of being" useful in this context. See Derrida, *Heidegger*, 11.

Hindutva's embrace of Being – "the whole Being" – is qualified, for it is an embrace of the "whole Being of our Hindu race."

The inclusion "of our Hindu race" is both important and problematic. It adds a new dimension to Savarkar's conceptualisation. Hindutva as an entity could only be known by understanding all the actions and thoughts that have happened in its human form – in other words, that have taken human shape as a Hindu, or, in the plural, in the shape of the Hindu race. It is important to note that, at this moment, Savarkar asserted himself as a Hindu too, staking a claim within and for "our Hindu race" as part of his conceptualisation of Hindutva. In sum, Savarkar was using the personal pronoun "our" on behalf of the Hindu race.

Conceptualising Hindutva could for Savarkar have been as close to an embrace of Being as was possible. His representation of the entity "Hindutva" in its human form – as a Hindu or as the Hindu race – marks the starting point of any study for Savarkar – and, one might add, *of* Savarkar. However, to suggest that Hindutva was the entity by which Being could be understood did not resolve how to interpret Hindutva. Savarkar pointed out that a single word, such as Hindutva, had the power to "imply an idea," but the word might function at the level of an "abstract generalisation."[16] In other words, language provided the possibility for conceptualising Hindutva, but language was also limited in providing a way to explicate its meaning. As a result, Savarkar explained that his purpose was to investigate the essentials of Hindutva as a word. He asserted that Hindutva had an "essential nature," an "essential significance," and an "essential meaning" because it had existed for over four millennia.[17] The task was to interpret the meaning of Hindutva's essentials – the essentials of a special word that had embraced Being, but which was nonetheless a word.

It was over this ongoing conceptual struggle that Savarkar tried to reveal his method for understanding Hindutva: namely, History. Perhaps the most audacious passage he penned appears in *Essentials of Hindutva*, where he states, "Hindutva is not a word but a history."[18] He explained that Hindutva was not a "spiritual or religious history,"

---

[16] Savarkar, *Essentials of Hindutva*, 2.
[17] Ibid., 3–4.
[18] Ibid., 3.

it was "a history in full."[19] Savarkar first identified Hindutva as a word in his text; he then asserted the negation of Hindutva as a word. This should not be seen as a negation of Hindutva *per se*, but as the negation of a word – and, by extension, language – that could not adequately represent the essence of Hindutva. And yet Savarkar knew he could not abandon the word "Hindutva" either; it was irreplaceable.

It is in this moment of what might be called an existential impasse for "Hindutva" – as a word and not a word – that Savarkar immediately offers "history" as an alternative to provide meaning to "Hindutva." To clarify matters once more: Hindutva is not simply "history," or "the history," but it is "a history," or more specifically "a history in full." Hindutva as *a history* is the singularity of Hindutva's history – a single and singular history that is finite. And yet simultaneously Savarkar's characterisation of it as a form of fulness suggests multiplicity, plurality, and completeness within that singularity or finitude. Savarkar concluded that the question of the meaning of Hindutva is not to be found in the word "Hindutva" itself, but within the multitude that is encompassed within *a history*. The essentials of Hindutva are truly the essentials of history.

<h1 style="text-align:center">III</h1>

*Hindutva and Violence* tells the story of the place of history in Savarkar's thought. The book is organised around Savarkar's formulation of "a history in full" as the central conceptualisation in his writings. In many ways, I have been guided by Savarkar's own argument. Hindutva may be indefinable, but the articulation that "Hindutva is not a word but a history" provides meaning to both "Hindutva" and "history." For Savarkar, the key point is that "a history in full" is Hindutva, too. In other words, he not only linked Hindutva to Being, he also made it clear that history was going to be his method of interpreting Hindutva: his "a history in full" was going to provide the ultimate interpretation of how Hindutva may be actualised, recovered, or approximated in language.

Even before Savarkar wrote *Essentials of Hindutva*, he had already conceptualised the centrality of "a history in full" in *The Indian War*

---

[19] Ibid.

*of Independence of 1857* (1909).[20] And even from that earlier book it seems that for Savarkar "a history in full" is not a complete history, a total history, a comprehensive history, or even a detailed history. Nor is it even a history that is necessarily archival or scientific. Rather, the purpose and practise of his own "history in full" seems to be to trace key historical events to a source – to a powerful unnamed source – which he defined as "desire" or "motive" within historical actors.[21] Whether this source was a manifestation of Being (or Being itself) in human subjects is not fully articulated in Savarkar's oeuvre. To begin to understand what Savarkar meant by Hindutva, I argue that it is necessary to trace the genealogy of his notion of "a history in full" in his writings on history, as well as in his historical writings.

I have also examined a corpus of Savarkar's other writings and speeches and unpublished texts that further illustrate the importance of the essentials of history in Savarkar's thought. A continuity in Savarkar's argument is found throughout his oeuvre: history is everywhere. Savarkar did however make a distinction between genres in his work. While he claimed that his poetry and dramas were inspired by history, and he wanted his histories to be aesthetically more like his poetry, he classified history as separate from his poetry, dramas, and novels. He was also aware of other disciplinary approaches for interpreting Hindutva. He began *Essentials of Hindutva*, for example, with a discussion of Shakespeare's *Romeo and Juliet* on the importance of naming: "We hope that the fair Maid of Verona who made the impassioned appeal to her lover to change 'a name' that was 'nor hand, nor foot, nor arm, nor face, nor any other part belonging to man' would forgive us for this idolatrous attachment to it when we make bold to assert that, 'Hindus we are and love to remain so!'"[22] He then turned to a brief discussion of the importance of understanding the links between language and meaning for the study of names, words, and concepts. He explained that "as the association of [a] word with the thing it signifies grows stronger," over time it becomes "impossible to separate" the word from what it signifies within the "two states of consciousness"

---

[20] An Indian Nationalist, *The Indian War of Independence of 1857*, 4. All references to this text are from the 1909 edition, unless otherwise specified.

[21] Ibid., 4–5.

[22] Savarkar, *Essentials of Hindutva*, 1.

experienced by humans.[23] At the level of what he called "secondary thoughts and feelings," the simple utterance of the word evoked an affective response which further reinforced these links.[24] Continuing to clarify matters, he said there are some words that not only signify "a complex idea or ideal," but they function like "living beings" that "grow like organisms."[25] Some words, such as "Hindutva", have longevity, or even immortality, because the ideas inscribed within words "live longer than [the] generations of man."[26] Savarkar appeared to be adopting a number of disciplinary practices to study Hindutva by engaging with concepts and ideas from literature, linguistics, semiotics, psychology, and biology. Yet he was clear that his disciplinary priority was history.

As a result, I have limited myself to writing about select texts; this book is not a complete or total analysis of Savarkar's entire work. His oeuvre is quite large, and there is even some uncertainty about its actual size. As early as 1933, the publisher of one of Savarkar's dramas included an advertisement for his Collected Works called *Savarkar Vanmaya*, listing all of Savarkar's published texts, including those he had written under various pseudonyms.[27] In 1963, his official Collected Works, entitled *Samagra Savarkar Vanmaya*, were published in nine volumes: seven volumes in Marathi and two volumes in English.[28] These, when reprinted in 1993, included select writings absent from the original edition.[29] In 2000, a Hindi translation was published in ten volumes as *Savarkar Samagra*.[30]

The works collected not only include Savarkar's main books, such as *Joseph Mazzini* (1907), *The Indian War of Independence of 1857* (1909), *Essentials of Hindutva* (1923), *Hindu Pad-Padashahi* (1925), *Majhi*

---

[23] Ibid., 1–2.

[24] Ibid.

[25] Ibid.

[26] Ibid.

[27] MSA, HD Spec File 60-D-V-1934, Advertisement for *Savarkar Vanmaya*, in Vinayak Damodar Savarkar, *Uttarkreya* (Ratnagiri: Balvant Press [1933]), S-112-114.

[28] Savarkar, *Samagra Savarkar Vanmaya*, 9 vols.

[29] Savarkar, *Samagra Savarkar*, 10 vols.

[30] Savarkar, *Samagra Savarkar*, 10 vols.

*Janmathep* (1927), and *Bharatiya Ithihastil Saha Soneri Pane* (1963), but also newsletters, speeches, poems, plays, memoirs, essays, and short stories. Even so, what is published as the Collected Works represents only part of his writings. For example, some of his journalism and one pseudonymous book are not included in the official Collected Works. According to Savarkar's personal secretary Balarao Savarkar, his employer was responsible for writing "3 dramas, 2 novels, ten thousand lines of poetry[,] 25 short stories, 4 books on history . . . and hundreds of articles that are compiled in about 20 books."[31] The problem is that Balarao Savarkar did not provide the titles or publication details of these works, making it impossible to work out whether some of the listed material was unpublished or merely uncollected or already published in the Collected Works or elsewhere.[32] More specifically, which four books Balarao Savarkar classified as works of history is unclear, as are the publication details of the twenty or so books he mentions.

The confusion is worse confounded by the evidence that Savarkar not only published books under various pseudonyms that have been identified – such as "An Indian Nationalist" and "A Maratha" – but that he may have also penned texts subsequently published under the names of his brothers Ganesh Damodar Savarkar and Narayan Damodar Savarkar.[33] This point was discussed by several British officials in the 1930s, when Savarkar was restricted to living in Ratnagiri. The subterfuge of publishing under the name of a trusted relative may have been necessary for Savarkar to shake off the government's censors at a time when he had agreed to refrain from writing on any topic related to politics. Since the colonial officials did not fully investigate the

---

[31] Savarkar, "Life Sketch of Veer Vinayak Damodar Savarkar," 16.

[32] Balarao Savarkar published writings as Bal Savarkar and S.S. Savarkar (Shantaram Shivram Savarkar). See Savarkar, *Historic Statements*, ii. The copyright page states, "S.S. alias Balarao Savarkar." Also, "3 Independents File Papers in City," *The Times of India*, December 4, 1979.

[33] Savarkar also used "A Maratha" as a pen name for select essays. See BL, L/P&S/12/484, A Mahratta, "Future Emperor of India," *Khyber Mail*, November 17, 1940. Officials suspected that a pseudonymous book by Durgatanaya titled *Rashtra Mimansa Va Hindusthanchen Rastriya Swarup* was written by Savarkar or Ganesh D. Savarkar. MSA, HD Spec File 60-D-V-1934, October 16, 1944. S-297-299, 316-318. (The signatures and initials are not legible in the document.)

authorship conundrum that they themselves had raised at the time, the difficulty of being able to pinpoint the authorship of certain texts has remained unresolved.

A large number of Savarkar's writings, including many hand-written letters and petitions, are in the Maharashtra State Archives (Mumbai). But the most substantial collection of Savarkar's work, most of it unpublished, makes up the "Papers of V.D. Savarkar" (hereafter, "Savarkar Papers") in thirty-four reels of microfilm at the Nehru Memorial Museum and Library (NMML), New Delhi. As each reel includes approximately 800–1000 pages of written work, the "Savarkar Papers" are roughly 25,000 to 30,000 pages in length. To complicate matters, this calculation does not consider writings by Savarkar in the "Hindu Mahasabha Papers," also housed at the NMML. Since the "Savarkar Papers" also include letters sent to Savarkar and letters written on behalf of Savarkar, exactitude of authorship in the "Savarkar Papers" remains unclear. On the other hand, some of the material in the "Savarkar Papers" includes early versions of Savarkar's writings that were subsequently published in newspapers, pamphlets, or elsewhere. The drafts of Savarkar's presidential addresses, for example, are in the "Savarkar Papers," but the final versions were published annually as pamphlets; these were later put together in two volumes. Savarkar's first three addresses were published as *Hindu Sanghatan, Its Ideology and Immediate Programme* (1940), while a second volume titled *Hindu Rashtra Darshan* (1949) included all his presidential addresses from 1937 to 1944.[34] A.S. Bhide, Savarkar's secretary in the Hindu Mahasabha, collated Savarkar's statements, messages, interviews, and extracts from Savarkar's diary from the "Papers" for 1937–41 into one large volume titled *Veer Savarkar's "Whirl-wind Propaganda."*[35] G.M. Joshi and Balarao Savarkar published a similar volume of Savarkar's writings over 1941–65, titled *Historic Statements*, but some of the material in it is not to be found in the "Savarkar Papers."[36]

Another collection of Savarkar's writings and speeches was put together by Satya Parkash as *Hindu Rashtravad* (1945).[37] More recently,

---

[34] Savarkar, *Hindu Sanghatan*; Savarkar, *Hindu Rashtra Darshan*.

[35] Bhide, ed., *Veer Savarkar's "Whirl-wind Propaganda."*

[36] Joshi and Savarkar, eds, *Historic Statements by V.D. Savarkar*.

[37] Parkash, ed., *Hindu Rashtravad*.

Himani Savarkar, the copyright holder of Savarkar's writings till her death in 2015, was responsible for publishing the *Selected Works of Veer Savarkar*.[38] She also appears to have been involved in starting www.savarkar.org – a website dedicated to promoting Savarkar's writings.[39]

## IV

Hindutva as "a history in full" is, as discussed, a conceptual conundrum because Savarkar did not provide an explanation for his choice of "history" as *the* central idea, discipline, or method in his work. He was not trained as a historian, but he wrote as if the concept "history" was always a central part of his thought. Indeed, for Savarkar most things were historical or had a history. Hindutva, however, is special: it *is* a history – or, in Savarkar's framing "Hindutva *is* . . . but a history." His coupling of Hindutva with history was now linked for posterity.

Savarkar's personal introduction to "history" had happened prior to his engagement with the concept of Hindutva. He was likely introduced to the concept of *itihaas* in Marathi even before he learned the English term "history." *Itihaas* is generally translated as "history," but its literal meaning is closer to "it so happened."[40] As has been noted, vernacular uses of *itihaas* often differ conceptually from uses of "history" in English.[41] The example of M.K. Gandhi is cited since he made a distinction by arguing that history is too limited a term that centres on wars and celebrates individuals engaged in acts of violence.[42] *Itihaas*, on the other hand, is a much more expansive concept for Gandhi; it allows for writing about *ahimsa* (nonviolence), especially satyagraha (soul force), which is not accurately captured when using "history."

[38] Savarkar, *Selected Works of Veer Savarkar*, 4 vols.

[39] Himani Savarkar was the daughter of Gopal Godse – a conspirator in Gandhi's murder and the brother of Gandhi's assassin Nathuram Godse. Himani married Savarkar's nephew, a son of Narayan D. Savarkar. See www.savarkar.org (accessed November 23, 2019).

[40] Gandhi, *Hind Swaraj*, 87.

[41] Skaria, "The Strange Violence of *Satyagraha*." Also, Suhrud, "Gandhi's Key Writings."

[42] Gandhi, *Hind Swaraj*, 89.

However, Savarkar's interpretation of *itihaas* functioned independently of Gandhi's critique of history and his interest in both *itihaas* and history followed a different intellectual trajectory.

Savarkar noted that, already in his childhood, he was well versed in "old events and heroic incidents out of [*sic*] Maratha history."[43] His father, Damodarpant Savarkar, had introduced him to a diverse body of writings, including Marathi chronicles and biographies known as *bakhars*.[44] These texts provided an initial framing for Savarkar's understanding of *itihaas* – and, by extension, history. Approximately two hundred *bakhars* had been written in Marathi, some dating back to the sixteenth century.[45] The greatest production of these texts had happened in the eighteenth and nineteenth centuries.[46] At the centre of the writings Savarkar was reading on Maratha pasts were debates about the importance of *bakhars* for scholars. It is clear that Savarkar selectively cited a few *bakhars*, such as the *Sabhasad Bakhar* (c. 1694) and the *Chitnis Bakhar* (c. 1811) but offered no lengthy engagement with these texts.[47] Some scholars have dismissed *bakhars* as unreliable because they combine facts with myths, while also violating temporal protocols of dates and chronology found in modern history-writing. *Bakhars* neither included enough factual evidence to be considered "scientific," nor were impartial or objective enough to be considered analytical. One argument is that *bakhars* provided local narratives connected to a bureaucratic strategy of Maratha statecraft while also playing a central role in the construction of knowledge of a Maratha past in the region.[48] They included diverse information – from discussions about taxes, land documents, and state administration, to detailed descriptions of battles and wars. They also provided accounts of key events, including biographical narratives of the lives of kings

---

[43] Gupta, *Life of Barrister Savarkar* (1926), 3. All reference are to the 1926 edition, unless otherwise specified.

[44] Ibid., 2.

[45] Deshpande, *Creative Pasts*, 20.

[46] Ibid.

[47] Savarkar, *Essentials of Hindutva*, 49–50; Savarkar, *Hindu Pad Padashahi*, (1925), 293, 296. All references are to the 1925 edition, unless otherwise specified.

[48] Guha, "Speaking Historically."

and genealogies of important and powerful men. Administrators also often turned to *bakhars* to settle land disputes or conflicts about status within the polity.

Another argument is that *bakhars* played a central role in the construction of a Marathi historical imagination.[49] Modern historiography of the Marathas was born out of a concatenation of social and political processes that witnessed the transformation of the very understanding of history-writing itself. If *bakhars* served as a convention of "pre-colonial history-writing,"[50] then the context of colonial modernity directly shaped both "historical consciousness" and "historical practice."[51] Standard conventions of disciplinary practice informed by positivist methods became normative in colonial India, but the impact of *bakhars* could not be ignored, and scholars continued to debate their veracity as historical narratives. In other words, modern historians debated the importance of *bakhars* as a source while continuing to underscore the epistemic and methodological limits of these texts in the creation of a modern historiography.

Savarkar later explained in his writings that he was familiar with a growing historiography that engaged with debates on whether *bakhars* were actual works of history, or sources for writing history. He had read the writings of major contemporary scholars in India, especially individuals who wrote about the history of the Marathas in English (and the *itihaas* of the Marathas in Marathi), such as Vishwanath Kashinath Rajwade, D.P. Parasnis, Govind Sakharam Sardesai, Mahadev Govind Ranade, and Jadunath Sarkar.[52] There was some continuity in using both history and *itihaas* to describe this historiography. However, he explained that he was not interested in subscribing to the scientific or positivist parameters or methods applied by some contemporary historians to his own writings. He further mentioned scholarship in the field of what he identified as "[O]riental research," but was also not concerned with explicitly engaging these debates in his work.[53]

[49] See Deshpande, *Creative Pasts*.

[50] Ibid., 203.

[51] Ibid., 2.

[52] Savarkar was likely familiar with the historical fiction of Bankimchandra, given that Bankim's "Vande Mataram" enjoyed a pan-India popularity.

[53] Savarkar, *Essentials of Hindutva*, 5.

Rather, he relied on the emergent historiography of the Marathas to construct his arguments about history, explaining that he did not want to replicate existing works on the Marathas within his own analysis. His purpose was to write "a history in full." Yet, in his writings in Marathi, and the official translations into Hindi, this category, "a history in full," was generally subsumed within the concept of *itihaas*. Savarkar's distinction between the two had become blurred: his use of *itihaas* appeared closer to his conceptualisation of "a history in full" rather than just another Maratha history.[54]

While Savarkar's understanding of history emerged out of these developments and debates about *bakhars*, he also explained that while attending Fergusson College in Pune he had read volumes of the "Story of the Nations" series, and they had influenced his thought.[55] T. Fisher Unwin started publishing books in the series in the 1880s, in London, and later collaborated with the New York-based publisher G.P. Putnam's Sons to bring out nearly seventy volumes – such as works on Greece, Holland, Mexico, Scotland, and the Tuscan Republics.[56] These were popular histories written by experts in the field for general audiences. The purpose of the series, as described in one of the books, was to produce "historical studies intended to present in a graphic manner the stories of the different nations that have attained prominence in history."[57] While the story of each nation was identified as "distinct," each volume was also meant to compare national history to "universal history."[58] (The idea of "universal history" is simply stated

[54] In the Marathi translation of *Essentials of Hindutva*, "a history in full" sometimes appears as *sarvangina itihaas* (literally, all-round history), while in the Hindi translation it is *sarva* (whole, entire, complete) *sangrahi* (collection, accumulation) *itihaas* (history). It is also translatable simply as *itihaas*, without any adjectives.

[55] Gupta, *Life of Barrister Savarkar* (1926), 19.

[56] The exact dates for the collaboration between the two publishers remain unclear. See http://www.public.coe.edu/~theller/soj/nor/nor-series.html (28 accessed November 28, 2019).

[57] This information is provided in an advertisement for "The Story of the Nations" series in Orne Jewett, *The Normans*. The page number for the advertisement is not printed in the book.

[58] Ibid.

in the copy of the advertisement, without further explanation.) On the other hand, the plan for each book was to narrate "the real life of the peoples," while also to interpret the "myths with which the history of all lands begin" and narrate "the actual history" of the nation.[59] In the late-1880s, libraries and bookstores in Bombay started receiving copies of books in this series, with advertisements and book reviews appearing in newspapers.[60] By 1893 Sayajirao Gaekwar III, Maharaja of Baroda, commissioned a Marathi translation of three volumes in the series for readers in western India.[61] Savarkar did not say which specific texts he read in this series, nor whether he read any of the Marathi translations available at the time. However, in his writings he noted their importance as "history was his special pursuit."[62] Moreover, they were different in form, structure, and methodology from the *bakhars*, providing him with an alternative framing for an interpretation of history where, at the end of the nineteenth century, the idea of a universal history was embedded in the writing of national histories.[63]

Savarkar's writings about his introduction to history are incomplete. He did not provide further information about his exposure to or interest in history as a subject or discipline. He says he was introduced to newspapers, poetry, novels, and religious texts, but little more about history *per se*.[64] The fact that he turned to history at this historical conjuncture in colonial India is not a surprise, for history as a form of knowledge was thriving.[65] Children were taught history as part of the new

[59] Ibid.

[60] Many advertisements and book reviews for the "Story of the Nations" series appeared in *The Times of India*, starting in the 1880s. One of the earliest was the Sassoon Institute's announcement of new books in the classified section of *The Times of India*, January 10, 1887.

[61] "The Story of the Nations," *The Publishers' Circular and Booksellers' Record of British and Foreign Literature*, 59, 1415 (August 12, 1893), 168. (The author's name is not given.) And, "Bombay Vernacular Literature," *The Times of India*, May 23, 1895.

[62] Gupta, *Life of Barrister Savarkar*, 18.

[63] By 1893, the series consisted of nearly forty volumes, ranging from histories of antiquity to the modern world. The advertisement is found in Boyesen, *The Story of Norway*.

[64] Gupta, *Life of Barrister Savarkar*, 1–32.

[65] There is debate about the origins of history or *itihaas* as an episteme

colonial education. Histories of Europe were introduced in select schools, as was the history of India. Public criticisms of English historians of Indian history were published in newspapers for not only using "derogatory" language, but also claiming that such works were "unworthy of the name history."[66] Already by the late-nineteenth century, a number of writers were arguing for "independent historiography" and "independent nationhood" from British colonialism.[67] History and *itihaas* were often used interchangeably, depending on the context and language of texts. As a law student at Fergusson College in Pune who was politically active in anti-colonial organisations, Savarkar was certainly aware of the emergent nationalist debates that critiqued colonialist interpretations of Indian history. The global spread of nationalism in this period also meant that histories of nations were fast proliferating. Debates about the practice of writing histories of the nation were part of the *zeitgeist*, especially in works that staked a claim to a national past to legitimate the nationalist present.[68] By the early decades of the twentieth century, the national imagination was intimately connected to the historical imagination. While the professionalisation of history as an academic discipline had not formed in India at this point in the early decades of the twentieth century – that would happen in the 1950s – an increasing number of scholars and writers produced works of history for popular consumption.[69] Savarkar was one of these figures.

He only started writing histories after his arrival in London, in 1906.

---

in India. For example, Sanjay Subrahmanyam, V. Narayana Rao, and David Shulman, in *Textures of Time*, argue that historical consciousness can be dated back to early-modern history by considering a range of texts that provide alternative interpretations for history in vernacular languages. By contrast, Dipesh Chakrabarty, in *Provincializing Europe*, locates the emergence of the history and the historical imagination as a part of modernity, while Audrey Truschke, in *The Language of History*, argues the need to consider Sanskrit histories of the twelfth to eighteenth centuries as a way to rethink the ways scholars interpret the origins of history and historical writings.

[66] "Bombay Vernacular Literature," *The Times of India*, May 23, 1895.

[67] Chatterjee, *The Nation and Its Fragments*, 109.

[68] Ibid., 106.

[69] Chatterjee, "Introduction," *History and the Present*, 5–8; Chakrabarty, *The Calling of History*, 1–12.

The fact that he was based in Britain is important, given that he now read a large number of works of history, especially books kept in the library of India House, London, where he resided, and in the British Library. He noted that the introduction to Giuseppe Mazzini's writings was transformative for his own understanding of the potential for writing revolutionary histories. Not only did Savarkar translate select essays from Mazzini's Collected Works in his first book, titled *Joseph Mazzini*, but he incorporated Mazzini's ideas for writing *The Indian War of Independence of 1857*.

Savarkar's first works of history were penned in Britain – not India – for an Indian audience. The years between 1906 and 1910 were when he wrote histories *before* incorporating "Hindutva" into his lexicon. After his arrest in 1910, and his period of incarceration in the Cellular Jail in the Andaman Islands between 1911 and 1921, he studied a number of books from the prison library, which had nearly 2000 volumes. The records of the Cellular Jail provide the dates that Savarkar borrowed a book or returned a book, but do not include the titles or authors of the books he borrowed. Savarkar was only permitted to write a few petitions and letters during his time in the Cellular Jail, but his productivity increased immediately after he was released from the Andamans on May 2, 1921 and transferred to prisons in western India. In May 1923, *Essentials of Hindutva* was published.

Savarkar may have been in uncharted intellectual territory when bringing together arguments for linking Being to both the essentials of Hindutva and the essentials of history. What inspired this shift remains unknown. Yet he was not alone in turning to "history" as a way to interpret Being in this period. The 1926 publication of Martin Heidegger's *Sein und Zeit* (later translated into English as *Being and Time*) provided the most comprehensive philosophical study of Being – what the philosopher calls "the most universal concept" – as part of "an historical inquiry."[70] Heidegger's conceptualisation of Being as possessing temporality marked a fundamental shift in the philosophical understanding of Being. For Heidegger, the insistence that time was central to interpreting the meaning of Being was the first step necessary in arguing that Being had a history. But Heidegger went further by

---

[70] Heidegger, *Being and Time*, 21.

suggesting that Being may best be understood as history – i.e. as time itself. In other words, what was required to conceptualise Being was a historical inquiry into history as Being.

For Savarkar, by contrast, Hindutva as "a history in full" did not transcend time; it was temporally bounded. Hindutva has a beginning, even if its moment of conception remains unknown. Savarkar says, "Forty centuries, if not more, had been at work to mould it as it is."[71] A history in full cannot, moreover, be a complete history of humankind; consequently, Hindutva's finitude is an aspect of its Being. In other words, for Savarkar Hindutva did not transcend time, but understanding its temporality was central to its conceptualisation.

I raise this parallel to suggest that the place of history was in the midst of radical reinterpretation for the study of Being. In this context, it is worth considering a lecture delivered by Jacques Derrida on this theme in 1964, in which he made an important observation about Heidegger's texts (though it is unlikely that Derrida had even heard of Savarkar, let alone read his work). Derrida states: "Never in the history of philosophy has there been a radical affirmation of an essential link between being and history."[72] He further notes that Heidegger's arguments fundamentally contradicted all philosophical writings, because history and time were generally not included in interpretations of ontology. He emphasises Heidegger's radical departure within the field: "Ontology has always been constituted through a gesture of wrenching itself away from historicity and temporality."[73]

To be clear: though some of Heidegger's work was done in the same period as Savarkar's, there is no reason to believe that either Savarkar or Heidegger was aware of the other's writings in this period. Nor is there evidence to suggest that they even knew of the other's existence. Given Heidegger's sympathies and alliances with Nazi ideology and politics, however, this may have changed in 1940, when the German Foreign Office translated Savarkar's *The Indian War of Independence of 1857* into German with the title *Indien im Aufruhr*.[74] It also appears that the Nazis were aware of some of Savarkar's activities, writings, and

[71] Savarkar, *Essentials of Hindutva*, 3.
[72] Derrida, *Heidegger*, 21.
[73] Ibid.
[74] An Indian Nationalist, *Indien im Aufruhr*.

speeches, especially as his name appeared in intelligence reports of the German Foreign Office. After Savarkar had published a celebration of Nazism and Germany's imperial expansion into the Sudetenland,[75] the Nazis reciprocated their admiration for Savarkar in a profile published in the official Nazi newspaper *Völkischer Beobachter*.[76]

In the end, Savarkar did not produce anything comparable to Heidegger's comprehensive philosophical work that examined the nexus of ontology and history. On the other hand, Heidegger did not write histories in the form, content, and style taken up by Savarkar. As will be discussed more fully in this book, Savarkar was a prolific writer of texts in which the importance of history, conceptualised as "a history in full," was at the centre of his corpus. Needless to say, so too was Hindutva.

**V**

The task of writing *any* history about Savarkar poses unique methodological and political challenges. This may in part help explain the paucity of writings about Savarkar in comparison to those on some of his Indian political contemporaries such as Gandhi and Nehru. The fact that Savarkar spent over three decades (c. 1906–37) writing under police surveillance or the prison censor helps to explain the sometimes inconsistent, incomplete, and fragmentary nature of his work. Extrapolating from what Savarkar read – or may have read – is a method commonly adopted when interpreting his thought. The secrets of Savarkar's ideas, in this approach, are said to lie in other texts. In other words, a sort of genealogy is demanded, even if it is not expected to emerge.

But the difficulties of knowing what Savarkar read, or how he may have interpreted what he read, raise obvious concerns for the purposes

[75] Savarkar, "India's Foreign Policy" (November 3, 1938), in Bhide, ed., *Veer Savarkar's "Whirl-wind Propaganda,"* 50–3.

[76] A copy of the article in *Völkischer Beobachter*, dated November 30, 1938, is in the NMML, Savarkar Papers, Reel 1. A commentary on the article is provided in "Hindu Mahasabha, The Most Important Hindu Association in India: Views of the Foremost German Daily," *The Hindu Outlook*, January 18, 1939.

of any interpretation. The adverse conditions he confronted need to be considered as central to critical readings of his work, especially as he conceptualised and produced his seminal writings during his incarceration. He says that, in one of his prisons, he had regular access to a limited number of books but not paper and writing instruments; in others he had paper and pens but no books. After his transfer to Yerwada Jail in Pune in 1923, Savarkar was prolific, but his writings were smuggled out and published under pseudonyms. Moreover, he was not explicit about the texts that influenced his writings. In some books he provided the names of authors and the titles of texts he had read, but the citations are usually incomplete: authors' names appear but not their book titles. Elsewhere, Savarkar assumes his reader is familiar with an idea or set of ideas and therefore does not provide context or explanation for subjects to which he refers. His citations are inconsistently deployed throughout, and bibliographies only appear in some of his publications. To see this as flawed is to miss the point: Savarkar was clear that his purpose was never to produce academic scholarship.

Savarkar, of course, was not alone in writing under the difficult circumstances of state surveillance and the prison censor. Prisons, it is evident, were often sites of productive thought, and knowledge formation as a byproduct of awful circumstances shows up in numerous instances. Some of the most important writings of the twentieth century emerged from political prisoners, the Italian Marxist Antonio Gramsci being the most noted example. Every study of Gramsci not only underscores the fact that he was imprisoned for over a decade (1926–1937) by the Fascist regime in Italy, but that his prison writings signalled a major intellectual achievement in political thought and revolutionary politics. Yet it has been noted that Gramsci is difficult to "read accurately or systematically," not only because he was closely monitored by prison censors but also because he "disguised" language in a way that makes it difficult to fully reconstruct and decipher his ideas.[77] Gramsci's work must therefore be read as being "censored twice over."[78] However, in another interpretation Gramsci's unorthodox use of terminology in his prison notebooks was not meant only to "evade" and "conceal" ideas from

---

[77] Anderson, "The Antinomies of Antonio Gramsci," 6.
[78] Ibid.

his censors, but also to "enhance" and "elaborate" complex thought.[79] The point is that Gramsci's political writings are almost always closely read and interpreted contextually – as the intellectual labour of a prisoner. It is also widely acknowledged that Gramsci made specific choices of language, style, form, and content despite, or rather because of, his peculiar circumstances. While Savarkar was not a revolutionary socialist like Gramsci, he too conceptualised his arguments for Hindutva while incarcerated. I am not suggesting that Savarkar was a "Hindutva-vadi Gramsci" or that Gramsci was a "Marxist Savarkar."[80] My point is merely that since Savarkar composed his foundational work on Hindutva as a political prisoner, it is necessary to identify and understand his aesthetic, literary, methodological, and linguistic choices in consonance with the interpretive strategies used to analyse Gramsci's writings. Only by doing this can we come closer to deciphering Savarkar's ideas.

In writing this book there have also been political challenges that make the task difficult. Representing Savarkar has been highly contentious across the political spectrum. For more than a century, the way Savarkar has been read has always been contingent on the history of politics: global, national, regional, anti-imperial, Anarchist, Fascist, or otherwise. The fact that he is now primarily interpreted through the optics of Hindutva is reflective of today's politics. So I would like to be clear from the outset that my book departs from many of the standard political critiques that dominate the academic and popular discourses on Savarkar. At one level, I am not interested in either establishing or perpetuating any claim that Savarkar was *veer* (heroic, brave) or *swatantraveer* (independent and heroic) – the common characterisations in the hagiographical and celebratory accounts of his life. Nor do I seek to substantiate Savarkar's bona fides as a patriot or a martyr. Conversely, I am not interested in condemning Savarkar on the grounds that he was an unoriginal thinker, or unpatriotic, or a British loyalist – accusations raised by many of his critics. Nor is my purpose to embark on some otiose project of providing a "middle path" to

[79] Arnold, "Gramsci and Peasant Subalternity in India," 33.

[80] This formulation comes from a discussion with Mike Davis, who described Savarkar as a "Right Wing Gramsci."

recuperate and understand the historical subject of Savarkar. Rather, I put forward a straightforward proposition: I try to make it thinkable that Savarkar contributed to political thought.

The celebrations and condemnations of Savarkar have created conditions for what a Marathi literary scholar and Marxist intellectual, G.P. Deshpande, called the "contemporary predicament" when writing about Savarkar's ideas.[81] Deshpande pointed out the polarising nature of scholarly and political debates about Savarkar while noting the paradox that Savarkar's writings, especially his vernacular texts, are not actually read by either his supporters or detractors. He further argued that many "secular intellectuals" regularly attack Savarkar's "positions" but rarely "quote from his writings."[82] He pointed out the irony that Savarkar, though iconic, is not cited in "Hindu nationalist circles" either. Deshpande himself was the only figure on the Left in India who actively urged a "Savarkar debate" in the twenty-first century.[83] In his argument, "a critique of Savarkar is sorely needed. But this critique will have to be directed at his world of ideas."[84]

Deshpande anticipated my problem in some ways: he was aware that his call for an intellectual history of Savarkar was likely to lead to dissatisfaction across the political spectrum in India – both among those who consider Savarkar a friend and those who see him as the enemy. In arguing the need for a close reading and critique of Savarkar's texts Deshpande foreshadows to a degree my own enterprise. Finally, as a Left intellectual his desire to get to grips with Savarkar as a thinker was crucially purposive: a textual strategy was absolutely necessary if Savarkar's "politics are to be opposed." Deshpande's prescription here marked a radical shift in academic and political debates: disagreement requires engagement, not peremptory or condescending dismissal.

In a parallel critique, the Marxist intellectual Perry Anderson argues that there is a natural tendency to take serious interest in ideas of one's own "political family," rather than consider oppositional ideas across the political spectrum.[85] He explains that intellectual landscapes are

81 Deshpande, *The World of Ideas in Modern Marathi*, 107.

82 Ibid., 85–6.

83 Ibid., 108.

84 Ibid.

85 Anderson, *Spectrum*, x.

necessarily porous; in them "ideas are rarely absolute values."[86] The circulation of ideas is not part of a "self-enclosed" political activity but varies across time and space. While these may be obvious points, Anderson provocatively suggests that the time has come for the Left to consider an "intellectual restoration" of its ideas through an engagement with adversaries, rather than by ignoring ideas that have gained ground and dismissing those that present opposing political allegiances.[87] To consider Savarkar's contributions to the history of ideas marks a beginning in this direction.

Anderson's formulation of a "zone of engagement" that encompasses what he calls "the world of ideas from right to left" provides an important framing for thinking about Savarkar's writings.[88] Rather than dismissing, ignoring, or refusing to read Savarkar's writings as a rejection of Savarkar's politics, it is necessary to take his writings seriously – not for the purpose of supporting his ideas but for the purpose of examining how they have influenced the making of modern political thought *writ large*. To consider Savarkar's ideas as separate from political thought is not only to underestimate them, but also to diminish a fuller understanding of political thought. The epistemic refusal to engage with Savarkar's ideas has not prevented the spread or growth of Hindutva in India or elsewhere.

Scholars are increasingly aware of the challenges they face when writing about politics in India today, especially any topic related to Hinduism, Hindu nationalism, and Hindutva. Lawsuits against academics and publishers are common, as is the banning of books. Sedition charges have been levelled against scholars for interpretations arbitrarily labelled "anti-national." Some scholars face threats of violence, others have been physically attacked, and in the most serious cases assassinated. Archives and libraries have been vandalised. This is not an easy climate to write about Savarkar, unless one chooses to write hagiography, the pressure in India being to hero-worship Savarkar. My purpose here is, instead, to stimulate interest in Savarkar's body of ideas on Hindutva and violence that have shaped modern political thought.

I begin with this discussion on the difficulty of writing about Savarkar because I am confronted with it nearly every time I discuss

---

[86] Ibid., xii.

[87] Ibid., xiv.

[88] Anderson, *A Zone of Engagement*.

Savarkar's ideas in the US, Europe, and India. There is often an assumption that reading Savarkar at all is an expression of political sympathy with his ideas – this point is often made to me by those antagonistic to Savarkar's politics. Needless to say, it is a point I reject. For many who oppose Hindutva, the subject of Savarkar is itself a problem, let alone the assertion that he was an intellectual: the impulse to dismiss his ideas because of hostility to his political allegiances is strong. There is also frequently an unwillingness to acknowledge the fact that the reception of Savarkar's ideas varied considerably through the twentieth century. The uneasy fact that his ideas were more influential than is generally acknowledged in the historiography raises questions about the nature of the production and circulation of ideas across the political spectrum.

A further claim often made about Savarkar is that he stole the title (and discourse) of "the Indian war of independence" from Karl Marx when writing his book on the events of 1857–8, *The Indian War of Independence of 1857* (1909). As one scholar said to me, "Savarkar's work cannot be taken seriously since he plagiarised Marx." The media reinforces the claim that Marx was responsible for the description of a war of independence. An example is an article in *The Times of India* in 2007, which, as part of the sesquicentennial commemorations of 1857, states, "It might be worth recalling what Karl Marx had to say on what he called the First Indian War of Independence."[89] In fact, the claim of plagiarism was made so often as a way of rejecting Savarkar (and thereby his ideas) that I thought it necessary to investigate the matter further.

Savarkar has long been accused of taking Marx's classification of the 1857–8 revolts and rebellions in India as a war of independence from Marx's articles in the *New York Tribune*. Yet nowhere in Marx's numerous articles does he actually use the phrase "the Indian war of independence" or "the war of Indian independence." However, in 1959 a volume of Marx's writings on these same events was published in Moscow, under the title *The First Indian War of Independence 1857–1859*, as a supplement to the *Karl Marx and Frederick Engels Collected Works* (*MECW*).[90] I turned to the first volume of the *MECW* for clues, as it

[89] Rup Narayan Das, "Marx and 1857," *The Times of India*, May 16, 2007.
[90] Marx and Engels, *The First Indian War of Independence 1857–1859*.

not only explains the methodology used in the massive project, but includes the names of the individuals involved.[91] As I went through the list of names, the only person I recognised, and who was alive at the time, was Eric Hobsbawm.

In 2010 I contacted Hobsbawm with the hope of getting clarification on this issue, especially as I had located an edition of Savarkar's book published in 1945 in Kuala Lumpur by the Indian National Army (INA), in collaboration with the Japanese Ministry of Propaganda, Sen-den Han, with a modified title: *The Volcano, or The First War of Indian Independence*.[92] I explained that Savarkar had never added "first" in his original book, and the adjective only appears in the INA edition of the book.[93] Moreover, there was a slight difference in the titles: *The First War of Indian Independence* in the INA edition, as against *The First Indian War of Independence*. I enquired if Hobsbawm had met any member of the INA – or anyone at all associated with the INA who may have been aware of Savarkar's book, and who happened to be based in Moscow, Berlin, or London – when he, Hobsbawm, was working on the *MECW*. Did someone take Savarkar's title (or the modified title) and adapt it for Marx's volume on the same nineteenth-century events? Was this the missing link between the titles? In response, Hobsbawm stated the following:

> Of course Marx could not have thought of the Revolt in India as "the first Indian war of independence." It does seem most likely that the title came from Savarkar's 1909 book and was subsequently adapted, presumably by an Indian comrade working in Moscow, for the Progressive Books edition of 1959. To the best of my memory there were no discussions in London on this title during the preparation of the *Collected Works*. The two people who translated the relevant texts in the *Collected Works of Marx and Engels* are now dead and therefore cannot be consulted.[94]

[91] "General Introduction," *Karl Marx and Frederick Engels Collected Works, Volume 1*, xxiv.

[92] Savarkar, *The Volcano, or The First War of Indian Independence 1857–1859*.

[93] For additional discussion on the title of the text, see Sharma, "History as Revenge and Retaliation," 1717; Basu, *The Rhetoric of Hindu India*, 102–3.

[94] Eric Hobsbawm, e-mail communication, February 3, 2010.

The "Publisher's Note" in *The First Indian War of Independence 1857–1859* provides one additional piece of useful information about the book: "This English edition of 'The First Indian War of Independence' is based on the Russian edition prepared by the Institute of Marxism-Leninism of the C.C.C.P.S.U. in 1959."[95] This is probably what Hobsbawm was referring to when he mentioned the two translators. However, the Russian edition of the book does not include "first" in the title.[96] In other words, the inclusion of "first" is only present in the title of the English edition of the book.

With Hobsbawm's death in 2012, I was left with few clues. The task of locating an "Indian comrade in Moscow" within the Russian archives without knowledge of Russian was not feasible. In any case, this line of inquiry was peripheral to my primary interest in writing about Savarkar. But what became apparent while I was engaged in this part of the research was the fact that political resistance to Savarkar and his writings functioned at many levels, including at the level of rumour. It has been shown in the case of M.K. Gandhi that public interpretations of the nationalist figure in India were often diverse, contradictory, and contingent.[97] The point made is that there was no way of controlling the public perception or interpretation of the life or work of an individual, especially a politically contentious individual in the national limelight. While some rumours allowed individuals to legitimate interpretations of a political figure, the circulation of others provided modes of resistance to the same figure. Maybe Hobsbawm's brief comments will not suffice for those who continue to maintain that Savarkar plagiarised Marx. Conversely, the idea that a Marxist was responsible for taking the title of Savarkar's book and modifying it to Marx's writings will strike some as anathema. I suspect rumours about Savarkar will continue to proliferate as long as Savarkar's life and work remain contentious in academic and public discourses.

[95] "Publisher's Preface," in Marx and Engels, *The First Indian War of Independence*, 4.

[96] Karl Marx and Friedrich Engels (trans. A.S. Dergunovoj), *O nacioal'no-osvoboditel'nom vosstanii 1857–1859 gg. v Indii* (Moscow: Gos. Izd. Polit. Lit, 1959). Special thanks to Lynn Mally for her help with the translation of the title.

[97] Amin, "Gandhi as Mahatma."

## VI

I include the reflections above to underscore the challenges that make it difficult to write about Savarkar. I also mention these concerns here in the spirit promoted by Deshpande: that is, the necessity of confronting the contemporary predicament that limits engagement with Savarkar's ideas. Deshpande raised an interesting paradox on this point: Savarkar's name often "crops up" in public debate, but Savarkar "the man" is "near forgotten."[98] But Deshpande was not interested in writing the story of Savarkar's life, or the life that Savarkar made. It is evident from Deshpande's writings that he possessed an insider's deep knowledge on the historical subject of Savarkar. It was his view that "[Savarkar] survives in Marathi consciousness in diverse ways."[99] And he believed that this consciousness of Savarkar in the region's social psyche was not known – and may not have been known – to most others, including those in Hindu nationalist circles.

Deshpande's claim also links an understanding of Savarkar's life to an interpretation of his work. While Savarkar's life may be a part of Deshpande's consciousness, allowing him to offer an interpretation of Savarkar's work, it certainly does not provide a way for reading Savarkar without this consciousness. Deshpande argued that the most complex understanding of Savarkar's work exists in Marathi debates, where his politics and aesthetics are taken seriously: in these Marathi debates Savarkar is not dismissed because of his politics; rather, his writings are considered contributions to the Marathi literary tradition. Deshpande cautioned that ideas and discourses within a given language – Marathi or otherwise – should not serve only as "source-material" for the writing of India's modernity or national discourse. Instead, the world of ideas within the language has a history of its own, independent of the conceptual or theoretical framings that dominate the writing of national and international histories. He argued that when it came to the study of the history of ideas of Marathi intellectuals, the tendency was to situate the individual (or individuals) within national or international contexts rather than within a Marathi framing. He does

---

[98] Deshpande, *The World of Ideas in Modern Marathi*, 86, 108.
[99] Ibid., 86.

not ask us to abandon the former, but emphasises the necessity of the latter.

To my mind, Deshpande's analysis provides some of the most significant insights into Savarkar's work but also raises a conceptual tension worth considering. Deshpande's point about interiority, which privileges "Marathi consciousness" as the ideal way into Savarkar's life and work, provides little accommodation for other languages in which Savarkar may be read and known. This then raises important concerns about interpreting "Marathi consciousness," especially given that Savarkar wrote about consciousness, ontology, and the question of the meaning of Being – to borrow Martin Heidegger's formulation – first in English, in *Essentials of Hindutva*; his Marathi, Hindi, and other vernacular translations appeared later. And the fact of the matter is that Savarkar's ontological explorations did not emphasise the centrality of either the Marathi language or Maratha identity (although these were not excluded either).

At another level, the distinction here is disciplinary as well as generic: Deshpande was mainly interested in writing about the history of ideas emerging out of Savarkar's literary canon, specifically his dramas and poetry, as opposed to Savarkar's histories or other writings. Savarkar wrote in diverse genres, for separate audiences, in different languages. His division of intellectual labour by writing in multiple genres had strategic, aesthetic, and political purposes, especially towards generating support for his ideas among varying audiences in India and beyond. For many of his texts he wanted an audience immersed in Marathi literary traditions. Equally, many others were written for a readership in English. He authorised some texts to be translated from Marathi to English, others from English to Marathi. Many of the works written in English included passages in Sanskrit, Marathi, and Hindi. During his lifetime, select texts were translated into languages such as Hindi, Gujarati, Kannada, Tamil, and Malayalam. New discoveries also suggest that Savarkar may have written some works in Urdu and Bengali. To be clear: my point is not to minimise the significance of Savarkar's Marathi writings, but rather to underscore the fact that Savarkar chose to write in multiple languages, including when writing about consciousness.

Of course, Savarkar was not unique in this context of bilingualism – not to mention trilingualism or quadralingualism. Partha Chatterjee's important observation is most relevant here, namely that by the mid-nineteenth century the intellectual formation of bilingual elites marked an important conjuncture in colonial India as the intelligentsia viewed its own language as central to "cultural identity."[100] He explains that the intelligentsia's literary work in the vernacular, especially dramas and novels, emerged in the "inner domain" – a sphere in which "the colonial intruder had to be kept out."[101] This inner domain not only remained largely impervious to European literary and aesthetic influences, but it was also the space that resisted and rejected "European conventions."[102] For Chatterjee, the inner domain was the space in which the nation was imagined into existence as sovereign, independent of colonial power. There seems no doubt that the argument about Marathi consciousness can be considered in consonance with Chatterjee's formulation of the "inner domain," given that Savarkar wrote his dramas and poetry in Marathi. However, Savarkar's circumstances were more complicated: not only did he write some of his major dramas when he was banned from taking up political writings, the additional problem was that colonial officials censored the dramas. There was extensive correspondence between Savarkar and various British government officials on questions of language, style, form, and politics – to the extent that Savarkar had to acquiesce and modify his writings.[103] In one case, Savarkar was required to withdraw a published play and submit all copies in his possession to the government.[104]

In other words, for Savarkar the "inner domain" was not a space in which the colonial official could be kept out. As a consequence,

---

[100] Chatterjee, *The Nation and Its Fragments*, 6–7.

[101] Ibid., 7.

[102] Ibid.

[103] MSA, HD Spec File File 60-D-IV-1927, Report on V.D. Savarkar's Play, District Magistrate, Ratnagiri, March 26, 1927, S-9-13; Ratnagiri Weekly Letter, April 8, 1927, S-27-29; "Usshap by V.D. Savarkar (after censoring)," S-41-43 (no name, no date given); Report of the *Shraddhanand*, April 8, 1927, S-211.

[104] MSA, HD Spec File 60-D-IV-1927, Letter from J. Monteath, Secretary to the Government of Bombay, to District Magistrate, Ratnagiri, May 14, 1927, S-285-287; Letter from V.D. Savarkar (no date given), S-291.

it is not possible to fully disentangle Savarkar's vernacular writings
from literary or aesthetic influences of European, British, or English
contexts, or his English writings from vernacular influences. It also
seems to me unclear how "Marathi consciousness" can be understood
as autonomous in such a context. Whether it is even possible to partition or compartmentalise any thinker into a singular/monlingual (or
binary/bilingual, tertiary/trilingual, and so on) framing is difficult at
best. This is not an issue specific to Savarkar but a conceptual hurdle
for interpreting the writing of all intellectuals.

<h1 style="text-align:center">VII</h1>

*Hindutva and Violence* is about the ideas of an individual who helped
shape the direction of modern political thought in India. It is not a
biography of Savarkar. Nor is it a political history of Savarkar's role
in the political movements of Hindu nationalism. Savarkar's writings
are considered within the temporal and spatial framings in which they
were produced. This means that the key historical contexts in which
Savarkar wrote are examined throughout the book. My analyses in it
are partial to Savarkar's ideas about history – and by extension to "a history in full" – as a way to interpret the meaning of Hindutva. The book
is also "partial" in the other sense of the word – it is not a total analysis
of Savarkar's entire corpus.

I have organised this book into four chronological parts rather
than chapters. Each part examines key concepts and texts published
by Savarkar in a given place: Part I – London (1906–1910); Part II –
Port Blair-Pune (1911–1923); Part III – Ratnagiri (1924–1937); Part
IV – Bombay (1937–1963). Each part consists of many sections, some
long, others short.

Savarkar's writings reflect what may be called an intellectual bricolage – as do those of many intellectuals of the time – this being an
aspect of what has been termed the "fluid intellectual economy" in the
making of modern thought in the early-twentieth century.[105] There
was much dynamism and interpenetration across languages, cultures,
and contexts within this process: intellectuals read across the political

---

[105] Bayly, *Recovering Liberties*, 311.

spectrum, engaging in scholarly debates that were important at the time but which became marginalised over the century. Many of the interlocutors were local or regional figures, while others were major intellectuals of their time. Taken together, all these factors represent the challenges of writing an intellectual history of a colonial subject who conceptualised his ideas under arduous circumstances in more than one language and for a variety of audiences. As a result, my chosen form in each part offers multiple methodological approaches for interpreting his ideas and concepts in order to situate his work within the fluid intellectual economy of the time. My purpose is to provide a perspective into the intellectual world in which Savarkar wrote, while also offering his interpretations of the making of Hindutva in the twentieth century. I have written each part to be read sequentially, but the book also allows readers to read each part (including the coda) as an autonomous essay.

Part I, "Principles of History," considers Savarkar's earliest published writings during 1906–1910, when he lived in London. He was prolific at this point, completing three books and dozens of essays before his arrest in 1910 for sedition and other crimes against the British government. This first part examines writings that help explain Savarkar's central concern with the principles of history. The key texts analysed are *Joseph Mazzini* (1907) and *The Indian War of Independence of 1857* (1909). The earliest influence in this period was the Italian thinker Giuseppe Mazzini, whose Collected Works Savarkar translated into Marathi. More important, he built on Mazzini's ideas of "principles of revolution" to conceptualise "a history in full," which he introduced for the first time in *The Indian War of Independence of 1857*. I offer an analysis of both texts, as also of a number of essays Savarkar produced while in London, in order to argue that these works serve as an important precursor to all his later writings on Hindutva.

"Hindutva is History" is the title of Part II, which examines Savarkar's key text on Hindutva: *Essentials of Hindutva* (1923). After his arrest in 1910, Savarkar was sentenced to two life terms. For the first ten years in the Cellular Jail in Port Blair, he was only allowed to write one letter a year to his family. However, once he was transferred to a prison in Pune, he reverted to being a prolific writer. This part of the book examines his argument in *Essentials of Hindutva* that "Hindutva is a history in full." It explains the importance of Savarkar's interpretations and conceptualisations in the text that served as the theoretical and methodological foundation for all his later writings. I also here examine Savarkar's conceptual histories of two additional terms that are required to understand Hindutva: "Hindu" and "Hindusthan." Finally, I look at Savarkar's interpretations of the three essentials of Hindutva that further clarified the meaning of "Hindu": that is, geography, blood, and civilisation.

Part III, "Modes of Hindu History," examines Savarkar's approaches to writing "a history in full" in two genres. The first section considers "Maratha History as Hindu History" through a study of *Hindu Pad-Padashahi* (1925), in which Savarkar argues for the importance of writing histories of pan-Hindu unity. It explains that Savarkar took key ideas from his writings on *The Indian War of Independence of 1857* and *Essentials of Hindutva* to write about the Hindu war of independence led by the Marathas. He also expanded key concepts to provide a new interpretation of the role of the Hindu Spirit in the making of Hindu History. The second section, "Autobiography as Hindu History," examines Savarkar's autobiographical writings as part of his understanding of "a history in full." In the 1920s and 1930s Savarkar contributed to the writing of multiple autobiographical texts: *Life of Barrister Savarkar* (1926), *Majhi Janmathep* (1927), and a series of autobiographical essays (1929–32). The genre of autobiography provided Savarkar a way to write about the "self" as a strategy of ontological integrity. In other words, Savarkar explained that it was his responsibility to narrate his life within the same parameters that he had used in examining the lives of past historical characters. Savarkar wanted to ensure that all narratives of his life evoked Hindutva. Part III also considers that Savarkar's turn towards autobiography occurred in a period of extensive correspondence with British officials during which he was required to stop all political analysis in his historical writings. Writing of the self was Savarkar's response.

"An Impossible History" is the title of Part IV. In 1937, after twenty-seven years as a political prisoner, Savarkar was finally released. In the same year he became President of the Akhil Bharatiya Hindu Mahasabha, the leading political organisation promoting Hindutva. This part of the book shows how Savarkar was consumed with taking his ideas about Hindutva and putting them into practice – a plan that proved difficult. In the 1930s and 1940s Savarkar was very prolific, but most of his writings centred on political work in which he repeated the arguments in *Essentials of Hindutva* within speeches and essays. The point of his activity now was to make the philosophical interpretations of Hindutva as a history in full accessible to the masses – as discussed in his book *Hindu Rashtra Darshan* (1949).

Savarkar's arguments were left unfulfilled and unfinished by the time India and Pakistan became independent from British rule in 1947. In 1948, M.K. Gandhi was assassinated by one of Savarkar's disciples, and Savarkar was one of the nine individuals arrested for the plot to murder Gandhi. He was acquitted due to lack of evidence and was largely shunned from public life till his death in 1966. But a few years before his death he produced the final volume of his Hindutva writings – a massive work entitled *Bharatiya Ithihastil Saha Soneri Pane* (1963; translated into English as *Six Glorious Epochs of Indian History* in 1971). Part IV discusses Savarkar's final text as an incomplete project in which he struggled with the idea that Hindutva was an impossible history.

# VIII

This book begins with an epigraph by Walter Benjamin from the "Theses on the Philosophy of History." His formulation that *"even the dead will not be safe from the enemy if he wins"* is a reminder of the power of history (and historians) to reclaim human subjects.[106] Although the context of Benjamin's statement is far removed from Savarkar's Hindutva, it has provided me with an important insight as I wrote this book – not least because Savarkar claimed to speak for the dead. What I have left out from the epigraph is Benjamin's sentence that immediately follows – "And this enemy has not ceased to be victorious."[107] For now, this is where I depart from Benjamin. Instead, I prefer his clarion call to historians to resist by maintaining a "spark of hope in the past," all the while recognising the conditions of the present.

It is in this spirit that I have written *Hindutva and Violence*.

---

[106] Benjamin, "Theses on the Philosophy of History," 255. Emphasis in original.

[107] Ibid.

# PART I

# Principles of History

... history attaches more importance to the exposition
of principles than to mere narrative

**Vinayak Damodar Savarkar,**
*The Indian War of Independence of 1857*

Prison Portrait of Vinayak Damodar Savarkar,
London (c. 1910/1911).
*Photo credit:* © The British Library Board (L/PJ/6/1069 6A).

# 1. Introduction

For nearly a century, there has been great speculation about Vinayak Damodar Savarkar's turn towards Hindutva. Implicit in this framing is the idea that Savarkar was not always interested in Hindutva, or that he had an alternative perspective on Indian society before his formal writings on Hindutva in the 1920s. Most scholars examine Savarkar's writings in London over the years 1906–10 in order to underscore a fundamental shift later. His *The Indian War of Independence of 1857* (1909: hereafter *Indian War*) is often cited as reflecting Savarkar's discussions of the historical solidarities between Hindus and Muslims in their struggle against the British. Pandits and "moulvies" were celebrated as heroes for their sacrifices, as were Hindu kings and the last Mughal emperor. Savarkar referred to Hindus and Muslims as *shahids* (martyrs) and celebrated the idea of jihad as part of a revolutionary war, while also arguing that Hindus and Muslims were fighting together to protect "our religion" – in the singular.[1] Such examples abound in this text.

There is also an argument about a bifurcation in Savarkar's political life, separating an early Savarkar *before* Hindutva – when he was a nationalist, a revolutionary, and an anti-imperialist – to the late Savarkar of Hindutva. Those who want to recuperate the early Savarkar insist on this separation and maintain that it is possible to celebrate this aspect of his life and work while remaining ambivalent or antagonistic towards his arguments for Hindutva.

By the time *Essentials of Hindutva* was published in 1923, Savarkar was considered *the* proponent of Hindutva. The emphasis on Hindu–Muslim unity had disappeared. He shifted from writing about arguments for "Indians" to a primary focus on "Hindus." He no longer wrote about Indian independence; instead, his work examined Hindu independence.[2] A number of explanations are offered for the transformation, and they centre on Savarkar's time as a political prisoner.

---

[1] Savarkar, *Indian War*, 8.

[2] See "Indian War of Independence," *The Indian Review* (August 1948), 416.

Savarkar was arrested in London on March 13, 1910 on multiple charges, including "procuring and distributing arms," "delivering seditious speeches," and "abetment of murder."[3] He was sent to India to be tried in the Bombay High Court along with thirty-seven others as part of a conspiracy against the government.[4] He was found guilty and sentenced to two life terms in the Cellular Jail in Port Blair in the Andaman Islands.[5]

Savarkar's prison experience is offered as a contributing factor, not least because his writings on Hindutva emerged immediately after he left the Andamans, when he was transferred to a prison in Ratnagiri in Maharashtra in 1921, and then to Yerwada Jail in Pune in 1923.[6] One explanation is that Savarkar was frustrated by the forced conversion of Hindus to Islam in the Andamans. Another is that he was apparently tortured and beaten by his Muslim warders in the Cellular Jail. Savarkar's writings about his prison years in the Andamans are cited as evidence for both arguments.[7] While he discussed the brutality and cruelty of the prison guards, he added that he objected to the differential treatment of prisoners based on religion. According to Savarkar, every Muslim prisoner was not only given a copy of the Quran, but warders allowed Muslim prisoners the opportunity to read the text in lieu of the required prison work.[8] Further, Muslim prisoners were allowed to celebrate holidays together. Savarkar explained that Hindus, in contrast, were often denied "any copy of their religious scriptures" and that it was "an offence to read them openly."[9] More generally, Savarkar's

[3] "Special Tribunal Under Act XIV of 1908, Before Sir Basil Scott, Kt., Chief Justice, Mr. Justice Chandavarkar and Mr. Justice Heaton, Emperor v. Vinayak Damodar Savarkar and Others," (October 6, 1910) in *Indian Law Reports*, Bombay Series, vol. XXXV, 1911, 225–31.

[4] BL, APAC, L/P&J/6/1058, File 284, "In the High Court of Judicature at Bombay. Judgment of Special Tribunal in Special Bench Cases Nos 2, 3 and 4 of 1910."

[5] Ibid. Also, MSA, Home Spec, File 60-D-(f)-1923, Letter from B. Scott, N.G. Chandavarkar, and J.J. Heaton, to The Superintendent of His Majesty's House of Correction, Bombay (no date given), S-13.

[6] Savarkar, *My Transportation for Life*, in *Selected Works of Veer Savarkar*, vol. 2, 529–30.

[7] Ibid., 224, 291.

[8] Ibid., 248–9.

[9] Ibid., 248.

objection was that Muslims were allowed to build communal bonds in prison; these privileges were not afforded to Hindus. Others have suggested that Savarkar was responding to prisoners who supported the pan-Islamic Khilafat movement in the new prison in Ratnagiri at the time.[10]

A further explanation is offered by Savarkar's contemporary Bhai Parmanand – a fellow prisoner in the Andamans, a comrade from London days in the India House, and former president of the Akhil Bharatiya Hindu Mahasabha. Parmanand said there was a public perception that he was responsible for influencing Savarkar because of their close relationship: "I have sometimes been accused of having lured my friend, Vir Savarkar, from the path of 'nationalism' to that of 'communalism', from being an arch-revolutionary to being an ardent Mahasabhaite."[11] He countered this view, arguing that Savarkar had already formed his ideas about Hindutva well before they met. In fact, he questioned the premise that there was a shift in Savarkar: "The simple fact is [that I make] a complete refutation of the accusation that I have been, in any way, responsible for any change in him[,] granting for argument's sake that a change has occurred. But has there been any change in him? I believe not."[12]

On this point Savarkar's detractors agree with Parmanand. Those who want to condemn Savarkar also insist that there was no bifurcation: he was always a Hindutva-vadi. Even if not fully recognised or formed, he was always so in the making. Another critique of an "early Savarkar" and a "late Savarkar" is on the grounds that this too closely echoes the taxonomy of Marx as "early Marx" and "late Marx."[13] To use the English adjectives in this context to describe Savarkar's writings is in itself anathema for some. For others there are passages in *Indian War* that indicate antagonism towards Muslims, confirming the notion of continuity in Savarkar's thought.[14]

Savarkar was aware of discussions about the shift in his work, but

[10] Jaffrelot, *The Hindu Nationalist Movement in India*, 25; Bakhle, "Country First?," 153–4.

[11] Bhai Parmanand, "Foreword," in Savarkar, *Hindutva* (1938), i.

[12] Ibid.

[13] Taneja, "The Myth of Early Savarkar," 224.

[14] Ibid. Also, Pincince, "V.D. Savarkar and *The Indian War of Independence*," 54–6.

he provided neither a full explanation nor acknowledgement of any transformation.[15] However, a clue can be found in his last major work, *Bharatiya Ithihastil Saha Soneri Pane* (1963; later translated as *Six Glorious Epochs of Indian History*, 1971), in which he states that that his early work, *Indian War*, was part of his writings on Hindutva's six glorious epochs. He explains that he has chosen not to repeat here the arguments of his writings on the events of 1857: "But I have already written some time in 1908–1909 a detailed history of this revolutionary war in my book of about five hundred pages named, '[The] Indian War of Independence of 1857'. In it I have reviewed that war from the standpoint of the Hindu nation. As such it is not necessary to repeat the same here again."[16] He recommends that readers simply read *Indian War*. These brief comments allow Savarkar to reclaim his early book as part of his oeuvre on Hindutva – a point often ignored when discussing Savarkar's writings. However, his own classification of his early work does not resolve the point that in *Indian War* he never claimed that the book reflected the perspective of the Hindu nation; this point was only made after the fact – perhaps only to silence those who would argue that there was a shift in his writings over the course of his career.

I begin with this discussion to suggest an alternative approach to interpreting Savarkar's work by considering an idea that exists throughout his writings: "a history in full." Savarkar's proposal for writing a history in full was actually first discussed in *Indian War*, not in *Essentials of Hindutva*. He then further built on this idea in his later writings from the 1920s to the 1960s. However, in *Indian War* Savarkar did not link it to Hindutva; the definition that "Hindutva is not a word [but] . . . a history in full" was a later development. In fact, Hindutva was not even mentioned in any of his writings in London. The conceptualisation of a history in full, therefore, was a precursor to Savarkar's writings on Hindutva. It is in *Indian War* that Savarkar explained what he meant specifically by a history in full: "[T]o write a full history . . . means necessarily the tracing of all events . . . back to

<hr>

[15] For example, Savarkar addresses this debate in a reply to C. Rajagopalachari in a Press Statement, August 24, 1944, in NMML, V.D. Savarkar Papers, Reel 28.

[16] Savarkar, *Six Glorious Epochs of Indian History*, 461.

their source – the motive."[17] He then defined motive as "the innermost desire" of individuals who initiated the event, or, in his words, those who "brought it about."[18] For Savarkar the task of the historian writing a full history was not only to conceptualise motive (or desire), it was also to trace that desire in the historical subject.

But who were these desiring subjects? Throughout *Indian War* he says his priority is to focus on individuals whom he called "chief actors," these being exemplary figures among the "people."[19] These actors formed a revolutionary vanguard of the most politically advanced sections of the masses. The vanguard was not made up of those individuals who were the most class-conscious – as in the Marxist use of the term. Rather, it referred to individuals who embodied an essence of *the* source that could be interpreted through a study of their actions. Savarkar also provides another important framing relevant for understanding his desiring subjects. He says he is speaking for the dead: "The spirits of the dead seemed hallowed by martyrdom, and out of the heaps of ashes appeared forth sparks of a fiery inspiration."[20] Once these "chief actors" were identified, the task was to clarify and codify their "countless actions." It is only then that a historian comes close to an understanding of the spirits of the dead – their actions, their motives, their inspirations, and their desires.

By the time Savarkar wrote *Essentials of Hindutva*, he had identified the motive or source for understanding a history in full as Being. As he put it: "Hindutva embraces all the department of thoughts and activity [actions] of the whole Being of our Hindu race."[21] However, the articulation of a history in full in *Indian War* was framed by what Savarkar called "principles." He states that "In all great religious and political revolutions, it is almost impossible to connect together links . . . without thoroughly understanding the principles which are at their root."[22] The foundation for any revolution in history is identifiable only by searching for its "hidden causes and the mysterious

---

<sup>17</sup> Savarkar, *Indian War*, 4–5.

<sup>18</sup> Ibid., 5.

<sup>19</sup> Ibid., 4.

<sup>20</sup> Ibid., vii.

<sup>21</sup> Savarkar, *Essentials of Hindutva*, 4.

<sup>22</sup> Savarkar, *Indian War*, 3.

forces that worked beneath."[23] These principles – his subterranean forces – were what he defined as "the essence of a revolution."[24] The task of the historian was to "search after principles."[25] By implication, it was also to search for the essences.

This was no easy task. The purpose of writing history was not to provide "a mere narrative" of the past; rather its importance was in "the exposition of principles."[26] In other words, Savarkar was not interested in producing narrative histories of revolutions – or any other history. The process of searching, identifying, and writing about principles allows the historian proximity to the essence that once served as the motive and desire of historical actors. This conceptualisation of a history in full helps explain Savarkar's interpretation of *Indian War* when writing about the events of 1857. It also serves as a precursor to his later definition of a history in full that was directly connected to the search for the essence of a different force: Hindutva.

Part I examines Savarkar's work in London in the years between 1906 and 1910. It is in this period that Savarkar penned key works that provide a foundation for interpreting his oeuvre, but also a time in which Savarkar emerged as a political figure in Britain at the centre of debates about empire, nationalism, and the epic traditions in India. While his writings reflect a commitment to investigating the principles of revolution for achieving independence in India, his activities in London also demonstrate Savarkar's interpretation and application of the same principles in daily life. His celebration of violence in his writings on wars of independence is related to his involvement in acts of violence by his supporters in India and England in this period. Moreover, Savarkar also had interlocutors in London who helped shape his ideas about the relationship between history and violence. Part I explains that *Indian War* was Savarkar's most prominent book written in this period, but its publication was also preceded by his first book, titled *Joseph Mazzini* (1907), in which Savarkar translated select essays from Giuseppe Mazzini's collected works into Marathi.[27] It is in the

[23] Ibid.
[24] Ibid.
[25] Ibid., 4.
[26] Ibid., 3.
[27] Savarkar, *Joseph Mazzini*, in *Samagra Savarkar*, vol. 8.

introduction of this book that Savarkar began to explain his interest in writing about the importance of bringing together religion and politics as a way to interpret the centrality of principles of revolutions.[28] He explains that he relied on arguments presented by Mazzini on the importance of writing histories of revolutions that considered the principles that motivated people. The Italian struggle for independence from the Austro-Hungarian empire in the nineteenth century, he says, served as his inspiration. As a result, Mazzini's influence was present throughout *Indian War*. In addition, Savarkar produced essays and pamphlets during his stay in London in which he brought together ideas from Mazzini's writings and a number of other texts to interpret India's history before the publication of *Indian War*. Part I is about Savarkar's early conceptualisation of a history in full – the conceptualisation that served as a precursor to all his later writings on Hindutva.

## 2.  Reading Mazzini in London

Savarkar arrived in London in early July 1906 to train as a barrister at Gray's Inn.[29] He had studied law as an undergraduate at Fergusson College in Pune, where he had become politically active, participating in debates on national and international politics with college mates. He became a student activist and founded an organisation called the Mitra Mela. He also wrote for a literate Marathi readership about current events. His political activities drew the attention of a number of major intellectuals, including the nationalist Bal Gangadhar Tilak, who recommended that Savarkar continue his studies in London. (Savarkar would later dedicate *Joseph Mazzini* to Tilak, a major influence in his intellectual formation.[30]) He received a scholarship to travel to Britain

[28] See V.D. Savarkar, "The Only Way Out: Hinduise All Politics!" in NMML, V.D. Savarkar Papers, Reel 30. No date is given for the essay.

[29] Savarkar, *Inside the Enemy Camp*, 20; Savarkar, *Shatruchya Shibirata*, 36. Savarkar wrote that he arrived on July 2 or 3, 1906, but he could not remember the exact date. For select references, I have cited Savarkar's Marathi original text and the official English translation: *Shatruchya Shibirata* and *Inside the Enemy Camp*, respectively. Direct quotations are taken from the English translation, unless otherwise noted.

[30] Savarkar actually had a dual dedication to Tilak and Shivram Mahadev

through the sponsorship of the former Dewan of Ratlam, Udaipur, and Junagadh, as well as the Oxford-educated Sanskritist Shyamji Krishnavarma.[31] In fact he was put up in Krishnavarma's residence, "India House," in north London, with a group of Indian students who had also been sponsored to study in Britain. Krishnavarma was keen that the students read broadly on the histories of empire, while also engaging and collaborating with others in the metropole to gain experience to fight colonial power at home.

Savarkar's political and intellectual career began in India, but it was in Britain that he emerged as an international figure. Most of what is known about his early life in India is based on his own recollections and autobiographical writings, published in the 1920s and after. This creates special challenges for writing about the period before Savarkar arrived in London. It is unclear if Savarkar's early writings from India have survived, so it is not possible to determine if they contained anything that might help interpret or contextualise his later work. What is evident is that, immediately after arriving in London, Savarkar was prolific. In the years between 1906 and 1910 he completed three books, a number of newspaper articles, a series of essays, and newsletters that were published and circulated in India. In addition, he was politically active in London, forming his own revolutionary organisation called the Abhinav Bharat Society – literally, Young India Society – as a way to agitate against empire. Not surprisingly, the British government closely monitored the activities of those resident at India House as well as members of the Abhinav Bharat Society. Savarkar was under constant surveillance, especially as many of his activities were public, including some of his writings and speeches.[32] Only after his arrest in

---

Paranjape, editor of the *Kaal*, a Marathi weekly newspaper. He wanted to thank Paranjape for publishing articles on Mazzini that influenced his thought and for encouraging him to continue his work. See Savarkar, *Inside the Enemy Camp*, 69; Savarkar, *Shatruchya Shibirata*, 142; *Legal Proceedings in the Case of Tilak v. Chirol and Another, vol. 1*, 196–7.

[31] See Yajnik, *Shyamaji Krishnavarma*.

[32] The Weekly Reports of the Director of Criminal Intelligence and other surveillance information for 1907–11 are in BL, APAC, India HD Pol Proceedings, A Series, IOR.POS.5944-5949, and B Series, IOR.POS.8959-

1910 did he learn that the authorities had been monitoring his activities as early as 1905 – a year before he even arrived in Britain.

Perhaps the greatest influence on Savarkar's thought in this early period in Britain was Mazzini. As noted, Savarkar translated select essays by Mazzini into Marathi and wrote a lengthy introduction on the importance of Mazzini's life story for Indians in *Joseph Mazzini*. It is this work that informed Savarkar's other writings of this period, especially those in which he conceptualised "a history in full." In an autobiographical essay he reflected on his introduction in India to the life and works of Mazzini: "I had read a biography of Mazzini in English and had realised that Mazzini's autobiography and a collection of his articles, translated into English, were available."[33] He did not provide a date for when he read the book, which he later identified in a separate essay as Bolton King's *The Life of Mazzini* (1902).[34] India House, where Savarkar resided, had a library with the first three volumes of Mazzini's collected works, which Savarkar said he read over a single week.[35] He acquired the remaining three volumes with the assistance of one Mr Mukherjee, the manager of India House.

Savarkar's discussion of Mazzini in his writings is extensive; it is also unique in his oeuvre. He provides details about the centrality of Mazzini and his ideas for his own conceptualisation of history. He also explains the reception of Mazzini in India, especially in Bengal and Maharashtra. More important, he includes a close reading of Mazzini's texts, while also discussing the importance of Mazzini's thought for an Indian audience. I underscore these writings about Mazzini to emphasise that Savarkar did not produce anything comparable for any other thinker throughout his career.

What explains this? At one level, it is important to note that when Savarkar started reading and writing about Mazzini, he did not have

8966. These are microfilmed records from the National Archives of India New Delhi), but there is a discrepancy when ordering these materials, which are not as listed in the catalogue in the APAC Room. For the B Series, it is necessary to replace "POS" with "NEG": such as, IOR.NEG.8959.

[33] Savarkar, *Inside the Enemy Camp*, 66; Savarkar, *Shatruchya Shibirata*, 136.

[34] Savarkar, *Inside the Enemy Camp*, 14; Savarkar, *Shatruchya Shibirata*, 17.

[35] Savarkar, *Inside the Enemy Camp*, 65; Savarkar, *Shatruchya Shibirata*, 132.

the government closely monitoring his activities. In part, the surveillance increased *after* Savarkar completed his book on Mazzini, which was immediately banned through the application of the Indian Press Act.[36] Savarkar's arrest in 1910, and the lengthy period of incarceration that followed, meant he did not have regular access to books when he wrote, especially in the 1920s and 1930s. The writings are more fragmented, and presumably this was a reflection of the fact that he was reading only what was available to him as a prisoner. At another level, reading Mazzini had a transformative impact – to the extent that he incorporated key ideas from Mazzini when writing *Indian War*, and these ideas continued to influence his later work on Hindutva.

The fact that Savarkar was interested in Mazzini is not a surprise. In the nineteenth century Mazzini was a central influence for radical liberals and nationalists in what has been called the "globalisation of democratic nationalism" in Asia, Europe, and the Americas.[37] He was already a global figure by the time Savarkar translated his writings into Marathi. In the 1840s–1850s Indian newspapers provided regular reports on Mazzini's activities and influence in Europe.[38] By the late-nineteenth century intellectuals in India were actively engaging with Mazzini's life and work. Surendranath Banerjea (1848–1925) was perhaps one of the first in India to analyse Mazzini's thought. On April 2, 1876 Banerjea delivered a speech to the Uttarpara Hitakari Sabha in which he explained the importance of Mazzini's ideas for interpreting contemporary conditions in India under British rule.[39] He drew parallels between India and Italy, especially as he had studied modern European thought and histories of nationalist movements in Europe. He was particularly impressed by the role of youth in the history of freedom movements, especially the example of Mazzini's

---

[36] "Proscribed Publications," *The Tribune*, June 7, 1910; "Burma News. Proscription of Publications," *The Leader*, May 10, 1910; "Seditious Publications. Forfeiture Notified in Burma," *Amrita Bazar Patrika*, May 9, 1910.

[37] See Bayly and Biagini, eds, *Giuseppe Mazzini and the Globalization of Democratic Nationalism*. Also, Flora, "The Changing Perception of Mazzini"; Fasana, "*Deshbhakta*."

[38] For example, "Letters on the State and Prospects of Italy," was one of the earliest discussions of Mazzini in *The Times of India* on August 17, 1839.

[39] Banerjea, "Joseph Mazzini," in *Speeches and Writings*, 391–416.

Young Italy, and celebrated Mazzini's "doctrine of self-reliance."[40] Banerjea had travelled to London in 1875 in an effort to petition the British government to restore his position in the Indian Civil Service after he had been wrongfully disqualified from taking up his job. His efforts had failed to convince the officials. Upon his return to India he was appointed professor at the Metropolitan Institution in Calcutta and began working closely with students in Bengal. The point was to take Mazzini's Young Italy as an inspiration to politicise India's youth, while also spreading Mazzini's message of "unification" as necessary for bringing Indians together.[41] Banerjea embarked on a lecture tour in which he spoke about the importance and relevance of Mazzini's work.

Between roughly 1880 and 1910 Mazzini's *The Duties of Man* was translated into several languages in India.[42] Biographies of Mazzini were also published in vernacular languages in this period, as were books on Mazzini's collaborator Giuseppe Garibaldi. As Mazzini's popularity grew, he was soon described as a "great figure" and "mahatma."[43] Newspapers not only published selections of Mazzini's writings, including his poetry, but also debated the importance of his life and writings for the Indian public. This is not to suggest that the reception of Mazzini was necessarily favourable, let alone consistent – there was disagreement over how to interpret his ideas. What complicated matters for those who were interested in Mazzini was the fact that British officials started banning vernacular writings about the Italian revolutionary as well as translations of his work. Newspaper editors were arrested and prosecuted for publishing Mazzini's writings that were seen as advocating violence against the government.[44]

---

[40] Ibid., 414.

[41] Banerjea, *A Nation in the Making*, 41–3.

[42] Smith, *Mazzini*, 219; also, see Srivastava, *Mazzini*.

[43] Gita Srivastava points out that Lajpat Rai was the first to refer to Mazzini as "Mahatma Mazzini." Srivastava, *Mazzini*, 16. Also, see Gokulji, *Mahatma Mazzini*. Gwilym O. Griffith later added, "Mazzini was in a sense the Mahatma of nineteenth-century Europe": Griffith, *Mazzini*, 12.

[44] "'Vihari' Sedition Case. Editor Sentenced," *The Times of India*, June 24, 1908. Also see Tilak's testimony on Savarkar's book: *Legal Proceedings in the Case of Tilak v. Chirol and Another, vols 1–2*; and Srivastava, "Historical Biographies of Italian Nationalist Leaders," 332.

Individuals committed to Mazzini's thought continued to celebrate his ideas – including in English – though some resorted to writing about him anonymously.

In India Mazzini's writings were interpreted by a number of individuals from diverse political backgrounds. For some intellectuals Mazzini's appeal was that there were parallels between the Italian anti-colonial movements against the Austro-Hungarian Empire of the late-1840s on the one hand, and on the other the rebellions against British rule in India in the late-1850s.[45] Similarities were seen, and what was inspiring was that the Italian movement had succeeded. Yet some Indian Moderates read Mazzini as a moderate, while Indian revolutionaries saw Mazzini's revolutionary potential.[46] In 1918, over three decades after he started advocating Mazzini's thought, Banerjea, in a speech delivered to the "All India Moderate Conference," argued that there was a proliferation of Mazzini's ideas that led to the creation of many "Indian Mazzinis."[47] Intellectuals interested in the convergence of religion and politics were attracted to the Italian's arguments about the conceptual nexus of the two. Others were attracted to Mazzini's description of secret societies and guerrilla tactics as justification for ethical violence. Still others emphasised his Republican ideas of democracy and national unification. On the other hand, many sympathetic to Mazzini also diverged from some of his ideas. Mazzini had supported the idea of universal franchise, but Banerjea opposed it on the grounds that the masses had often threatened "turbulence" and "tyranny."[48] Another instance of divergence is M.K. Gandhi, who wrote an essay in 1905, titled "Joseph Mazzini: A Remarkable Career," in which he argued that Mazzini proposed a "non-violent form of democratic nationalism"; this combined Mazzini's arguments about duty and self-rule with Gandhi's own conceptualisation of *swaraj* (self-rule).[49] It has been pointed out that the publication of this essay corresponded with the centenary celebrations of Mazzini's birth and emphasised the religious and spiritual

[45] Bayly, "Mazzini and Nineteenth-Century Indian Thought," 358.

[46] Ibid.

[47] "Presidential Address. Men of Yesterday," *The Times of India*, November 2, 1918.

[48] De Donno, "The Gandhian Mazzini," 376.

[49] Gandhi, "Joseph Mazzini," 366–7.

ideas in Mazzini's writings that were useful for Indians to consider. Gandhi's interpretation of Mazzini was a radical departure from all contemporary analyses of Mazzini's thought in moving away from the centrality of violence as a necessary condition for freedom, thereby promoting the idea of "the Gandhian Mazzini."[50]

Savarkar's analysis of the literature on Mazzini emphasised the importance of two thinkers, Banerjea and Bipin Chandra Pal: "After the unsuccessful war of 1857–59, there was a period of lull in Indian politics. But the next generation of English educated Indians like Surendranath Banerjea had taken inspiration from Mazzini's biography."[51] Banerjea became a figure of much discussion among Indian nationalists in the late-nineteenth century, being viewed as a victim of discrimination by British authorities, who had failed him in his examination for the Indian Civil Service due to a technicality despite the fact that he had excelled in the entrance exams. "Surendranath was forced to resign," says Savarkar, "and then decided to devote his life for the service of India."[52] Banerjea was an important figure for Savarkar not only because of his commitment to the Indian nation but also because he was "deeply impressed" by Mazzini: "During 1875 to 1878, [Banerjea] delivered public speeches on the subject [of] Mazzini and his secret society . . . Surendranath inspired hundreds of Bengali youth in their twenties and thirties."[53] As evidence of Banerjea's success, Savarkar cites the example of Bipin Chandra Pal, who heard Banerjea's speeches when he was young and became a nationalist. Savarkar quotes Pal's autobiography as evidence of this influence: "I was inspired by Surendranath's speeches on Mazzini and was determined to take part in political movements to achieve our freedom."[54]

Pal emerged as a major nationalist in his own right in this period. Like Savarkar, he was the recipient of one of Krishnavarma's scholarships in London.[55] He wrote extensively about Banerjea's work among Bengal's students, noting that Banerjea was able to spread "patriotic

[50] See De Donno, "The Gandhian Mazzini."

[51] Savarkar, *Inside the Enemy Camp*, 65; Savarkar, *Shatruchya Shibirata,* 133.

[52] Savarkar, *Inside the Enemy Camp*, 65; Savarkar, *Shatruchya Shibirata,* 133.

[53] Savarkar, *Inside the Enemy Camp*, 65; Savarkar, *Shatruchya Shibirata,* 133.

[54] Savarkar, *Inside the Enemy Camp*, 66; Savarkar, *Shatruchya Shibirata,* 135.

[55] BL, APAC, India HD Pol Proceedings, B Series, IOR.POS.8963, *Berar*

fervour" as one of the "most powerful orators of his generation."[56] He says "the greatest and most inspiring message of Surendra Nath's early propaganda was delivered through his lectures on Joseph Mazzini and the Young Italy movement organised by him."[57] Pal explained that the result was that he and other students started to read Mazzini's writings and study the history of Italian nationalism, especially the role of Young Italy in the struggle against the Austro-Hungarian empire.[58] Pal emerged as a revolutionary and was a major figure in the 1905 Swadeshi movement; he was responsible for influencing the direction of nationalist politics at the start of the century, along with his collaborators Lajpat Rai and Bal Gangadhar Tilak.

Interestingly, the primary Indian interpreters of Mazzini's writings were all present in London at the same time. In fact, Banerjea, Pal, and Savarkar were in a meeting together following the assassination of a colonial soldier-official, Curzon Wyllie, by an India House student, Madan Lal Dhingra, in July 1909. Gandhi, who had penned two essays on Mazzini, was also in London shortly after this point, as was Lajpat Rai, who provided the most comprehensive reception of Mazzini's life and work in India by writing a biography of Mazzini and translating his *The Duties of Man* into Urdu.[59] While there has been growing scholarly interest in the London intellectual milieu within which Indian intellectuals were discussing and debating the meaning of the Ramayana and the Bhagavad Gita, there is little on the place of Mazzini's writings as part of these conversations.[60]

---

*Samachar,* July 26, 1909, in *Report on Native Newspapers Published in the Central Provinces and Berar for the Week Ending 31ˢᵗ July 1909.*

[56] Pal, *Memories of My Life and Times,* 243.

[57] Ibid., 245.

[58] Ibid., 246. Also, Das Gupta, "Mazzini and Indian Nationalism," 68.

[59] Lajpat Rai's *Giuseppe Mazzini* (Lahore, 1896) was one of five biographies he wrote for the "Great Men of India Series." The English translation of the book is published in Nanda, ed., *The Collected Works of Lala Lajpat Rai, vol. 1,* 283–310.

[60] Savarkar, Rai, and Pal also attended a meeting in London in October 1908 to discuss the condition of Indians in South Africa. See "The Caxton Hall Meeting. Indignation Against the Transvaal," *Indian Opinion,* November 21, 1908. Another meeting with the three was held to celebrate Guru Gobind

Savarkar provided an extended discussion of Mazzini's reception in Bengal. His treatment of Banerjea was tempered, however, as he claimed that Banerjea wanted his supporters to "avoid the revolutionary methods of Mazzini," in favour of "legal, constitutional and absolutely peaceful" means.[61] Savarkar was disappointed that Banerjea was not interested in revolutionary tactics or "secret assassinations" for achieving independence. Moreover, he wanted to follow an alternative strategy to the one espoused by Banerjea, who delivered many lectures in which he argued that while an armed revolution was effective in Italy's struggle against the Austro-Hungarian empire, it would have detrimental consequences for India. Banerjea did not write a book; that goal was Savarkar's. What Savarkar did see was the importance of Banerjea's commitment to Mazzini, which seemed to Savarkar connected to the foundation Banerjea laid for Bengal's revolutionary movement in later decades.

According to Savarkar, Mazzini's reception in Maharashtra was possible because it was where "the revolutionary spirit was ever present since 1857."[62] Further, he says the "Anti-British revolutionary movement was already deeply rooted. Those feelings were not to be imported from outside."[63] So, Mazzini was important in Maharashtra, but the revolutionary movement existed *before* any formal publication of texts about Mazzini in Marathi. This was an important distinction for Savarkar: "As far as I can remember, the first biography of Mazzini was written by one Mr. Ghanekar in 1900. Mr. S.M. Paranjape in his paper [*Kaal*] also wrote histories of various freedom movements in modern Europe . . . [including] an article about the Young Italy

---

Singh in December 1908 at Caxton Hall: BL, APAC, L/P&J/6/1058, File 284, Testimony of Harishchandra Krishna Kergaumkar, date not given. (I have maintained the spelling "Kergaumkar" as it appears in the court document, but it is also spelt "Koregaonkar" in the Weekly Report of the Director of Criminal Intelligence, July 31, 1909, BL, APAC, India HD Pol Proceedings, B Series, IOR.POS.8962.)

[61] Savarkar, *Inside the Enemy Camp*, 66; Savarkar, *Shatruchya Shibirata*, 134.

[62] Savarkar, *Inside the Enemy Camp*, 66; Savarkar, *Shatruchya Shibirata*, 136–7.

[63] Savarkar, *Inside the Enemy Camp*, 66; Savarkar, *Shatruchya Shibirata*, 136–7.

movement of Mazzini."[64] He explained that in reading these works he saw historical parallels between India and Italy. Inspired by the connections and potential to expand a revolutionary base, Savarkar began delivering lectures on the importance of Mazzini's ideas and methods. By 1906 he was committed to not only translating Mazzini's writings into Marathi, but also to writing an introduction analysing the revolutionary potential of Mazzini in the twentieth century. His focus in Mazzini's writings was on the centrality of the principles of revolution that would have universal appeal for the Marathi reader in India. As a result he selected specific texts within Mazzini's corpus that allowed him to draw historical parallels between Italy and India, but also to argue the universality of the principles. Savarkar noted that he was not interested in history only as narratives of the past; his purpose was to write about historical figures whose political actions reflected revolutionary principles: "After all I wanted [the] people of Maharashtra to study and follow the revolutionary path of Mazzini. That was the purpose of my book."[65]

## 3.  Interpreting Mazzini for Maharashtra

On September 28, 1906 Savarkar finished his translation. The process had taken him about ten weeks.[66] However, Savarkar's book was not a complete translation of the six-volume edition of Mazzini's Collected Works in English: *Life and Writings of Joseph Mazzini*. (It is likely that Savarkar relied upon the 1890s edition of Mazzini's writings.) Instead, he translated most of the first volume and selections from other volumes.[67] In addition, he wrote an introduction to the book in which

---

[64] Savarkar, *Inside the Enemy Camp*, 67; Savarkar, *Shatruchya Shibirata*, 137.

[65] Savarkar, *Inside the Enemy Camp*, 68; Savarkar, *Shatruchya Shibirata*, 138.

[66] Savarkar, *Inside the Enemy Camp*, 68; Savarkar, *Shatruchya Shibirata*, 138.

[67] Savarkar translated most of *Life and Writings of Joseph Mazzini*, vol. 1, which consisted of eighteen separate essays. However, in the Marathi original (and the official Hindi translation), not all the essays that were translated were actually included in the table of contents. Only the following titles were listed: "Autobiographical Notes" (1861); "General Instructions for the Members of Young Italy" (1831); "Manifesto of Young Italy" (1831); "Appendix – Rules for the Conduct of Guerrilla Bands." Savarkar also translated two essays from

he explained that he chose to translate fragments of selected essays in one volume to provide a general introduction to Mazzini's life, strategies, and political thought in the hope readers would be inspired in their own lives – as he himself had been.[68] He acknowledged that such a strategy was likely to make it difficult for readers to fully interpret Mazzini's thought. However, he added that the introduction was meant to provide a foundation for Mazzini's teachings which would make it easier for readers to interpret his ideas; and that throughout the text he had cited Mazzini's own words to help clarify specific concepts relevant for the Indian reader.

Savarkar says he has been careful to write his book in a way which would avoid legal trouble with the British authorities. Its purpose was to share the revolutionary potential of Mazzini's arguments with the Marathi reader. Being aware that writing a book or translating articles that promoted revolutionary violence could be interpreted as a criminal act, he states: "I had taken extreme care not to be caught in any Law in India. I simply translated Mazzini's [auto]biography and his thoughts. Nowhere did I preach rebellion against the British Rule in India. There was no mention of enslavement of India at all."[69] The point about enslavement is not in fact correct, for Savarkar discussed the topic of slavery in his introductory essay. And Savarkar also appears to contradict himself in a later analysis of the text when he argues that the purpose of the book was to inspire revolution:

> My book was not just worth reading as History, or just a readable work. I wanted to emphasise that people should follow Mazzini's example. Otherwise ordinary people would not have got the message. I therefore decided to add a preface to show parallels between Italy and India, add some suggestive lines that the readers would be thrilled and inspired to carry out armed revolution in India also.[70]

---

vol. 3: "Persecution of Exiles" (1834), and "Records of the Brothers Bandiera and Their Fellow-Martyrs at Cosenza" (1844); and one essay from vol. 6, "On the 'Theory of the Dagger'."

[68] I have consulted Savarkar, *Joseph Mazzini*, in *Samagra Savarkar, vol. 8* (1993); Savarkar, *Mazzini Charitra*, in *Savarkar Samagra, vol. 8* (2003). I have relied on Prakash, trans., "Preface," *Mazzini Charitra*, for direct quotes in this part.

[69] Savarkar, *Inside the Enemy Camp*, 74; Savarkar, *Shatruchya Shibirata*, 145.

[70] Savarkar, *Inside the Enemy Camp*, 68; Savarkar, *Shatruchya Shibirata*, 140.

The manuscript, he says, was sent to India from London in December 1906, and the book was published in June 1907, with a first print run of 2000 copies, followed by a second printing a month later.[71] According to Savarkar the book quickly circulated, while summaries of its arguments about the importance of reading Mazzini's ideas were published in Marathi newspapers, such as *Vihari*, *Kesari*, and *Kaal*.[72] The authorities soon became aware of the text, especially as a review of Savarkar's book, published in *Vihari* on June 17, 1907, was translated into English by the Home Department in the Bombay Presidency. The review states that "The study of Mazzini's autobiography is useful to those who are anxious to regain their independence and to be rid of foreign rule."[73] The reviewer encourages parents to share the book and its ideas with their children to inculcate in them a spirit of patriotism and introduce them to armed resistance and political agitation. A plan to translate the book into Gujarati and Hindi is also outlined in the review, but it never came to fruition as the government immediately proscribed the book. Select copies were apparently confiscated by the authorities, but the ideas presented in it continued to circulate. Savarkar says the underground network of the Abhinav Bharat Society was responsible for circulating the text and its ideas throughout the country; he cites examples of the book appearing in Gwalior in central India, and Marathawada in eastern Maharashtra.

Savarkar's introduction begins with a provocative statement: "Theorems of the shastras (*shastrachi prameya*) are not bound by the time of the nation (*deshkaal*)."[74] These theorems he believes are important for *all* individuals to understand as they transcend time and space. Their applicability is neither limited by specific years nor centuries, nor are

[71] Savarkar, *Inside the Enemy Camp*, 69; Savarkar, *Shatruchya Shibirata*, 143.

[72] "Italian Deshbhakta Mazzini," *Kesari*, July 23, 1907; "Reviews and Notices," *Mahratta*, December 23, 1923.

[73] "Review of a Marathi translation of the 'Autobiography of Joseph Mazzini'," in *Vihari* (June 17, 1907), *Report on Native Papers Published in the Bombay Presidency for the Week Ending 22nd June 1907*, 22.

[74] Savarkar, *Joseph Mazzini* (1993), 24. The difficulty here is translating the meaning of *shastras* in this context, which can be defined as a scriptural text, teaching, or a science. The Hindi translation *Mazzini Charitra*, 25, *vigyaan* replaces *shastra* in the sentence to emphasise "scientific theorem" in this context.

they specific to one nation or land. Rather what these theorems demonstrate is their universality for humankind.

Implicit in this framing is the idea that the time of the nation is specific to only *that* nation. This then meant that one *deshkaal* was not necessarily the same as another *deshkaal*. In other words, there were multiple *deshkaals* that functioned at any one time: a plurality of nations meant a plurality of *deshkaals*. At another level, Savarkar is also suggesting that any given *deshkaal* is different from every other time. There may be lands, spaces, territories (that are not nations) that function in an alternative time not defined by *deshkaal*, especially a time not associated with a given nation. Not only did *deshkaal* have the characteristic of finitude – it was bounded, not limitless – but there is also a measure of time beyond the time of the nation. Although Savarkar begins with a discussion of *deshkaal* in this text, his primary interest is to underscore the importance of the applicability of generalised laws that can be theorised to discuss global universalities. (He returned to the importance of understanding temporalities in his later writings on Hindutva, but he introduced some key ideas here.) Savarkar explains that the specific purpose in his introduction was to build upon scientific forms of knowledge that were based on "detailed experiments" and "discoveries" that could claim "universally proven and accepted principles (*tattva*)."[75] For him these principles were important for the study of politics and political science.

Savarkar argued that Mazzini's writings provided "universally accepted principles" for the study of politics that were "true" for all places across all time periods. He further claimed that philosophers who studied politics historically understood the importance of the "experiences accumulated in the past" as a way to argue for interpreting politics as a science with "universal principles."[76] He believed "This fact holds as true for astronomy, chemistry, and geography, as it does for political science."[77] Like other sciences, political science has assumed the status of a seminal truth unbounded by nation-time. Savarkar further posited that by the start of the twentieth century it was possible to argue that

---

[75] Savarkar, *Mazzini Charitra*, 25; and Savarkar, *Joseph Mazzini*, 24.

[76] Ibid.

[77] Ibid.

the claims made by Mazzini could be considered a scientific theorem: Mazzini's statements had been proven to be true, meaning that they were true for all contexts. In other words, in Savarkar's view Mazzini's arguments about politics were not historically specific to Italy in the nineteenth century: other nations, such as India, could learn from the example set by Italian independence from the Austro-Hungarian empire. For Savarkar, these principles also formed the basis for his understanding of "a history in full."

He says the key argument in Mazzini's work was that "politics is a God-ordained duty."[78] For Savarkar it was important to highlight Mazzini's claim that there was no "antagonism between politics and religion."[79] This was a necessary intervention, according to Savarkar, as Mazzini helped to redefine the meaning of politics in the nineteenth century by arguing that the foundation for all revolutions were "principles." Needless to say, his interpretation of Mazzini's arguments about politics – and by extension political thought – was specifically about the history of revolutions. In other words, the claim that "politics is a God-ordained duty" could also be read as revolution is a God-ordained duty. It was a shift in the study of politics away from claims that politics was based on "selfishness" and "guided by the lathi."[80] It was also a departure from defining politics as the invasion and enslavement of nations. In Savarkar's view Mazzini's example of studying the principles of a revolution provided a moral centre for the interpretation of politics: the Italian revolution was not only virtuous, it was also founded on important principles. As a result, Savarkar argued that Italy's revolution was a "holy war of independence."[81]

Savarkar was most impressed with Mazzini's example of making a revolution by adhering to ethics, morality, and the sanctity of religion.

[78] Savarkar, *Mazzini Charitra*, 28; and Savarkar, *Joseph Mazzini*, 27.

[79] Savarkar, *Mazzini Charitra*, 29; and Savarkar, *Joseph Mazzini*, 28.

[80] Savarkar, *Mazzini Charitra*, 28; and Savarkar, *Joseph Mazzini*, 27. For a parallel discussion of the use of the stick (*danda*) as a form of extra-economic coercion, see Guha, *Dominance Without Hegemony*. Savarkar further developed the idea of using the *lathi* to defend Hinduism later in his career. See MSA, HD Spec File 60-I-1933, "Home Department Note," October 28, 1924, S-137-138. (The initials of the author are unclear.)

[81] Whereas Mazzini often used "sacred war" and "sacred fight" in his writings, Savarkar translated "holy war of independence" as *pavitra swatantryayuddha*

He celebrated Mazzini's claim that religion and politics were synonymous. This point was extremely relevant for Savarkar, especially later in his career, when British officials restricted his political activities but allowed him to participate in religious ones. He cited Mazzini to underscore that "There is religion in politics and there is politics in religion."[82] Savarkar was also convinced by Mazzini's claim that a political intervention in religion was essential. It was not enough to understand the centrality of religion in politics, especially when interpreting revolutions; it was also necessary to consider the place of politics in religion. Moreover, it was a religious duty to establish politics in religion.

Mazzini's interpretation of politics was transformative for Savarkar. He argued that Mazzini's move away from viewing politics as a form of "self-seeking behaviour" provided an opportunity to rethink the centrality of religion. He interpreted Mazzini as saying, "The intervention of politics in religion is necessary. In fact, to do so is a religious duty."[83] In fact he also found Mazzini compelling on the issue of compassion for other humans, especially those who were enslaved. He pointed to Mazzini's claim that one's own self-liberation was only possible by liberating others from slavery, especially individuals living in a politically enslaved nation. In other words, the liberation of the self was directly connected not only to compassion for the enslaved but also to their liberation from slavery. This was a God-ordained duty in which every individual would be judged by God. Savarkar underscored the point that heaven was only open to individuals who had paid their debt to the nation of their birth. He built upon Mazzini's argument about slavery by positing that politics was *the* means for redemption of a society or nation from slavery. In fact he claimed that it was a religious duty to intervene politically in order to ensure the liberation of all individuals from enslavement: "Till the time a man is kept imprisoned, it is impossible for him to progress . . . and it is impossible to secure any sort of help for the progress of humankind from a political[ly] enslaved nation."[84] He adds that "To ignore this

---

in Savarkar, *Joseph Mazzini*, 26. For comparison, the Hindi translation in Savarkar, *Mazzini Charitra*, 27, is *pavitra swatantrata sangrama*.

[82] Savarkar, *Mazzini Charitra*, 30; and Savarkar, *Joseph Mazzini*, 28.

[83] Savarkar, *Mazzini Charitra*, 28; and Savarkar, *Joseph Mazzini*, 27.

[84] Ibid.

duty and to silently watch human species endure through miseries unleashed on it is an unforgiveable sin."

Savarkar did not discuss the processes of how an individual or a nation became enslaved. His focus in the introduction is to explain the necessity of ending slavery as an act of religious and political duty. Throughout his introduction he provided interpretations of Mazzini's arguments about humanism by referring to slavery. Implicit in Savarkar's argument was that the process of becoming enslaved was a long one, as individuals had forgotten the centrality of politics and religion. Slavery in this context was not about the historical practices of bonded labour (although it did not exclude it); instead, it was in reference to the individuals or peoples who lacked consciousness of their own subjugation within an empire. However, individuals who refused to reject their circumstances even after becoming conscious of their own enslavement were not worthy of being interpreted as human: "A person who refuses to budge in slavery cannot be considered a human. He is a lifeless and worthless lump of clay."[85] What Mazzini offered was a reminder of the importance of the duties expected of each individual to not only end slavery, but also to achieve the betterment of each individual self *and* the nation. He had pointed out the existence of select individuals conscious of the need to end enslavement across the globe. The first task for Mazzini was to attain "self-rule for one's own country," followed by ending slavery for the human race; these human duties were both political and religious: "Politics means securing the redemption of our society, country and nation from slavery and setting them upon a path of improvement."[86] Only through a revolution would the bonds of slavery be broken.

## 4. From *Principio* to *Tattva*

It is worth considering the significance of the word "principle," especially as Savarkar used it in his writings to conceptualise a history in full, but also because it is found throughout all the volumes of Mazzini's *Life and Writings*. In Mazzini's English-language publications,

---

[85] Savarkar, *Mazzini Charitra*, 30; and Savarkar, *Joseph Mazzini*, 29.
[86] Savarkar, *Mazzini Charitra*, 28; and Savarkar, *Joseph Mazzini*, 27.

"principle" is generally the translation of *principio* in Italian. When "principle" appears in Mazzini's translated texts, it generally corresponds with the normative English definitions of the word: namely, a comprehensive and fundamental law, doctrine, or assumption.[87] There are select places in the English translation in which the word is capitalised as "Principle" to emphasise the importance of the concept in the specific context. This is perhaps best exemplified in *The Duties of Man*, Mazzini's best-known text in India – and the most frequently translated into vernacular languages such as Urdu, Hindi, Marathi, and Tamil – which begins:

> To you, sons and daughters of the people, I dedicate this book. In it I have traced for you the *Principles*, in the same name and by the aid of which, you may, if you will, fulfil your mission in Italy; a mission of Republican Progress for all your Countrymen, and of emancipation for yourselves. Let those among you whom favourable circumstances or superior ability have rendered more capable of penetrating the deep meaning of these *Principles*, explain them to the others in the same loving spirit in which I thought, while writing of your sufferings . . .[88]

One of the purposes of his book, he said, was to outline and trace the principles for "improvement" and "self-sacrifice" as a way of "uniting mankind" for the purpose of liberating enslaved Italians from their oppressor. He provided numerous examples to illustrate the importance of principles that would guide readers of his text in their lives, underscoring the centrality of what he called the "Principle of Duty:"

> We must convince men that they are all sons of one sole God, and bound to fulfil and execute one sole law here on earth: – that each of them is bound to live, not for himself, but for others: – that the aim of existence is not to be more or less happy, but to make themselves and others more virtuous: – that to struggle against injustice and error, wherever they exist,

---

[87] I owe special thanks to Vinita Chaturvedi for her discussion and translation of the meaning of *principio* from the Italian: that is, an idea indigenous or native to criteria from which is derived a system of ideas, or upon which are based the elements of speculation, vital or fundamental. I also appreciate her translation of a selection of Mazzini's *Dei doveri dell'uomo*. (Emphasis added.)

[88] Mazzini, "Preface to the Italian Working Class," in idem, *The Duties of Man*, ix.

in the name and for the benefit of their brothers, is not only a *right*, but a Duty: – a duty which may not be neglected without sin: – the duty of their whole life.[89]

This "principle of duty" was conceptualised as part of a commitment to religion – in his case Christianity – but also provided a political foundation for what he called the "struggle against injustice." A "republican progress" for the people of Italy was part of Mazzini's framing, as was the centrality of revolution for Italy's independence, unification, and republicanism in the form of a radical democracy.

Savarkar interpreted Mazzini's arguments as directly addressing the concerns facing colonial India because they provided "universally accepted principles."[90] In Savarkar's translation of Mazzini's "principle," he chose two separate but related terms: *tattva* and *siddhanth*. Looking at the Marathi text, or the official Hindi translation, it is clear that there were conceptual challenges to the translation of Mazzini's work on this point. Savarkar made a distinction – which is not reflected in the English-language versions of Mazzini's work – between *siddhanth* and *tattva*. He certainly used the word *siddhanth* (principle) in his translation of *Life and Writings*, but it does not appear with frequency or uniformity in the original text, or its cognate translations. Instead, Savarkar tended to use *tattva* (essence, element, essential) with greater frequency throughout, but especially in his later writings. This is not to say that *tattva* cannot be translated as "principle," as it is throughout Savarkar's writings, but that this is also not the primary meaning of *tattva*. In other words, Savarkar's interpretation of principle functioned between *tattva* and *siddhanth*: in specific places "principle" exists in the vernacular works as essence, element, or essential, while in others it is principle.

When these works were translated into English, *tattva* was generally identified as principle. In other works, principle was predominantly translated as *tattva*. Savarkar complicated these interpretations by arguing that the principles of a revolution were defined by "the essence of a revolution."[91] Was Savarkar saying thereby that the *siddhanth*

---

[89] Ibid., 19.

[90] Savarkar, *Mazzini Charitra*, 25; and Savarkar, *Joseph Mazzini*, 24.

[91] Savarkar, *Indian War*, 3.

(principle) of a revolution was defined by the *tattva* (essence) of a revolution? Or was he saying that the *tattva* of a revolution was defined by the *tattva* of a revolution – i.e. was there a *tattva* of *tattva*, or an essence of the essence? No satisfactory answers to these questions are available in Savarkar's writings. He seems to assume his reader will decipher the links between the essence of a revolution and the principles of a revolution. By adding these distinctions in his translation of Mazzini's writings, he also added complexity to the understanding of "principle" in all his later writings. The meaning of *tattva* also changed, as it was now understood by Marathi and Hindi readers as a universal category promoted by Mazzini – albeit as mediated by Savarkar.

## 5. From Duty to Dharma

Savarkar provided an introduction to the history of Italy in the nineteenth century. His purpose he says was to answer a key question for the Marathi reader: "What is the path to fulfilling our duty for achieving political independence?"[92] He outlines the general condition of Italy as a slave market under the sovereignty of Austria. Places like Venice and Milan, once considered prosperous, were now destitute and Rome was "dead." Education and commerce were controlled by the Austrian empire, Italians had lost their freedom, and "the name of 'Italy' was wiped off the map."[93] For all purposes, Italy was a "horrific jail" with Austrian soldiers serving as guards: "All is quiet in Italy today, but this is not the silence of living beings. This is the silence of death. How does one salvage national pride from such humiliating plight? How to achieve independence again?"[94]

For Savarkar the task was to write a history that would provide an "extraordinary analogy" for interpreting India's history, and which would simultaneously show "universally accepted principles" – i.e. the universal relevance of the struggle for Italian freedom wherein the people of Italy had experienced a "new awakening" that marked the start of their national independence movement.

[92] Savarkar, *Mazzini Charitra*, 31; and Savarkar, *Joseph Mazzini*, 30.
[93] Savarkar, *Mazzini Charitra*, 32; and Savarkar *Joseph Mazzini*, 30.
[94] Savarkar, *Mazzini Charitra*, 32; and Savarkar *Joseph Mazzini*, 30.

The challenge of interpreting Savarkar's text is the difficulty of disentangling his own interpretation of Mazzini's writings with Mazzini's interpretations of Italian history. There are no citations or references, with the result that the vernacular translation blends the translation of Mazzini's interpretations with Savarkar's writing on the subject. This is not to suggest that Savarkar simply translated Mazzini's writings without a critical interpretation or reclassification of categories important to his Marathi readers; in fact his analysis of the first stage in the struggle for independence in Italy is classified as a "Swadeshi movement."[95]

Savarkar points out that Italy's awakening was marked by boycotts of foreign industries and goods, such as clothing, tobacco, and tea. All "Swadeshi movements" had the dual purpose of protecting the rights of protesters and limiting the oppressor's tactics to control the economy and society. "Swadeshi" is of course not a category in Mazzini's writings, it was inserted by Savarkar in his analysis of the Italian boycotts. For the Marathi reader Savarkar's history by analogy was a likely reminder of the countrywide protests and boycotts against British clothing and goods in 1905 over the Swadeshi movement. The use of the same terminology was a discursive strategy to signal the common ground in histories of India and Italy and nations generally, including the United States.

For all the similarities he saw across national boycotts, Savarkar found Swadeshi movements structurally limited in creating social transformation because those in power often reacted by persecuting protesters through increased violence:

> It began to dawn upon them that it is futile to boycott lifeless objects. What is the point in taking out one's anger over lifeless things? The ones really deserving our wrath are the people who make use of these lifeless objects to advance their interests. Austrian people, not Austrian tea, and the English people, not the English tea must be driven out of this country. This thought transformed the Swadeshi movements waged by American and Italian peoples into wars of national independence.[96]

Savarkar attributed the transformation to a growing frustration among Italians against Austrians, leading to widespread public discontent

[95] Savarkar, Mazzini Charitra, 32–3; and Savarkar *Joseph Mazzini*, 30.
[96] Savarkar, *Mazzini Charitra*, 33; and Savarkar *Joseph Mazzini*, 32.

in which individuals and groups discussed the idea of "Italian independence" and the need for a "war of independence." In this context, Savarkar explained, Mazzini had worked to end foreign rule through a number of tactics and strategies. His goal was not simply removing all Austrians from Italy, but rather creating an epistemic rupture in society. Italy's youth had to be worked on, for their "minds were not shackled by older thoughts, whose souls have not been afflicted by the communicable disease of slavery."[97] Mazzini's focus on alerting the young was important so that "Italy could smash foreign rule," but also to inculcate the idea of the "love of self-rule" and "love of one's country" as a way to prepare them for war.[98] To "transform the Italians' minds" was the best path to a war of independence.

Savarkar's introduction also explores Mazzini's ideas about the place of morality in politics as a way of achieving independence. There is no full description of Mazzini's political life, nor a comprehensive exploration of his thought. In fact, the introduction does not even discuss the contents of the essays in the translated volume. Savarkar offers a general overview of Mazzini's thought to establish a connection with local context in the Marathi reader. At another level, the process of establishing connections with Mazzini's politics provided a rationale for Savarkar's own activities: the convergence between Mazzini's conceptualisations and political praxis provided a template for Savarkar. Mazzini's formation of Young Italy inspired Savarkar to form the Abhinav Bharat Society, and also to take up Mazzini's argument that Italy's independence and unification were a direct result of the contributions of Young Italy. He was particularly interested in Mazzini's description of the strategies necessary for Italian independence: "I am preparing a two-pronged plan to secure the help of Young Italy. Education and war training would support the war, and the war would support education."[99] From Mazzini it was possible to learn that Young Italy functioned like a secret society in the struggle against foreign rule, educating youth primarily about the four stages of independence: freedom, equality, national unification, and rule by the people. A second duty was to prepare the young for a holy war, using guerrilla

---

[97] Savarkar, *Mazzini Charitra*, 34; and Savarkar *Joseph Mazzini*, 32.

[98] Savarkar, *Mazzini Charitra*, 34; and Savarkar *Joseph Mazzini*, 33.

[99] Savarkar, *Mazzini Charitra*, 36; and Savarkar *Joseph Mazzini*, 34–5.

tactics when necessary. The goal was not simply to win independence, it was to stay united *after* the war with the aim of achieving "people's rule" as a republican form of government.[100]

While Savarkar provided a rationale for translating Mazzini's book, he did not offer an explanation for the specific texts that he translated from the six volumes of *Life and Writings*. The only essay Savarkar specifically discussed in the introduction was *The Duties of Man*:

> Mazzini's speculation about duty is based on very noble principles, but I am only trying to present a part of his political thought . . . I intend to translate a superior and extremely interesting portion of Mazzini's essay *Duties of Man*. If I am successful in this endeavour then readers would get to read Mazzini's philosophy in his own words. It is enough to say here that according to Mazzini once a person recognises a task as his duty, he must fulfil it [at] all costs, regardless of the perils involved. Do your duty as a matter of duty.[101]

The task for an individual was not only to "recognise" his duty, but to complete his duty for its own sake.

Mazzini's conceptualisations of "sacred war," "self-improvement," and "self-liberation" as part of one's duty were analogous themes discussed by a number of nationalists in this period, albeit in relation to a different text: the Bhagavad Gita. Savarkar pointed out a similar parallel in the newspaper *Kaal*: "We believe that recitation of the Bhagavad Gita everyday gives us salvation. Mazzini's articles also have similar powers."[102] Gandhi too connected Mazzini's concept of duty with ideas found in the Gita, especially relating to *swaraj*. He saw parallels between his own thinking about *swaraj* and Mazzini's argument that "self-improvement" and "self-liberation" were central to any understanding of duty. Gandhi says in *Hind Swaraj*: "Mazzini has shown in his writings on the duty of man that every man must learn to rule himself."[103] It was also noted that emerging out of the writings of both Banerjea and Pal was the idea that the "Gita became the divine

---

[100] Savarkar, *Mazzini Charitra*, 39; and Savarkar *Joseph Mazzini*, 38.

[101] Savarkar, *Mazzini Charitra*, 30–1; and Savarkar *Joseph Mazzini*, 29.

[102] Savarkar, *In the Enemy Camp*, 70.

[103] Gandhi, *Hind Swaraj*, 73.

avatar of the *The Duties of Man*."[104] This was an important – and perhaps unexpected – convergence of texts for these thinkers, reflecting the emergence of a conceptual grammar for rethinking critiques of and strategies for opposing the British empire around the turn of the century.

More specifically, the two texts seemed linked: Mazzini's "principle of duty" connected with the Bhagavad Gita's central concern with duty in the form of dharma.[105] The affinity of Mazzini's "duties" with dharma is close enough for the two texts to seem to overlap and converge at many points. Savarkar however was careful not to equate Mazzini's idea of "duty" with dharma, and he translated duty as *kartavya*. Dharma, of course, means more than just duty (*kartavya*) in the context of the Bhagavad Gita. However, after completing the translation of the essays in the first volume of *Life and Writings* in his book, Savarkar cited verses from chapter 2, lines 33 and 37 of the Bhagavad Gita as a way to help interpret the history of Young Italy presented by Mazzini for readers in Marathi:

> Or suppose you will not engage in this lawful war:
> then you give up your Law and honour, and incur guilt [line 33]

> Holding alike happiness and unhappiness, gain and loss, victory and defeat, yoke yourself to the battle, and so do not incur evil [line 37][106]

Mazzini's argument that the "principle of duty" sanctioned individuals to fight in a "sacred war" certainly resonated with Savarkar for its obvious connections with the ultimate war described in the Bhagavad Gita. In his writings he frequently refers to revolutions as *pavitra sangrama* (holy wars). The earliest discussion of this distinction appeared in his writings on Mazzini because the Italian provided him an understanding of "sacred wars" as revolutions when they were fought for religion: "This is Mazzini's special contribution."[107] The ultimate

---

[104] Bayly, "India, the Bhagavad Gita and the World," 287.

[105] De Donno, "The Gandhian Mazzini," 383–4. Also, Ragni, "From 'The Duties of Man' to Dharma."

[106] Savarkar, *Mazzini Charitra*, 154; Savarkar, *Joseph Mazzini*, 148. For the translation of the verses from the Bhagavad Gita, I have relied on van Buitenen, *The Bhagavadgita*, 77.

[107] Savarkar, *Mazzini Charitra*, 29; Savarkar, *Joseph Mazzini*, 28.

expression of Mazzini's "principle of duty" was justifiable, necessary, and divinely sanctioned warfare to end oppression. Mazzini's writings were in this way an analogue of Krishna's dialogue with Arjuna in the Bhagavad Gita, in which Krishna not only sanctions Arjuna killing his cousins on the battlefield of Kurukshetra but states that Arjuna, and indeed all men, should follow their own duty without being attached to desires, pleasures, or thoughts of reward. An individual's actions – including killing in war – should be in the service of God (Krishna), a commitment to fulfilling one's own duty that will lead to self-improvement and self-rule.

The Bhagavad Gita was central to *all* of Savarkar's writings, but it is not a text that he wrote about extensively. He only made minor references to the Bhagavad Gita without providing direct interpretations of the text or its ideas. Unlike some of his contemporaries in the first half of the twentieth century – such as Gandhi, Bal Gangadhar Tilak, Lajpat Rai, or Aurobindo Ghose – he did not produce a systematic critique of the text.[108] Nor did he turn to the existing hermeneutical traditions to interpret the Bhagavad Gita, such as *bhasya* (commentary) or *tika* (criticism), which were distinct literary forms of engaging with the text that dated back at least a millennium.[109] Authors of *bhasya* and *tika* followed specific guidelines that were required within each literary form.[110] This not only helped to distinguish between formal commentary and criticism, it also established links with earlier authors and their writings on the Gita. Savarkar departed from these traditions of interpreting the Bhagavad Gita; instead, he adopted

[108] The historiography of the reception of the Bhagavad Gita in modern India has generally neglected to even consider Savarkar and his writings. In fact, it may appear that Savarkar really did not have much to contribute to the scholarship and debates on the Bhagavad Gita. There are, of course, important factors that help to explain the nature of the scholarship. Perhaps the main reason Savarkar is overlooked in this context is that he did not adopt the existing hermeneutical traditions to establish a critique of the text. While there is no systematic analysis of or engagement with Savarkar's interpretation of the Gita, some scholars have briefly mentioned the impact of the text on Savarkar. For example, see Minor, ed., *Modern Interpreters of the Bhagavad Gita*, 223; Keer, *Veer Savarkar*, 78, 458; Bhatt, *Hindu Nationalism*, 104.

[109] Tilak, *Srimad Bhagavadgita Rahasya, vol. 1*, 15–16.

[110] Ibid.

history as the main literary form for his engagement with the text and its principles. In his writings in London he continued to incorporate key concepts from the Bhagavad Gita – often concepts that had parallels with Mazzini's writings – for writing histories.

To what extent Savarkar was building upon the arguments of others when writing about the Bhagavad Gita in the late-nineteenth and early-twentieth centuries also remains unclear. However, it is likely that as early as 1902 Savarkar was familiar with Tilak's interpretations of the Gita, which were initially delivered as speeches in Nagpur before being published in regional newspapers in western India. Tilak had later completed his *Bhagavadgita Rahasya, or Karma-Yoga-Sastra* (1915), arguing that the Bhagavad Gita encouraged the discipline of action, or *karma yoga* (the subtitle of Tilak's book), rather than simply advocating renunciation or devotion, as had been suggested by other contemporary interpreters of the text. Further, Tilak claimed that it was the dharma or duty of individuals to take up forms of political action to defend the nation from oppression, exploitation, and injustice.[111] Many individuals, especially revolutionaries and extremists, were influenced by Tilak's interpretation and embraced the idea that Krishna's instructions to Arjuna to take up arms and fulfil his dharma as a *kshatriya* (warrior) was an ethical justification for violence against the British empire. Tilak had an impact on Savarkar's ideas, and the two appear to have similar interpretations of the Bhagavad Gita, even if Savarkar did not fully elaborate Tilak's influence on his writing. Instead, he dedicated his book on Mazzini to Tilak – perhaps confirming the convergence of ideas that influenced his thought.

## 6. Reading History and Political Action

Shortly after arriving in London, Savarkar founded a branch of the Abhinav Bharat Society after having read of Mazzini's secret society, Young Italy. He clearly saw a direct connection between Mazzini's writings about "principles" and people who took up arms in their name. But while Savarkar considered Mazzini seminal, he also says, "When

[111] Brown, "The Philosophy of Bal Gangadhar Tilak," 198.

I studied Mazzini's political thoughts, I also studied biographies of others and read extensively books on history of the Italian freedom struggle."[112] Garibaldi, Victor Emmanuel II, and Camillo Benso (Count Cavour) also provided him evidence of the need for Indians to study the parallels with Italian history. What is also important to consider is Savarkar's revelation – establishing a methodological framework not only for writing about Mazzini but also developing an intellectual strategy that combined reading biographies with works on political thought. It was not enough to identify the principles of a revolution, it was necessary to teach the principles and train the minds of youth in preparation for revolution: "The principles on which the foundations of this sacred war of independence were laid were first taught to Italy by Mazzini. Almost all Italian patriots fighting for independence had been trained by Mazzini's 'Young Italy'."[113] Savarkar clarified that when individuals took up arms and participated in acts of violence – often brutal violence – this was made possible by a commitment to principles that had a foundation in religion.

Savarkar was inspired by Mazzini's recruitment of Italian soldiers in the Austrian army to join the struggle for Italian freedom from imperial rule. He was also impressed by Mazzini's ability to bring together people from various principalities to work together against the oppression of "foreign rule." The fact that Young Italy was an underground organisation meant that it required a great deal of commitment from both organisers and participants, especially as government spies were working against resistance movements. Savarkar said he was aware of the dangers of his work with the Abhinav Bharat Society, but it did not stop him from applying Mazzini's principles to his own activities in London: "I was busy with writing my books. I was in search of bombs and other explosives and also arranging training for how to use them."[114] The challenge for him was figuring out a way of applying Mazzini's principles to a war of independence in India. He had expectations that with proper education, it would be possible for Indian

[112] Savarkar, *Inside the Enemy Camp*, 75; Savarkar, *Shatruchya Shibirata*, 155.

[113] Savarkar, *Mazzini Charitra*, 27; and Savarkar, *Joseph Mazzini*, 26.

[114] Savarkar, *Inside the Enemy Camp*, 76; Savarkar, *Shatruchya Shibirata*, 156–7.

soldiers in the British Indian Army to rebel against their British officers, following the example set by Mazzini in Italy: "The arms being borne by Indian soldiers under the British command are *our* arms. True, our Indian soldiers are illiterate, but they too must have some desire to make our country independent. Spread the fire of movement of freedom among them and see how the same soldiers turn against the English with the same arms and ammunitions."[115]

However, while in London, Savarkar's initial goals were modest. He turned his attention to holding weekly meetings with members of the Abhinav Bharat Society to "talk about Mazzini" and "discuss what we could do to free our country."[116] He also embarked on a study of the mutiny and rebellions in India in 1857. If Indian soldiers were going to rebel against the British, he needed to illustrate that this idea was not new: "I was firm on my stand and wanted to write a detailed, fully supported by evidence, and inspiring account of the 1857 war."[117] He began this research by reading the first volume of John William Kaye's *The History of the Indian Mutiny* (1890; six volumes), a book that was part of the India House Library collection. Upon finishing it, Savarkar requested Mr Mukherjee, the India House manager, to locate the remaining five volumes (which were co-authored by G.B. Malleson).

After reading all the volumes, Savarkar says he arrived at an entirely new interpretation of the events of 1857. For him, most Indians simply did not understand the significance of this movement of the people: Indians were ignorant of the details and they considered that the "rebellious Indian soldiers were brutes and a blot on our history, and a disgrace to our culture."[118] The information presented in the volumes by Kaye and Malleson were instructive as the authors provided extensive details about the revolts. Savarkar says: "As I read them the whole picture unfolded in front of me. The battles were extensive; there were mentions of deeds of our heroes, Nanasaheb, Tatya Tope, Rani Laxmibai of Jhansi, Maulavi Ahmadshah, Veer Kurarsingh of Bihar and others. I could imagine their bravery and audacity."[119]

[115] Savarkar, *Inside the Enemy Camp*, 77.
[116] Ibid., 76.
[117] Ibid., 77.
[118] Ibid.
[119] Ibid.

Savarkar found Kaye and Malleson biased, especially in their condemnation of Indian heroes in every volume, but they also included a lengthy bibliography that inspired Savarkar to go deeper into the subject.

After completing his book on Mazzini, and reading the available books in India House, Savarkar began researching the events of 1857 in the India Office Library in London. He read a number of books on the subject while also looking at official documents, such as the British Parliamentary Papers, the letters of British officers, and political speeches.[120] These materials made it clear to him that all British authors were biased; there was an epistemic refusal to acknowledge that Indian soldiers were "fighting for their religion and country and wanted to overthrow foreign rule."[121] The idea for Savarkar's decision to write a revisionist history about the events of 1857 was born: "I was convinced that in 1857, Indian soldiers, princes, and the general public of various provinces came together and fought a tenacious, pre-planned war to overthrow the rule of the East India Company. It did not succeed, but gave a big jolt to the British Empire. It did not hinder our progress, but left a guide for similar action in [the] future. That was the outline of my book."[122]

Savarkar began sharing his findings of the events of 1857 with members of the Abhinav Bharat Society in India House. Over secret meetings he discussed the importance of studying "1857" as a revolutionary war with the idea of inspiring individuals to take up arms against the British. The principles of revolution, he believed, were as relevant for the Abhinav Bharat Society in London as for revolutionaries in 1857: "I used to explain the heroic deeds of our heroes of 1857 and induce the youth to try a similar uprising in [the] future and be ready for self-sacrifice."[123]

Government officials were aware of Savarkar's research and Savarkar suspected there was a spy planted in India House who was not only reporting his findings but also sharing drafts of Savarkar's writings about "1857." The immediate consequence of this surveillance was

[120] Ibid., 78–80.
[121] Ibid., 79.
[122] Ibid.
[123] Ibid.

that officials demanded that the India Office Library revoke Savarkar's reader's pass, thereby denying him access to books. In an essay titled "I was banned from the India Office Library," Savarkar says, "The British Secret Service was alarmed and warned the Librarian at the Indian Office Library that I should not be admitted to the library. He was stunned and informed me accordingly."[124] Savarkar believed that officials were unaware at this point that his book was near completion; in fact he believed they were unsure whether he was writing a book, or a pamphlet based on his research.[125] In any case, the additional research that remained was done by a member of the Abhinav Bharat Society.

Officials in India were informed of the dangers of Savarkar's writings, especially if the text were smuggled into the country. Part of the confusion was due to the fact that on May 10, 1908 Savarkar circulated a pamphlet entitled "Oh Martyrs" at an event organised at India House to celebrate the anniversary of the start of the 1857 battles against the British in India.[126] Although "Oh Martyrs" was published anonymously, Savarkar was immediately identified as its author. The pamphlet was the first public proclamation of the conflict as a war of independence. This marked an important taxonomic shift away from the official British classification of the events as the "1857 Mutiny." It began with a statement addressed to the individuals who had fought and died in the battles of 1857: "Today is the tenth of May; it was on this day, that in the ever memorable year of 1857, the first campaign of the War of Independence was opened by you[:] Oh Martyrs, on the battlefield of India."[127] It continues, "It was on this day that the war-cry

---

[124] Ibid.

[125] BL, APAC, India HD Pol Proceedings, Part A, IOR.POS.5944, "Interception of a Book or Pamphlet by V.D. Savarkar on the Indian Mutiny," Proceedings, February 1909, nos 13-13A. See Savarkar's public letter to government regarding the surveillance related to his book: "Deshbhakta Savarkar ka patra," September 17, 1909, *Savarkar Samagra*, vol. 1, 609; and *Samagra Savarkar, vol. 1*, 116.

[126] "Seditious Indian Propaganda in London," *The Times* (London), May 23, 1908. Also, see Shyamaji Krishnavarma's letter to the editor in response to the May 23rd article: *The Times* (London), June 2, 1908.

[127] Savarkar, "Oh Martyrs," *Samagra Savarkar Vanmaya, vol. 5*, 443.

'*Maro Feringhee Ko*' [Kill the Foreigners] was raised by the throats of thousands."[128] The first battle is described as a "terrible uprising" by sepoys who introduced a "new epoch" that "converted the mutiny into a national and religious war."[129] Perhaps the most significant claim was that this battle was the first in an emergent permanent war that would be defined by vengeance and bloodshed. The pamphlet ended: "Indians, these words must be fulfilled! Your blood, oh Martyrs, shall be avenged."[130]

The small number of guests who arrived at India House received copies of the pamphlet. However, it quickly spread to government officials and the news media. The speculation was that British intelligence had put an agent in attendance.[131] The appearance of "Oh Martyrs" was confirmation of their suspicions and its contents caused great alarm. *The Times* (London) declared it "inflammatory," "violent," and "seditious" – which ironically helped to circulate the key ideas of "Oh Martyrs" because the newspaper published a summary of the pamphlet and excerpts from the text.[132] Within a few months, copies of "Oh Martyrs" were also circulating in India, despite the fact that the government had proscribed the pamphlet by applying the Sea Customs Act of 1878 which prohibited transport of the text into India.[133] Newspapers, such as *Amrita Bazar Patrika* (Calcutta), *The Indian People* (Allahabad), and *The Tribune* (Lahore), carried reports about the pamphlet in India and its potential to create unrest.[134] What remained unclear in the press was whether this pamphlet was the only

[128] Ibid.

[129] Ibid.

[130] Ibid., 446.

[131] BL, APAC, L/P&J/6/926, File 924, "Parliamentary Notice: Question by Claude Hay," March 11, 1909.

[132] "The Unrest in India. The Inflammatory Leaflet," *The Times* (London), June 27, 1908.

[133] "Proscribed Publications," *The Tribune* (Lahore), December 7, 1910. Also, see BL, APAC, L/P&J/6/1058, File 284, Testimony of Chaturbhuj Javerbhai Amin, January 24, 1911.

[134] "Dissemination of Pamphlets," *Amrita Bazar Patrika*, August 17, 1908; "Speech Delivered by Sir John Hewett at Lucknow, Allahabad and Agra During His Monsoon Tour of 1908," *The Indian People*, August 20, 1908; "Dissemination of Pamphlets," *The Tribune* (Lahore), August 26, 1908. A copy headed Kashmir was confiscated in Karachi: BL, APAC, India HD Pol

text that Savarkar was going to produce on "1857," or if there was a larger project in progress.

The circulation of "Oh Martyrs" had an impact on the official perception of Savarkar's writings, for his work was banned even before it was published. In fact, from this point forward, most of Savarkar's key writings were officially proscribed on account of their potential for inciting violence. But the pamphlet also served an important purpose in introducing the ideas of Savarkar's first two books in the English language. His book on Mazzini having been written in Marathi, this was the first time he had applied Mazzini's concepts to interpret Indian history in English. It is possible to suggest that this short work served as a preview to *Indian War*. Savarkar not only identified the events of 1857 as a war of independence in "Oh Martyrs" – a point often not considered when examining Savarkar's work – it also includes references to Mazzini's principles which serve as the foundation for conceptualising a history in full. The title "Oh Martyrs" was homage to Mazzini's extensive discussion of martyrs and martyrdom in his own work which Savarkar expanded in the pamphlet. Savarkar also built on Mazzini's idea that revolutionaries played a central role in bringing "the people" together against "the foreigner" in the struggle to eradicate slavery. The revolutionaries who fought and died in the war of independence were Savarkar's martyrs. He did not discuss the argument that these individuals embody the source or motive for his conceptualisation of a history in full, as these are themes more fully developed in *Indian War*.

However, he provided a key argument in "Oh Martyrs" that the actions of these revolutionaries (and martyrs) motivated others during their lifetime to participate in the war, while also continuing to inspire the next generation of Indians. A study of the actions of these revolutionaries was important for Savarkar as they exemplified the principles of religious and political revolutions. His discussion in the pamphlet is brief; it was a preview of the book that he was writing. Yet he brought together themes to not only rethink the mutiny of 1857 as a war of independence, but also to motivate people to participate

---

Proceedings, B Series, IOR.POS.8964, Letter from Chief Collector of Customs, Karachi, to the Resident in Kashmir [1910]. (Names are not included in the letter.)

in an ongoing revolutionary war. The martyrs were part of a "pious struggle" that was "magical" and part of a "grand unity."[135] It had brought Hindus and Muslims together, while also uniting castes and classes (e.g. Brahmins and Shudras) throughout India, a unity only possible through a revolutionary war. Moreover, the "spirits of the dead" were also important as their "blood" needed to be "avenged":

> For the bones of Bahadur Shah are crying vengeance from their grave! For, the blood of the dauntless Laxmi is boiling with indignation! For the Shahid Peer Ali of Patna, when he was going to the gallows for having refused to divulge the secrets of the conspiracy whispered defiance to the Feringhee and said in prophetic words "You may hang me today, you may hang such as me everyday, but thousands will still rise in my place – your object will never be gained." Indians, these words must be fulfilled! Your blood, oh Martyrs, shall be avenged.[136]

"Oh Martyrs" provided an important theme that continued throughout Savarkar's writings: the idea of a permanent war in India whose primary "mission" was to rid India of foreigners. The battle chants of "kill the foreigner" or "away with the foreigner" were central to a revolutionary war.[137] Also, "the War of 1857 shall not cease till the revolutionary arrives, striking slavery into dust, elevating liberty to the throne."[138] And extending beyond him, the war would persist until the "people" achieved "liberty or death."[139]

Savarkar also outlined the role of the "people" in the war, explaining how they might reach the goal of liberty (he also used "freedom"

---

[135] Savarkar, "Oh Martyrs," *Samagra Savarkar Vanmaya, vol. 5*, 446.

[136] Ibid. In the 1986 edition of Savarkar's *Indian War*, "Oh Martyrs" is included at the end of the book and it differs from the version published in *Samagra Savarkar Vanmaya*. There may have been multiple versions of "Oh Martyrs" that were written, but it is not clear if either is the original. For purposes of comparison, the following are the changes in the later edition after the first sentence of the quote: "The spirit of Mangal Pandey is still betokening from the scaffold for the fulfilment of the sacred mission. The solemn affirmation of Kumar Singh to shatter to pieces the British rule is still echoing in the air of Hindusthan. The streaks of blood that flowed from Azim-Ullah and Pir Ali Shah have left an indelible impression on the pages of history."

[137] Ibid., 443–4.

[138] Ibid., 444.

[139] Ibid.

and "*swaraj*" in his discussion of liberty): "Whenever a people rises for its freedom, whenever that seed of liberty gets germinated in the blood of its father[,] and whenever there remains at least one true son to avenge that blood of his father, there can never be an end to such a war as this."[140]

Savarkar's brief discussion of blood in the pamphlet was another theme taken from Mazzini and discussed more fully in *Indian War* (and later in *Essentials of Hindutva*). But it is worth considering the key points here. The "seed of liberty" was equated with "freedom" that existed in the blood of the father of every revolutionary. But when that blood was shed on the battlefield – transforming the revolutionary father into a martyr – it was absorbed into "the Motherland."[141] What May 10, 1857 represented was the "awakening of the Motherland," in which the blood of many revolutionaries was spilt on the battlefield. Any blood that was shed by the revolutionary was never in vain; rather the son, who inherited the seed of liberty from the father would seek vengeance in the name of the father, while also defending the Motherland. In other words Savarkar's conceptualisation of the revolutionary functioned in a patrilineal system in which the blood of the revolutionary was passed from father to son with the help of the body of the Motherland.

"Oh Martyrs" introduced key themes from Savarkar's writings that appeared to inspire a number of individuals. At the same time it alerted British authorities that his writings had the potential to create law and order problems in the UK and India. The assassination of a British official by a member of the Abhinav Bharat Society signalled a shift from writing and discussing history inspired by Mazzini to taking up revolutionary violence as a practice of anti-colonialism.

# 7. The Assassination and the Debate

On the evening of July 1, 1909 Madan Lal Dhingra, a member of the Abhinav Bharat Society, attended a function of the National Indian Association held at the Imperial Institute. The association was established to promote "social engagement" between the English and Indians

140 Ibid.

141 Savarkar, *Indian War*, 89.

residing in London.[142] Curzon Wyllie was a member of the council and treasurer of the association, but he also worked for police intelligence and served as an assistant to the Secretary of State for India. Dhingra had completed his studies at University College, London, and planned to sit for the I.C.E. examination later in the year. Around 11 p.m. Dhingra walked up to Wyllie and shot him four times in the head, killing him. When Dr Cawas Lalcaca, a guest at the function, tried to stop the attack Dhingra fired another two rounds and killed Lalcaca as well. Dhingra was captured and handed over to the police.

On July 5th a public meeting was held to condemn the murder of Wyllie.[143] It was a crowded event attended by many individuals, including Savarkar, Surendranath Banerjea, Bipin Chandra Pal, and the Aga Khan. Savarkar described the meeting: "Speaker after speaker denounced the murder, the man, the motive, the revolutionary rascals and their tenets."[144] The president of the meeting proposed a resolution to formally condemn Dhingra. According to Savarkar, the president announced that the resolution had passed unanimously, though there was no actual vote. Savarkar objected, stating he had voted against the resolution; he says some individuals at the meeting then responded by attacking him. The following day *The Times* (London) published a letter titled "Mr. Savarkar's Statement" in which Savarkar clarified that he was arguing for proper procedure for voting at the meeting.[145] But he also wanted Dhingra to be treated fairly before being condemned as a criminal by a group that had committed a crime in attacking him at the meeting.

At Dhingra's trial, held on July 19th, he read the following as part of his explanation for the murder: "I do not want to say anything in defence of myself, but simply to prove the justice of my deed."[146] He continued:

[142] OBP, Trial of Madan Lal Dhingra, July 19, 1909 (Reference Number t19090719-55), www.oldbaileyonline.org, version 8.0 (accessed February 16, 2019).

[143] As reported in *The Times*, two meetings were held, but Savarkar's attendance is only noted in the second meeting: *The Times* (London), July 6, 1909.

[144] Gupta, *Life of Barrister Savarkar*, 60–1.

[145] Savarkar, "Mr. Savarkar's Statement," *The Times* (London), July 6, 1909.

[146] OBP, Trial of Madan Lal Dhingra.

I maintain that if it is patriotic in an Englishman to fight against the Germans if they were to occupy this country, it is much more justifiable and patriotic in my case to fight against the English. I hold the English people responsible for the murder of 80 millions of Indian people in the last fifty years . . . It is perfectly justifiable on our part to kill the Englishman. I wish that the English people should sentence me to death, for in that case the vengeance of my countrymen will be all the more keen."[147]

Dhingra was found guilty of killing Wyllie, and on August 17th he was executed. The Abhinav Bharat Society, led by Savarkar, organised the printing of a postcard commemorating Dhingra as a revolutionary; the postcard included excerpts from Dhingra's statement at his trial about the "justifiable" use of violence. It also included the text of an oath taken by all members of the Abhinav Bharat Society who swore a commitment to the "bloody, relentless war against the foreigner."[148] One purpose of celebrating Dhingra's death was to make clear that Wyllie's killing was part of a larger effort to wage war against colonial rule in India. It was to underscore the point that Dhingra's assassination of Wyllie was not a random act of violence, or a single killing. The British government came to be doubly aware that revolutionary activity posed a threat at home and in India.

Savarkar's public defence of Dhingra drew a great deal of attention. The revolutionary tactics promoted by Savarkar, the India House, and the Abhinav Bharat Society were heavily criticised by Indians and British alike. Perhaps the most trenchant comments were made by M.K. Gandhi. In July 1909 Gandhi had travelled from South Africa – where he was settled at the time – to London for the purpose of lobbying the government on behalf of Indians in South Africa. He also wanted to meet Indians based in Britain to better understand their concerns about nationalism and colonialism. He had followed the newspaper coverage of Wyllie's murder and Dhingra's trial, and he produced analyses of the events: "Every Indian should reflect thoroughly on this murder . . . Mr. Dhingra's defence by Indian revolutionaries was inadmissible . . . He was egged on to do this act by ill-digested reading of worthless writings . . . It is those who incited him to this

---

[147] Ibid.

[148] BL, APAC, EPP 1/46, "The Oath of the Abhinava Bharat," March 13, 1910.

that deserve to be punished."[149] Needless to say, this was a serious indictment of all revolutionaries who had supported Dhingra, but especially Savarkar, whose writings and principle of revolution were said to have directly influenced Dhingra. More important, according to government surveillance, members of Savarkar's inner circle in London were reported to have discussed that "Dhingra was the product of Savarkar's sound teachings."[150] Savarkar's close comrade V.V.S. Aiyer is said to have stated, "Dhingra had done a glorious act, but there was someone . . . who was the real guru, the Avatar of Krishna, who had produced a man like Dhingra."[151] Aiyer's reference was to Savarkar.

The roots of the earliest disagreement between Gandhi and Savarkar began in the shadow of the assassination of Curzon Wyllie. The first – and perhaps only – public meeting between the two figures was held in the aftermath of the execution of Dhingra. On October 24, 1909 Gandhi was invited as guest of honour at a Vijayadashami function in which he was asked to speak to an audience of sixty or seventy people, which included Savarkar.[152] Gandhi delivered a speech in which he discussed the importance of honouring the king of Ayodhya, Ramachandra, by all Indians – Hindus, Muslims, and Parsis.[153] Two other individuals spoke after Gandhi, who then turned to Savarkar and invited him to speak. Savarkar thanked Gandhi and said: "You have requested me not to speak on any aspect of current affairs but only about our ancient past. What can we say of today? Plague, slavery, bondage. How wonderful it is to think of the past!"[154] As Gandhi had met a number of Indian revolutionaries in London – namely, members of Shyamji Krishnavarma's India House and the Abhinav Bharat Society – he had decided against a public discussion about *all* forms of politics at the event.[155] Savarkar then recited passages from

---

[149] Gandhi, "Curzon Wyllie's Assassination," in *CWMG, vol. 9*, 428.

[150] BL, APAC, India HD Pol Proceedings, B Series, IOR.POS.8962, Weekly Report of the Director of Criminal Intelligence, Simla, July 31, 1909.

[151] Ibid. Also, Parel, "Editor's Introduction," *Hind Swaraj*, xxvii.

[152] Parel, "Editor's Introduction," *Hind Swaraj*, xxvii–xxviii.

[153] Gandhi, "Vijaya Dashami," in *CWMG, vol. 10*, 189–90.

[154] Savarkar, "Vijayadashami," November 26, 1909, in *Savarkar Samagra, vol. 1*, 611–12; and *Samagra Savarkar, vol. 1*, 118–19. Also, see "A Great Speech," in Gupta, *Life of Barrister Savarkar*, Appendix I, 134–5.

[155] See Fischer-Tiné, "Mass-Mediated Panic in the British Empire?"

the Ramayana and discussed the nature of violence in the epic, especially as the function was meant to celebrate Ramachandra's killing of Ravana. Gandhi described Savarkar's lecture as "a spirited speech on the excellence of the *Ramayana*."[156] The official surveillance report of the Criminal Intelligence Department (CID) provided a different rendering of the meeting:

> The Dassera celebration organised by Savarkar . . . was held on October 24th in the shape of a dinner party. M.K. Gandhi presided and somewhat surprised the audience by commencing his after-dinner speech with the remark that he belonged to a different school of thought from Savarkar. He said he considered Savarkar's teaching injurious to the well-being of the country, and that the real oppressor – the ten headed monster [Ravana] – was within them and not without. His speech caused considerable dissatisfaction . . . Savarkar was called upon and he also criticised [Gandhi's] remarks. He disagreed with [Gandhi's] interpretation of the Ramayana; Ram did not invade Ceylon, the island of the tyrant, for the sake of peace, and did not carry war abroad to kill the ten-headed monster within himself. He fought for Sita the chaste, for Sita the freedom of India. His speech is said to have been very effective and well received. Savarkar afterwards, referring to this meeting, complained of the underhand tricks of his enemies.[157]

It appears that Gandhi and Savarkar had other conversations too, including discussions about the Bhagavad Gita. Gandhi writes: "When I was in London, Savarkar and others used to tell me that the Gita and *Ramayana* taught quite the opposite of what I said they did."[158] For Gandhi, the violence in the Ramayana and the Gita served as allegories for the internal conflict in all humans. For Savarkar, the necessity of violence in both texts was meant to be interpreted literally, as an essence of the human condition. Moreover he argued that violence was a central feature of all human history. Their divergent interpretations of violence set them apart from this moment forward.[159]

In mid-November, a few weeks after the Vijayadashami function,

---

[156] Gandhi, "Vijaya Dashami," in *CWMG, vol. 10*, 189.

[157] BL, APAC, India HD Pol Proceedings, B Series, IOR.POS.8963, Weekly Report of the Director of Criminal Intelligence, Simla, November 20, 1909.

[158] Gandhi, "Discourses on the 'Gita'," in *CWMG, vol. 37*, 82.

[159] See Pinney, "The Tiger's Nature, But Not the Tiger."

Gandhi boarded a ship back to South Africa. On the return journey he felt the urgency to write what became his best-known work, *Hind Swaraj, or Indian Home Rule* (1909), in which he presented arguments against an unnamed revolutionary. By not specifically identifying Savarkar, or any other individual, *Hind Swaraj* may be considered Gandhi's response to emergent revolutionary thought, but there are passages that look like direct responses to Savarkar. It is worth considering the following dialogue in *Hind Swaraj*:

> READER (The Revolutionary): At first, we will assassinate a few Englishmen and strike terror; then, a few men who will have been armed will fight openly. We may have to lose a quarter of a million men, but we will regain our land. We will undertake guerrilla warfare, and defeat the English.
>
> EDITOR (Gandhi): Do you not tremble to think of freeing India by assassination? What we need to do is to kill ourselves. It is a cowardly thought, that of killing others. Whom do you suppose to free by assassination? The millions of India do not desire it. Those who are intoxicated by the wretched modern civilisation think these things. Those who will rise to power by murder will certainly not make the nation happy. Those who believe that India has gained by Dhingra's act and such other acts in India make a serious mistake.[160]

For Gandhi, the idea of the assassination was directly linked to his understanding of modern civilisation, which was antithetical to Indian civilisation. It was also a serious indictment against Indian revolutionaries like Savarkar who were not only celebrating assassination as legitimate but also promoting it as an ethical mode of conduct. When reflecting on meeting Gandhi in London in 1909 Savarkar says: "I happened to be closely acquainted in a friendly way when he had come to England where he was then known simply as Barrister Gandhi and thereafter throughout our lives came together and many times in conflict – in the political arena in India."[161] Gandhi's refusal to speak about politics at the meeting meant that their public discussion centred on warfare, violence, and the conflicts of the gods in the Ramayana. Gandhi saw this discussion as reflecting the internal conflict of all

---

[160] Gandhi, *Hind Swaraj*, 75.
[161] Savarkar, *Six Glorious Epochs of Indian History*, 468.

humans, while Savarkar viewed it as relevant to interpreting the world in the twentieth century. Perhaps Gandhi overlooked Savarkar's argument, taken from Mazzini, that religion and politics were inextricably entangled, so it did not matter to Savarkar if he only spoke about the epics. The more Gandhi wanted to move away from a literal reading of the texts, the more Savarkar appeared to rely on them to interpret the contemporary condition.

## 8. Writing a Banned History

Dhingra's assassination of Wyllie resulted in a growing concern among officials about further acts of violence by the Abhinav Bharat Society.[162] There was suspicion of Savarkar's work and information was sent to India about its potential for danger. The primary task was to confiscate the text and prevent its circulation, but this proved more difficult than anticipated. On July 21, 1909 H.A. Stuart, Director of the CID in Bombay, sent a telegram to officials in the Government of India urging application of the Sea Customs Act and the Indian Post Office Act to intercept and confiscate copies of a text written by Savarkar.[163] Stuart explained that he believed there were two versions of the text – the original in Marathi and a translation in English – that would be arriving in Indian ports from England. He thought the English translation was published in London and the Marathi edition in Germany, but said he was not certain. He did not know if Savarkar had written a book or a pamphlet, or how many copies were expected to arrive by ship. Nor did he know the title of the work or the name of its publisher. In fact, all he knew was that the subject of the text was the "Indian Mutiny . . . That is, I think, as wide as we can make the description."[164]

The incomplete nature of Stuart's information created bureaucratic

---

[162] BL, APAC, Mss.Eur.D573/4, Papers of John Morley as Secretary of State for India, Correspondence with the Viceroy, Letter from Morley to Lord Minto, August 26, 1909.

[163] BL, APAC, Home Pol Proceedings, Part A, IOR.POS.5945, Telegram from H.A. Stuart, Director, Criminal Intelligence, July 21, 1909.

[164] Ibid.

problems in India. Officials complained that neither the Sea Customs Act nor the Indian Post Office Act could be applied without a complete citation: how could they be expected to confiscate a text without accurate details.[165] Despite this the government took the potential threat seriously, so much so that even the viceroy, Lord Minto, agreed confiscation was necessary.[166] What officialdom did not know was that the first edition was already published as a 451-page book entitled *The Indian War of Independence of 1857* with the author simply listed as "An Indian Nationalist."

The CID planned to intercept copies arriving on ships at the port of Bombay but did not want government to reveal details of the strategy to lower-level officials until it could figure out which ships might be carrying the contraband. The explanation offered was that in order to inform customs and postal inspectors, detailed information about Savarkar's text and instructions for its confiscation would need to be printed in the *Bombay Gazette Extraordinary*. The CID was concerned that once the information was published, it would be impossible to control its circulation, especially given the existence of global networks linking Indian nationalists and revolutionaries from Bombay to London and beyond. Officials explained that if Savarkar and his comrades became aware of the government's confiscation strategy they would hatch new plans for its dispatch. Not surprisingly, alternative strategies to smuggle copies of Savarkar's writings were already under way well before the publication of the *Gazette*. Even the government knew it would be impossible to prevent all copies from entering Bombay and every other port. What the government, and perhaps Savarkar himself, did not anticipate was how widely *Indian War* would eventually circulate in India and beyond in later decades of the twentieth century.

The history of the production and circulation of *Indian War* has received a great deal of attention because of its unusual origins, including the fact that the British government banned the book even before it

---

[165] "A Loathsome Book," *The Academy*, June 24, 1911. This is a review of the book by an anonymous author who was clearly aware of the government's problems in identifying the seditious text.

[166] BL, APAC, GOI, Home Pol Proceedings, Part A, IOR.POS.5945, Telegram from Lord Minto, July 21, 1909.

was published. It is as if the book served as a metaphor for the circulation of *chapatis* by rebels from village to village in 1857 to spread the news of a forthcoming revolt. Savarkar's book was circulated through an underground global network of revolutionaries who wanted it to serve as a catalyst for a revolution in Britain and India.

In the 1947 edition of *Indian War* – the first edition published in post-colonial India – G.M. Joshi authored an essay titled, "The Story of this History."[167] Savarkar himself encouraged readers interested in the "true history" of the book to turn to this essay, which may have been the first authorised history of *Indian War*. Select details of the book were already publicly available before it appeared: after Savarkar's arrest in London an article in *The Times*, titled "The Savarkar Case: Text of the Judgment," published extensive details on January 14, 1911. A key point discussed in "The Story of this History" was the difficulty that Savarkar had faced in getting the book published.[168] *Indian War* was apparently completed in 1907, but Savarkar could not find a publisher in London or elsewhere in Europe as it was written in Marathi. Thus a decision was made to translate the book into English, especially as the British authorities were eager to confiscate and destroy the original manuscript. Savarkar's first book on Mazzini was written in Marathi and, being immediately banned by the government, had limited circulation in India. His second book manuscript, on the history of the Sikhs, was apparently lost in the post or destroyed by officials, with the result that it was never published.[169] It is also unclear how many individuals were actually involved in translating Savarkar's text. "Text of the Judgment" says "He completed, while he was there [at India House], a history of the Indian Mutiny, or, as he calls it, 'the Indian War of Independence,' in Marathi, which was translated into English by other residents at the India House."[170]

While the discussion of the translation is now part of the official

[167] In a later edition of Savarkar, *The Indian War of Independence, 1857* (1986), G.M. Joshi and Bal Savarkar are listed as the authors of "The Story of this History."

[168] See Joshi, "The Story of this History."

[169] Savarkar, *Six Glorious Epochs of Indian History*, 458.

[170] "The Savarkar Case: Text of the Judgment," *The Times* (London), January 14, 1911.

story of *Indian War*, it is worth considering the language in the book. The book does not read like a collaborative translation project hastily put together, despite the anonymous publisher's statement in the preface that

> the publishers have not waited till the language of this translation could be rendered elegant, which would be more shameful – to let hideous calumny hover over and smother down the spirit of martyrdom, or to let some mistake creep into a book admittedly translated into a foreign tongue? Therefore, the publishers owe no apology to, nor would one be asked for, but the Indian readers for whose special benefit, the work is published.[171]

In fact the language is quite consistent throughout the book. Nor is it clear how many of Savarkar's inner circle in London had the required fluency in Marathi to serve as translators of the massive handwritten manuscript.[172] Perhaps an editor standardised the language; perhaps Savarkar himself served in this role, especially since the English translation shares phrases, word choices, and patterns of writing found in Savarkar's other English-language publications. Savarkar was not a literary stylist in any of his English writings – his writing is polemical, repetitive, and euphemistic. It is also dramatic, sometimes melodramatic, and vivid in its descriptions; in other places it is formal. But the writing appears normalised throughout *Indian War*. In contrast, Savarkar was celebrated for the quality and aesthetics of his Marathi compositions, especially his poetry. The fact that Savarkar researched and wrote *Indian War* under surveillance also complicated a proper reception of his book – not only in terms of its contents, but also its language and style. I raise the issue of translation here to indicate that the collective translation of *Indian War* opens further questions for which Savarkar did not provide a clear explanation. But one point of aesthetics that he did articulate was that he wanted his historical writings to

---

[171] "Publisher's Preface," in Savarkar, *Indian War*, vi.

[172] BL, APAC, L/P&J/6/1058, File 284, Testimony of Harishchandra Krishna Kergaumkar, date not given. Kergaumkar claimed that he was the translator of approximately half of Savarkar's *Indian War*. I have not been able to locate other information corroborating this claim, or the names of others involved in the translation.

look more like his poetry. Perhaps this helps to explain his literary choices in *Indian War* and his other works of history.

In the "Author's Introduction" to this work Savarkar started by positing that the "War of 1857" could now be "relegated to the realms of history." He described the events of 1857 as not only an "instructive and magnificent spectacle," but also "the brilliance of a War of Independence shining in the 'mutiny of 1857'."[173] He was "disappointed" by the fact that the events of 1857 were not only "buried" but also "neglected" aspects of what he calls "our history." The point was to create a "faithful picture" through research aimed at creating a national consciousness. In Savarkar's view there was a direct connection between writing a history of a revolutionary war of independence and establishing a popular demand for "absolute political independence" from the British empire. All nations needed to "develop a capacity" for claiming the past while adopting a strategy of knowing how to use these claims for the nation's future.[174]

Savarkar's assertion that independence could only be achieved through writing a history of revolutionary war is what sets him apart from others who had engaged with the idea of independence throughout the nineteenth and early-twentieth century. He was also aware, of course, that other nationalists in India were advocating the use of violence and revolution to challenge colonial power, especially during the Swadeshi movements of 1905. However, these "extremist" nationalists – as they were popularly known – and revolutionaries were not putting forward a specific argument for the necessity of writing histories of revolution *per se*. Further, and perhaps more important, Savarkar argued that political independence from British rule could only be achieved once the principles of past revolutionary wars were known by India's masses. The publication and circulation of *Indian War* served the initial purpose of creating such awareness.

Savarkar explained that *Indian War* provided an important corrective to historical analyses that only considered the events of 1857 as a sepoy mutiny. To classify them so was to ignore the principles that inspired revolutionaries to take up arms as an ethical duty. The

---

[173] Savarkar, *Indian War*, vii.
[174] Ibid.

point of articulating a discursive shift in reclassifying 1857 as a "war of independence" or a "revolutionary war" – Savarkar used both interchangeably – was to disrupt the existing historiography on the subject dominated by colonialist knowledge. In the "Author's Introduction" he says he primarily read English-language books in order to write *Indian War*.[175] He included a bibliographic section called "List of Books Consulted" to identify these texts.[176] (Interestingly, later editions of the book also include Marathi and Bengali texts in the list, not mentioned in the original edition.) By basing his work on English sources, Savarkar argued that inscribed within the works of colonial officials and historians was a history of the Indian war of independence ignored or silenced because of prejudice and perspective. English historians – and what he called their "Indian sycophants" – typically wrote histories that were not only "misleading" and "unjust," but also based on "a wicked and partial spirit."[177] These historians simply ignored major evidence that contradicted their own perspective, because "it [was] against their interests to admit the truth."[178]

A further problem for Savarkar was that most Indian historians had accepted and incorporated the interpretations and perspectives of their English counterparts. These individuals, whom he did not identify by name, reproduced incorrect explanations of 1857 which simply "change[d] or distort[ed] the whole spirit of the Revolution."[179] All the details and evidence needed to write about the revolution were present in the existing historiography, including the principles that guided, motivated, and inspired the historical actors. To use a phrase common to explain the methodology of *Indian War*, Savarkar opted to read "against the grain" of colonial historiography to write his own nationalist

---

[175] Ibid., viii.

[176] "List of Books Consulted," in Savarkar, *Indian War*, ix–x. Savarkar lists one exception: Mu'in Al-din Hasan Khan's *Two Native Narratives* (publication details are not given in the original). However, the text was translated into English by Charles Metcalfe and edited by Esther G. Eddis Metcalfe. The citation for the text Savarkar likely used is *Two Native Narratives of the Mutiny in Delhi* (Lahore: Al-biruni, 1889).

[177] Savarkar, *Indian War*, 5.

[178] Ibid.

[179] Ibid.

history. He argued that the smallest "references" and "most minute
details" of the events discussed in *Indian War* illustrated the existence
of a war of independence that could actually be found in texts that are
considered "authoritative works" in the field: that is, English language
histories of 1857.[180] For Savarkar, *Indian War* was only a starting point
for providing alternative methodologies for writing history; future
histories needed to be based on oral sources:

> if some patriotic historian would go to northern India and try to collect
> the traditions from the very mouths of those who witnessed and perhaps
> took a leading part in the War . . . Within a decade or two, the whole
> generation of those who took part in that war shall have passed away . . .
> not only would it be impossible to have the pleasure of seeing the actors
> themselves, but the history of their actions will have to be left permanently
> incomplete.[181]

Since he relied on English authors, he saw there were possible historical actors or moments in the past ignored or forgotten, and others
"unstated" or "wrongly described."[182] A study of the "history of actions" of all who rebelled was for Savarkar the single best way of understanding the principles of individuals who took up arms against the
British.

## 9.  A Mazzinian History of India

In writing *Indian War* Savarkar says he relied on Mazzini's argument
that histories of revolutions must take into consideration the principles
and motives of the people involved. He referred to the "rising of 1848
in Italy" as an example for Indian historians to consider when writing
about the "Revolutionary War of 1857."[183] What Mazzini showed was
that it was possible to organise the masses, even in very difficult circumstances.[184] While in London, Savarkar also read widely on global

---

[180] Ibid., viii.
[181] Ibid.
[182] Ibid.
[183] Ibid., 11.
[184] Gupta, *Life of Barrister Savarkar*, 43.

histories of imperialism and nationalism. Needless to say, he was also engaged in the study of diverse methodological approaches to writing history to equip himself with a corrective to colonialist historiography.[185] He claimed that without his intervention histories of Indian revolutions and revolutionaries would eventually be "erased from the pages of our history."[186]

> [Mazzini] has said that every revolution must have a fundamental principle . . . A revolutionary movement cannot be based on a flimsy and momentary grievance. It is always due to some all-moving principle for which hundreds and thousands of men fight . . . The moving spirits of revolutions are deemed holy or unholy in proportion as the principle underlying them is beneficial or wicked . . . In history, the deeds of an individual or a nation are judged by the character of the motive . . . To write a full history of a revolution means necessarily the tracing of all the events of that revolution back to their source – the motive.[187]

Savarkar's articulation of a "full history" in this context is directly linked to Mazzini's argument about the fundamental principle of a revolution. (It is this "full history" that Savarkar developed into "a history in full" to define Hindutva in the 1920s. He used "full history" in later writings as well, and synonymously with "a history in full.") He conceptualised a history in full by explaining the centrality of understanding the principles of all revolutions and wars of independence, principles directly connected to an unnamed "source" that inspired historical actors. The entire historiography of 1857 had neglected to study the "true" motives of the historical actors who took up arms by focusing on what Savarkar called "temporary" or "accidental" causes that simply deny the "real spirit of the Revolution."[188] He suggested that the historiography provided two general explanations: individuals revolted because their lands were annexed, or participated in the sepoy mutiny because of a rumour that the British had greased cartridges with animal fat. These arguments may have helped clarify some incidents that took place in 1857 but did not explain the motives of the "whole Revolution."[189] The "holy work" of the historian

---

[185] Savarkar, *Indian War*, 8.
[186] Ibid.
[187] Ibid., 4.
[188] Ibid., 7.
[189] Ibid.

was to articulate the "all-moving principles" of a revolution, only then could a "full history" be written.

When considering the official Marathi or Hindi editions and translations of Savarkar's writings, the terms used to convey a history in full add complexity to Savarkar's conceptualisation. In both the Marathi and Hindi editions of *Indian War* the discussions centre around the importance of searching for *tattva* in historical actors. In fact in the Hindi edition Savarkar says a central objective in writing any *itihaas* was to search for the *mul tattva* (original essence, or prime essence).[190] Perhaps a more revealing statement in the text is that a historian is required to not only understand the motive (*hetu*) of a historical actor, or foundation (*neenv*) of a historical movement, but also the "evolution" of a historical actor's transformation by what is called *tattva darshan*.[191] In other words, Savarkar's claim was that historians must search for figures from the past who not only experienced, visualised, and witnessed the essence (or an essence) in the making of historical events, but who were existentially transformed in the process.

At the centre of *Indian War* are themes Savarkar developed further from Mazzini's *Life and Writings*. There is an overlap with his writings in *Joseph Mazzini*, but also an expansion of ideas to interpret the Indian war of independence. There is a discussion of enslavement (and slavery) which continues throughout the book, as does the idea that liberty is divinely ordained: "[I]t was evident that the chains of political slavery had been put around them and their God-given liberty wrested away by subtle tricks."[192] The point for Savarkar – as for Mazzini – was to underscore the idea of enslavement within an epistemic framing rather than a literal discussion of bonded labour. For example, in the "Author's Introduction" Savarkar states: "The nation ought to be the master and not the slave of its own history."[193] By writing *Indian War* he was liberating the enslaved history of India. He uses disease as a metaphor to argue that the condition of the people was a direct consequence

[190] See Savarkar, *1857 ka swatantra sangrama*, in *Savarkar Samagra, vol. 5*, 21.

[191] Perhaps there is no proper English translation for this formulation, except to suggest that it comes close to the idea of seeing or experiencing *tattva* – the essence.

[192] Savarkar, *Indian War*, 8.

[193] Ibid., vii.

of "the plague of slavery . . . [which is] destroying India."[194] The fault lay in "the people" who had lost their ability to "defend religion," and adds: "The command of God, is, Obtain Swaraj, for that is the chief key to the protection of Dharma. He who does not attempt to acquire Swaraj, he who sits silently in slavery, he is an atheist and hater of Religion. Therefore, rise for Swadharma and acquire Swaraj!"[195]

Mazzini's articulation of the centrality of "God-given liberty" as a way to break the chains of slavery is qualified in Savarkar by adding vernacular terms that were part of contemporary debates in India: *swaraj* and *swadharma*. The concept of "liberty" is defined as a "love of one's country" combined with a "love of one's religion."[196] This represents a modification by Savarkar of the links between religion and politics in Mazzini's writings: that is, "there is religion in politics and there is politics in religion." The concepts of *swaraj* and *swadharma* were intimately connected for Savarkar, and both together defined the principle of revolution: "Our idea of swadharma is not contradictory to that of swaraj. The two are connected as a means and end. Swaraj without swadharma is despicable and swadharma without swaraj is powerless. The sword of material power, swaraj, should always be ready drawn for our object, our safety is the other world, swadharma."[197] He further complicates the principle of revolution borrowed from Mazzini by arguing that the principle has been present in India for centuries. Mazzini's argument was the most recent formulation of the principle of revolution, but, since it was a universally accepted principle, it had antecedents before the nineteenth century (and outside Europe). Savarkar claimed that the poet-saint and philosopher Ramdas (1608–1681) was the first to articulate the links between *swaraj* and *swadharma* when he stated, "Rise for Swadharma and acquire Swaraj!"[198] Ramdas had instructed the Marathas to realise the power of principle in their battles. Savarkar quotes Ramdas in *Indian War*: "Die for your Dharma, kill the enemies of your Dharma while you are dying; in this way fight and kill, and take back your kingdom! This alone is the principle in

<hr>

194 Ibid., 10.
195 Ibid., 9–10.
196 Ibid., 8.
197 Ibid., 9.
198 Ibid., 10.

the Revolutionary War of 1857."[199] Reading Mazzini and Ramdas led Savarkar to the same conclusion about the importance of the principle of revolution. In fact he went so far as to argue that since their ideas were similar, the two were often considered synonymous in Maharashtra: "The Italian-born Ramdas is called Mazzini and the Hindusthani-born Mazzini is Ramdas."[200] Both, in his view, advocated the principle of revolution and the necessity of violence.

*Indian War* was written at a time when *swadharma* and *swaraj* were already central to debates on nationalism and religion, especially by focusing on interpretations of the Bhagavad Gita within nationalist thought.[201] Tilak famously adopted a slogan that circulated widely in India, "Swaraj is my birthright and I shall have it." He also delivered speeches on and published interpretations of the Bhagavad Gita which influenced Savarkar's thought. Without attempting a commentary or critique of the Bhagavad Gita, Savarkar incorporated key concepts and themes from the text into all his major writings. *Indian War* may be interpreted as part of an emergent historiography on *swaraj* and *swadharma*, but its primary focus was a "full history" incorporating these twin concepts in the principle of revolution.

At the centre of Savarkar's major writings was an analysis of warfare in India. This allowed him to engage with the Bhagavad Gita by examining themes relating to the ethics of violence within the act of killing in battles. An analysis of the embodiment of the Bhagavad Gita and its ideas in Savarkar's work provides necessary context for the intellectual and political development of religion and nationalism in colonial and post-colonial India. Perhaps this explains why Savarkar attributed great power to historical texts, claiming that they allow readers access to knowledge that was ontologically transformative. Though engaging with key concepts in the Bhagavad Gita in his histories, his interpretation of "knowledge" did not centre on knowing Krishna. I raise this point to question whether Savarkar saw himself departing from the ultimate form of knowledge as prescribed in the Bhagavad

---

[199] Ibid.

[200] Savarkar, *Mazzini Charitra*, 30; and Savarkar, *Joseph Mazzini*, 29.

[201] See Ray, "Moderates, Extremists, and Revolutionaries." Also, see Minor, ed., *Modern Indian Interpreters of the Bhagavad Gita*.

Gita, namely Krishna, or whether he considered his approach a modification of the message of the Bhagavad Gita. Savarkar himself did not clarify this point directly. After all, the purpose of Krishna's dialogue with Arjuna in the Bhagavad Gita is not to reveal the importance of historical knowledge *per se*, but rather that Krishna embodies *all* knowledge. For example, Krishna states:

> Hear how you, fixing your mind on me and finding shelter in me, shall find me entirely beyond doubt . . . I shall propound to you more fully that insight and knowledge, after acquiring which nothing more remains to be known in this world. Among thousands of people there is perhaps one who strives toward success, and even among those who have striven successfully, perhaps only one really knows me.[202]

It may be argued that Savarkar had accepted the idea that seeking knowledge as discussed by Krishna was difficult, if not impossible, for anyone other than Arjuna. Or else Savarkar believed that historical knowledge was in fact a component of the "true" knowledge prescribed in the Bhagavad Gita. He did situate his interpretation of the Bhagavad Gita's central concepts within the debates on karma yoga, especially those from Tilak. And, rather than write on the text, he produced histories that he believed would transform the individual and the nation.

## 10. Violence in the Revolution

In *Indian War* Savarkar provided descriptions and analyses of unrelenting violence. Most chapters of the book are organised around places of revolutionary activity (Meerut, Delhi, Rohilkhand, Benares, Jhansi), and individual actors who took up violence as revolutionaries (Nana Sahib, Tatia Tope, Kumar Singh, Lakshmi Bai). The only exceptions are chapters that appear in the first part of the book based on themes such as "Swadharma and Swaraj," "The Chain of Causes," or "Secret Organisation." Moments of violence and individuals who perpetrated violence were important for Savarkar throughout the book: he argued that the principles of revolution were expressed in

---

[202] van Buitenen, trans., *The Bhagavadgita*, 99. The reference is from chapter VII, lines 1–4, of the Gita.

the very moment of violence. The task of the historian was not only to recognise the link between the moment of violence and the principle of revolution, but to write "a history in full" tracing the events of the revolution back to its source. Scores of individuals discussed in *Indian War* represent the "people" in the war, but he only discusses the select few who embody the principle of revolution. This was largely due to the limitations of the English sources he relied upon. A further difficulty for him was the fact that secret societies proliferated in the country, which meant that many individuals were involved in guerrilla tactics that remained hidden or silent. The success of underground revolutionaries meant that they did not appear in colonial historiography, adding to the challenge of writing about them.

Throughout *Indian War* Savarkar underscores his view that the war unified the people, creating a solidarity within society that transcended earlier conflicts: "Private enmity, differences of religion and caste and rank were all absorbed in the love of country."[203] He particularly emphasises the unity of Hindus and Muslims, who he says worked together for the purpose of "freeing *their* country."[204] In the "Author's Introduction" he makes an important point regarding historical enmity against Muslims by arguing that it is "unwise" for Hindus to repeat the actions of past centuries in the present day: "The feeling of hatred against the Mahomedans was just and necessary in the times of Shivaji – but, such a feeling would be unjust and foolish if nursed now, simply because it was the dominant feeling of the Hindus then."[205] Instead, Hindus and Muslims needed to unify against the foreigner. Savarkar provided several commentaries in *Indian War* on the solidarity of Hindus and Muslims in the nineteenth century, even as he reminded the reader that the long-standing religious conflict should be forgotten. In specific places in the text he expressed reservations about the coming together of Hindus and Muslims as an "inconceivable unity" or "an unnatural confederacy."[206] On the other hand, he also offered a message of unity:

---

[203] Savarkar, *Indian War*, 209.
[204] Ibid. Emphasis added.
[205] Ibid., viii.
[206] See, e.g., ibid., 419 and 337.

So, now, the original antagonism between Hindus and Mahomedans might be consigned to the Past. Their present relation was one not of rulers and ruled, foreigner and native, but simply that of brothers with the one difference between them of religion alone. For, they were both children of the soil of Hindusthan. Their names were different, but they were all children of the same Mother; India therefore being the common mother of these two, they were brothers by blood.[207]

This was a radical statement that signalled a new beginning, especially in a time of great conflict. Savarkar explained that to announce the unification of Hindus and Muslims, handbills were circulated throughout the country with messages about religious solidarity: "To all Hindus and Mahomedans! We, solely on account of religious duty, have joined with the people . . . It is further necessary that all Hindus and Mahomedans, unite in this struggle."[208] Thousands of religious men – Moulvies and Pandits – worked together to preach a "sacred" and "holy" war against the British. When describing Muslim participation in the revolution, Savarkar turned to the concept of jihad to argue it was an equivalent of the war of independence.[209] Not only was this jihad characterised as a "religious war for justice," but it was a "Jehad for freedom for the Hindu and Islamic religions."[210] (The Indian war of independence of 1857 was now the Indian jihad of 1857.) For Savarkar, Hindu–Muslim unity was successful because the revolutionaries who reached Delhi agreed to place Bahadur Shah Zafar on the throne as the Mughal emperor and leader of the war of independence. It was the "voice of the people" that was expressed in selecting Bahadur Shah Zafar, for "the people of the soil were once more free to choose their own monarch."[211] Moreover, it also signalled the end of the war between Hindus and Muslims.

Savarkar's incorporation of Mazzini's concepts is clear also in the chapters on revolutionaries, especially in his conceptualisation of "the people," whom he defines as including sepoys, police, zamindars, civil officials, peasants, merchants, bankers, gypsies, actors, poets, servants, and

---

[207] Ibid., 63.
[208] Ibid., 235.
[209] Ibid., 72.
[210] Ibid., 73, 198.
[211] Ibid., 234.

religious men. The war not only represented the unification of Hindus and Muslims, but of all sections of society: "Hindu and Mahomedan, Brahmin and Sudra, Kshatriya and Vaisha, prince and pauper, men and women, Pundits and Moulvies, Sepoys and the police, townsmen and villagers, merchants and farmers – men of different religions, men of different castes, people following widely different professions – So, universal was the agitation!"[212]

He says thousands contributed to the war effort: some provided support and shelter to revolutionaries and helped in spreading news of the war, others took up arms. He celebrates quotidian efforts to inculcate a revolutionary spirit among the people, from mothers informing their children of the need to destroy the English, to the circulation of poetry and ballads (*powadas*) about revolutionary discontent.[213] He extols the power of oral culture as a way to bring people together: "To instil into every heart the one great desire for independence, and rouse it to action, there could be no more effective weapon than poetry."[214] He points out that wandering groups of singers, storytellers, and performers (*tamashgars*) who travelled from Calcutta to Panjab escaped surveillance and were central in circulating information about the principle of revolution among the people. Itinerant religious men – moulvies, pandits, fakirs, and *sanyasis* – were among those who played this role. There was also the awareness that, in order for the revolution to succeed, women not only needed to be informed about the principle of it but should be included in the war. Leaders turned to female gypsies to assist in contacting women who would otherwise not have access to information: "Thus, the war was preached in temples and Tirthas, in *Kshetras, Jatras*, and in festivals, on the road and in the house, amongst Sepoys and the citizens, in *Natakas* and in *Tamashas*, to men as well to women."[215] Resistance against the English proliferated as well: ayahs abandoned their jobs, chefs refused to dress properly, Indian messengers dragged their feet when tasked with an assignment.[216]

---

[212] Ibid., 227.

[213] Ibid., 69.

[214] Ibid., 70.

[215] Ibid.

[216] Ibid., 68. These are reminiscent of everyday forms of peasant resistance discussed in Scott, *Weapons of the Weak*.

The proliferation of these activities exemplified "the revolutionary spirit among all the classes of the people."[217] In other words, there existed an autonomous space in which the people communicated with each other in the vernacular that allowed anti-colonial ideas to spread. The war of independence was not simply a "spontaneous" or "unpremeditated affair" but the concatenation of people's activities in a solidarity that shaped the revolution.[218]

*The people* throughout India adopted violence as members of "secret organisations" that were sometimes involved in guerrilla tactics against the British. These moments of violence were important for the historian when interpreting the principle of revolution, especially because colonial historiography had refused to acknowledge the role of the revolutionary: "Order appears in the apparent chaos of inconsistent facts, crooked lines become straight, and straight lines appear crooked, light appears where darkness is, and darkness spreads over light, what appeared ugly becomes fair and what looked beautiful is seen to be deformed. And expectedly, or unexpectedly, but in a clear form, the Revolution comes into the light of real history."[219]

However, Savarkar noted that there were moments of violence perpetrated by revolutionaries that appeared to violate the very principle of revolution: that is, actions that were unethical or immoral. He acknowledged the acts of cruelty and brutality committed by revolutionaries but attributed blame to the British – the root of unethical violence lay in the British conquest. Mazzini's message about cruelty also resonated in Savarkar's writings: the Italian thinker had argued that "noble causes" can be tainted by "cruel reactions" in moments of impetuosity in battle.[220] He had suggested that cruelty in battle was universally condemned but was a sign of "the cries of despairing men" frustrated and disillusioned by oppressors. If the war was fought for

[217] Savarkar, *Indian War*, 86.

[218] There are important parallels with Savarkar's work on 1857 with the writings of Ranajit Guha on this point, albeit with different purposes. See Guha, "The Prose of Counter-Insurgency," and Guha, *Elementary Aspects of Peasant Insurgency in Colonial India.*

[219] Savarkar, *Indian War*, 5.

[220] Mazzini, "On the Encyclica of Pope Pius IX," in idem, *Life and Writings of Mazzini,* vol. 5, 356.

a principle, the moments of cruelty would simply "die away on the day of victory."[221]

What appeared to intrigue Savarkar in the colonial historiography was an admission that the British were not only cruel in their treatment of Indians but also of the Irish. He turned to Irish history to discuss the typology of cruelty perpetrated by the British throughout their colonies. He used three classifications: "cruel oppression"; "cruel vengeance"; and what he called "the cruellest of all" – bloodshed.[222] Savarkar mostly discussed examples of cruel vengeance and bloodshed, often blurring the line between the two and thereby making it difficult to distinguish one from the other, but the main distinction made is that one was about the literal shedding of blood while the other was not.

Before discussing these two main forms of cruelty, it is worth looking at his interpretation of "cruel oppression." The application of British agrarian policies in India that led to the structural transformation of property rights is at the centre of Savarkar's understanding of cruel oppression. The loss of hereditary rights among landowners led to deterioration in the everyday lives of peasants, which led to widespread poverty in the countryside. According to Savarkar, the government claimed that its purpose was to protect peasants from the "tyranny" of landlords; instead, a new form of tyranny was established that sought to destroy both self-rule and self-government in India. The new extractive land policies of the British government had led to "cruel oppression."

Savarkar's second category was "cruel vengeance." As perpetrated by the British, this is distinct from the justifiable vengeance of Indians. Savarkar began by explaining that the discourse of cruel vengeance was found throughout colonial historiography: narrators had acknowledged that the British were cruel in their treatment of Indians in 1857 because they were seeking revenge against Indians for the sake of humanity, or for the betterment of humankind. This double move intrigued Savarkar: that is, there was a collective agreement to declare Indians inhuman for taking up violence (or participating in rebellions) against the British, and then arguing the need for cruelty to improve

---

[221] Ibid.
[222] Savarkar, *Indian War*, 225.

humanity. While Savarkar did not fully develop a critique of this "humanism" propagated by British authors, he regularly returned to arguments about how cruel vengeance was perpetrated as central to the imperial project under the guise of improving the human condition – all the while repeating that this could only happen once Indians were declared inhuman. *Indian War* is full of references to cruel vengeance, but Savarkar made a distinction between this second category and bloodshed. Cruel vengeance was defined as physical torture, but also included the forcible stuffing of pork or beef into the mouths of Indian soldiers who did not eat meat, sexual violence against women and children, and the burning and destruction of villages. An aspect of cruel vengeance was that its victims were innocent.

Most of Savarkar's book is concerned with bloodshed – his third form of cruelty – and descriptions of the orgy of killing of Indians. One figure in particular exemplifies the cruellest form of cruelty: General James George Smith Neill: "It is difficult to find a parallel, even in the history of savages, to the cruel brutality which Neill showed . . . Hundreds . . . have been burnt alive by Neill. Neill has killed as many people in Allahabad alone as all Englishmen, women, and children who had been killed throughout India put together! And tens of such Neills were conducting such massacres in hundreds of places!"[223] Savarkar provided a historiographical review of how Neill was remembered by colonial historians, concluding that Neill was not only celebrated as "bold and brave", but that he was "merciful" in what was called "timely cruelty . . . Some say that this cruelty on [Neill's] part shows the great love of humanity in Neill's heart."[224] At one level, he says, "of what use is philosophy now? Neill has sowed the seeds of cruelty and horror. Their abundant crops are already rising in the fields. Let us, then, behold them in their full season."[225] At another level, he provides a context for cruelty in the form of "justifiable vengeance." He narrates in detail the brutal killing of British men, women, and children by what he calls Indian "butchers." However, these individuals were far more ethical than the real perpetrators of cruelty.

[223] Ibid., 167.
[224] Ibid.
[225] Ibid., 168.

The culpability of the "sin of cruelty" was with the "original evil-doer," and "The sin of brutality falls heavily on the heads of those who committed the provoking injustice."[226] The victims of cruelty were justified in seeking vengeance via cruelty: "Revolt, bloodshed, and revenge have often been instruments created by Nature to root out injustice and introduce an era of justice."[227] After all, violence in warfare had even been justified in the textual tradition, including in the epics, the Puranas, and the Bhagavad Gita. The English, an unethical enemy, were an "oppressive Demon."[228] In a battle in Meerut, he feels the revolutionaries needed to show more cruelty in their attacks than they did: "the Indians no doubt killed the alien English but it was not done savagely enough. They simply cut off the heads with a blow of the sword."[229] Indian revolutionaries were always more ethical before they killed any Englishman, even in mass killings: "In the massacres ordered by the Revolutionaries, not only no religious injuries were inflicted on the English, but they were always given time, when they requested so, to read the Bible before they were killed."[230] Consistent with his argument on the need for cruelty, Savarkar says Krishna counselled Arjuna that it was necessary to abandon a code of ethics with an enemy who is unjust or unethical. Savarkar explains that Krishna's instruction to Arjuna, "*Tasmat yuddhaya yujyaswa*," which he translated as "Therefore, get ready for battle," is repeated in every part of the country, and in every attack by a revolutionary.[231] All the locations for conflict in 1857 – such as the United Provinces, Oudh, Rohilkhand, Bihar, Bengal, Bundelkhand, and Central India – formed the battleground for a contemporary Kurukshetra.

Whether Savarkar was using Kurukshetra only as a metaphor is unclear, but *Indian War* served as the modern embodiment of the Gita at multiple levels. The 1857 war was for justice, making cruelty against an unethical enemy justified and often necessary. All revolutionaries recited the words of Krishna in preparation for battle, and the principle

226 Ibid., 222.
227 Ibid.
228 Ibid., 8.
229 Ibid., 111.
230 Ibid., 255.
231 Ibid., 61, 451.

of revolution was present in the actions of every individual. Writing about 1857 in this framing allowed Savarkar to assert that he was producing a history in full that would transform the reader to take up arms in a colonial world.

## 11. The Revolutionary

For Savarkar the most important figure in India in this period was Mangal Panday: he truly embodied the principle of revolution. An entire chapter is devoted to "Shahid Mangal Panday" (Martyr Mangal Panday), in which Savarkar examines the first sepoy to rise up in the war of independence.[232] He begins with a brief biographical statement about Panday's caste and occupation: "Mangal Panday was a Brahmin by birth. He took up [the] duties of a Kshatriya and was [a] valiant young soldier."[233] Panday's whole life story is not narrated since its importance for Savarkar lies mainly in the moment Mangal Panday exhibited *swaraj* and *swadharma* through his actions. Savarkar's primary interest was in interpreting Panday's motive for killing a British officer as the first act in the war. Savarkar was not deterred in his analysis by the fact that Panday did not explain his motive for the killing. He offered an alternative to the analyses provided by English writers who referred to Panday as a mutineer, an assassin, a criminal. The mutiny could not be a mutiny without Panday as a soldier perpetrating acts that British historiography classified as mutinous.

Savarkar opted to switch the discursive code by selecting antonyms that signalled a counter-message.[234] The classification "Indian War of Independence of 1857" was in itself a counter-message; he also stated that reading colonial historiography required judgement on the part of the historian to interpret which historical acts were "just or unjust."[235] English writers had long considered the concept of

---

[232] Ibid., 85–9. Panday is spelt in multiple ways in sources – Pandy, Pandey, Pandie – but I have maintained the spelling used by Savarkar in this text.

[233] Ibid., 87.

[234] Guha, "The Prose of Counter-Insurgency," 58. My debt to Ranajit Guha is obvious here. I borrow his ideas of switching code signs from colonial discourses by selecting antonyms to produce a counter-message.

[235] Savarkar, *Indian War*, 222.

"rule" – colonial rule over India – as just, while arguing that revolts, bloodshed, and revenge by Indians were unjust. Countering this meant saying: "As long as the word 'rule' is . . . both just and unjust, so long its antonym 'rebellion' can also be just as well as unjust."[236] This opened the discursive space for rethinking rebellion within a different history where the revolutionary was the subject, and the act of rebellion necessary. Savarkar's characterisations of Panday were naturally therefore the reverse of those in official histories; Panday was for Savarkar a revolutionary, a martyr, and a hero. The reclaiming of Panday from colonial history was part of a reclaiming of the official history.

Savarkar neither adhered to normative contemporary approaches to history writing, nor was his purpose to produce a narrative of all the events. His anti-colonial history was meant simply to disrupt the normative interpretations of the most important event of British imperial history in the nineteenth century. And by claiming to understand the consciousness, motive, and desires of his subjects via reading against the grain, Savarkar produced a work that was as much about claiming the past as it was a manual for thinking about the future.

Savarkar says Mangal Panday, a soldier in the 34th Regiment of the Bengal Army stationed in Barrackpore, was, like his fellow soldiers, upset by the forced introduction of greased cartridges to be used by soldiers when loading their rifles. The cartridges were apparently dipped in beef and pork fat, and it was rumoured that their purpose was to pollute and insult both Hindu and Muslim soldiers. Savarkar says that the soldiers were already "infused with the revolutionary spirit" and united with a "sacred purpose of freeing the motherland" even before the controversy about the cartridges.[237] The greased cartridge was incidental to the larger principle that motivated the soldiers: that is, "the love of their country" (*swaraj*) and the "love of their religion" (*swadharma*). Panday was hurt and enraged, "the young man's spirit became uncontrollable, and he at once snatched and loaded his gun, and jumped on the parade-ground shouting, 'Rise! Ye brethren, rise! I bind you by the oath of your religion! Come, let us rise and attack the treacherous enemies for the sake of our freedom.'"[238] Panday then fired

[236] Ibid.
[237] Ibid., 86.
[238] Ibid., 87.

his gun and killed Sergeant-Major Hughson: "a bullet from Panday killed the officer, and his corpse rolled on the ground!"[239] He then drew his sword and attacked a second officer, Lieutenant Baugh. Savarkar provides a discussion of Panday's affect and emotion in his acts of violence: "Into the heart of this young and brilliant Brahmin who loved his religion more than his life, and who was pure in his private life and undaunted in battle, the idea of freedom of his country had entered and electrified his blood."[240] Panday is described as impatient and "hot-blooded," the celebrated characteristics of "martyrs." Panday kept shouting, "Rise! Brethren, rise!" but with little effect. In Savarkar's description, a group of British soldiers on horseback started moving towards Panday, who saw he would be soon captured and decided to shoot himself in the chest as his final act of sacrifice and defiance. He lay injured on the battlefield but did not die. He was arrested and eventually tried for his crimes, for which he was sentenced to be hanged.

Panday serves as the exemplary revolutionary in Savarkar's book because he took the initiative to attack the officers of his regiment when others were either indecisive or unwilling to take up arms. Savarkar says Panday had the message of the Bhagavad Gita in mind. Like Arjuna, he had "no personal malice" against the British officers: it was a matter of duty that was fulfilled out of "devotion to a high and noble principle" of *swaraj* and *swadharma*.[241] Panday was exemplary because he was inspired by Krishna's message to Arjuna and was "thinking alike of victory and defeat."[242] His was an act committed for the sake of duty, a killing for the principle of revolution.

Savarkar ends the chapter with a description of Panday's death. After the trial, a date was set for Panday's execution, but no Indian was willing to serve as hangman because all the soldiers witnessing the execution had "divine love" for Panday: "Not even a low-class man could be found in the whole of Barrackpore to act as executioner! At last four

[239] Ibid.

[240] Ibid.

[241] Ibid., 88.

[242] Ibid. Savarkar appears to have taken a selection from chapter 2, verse 38 of the Bhagavad Gita and incorporated it into his discussion, citing Krishna: "Holding alike happiness and unhappiness, gain and loss, victory and defeat . . ." van Buitenen, trans., *The Bhagavadgita*, 77.

hangmen had to be brought from Calcutta to do the dirty work!"[243] Before the noose was placed around Panday's neck, he was offered an opportunity to reveal the names of collaborators. He refused and was hanged, making him the "first martyr" in the war of independence, the man who planted the "seed of freedom . . . sown for three years."

The loss of a revolutionary's life was always productive. Metaphorically, it was also reproductive: Savarkar noted that the seed was passed from a revolutionary father to a revolutionary son. If one revolution did not succeed, the principle of revolution would be passed in a patrilineal descent inspiring future revolutionaries: "The seed of revolutionary martyrdom soaked in the blood of Mangal Panday was not long in taking root."[244] Savarkar's discussion focuses less on the event than on the power of the revolutionary's spirit: "Mangal Panday is gone, but his spirit has spread all over Hindusthan; and the principle for which he fought has become immortal!"

The fact that Savarkar mentions Panday's caste identity as a Brahmin several times in the chapter may be relevant for thinking about his interpretation of the revolutionary within the caste system. If Panday's spirit as a Brahmin served as the seed for the revolution, did it mean this war of independence was not only inspired by but also defined by the Brahmin spirit? There is no answer to this question in Savarkar's text beyond Panday's celebration as a Brahmin. He ends by noting that the martyrdom was so powerful that "Panday" became synonymous with any revolutionary who fought for *swaraj* and *swadharma*.

Savarkar included a footnote that identified two books he had read in order to write about Mangal Panday: Charles Ball's *The History of the Indian Mutiny* (1811), and Frederick Sleigh Robert's *Forty-one Years in India* (1897). References are often not included in *Indian War*, but in this chapter they provide important insights into Savarkar's method of reading against the grain in the process of writing a history in full. He was selective in the passages he summarised and included in *Indian War*: the description of events leading up to Mangal Panday's attack on the officers is not only shorter in his text, it also lacks many of the details included in Ball and Robert. Using antonyms provided in of-

---

[243] Savarkar, *Indian War*, 88.
[244] Ibid., 90.

ficial classifications, Savarkar also changed the dialogue in Ball's book. Ball says Panday shouted, "Come out, men! Come out, men! You have sent me out, why don't you follow me? You will have to bite the cartridges! Come out for your religion!"[245] Savarkar changes this to "Rise! Ye brethren, rise! I bind you by the oath of your religion! Come, let us rise and attack the treacherous enemies for the sake of our freedom."[246]

In the Bhagavad Gita, there is a passage in which Krishna encourages Arjuna to "Rise up" in battle. It does not fully parallel Savarkar's modification of Ball's text, yet when considering the same sentence in the vernacular text, "your religion" is translated as *swadharma*, and "freedom" as *swaraj*. Savarkar's revision suggests that he inserted the principle of revolution as part of Panday's speech. This is a pattern he followed throughout the text, especially when arguing that every revolutionary in 1857 repeated Krishna's words on the battlefield of Kurukshetra. Panday's quote has many different versions that appear in nearly every narrative description of his attack on British officers.[247] Savarkar's purpose was to underscore that his interpretation of Panday's speech was consistent with the principle of revolution. There are other concerns as well: Savarkar described Panday as killing Sergeant-Major Hughes as the first act of the revolution, but according to Ball's writings Hughes was only injured and survived the attack.[248] When Ball explained that four "low-caste" men had to be brought from Calcutta to serve as hangmen, Savarkar changed the description to "low-class."[249] This point is particularly curious as he restated Panday's Brahmin identity multiple times in the chapter. The idea that people identified as low caste would execute Panday was something that Savarkar likely wanted to avoid mentioning. There are naturally no full or satisfactory explanations for Savarkar's choices. His strategy of writing a history in full did not adhere to the normative conventions of the discipline of history. His point was that colonial writers were never interested in accuracy in their narration; in fact the entire colonial

---

[245] Ball, *The History of the Indian Mutiny*, vol. 1, 45.

[246] Savarkar, *Indian War*, 90.

[247] For a recent revision of this statement, see Wagner, *The Skull of Alum Bheg*, 45.

[248] Ball, *The History of the Indian Mutiny*, 50; Savarkar, *Indian War*, 88.

[249] Savarkar, *Indian War*, 88.

historiography of 1857 had violated the protocols of history writing in the first instance by calling it the "Mutiny of 1857" and Panday its first "mutineer." Savarkar was far from deterred in writing histories with interpretations antithetical to colonial histories (or dominant narratives). This was, on the contrary, a discursive strategy he also adopted in his later writings which privilege the principles of history.

## 12.  The Spirit of Revolution

The spirit of revolution was important in Savarkar's *Indian War*. Every revolutionary in the book is described as having *this* spirit. The original story of the revolutionary in 1857 is Panday's, which is then said to be replicated by all other revolutionaries, who are also called "Panday." It is in these descriptions that Savarkar comes closest to clarifying the conceptualisation of a history in full. The task of the historian was to identify figures like Mangal Panday and study their actions; the historian then comes close to articulating the original essence (*mul tattva*) at the centre of history.

If Panday's was indeed the original story of the revolution that got reproduced, then was it even necessary to study any other revolutionary? On this point Savarkar was clear: the task of the historian was to write every story about every revolutionary. *Indian War* is organised into chapters that focus on the location of battles and individual revolutionaries. Panday's is the original revolutionary story, while all the other revolutionaries represent replication, a kind of mimesis. The revolutionary had a moment of awareness (a spiritual awakening), participated in a violent action (typically a killing), shouted a slogan (often "Maro Feringhiko!" or "Kill the Foreigner"), inspired fellow revolutionaries (usually with an excerpt from the Bhagavad Gita), participated in a battle, performed an act of bravery (valour, manhood, or heroism), died in the battle (achieving martyrdom), and inspired others to take up arms (either through the seed of liberty in the blood or through his spirit travelling to another individual). If the revolutionary did not die in the first battle, he escaped capture (usually due to a secret organisation or guerrilla tactics), and the pattern was repeated in a second or third battle (in which the revolutionary cited the importance of *swadharma* and *swaraj*). There were, of

course, exceptions to these patterns, as there were instances with some
deviations (usually moral or ethical dilemmas) that were resolved by
more killings (usually in the name of justifiable cruelty or super-savage
cruelty). In the end, the outcome for nearly all the figures that Savarkar
discussed in *Indian War* was death (either in battle or through an execution), followed by being declared a martyr, a *shahid*, or a hero. The
spirit of the revolutionary was released at the moment of death – either
it went to heaven or travelled to influence another individual – and
the pattern was repeated again. Savarkar describes all his figures in
this framework: Nana Sahib, Tatia Tope, Kumar Singh, Amar Singh,
Ahmed Shah, Rani Lakshmi Bai, and the dozens of minor figures
mentioned in the book.

To track and document the actions of these revolutionaries was
to confirm that the principle of revolution was universal. The descriptions of killings, mutilations, beheadings, stabbings, bleeding, burnings,
tortures, rapes, and annihilation were just a select number of revolutionary actions. Each action was unique in its own way and yet exemplified the principles of *swaraj* and *swadharma*. Each killing in the name
of the principle of revolution was worthy of separate recognition, just
as every death of each revolutionary was unique.

To study each action (as a revolutionary action) was necessarily a
practice in repetition. Savarkar embraced this repetition in *Indian War*.
The metaphoric seed of liberty or freedom had the potential to create a
field of crops – a luxuriant expanse, in Savarkar's words. The task was
to write about *each* seed, with the hope that the entire nation would
be full of crops – revolutionaries. Savarkar's point was to celebrate the
repetition in order to argue that the revolution never actually ended.
To read against the grain of colonial historiography only marked the
beginning of his project, especially as he hoped future writers would
turn to alternative methods of documenting and recording the actions of revolutionaries. What Savarkar wanted to show was that there
existed a foundation for permanent revolution in India, a revolution
that *Indian War* was meant to inspire.

## 13.  A Failed Revolution

In the end, the Indian war of independence of 1857 did not succeed.
Savarkar described it as a "failure." In a separate text he also noted

Mazzini's view that the Italian revolution had not immediately succeeded in fulfilling its objectives either. But for Mazzini failure did not mean that the revolution should be viewed negatively.[250] In the Indian case, many revolutionaries were captured and executed, while others escaped India altogether. The problem was not with the principle of revolution – there was absolute agreement that the English had to be defeated: "Nobody was *against* destroying the English power."[251] But, "Then, why was there the defeat?" The answer, Savarkar believes, has less to do with the actual attacks and violence necessary for defeating the English and more to do with the fact that there was no clear articulation of a future after the war of independence. Savarkar provides a Biblical reference to explain the necessity of destruction in a war: "creation comes only after the Deluge."[252] And further: "the Revolution worked out successfully as far as the destructive part was concerned; but, as soon as the time for construction came, indifference, mutual fear, and want of confidence sprang up."[253]

Savarkar here basically repeats Mazzini's argument in *Life and Writings* on the same theme that he had discussed in *Joseph Mazzini*, where he had argued that what Young Italy illustrated was that the task was not simply destruction, but to construct the world anew after the destruction. This was the larger problem facing *all* revolutions: that is, at the height of destruction a doubt sets in among those who do not fully understand the principle of revolution. All the same, Italy was fortunate in having Mazzini, who could take up the task of rebuilding Italy by ensuring national unity. In the India of 1857 there had been no single figure capable of fulfilling this role. Moreover, many had not only wavered in their commitment to the revolution, they had been "ignorant" in abandoning violence for the *status quo* without realising that English domination was more destructive than any *swaraj* that would emerge after the revolution.

For the first time in *Indian War*, on the penultimate page of the book, Savarkar provided a typology of *swaraj* in India: democratic, monarchical, and anarchical. This is a curious inclusion, given that

---

[250] Mazzini, *On the Duties of Man*, 174.
[251] Savarkar, *Indian War*, 442.
[252] Ibid.
[253] Ibid.

*swaraj* is central to understanding the principle of revolution in the process of writing a history in full. There is no further discussion of the types of *swaraj*, or the place of each type of *swaraj* in understanding the principle of revolution. Savarkar merely asserts any form of *swaraj* as preferable to foreign rule.

He returned to the theme of cruelty at the end of *Indian War* to further explicate the failure of the revolution. "Mother India" was awakened from her deep sleep at the onset of the war of independence with the goal of smashing slavery in India. In order to illustrate the basic failure, he says Mother India had two sons: the first was an exemplary son who "gave a terrific blow on the head of Tyranny," and the second a traitorous son who "thrust a dagger in her own heart."[254] Savarkar asks: "Now, which of these two sons was wicked, cruel, treacherous, and accursed?" The answer, of course, is the son who betrayed the mother by stabbing her in the heart. The exemplary son is obviously the polar opposite and thus the ideal revolutionary.

Individuals who were like Mother India's exemplary son not only "understood" the principle of revolution, they also "fulfilled their duty to their religion and to their country" as part of a holy war.[255] For those like the traitorous son "the fault of failure lies with the idle, effeminate, selfish, and treacherous men who ruined it."[256] Whereas in early parts of *Indian War* Savarkar celebrated the role of the people as revolutionaries – men, women, and children – by the end of the book women and children simply disappear from the analysis. Here in the conclusion the idea of the "effeminate" man is juxtaposed with the "brave" man (the revolutionary).[257] The effeminate man is only discussed within the context of the failure of the war of independence as the negation of the characteristics of the revolutionary; the effeminate man, like the traitorous son, is responsible for the ultimate betrayal of Mother India. In *Indian War* Savarkar argued that the effeminate man would eventually be forgotten for his failings. In his later writings, he advocated that such men should be annihilated and suffer super-savage cruelty. There was then hope for a future revolution. For Savarkar, as

[254] Ibid., 444.

[255] Ibid., 443.

[256] Ibid.

[257] I have benefited from the discussion in Sinha, *Colonial Masculinity*, to help me conceptualise this binary in Savarkar's writings.

long as there was a trace – however minor – of the principle of revolution embraced by any brave man, it was possible to rise up once again.

# 14. Conclusion

I underscore the point that Savarkar's writings need to be considered as engagements with Mazzini's thought. Key ideas conceptualised by Mazzini in his *Life & Writings* were translated, analysed, and incorporated into Savarkar's work. But Savarkar was also critical in his approach: he modified concepts by turning to vernacular ideas that added complexity to Mazzini's formulations. At another level he also used vernacular terms to interpret Italian, European, and US history, while also being inspired by the Bhagavad Gita. The key argument that Savarkar proposed in this period was understanding that *all* histories of revolution were founded on a universally accepted principle. The task of the historian was to write about actions that reflected this principle in what Savarkar called "a history in full." For the purposes of his own historical project, Savarkar fruitfully violated the normative methodological and disciplinary protocols of contemporary history writing by focusing on a universally accepted principle as the driving force for all history, and by linking this principle to an unnamed source. In this sense he offers a major intervention – writing about the past to serve as an inspiration for future revolutions. Dhingra was only one revolutionary in the ongoing struggle against the foreigner; for Savarkar there was great potential for many more such in writing about the history of the present. What Savarkar accomplished was a discursive rupture that challenged colonial knowledge formation. The "Mutiny of 1857" was from this point forward always contrasted with the "Indian war of independence of 1857." More important, the foundation for Savarkar's long-term conceptualisation of a history in full had been set.

However, Savarkar's ability to develop his idea was restricted for more than a decade. On March 13, 1910 he was arrested at Victoria Station in London on multiple charges, including "procuring and distributing arms," "waging war," and "delivering seditious speeches."[258]

---

[258] "Emperor v. Vinayak Damodar Savarkar and Others," *Indian Law Reports*, 225; "Nasik Conspiracy, Tribunal's Findings. Case Against Savarkar," *The Times of India*, December 28, 1910.

He was also accused of leading a conspiracy to murder officials in India with the aim of overthrowing the government. Most members of the Abhinav Bharat Society and India House had left Britain over the previous weeks for fear of being arrested for sedition. Savarkar had fled with some individuals to France but decided to return – against the advice of his comrades. At the time of his arrest he was carrying a number of texts, including copies of his own banned books: two copies of *Indian War*; one copy of his book on Mazzini; seven copies of a manuscript titled "Choose Oh, Indian Princes"; one copy of a pamphlet on Garibaldi; a scrapbook of vernacular newspaper articles; articles from English newspapers (primarily on Dhingra's assassination of Wyllie); several copies of the *Indian Sociologist* edited by Krishnavarma; one copy of a booklet celebrating Dhingra entitled "Bande Matram"; a number of vernacular manuscripts; one photo zinco block of Mazzini; two photographs of Mazzini; and several badges commemorating the anniversary of 1857.[259]

The British government had evidence of Savarkar's role in the December 21, 1909 murder of A.M.T. Jackson, a district collector in Nasik, in the Bombay Presidency. Savarkar had organised the smuggling of twenty Browning handguns into India, one of which was used by Anant Laxman Kanhere to assassinate Jackson. (Dhingra had also used a Browning to kill Wyllie.) What Savarkar did not anticipate when he returned to London was that the government had no plans to set his trial in Britain and instead transported him to Bombay. When the ship carrying Savarkar docked in Marseilles, France, he escaped by jumping through a ship's window and swam to the shore. He found a French policeman and asked him for political asylum, but the policeman did not understand Savarkar's request. Instead, he handed Savarkar back to the British authorities. The French government filed a case in the International Court of Arbitration at The Hague on behalf of Savarkar, demanding that the British government return him to French custody.[260] News of Savarkar's escape and trial spread globally

[259] "Nasik Conspiracy Case. Evidence from London," *The Times of India*, October 8, 1910. Also, BL, APAC, L/P&J/6/1058, File 284, Judgment of Special Tribunal in Special Bench Cases Nos 2, 3, and 4 of 1910, Emperor versus Shankar Balwant Waidya, *et al.*

[260] *Savarkar Arbitration. Counter-Case Presented on Behalf of the Government of His Britannic Majesty to the Tribunal Constituted under the Agreement*

as newspapers carried stories about the case. French anti-imperialists publicly advocated for Savarkar's release; they included the socialist Jean Longuet (Karl Marx's grandson), who not only wrote an article for the newspaper *L'Humanité* defending Savarkar, but also published a 24-page booklet arguing for his release.[261] Savarkar also had defenders in Britain, especially the Scottish anarchist Guy Aldred who had to spend a year in prison for defending Savarkar and members of the Abhinav Bharat Society.[262] His newspaper *The Word* also carried articles demanding Savarkar's release from British custody. On this point Aldred stated:

> I was imprisoned with Savarkar in Brixton Jail, London, in 19[10], for defending freedom of speech and writing for Indians, and for proclaiming my belief in the coming Indian Republic . . . Savarkar and I, not allowed to speak or see each other, passed like ships in the night. He was *en route* to his terrible Andamans imprisonment. I defended him when he was prosecuted here and in India.[263]

Further news coverage of Savarkar's escape and court case at The Hague elevated his status as the anti-imperialist *extraordinare*. A member of the Abhinav Bharat Society who had settled in Paris advertised and sold copies of *Indian War*, which helped circulation of the book in

*Signed in London on the 25ᵗʰ Day of October, 1910, between the Government of His Brittanic Majesty and the Government of the French Republic* (London: The Foreign Office, 1911). Also, "Award of the Permanent Court of Arbitration in the Case of Savarkar, between France and Great Britain, February 24, 1911," in *The American Journal of International Law*, 5, 2 (1911), 520–3; BL, APAC, Mss.Eur.D573/4, Papers of John Morley as Secretary of State for India, Correspondence with the Viceroy, Letter from Morley, to Lord Minto, August 23, 1910.

[261] Longuet, *Mémoire présenté àla Cour d'Arbitrage de La Haye au nom de M. Vinayak Damodar Savarkar*. Also, Jean Longuet, "Une Violation du Droit d'asile," *L'Humanité*, July 13, 1910; "Another Leading French Newspaper on India: An Interview with the Editor of this Journal," *The Indian Sociologist*, 5, 5 (1909), 18–19.

[262] BL, APAC, EPP/1/3, Guy Aldred, "The White Terror in India: Being the Second Appeal of the Savarkar Release Committee"; Aldred, "To the English Proletariat!" 31–2; Aldred, "The Savarkar Infamy."

[263] Aldred, "Savarkar Arrested," *The Word*, 11, 7 (1950), 65.

Europe, the US, and India. In the end, the French government ended up losing the case, and Savarkar was brought to trial in the Bombay High Court – in which dozens of men were tried as part of what became known as the "Nasik Conspiracy Trial."[264]

The government presented evidence against Savarkar that led to his conviction and a sentence of two life terms to be served in the Cellular Jail in Port Blair, in the Andaman Islands. At the start of the trial Savarkar declared he was not guilty and refused to participate in the proceedings. He requested that the case be dismissed as he considered his arrest illegal. Chaturbhuj Amin, the cook in India House, testified that he himself was a member of the Abhinav Bharat Society in London, and that Savarkar had instructed him to smuggle the twenty handguns back with him to India.[265] In addition to the weapons charges, the government presented evidence to the effect that, before leaving for London in 1906, Savarkar had delivered several speeches in Nasik and Pune as part of a revolutionary organisation called the Mitra Mela, which later became the Abhinav Bharat Society. The speeches were described as "inflammatory." In them Savarkar discussed the importance of Mazzini, but also the need to gather arms for organising a rebellion and circulate literature about revolution.[266] Savarkar's writings in London were introduced in court as promoting violence in India and Britain. The Dhingra case was presented as further evidence of the impact of Savarkar's ideas on violence, as were copies of a bomb manual that Savarkar had sent from London to various people in India.

Witnesses at the trial provided details about Savarkar's book on Mazzini and its impact in the Bombay Presidency. From London Savarkar had sent the manuscript of the book to his brother Ganesh Damodar Savarkar, who resided in Nasik. Ganesh Savarkar was an important

---

[264] "The Nasik Conspiracy Case. Tribunal's Findings. Case Against Savarkar," *The Tribune*, January 5, 1911.

[265] "Bombay Law Courts. High Court. The Savarkar Trial," *The Times of India*, January 30, 1911.

[266] "The Savarkar Trial: Sentence Passed," *The Times of India*, January 31, 1911. Also, BL, APAC, L/P&J/6/1058, File 284, Testimony of Raghunath Venkatesh, January 24, 1911, and Testimony of Harishchandra Krishna Kergaumkar, date not given.

political figure at this point, especially within the Abhinav Bharat Society.[267] He hosted secret meetings at his house, where it was reported that the handwritten manuscript of the Mazzini book was circulated amongst members of the Abhinav Bharat Society.[268] To raise political funds, Ganesh Savarkar promoted the idea for the need to sell his brother's book, which in the official records was identified as *Life of Mazzini*.[269] But Ganesh Savarkar needed to get the book printed before copies could be sold. He soon secured the printing of 2000 copies at the Jagat Hitechu Press in Pune.[270]

A member of Ganesh Savarkar's organisation named Balwant Ramachandra Barve explained that he started a branch of the secret organisation. Barve delivered speeches in the Bombay Presidency based on Savarkar's writings and urged members of the audience to read *Life of Mazzini*.[271] In his court testimony he explained that he discussed the need for a "Mazzini for India," while also establishing comparisons between Ramdas and Mazzini, paralleling Savarkar's argument. One of the prosecutors in the case cited Savarkar's speeches as further evidence connecting his ideas with the violence of his supporters. He pointed to the fact that there was "a great similarity between the acts committed by the accused and the acts urged in the *Life of Mazzini* and the preface to that book written by Savarkar."[272] But when the prosecutor asked one of the witnesses to describe the method advocated in the secret organisation for achieving independence, he replied, "By following the methods of 1857."[273]

[267] "Nasik Conspiracy Case. Speeches by the Accused," *The Times of India*, October 5, 1910.

[268] "Nasik Conspiracy, Tribunal's Findings. Case Against Savarkar," *The Times of India*, December 28, 1910.

[269] *Life of Mazzini* is also the title of Bolton King's biography of Mazzini, but for the purposes of the court case the English translation of the Marathi title of Savarkar's books was used. To be clear: this was not a reference to King's book.

[270] "Nasik Conspiracy Trial. A Printed Handbill," *The Times of India*, October 4, 1910.

[271] "Nasik Conspiracy Case. Speeches by the Accused," *The Times of India*, October 5, 1910.

[272] Ibid.

[273] Ibid.

An unintended consequence of the Nasik Conspiracy Case was that the government's arguments against Savarkar actually confirmed his idea that histories of revolutions and wars of independence actually had the potential to inspire new revolutionaries. The fact that newspapers published reports of and excerpts from the daily testimony helped spread the news about the importance of Mazzini's writings for Indian revolutionaries. As reported in the *The Times of India* article on September 28, 1910, the advocate general presented a speech in court in which he discussed the publication of Savarkar's *Life of Mazzini*: "[It was] published for distribution and broadcast throughout India, with the view of inculcating in the minds of the people the principle set out in that book."[274] His articulation provided as good a summary of Savarkar's argument as Savarkar might himself have provided. The principle of history that Savarkar conceptualised was now circulating throughout India – at the very moment that Savarkar was beginning his prison sentence of two life terms.

[274] "Nasik Conspiracy Case. Advocate-General's Speech," *The Times of India*, September 28, 1910.

# PART II

# Hindutva is History

The critical eye will find in *Hindutva*, too, the same
passion for liberty which inspired Shriyut Savarkar's
*[The Indian] War of Independence [of 1857]*
**Indra Prakash, 1938**

Vinayak Damodar Savarkar, photographed by
Narayan Vinayak Virkar (c. 1924).
*Photo credit:* This image was previously published in
Christopher Pinney, "The Tiger's Nature, but Not the
Tiger: Bal Gangadhar Tilak as Mohandas Karamchand Gandhi's
Counter-Guru," *Public Culture*, 23, 2 (2011), 395–416.

# 1. Introduction

Savarkar was celebrated as an anti-imperialist for most of the twentieth century – a legacy that persists. During his lifetime even his detractors praised Savarkar as a leading figure who spent his career fighting empire, arguing that he had sacrificed twenty-seven years as a political prisoner. Implicit in popular characterisations of him as a "freedom fighter" is the idea that he fought for freedom against the British empire as a patriot and nationalist. Yet in the 1920s, in his writings on Hindutva Savarkar argued precisely for the centrality of empire – for all Hindus. This seems on the face of it quite a paradox, but it was not a paradox for Savarkar. He explained that Hindus had once participated in the violent colonisation of land that had eventually led to the creation of a Hindu nation, followed by the establishment of a Hindu empire. He clarified that he himself was a proponent of empire, not an anti-imperialist *per se*. In *Hindu Pad Padashahi* he says, "we grudge not England her victory . . . we admire her skill and might that, stretching her hand over oceans and seas, over continents and countries, snatched an Indian Empire from our struggling hand and on that foundation has raised a magnificent World-Empire."[1] In fact, Savarkar lamented the decline of empire – the Hindu empire, that is – even as he opposed the impact of Islamic empires and the dominance of the British empire in India. The conundrum for him was not only to understand the loss of the Hindu empire over the course of many centuries, but also to frame a future for its return. He pointed out that the Marathas represented the "last great Hindu Empire" and "the most glorious of our Hindu Empires." His goal was to look forward and inspire Hindus to fight for a new Hindu empire.[2] He even provided a Biblical reference in *Hindu Pad Padashahi* on this point: *"For who knows when the Resurrection comes!"*[3]

[1] Savarkar, *Hindu Pad Padashahi* (1925), 287.

[2] Ibid.

[3] Savarkar, *Hindu Pad Padashahi* (2003), 241 (italics in original). This sentence does not appear in the first edition (1925) but was added in a later edition.

In *Essentials of Hindutva* Savarkar also argued that the hundreds of thousands of Hindus who had travelled as merchants and traders to the farthest reaches of the globe were actually colonisers. His point was that these Hindus who had settled all over the world had the potential to "own a whole country" and "form a separate state."[4] In other words, diasporic Hindus had the potential for establishing a new world empire: "Let our colonists continue unabated their labours of founding a Greater India, a Mahabharata, to the best of their capacities and contribute all that is best in our civilisation to the upbuilding of Humanity."[5] The processes of colonisation meant that Hindus would be able to contribute and improve the lives of people on a global scale, especially by expanding into multiple territories with a planetary ambition – "from Pole to Pole."[6] If the Maratha empire represented the last Hindu empire, it was clear that Savarkar had earlier Hindu empires in mind as he constructed his argument. The reference to Greater India, for example, was likely not an accident, as the 1920s also saw the founding of the Greater India Society, which sought to examine the history of India's influence in South East Asia, dating back to antiquity.[7] This early period was considered central to understanding the power and influence of Hindu empires. However, in *Essentials of Hindutva* Savarkar provided an argument for the future: "The only geographical limits of Hindutva are the limits of the [E]arth!"[8] His point was not simply that Hindus needed to unify or rebuild an old territoriality – what would later be called Akhand Bharat (or Unified India) – but to have the greater ambition of colonising parts of the world with the aim of establishing a new and global Hindu empire.

Savarkar's conceptualisation of a Hindu colonisation of the planet was formed in the period of his incarceration. His idea that Hindus were travelling across the world and could establish a Hindu empire was taking place at a time when Savarkar's own movements were restricted. The core idea was part of a fantastic programme of spreading Hindutva through the imagining of a Hindu empire when he was a prisoner. As if referring to himself metaphorically, Savarkar says,

---

[4] Savarkar, *Essentials of Hindutva*, 106.

[5] Ibid.

[6] Ibid., 79, 106.

[7] Bayly, "Imagining 'Greater India'," 703–44.

[8] Savarkar, *Essentials of Hindutva*, 106.

"Hindutva does not clip the wings of the Himalayan eagles but only adds to their urge . . . Nothing can stand in the way of your desire to expand [Hindutva]."[9] Paradoxically, while imprisoned, Savarkar's mind was in full flight.

I begin with this discussion of what may be called Savarkar's imperial ambitions to argue that the very idea of a Hindu nation can only be understood within his own articulation that Hindus were *the* original colonisers of the land. Savarkar described this as a violent process in which people had an impact on the lives of populations that resided on the land *before* the arrival of the Aryans: "They [the Aryans] soon reclaimed the vast, waste and but thinly populated lands. Forests were felled, agriculture flourished, cities rose, kingdoms thrived – the touch of the human hand changed the whole face of the wild and unkempt nature."[10] He pointed out that the process of colonisation was not simply a conquest of the land, it was also cultural imperialism. As the number of colonies increased over time, earlier inhabitants of these territories came to be culturally dominated by the Hindus. The key characteristic that marked this form of power occurred when, after a time, the colonised populations abandoned their old customs, attachments, and names to create a new "national and cultural unity."[11] In other words, Hindu colonisation had proven itself a success in establishing a Hindu nation.

The ability to expand and create Hindu empires was further evidence of Hindu power. Yet the task for the present was also to interpret the decline of the Hindu empire (and the rise of Islamic empires and European empires), while simultaneously providing a framework for reviving or resurrecting the Hindu empire and colonising the world with Hindu states. Not only was an analysis of empire at the centre of Savarkar's thought, his imperial ambitions were grand. This was a secret little known among those who continued to celebrate Savarkar as an anti-imperialist.

In reading *Essentials of Hindutva* it is evident that Savarkar's terminology was analytically imprecise. His uses of "Hindu nation" and "Hindu empire" are often overlapping and indistinguishable. In other instances, the Hindu empire – as in the case of the Marathas – is

[9] Ibid.
[10] Ibid., 10.
[11] Ibid., 6, 8.

inscribed within the boundaries of the idealised Hindu nation (or the land of the Hindus). In specific contexts he argued that Hindus had created a nation and then colonised lands to establish *the* Hindu nation. The nation was formed in the process of imperialism itself. Boundaries were typically not fixed, resulting in some uncertainty about the limits of both Hindu nation and Hindu empire. On the other hand Savarkar's blurring of "nation" and "empire" is not necessarily unique, especially when considering the formation of nations and empires in Europe, but especially in Britain, with its own four nations that were united under one kingdom and its simultaneous world empire. It has been pointed out that "empire" was a form of state that existed historically, but empires in world history were never consistent or normalised in their structures or forms of governance.[12] The idea of "making nations on imperial terrain" was a common feature of nineteenth-century Europe.[13] The idealised formation of a nation with a unified population and territory under one state was often discussed by nationalists seeking to carve nations out of existing empires. By the early-twentieth century the nexus of nation and empire was certainly rethought globally – not just in India – with the many wars and revolutions that sought the destruction of world empires and the creation of new postcolonial nation-states.

Savarkar was consistent with nineteenth- and twentieth-century nationalists in arguing that the origin of the nation dated back to antiquity – an aspect of nationalism noted by Benedict Anderson.[14] There were contemporary intellectuals in India who had similarly interpreted the formation of nationalism in Hindu culture as a pre-modern phenomenon before the publication of Savarkar's book. At the centre of these interpretations was the idea that Hindus were territorially and culturally united in the past – the distant past. It has been shown that the desire to trace the origins of the Hindu nation to ancient India was part of an emergent historiography that converged on the idea that the greatness of India's past was in a "golden age" when Hindus ruled before the arrival into the subcontinent of Muslims.[15]

[12] Burbank and Cooper, *Empires in World History*.

[13] Ibid., 336.

[14] Anderson, *Imagined Communities*, 70–1.

[15] See Thapar, "Imagined Religious Communities?"; Trautmann, *The Aryan Debate*; Thapar, "The Theory of Aryan Race in India."

The construction of this argument was also a response to British historians who argued that Hindus had no history. People like Savarkar wanted to demonstrate the opposite by turning to nineteenth-century Orientalists who had celebrated the imagined Hindu past. Savarkar's arguments reflect familiarity with this body of work.

My primary focus here is Savarkar's *Essentials of Hindutva* (1923). He completed this text during his period of incarceration but was able to smuggle the manuscript out of prison at some point. Between 1910 and 1921 he was only permitted to write an annual letter to his family and submit written petitions to the government. But in his shorter writings, which are also considered here, Savarkar sometimes provided important ideas that were developed in his later writings. *Essentials of Hindutva* was his first major work since completing *Indian War*. I try to analyse and contextualise Savarkar's method of writing "a history in full" in part because he himself asserted that Hindutva is indefinable. He was convinced that his approaches to the study of texts made it possible to approximate Hindutva by first seeking out the conceptual histories of "Hindu" and "Hindusthan." I argue that Savarkar interpreted the formation of these words as a direct outcome of the colonisation of the people and the land. It was for him a dialectical process in which coloniser and colonised both became "Hindu" through conquest and violence. The territory created from this process was called the land of the Hindus, or Hindusthan. The unification of Hindus under one territory (and one name) also meant that the plurality of existing names of lands were either discursively marginalised or subsumed within "Hindusthan." His was an idealised and imagined and unified nation *of* Hindus, marking a territory that was finally conquered *by* Hindus, and a holy place in the world meant only *for* Hindus.

In *Essentials of Hindutva* the principles of history that Savarkar outlined in *Indian War* are actually violated first of all by Hindus. Savarkar says the "original evil-doer" initiated the cruelty, so that victims of this cruelty were justified in seeking vengeance through acts that he characterised as forms of cruelty.[16] Savarkar explains that Hindu colonisers inflicted violence on the land and existing inhabitants. These colonisers were not motivated by *swaraj* and *swadharma* – but nor were the people of the newly conquered territory. The motives and

---

[16] Savarkar, *Indian War*, 222.

desires of the historical actors in *Essentials of Hindutva* are different from those discussed in wars of independence. Implicit in Savarkar's articulation of the process of colonisation is that the original Hindus were moral or just in their conquests, whereas the British colonisers were not. This is not to suggest that Savarkar abandoned writing about the principles of history; rather, the point is that these principles were now revised as a way to understand Hindutva.

In other words, there was no period of vengeance against the Hindus in this phase of their expansion. Instead, the local population was not only dominated by Hindus, it was also persuaded to adopt Hindu culture as its own. As a result, people already long resident in the territory were transformed or converted into Hindus. This process of colonisation expanded from the Indus river towards what is now known as the Bay of Bengal and the Indian Ocean; it became a pattern which was repeated, leading to many diverse populations calling themselves Hindus. For Savarkar, a conceptualisation of "Hindu" must recognise *this* history of colonisation. The history of Hindus was both a history of conquest over large populations *and* a history of such populations being dominated in the process of becoming Hindu. The Hindu was therefore formed (or transformed) in the very act of violence itself. *Essentials of Hindutva* marks an important epistemological shift in Savarkar's writings by reconceptualising a history in full as Hindutva. Moreover, in it he provides a methodology for reading diverse sources to investigate the motives and desires of Hindus in the making of Hindusthan.

## 2. The Writings of Prisoner Number 32778

By the time *Essentials of Hindutva* was published in May 1923, Savarkar had spent nearly thirteen years in custody. After his conviction in the Nasik Conspiracy Case in Bombay, he began his life sentence in the Cellular Jail in the Andaman Islands on June 30, 1911 as Prisoner Number 32778.[17] The period of incarceration between 1911 and 1921

[17] MSA, Home Spec, File 60-D-(f)-1923, "Cellular Jail History Ticket for Vinayak Damodar Savarkar (No. 32778)," S-33.

in the Cellular Jail was a difficult one. For over a decade Savarkar, like other prisoners, was subjected to hard labour, solitary confinement, torture, illness, and violence. His ability to write was initially restricted: he was only allowed to send one or two letters a year to his family. The fact that Savarkar's older brother Ganesh D. Savarkar was also in the Cellular Jail allowed him some connection with family during his lengthy prison sentence. On December 15, 1912 Savarkar penned a letter to his younger brother Narayan D. Savarkar. He began: "Thus it is after 18 months I have a chance to touch pen and ink again: At this rate one can quickly unlearn the art of writing altogether!"[18] In the letter Savarkar discusses his daily routine, which included getting up at 5 a.m., working till 10 a.m., lunch at noon, followed by a second round of work till 4 p.m. He was able to rest and read once he returned to his cell. He was allowed to receive books from his family; this provides clues as to what Savarkar was reading in the Cellular Jail. In contrast, the official prison records only include the dates Savarkar checked out books from the library, which, as noted earlier, was said to have a collection of 2000 volumes; the records do not provide the titles or authors of the books that Savarkar read.

In his letter Savarkar thanks his brother for sending works by Moropant, Bharat, and Vivekananda (the titles are not given) but complains that two books he had requested never arrived: *Jneya mimansa* and *Ajneya mimansa*.[19] In the absence of other information it is difficult to be definite, but it is likely that *Ajneya mimansa* was a Marathi translation of selections – notably the part entitled "The Unknowable" – from Herbert Spencer's (1820–1903) *First Principles* edited and translated by Narayan Laxman Phadke.[20] In London Savarkar had engaged with Spencer's works via Shyamji Krishnavarma and the residents of India House. Spencer was not only an influence on Krishnavarma's thought – *The Indian Sociologist* often began with epigraphs from Spencer's writings – but the two were personally close as well.[21] Newspapers noted that Krishnavarma attended Spencer's

---

[18] Letter from V.D. Savarkar to N.D. Savarkar, December 12, 1912, in Savarkar, *Letters from the Andamans, Selected Works of Veer Savarkar*, vol. 3, 426.

[19] Ibid.

[20] Phadke, *Ajneya mimansa*.

[21] For example, the following is an epigraph by Herbert Spencer from

funeral and publicly announced there the establishment of an endowment for the Spencer Lectureship at the University of Oxford.[22] If
indeed the *Ajneya mimansa* mentioned in Savarkar's letter was Phadke's
book, it may provide a new framing for Savarkar's conceptualisation
of "principles" in his own writings, in *Indian War*, and in his later
works, especially as *Ajneya mimansa* was the first volume in a series
titled "Adi Tattvem" (The Origin of Principles).[23] The reference to
*Jneya mimansa* is less clear, including whether it was part of the same
series. What is interesting about these references is that they indicate
works on Mimansa – epistemology, ontology, and philosophy more
generally, subjects that Savarkar developed in *Essentials of Hindutva*
to conceptualise Hindutva.

Subsequent letters give no evidence of Savarkar eventually having received these two books, although in his annual letters of 1914 and 1915
he mentions additional books that he enjoyed reading, including novels and works of philosophy. Prison records list four separate dates in
1913, 1914, 1916, and 1919 when Savarkar received packages of books
and magazines totalling sixty-eight items; their details are not given.[24]

Many facts about Savarkar's time in the Cellular Jail are provided
in the "Cellular Jail History Ticket." This is a document in which jail
officials chronologically itemised notes about Savarkar from the day
of his arrival in 1911 till his departure on May 2, 1921. It records everything from the nature of his prison work to the days he borrowed
library books; from the days he received special punishments to the
dates he sent letters. A topic that attracted a great deal of official attention were petitions that Savarkar filed during his time in the Cellular
Jail. Within two months of his arrival, Savarkar submitted his first

---

*Principles of Ethics* in *The Indian Sociologist: An Organ of Freedom, and of Political, Social, and Religious Reform*, vol. 3, no. 1, January 1907: "Every man is
free to do that which he wills, provided he infringes not on the equal freedom
of any other man."

[22] "The Funeral of Herbert Spencer," *The Times* (London), December 15,
1903.

[23] Phadke, *Ajneya mimansa*, "Title page." "The Source of the Essence" is an
alternative interpretation for the title of the book series.

[24] MSA, Home Spec, File 60-D-(f)-1923, "Cellular Jail History Ticket for
Vinayak Damodar Savarkar (No. 32778)," S-33.

petition for clemency, which was rejected on September 3, 1911.[25] He filed a second the following year, on October 20, 1912, arguing that he should be released from the Cellular Jail as his conduct was better than that of other prisoners who had been shown clemency. A third was submitted to the Home Department of the Government of India on November 11, 1913, which attracted a great deal of attention, including by Members of Parliament in Britain. As in the earlier petitions, Savarkar had requested a remission of his sentence. According to the reports received by the Home Department from the prison officials, Savarkar was a co-operative prisoner for the first two and a half years of his sentence, but on December 18, 1913 he refused the mandated work required of inmates. In the "History Ticket" officials simply noted, "Absolutely refusing to work."[26] As punishment Savarkar was put in solitary confinement for a month. His behaviour was reported to have improved, until he went on strike three times in June 1914. For each protest Savarkar received a different punishment; according to the Secretary to the Government of India: (1) seven days in standing handcuffs; (2) four months chain-gang (with chain fetters); and, (3) ten days in crossbar fetters.[27] The information in the "History Ticket" indicates that between 1911 and 1912 Savarkar was placed in solitary confinement on four separate occasions, as well as received a punishment of seven days in standing-position handcuffs.[28] However, it appears that this earlier information was not forwarded to the Home Department during its inquiry in 1914.

As Savarkar completed the punishments for his protests, government officials discussed his petition. Officials were also concerned by the information that Savarkar was regularly kept in chains well before Savarkar's first refusal to work. The inquiry into the extra-legal use of chains was dismissed: prison officials simply stated, "No convicts are regularly kept in chains in the Andamans, but as punishment for prior offences a convict may be placed in a punishment chain-gang."

[25] Ibid., S-35.

[26] Ibid., S-39.

[27] BL, IOR, L/P&J/6/1341, File 2286, Letter from Secretary to the GOI, to T.W. Holderness, Under Secretary of State for India, September 24, 1914.

[28] MSA, Home Spec, File 60-D-(f)-1923, "Cellular Jail History Ticket for Vinayak Damodar Savarkar (No. 32778)," S-33–5.

Savarkar's petition was rejected with the explanation that since he had been convicted for "the abetment of the murder" of A.M.T. Jackson, there was "no reason for clemency in this case."

Savarkar submitted a fourth petition to the Government of India on October 5, 1917 in which he requested amnesty for all political prisoners. He acknowledged that while the government had rejected his 1914 petition, he argued that the First World War had transformed the circumstances for everyone globally, so it was possible to reconsider the role of prisoners anew:

> The war, and all that it means, has definitely and materially changed the political relations of almost all peoples and states. A new spirit has manifested itself in man and whole nations are being roused and animated by new visions and new hopes, which have found responsible and glowing expressions in the utterances of Republics and Ministers of Empires. Neither India nor the British Empire as a whole could have remained unaffected by this great Democratical [*sic*] upheaval in the world.[29]

Britain should follow the policy of "Co-operation and Commonwealth" with Indian political prisoners, as it had in Canada and South Africa: that is, either release the prisoners or give them autonomy.[30] He cited that prisoners had been granted amnesty in Russia, France, Ireland, and Austria. Most Indian political prisoners were convicted on "conspiracy" charges, rather than individual acts of violence, for which many had already served up to ten years' hard labour.[31] In contrast, he said the Suffragists in Britain who had been convicted for "individual acts" of violence had been released from prison and granted amnesty immediately after the start of the war. If the British empire really wanted to treat all nations equally with the aim of working towards a "Human State" – a category that Savarkar also mentions in *Essentials of Hindutva* – then the Indian resistance to empire was likely to subside. In fact, on this point Savarkar also stated: "I can have nothing but sympathy with an Empire that binding a vast portion of mankind

---

[29] BL, IOR, L/P&J/6/1525, File 806, Petition by Vinayak Damodar Savarkar for Amnesty to all Political Offenders, to Secretary to the GOI, Home Department, October 5, 1917.

[30] Ibid.

[31] Ibid.

together takes us nearer to such an Ideal."[32] Savarkar concluded that his primary purpose in writing to government was not to seek his own release; rather it was for government to grant amnesty to all the other political prisoners, even if it meant that he still remained in the Cellular Jail. Savarkar's petition was denied once again.

As we can see, official government records only provide select information about Savarkar's time in the Cellular Jail, with a focus on Savarkar's violations of his prison sentence and punishments. Savarkar's own writings about the Cellular Jail indicate that prisoners were subject to a great deal of everyday violence. Even the government's inquiry suggested that Savarkar was required to wear chains on a daily basis without that information being noted in the "History Ticket." The only petition approved during Savarkar's stay in the Cellular Jail was his request to be promoted to a 2nd Class prisoner (from 3rd Class) in 1916.[33] This shift in classification was due to good behaviour and allowed Savarkar to have greater access to books and permitted him to meet family members who visited the prison. Savarkar's wife and his brother travelled to the Andamans to meet him in 1919.

Over the years 1917–19 Savarkar's health deteriorated significantly due to chronic dysentery, malaria, and pulmonary tuberculosis. This was also the period of the influenza pandemic in which an estimated twelve to thirty million Indians lost their lives; Savarkar does not mention suffering from influenza.[34] He was placed in a "convalescent gang" on eight different occasions for a total of approximately nine months.[35] Individuals who were discharged from the hospital or who needed extra time to recover from an illness were transferred to "convalescent gangs" in which they were served higher-quality food and given extra rations of milk.[36] These prisoners were generally made to do light work, such as

[32] Ibid.

[33] MSA, Home Spec, File 60-D-(f)-1923, "Cellular Jail History Ticket for Vinayak Damodar Savarkar (No. 32778)," S-41.

[34] See Arnold, "Death and the Modern Empire."

[35] See MSA, Home Spec, File 60-D-(f)-1923, "Cellular Jail History Ticket for Vinayak Damodar Savarkar (No. 32778)."

[36] *Report on the Administration of Andaman and Nicobar Islands and the Penal Settlement of Port Blair for 1904–05* (Calcutta: Office of the Superintendent of Government Printing, India, 1906), 39.

"rope making," and provided with daily medical care. Once a prisoner's health improved, he was transferred back to the general prison population. In his letter of August 4, 1918 to his brother Narayan, Savarkar explained his declining health in detail. The Cellular Jail was "bearable" when he was feeling well, but with his illness he was "utterly broken."[37] He felt obliged to inform Narayan about the seriousness of the situation as a "duty" to his family. He felt great "joy" on the one day each year that he was allowed to write an annual letter to the family, but he was barely well enough to write:

> Yet [I] am feeling the strain of penning even such a letter as this! The flesh complains and I could not go on without a rest! Last year March, I weighed 119 [pounds] – this year I weigh 98! Chronic dysentery due to disregard of the medical treatment in the beginning has reduced me to a skeleton. Eight years I bore the burden well . . . But now I feel the flesh has received wounds that are hard to heal and day by day pining away . . . But what is likely is that this constant debility may end in some fatal malady or that inevitable friend so well known in jails, especially in the Andamans – the Pthysis. Only one thing and one thing alone could assure me of my recovering and that is a change . . . to a better climate in some Indian jail.[38]

In Savarkar's letter to his brother on September 21, 1919 he explains that his health has deteriorated further with malarial fever and dysentery. His weight has dropped to 95 lbs, resulting in his being removed from rigorous work in the prison. The situation is dire; he urges his brother to help transfer him to another prison: "it is therefore all the more necessary and is all the more forcibly demonstrated how necessary it is to remove me from this unhealthy and malarious climate."[39]

On January 24, 1920 and March 30, 1920 Savarkar submitted two final petitions to the Jails Committee and the Chief Commissioner of the Andamans, respectively. By this point he was aware that the government was in serious discussions about granting amnesty to political prisoners, especially as various individuals and organisations

[37] Letter from V.D. Savarkar to N.D. Savarkar, August 4, 1918, in Savarkar, *Letters from the Andamans, Selected Works of Veer Savarkar*, vol. 3, 466.

[38] Ibid., 466–7.

[39] Letter from V.D. Savarkar to N.D. Savarkar, September 21, 1919, in Savarkar, *Letters from the Andamans, Selected Works of Veer Savarkar*, vol. 3, 469.

in India were advocating for their release. In his petition of March 1920 Savarkar began by citing the Home Department's statement that government was open to reviewing the documents and papers of any political prisoner under the condition that the individual no longer posed a danger to the state. Savarkar cited the official statement in his letter stating that "the Government would extend the Royal clemency to that person."[40] He added, "the undersigned most humbly begs that he should be given a last chance to submit his case, before it is too late." He cited his declining health and desire to lead a retired life away from active politics; these factors provide Savarkar with a context in which to explain the purpose of the petition, especially the point that the matter of his request for amnesty be reviewed in a timely manner. Presumably Savarkar was thinking of his own mortality when writing this petition, as he had been when he composed the letter to Narayan Savarkar about his deteriorating health.

Savarkar argues that he and Ganesh Savarkar have met the criteria set for "Royal clemency" based on the government's own reports, especially the Sedition Committee Report (1918), which stated that the period between 1899 and 1909 witnessed a great deal of political activity, with books written on Mazzini, the establishment of secret societies, and shipment of arms to India that were independent of Savarkar and his brother.[41] They were not the only ones responsible for all anticolonial activity in this period, and for that reason they should not be held accountable for the actions of others. He cites the circulation of a petition signed by over 5000 individuals calling for his release. He says the reason he broke the law was for "political progress," but in no way was he or his brother responsible for the murder of A.M.T. Jackson. He mentions other political assassination cases in which the government had granted clemency to the murderers – even to those who had done the killing; whereas he and his brother had only been convicted of a conspiracy, not for the actual assassination; and moreover, unlike the Russian Peter Kropotin they were not anarchists. Savarkar explains

[40] MSA, Home Spec, File 60-D-(b)-1919, Petition from V.D. Savarkar to the Chief Commissioner of Andamans, Cellular Jail, Port Blair, March 30, 1920.

[41] *Sedition Committee Report, 1918* (Calcutta: Superintendent Government Printing, 1918).

that his petition is an attempt to express his "despair" at his circumstances, but also to offer that he and Ganesh are willing to pledge that they will refrain from politics for "a definite and reasonable period." In addition, he reiterates his willingness to "abide by the constitution and stand by it" – this being what he also stated in his petitions of 1914 and 1918. He concludes: "Therefore I humbly submit that the Government be pleased to extend the clemency to me."[42]

Yet in Savarkar's final letter to his younger brother, dated July 6, 1920, he explains that he does not anticipate the government approving his petition for him or Ganesh Savarkar – presumably this was in reference to the March 30, 1920 petition: "Please do not hope much from this petition so far as our release is concerned . . . we shall not be very much disappointed."[43] As anticipated, the Government of India once again rejected Savarkar's petition while continuing to grant amnesty to other political prisoners. An official in the Cellular Jail added a note on Savarkar's "History Ticket": "The Viceroy is not prepared at present to extend to him the benefit of the amnesty."[44] This was despite the fact that Savarkar's last petition expresses willingness to declare his loyalty and co-operate with the British:

> The danger that is threatening our country from the north at the hands of the fanatic hordes of Asia who have been the curse of India in the past when they came as foes, and who are more likely to be so in the future now that they want to come as friends, makes me convinced that every intelligent lover of India would heartily and loyally co-operate with the British people in the interests of India herself.

This was an important declaration, given Savarkar's long-standing antagonism to the British. More important, this is perhaps the first piece of writing in which Savarkar shows a shift from his writings in London in relation to his interpretation of Muslims – though without actually

[42] MSA, Home Spec, File 60-D-(b)-1919, Petition from V.D. Savarkar to the Chief Commissioner of Andamans, Cellular Jail, Port Blair, March 30, 1920.

[43] Letter from V.D. Savarkar to N.D. Savarkar, July 6, 1920, in Savarkar, *Letters from the Andamans, Selected Works of Veer Savarkar*, vol. 3, 479.

[44] MSA, Home Spec, File 60-D-(f)-1923, "Cellular Jail History Ticket for Vinayak Damodar Savarkar (No. 32778)," Entry for August 8, 1920, S-45.

mentioning Muslims by name: he opts to refer to them as "the fanatic hordes of Asia."[45] Savarkar wrote his petition to the Government of India when Gandhi was organising a mass movement of non-cooperation. Gandhi had established an alliance with Muslim leaders of the Khilafat movement, such as Shaukat Ali and Mohammad Ali, in support of their view that the the Ottoman Sultan was the Caliph of Islam. News of these political developments had filtered through into the Cellular Jail. Savarkar's argument that India needed to "loyally co-operate" with the British occurred even as the Non-Cooperation movement was emerging in solidarity with Muslims committed to the Khilafat movement. The idea of maintaining "India's interests" by declaring loyalty to the British marked a radical departure from his earlier writings – the urgency for Savarkar seems to have been to argue against co-operation with Muslims in India, rather than oppose the domination of the British. All the same, by rejecting Savarkar's petition British officialdom made it clear it was not convinced about Savarkar's pledge to co-operate.

Savarkar's last letter to Narayan also reveals that he was engaged with Humanist thought and ideas which he had first articulated in his book on Mazzini. Savarkar's prison writings – the letters and petitions – provide a glimpse into his thought over this period of incarceration. As Savarkar noted in his first letter to Narayan, his writings had by necessity to have the quality of being generic or formulaic, given that the prison authorities reserved the right to read and censor letters.[46] Yet his inclusion of a discussion of the value of creating a "Human state" was certainly unusual in the context of his letters. These developments in Savarkar's thought are particularly important, especially because they were later incorporated into his conceptualisation of Hindutva in *Essentials of Hindutva*. What was not clear at the time was that, in his correspondence with his brother as well as in the last petition, Savarkar provides a preview of his arguments that were published only a few years later. In his letter Savarkar says: " We believe in a universal state embracing all mankind and wherein all men and

[45] Cf. a similar earlier reference: "The *Mussulman hordes* began to receive them in a terrible manner," in Savarkar, *Indian War*, 123.

[46] Letter from V.D. Savarkar to N.D. Savarkar, December 12, 1912, *Letters from the Andamans, Selected Works of Veer Savarkar*, vol. 3, 429.

women would be citizens working for and enjoying equally the fruits of this earth and this sun, this land and this light, which constitute the real Motherland and the Fatherland of man."[47] He argues that the "ideal" is the concept of a "Human state" in which all nations can emerge and coexist.[48] The point was for every nation to have the ability to thrive as a political entity for its own fulfilment and promise. The principle of humanity was the highest form of patriotism in bringing "conflicting races and nations" under one unified entity, even if it meant constructing an empire or commonwealth.[49] Savarkar explained that he had turned to revolutionary violence as a necessary strategy because a "virulent cancer" had grown in India that threatened not only the country's existence but humanity itself. As a result there was a need to excise the disease by any means necessary to save the ideal of the Human state. (Although, he did not specify the cancer as British rule, it is implicit in his letter.) This is perhaps the only text in which Savarkar clarified his position on violence, all the while recognising that his writing was being monitored:

> But even while combatting force with force we heartily abhorred and do yet abhor all violence. For violence is force aggressively used – force that is life killing. I never cherished it not even in my dreams any aggressive ambition for personal or national aggrandizement, and so far was I from being a party to violence that I actually kept opposing it.[50]

In short, he explained that he was fundamentally opposed to violence itself; however, he added an important caveat: he "abhorred" violence when it was inflicted by "powerful combinations against their weaker but righteous rivals."[51] The argument was meant to attract sympathy for the victims of violence by strong perpetrators, but it was also a justification for victims of violence to use violence against their oppressors. This justified 1857, but, more important, Savarkar is also here providing the justification he would later adopt for Hindu

[47] Letter from V.D. Savarkar to N.D. Savarkar, July 6, 1920, *Letters from the Andamans, Selected Works of Veer Savarkar*, vol. 3, 476.

[48] Ibid., 475.

[49] Ibid.

[50] Ibid., 477.

[51] Ibid.

violence against Muslims. As he states in the letter, his goal is to promote a new form of empire or commonwealth for the betterment of humanity. Implicit in his argument is that the British have failed in their imperial project to create a Human state. For him, the ideal was to now unify all humans under a new framework, which he called the Hindu commonwealth – or, to put it differently, a new Hindu empire.[52]

On May 2, 1921 Savarkar and his brother Ganesh were finally released from the Cellular Jail and transferred to prisons in the Bombay Presidency.[53] Savarkar was placed in jail in Ratnagiri while Ganesh was sent to Bijapur.[54] Initially, Savarkar was kept in solitary confinement in Ratnagiri, where he did not have access to books. He remarked that he had not realised that jail conditions in the Bombay Presidency were actually worse than in the Cellular Jail.[55] By 1923 he was transferred to Yerwada Jail in Pune, which he found more conducive to work as it had a library.

A few months after his arrival in May 1923, Savarkar's *Essentials of Hindutva* was published under the penname "A Maratha." Copies of the manuscript were smuggled out of the jail and delivered to V.V. Kelkar, the publisher of the book. Savarkar stayed in Yerwada Jail till January 5, 1924, when he was released and allowed to live in Ratnagiri District, also in the Bombay Presidency. Under his agreement with the government, he was allowed to live in a residence with his family but his mobility was restricted and he could not participate in political activity.[56] He was permitted to write as long as the topics were apolitical. Savarkar agreed to these conditions; the government stated it would review Savarkar's status after five years.[57] It was in the second half of

[52] Savarkar, *Essentials of Hindutva*, 105.

[53] MSA, Home Spec, File 60-D-(f)-1923, "Cellular Jail History Ticket for Vinayak Damodar Savarkar (No. 32778)," Entry for May 2, 1921, S-45.

[54] Savarkar, *My Transportation for Life*, in *Selected Works of Veer Savarkar*, vol. 2, 527.

[55] Ibid., 516–17.

[56] BL, IOR, L/P&J/6/1871, File 515, Letter from Secretary to the Government of Bombay, Home Department, to Secretary to the GOI, Home Department, January 15, 1924.

[57] See Savarkar Special Issue, *Mahratta*, January 6, 1924; "Release of

the 1920s that Savarkar returned to writing regularly and produced a number of works related to his interest in Hindutva.

## 3. The Word: "Hindutva"

The publication of Chandranath Basu's *Hindutva* in 1892 started a debate on the conceptual history of the word "Hindutva." Basu is recognised as having conceptualised "Hindutva" to signify the central characteristics of "Hinduness" as part of his extensive writings on topics related to Hindus and Hinduism.[58] It has been pointed out that Basu was a prolific writer of English and Bengali texts on a number of topics, from the Bengali peasantry to Indian manufacturing.[59] By the end of the nineteenth century he was identified by one Bengali reviewer as "one of our best Bengali poets."[60] The primary focus of Basu's writings shifted to topics related to Hindu society with an emphasis on explaining the centrality of Hindu dharma.[61] As part of his analyses, Basu celebrated the importance of the land of the Hindus since antiquity and pointed out that Hindu dharma had survived while other ancient civilisations had faded over millennia.[62] Hindus had survived and thrived as a direct consequence of the unique nature of their dharma, despite the long periods of conflicts and turmoil that had confronted them for centuries. At the same time, Basu challenged the superiority of European thought and institutions by providing counter-examples from Hindu philosophy.[63] By 1892 he had turned to the concept of

---

Mr. V.D. Savarkar," and "Conditions of His Release," *Mahratta*, January 13, 1924.

[58] Sen, "A Hindu Conservative Negotiates Modernity," 178. Ashis Nandy has pointed out that the term was also used by figures like Brahmabandhab Upadhyay (1861–1907), but he does not attribute the founding of the term to Upadhyay. See Nandy, "A Disowned Father of the Nation in India," 95.

[59] Sen, "A Hindu Conservative Negotiates Modernity," 179.

[60] "Vernacular Literature in India," *The Academy*, no. 1161 (August 4, 1894), 89. The author's name is not given.

[61] Ibid.

[62] Barua, "Vedantic Variations in the Presence of Europe," 5.

[63] Ibid.

Hindutva to capture the essential qualities and characteristics of Hindu dharma.[64] He also believed there was inscribed within Hindutva a critique of the practices and interpretations of contemporary Hinduism at the end of the nineteenth century in Bengal.

An early English-language reception of Basu's book – and by extension the concept of Hindutva – appeared in *The Calcutta Review* in 1894.[65] The work was described as part of a "Hindu revival," but there was no engagement with or analysis of the author's newly coined term Hindutva. Basu was described as selecting the "noblest doctrines of Hinduism" while not ascribing to any of the "ancient schools."[66] His "sole object is to compare . . . the leading doctrines of the Hindu faith with those of other religions."[67] His *Hindutva* was viewed as celebrating Hinduism by providing a treatise on "Hindu articles of faith" – from a study of texts such as the Upanishads, to an analysis of key ideas like karma and *jnana*. The review ends by arguing that *Hindutva*'s impact on the "Hindu revival movement" would be experienced by "sav[ing] thousands" of young Bengalis from the negative and deleterious effects of "European manners" and "European modes of thought" with the rise of English education.[68] In one argument, inscribed within Basu's conceptualisation of Hindutva was a critique of European modernity which sought to offer an alternative to Hindus.[69] Needless to say, Basu's *Hindutva* also provided a foundation for anti-colonial thought at the turn of the century that also celebrated the essence of Hinduness in the formation of nationalism in Bengal.

The term Hindutva started circulating in Bengali debates after the publication of Basu's book. The *Arjyadharma pracaraka*, a Bengali-language monthly newspaper which began life in 1889, stated its

[64] Sen, "A Hindu Conservative Negotiates Modernity," 178.

[65] "Vernacular Literature: *Hindutva* by Babu Chandra Nath Basu," *The Calcutta Review*, 99, 197 (July 1894), xxv–xxvii. (The reviewer's name is not given.) In 1894, Basu's book was also included in a list of new publications in *Orientalische Bibliographie* (Berlin: Verlag Von Reuther & Reichard, 1894), 228.

[66] "Vernacular Literature," *The Calcutta Review*, xxvi.

[67] Ibid.

[68] Ibid., xxvii.

[69] Sen, "A Hindu Conservative Negotiates Modernity," 187.

purpose was to "rescue Hindutva from the 'evil of Brahmoism'."[70] The newspaper survived only a year, but it helped spread the idea of Hindutva.

Independent of Basu's text, one of the first uses of "Hindutva" in an English-language publication appeared in 1913 – in an article in *The Journal of the Royal Asiatic Society of Great Britain and Ireland*. J.D. Anderson, its author, argued that Bengali was a language "wholly Hinduised and Sanskritised."[71] And "As Frenchmen are justly proud of their Latinity, so are Bengalis justly proud of their Hindutva, of the fact that almost every Bengali word can be traced to a Sanskrit origin." Basu's *Hindutva* received further attention in a 1915 article entitled "The Religious Quest of India" in *The Athenaeum*.[72] He was described as the "most amiable and tolerant of Hindus" who "strove to explain the faith of Bengal in his admirable *Hindutva*."[73] His book was compared to the writings of Rabindranath Tagore and Bankim Chandra Chatterjee, all three being described as "compelled to take the Hindu view" during a period that witnessed the increasing influence of Christianity in Bengal.[74] Reception of Basu's *Hindutva* appears to have been limited to Bengali debates in the first two decades after its publication.

Savarkar did not explain when he came across this concept that became central to his own thought. He turned to writing about Hindutva *after* his period of incarceration in the Andamans. In the Cellular Jail Savarkar says he engaged with a number of Bengali intellectuals who were also serving sentences related to political and seditious activities, and that he was also reading Bengali texts.[75] Whether the Cellular Jail was where Savarkar first read Basu's book or learned the word "Hindutva" remains unknown, but in his publications prior to his arrest in 1910 the concept is not part of his lexicon.

[70] See *Arjyadharma pracaraka*, vol. 1 (1889), https://crossasia-repository. ub.uni-heidelberg.de/1589/ (accessed May 11, 2021).

[71] Anderson, "Stress and Pitch in Indian Languages," 871.

[72] "The Religious Quest of India," *The Athenaeum*, no. 4580 (August 7, 1915), 89–91. The author's name is not given.

[73] Ibid., 89.

[74] Ibid.

[75] Savarkar, *My Transportation for Life*, in *Selected Works of Veer Savarkar*, vol. 2, 256–7.

What is the etymology of the word? Scholars have typically explained Hindutva as a compound of "Hindu" and the Sanskrit suffix "-*tva*" that results in the construction of an abstract noun.[76] Since Basu is credited with coining the term, it is worth considering an alternative interpretation that may help explain Savarkar's interest in the concept. Basu wrote extensively about the concept of *tattva* (essence, principle), as illustrated by his two major works on the subject: *Shakuntala Tattva* (1881) and *Savitri Tattva* (1901). The fact that he had expertise in writing about *tattva* suggests the possibility that his conceptualisation of Hindutva was a combination of "Hindu" and "*tattva*."[77] The compound certainly comes closer to the meaning of Hindutva as it was used in the twentieth century: that is, literally, the essence of the Hindu, or the Hindu's essence.

After 1923, Savarkar's *Essentials of Hindutva* was viewed as the most important contribution to the understanding of Hindutva, to the extent that Basu's writings on Hindutva were not only ignored but also forgotten. Savarkar's interpretation of Hindutva entirely overshadowed Basu's earlier conceptualisation. Many twentieth-century observers assumed that Savarkar invented the term for his arguments about Hindu India without realising that Hindutva was already a part of Bengali debates. The spread of Savarkar's *Essentials of Hindutva* was facilitated by the fact that it was written in English, making it widely accessible. Yet, even after the publication of Savarkar's *Essentials of Hindutva*, the Bengali debates continued along the lines proposed by Basu. In 1929 another Bengali newspaper titled *Arya-prabara* appeared, its stated objective being "to save Hindutva and its religious practices and social customs from its present decadence."[78] Like its nineteenth-century predecessor, it survived only a year. But the point here is that both papers, despite being separated by four decades, were interested in saving or rescuing Hindutva from what were perceived as the problems of emergent forms of religious practice in Bengal. By the late 1920s to 1930s Hindutva as a concept was certainly spreading in a number of texts beyond Savarkar's *Essentials of Hindutva*, but

[76] For example, Bhatt, *Hindu Nationalism*, 77. Bakhle, "Country First?", 181.

[77] See Paranjape, "Hindutva before Savarkar."

[78] See *Arjya prabara*, vol. 1 (1929), https://crossasia-repository.ub.uni-heidelberg.de/1462/ (accessed May 11, 2021).

his argument was the most influential articulation of Hindutva in the twentieth century.[79]

# 4. Intellectual Bricolage

Savarkar's decision to write *Essentials of Hindutva* in English rather than Marathi was strategic and marked an important linguistic shift. Given the sheer number of people with an English-language education in colonial India, writing in English meant the book could have a national readership. It also had the potential for an international audience, following the example of *Indian War*. This did not mean that Savarkar stopped writing in Marathi; rather, he opted to write in both languages depending on his target audience.

Savarkar was not alone in having to make such linguistic choices. Once English achieved global hegemony as a language, it was easier for texts in English to circulate widely, while books in vernacular languages often had a limited readership.[80] Savarkar knew this. He was also familiar with the English literary canon. He began *the* key work on Hindutva by citing "What is in a name?" from Shakespeare's *Romeo and Juliet*.[81] Shakespeare was taught in schools and his plays had been translated into vernacular languages and performed publicly in India since the eighteenth century.[82] Savarkar's purpose in including Shakespeare's question was to underscore the significance of names, especially the importance of the name "Hindutva."

[79] The publication of an English-language newspaper called *Hindutva* in the late 1920s further promoted the concept. I have not been able to locate copies of this newspaper, although there are several articles in *The Times of India* in 1928–9 that discuss the newspaper and cite passages from it. By the late 1930s the concept was part of the political lexicon in public debates beyond Savarkar's growing body of work at this point. For example, Ramadasa Gaura wrote a Hindi-language book called *Hindutva* that was published in Varanasi, in 1938. In later decades of the twentieth century, several authors used the title *Hindutva* for their writings, while the concept Hindutva acquired a normative presence in political discourses in India.

[80] Anderson, *Imagined Communities*, 207.

[81] Savarkar, *Essentials of Hindutva*, 1.

[82] See Trivedi and Bartholomeusz, eds, *India's Shakespeare*.

He argued that "things do matter more than their names," especially in instances when the association of the *thing* with its *name* is "new or simple."[83] In other cases it is also possible that "a *thing*" has many names (in many languages), which then leads to an interpretation that the thing and its name are not necessarily linked: "The very fact that the thing is indicated by a dozen names in a dozen human tongues disarms the suspicion that there is an invariable connection or natural concomitance between sound and the meaning it conveys."[84] Over time, he says, there was a transformation of the habitus in which there was a convergence between the thing and its name; once they were no longer distinct from one another, they became part of the collective consciousness: "[A]s the association of the word with the thing it signifies grows stronger and lasts long, so does the channel which connects the two states of consciousness tend to allow an easy flow of thoughts from one to the other till at last it seems almost impossible to separate them."[85] Savarkar's main purpose was to underscore that the association of Hindutva and its meaning evolved over a long period of time. Inscribed within the name was a specific history that helped define what it meant to be a Hindu. This process resulted in the formation of a "natural concomitance" between the name and its meaning. Ultimately, their convergence resulted in the unity of "the two states of consciousness." However, the process did not end at this point. For Savarkar the name had the potential to evolve into a complex idea or a system of thought: it could "live and grow as an organism."[86]

Savarkar's formulations and uses of terminology are important because they suggest familiarity with specific conceptualisations in a number of contemporary debates. Yet he did not provide any clarification or clues about these debates in his analysis. First, Savarkar's use of consciousness does not have a reference or context, and it opens up many questions, especially considering that he returned to the topic of consciousness later in the text. Interpretations of Freud's three stages of consciousness and Advaita Vedanta's four stages of consciousness were already widely discussed. But, more likely, Savarkar was referring

[83] Savarkar, *Essentials of Hindutva*, 1. My emphasis.
[84] Ibid.
[85] Ibid., 1–2.
[86] Ibid., 2.

to Herbert Spencer's *Principles of Psychology* (1855), in which he discussed two stages of consciousness, making a distinction between "self" and "non-self." Savarkar had quite evidently incorporated this characteristic of consciousness into his way of thinking: "Nothing makes self-consciousness of itself so much as a conflict with non-self."[87] He was familiar with Spencer's writings in London because of Krishnavarma's close personal and intellectual relationship with Spencer, but also because, as earlier noted, Savarkar had almost certainly requested the Marathi translations of his writings in the Cellular Jail.

Second, Savarkar's discussion of the relationship and associations of names (and words) with their meaning evoked a number of contemporary debates in linguistics and Sanskrit. Within schools of Indian philosophy there were divergent interpretations of the signification functions of words and their meanings discussed by Sanskritists.[88] To what extent Savarkar was familiar with specific debates among Sanskritists is difficult to say, but he had studied Sanskrit. Krishnavarma, to whom he was close, was a Sanskritist who had interacted with the leading Sanskrit scholars and Orientalists in Europe.[89] Krishnavarma had also collaborated with Monier Monier-Williams, Boden Professor of Sanskrit at Oxford University, the best-known Sanskritist in Britain at the time. Debates on language and meaning were also emerging in linguistics and semiotics, especially in the work of Ferdinand de Saussure, who had conceptualised his theory of the linguistic sign after having studied a number of subjects and languages, including Sanskrit and Indo-European philology.[90] The idea that names (and words) functioned as living organisms was also part of an emergent debate in Indo-European linguistics in the mid-nineteenth century. The

[87] Ibid., 37.

[88] Deshpande, trans., *The Meaning of Nouns*, 2.

[89] Krishnavarma translated a text entitled "A Sanskrit Ode Addressed to the Congress of Orientalists at Berlin" written by Rama Dasa Sena, Zamindar of Berhampore, who was the author of *Aitihesika Rahasya*. Sena was invited to the 1881 Congress of Orientalists in Berlin but was unable to attend. Krishnavarma, who was based at Balliol College, translated Sena's essay, which was then published in *The Journal of the Royal Asiatic Society of Great Britain and Ireland*, New Series, 13, 4 (1881), 573–6.

[90] See de Saussure, *Course in General Linguistics*.

German Orientalist August Schleicher (1821–1868) had put forward the idea that there were similarities between linguistics and Darwin's theory of evolution.[91] He argued that language had the characteristics of an organism and constructed a system of taxonomy that paralleled biological classifications. Savarkar's selection of terms and concepts was very specific, even if he did not provide references to a diverse range of ideas and concepts that were part of the *zeitgeist* and useful in writing *Essentials of Hindutva*.

Third, Savarkar's inclusion of the phrase "natural concomitance" to describe the unity or connection between the sound of a name and its meaning is worth considering. The conceptualisation of "natural concomitance" was a normative reference to the Eucharist, a rite in the New Testament in which Christ provides his disciples with bread and wine as symbols of his body and blood, respectively. Commentaries on the Eucharist noted that while there are two parts to the sacrament, the body and blood should not be viewed as separate from one another for Christ is present in both. Moreover, the interpretation that Christ's blood could not be separated from his body was due to the fact they were joined by natural concomitance.

I raise these specific passages in relation to *Essentials of Hindutva* – all from the first two pages of the text – to underscore the complexity of interpreting Savarkar's key work, given the many texts and ideas that may have informed his thought. The fact that he did not have full access to sources as a prisoner helps explain the structure and form of the work, especially as he says he often wrote from memory. Savarkar certainly had read the Bible in prison. In fact he says it was the only book offered to him at one point in his incarceration.[92] There are Biblical references throughout Savarkar's writings, so it is not surprising that he should have turned to concepts or ideas from it to help conceptualise the meaning of "Hindutva." In fact, says Savarkar, "The life of Jesus Christ and his Sermon on the Mount had always appealed to me, and I had cherished them both with deep reverence."[93]

On the other hand Savarkar's writings were full of diverse references

[91] Richards, *Darwin and the Emergence of Evolutionary Theories*, 202–3.
[92] Savarkar, *My Transportation for Life*, in *Selected Works of Veer Savarkar*, vol. 2, 26.
[93] Ibid.

that formed an intellectual bricolage of his eclectic readings. But this bricolage was also a direct consequence of Savarkar's claim that Hindutva as a word "defies all attempts at analysis." No matter how many different texts Savarkar consulted and interpreted, defining Hindutva was epistemologically an impossibility. Yet this did not mean that Hindutva should not be approximated in language – English, Marathi, or otherwise – by turning to history as a way to document the thoughts and actions that reflected the principles of history. The first step in writing this history was to assert that Hindutva had a temporality; he made it clear that a history in full was not infinite: "Forty centuries, if not more, had been at work to mould it as it is."[94]

To clarify, for Savarkar history existed "within-time," but not all time was within history.[95] A history in full had a temporality that could be measured by certain normative measures of time which appear in his writings: second, minute, hour, day, year, century, and so on. Moreover, he deferred to the Gregorian calendar, as against the multiple calendars or temporalities used in India during his lifetime, including discussions of periods of time made up of millions or billions of years. He also adopted classifications of time that did not have a fixed measure, such as an epoch and *deshkaal* (national time), but defined them in very specific ways that were unique to his interpretations of history. There was of course nothing exceptional in his adoption of these temporal conventions which he used to discuss history "within-time."

On the other hand, throughout Savarkar's writings we find him sensitive to conceptions of time that could not be accounted for by history. While Hindutva had to be understood in terms of its temporality, he pointed out that there was a time before Hindutva – before history – that needed to be considered. He explained that this time (the time *before* history) was characterised by its remoteness. It was a period so far removed from measurable time that "even mythology fails to penetrate – to trace to its source."[96] This was, as it were, a time before time, a time that could not be imagined. But if the time could not be imagined or conceptualised, then was it necessary to even

[94] Savarkar, *Essentials of Hindutva*, 3.
[95] Heidegger, *Being and Time*, 456.
[96] Savarkar, *Essentials of Hindutva*, 9.

consider it a temporality? Savarkar did not provide an answer but suggested the presence of an unnamed "source" before Hindutva. This was a source that existed in the time before time. Whether there was a convergence – a natural concomitance – of the source and time he did not say. This was as close as Savarkar came to saying that the time before time might very well be Being itself. He did not explore this idea further; instead, he shifted back to examining Hindutva as a history in full and within-time.

In Savarkar's conceptualisation Hindutva existed in a temporality that could be measured – forty centuries – but time itself had also shaped Hindutva into its form. Hindutva as an entity did not have its present shape when it came into being – it developed and evolved over time. There is a conceptual tension here: Savarkar did not fully explain what he meant by the claim that time – measured in forty centuries – "had been at work to mould" Hindutva. He only asserted that the "countless actions" of individuals were responsible for Hindutva, and that those actions themselves reflected the principles of Hindutva.[97] The coupling of human activity with time provided a means for him to give meaning to Hindutva.

Savarkar's "forty centuries" as marking the start of Hindutva is worth considering further. To begin with, it is unclear why he broke time down into centuries, as opposed to years, millennia, or other classifications, especially given the number of existing calendars used in India. There has also been no explanation for Savarkar's reference to "forty" as the number of centuries for dating Hindutva. His reference to four thousand years – four millennia – was significantly shorter than what he argued in his later works about the origins of India's history. Hindutva, it seems, was a recent entity in Savarkar's conceptualisation of time. Why forty centuries? I return to this conundrum to suggest that Savarkar's figure was not random. There may have been a context independent of Hindutva, and which had more to do with Savarkar's familiarity with contemporary global debates about the specific temporality of "forty centuries."

In the nineteenth century a number of authors had incorporated forty centuries as a unit of time in their writings. Napoleon Bonaparte's

---

[97] Ibid., 3.

speech delivered to his troops in Egypt on July 21, 1798 was perhaps one of the best-known instances, its content being reproduced in several publications. Napoleon is reported to have stated: "From the heights of these pyramids, forty centuries look down upon us."[98] Egyptologists had also estimated forty centuries as the date of some of the key monuments in Egypt.[99] But the most significant debate that centred on forty centuries was among Biblical scholars involved in estimating the date of Creation. In the seventeenth century James Ussher calculated that Creation occurred in 4004 BCE. Ussher's date was a modification of the views of earlier scholars, such as Johannes Kepler and Isaac Newton, who had estimated the date within a couple of decades of Ussher's calculation. By the early-nineteenth century Ussher's view had been included in school textbooks, as noted by William Pinnock in a work published in 1834 in London. Pinnock states: "Sacred History is so called, because it treats of the works of God, and gives the history of his favoured people, the Jews. It includes 4004 years, or forty centuries, without interruption; namely from the Creation of the world to Jesus Christ."[100] In the early-twentieth century authors continued to use "forty centuries" in their historical analyses: David Carvalho's *Forty Centuries of Ink* (1904); H.O. Lock's *The Conquerors of Palestine Through Forty Centuries* (1920); and F.H. King's *Farmers of Forty Centuries* (1922).[101]

The point of providing this context is to underscore that by the time Savarkar had conceptualised the temporal origins of Hindutva, "forty centuries" had become a metaphor much used. Having read the Bible and the seminal texts of Christianity, Savarkar is very unlikely to have

---

[98] Since the nineteenth century, this statement has been cited in many texts that discuss Napoleon Bonaparte's conquest of Egypt. For a recent work, see Cole, *Napoleon's Egypt*, 63.

[99] R.S.P., "The Egyptian Galleries at the British Museum," in *Temple Bar: A London Magazine*, vol. IV (March 1862), 228. (The author's full name is not given in the text.) In addition, the period of 4000 years was often cited by scholars of Egypt to date monuments, likely due to the age of written history. See Lopriano, *Ancient Egyptian*, 238.

[100] Pinnock, *Comprehensive Grammar*, 2.

[101] Nineteenth-century studies of the Bible have also noted forty centuries as a measure of time. See Halsey, *Life Pictures from the Bible*, 48.

been ignorant of "forty centuries" within Christian and Jewish traditions linked to debates on Creation. What is important to note is that Hindutva's temporality was conceptualised as the analogy of another temporality popular at the time, rather than a temporality of its own.

# 5. The Methods for Writing a Conceptual History

One of Savarkar's main objectives in writing *Essentials of Hindutva* was to explain these essentials by providing a conceptual history of "Hindu" and "Hindusthan." The slim text detailed a number of themes and concepts that served as a foundation for all of Savarkar's later writings on Hindutva: over the rest of his career he expanded and developed the essentials outlined here. He also provided an analysis of three methodological approaches for writing a history in full.

First, he turned to a number of sources in the field of "Oriental research" as a starting point, stating that they provided a foundation for "treading on [the] solid ground of recorded facts."[102] However, he found the research epistemologically limiting for his purpose. He argued that scholars conducting Oriental research had concluded that only those details in the Hindu epics and textual tradition which could be empirically proven must be true. He proposed the exact opposite: that is, these ancient texts must be considered as representing the truth, unless specific details in them could be shown to be demonstrably false. The longevity of the texts and the fact that they continued to have meaning for Hindus for millennia indicated their validity. Second, Savarkar explained that he turned to a "borderland of conjecture" as a way to interpret the meaning of Hindutva through his reading of select Hindu epics and related texts. The idea of "borderland" here is epistemologically ambiguous, given that Oriental research itself was "treading" on facts, no matter how solid the nature of the facts. And third, Savarkar provided a genealogy of "Hindu" based on vernacular sources in Marathi, Hindi, and Braj Bhasha as a way to underscore the circulation and reception of the word over several centuries. He was also aware that alternative interpretations of "Hindu" were concur-

---

[102] Savarkar, *Essentials of Hindutva*, 8.

rently being used in India and neighbouring regions, and his text was meant as an important corrective to what he considered fundamentally disparaging uses of "Hindu."

By the time Savarkar wrote *Essentials of Hindutva* the larger field of Oriental Studies was thriving in Europe, the US, and India. Although he did not cite specific authors or texts to substantiate his interpretations, Savarkar was very familiar with the key concepts and debates, especially as he had access to a large library of books in and on Sanskrit in the India House in London.[103] Also, since the founding in 1784 of the Asiatick Society by William Jones, Oriental research had seen continuous developments. In the first volume of the society's journal, *Asiatick Researches*, Jones published "A Discourse on the Institution of a Society," in which he explained that the society had decided to use "Asiatick" as part of its name rather than "Oriental."[104] Jones considered Asiatick to be "classical and proper" and "preferable to *Oriental*," because the latter "convey[ed] no very distinct idea."[105] Despite this clarification, Jones still opted to use the term "Oriental" in his writings in *Asiatick Researches*.

Oriental research continued to grow in the nineteenth and twentieth century with the addition of new societies and publications – the Royal Asiatic Society established in 1824 and the *Indian Antiquary* founded in 1872 being prominent examples. The "Prefatory" of the first issue of *Indian Antiquary* explained that the purpose of the journal was to supplement the publications of Asiatic Societies in India by including topics often not discussed in other journals.[106] The point was to spread knowledge about Oriental research to general readers – Europeans and Indians – independent of the formal structures of the societies. Perhaps best known to Savarkar was the Bhandarkar Oriental Research Institute (BORI) in Pune, the city where Savarkar was jailed in 1923. BORI, founded in 1917, was named after Ramkrishna Gopal Bhandarkar for his services to Sanskrit literature. The institute became

---

[103] Like the other members of the India House, Krishnavarma fled to Paris to escape arrest in Britain. He took with him his entire library, which was posthumously donated to the College of France, where his books are still kept.

[104] Jones, "A Discourse on the Institution of a Society," xii.

[105] Ibid.

[106] "Prefatory," *The Indian Antiquary: A Journal of Oriental Research*, vol. 1 (1872), 1.

one of the major centres in Western India for bringing Orientalists together for research and conferences – including the first All-India Conference of Orientalists in 1919 – and publishing a journal, *Annals of the Bhandarkar Institute*.[107] The one individual Savarkar actually cited in *Essentials of Hindutva* (and later in *Hindu Pad Padashahi*) was Vishwanath Kashinath Rajwade, an influential scholar of Maratha history and executive member of BORI.

The fact that Savarkar wrote *Essentials of Hindutva* in prison without full access to texts helps explain the fragmentary nature of his arguments. But he was familiar with some of the key debates of the nineteenth century on the relationship of languages (Indo-Aryan, Indo-European, Sanskrit), races (Aryan and non-Aryan), and texts (Vedas, Avesta, Puranas) that had dominated the historiography of Orientalists, especially among scholars who specialised in Sanskrit. There was great interest in studying the language and culture of "Aryans," who were identified as part of a linguistic family *and* a racial category. Philologists argued that there were links between Sanskrit, Latin, and Greek, which meant that all three were related languages that needed to be studied together. There was a sense that these linguistic commonalities meant that there had existed an "Indo-European" homeland, possibly located in Central Asia. Others argued that "Aryan" could also be appropriated as a racial category, Aryans being identified as "fair-complexioned Indo-European speakers."[108] Another set of debates emerged on the migration patterns of these Aryans from Central Asia to Europe and Asia. Some argued that Aryans entered India in 1500 BCE to create an "Aryan nation" that conquered the non-Aryan inhabitants of the region, who were described as dark-skinned. Intensive studies of Vedic texts, like the Rigveda, were also published in this period to provide textual evidence supporting a nexus of language and race at the centre of such interpretations. Much literature was produced in this period to reconstruct the history of an "idyllic society" which was believed to have formed with the arrival of Aryans.[109] Savarkar's interpretations of Oriental research engaged with many of these ideas, but he adopted a strategy to write a history that did not necessarily

---

[107] *Proceedings & Transactions of the First Oriental Conference, Poona*, vol. 1 (Poona: Bhandarkar Oriental Research Institute, 1920), 1.

[108] Thapar, "The Theory of Aryan Race," 5.

[109] Thapar, *Ancient Indian Social History*, 225.

adhere to normative readings of these texts. He provided revisionist interpretations that were unorthodox and eclectic in their approach by reinforcing the idea that Hindutva was an emanation out of Being.

He began his conceptual history by articulating some uncertainty about the origins of "Hindu." No one actually knew its beginning, not even scholars engaged in Oriental research. However, Savarkar dated "Hindu" to the "source" (Being?) in the time before time – following the pattern for dating "Hindutva." The fact that it was the etymological root of Hindutva meant that it likely preceded the formation and naming of Hindutva. But if both "Hindu" and "Hindutva" were coeval with the "source," was it even necessary – or possible – within Savarkar's conceptualisation to measure their existence in time? (To evoke a question raised by Heidegger: did Being have a temporality?) Savarkar explained that contemporary research could only go back to the civilisation of the "Aryans" who resided on the banks of the Sindhu – also known as the Indus.[110] (Savarkar noted that Sindhu literally meant river, but it was later called the Indus River.) This was a civilisation that Savarkar believed pre-dated the ancient Egyptians and Babylonians. These Aryans soon moved into the neighbouring land of seven (*sapta*) rivers called Sapta Sindhu.[111] He says that in the process of expanding into this new territory, the Aryans developed a new nation and nationality based on common land and a common culture.[112] These Aryans felt a sense of unity and attachment to Sapta Sindhu, to the extent that they started identifying themselves as "Sindhu." This was a crucial discursive shift for these Aryans, whose primary identity was Sindhu from this moment forward. At another level, the formation of their national and cultural identity as Sindhus was intertwined from its conception with a geographical context. In order to substantiate his claims, Savarkar turned to the Rigveda as textual evidence of the existence of Sapta Sindhu, though he also pointed out that the neighbouring ancient Persians referred in the *Zend Avesta* to the inhabitants of this area as Sindhu.[113]

[110] Savarkar, *Essentials of Hindutva*, 5.
[111] I have modified the spelling of "Sapta Sindhus" to "Sapta Sindhu" to reflect the Marathi spelling of the name in the text, which is actually more accurate than the English original.
[112] Savarkar, *Essentials of Hindutva*, 12.
[113] Ibid., 5, 63.

Savarkar says that while Sanskrit was the language of the Sindhus, a number of languages known as Prakrits developed in India that then led to the emergence of "Hindu" in the lexicon.[114] He focused on the transition from classical Sanskrit to the formation of Prakrits to help describe the etymological development of the term.

Some contextual information may be of help here. Prakrits have been historically difficult to classify as languages. While some scholars have argued that they emerged as vernacular languages, others have simply classified any language that diverged from Sanskrit as Prakrit. What further complicates an understanding of the term Prakrit, according to Andrew Ollett, is that it was used to retroactively describe languages that were not known as Prakrit in premodern India.[115] Prakrit functioned in a liminal space between Sanskrit and a vernacular language,"neither Sanskrit . . . nor a regional vernacular."[116] Yet the history of "Prakrit" illustrates important distinctions in the formation of languages that were part of a process of vernacularisation from forms of classical Sanskrit.[117] While Savarkar noted the existence of multiple Prakrits in his discussion, he had a singular purpose in highlighting the linguistic transition from Sanskrit to Prakrits as part of the etymology of Hindu: "The letter 's' in Sanskrit is at times changed to 'h' in some Prakrit languages, both Indian and non-Indian."[118] The result: "Sindhu" was now called "Hindu." The time frame for this transition is never mentioned in his text, but at least Savarkar could now identify a period of a few millennia in which "Hindu" formally emerged as a word.

Based on Savarkar's analyses, the word "Hindu" began as a geographic reference (river) but was also the name adopted by people who lived in the territory of Sapta Sindhu after the Aryan movement, conquest, and colonisation of lands and tribes in the area.[119] Both the

---

[114] Ibid., 6.

[115] Ollett, *Language of the Snakes*, 13.

[116] Ibid., 15.

[117] There appear to be parallels with arguments proposed by Benedict Anderson on the importance of the transition from classical languages to vernaculars as central to his conceptualisation of the nation as an "imagined community." See Anderson, *Imagined Communities*.

[118] Savarkar, *Essentials of Hindutva*, 6.

[119] Ibid., 7–9.

Aryans (as conquerors) and the tribes (as conquered) came together to form the national and cultural unity reflected in the name "Hindu." Inscribed within the historical formation of "Hindu" (as a name and a people) were acts of violence through colonisation. This was an argument that Savarkar repeated in *Essentials of Hindutva* and throughout his writings on Hindu history. By extension, the idea of "Hindu unity" within Savarkar's writings had a different resonance when read in the context of unity through violence as a foundational characteristic of the very meaning of "Hindu." The idea of Hindu unity was also central to the naming practice of the territory controlled by Hindus. Savarkar says Sindhusthan replaced Sapta Sindhu as the name of the land:

> the name that associates and identifies our nation with a river . . . enlists nature on our side and bases our national life on a foundation, that is, so far as human calculation are concerned, as lasting as eternity. All these considerations must have fired the imagination of the then leaders of *thought and action* and made them restore the ancient Vedic name of our land and nation Sindhusthan.[120]

While Savarkar argued that Aryans identified themselves as Sindhu after taking over the land, he periodically maintained the original category "Aryan" in his discussions in the text. For him the dominance of Aryans was still a feature of the Sindhu if Sindhusthan was considered an Aryan nation. In his discussion of Sindhusthan a secondary definition of "Sindhu" in Sanskrit is added to clarify the meaning and scope of the word. Sindhu is no longer only a reference to "river," it also means "sea" – especially the sea around the "southern peninsula" of the subcontinent.[121] He says Sindhu was "like the vital spinal cord that connect[ed] the remotest past to the remotest future."[122] This corresponded with Savarkar's idea that Sindhu – the name and the idea – were connected to the "source" in the time *before* time, but the potential for Sindhu – the people and the nation – was also spatially infinite on the planet. Sindhusthan was geographically bounded within Savarkar's discussion: that is, it was the land between "Sindhu

120 Ibid., 27. Emphasis mine.
121 Ibid.
122 Ibid.

and Sindhu – from the Indus to the Seas."[123] The name "Sindhusthan"
signalled the colonisation and conquest of this territory, but it also
meant the cultural imperialism by which people had developed an
identity based on "common culture, common blood, common country, and common polity."[124]

Savarkar noted a linguistic shift away from Sanskrit to the vernacularisation of languages by which the spelling of Sindhusthan was
eventually changed to Hindusthan – the land of the Hindus. The new
hegemony of Hindusthan as a name also involved discursive ruptures
(and erasures) of other names that had existed for centuries or millennia.[125] The process of colonising the land between the Indus and the
seas meant that Hindus, as their expansion took place from the starting
point of Sapta Sindhu, replaced existing geographical names – such as
"Aryawarta" and "Daxinapatha" used since antiquity – with the grand-
er title "Bharatkhanda" (or "Bharat Varsha").[126] While Bharatkhanda
may have been successful initially, it only served as a heuristic till it
was replaced by Sindhusthan.[127] Savarkar says the people longed for a
name which reflected the land of the Sindhu based in Sanskrit, which
constantly evoked "Sindhu" as a key word. Perhaps more important
for Savarkar, the inhabitants of lands beyond the Sapta Sindhu, such
as the Persians and the Greeks, continued to refer to such people as
Sindhu; very rarely did foreigners refer to the land as Bharatkhanda,
they preferred the name Hindusthan.

In order to write this conceptual history Savarkar provided a clarification to prevent confusion: he said his purpose was not to link Hindu
to Hinduism – a term that he found objectionable and characterised
as "limited, less satisfactory and essentially sectarian."[128] He argued
that his book was about Hindutva – *not* Hinduism. While early in the

[123] Ibid., 39.

[124] Ibid., 28.

[125] Manan Ahmed Asif provides an important insight into placing Savarkar's
redefinition and reimagination of "Hindusthan" as part of a political process
of erasure of "Hindustan." See Asif, *The Loss of Hindustan*, 1–13.

[126] Savarkar, *Essentials of Hindutva*, 12.

[127] See Chattopadhyaya, *The Concept of Bharatavarsha*, for a discussion of
geographic names related to this discussion.

[128] Savarkar, *Essentials of Hindutva*, 4.

text Savarkar says Hinduism is a part of Hindutva, later he provides an intellectual distinction: "if there be really any word of alien growth it is this word Hinduism and so we should not allow our thoughts to get confused by this new-fangled term."[129] The claim that "Hinduism" was not only new but also alien was provocative, except for those who had followed the Orientalist debates on the use and conceptualisation of "Hinduism" as a category for interpreting society. By the late-eighteenth century, "Hindooism" was already a category of analysis in the writings of English administrators. The category continued to be used widely throughout the nineteenth century by missionaries, administrators, and Orientalist scholars. This is not to suggest that Indian writers did not also adopt the term or use it synonymously with "Hindoo faith" and "Hindu religion."

It has been suggested that within the vast literature produced in the nineteenth century, Monier Monier-Williams' *Hinduism* (1877) was one of the most influential texts published on the subject.[130] It was written for the Society for Promoting Christian Knowledge in London. Monier-Williams argued that Hinduism as a system was divided along lines of education, caste, region, rank, and creed. He made distinctions between the "uncompromising" and "sterner" forms of Hinduism practised by "educated Hindus" known as Brahminism, and what he called "popular Hinduism."[131] His descriptions of and differentiations within Hinduism were many, given the complexity of having to explain the term to his audience. He argued that Hinduism was difficult to define: "no description of Hinduism can be exhaustive which does not touch on almost every religious and philosophical idea that the world has ever known."[132] As he provided more complexity to his argument, he also alerted the reader that "the religious belief of the Hindus has really no single succinct designation." He asked a rhetorical question: "If, then, such all-comprehensive breadth and diversity are *essential* features of Hinduism, is it possible to give a concise description of it which shall be intelligible and satisfactory?"[133] The

[129] Ibid., 70.

[130] Hawley, "Naming Hinduism," 20–1.

[131] Monier-Williams, *Hinduism*, 11.

[132] Ibid., 12.

[133] Ibid., 13. Brian Pennington has pointed out that the emergence of modern Hinduism was a consequence of a dialectical process that involved Britons

taxonomy that he had introduced in his text, he said, would not be acceptable to those who were practising Hinduism, for "these are not names recognised by the natives."[134]

My purpose in discussing Monier-Williams is to provide a context in which Savarkar constructed his argument *against* Hinduism, especially since this text had a popular reception that defined the term as a name and as a practice. While *Essentials of Hindutva* relied on Orientalist scholarship, Savarkar also "read against the grain" of this body of work in order to show how "Hindutva" provided a discursive unity for all Hindus that simply could not be grasped by scholars of Oriental research – who argued for Hinduism as the religion of Hindus. It is doubtful that Savarkar met Monier-Williams, who died in 1899, but the fact that Monier-Williams was close to Krishnavarma certainly layers the context. It seems likely to me, if only for that reason, that Savarkar was familiar with the arguments of Monier-Williams' book, especially given its popularity. His articulation of the "essential features of Hinduism" may have influenced others to write about this theme in the early decades of the twentieth century. For example, in 1911–12 the English-language newspaper *The Leader* (Allahabad) published a regular symposium called "Essentials of Hinduism." The essays from *The Leader* were published in a 1913 volume in Madras with the title *Essentials of Hinduism*.[135] Coincidentally, in 1923 some copies of *Essentials of Hindutva* were published with a cover that had the title *Hinduism*. This was corrected for all later printings with the appropriate title. A copy of Savarkar's text with the incorrect title is in the British Library.[136]

Savarkar explained that "Hinduism" was simply another "-ism" that was imprecise (and incorrect) in representing the history of Hindus.[137] He maintained that Hinduism was conceptually limited as a term

---

and Indians alike. But it was a process for which there was no agreement on the meaning of "Hinduism" (as a name and practice). Moreover, he argues that the debates about the origins of Hinduism continue to persist today. See Pennington, *Was Hinduism Invented?*

[134] Monier-Williams, *Hinduism*, 13.

[135] Banerjee, *Essentials of Hinduism*.

[136] See Savarkar, *Hinduism*, in the BL, APAC, JRW.1986a.2382.

[137] Savarkar, *Essentials of Hindutva*, 4, 70, 91–2.

and functioned as a "dogma."[138] It simply was not inclusive for the number of individuals who called themselves Hindus, such as Jains, Sikhs, and Buddhists. This was not a paradox for Savarkar. In fact he argued that to ask all Hindus to identify as "believers of Hinduism" was a mistake which would lead to "hurt feelings" for *all* Hindus.[139] He states: "All this bitterness is mostly due to the wrong use of the word, Hinduism, to denote the religion of the majority only."[140] He said the term "Hinduism" needed to be rethought or simply abandoned: "Either the word should be restored to its proper significance to denote the religions of all Hindus or . . . it should be dropped altogether."[141] "Hinduism," Savarkar says, was a modern construction that emerged in the context of British colonialism. It also became a term of colonial governmentality that negated the diversity among Hindus, whereas "Hindu" and "Hindusthan" were terms of antiquity – of the Vedic Age. Savarkar's solution was to prioritise "Hindu dharma" and clarify that it was incorrect to translate "Hindu dharma" as "Hinduism," even if it was sometimes necessary to use Hinduism as a heuristic. He argued that dharma was "not merely religion": that is, Hindu dharma was more than the religion of the Hindus.[142] For him, it constituted all the thoughts and actions of Hindus – it was closer to his conceptualisation of Hindutva. In other words, "Hindutva" was not "Hinduism."

He also argued that Oriental research had created circumstances whereby ancient Hindu texts were frequently ignored or marginalised as sources, being deemed imprecise or unverifiable: "The habit of doubting everything in the Puranas till it has been corroborated by some foreign evidence is absurd."[143] His critique of Oriental research was also connected to the validation of the Hindu past by facts from outside India. (Savarkar appears to have directed his comment at a specific individual, but he did not identify this scholar in the book.) Instead, Savarkar offered a process other than the one taken up by Oriental research: that is, the Puranas and Hindu epics should be interpreted as representing Hindu history, unless they were proven

138 Ibid., 4.
139 Ibid., 70.
140 Ibid., 95.
141 Ibid.
142 Ibid., 97.
143 Ibid., 31.

inaccurate; and what constituted proof should be based on substantial evidence.

The challenge of interpreting Savarkar's critique is that he does not provide enough detail. At one level he rejects Oriental research (or select researchers) as he finds their interpretations of texts not based on evidence. At another level he provides interpretations of the same texts as representative of the past – also without evidence. However, he clarifies his position:

> Their details may be challenged, their dates determined and rejected, but on account of discrepancies here or miraculous colouring there which are in fact common to all ancient records of mankind, we cannot dismiss them altogether, especially where the acts recorded have not an impossible or unnatural element in them or when they do not contradict events otherwise proved to be indisputably true.[144]

Savarkar's explanation was that the Puranas and epics had been preserved and survived since antiquity. It was undeniable that these were "*the records of our people.*"[145] As records they were reliable accounts of revolutions that provided an *itihaas* (history) of Hindus; and in his view comparable records were not available for other civilisations.

What is worth noting are the continuities from his writings about the centrality of the *people* in creating a revolution in *Indian War*, and the traces of Mazzini's thought more generally. The role of *itihaas* in this context is also important because Savarkar discussed it in the framework of texts that could be read as history within the realm of conjecture – without evidence and facts. His argument was that these texts as *itihaas* could only be negated with evidence. This is a point not discussed in Savarkar's conceptualisation of his work; it is also an indication of his view that Oriental research was limited in not being able to address the concept of Hindutva as a history in full. Not that it was possible for Savarkar to negate Oriental research in its entirety – he was dependent on the work of Sanskritists, many of their findings being central to his interpretations.

Especially among scholars engaged in the study of Persian within the field of Oriental Studies, there was no agreement on the meaning of "Hindu" and "Hindusthan." As part of Savarkar's discussion of the

144 Ibid., 30.
145 Ibid., 31. Emphasis added.

conceptual history of "Hindu," he says that in the Persian language "Hindu" was defined as "thief" or "black man."[146] He added that these definitions were used by "Persian Mohammadans" as a way of expressing their "contempt" for Hindus. In *Essentials of Hindutva* Savarkar rejected these definitions in order to reclaim the "original" meaning of Hindu that served as the root for Hindutva – etymologically and discursively. Implicit in his assertion was the idea that non-Muslims who spoke Persian would not have considered the Hindu a thief or a black man. To substantiate his claim he pointed out that within Iran's ancient language of Zend – in the Middle Persian commentaries of Zoroastrian texts – the term Hindu did not have the meanings that it had in the contemporary Persian used by Muslims.[147] Savarkar was consumed with disproving that Hindus were black. He says that the Hindus were described as being as "fair" as the Persians in the Sasanian empire of Late Antiquity. And "Even so late as the dawn of the Christian era the Parthians used to call our frontier province as Shvetabharat or White India. Thus[,] originally Hindu simply could not have literally meant a black man."[148] This was further indication that the meaning of the word Hindu had only changed after the arrival of Islam in Iran. In the process of providing this specific critique of the history of the word and reclaiming it, Savarkar also asserted a racial component to Hindu as the negation of black, and in favour of fair or white.

The late-eighteenth-century publication of Persian–English dictionaries by the British included definitions of "Hindu" that he found problematic. For example, John Richardson's *A Dictionary, Persian, Arabic, and English* (1777) has an entry for "hindu" saying "See Hindi." The definitions for "Hindi" are the following: "One Indian. ²Any thing Indian, or belonging to India. ³A negro, a black Arabian, Indian or Ethiopian."[149] In the second edition of Richardson's dictionary (1806), the definition of "hindi" is simplified to "One Indian. Anything Indian, or belonging to India."[150] The same definition is maintained in the 1829 edition of *A Dictionary*, but when it was

---

[146] Ibid., 63.

[147] Ibid.

[148] Ibid.

[149] Richardson, *A Dictionary, Persian, Arabic, and English* (1777), 2117. Also, see Hakala, *Negotiating Languages*, 245, n. 41.

[150] Richardson, *A Dictionary, Persian, Arabic, and English* (1806), 1141.

revised again in 1852 by Francis Johnson, and published specifically for the East India Company, the entry for "hindu" came to be "An Indian. Black. A servant. A slave. A robber. An infidel. A watchman."[151] But there is now no entry for "hindi"; instead, "hindurvi" is defined as "One Indian. Anything Indian, or belonging to India."[152] The fact that the definition of Hindu found in the 1852 edition was reproduced in a dictionary by Maulawi Fazl-I-Ali in 1885 for the use of British officers was further indication that these definitions of Hindu were part of an official colonial discourse at the end of the nineteenth century.

Savarkar also rejected the idea that Hindusthan had its roots in Persian, as was argued by philologists who explained that the word was a compound of "Hindu" and the suffix -*stan* (place). Savarkar's distinction was to spell the word differently in order to demonstrate that the word actually had its roots in Sanskrit. Whereas the common spelling was "Hindustan," he chose "Hindusthan" (in English and its equivalent in Marathi): the suffix here was the Sanskrit -*sthan*, meaning abode, dwelling, or place — but it could also mean "sphere of god." He was concerned with the issue of spelling the word (and its pronunciation), but also with the history of the word itself. Select nineteenth-century dictionaries maintained that -*sthan* was a Sanskrit root, an example being "Hindusthan" in John T. Platts' *A Dictionary of Urdu, Classical Hindi, and English* (1884). However, there was an important distinction between Savarkar's interpretation and that in Platts' dictionary, where "Hindu" and -*stan* were both identified as of Persian origin.[153] Savarkar's own writings are not consistent on this point either: whereas in *Essentials of Hindutva* "Hindusthan" is used throughout the text, in *Hindu Pad Padashahi* the spelling is "Hindustan." However, it is worth noting that in his Marathi writings and in the Marathi translations of his English writings "Hindusthan" is the preferred spelling. The main point for Savarkar was to revise the etymology

---

[151] Johnson, *Dictionary, Persian, Arabic, and English*, 1403. The exact same definition is also found in Fazl-I-Ali, *A Dictionary of the Persian and English Languages*, 653.

[152] Johnson, *Dictionary, Persian, Arabic, and English*, 1403.

[153] See Platts, *A Dictionary of Urdu, Classical Hindi, and English*. For a recent comparison, in McGregor, *The Oxford Hindi–English Dictionary*, "Hindustan" is listed as having Persian roots, while "Hindusthan" is identified as having Sanskrit origins.

by placing the words within the classical tradition of Sanskrit. Ultimately, he blamed Muslims for having initially appropriated the words and their meanings to denigrate Hindus. His was a discursive battle to reclaim both terms from Orientalists who had codified the meaning and spelling of key words based on their interpretations of the links of such words with Persian.

What troubled Savarkar considerably was that negative definitions and associations had influenced some Hindus to doubt their own identity as Hindus. The introduction of the Census of India had, he believed, exacerbated the situation for some individuals who refused to classify themselves as Hindus: "The first result of our enquiry is to explode the baseless suspicion which has crept into the minds of some of our well-meaning but hasty countrymen that the origin of the words Hindu and Hindusthan is to be traced to the malice of the Mohammedans!"[154] Savarkar says he once met a man — whom he describes as "well-meaning and patriotic" — who wanted to be officially registered as "Aryan." This in itself may not have been a problem, but Savarkar said the man had chosen to identify as an Aryan because he did not want to be classified as a Hindu — this was the man's main concern: "He had been a victim to the wide-spread lie that we were first called Hindus by the Persian Mohammedans out of their contempt — that the word meant thief or a black man."[155] In other words when a Hindu, by identifying himself as an Aryan, went so far as to negate his identity as a Hindu because of a misconception or deception, it showed that the very meaning of the word "Hindu" had been historically altered.[156] For Savarkar it was urgent to reclaim "Hindu" by rejecting both Persian and English definitions of the word proposed in Oriental research.

In many ways Savarkar had already set out to define Hindusthan *before* writing *Essentials of Hindutva*. In *Indian War* he had introduced the term to describe the land of the Hindus.[157] Although he did not there provide a history of the concept of Hindusthan, as he did in *Essentials of Hindutva*, he had provided a brief history of "Hindustan" that appears to serve as the foundation for his later writings. In *Indian War*

[154] Savarkar, *Essentials of Hindutva*, 61.

[155] Ibid., 66.

[156] See NMML, V.D. Savarkar Papers, Reel 30, Press Note by V.D. Savarkar, "An Appeal to My Aryasamajist Brethren Regarding the Census Question."

[157] Savarkar, *Indian War*, 234.

he had acknowledged the need for Hindu–Muslim unity during the war of independence of 1857, arguing against "the feeling of hatred against the Mahomedans" even if this had been "just and necessary" in earlier centuries.[158] The point was that Islam after its founding was a "rising power" that conquered territory in the "East and West . . . [It was] irresistible and unchallenged, country after country and people after people had been made to prostrate in submission to this martial voice of God."[159] It was only in "the land of Bharat" that, for the first time, Islam was challenged: "For more than five centuries the struggle continued; for more than five centuries the Hindu civilisation had been fighting a defensive war against the foreign encroachment on its birth-rights."[160] Savarkar's purpose in including this view in *Indian War* was to emphasise that "Hindu power" re-emerged in the middle of what he called a "gory struggle of countless years."[161] The point he was making even in that early work was that "the honour of the Hindu civilisation" was restored, the "conqueror was conquered," and the "blot of slavery" had finally ended: "Hindus again were the masters of the land of the Hindus."[162]

Not only was this a victory in which Savarkar claimed that Hindusthan was restored to its glory by Hindus on the battlefield, it was also a revision of the history of "Hindus" and "Hindusthan." He went on to offer additional methodological approaches that were central to interpreting Hindutva – beyond his interpretations of Oriental research. His turn to "conjecture" as a strategy was a radical shift as it provided him with infinite possibilities for writing histories.

## 6. Conjecture as Method

*Essentials of Hindutva* was organised to consider the importance of each type of source within a history of concepts, but in the process of writing his book Savarkar often blurred the distinction between sources, making them difficult to distinguish in the arguments he made. Over his attempt to define the meaning of Hindutva, he assumed within his

[158] Ibid., vii.
[159] Ibid., 233.
[160] Ibid.
[161] Ibid., 234.
[162] Ibid.

readers a basic understanding of both the plurality of sources as well as of the realm of conjecture that he used as his archive. Despite the limits of "Oriental research," he says it provided a foundation for "treading on [the] solid ground of recorded facts." Given his reminders of the epistemic limits of Oriental research, his formulation adds uncertainty to the very meaning of Hindu; at the same time, he acknowledges that, despite these constraints, this is a body of knowledge containing facts that support his claims about the term. In other words, Savarkar opted to remain ambivalent about research as part of his argument that *Essentials of Hindutva* also includes conjecture as a strategy: "[W]e cannot refrain ourselves from making an occasional excursion into the borderland of [conjecture]."[163] His declaration about relying on conjecture – whether that meant guesswork, speculation, or even imagination – provides an important insight into his approach when writing about Hindutva.

Savarkar's effort was to provide an alternative approach in his conceptualisation of a history in full: this alternative meant turning to mythology and the epic tradition. He cited numerous examples from the epics in *Essentials of Hindutva* to substantiate his interpretation of Hindutva but does not clarify whether the examples are based on research or conjecture (or something else altogether). This creates a challenge in understanding Savarkar's critiques of methodology. His most important discussion in *Essentials of Hindutva* to illustrate his argument is from the Ramayana. He says that Ramchandra, Prince of Ayodhya, was responsible for "founding a nation and a country" that "reached its geographical limit."[164] Ramchandra's victory over the king of Lanka, Ravana, represented the final stage in the colonisation of land that had started with the entry of Aryan tribes. This is also an indication of Savarkar's interpretation of the colonial process by the early Hindus. He sees it as a brutally violent takeover of territory, in which large armies devastated the landscape by burning it to the

---

[163] Savarkar, *Essentials of Hindutva*, 8. The sentence in the first edition of the text ends with "conjuncture." In subsequent editions of the book, the word is replaced by "conjecture." In the context of this sentence (and paragraph), the use of "conjuncture" in the first edition appears to be an error. As a result, I have followed the recommended modification. For comparative purposes, see Savarkar, *Hindutva* (2003), 8.

[164] Savarkar, *Essentials of Hindutva*, 11.

ground and massacring the local population. This form of colonisation is justifiable because Ramchandra thereby brought the entire territory under a single imperial rule: "the valorous Prince of Ayodhya made a triumphant entry in Ceylon and actually brought the whole land from the Himalayas to the Seas under one sovereign sway."[165] (Lanka in the Ramayana was assumed to be Sri Lanka, which explains Savarkar's use of "Ceylon" in this context.) In the process of establishing imperial rule, Ramchandra united *all* Hindus: "That day was the real birth-day of our Hindu people."[166]

The conceptualisation of Hindu (or Hindu people) was therefore in the crucible of the violent colonisation and annihilation of Lanka – a moment to celebrate as "a national day" since it also brought Aryans and Anaryans (literally, non-Aryans) together under the classification "Hindu." He calls this process the "knitting" of Aryans and Anaryans: it was the coming together of Ramchandra, Hanuman, Sugriva, and Bibhishana.[167]

The Anaryan in Savarkar's framing was not only the non-Aryan human but also the animal. While Hanuman and Sugriva were part of the army of monkeys devoted to Ramchandra, Bibhishana was Ravana's brother, installed as heir to the throne of Lanka after Ramchandra killed Ravana. What remains unclear in Savarkar's discussion is the conceptualisation of animals as Hindus – unless, of course, he was only referring to Hanuman and Sugriva as *the* exceptional and devoted monkeys. This point is never clarified in the text; nor is it clear whether Savarkar classified other animals as Hindus in his work. However, Savarkar's point of highlighting this narrative from the Ramayana was to argue that violence was at the centre of the formation of the Hindu as a Hindu.

Colonisation of the vast territory was a multi-generational process that necessarily involved destruction and annihilation: this was the process by which the Hindu nation was formed. Ramchandra was its founding father and the Ramayana the text that explained the nation's formation. In other words, the Ramayana was no longer only an epic, it was being reclaimed as *the* nationalist history in which the final battle for the conquest of the land was completed. Savarkar did not rely

---

[165] Ibid.

[166] Ibid.

[167] Ibid.

on research as part of his interpretation of the Ramayana; he simply asserted the nexus of what he called conjecture with mythology. It is also evident that he was narrating Ramchandra's story from the most prominent version of the epic composed by Valmiki. *Essentials of Hindutva* prioritises the most popular Ramayana, it does not consider the "many Ramayanas" that have existed for centuries, if not millennia, in India.[168] Savarkar was not interested in tracing the plurality of Ramayana narratives as part of his argument; his purpose was very specific in underscoring the moment of conception of the Hindus and their nation.

This interpretation of the Ramayana also gave a new meaning to the annual celebrations of Ramchandra's killing of Ravana on Vijayadashami as the first national holiday, or what Savarkar called "Hindu Nation Day."[169] It signified the killing of Ravana every year as a reaffirmation of the national formation of Hindus and the completion of colonisation of the land of the Hindus – of Hindusthan. The killing of Ravana signalled the consummation of Hindu identity.[170] What made Vijayadashami special was that every single Hindu could symbolically kill Ravana as part of the celebration – ritually repeating Ramchandra's original act.

The discussion in *Essentials of Hindutva* was not the first time that Savarkar had discussed the importance of the Ramayana. In London in 1909, as earlier noted, Savarkar and Gandhi had shared a stage delivering speeches to a group of Indians celebrating Vijayadashami. Savarkar had offered a lengthy provocation about the Ramayana as part of his agreement that he would not discuss politics. Gandhi later said Savarkar's interpretation of the Ramayana was literal, whereas he, Gandhi, saw the epic as allegorical. Details of Savarkar's 45-minute speech are not known, but there is room for the view that Savarkar's interpretation of the Ramayana in *Essentials of Hindutva* had brewed in his mind since at least his days in London.

From the above it is clear that for Savarkar there existed systems of knowledge to interpret Hindutva that could dispense with absolute reliance on research. We have seen that he was also familiar with tradi-

---

[168] See Richman, ed., *Many Ramayanas*.

[169] Savarkar, "Celebrate the Hindu Nation Day," September 1, 1939, in Bhide, ed., *Veer Savarkar's "Whirl-wind Propaganda,"* 130–3.

[170] NMML, V.D. Savarkar Papers, Reel 25, "Veer Savarkar's Message to Hindudom on Vijay Dashmi Day," August 12, 1942.

tions of writing about the past, such as the *bakhars*, which incorporated alternative forms of knowledge in their construction. In *Indian War* a history in full was already framed as reading against the grain of colonialist historiography; now in *Essentials of Hindutva* Savarkar provided another dimension for his "history in full" which allowed him to conceptualise Hindutva free from the constraints of Oriental research, and perhaps all research.

In providing a critique of Orientalist knowledge formation, or simply moving away from Orientalist knowledge towards conjecture, Savarkar was engaged in the construction of knowledge formation that placed Hindutva as a history in full at its centre. This was a departure from previous engagements with the concept of Hindutva inasmuch as Savarkar was conceptualising it anew within parameters that did not fit straightforwardly within any framework. Hindutva emanated from "all the departments of thought and activity of the whole Being of our Hindu race," signalling an approach methodologically plural.[171] This conception of Hindutva as a history in full, within a framing comprising all departments of thought and activity, meant in effect that Hindutva as a history in full could be infinite: "The ideas and ideals, the systems and societies, the thoughts and sentiments which have centred round this name are so varied and rich, so powerful and so subtle, so elusive and yet so vivid that the term Hindutva defies all attempts at analysis."

Despite providing this caveat about Hindutva's taxonomic defiance, Savarkar spent the rest of his career analysing it. Every action and every activity provided further confirmation of Hindutva's links to Being. *Essentials of Hindutva* was an articulation of the methodological difficulties and epistemological limits of Hindutva as a concept, but also the start of a process of interpreting Being as a regional ontology in the form of the whole Being of the Hindu race.

## 7. From Buddhism to the Vedic Church

The emergence and spread of Buddhism played an important role in Savarkar's argument about the history of the word "Hindu," even if

---

[171] Savarkar, *Essentials of Hindutva*, 3.

his purpose in *Essentials of Hindutva* was not to provide a history of the Buddha (c. sixth century BCE) or his thought. Nor is there any specificity to his description of the Buddhists or Buddhism in the centuries after the Buddha's death. In fact, there is no temporal reference in Savarkar's discussion with the exception of his statement that "the international life of India *after* the rise of Buddhism requires chiefly to be considered."[172] He says: "it was about this time when political enterprise having exposed or exhausted all possibilities of expansion in our own land naturally began to overflow its limits to an extent unevidenced before."[173] This was again a reference to the Hindu colonisation of land. But here Savarkar argues that the "expansion" exceeded "our own land" – presumably the land of the Hindus. The point of when (or where) Hindu colonisation stopped territorially only reflects one concern. At another level it is unclear when Hindu conquests were no longer about the formation of more Hindus in the processes of colonisation – as argued by Savarkar in his conceptualisation of the first wave of Hindu colonisation completed with the victory over Lanka in the Ramayana. My point here is not that Savarkar presented an argument that followed the disciplinary protocols of history, but to emphasise that this conceptualisation was part of an emergent argument about reclaiming the Hindu past as a history in full. Inscribed within Savarkar's framework was his view that historical subjects – the Hindus – were acting and thinking as Hindus for Hindus and Hindusthan. For him it was necessary to trace these moments – even moments based on conjecture – in order to argue the centrality of Hindutva.

A consequence of this process of colonisation beyond the land of the Hindus was the entry of people into Hindusthan: "the outsiders began to knock at our doors more imprudently and even imperatively than they ever had done."[174] Once Hindu colonisation ceased, the rise of Buddhist efforts to spread Buddhism started. The Mauryan emperor Ashoka abandoned warfare and adopted Buddhism, and soon Buddhists were travelling across the globe to share with the world the teachings of the Buddha, promoting "the wheel of the law of Righteousness."[175] Through this process, Savarkar says, people all over

---

[172] Ibid., 15. Emphasis added.
[173] Ibid.
[174] Ibid.
[175] Ibid.

the world learned the name "Sindu" or "Hindu." When these wandering Buddhists had to explain where they were from, they had to repeat Hindu, Hindusthan, or Indus in every interaction, especially in explaining the place where the Buddha was born or the start of Buddhism.

The growth of Buddhism meant that Hindus became more conscious of themselves as Hindus. Savarkar says that once Buddhism spread globally, millions of individuals not only learned about the land of the Hindus, thousands of pilgrims also arrived in India and interactions with these global travellers made Hindus more aware of what distinguished them from non-Hindus: "[It] made us more and more conscious of ourselves as Hindus, then strange to say the fall of Buddhism only carried this process further than ever."[176] Inscribed within the story of the rise of Buddhism was its eventual demise. For Savarkar the Buddhist desire to create a "universal religion" by spreading Buddhism was "disastrous to the national virility and even the national existence of [the Hindu] race."[177]

As the Buddhists spread, they informed the world of the vows of *ahimsa* (non-violence) taken by the leaders of the state. The problem then became that Hindusthan no longer had a theory of warfare or a strategy to resist attacks. Savarkar says scholars had overlooked Buddhism's role in creating the circumstances that transformed the land of the Hindus. Foreign invasions became commonplace over the centuries, while the Buddha himself was not bothered: "the whole of Bharatvarsha itself . . . fell an easy prey to the strong and warlike[:] the Lichis and Huns. Of course the Enlightened [i.e. the Buddha] would perhaps remain unaffected as ever, if this news could ever reach him."[178] Hindus grew resentful of the increasing "barbarous violence" from outside, even as Buddhists continued to promote non-violence – Savarkar refers to these teachings as "the opiates of Universalism and non-violence."[179] The result was further invasions and raids:

> the Huns and Shakas poured like volcanic torrents and burnt all that thrived. Indians saw that the cherished ideals of their race . . . were trampled underfoot, the holy land of their love devastated and sacked by hordes of

[176] Ibid., 16.
[177] Ibid., 17.
[178] Ibid., 17–18.
[179] Ibid., 22.

barbarians, so inferior to them in language, religion, philosophy, mercy and all the soft and human attributes of man and God – but superior to them in strength alone.[180]

Savarkar's discussion of Buddhism provides a caveat worth noting: "we cannot treat [Buddhism] here in full."[181] He seems to be allowing some room for virtue in Buddhism, but centrally he is arguing against a contemporary interpretation that the rise of Buddhism represented "the most glorious epoch" of Indian history.[182] There is no doubt that in Savarkar's mind the turn to Buddhism – and by extension non-violence – not only threatened the virility and masculinity of Hindus, it represented an existential threat to all Hindus.

Moreover, even if Hindutva was indefinable, as argued by Savarkar, what Buddhism posed was the ultimate negation of Hindutva. Therefore he could not ignore or abandon the impact of the Buddha or Buddhism, either as it emerged or as part of Hindu civilisation: "the Buddha – the Dharma – the Sangha[:] They are all ours. Their glories are ours and ours their failures."[183] Technically, Buddhism could not be separated from Savarkar's definition of Hindutva as a history in full. But he chose to clarify that his writings on Buddhism were not a history in full of that worldview.

Savarkar's interpretation that Ashoka's conversion to Buddhism was responsible for Hindus lacking a theory of warfare emerged in the period following the rediscovery of Kautilya's *Arthashastra* – a political treatise on statecraft that was said to have been composed (or compiled) during the Mauryan period (c. 321–187 BCE).[184] There remains uncertainty over whether Kautilya (also known as Chanakya and Vishnugupta) was the figure who served as a minister with Chandragupta Maurya – Ashoka's grandfather – and authored the *Arthashastra*.[185]

---

[180] Ibid., 19.

[181] Ibid., 16.

[182] Ibid., 18.

[183] Ibid.

[184] I owe special thanks to Chris Bayly for this insight. (Personal communication.) The approximate dating of the *Arthashastra* as composed or compiled during the Mauryan period is given in Singh, *A History of Ancient and Early Medieval India*, 321.

[185] Banerjee, "Chanakya/Kautilya," 31–2.

Regardless, Kautilya saw himself as part of a tradition of theoreticians writing about *artha*, making certainty impossible on whether he was the sole author or part of a genealogy of authors involved in writing the *Arthashastra*. The fact that the text apparently went missing or was marginalised for centuries was likely further confirmation of Savarkar's concern with the impact of Buddhism on Hindu history. R. Shamasastry's finding and identification of a copy of the *Arthashastra* on palm leaves in the Oriental Library in Mysore in 1905 had revived a debate about the centrality of the text for understanding state formation in ancient India. Shamasastry started publishing his findings in the *Indian Antiquary* (1905) and the *Mysore Review* (1907) before publishing the entire text in Sanskrit in 1909. His English translation was published in 1915 as *Kautilya's Arthashastra* by the Government Oriental Library Series. His translation of the *Arthashastra* served as a reminder that the text was full of insights about numerous topics related to statecraft, such as the duties of kings and officials, methods of diplomacy, economics, land and revenue policy, and commentaries about warfare. The text not only existed during Ashoka's lifetime, it is likely to have influenced his own state policies. Shortly after Shamasastry's work was published, a number of other scholars identified other versions of the *Arthashastra* in other libraries and published additional research and translations of the work. By the 1920s a vibrant debate about the text was visible in a number of venues, including the *Indian Historical Quarterly*.[186] Shamasastry's first publication on the *Arthashastra* began with a quote from the text: "This Sastra has been written by him who, with knowledge in his head and weapon in his hand, snatched with irresistible force the earth from Nanda."[187] This was a reference to Chandragupta's victory over the Nanda dynasty, but also indicated Kautilya's own role as mastermind of the plan that led to the founding of the Mauryan empire.

For early-twentieth-century scholars, Shamasastry's *Arthashastra* raised important questions: did Ashoka's conversion to Buddhism lead to the eventual marginalisation of the *Arthashastra* and its ideas? Was this the explanation for the lack of a theory of warfare? Although Savarkar did not address these questions directly in *Essentials of Hindutva*,

[186] Ibid., 28.
[187] Shamasastry, "Chanakya's Land and Revenue Policy," 5.

he suggested that Ashoka's turn to Buddhism meant that the land of the Hindus could no longer defend itself. By abandoning warfare, Buddhists had no response to invasions and attacks.

He pointed out that despite the impact of Buddhism there were "valorous" Hindus whose "thought and action" were inspired by the need to take up arms against "foreigners."[188] Savarkar's "thought and action" is an abbreviation for Hindutva. He sees Buddhists as lacking virility, and the Hindus as returning to bravery and masculinity: they came together politically with a clarion call for "Up with the Vedic Dharma! Back to the Vedas!"[189] Hindutva, he says, was central for all Hindus at this moment and it was "politically necessary" to understand the thoughts and activities of Hindus for a history in full: "Once more the people rose to the heights of greatness that shed its lustre on all departments of life. Poetry and philosophy, art and architecture, agriculture and commerce, thought and action felt the quickening impulse which consciousness of Independence strength and Victory alone can radiate."[190]

Witnessing the rise and demise of Buddhism and surviving foreign invasions, Hindu identity came to be further consolidated. Savarkar is emphatic that Hindus understood themselves as Hindus through acts of violence. The example he provides is of the legendary king Vikramaditya, who "drove the foreigners from the Indian soil."[191] Details of Vikramaditya's life are not known, but he may have lived in the first century BCE and there are numerous legends based on his life in many regions of India. For Savarkar, Vikramaditya was important for another reason: he recolonised land near the Indus. A further factor for Vikramaditya's significance, says Savarkar, was that Hindus were marrying non-Hindus: "on the north-western side of our nation the commingling of races was growing rather too unceremonious to be healthy and our frontiers too shifty to be safe."[192] Vikramaditya provided a new direction for this population in his battles for recolonisation

---

[188] Savarkar, *Essentials of Hindutva*, 20–1.

[189] Ibid., 20.

[190] Ibid.

[191] Ibid.

[192] Ibid., 25.

of the land, with his warriors inspired by the clarion call "Back to the Vedas." Just as Ramchandra's victory over Lanka represented one important moment in the formation of "Hindu," so Vikramaditya's return to arms, and his forcing foreigners to leave, was another important moment.

Once the population on the "frontier" of the Indus had been "assimilated" (or reassimilated) as Hindus, a "Vedic State" was established and supported by the "Vedic Church."[193] Vikramaditya's grandson Shalivahan, Savarkar says, proclaimed that the Indus was the official border separating India from other territories; he wanted to incorporate the word "Arya" as part of his discussion of the creation of Sindhusthan: "All these considerations must have fired the imagination of the leaders of *thought and action* and made them restore the ancient Vedic name of our land and nation Sindhusthan."[194] As in *Indian War*, here again Savarkar argues that the thoughts and actions of its leaders exemplified Hindutva. To write this history was to confirm each thought and action as essential to understanding the motive and source that inspired every Hindu.

Savarkar says he turned to the ancient text Bhavishya Purana to substantiate his arguments about this period. However, there was another contemporary influence that Savarkar did not explicitly discuss in *Essentials of Hindutva*: Dayananda Saraswati – founder of the Arya Samaj reform movement which started in 1875. Dayananda was a Sanskrit scholar who emphasised the centrality of the Vedas as books of "true knowledge."[195] His purpose was to re-establish the "Vedic religion" and institute social reform among Hindus. As pointed out by Lajpat Rai in his book *The Arya Samaj* (1915), Dayananda's goal was to "reform the abuses that had crept into Hindu society" rather than start a new religious tradition.[196] Ultimately, Dayananda wanted Hindus to return to the Vedas and Vedic thought as it existed *before* the emergence of Buddhism.[197] He argued that this Vedic time was when "Hindu culture" and "Hindu thought" exemplified the very best in

[193] Ibid., 26.
[194] Ibid., 27.
[195] Rai, *The Arya Samaj*, 102.
[196] Ibid., 106.
[197] See Prasad, *An English Translation of the Satyarth Prakash*.

society.[198] Dayananda had begun advocating "Back to the Vedas" for all Hindus at the end of the nineteenth century.[199] In *My Transportation for Life* Savarkar says he was aware of Lajpat Rai's writings on the Arya Samaj when he wrote *Essentials of Hindutva*.[200] He says that in writing this text he wanted to bring all Hindus together, including the Arya Samajis. While Dayananda had argued for going back to the Vedas and establishing a "Vedic State" and a "Vedic Church" in modern India, Savarkar appears to have taken these concepts and formulations from the Arya Samaj and inserted them into his discussion of Vikramaditya's recolonisation of Hindusthan without specifically citing Dayananda or the Arya Samaj or Lajpat Rai's *The Arya Samaj*.

## 8. Uses of Vernacular Sources

We have seen Savarkar introducing a method for pursuing a history of the word "Hindu" independent of Oriental and other research. Having provided an etymology of "Hindu" in the first half of *Essentials of Hindutva*, he now shifts his focus to an excavation of texts that demonstrate the centrality of the word "Hindu" (and its derivations) in diverse genres written between 1300 and 1800 CE. His purpose in investigating these texts is to examine not only the "activity" of Hindus, but also their "thought" in a period of violence, conflict, and existential threat. Usage of the word "Hindu" and celebration of "Hindu" in texts of this era was a sign that their authors not only saw themselves as Hindus, they also viewed others as Hindus. Every appearance of "Hindu" in vernacular texts is for Savarkar a confirmation that, discursively, Hindus refused to abandon the term and capitulate to Muslim demands, while also demonstrating their willingness to struggle in solidarity for other Hindus. Savarkar's narrative strategy here shows him moving towards vernacular sources to provide a history of the word "Hindu" in order to complement texts in Sanskrit

---

[198] Rai, *The Arya Samaj*, 107.

[199] Dayananda repeated "Back to the Vedas" into the twentieth century as well. For example, see "Missionary Conference: Revival of Hinduism," *The Times of India*, June 10, 1909.

[200] Savarkar, *My Transportation for Life*, in *Selected Works of Veer Savarkar*, vol. 2, 303.

and the Prakrits. All these words, thoughts, and actions put together
was to write a history in full – this was Hindutva:

> This one word, Hindutva, ran like a vital spinal cord through our whole
> body politic and made the Nayars of Malabar weep over the sufferings of
> the Brahmins of Kashmir. Our bards bewailed the fall of Hindus, our seers
> roused the feelings of Hindus, our heroes fought the battles of Hindus,
> our saints blessed the efforts of Hindus, our statesmen molded [sic] the
> fate of Hindus, our mothers wept over the wounds and gloried over the
> triumphs of Hindus.[201]

To Savarkar it was clear that Hindus had suffered for centuries,
and in the process had left traces in the historical record that exemplified what he posited as Hindutva. His strategy for reading texts from
the 1300–1800 CE period was to argue that there was a lacuna in the
literature: scholars had neglected to discuss the writings and activities
of Hindus over these centuries.

Savarkar returns here to the idea that he introduced at the start
of his text: "Hindutva embraces all the departments of thought and
activity of the whole Being of our Hindu race." This period of conflict
with Muslims allowed *all* Hindus to see themselves as Hindus in every
act of violence. Muslims had persecuted Hindus as non-Muslims, irrespective of differences among Hindus based on region, language, or
caste. In the various moments of conflict with Muslims, Hindus from
these diverse backgrounds had consolidated their identity as Hindus:
"The enemies hated us as Hindus and the whole family of peoples and
races, of sects and creeds that flourished from Attock to Cuttack was
suddenly individualised into a single Being."[202] This is yet another
moment in *Essentials of Hindutva* for Savarkar to argue that it was
through violence – collective violence – that Hindus saw themselves
as Hindus: "Sanatanists, Satnamis, Sikhs, Aryas, Anaryas, Marathas
and Madrasis, Brahmins and Panchamas – all suffered as Hindus and
triumphed as Hindus."[203] For which reason, he says, "We cannot help
dropping the remark that no one has up to this time taken the whole

---

[201] Savarkar, *Essentials of Hindutva*, 40.
[202] Ibid.
[203] Ibid., 39.

field of Hindu activities from A.D. 1300 to 1800 into survey from this point of view."[204]

This is an indictment of Hindus who failed to recognise their moment of coming together as a single Being. Implicit in Savarkar's formulation is that the moment did not last; the epiphany, the euphoria, and the light of Being disappeared. What remained was the possibility and hope that Hindus could be reminded of the moment. Savarkar's task was to show that Hindus had forgotten neither the meaning of Hindu nor how they came to be Hindu – to give them a history in full. To glimpse Hindutva in these activities was to be reminded of the possibility of another moment, another embrace of Being.

Bringing all this material together was not easy, given the prison conditions in which Savarkar produced *Essentials of Hindutva*: "It would require a volume if we were to substantiate these remarks by quoting all the words and writings of our forefathers that bear on this point."[205] Instead, he would offer "a few eloquent lines" of what he called "the foremost representatives of our Hindu race."[206] Savarkar did not explain his selection of texts, but they included poetry, autobiography, *bakhar*s, and letters in at least three languages: Hindi, Braj Bhasha, and Marathi.

Perhaps this choice of texts was determined by the circumstances of being in prison and the limitations of memory; he pointed out that his selections were fragmentary. For all that, Savarkar's strategy was very specific: he simply identified passages that exemplified the highest quality of Hindus in this period, which he designates a period of conflict with Muslims. He searched for texts that included the word "Hindu," or any of its roots or derivations, such as Hind, Hindawan, and Hindupati. Most of his quotes are related to the Maratha king Shivaji Bhonsle's reign, including Shivaji's own letters, and writings about Shivaji. The others are from Rajasthan, North India, and Punjab. Savarkar included brief analyses of specific authors, such as Chand Bardai, who is attributed as the author of the *Prithviraj Raso*, a series of poems about the eleventh-century warrior Prithviraj Chauhan: "Chand Baradai . . . may justly be called the first poet of Hindi

---

[204] Ibid., 40.
[205] Ibid.
[206] Ibid., 41.

Table 1

| Author | Text | Year |
| --- | --- | --- |
| Chand Bardai | *Prithviraj Raso* | c. 13th–16th century? |
| [Samrath] Ramdas | Not Given | 17th century |
| Bhushan [Tripathi] | Not Given | 17th century |
| Lal Kavi [Gore Lal Purohit] | *Chhatra Prakash* | 18th century |
| [Rattan Singh] | *Panth Prakash* | 1809 |
| [Bhai Santokh Singh] | *Surya Prakash* [Gurpartap Surya] | 18th century |
| Guru Gobind Singh | *Bachittar Natak* | c. 18th century |
| [Krishnaji Anant Sabhasad] | *Sabhasad Bakhar* | c. 1694 |
| [Malhar Ramrao Chitnis] | *Chitnis Bakhar* | c. 1811 |
| [G.S.] Sardesai | *Madhyavibhag* | 1925 |
| Shivaji [Bhonsle] | Letter 1 | 1646 |
| | Letter 2 (to Jaisingh) | [17th century] |
| | Letter 3 | [17th century] |
| Jai Singh | Letter 1 (to Shivaji) | [17th century] |
| | Letter 2 | October 26, 1721 |
| Author not given | Letter (to Shivaji) | [17th century] |
| Rajaram [Bhonsle] | Letter | [17th century] |
| Baijirao | Not specified | [18th century] |
| | Letter 1 | [18th century] |
| | Letter 2 | [18th century] |
| Mathurabai [Angre] | Letter (to Brahmendra Swami) | [c. 18th century] |
| Dhondo Govind | Letter (to Bajirao) | [18th century] |
| Nanasaheb [Balaji Baji Rao] | Letter (to Tarabai) | [18th century] |
| Govindrao Kale | Letter (to Nana Fadnavis) | 1793 |

literature, [he] uses the words Hindi, Hindawan, Hind so often and so naturally as to leave no doubt of their being quite common and accepted terms as far back as the eleventh century, when Mohammedans had not secured any permanent footing."[207] He cites several stanzas and lines from *Prithviraj Raso* to illustrate his point; each instance is of Chand Bardai's use of "Hindu" and related words. Short commentaries are included about Prithviraj's battle with Shahabuddin, abruptly ending in Prithviraj's death. The purpose is not to provide a summary

---

[207] Ibid.

or analysis of *Prithviraj Raso* but emphasise the presence of "Hindu" in a text that narrates a Hindu king's struggle against a Muslim enemy.

Savarkar concludes his discussion of Prithviraj by highlighting another word that appears frequently in the poem: Bharat. It is another indication to him that the language of the text itself – its word choice – is evidence of Hindus truly seeing themselves as Hindus in the struggle against Muslims: "What we find in this earliest of our northern vernacular composition[s] holds good in the latter development of our vernacular literature down to the day of the great Hindu revival and the war of Hindu liberation."[208]

Savarkar then shifts his focus to a poem by Samrath Ramdas, the seventeenth-century figure he had compared with Mazzini in *Indian War*. There is no analysis of the poem, nor any discussion of the historical Ramdas.

Savarkar's next interest is in a stanza of a poem by Bhushan Tripathi, another seventeenth-century poet. He simply states, "Bhushana, the Hindu poet was one of the most prominent of our national bards that went up and down the country and roused 'Hindawan' to action[,] an achievement in those days of the war of Hindu liberation."[209]

This pattern of brief references is repeated for other authors cited in *Essentials of Hindutva*; sometimes, translations of the text are provided, in other instances he leaves the passages in the vernacular. Authors are sometimes identified by their full name, in other places only a part of their names are given. Most dates are also incomplete or missing: his priority is clearly to excavate select texts which will reinforce the argument he is making for "Hindu." While he did not analyse any of the texts that he cites in *Essentials of Hindutva*, later when he wrote *Hindu Pad Padashahi* and *Bharatiya Ithihastil Saha Soneri Pane* he turned to the same sources to substantiate his claims. Some of these sources also became central to Savarkar's speeches when he served as president of the Akhil Bharatiya Hindu Mahasabha (1937–44).

Needless to say, Savarkar's method in *Essentials of Hindutva* contrasts with the one in *Indian War*, in which he reads colonial history against the grain. In *Essentials of Hindutva* Savarkar privileges authors

---

[208] Ibid., 43.
[209] Ibid., 45.

who wrote of Hindus as Hindus. However, he not only returned to the idea of a war of independence, he also expanded it to cover a period of five centuries. This was not an Indian war of independence against the British, but a Hindu war of independence against Muslims. It marked an important shift in Savarkar's writings that became central to his understanding of Hindutva.

## 9. Geography, Maps, Motherland

After describing the methods of writing a conceptual history of "Hindu" and "Hindusthan," Savarkar shifts attention to what he calls "the main task of determining the essentials of Hindutva."[210] It should be remembered that he claimed Hindutva was indefinable, but this did not mean that it could not be conceptually approximated in language. Since the word Hindutva was a "derivative" of Hindu, it was important to first understand its characteristics. Not only was "Hindu" coeval to a "source" in a time that could not be measured, it was "the most comprehensive and bewilderingly synthetic concept known to the human tongue."[211] Paradoxically, "Hindu" had a materiality primarily geographical – the river – but expanded with Hindusthan as the area or country between "the Sindhu and the Sindhu from the Indus to the Seas." These names, "Hindu" and "Hindusthan," became powerful over time in evoking a visual aesthetic about the landscape and nature. Hindus had a "geographical sense" of their land. In other words, within Savarkar's narrative the movement of and colonisation by Hindus across the territory created an idyllic land for Hindus: "Hindusthan meaning the land of Hindus, the first essential of Hindutva must necessarily be this geographical one."[212]

Even just simply saying "Hindusthan" evoked images of a territory in the minds of Hindus: this was the Hindusthan imagined into existence after its complete colonisation by Hindus. And Hindus had continued to hold on to *this* imagination of their territory for millennia. This was a spatial imagination of territoriality that he claimed he

[210] Ibid., 61.
[211] Ibid., 70.
[212] Ibid., 71.

himself shared with all Hindus – past and present. Savarkar provides textual (and conjectural) methods for interpreting the conceptual histories of "Hindu" and "Hindusthan" that were discursively produced into what has been called "geo-body."[213] It is clear that Savarkar was informed by the development of cartography – he refers to maps and discusses a "map of the world" in *Essentials of Hindutva*. This is not surprising because the publication and circulation of British imperial maps played an important role in conceptualising spaces that were being scientifically measured at this point in time.[214] It has been argued that the British were successful in representing *their* interpretation of India based on epistemologies of science and technology of the time.[215] Most educated colonial subjects studied geography in schools and likely had map literacy. This is not to suggest that cartographic knowledge or the ability to read maps only emerged with the construction of imperial knowledge formation. After all, given Savarkar's engagement with the historiography and methodology of writing Maratha histories – a topic that will be discussed in Part III – it is likely that Savarkar was familiar with Maratha maps of the seventeenth or eighteenth century.[216] He sometimes referred to maps in his speeches later in his career and cited them as a way to study Hindu history:

> Just take up the map of Hindusthan about 1600 A.D. The Moslems ruled all over Hindusthan unchallengeably . . . Hindusthan as such was simply wiped out. Then open out the map of India about 1700 to 1798 A.D. and what do you see? Beating the Moslem Army to a chip in hundreds of battlefields the Hindu forces are marching triumphantly throughout India.[217]

A comparative analysis of these maps revealed "historical facts" and "historical truths" that could be "validated" by studying representations of geography that visually told the story of Muslim decline and

---

[213] Winichakul, *Siam Mapped*.

[214] Savarkar, *Essentials of Hindutva*, 64.

[215] See Edney, *Mapping an Empire*.

[216] See Gogate and Arunachalam, "Area Maps in Maratha Cartography"; Deshpande, "A Note on Maratha Cartography"; Schwartzberg, "South Asian Cartography: Geographical Mapping."

[217] Savarkar, "Protest Against the Vivisection of Hindusthan" (July 1, 1947), in Joshi and Savarkar, eds, *Historic Statements*, 168.

Hindu ascendancy.[218] Savarkar provided no analysis of cartography in his major writings, nor identified the specific maps he was reading. The only map included in any of Savarkar's early texts is found in the 1909 edition of *Indian War*. It is a foldout entitled "India" which was attached inside the front cover of the book; there is no information on the cartographer or publisher of the map. The first volume of *The British Empire Series* (1899) on India and Asia includes a map identical to the one in Savarkar's text, with one exception: all the main rivers are painted red in the map in *Indian War*.[219] The maps are not extraordinary or unusual for British imperial maps of the late-nineteenth or early-twentieth century, except that India is represented entirely in pink.

Benedict Anderson pointed out that the colours of territories and colonies were important to consider when examining imperial maps.[220] Each European nation had a select colour for their colonies that was generally standardised by mapmakers. Mapping the territory was a discursive strategy of colonial power, and putting colour into maps was a representative act of conquest as well. Pink was the designated colour for Britain's colonies – it was the colour used for India in world maps representing the entire British empire. However, for specific maps of India, mapmakers generally distinguished between "Native States" (or princely states), which were typically demarcated and identified by a colour other than pink (often yellow), and British-administered lands that were in pink. The map titled "India" (Map 1) appears to violate these parameters as all of India is coloured pink. In other words, *these* maps did not properly represent the British administration of India at the turn of the century. In many ways, the maps can be interpreted as a colonial fantasy of complete British conquest of the entire territory, including all the princely states, but also the Portuguese- and French-controlled areas of India. They represent an anticipatory future in a visual form – a fiction created by imperial mapmaking.

[218] Ibid.

[219] *The British Empire Series, vol. 1 – India, Ceylon, Straits Settlements, British North Borneo, Hong Kong, with Two Maps* (London: Kegan Paul, Trench, Trubner & Company, 1899). The map is attached to the back cover. An author or editor is not given.

[220] Anderson, *Imagined Communities*, 179.

Map 1:  "India," by An Indian Nationalist,
*The Indian War of Independence of 1857* (1909).

The same maps could of course serve a different function: that is, they could be read as the geo-body of Hindusthan. They provided a representation of Savarkar's imagined Hindu nation that was formed out of the different type of colonisation discussed in *Essentials of Hindutva*.

The map shows blurred (pink) boundaries rather than the "hard" territorial borders of modern maps. These are important considerations for contextualising Savarkar's spatial imagination, given that he also focused on the lack of fixity of borders or boundaries. Sometimes the territory of Hindusthan begins in his imagining on the eastern frontiers of the banks of the Indus, at other times in the Indus, and sometimes it includes lands west of the river. For the north-western border Savarkar simply says, "our frontiers were [growing] too shifty to be safe."[221] The same problem emerges on the eastern frontier with the Brahmaputra. In the case of the Himalayas (and the Hindu Kush) there is no clarity about which parts of the mountains were included or excluded, or which elevations were integral to Hindusthan. It has been argued that the elevations of hills and mountains have been important for thinking about the historical limits of nations and states.[222] This was also a consideration raised by Savarkar in reference to holy men who resided in the mountains; presumably these individuals lived within Savarkar's conceptualisation of the borderlands of Hindusthan.

Savarkar's analysis of geography also examined the sacred geographies found in the Rigveda, Ramayana, and Vishnu Purana – to name a few works he cited. In consonance with his approach to writing the conceptual history of "Hindu" and "Hindusthan," he relied on official British maps, vernacular sources, and classical texts within the Hindu tradition for interpreting geography as an essential of Hindutva. Perhaps there is another context. Sumathi Ramaswamy has pointed out that by the late-nineteenth century nationalists were engaged in disrupting analytical narratives of British representations of space and territory.[223] The scientific map that rationalised India as a colonised land for administration, taxation, and law and order was challenged at many intellectual levels. Discursive strategies for remapping India were adopted by various mapmakers, artists, and nationalists. The idea of the scientific map was reconstituted in the period following the 1880s: various intellectuals, according to Ramaswamy, "embraced another vision and version of the . . . territory."[224] Instead of the "gridlines of power" of British imperial maps, these individuals advanced a "sensuously qualified place-world."[225] One of the primary strategies for "remapping" India in this period was naming the geo-body

[221] Savarkar, *Essentials of Hindutva*, 25.
[222] Scott, *The Art of Not Being Governed*.
[223] Ramaswamy, *The Goddess and the Nation*.
[224] Ibid., 9.
[225] Ibid.

Mother India (Bharat Mata), while also publishing images of Mother India standing or sitting on maps of India (or planet Earth). These representations of Mother India were diverse, as were the maps of India. For example, Mother India was sometimes depicted sitting on topographical maps; in other images she stood on top of silhouettes of India's map; in yet other instances Mother India's body was the geo-body itself, or her sari was shown as the shape of India – her body was depicted as one with the land of Hindusthan and she emerged as *the* motherland. These visual representations of Mother India corresponded with textual arguments for the motherland that went beyond the contours of imperial maps.

Savarkar was influenced by this emergent discourse of Mother India. In "Oh Martyrs" and *Indian War*, Savarkar had introduced the idea that Hindusthan *was* Mother India: 1857 represented the "awakening of the Motherland" when the land of the Hindus was finally freed – albeit briefly.[226] The Motherland was described as "sacred" and as needing to be "liberated" from British control, but Mother India was not specifically mentioned, except in an entry in the Glossary that simply reads "BHARATA-Mata – Mother India."[227] However, it is worth noting the last two words of *Indian War*: "Vande Mataram" (I worship the mother).[228] This pattern was to be found in texts by other writers as well. By the late-nineteenth century the poem "Vande Mataram" became Mother India's "signature hymn" – it was part of public nationalist performances, and recitations of the phrase became common throughout India.[229] The poem and the discourse of "Mother India" also travelled internationally with Savarkar, members of the Abhinav Bharat Society, and other Indians. The publications of the Abhinav Bharat Society generally mentioned "Vande Mataram" as a salutation to readers. And it was reported that Madan Lal Dhingra's last words before his execution were "Vande Mataram."[230]

Savarkar, it would seem, had expanded his early conceptualisation of Hindusthan as the Motherland in *Essentials of Hindutva*. Such expansion had come about only after the formation of Hindusthan,

---

[226] Savarkar, "Oh Martyrs," *Samagra Savarkar Vanmaya*, vol. 5, 443.

[227] Savarkar, *Indian War*, 447.

[228] Ibid., 444.

[229] Ramaswamy, *The Goddess and the Nation*, 117–18.

[230] Ibid., 120.

with Hindu colonisation of the entire territory and with victorious Hindus replacing the existing names of the conquered territories with "Hindusthan." In Savarkar's view a new, hegemonic epistemic formation then came to dominate the spatial imagination of Hindus: "The first image that [Hindustan] rouses in the mind is unmistakably of our *motherland* and by an express appeal to its geographical and physical features it [vivifies] it into a living Being."[231]

Savarkar was not alone in writing about the motherland – it was a concept that in English dated back at least to the mid-sixteenth century. Radhakumud Mookerji, in *The Fundamental Unity of India* (1914), argued that there was a "fundamental unity of India" directly connected to a knowledge of geography based on the history of religion and politics.[232] He explained that he was primarily interested in using "Hindu sources" to write an account of what he called "the making of a nation" based on "a common language, a common religion, a common government and a common culture and social economy."[233] But his key argument was that there existed "a common country" that was a "fixed" homeland for Hindus.[234] Turning to Hindu texts, he argued that there was a long history of Hindu unity that existed with a "geographical consciousness."[235] His book included a contemporary map that represented a unified India, entitled "Map of Ancient India," produced by the London Geographical Institute.[236] Mookerji was also interested in "re-mapping" the territory by turning to the Hindu imagination that linked the geo-body to Mother India: "It was in a real sense the conquest of matter by mind; the subjection of the physical to the spiritual. India as a whole was realised as the mighty motherland by the popular mind in every part of India."[237]

---

[231] Savarkar, *Essentials of Hindutva*, 71. The term in the first edition of the text is "verifies," but later editions substitute it with "vivifies." Savarkar uses "vivifying" in the first edition (pages 27, 84), so this was likely an error corrected in later editions.

[232] See Mookerji, *The Fundamental Unity of India*.

[233] Ibid., 1.

[234] Ibid., 2–3.

[235] Ibid., 4.

[236] Ibid. "Map of Ancient India" is placed at the end of the book, but it does not have a page number in the edition I consulted.

[237] Ibid., 133.

Given their extensive overlapping themes and shared concepts, Mookerji's text offers important parallels for interpreting Savarkar's *Essentials of Hindutva*. Both provided challenges to and critiques of colonial knowledge formation on geography and history, while simultaneously addressing nationalist concerns about reclaiming the land and its history. Mookerji's interest was in establishing India's unity using Hindu sources, whereas the centrality of Savarkar's work had a different purpose – namely, claiming the geography of Hindusthan as the first essential of Hindutva.

While Savarkar underscored the importance of geography, he clarified that the meaning of Hindu was not only geographical. It was incorrect to assume that "Hindu" was synonymous with "Indian" only as a geographical category, without considering a common religion and common culture. To equate "Hindu" with "Indian" via geography would mean that Muslims too could be identified as Hindus – as those who lived between the Indus and the seas. It is in this context that Savarkar added a further qualification of patriliny for Hindus: "A Hindu is primarily a citizen either in himself or through his forefathers of 'Hindusthan' and claims the land as his motherland."[238] To understand the importance of patrilineal descent, Savarkar turned to an analysis of blood as the second essential of Hindutva.

## 10. Blood, Census, Fatherland

Hindus were united by "the bonds of *a* common blood."[239] Further, Hindus were "not only a rashtra [nation] but also a jati"; they could collectively trace themselves to a "race" with a "common origin."[240] Throughout his text, Savarkar used race and jati interchangeably and as equivalents. This marks a continuity from *Indian War*, where Savarkar had already used "race" as a fluid category of analysis to describe Moors, Muslims, and Rajputs. I suggest that both terms functioned as heuristics to underscore the tentative nature of Savarkar's arguments about blood as well as shifting interpretations of the very meaning of

<hr>

238 Savarkar, *Essentials of Hindutva*, 71–2.
239 Ibid., 73. Emphasis added.
240 Ibid.

race and jati. He says, "All Hindus claim to have in their veins the blood of the mighty race incorporated with and descended from the Vedic fathers, the Sindhus."[241] This was an important assertion for Savarkar's argument that Hindusthan was also the fatherland of all Hindus. It signalled a "flow of blood" from the "Vedic fathers" – the Aryans – to *all* Hindus in the twentieth century.[242]

The idea of the fatherland was a well-established patriotic and patrilineal reference used globally to identify a person's country. Interpretations of "fatherland" in nineteenth-century India were diverse. Some Anglo-Indians raised in India referred to Britain as their fatherland.[243] Individuals residing in the Hyderabad State identified the Nizam's territory as the "beloved fatherland."[244] "A Brahman," the pseudonymous author of a book titled *The Thoughts on India* (1881), considered the lands of the Marathas as his "fatherland" and says, "It was the poverty of the Maharattas which made them, a bold and hardy race, and helped them to recover their fatherland from the foreigners."[245]

Discourses relating to the fatherland were proliferating in India and corresponded to patriotic attachments to the land. Very possibly, discourses of the motherland (and Bharat Mata) had greater popular appeal than fatherland in India at this time.[246] But Savarkar turned to both fatherland and motherland in *Essentials of Hindutva* when interpreting the meaning of Hindutva. The fact that Mazzini's writings were full of references to the fatherland likely influenced Savarkar's conceptualisation. Mazzini's *The Duties of Man* begins: "I intend to speak to you of your duties . . . to speak to you of God, of Humanity, of the Fatherland, and the Family."[247] I return to Mazzini here to underscore that his writings influenced Savarkar throughout his career, and often in unexpected ways.

[241] Ibid., 74.

[242] Ibid.

[243] Blunt, *Domicile and Diaspora*, 23–4.

[244] Mirza Mehdy Khan, *Report on the Census Operations, Part I, in Census of India, 1891, vol. XXIII. His Highness the Nizam's Dominions* (Bombay: Jehangir B. Marzban & Co., 1893), 109.

[245] "A Brahman," *The Thoughts on India*, 38.

[246] Ramaswamy, *The Goddess and the Nation*, 113.

[247] Mazzini, *On the Duties of Man*, in *Life & Writings*, vol. 4, 204.

Race and jati were equally useful categories that helped to illustrate what Savarkar called the "common flow of blood" among Hindus.[248] He pointed out that scholars were unsure if Hindus could actually be identified as a race *per se* and opted to address this concern rhetorically: "Are the English a race? Is there anything as English blood, the French blood, the German blood or Chinese blood in this world?"[249] He added that no matter how much one nation's blood came to be mixed with "foreign blood," it still retained the name of the nation's blood and substantiated the claims of a given race.

The implication of Savarkar's argument was that race was socially constructed by those who claimed the category to be true. The conflation of race with jati or caste – or the use of race and caste as concepts – had its origins in discourses about the organisation of Indian society by Europeans. One scholar has pointed out that the Portuguese term *casta* was initially used to identify the lineages of Amerindian groups in the Americas, but was also used to classify the purity of strains of flora and breeds of fauna.[250] Europeans in India used *casta* as an "ambiguous" concept to identify "community, blood-line or birth group."[251] European ethnographers, writers, and administrators later used a number of additional terms without rigour or analytical precision as analogues or equivalents of *casta* – including race, tribe, nation, and sect.[252]

Among writers in India, the categories of analyses centred on jati, and the original category of social division called *varna*, that were based on Sanskrit textual traditions. The caste system emerged as a category through discursive interactions and struggles to define the meaning of "Hindu" – and by extension the society of Hindus. In other words, there was a social and cultural system (or a plurality of systems) that existed which enabled identifying Hindus as those within the caste system. The fact that Brahmin intellectuals were involved in the construction of discourses of caste certainly adds an important dimension to how jatis were represented and translated into the caste

[248] Savarkar, *Essentials of Hindutva*, 74.
[249] Ibid.
[250] Bayly, *Caste, Society, and Politics in India*, 106.
[251] Ibid.
[252] Ibid.

system, including the representation of those who were on the margins of society or who lived outside society. The impact of colonial governmentality on society had further complicated the process of interpreting caste as a system. Whether caste is even the right term, or if it is a heuristic for interpreting the complexity of social structures in India, remains a topic of heated debate. Nicholas Dirks reminds us that caste has not only come to "define the core of Indian tradition," but any interpretation of modernity in India must account for the *place* of caste.[253] In this view, caste emerged as a singular term to represent the plurality of identities, communities, and organisations as a direct consequence of the "historical encounter between India and Western colonial rule."[254] However, Sumit Guha provides an alternative interpretation that seeks to understand caste as a type of ethnicity formed through political, economic, and cultural practices in the *longue durée*, rather than via colonial encounters.[255] In this argument, both state power and political economy helped shape the social organisations of society within particular geographies that were identified as "castes" over centuries, if not millennia. What appears evident is that commentators on "caste" have relied on contemporary categories of analyses to approximate the very meaning of the term as a way to interpret India. Needless to say, this was always an enormous intellectual task, not to mention an administrative one for states interested in using caste to govern.

In colonial India the role of Orientalists in turning to Aryan race theory and ethnological race science added another dimension to debates on caste (and jati).[256] There was no agreement on whether there was "racial unity" or "shared blood" that could be connected from antiquity to the present. Debates on Aryans that centred on the philology of Indo-European (or Indo-Aryan) languages were replaced by theories of the Aryan race and "the pride of blood." In one account, the "unity of the Indian race" was linked to the conquest of the land by a race of "white-complexioned foreigners" called Aryans.[257] The

[253] Dirks, *Castes of Mind*, 3.

[254] Ibid., 5.

[255] See Guha, *Beyond Caste*.

[256] Bayly, *Caste, Society, and Politics in India*, 126–7.

[257] Risley, *The Tribes and Castes of Bengal*, xx–xxi.

blood of the conquerors was eventually diluted by mixing with the indigenous population. In other accounts the blood of the Aryans persisted, reflecting the dominance of the superior race. A consequence was that the category of race superseded the categories of jati, caste, *varna*, and tribe. In other words, the racial aspects of caste were formalised in ethnographic discourses that influenced the ways Hindus were interpreted. This is not to suggest that Indian intellectuals were not involved in the production and circulation of these ideas in their own writings. Savarkar's conceptualisation of the essentials of Hindutva served as a critique of the dominant narratives of race and blood that were produced in the nineteenth century by placing the Hindu at the centre of the history. Savarkar did not abandon the key aspects of these narratives, but he reclaimed them as his own as the essentials for interpreting Hindutva.

For elaborating on the importance of the nexus of race and blood in Hindu history, Savarkar turned to the *Manusmriti* (Laws of Manu), a Sanskrit text composed around the start of the Common Era. The *Manusmriti*, it has been shown, is a seminal text that has influenced the construction of "Hindu religion and Indic society."[258] It has been called "the most celebrated and best known legal text from ancient India."[259] The topics it covers are diverse and include the ethical behaviour of Hindu kings and instructions on the practices of everyday life. The expectations of husbands and wives at home, caste rules, the treatment of animals, the payment of taxes, and the legal system are all examined. A comprehensive work that provides guidelines for all levels of society, it also lists punishments for digressions and violations. The text gained importance in colonial India: British officials treated it as a "canonical text" for interpreting the law and understanding "the foundational nature of Indian society."[260]

While Savarkar did not provide a commentary on the entire text, his specific purpose in citing the *Manusmriti* was to examine the analysis of two forms of marriages, known as Anuloma and Pratiloma, between different castes. He was interested in the discussion of rules relating to children of "mixed classes" who were born of a higher-caste father

[258] Doniger and Smith, trans., *The Laws of Manu*, xvii.
[259] Olivelle, trans., *The Law Code of Manu*, xvi.
[260] Dirks, *Castes of Mind*, 34.

and lower-caste mother (Anuloma), and a lower-caste father and higher-caste mother (Pratiloma). Citing specific cases, he says that among Hindus intermarriage between castes has been long-standing and normative. The formations of new castes, jatis, and classes were the unintended outcomes of these marriages: "Even a cursory glance at any of our Smritis would conclusively prove that the Anuloma and Pratiloma marriage institutions were the order of the day and have given birth to the majority of the castes that obtain amongst us."[261]

He added that marriages often led to individuals being "outcast from a caste"; this was a "daily occurrence" as the individuals formed a new caste or merged into an existing one.[262] He states: "A Hindu marrying a Hindu may lose his caste but not his Hindutva."[263] In other instances, certain behaviours and actions resulted in losing one's caste or being relegated to a different caste: "A Shudra can become a Brahman and a Brahman can become a Shudra."[264] There was also fluidity across the sectarian divide, shown in the intermarriages between Hindus, Buddhists, Sikhs, and Jains that historically led to new social formations within these groups. For Savarkar these processes were important as they showed dynamic exogamy among Hindus; these individuals remained "Hindus" and retained the flow of what he called "common blood."

Inscribed within Savarkar's analysis of blood was a trenchant critique of any argument about the purity of blood – and by implication the purity of any given race. He asserted that all humans have the same blood – human blood – as it is the essential biological characteristic of all humans.[265] He rejected the claim that some human blood was "pure," arguing that this was not possible based on the libidinal urges of all humans through history: "Sexual attraction has proved to be more powerful than all the commands of all the prophets put together."[266] Rather, he argued, all blood is necessarily tainted or polluted. But while it may be true *analytically* that there is no pure blood and

[261] Savarkar, *Essentials of Hindutva*, 74.
[262] Ibid., 76–7.
[263] Ibid., 79.
[264] Ibid., 76.
[265] Ibid., 78.
[266] Ibid.

all humans have impure blood, *affectively* it was necessary for Hindus to assert that they *"feel"* their blood is pure in comparison to all other blood.[267]

Savarkar's argument was not only strategic, it was also essential in providing a critique of the purity of races and jatis. His point in this critique was that his arguments had come under scrutiny for being partial or prejudiced in favour of Hindus. This he felt should not be surprising because no Indian political party or organisation was making universal claims for the creation of a Human State or a global Human Community. National or racial resolutions to the problems facing all humans were universally posited, so those in favour of Hindus could hardly be faulted. All forms of identity were "provisional," "makeshift," and "only relatively true."[268] All distinctions between "races" (or jatis and nationalities) were really obstacles created throughout the world to prevent the interactions and "commingling" of people.

Savarkar was able to accomplish two things in arguing for both an analytical and affective interpretation of blood. Analytically, he acknowledged the idea of the universal human. Hindus have "impure" blood, just like every other human being: there is no such thing as pure blood, just human blood: "Truly speaking all that any one of us can claim, all that history entitles one to claim, is that one has the blood of all mankind in one's veins. The fundamental unity of man . . . is true, all else is relatively so."[269] And yet globally no "race" actually accepted the idea of the universal human.

Affectively, Savarkar's claim that Hindu blood was pure had a powerful consequence for uniting all Hindus. It allowed Savarkar to argue that Jains, Buddhists, and Sikhs all shared the same blood as "Hindus," but so did all "untouchables," low-castes, and tribals. Needless to say, this was a radical assertion that challenged the essence of social hierarchies encompassed within the existing caste system. It allowed Savarkar to establish a bloodline between all Hindus – across time – and thus the argument that historically all individuals sharing Hindu blood were responsible for creating a unified race or jati. In fact, Savarkar suggested that his turn to Hindutva was to create a new Hindu universal that conceptualised caste and class differences in ways

[267] Ibid. Emphasis in original.
[268] Ibid.
[269] Ibid.

that were inclusive for all Hindus. To accomplish this goal, Hindus only needed to *feel* that they shared their blood with all other Hindus.

Savarkar had discussed the importance of blood in *Indian War*. His argument there was that the blood of every martyr served as a seed absorbed by the motherland to create new revolutionaries. As a result, blood was mentioned in nearly every death of a revolutionary as having been spilled on the geo-body of Hindusthan. Savarkar's analysis of blood in *Essentials of Hindutva* was an extension of his descriptions of the war in 1857. Now, in *Essentials of Hindutva*, he saw additional intellectual contexts for arguing that Hindus shared common blood. His idea of linking diverse races and jatis together as a composite form of Hindus happened in a period of debates about the colonial census, in which the category "Hindu" was contested. Savarkar pointed out that the colonial census had fragmented Hindus by demanding that they classify themselves under multiple categories.[270] The problem for him was that some Hindus had stopped identifying as Hindus in the government's taxonomies. What the census had accomplished, in the effort to enumerate population sizes, was disaggregate Hindus into castes and tribes. He saw the census as a fissiparous exercise that had bifurcated and fragmented Hindus, and created tensions and divisions within what he saw as a singularity. Individuals and communities who had long identified as Hindus now had the opportunity to select categories that privileged caste, sub-caste, tribe, and sub-tribe.

A number of writers claimed that, based on the demographic data compiled by the government, Hindus were eventually going to become extinct. This argument was proposed by Lieutenant Colonel U.N. Mukerji in his book called *A Dying Race* (1909). He explained that, based on the Census of India for 1872, 1881, 1891, and 1901, the Hindu population was likely to completely disappear from Bengal because the Muslim population was growing at a significantly faster rate.[271] Mukerji explained that Muslims demonstrated greater solidarity in their effort to create what he called a "united Mahomedan

---

[270] NMML, V.D. Savarkar Papers, Reel 30, Letter from V.D. Savarkar to Lala Narayan Duttaji, regarding the importance of the census, January 12, 1941. Also, see Savarkar, "Hindu Sabhas, Watch Out: The Coming Census & Your Duty," "The Census Week," and "The Census & The Pan-Hindu Fold," in Bhide, ed., *Veer Savarkar's "Whirl-wind Propaganda,"* 266–76, 293–6, 311–15.

[271] Mukerji, *A Dying Race*.

world."[272] In contrast, Hindus were "crumbling to pieces" due to the fact that Hindus were in constant conflict with other Hindus based on caste hierarchies and class conflict.[273] He lamented: *Disunion is the cornerstone of our community.*"[274] Why had this come about? Mukerji argued that "disunion" was a consequence of British policies that had directly affected the social and economic structures within Hindu society. He also argued that some Muslims had introduced the idea that low-caste Hindus should no longer be considered Hindus in the census, and the government had endorsed this separatist notion. The total Hindu population in the census, when "low-caste Hindus" identified themselves as "non-Hindus," had fallen.[275] Hindu unity was fractured; "cooperation" was not possible as individuals of different backgrounds refused the "idea of [a] combination" to unite Hindus.[276] His view was that "In our treatment towards our co-religionists lies the germ of our self-destruction. This is the history of the Hindus."[277]

There were also on the other side of this argument figures like B.R. Ambedkar who had argued that the census should have separate categories for "Depressed Classes," independent of upper-caste and elite Hindus.[278] Ambedkar pointed out that upper-caste Hindus had historically not only oppressed "untouchables," "tribals," and others considered "depressed" members of society, but also that these communities and groups were viewed as "impure." The task was to create a new taxonomy for the census that would distinguish between Hindus and Depressed Classes.[279] Ambedkar pointed out that there were no

---

[272] Ibid., 97.

[273] Ibid.

[274] Ibid., 40. Italics in original.

[275] Ibid., 78.

[276] Ibid., 55.

[277] Ibid., 97.

[278] B.R. Ambedkar, "Statement Concerning the Safeguards for the Protection of the Interests of the Depressed Classes as a Minority in the Bombay Presidency and the Changes in the Composition of and the Guarantees from the Bombay Legislative Council Necessary to Ensure the Same under Provincial Autonomy" (May 29, 1928), in Narke, ed., *Dr. Babasaheb Ambedkar Writings and Speeches*, vol. 2, 435.

[279] "Evidence of Dr. Ambedkar before the Indian Statutory Commission on 23rd October 1928," in Narke, ed., *Dr. Babasaheb Ambedkar Writings and Speeches*, vol. 2, 459–89.

special categories for "Untouchables" or any attempts to distinguish between "different Hindu castes" in the Census of India between 1881 and 1901.[280] However, there was a shift in the 1911 census that included a number of questions to establish the distinctions of caste: "There was no doubt that those tests were such as would mark off the Depressed Classes from the Caste Hindus."[281] Ambedkar saw this as a major development in allowing the government to include new classifications that accounted for the differentiation within the category "Hindu," enabling possible legally egalitarian provisions. He also saw that "Caste Hindus" were not only concerned that the disaggregation of "Hindu" would "reduce the strength of the Hindu Community and its importance," but that they would suggest this was a conspiracy orchestrated by Muslims to weaken the position of Hindus.[282] The distinction between "Untouchables" and Hindus was for Ambedkar not "a matter of blood," but rather the "modes of treatment and observance of certain practices."[283] Hindus and "Untouchables" were separate and needed to be classified and counted so to account for their differences. Needless to say, there were Hindus who opposed these census developments and lodged protests against the census commissioner.

Savarkar's construction of "Hindu" through an argument of common blood (in which all blood was impure) was a strategy to build a solidarity at a time when there was this clear perception of the fragmenting of Hindu identity at multiple levels. He specifically targeted colonial governmentality as a source of this problem but did not address Ambedkar's critique in *Essentials of Hindutva*. His argument about blood did, however, at least conceptually, serve as a rejoinder to the idea that Hindus were a dying race. While Savarkar agreed that the Census of India had fragmented the Hindu population with its classifications of castes and tribes, he was optimistic about the unity of Hindus and their history: "This definition [of Hindu] should be recognised by the Government and made the test of Hindutva in enumerating the populations of Hindus in the Government Census to come."[284] His argument for rethinking Hindu blood as the second

---

[280] Ambedkar, "From Millions to Fractions," 334.
[281] Ibid., 333.
[282] Ibid.
[283] Ibid., 336.
[284] Vinayak D. Savarkar, "Presidential Address, 21ˢᵗ Session of the Akhil

essential of Hindutva was central to his desire for establishing Hindu unity. The issue of blood had, he said, prevented Hindus of different jatis or races from coming together in the past; the imperative now was to show that blood across castes and Hindu divisions was both impure in a purely analytical sense, while capable of being entirely pure if Hindus felt it so in the affective sense. By this assertion Savarkar provided a major argument for solidarity in the name of Hindutva.

However, Savarkar's interpretation of blood still did technically allow Hindu converts to Islam and Christianity to claim that Hindusthan was their motherland (as they also lived between the Indus and the seas) and their fatherland (as they still possessed the blood of Hindus). How then were Muslims to be shown as not really belonging to the land of the Hindus – Hindusthan? Savarkar's solution to this problem was that Muslims did not consider Hindusthan their "holyland." This was a key point. Savarkar developed this view as part of his analysis of civilisation – as the third essential of Hindutva.

## 11. Civilisation, History, Holy Land

Of the three essentials of Hindutva that Savarkar analysed in his book, civilisation was the least developed, perhaps because it was the most conceptually challenging. He struggled with its definition, resulting in multiple explanations of its significance and meaning. It was also the most contentious essential, given that Savarkar was interpreting "civilisation" by negating the Muslim and Christian claim to see Hindusthan as their motherland and fatherland. Savarkar recognised that these were legitimate assertions within the parameters he had established for defining "Hindu." Therefore, clarifying the meaning of "civilisation" was crucial for interpreting Hindutva.

First, Savarkar turned to the word "Sanskriti" as the definition of civilisation. He explained that since the language of Sanskrit was "the chosen means of expression and preservation of [Hindu] culture," inscribed in "Sanskriti" was the "history of our race."[285] In other

---

Bharatiya Hindu Mahasabha, Calcutta, 1939," in Savarkar, *Hindu Rashtra Darshan.*

[285] Savarkar, *Essentials of Hindutva*, 80.

words, Hindu civilisation could be dated back to the first speech act in Sanskrit, but there was also his assertion that every concept and idea conceptualised in Sanskrit reflected the Sanskriti of all Hindus. For Savarkar, the vernacularisation of languages that emerged from the classical Sanskrit also signalled the furtherance of Sanskriti into contemporary India.

Second, Savarkar provided an answer to his own rhetorical question "what is civilisation?" by stating: "Civilisation is the expression of the mind of man. Civilisation is the account of what man has made of matter. If matter is the creation of the Lord, then civilisation is the miniature secondary creation of man."[286] In this definition it is clear that Savarkar was reflecting on an existing contemporary literature that examined the "mind of man" without providing further discussion of the texts or ideas that may have influenced him. There is a large literature in European thought that assesses these concepts as central to the fields of philosophy, natural history, and psychology – from Bacon to Hegel and Spencer and beyond. There was a proliferation of commentaries on the meanings of "mind" for understanding the human condition. Where and when precisely Savarkar intellectually engaged with this body of work is unclear, but the fact that his interpretation of Hindu civilisation was a direct consequence of linking the "mind of man" to Hindus was an important step for reclaiming Hindu history – as was the idea that civilisation is also "*the* account" of Hindus remaking "matter."[287] In this context Savarkar appears to begin by assuming the correctness of the Biblical *creatio ex nihilo*: that is, the Lord created the world (matter) out of nothing. In Savarkar's formulation, Hindus, following the Lord, had created Sanskriti, or what he refers to as "the miniature secondary creation of man."[288] In other words, a history in full was an account of these Hindu creations that formed civilisation.

Third, Savarkar defined civilisation in the exact terms he defined Hindutva: that is, it is the story of the culmination of all Hindu "Thoughts, Actions, and Achievements."[289] He continues: "Literature and art tell

---

[286] Ibid.

[287] Ibid. Emphasis added.

[288] Ibid.

[289] Ibid., 81.

us of its thoughts; history and social institutions of its actions and achievements."[290] Although Savarkar used the same terminology to define both civilisation and Hindutva, he also made a distinction: the two were not identical. At the centre of Savarkar claiming Sanskriti as Hindu civilisation was an assertion that Hindus *had* history. Sanskriti showed that Hindus formed a "cultural unit" with a common mother tongue, common institutions, common law, common art, common architecture, common literature, common inheritance, and common treasure: "If Hindus do not possess a common history, then none in the world does."[291] Throughout his discussion of civilisation, Savarkar argued for the longevity of Hindu history. It has been pointed out that the interpretations of eighteenth-century Orientalist scholars who provided positive views of India's ancient civilisation were rejected by later writers.[292] For example, James Mill in his *History of British India* argued that Hindus had always been in a "low stage of civilisation" and believed their claims of a glorious ancient past were overstated.[293] For Mill the idea of Hindu civilisation was an oxymoron that simply could not have existed, especially as Hindus had "a rude state of the human mind" incapable of complex thought.[294] Mill's infamous denigration of Hindu civilisation was backed up by his profound ignorance of Sanskrit and Indian languages generally. Hindus, he said, not only lacked culture, they did not have the "intellectual maturity" to produce works of history.[295] This made them uncivilised. It has also been remarked that ethnologists had conflated civilisational achievements with "advanced races" in the nineteenth century.[296] In this argument, Hindus had never achieved a civilised state because of their racial inferiority and backwardness. Savarkar's arguments in favour of Hindu civilisation are clearly situated within the context of Mill and other British writers who held a hostile view of Hindu history and achievements. They provide a counter to the assertion that Hindus had no history.

[290] Ibid.

[291] Ibid., 83.

[292] Bhattacharya, *Talking Back.*

[293] Mill, *History of the British Empire*, vol.1, 337.

[294] Ibid., 134.

[295] Ibid., 374.

[296] Bayly, *Caste, Society, and Politics in India*, 113.

On the other hand it is also clear that Savarkar did not want to cede the conceptual history of Sanskriti to any of his Indian contemporaries who were providing alternative interpretations of civilisation. By the time Savarkar wrote *Essentials of Hindutva*, Gandhi had already provided an interpretation of Indian civilisation in *Hind Swaraj* that he had been promoting for over a decade while Savarkar was in prison. Gandhi had condemned the modern civilisation that had emerged out of the industrial revolution. His dialogue with the unnamed revolutionary in *Hind Swaraj* has been noted earlier; when the revolutionary asks Gandhi to explain what he means by civilisation, Gandhi has no clear definition; he offers instead some characteristics of modern civilisation – doctors, lawyers, and the railway – and says modern civilisation is like a disease.[297] People lured by modern civilisation have become "irreligious," "immoral," "cowardly," and "effeminate." The revolutionary persists with "What, then, is civilisation?" Gandhi finally answers: "Civilisation is that mode of conduct which points out to man the path of duty. Performance of duty and observance of morality are convertible terms. To observe morality is to attain mastery over our mind and our passions. So doing, we know ourselves. The Gujarati equivalent for civilisation means 'good conduct'."[298] For Gandhi, modern civilisation had radically changed systems of knowledge and thought, but Indian civilisation – or what he called "true civilisation" – still existed in India as it had managed to remain autonomous and avoided the negative impact of modern civilisation.[299] He tells his interlocutor: "I would certainly advise you and those like you who love the motherland to go into the interior that has yet not been polluted by the railways."[300] His use of the metaphor of India as mother is clear in his claim that "it behoves every lover of India to cling to the old India civilisation even as a child clings to its mother's breast."[301]

Gandhi's interpretations of Indian civilisation provide an important point of reference when thinking about Savarkar's argument about Hindu civilisation as the third essential of Hindutva. This was

[297] Gandhi, *Hind Swaraj*, 34–65.
[298] Ibid., 67.
[299] Ibid., 66–71.
[300] Ibid., 70.
[301] Ibid., 71.

an epistemic battle over which interpretation of civilisation would become normative in postcolonial India. Needless to say, it was also a discursive fight to represent the motherland. Both celebrated the idea of civilisation *before* modern civilisation, but centrally theirs was a clash of civilisations between Gandhi's "Indian civilisation" and Savarkar's "Hindu civilisation." Whereas Savarkar turned to "a full [Hindu] history" to substantiate his civilisational claims, Gandhi opted to reject history as "a record of the wars of the world."[302] For Gandhi, a history that centred on the battles and wars of kings and emperors could not account for Indian civilisation as a mode of conduct, or good conduct. In contrast, Savarkar's argument for the formation of Hindu civilisation – of Hindusthan – was only possible through a complete Hindu conquest and colonisation of the land which had of necessity involved violence. *This* history of violence was at the centre of the very meaning of civilisation as the third essential of Hindutva.

Savarkar's analysis of Sanskriti was vital: it allowed him to negate all Muslim and Christian claims of their being "Hindu" based on the criteria for the first two essentials. By asserting that Hindusthan was the cradle of Hindu civilisation, he was saying that the land of Hindus was *their* Holy Land. It was the land on which *all* the thoughts, actions, and achievements of Hindus had been accomplished. As a result, Sanskriti required "special treatment and analysis" which truly reflected its "multitude" – its Hindutva.[303] The articulation of Hindusthan as Hindu Holy Land was a radical step in establishing a fundamental distinction between "Hindus" and others. For Savarkar, the assertion of this third essential meant "Hindu" was no longer only a geographic identity or a racial one; rather, Sanskriti was at the centre of what he called the "religious aspect of Hindutva."[304] He was willing to acknowledge that Hindusthan could be recognised as the motherland and fatherland of Muslims and Christians, but the objects of their worship lay elsewhere and so they would never consider it their Holy Land. This, centrally, was Savarkar's distinction in defining Hindutva via Hindu civilisation.

---

[302] Ibid., 89.
[303] Savarkar, *Essentials of Hindutva*, 89–90.
[304] Ibid., 90.

Savarkar's main concern with Muslims who lived in Hindusthan was that they had an extra-territorial allegiance to a holy land that was not Hindusthan: "Look at the Mohammadens. Mecca is a sterner reality than Delhi or Agra."[305] He raised similar critiques about Zionists, who were at the time seeking to create a Jewish state. He argued that Jews were necessarily divided in their allegiance to the "land of their birth" and the "land of their Prophets."[306] In other words, no matter where Muslims or Jews resided, both would adhere to a principle of extra-territorial allegiance. He adds that, historically, Muslims and Jews were not the only religions to turn to the idea of a holy land – Christians, too, had exemplified such an allegiance during the Crusades, and also in the context of the arguments of Christian Zionism:

> If the Zionists' dreams are ever realised – if Palestine becomes a Jewish State and it will gladden us almost as much as our Jewish friends – they, like the Mohammadans would naturally set their interests of their Holyland above those of their Motherland in America and Europe and in the case of war between their adopted country and the Jewish State would naturally sympathise with the latter.[307]

The idea of the holy land originated as a reference to Jerusalem (Western Palestine) as the place where Jesus Christ lived and died, but also as the location of the development of Christianity and Judaism. In the nineteenth century Christian Zionists in Britain had, on scriptural grounds, led the Zionist movement to return the Jewish people to their Holy Land for the purpose of establishing a Jewish state.[308] It has been argued that the English context is important to consider, given that these Christians saw themselves as being "chosen" to "restor[e] the Jews to Palestine."[309] The establishment of Theodor Herzl's First Zionist Congress in 1897 in Basel, Switzerland, further globalised the

---

[305] Ibid., 122.

[306] Ibid., 123.

[307] Ibid., 124. Also, Savarkar, "Independent Jewish State," *Samagra Savarkar Vanmaya*, vol. 6, 558–9; Savarkar, "A Statement on the Jewish International Question," in Bhide, ed., *Veer Savarkar's "Whirl-wind Propaganda,"* 70–2.

[308] Crome, *Christian Zionism*.

[309] Ibid., 79.

idea of Zionism and the return of Jews to the Holy Land.[310] Savarkar seems well aware of these debates, which he discusses in *Essentials of Hindutva.*

My general point is that Savarkar was here incorporating another Biblical reference in conceptualising Hindusthan, illustrating the wide range of ideas that influenced or inspired his thought – including those coming from the direction of Islam. Over the time he conceived and wrote *Essentials of Hindutva*, the leaders of the Khilafat movement had been demanding the restoration of the Caliph within the Ottoman empire, the Caliph's responsibility having been to control Muslim lands, including Islam's holy places. The attention Indian Muslims bestowed on pan-Islamism confirmed in him the need to articulate the idea of a "Hindu Holy Land." Perhaps most important, Savarkar clarified the meaning of Hindu in this context: "Everyone who regards this Hindusthan from the Indus to the Seas as his *fatherland* and *holy-land* is a Hindu."[311]

# 12. Conclusion

*Essentials of Hindutva* emerged as *the* most important articulation of Hindutva in its time. Savarkar's audacity in linking Hindutva to history allowed him to not only engage with the seminal scholarly debates of the late-nineteenth and early-twentieth centuries, but also revise them based on his arguments for conceptualising "Hindu" and "Hindusthan." This text provides a clear outline for writing Hindutva as a history in full. It is as much a work that provides methodological approaches for writing history as for providing a history of key words that interpret the essentials of Hindutva. At the same time, it is a bricolage which reflects the intellectual milieu in which it was written by drawing from and building on diverse ideas and concepts. The fact that Savarkar was in prison when he wrote this work provides context to the challenges he faced in its production. But this fact of his circumstances also adds complexity to interpreting a text influenced by a constellation of ideas – often unexpected. *Essentials of Hindutva* is the

---

[310] Ibid., 8.
[311] Savarkar, *Essentials of Hindutva*, 124.

Savarkar opus that serves as the foundation for all his work. He spent the rest of his career expanding, developing, and refining the ideas that he produced in this book. It was, within his life, the exemplary work of Hindu history – "a history in full" – that would change all interpretations of Hindutva in the twentieth century.

# PART III

# Modes
# of Hindu History

Vinayak Damodar Savarkar, photographed by
Narayan Vinayak Virkar (c. 1924).
*Photo credit:* This image was previously published in
*Samagra Savarkar Vanmaya*, vol. 7
(Poona: Maharashtra Prantik Hindusabha, 1965).

# MODE 1: MARATHA HISTORY AS HINDU HISTORY

The book is . . . meant, not primarily to tell a detailed story
of the Hindu Empire of Maharashtra, but to bring out the
salient principles and ideals that animated it.
**Vinayak Damodar Savarkar, *Hindu Pad Padashahi***

## 1. Introduction

In *Six Glorious Epochs of Indian History*, Savarkar says that one morning an elderly man arrived unannounced at his house, asking to meet him. Savarkar was living in Ratnagiri at the time, with his movements restricted to the locality as part of an agreement with the government in 1924 – but the exact date of this meeting is not given.[1] Savarkar inquired, "Whom have I the pleasure to receive?" The man replied, "I am Sardesai from Baroda . . . whom you know as the writer of Indian history."[2] Savarkar says he was surprised: "What? Riyasat-kar Sardesai?" The individual visiting Savarkar was Govindrao Sakharam Sardesai, a prolific historian who published extensively from the 1890s to the 1940s. But he was best known as the author of an eight-volume history of the Marathas entitled *Marathi Riyasat*; thus, he was popularly called Riyasatkar.[3] Savarkar had apparently sent messages to Sardesai via mutual acquaintances after his return from the Cellular Jail in the Andamans but not received a reply, though he had heard that Sardesai was fond him: "I learn[ed] from other people that Sardesai praised my revolutionary activities as brave deeds."[4]

Savarkar's description of the meeting with Sardesai is brief. Sardesai had voluntarily retired from service of the Baroda State in 1925, so it

---

[1] Savarkar, *Six Glorious Epochs of Indian History*, 407–8.

[2] Ibid.

[3] Rao, "Govind Sakharam Sardesai," 222–34; Chakrabarty, *The Calling of History*, 16.

[4] Savarkar, *Six Glorious Epochs of Indian History*, 407.

is likely that the meeting took place before his retirement. Savarkar told Sardesai he had read all of his books, and especially appreciated the "big volumes on Muslim Riyasat."[5] He encouraged Sardesai to write a history of the Marathas in English for "non-Marathi scholars" who, according to Savarkar, had "no knowledge of the greatness of, nor even a nodding acquaintance with, the *essence* of Maratha history."[6] He tells us: "So I said . . . at least today you are the only authoritative writer who can possibly do it. At least you should begin at once and write such a history in English'."[7] Sardesai's response was that the task needed to be taken up by someone else. As the visit came to an end, Savarkar thanked Sardesai and expressed gratitude, with the latter politely demurring – "No, No, the real pleasure is mine! We are all the writers of history; but you are the maker [*sic*] of history! When you make history we note it down and I came here with a sincere desire to see you as the maker of history!"[8]

Based on Savarkar's recollection of the meeting, Sardesai articulated a distinction between "makers of history" and "writers of history." Perhaps worth noting are the parallels, in this exchange between Sardesai and Savarkar, with Karl Marx's famous claim in the *Theses on Feuerbach*: "The philosophers have only interpreted the world, in various ways; the point is to change it."[9] Of course, in the context of the dialogue between Sardesai and Savarkar the distinction was between the historian as interpreter, and the maker of history as the individual striving to change the colonial world. Whether Sardesai had read Savarkar's *Indian War*, *Joseph Mazzini*, and *Essentials of Hindutva*, or even considered the books works of history, is unclear, but he was familiar with the political activities that had landed Savarkar in legal trouble with the British. The distinction between interpreter and maker of history may have been irrelevant to Savarkar, who saw writing history and making history as congruous and entangled processes. To write history as a history in full did not simply mean interpreting the world, but also effecting revolutionary political change.

[5] Ibid., 408.
[6] Ibid. Emphasis mine.
[7] Ibid.
[8] Ibid.
[9] Marx, "Theses on Feuerbach."

The meeting left a definite impression on Savarkar because he himself took up the task of writing a Maratha history in English that he says he suggested to Sardesai. By February 1925 Savarkar completed this work, entitled *Hindu Pad Padashahi*.[10] The book was published in Madras by B.G. Paul & Company in November 1925 with the subtitle *A Review of the Hindu Empire of Maharashtra.*

Here, in Part III, I examine Savarkar's writings between 1925 and 1931 that further extended his conceptualisation of a history in full. I begin with *Hindu Pad Padashahi* as it brings together themes and concepts related to the principles of history that Savarkar had addressed in *Indian War*, even as it had incorporated the arguments articulated in *Essentials of Hindutva*. Hindutva as a history in full now meant applying his interpretations in *Essentials of Hindutva* to Maratha history. This was an important shift – from writing about historical actors as Indian revolutionaries in the Indian war of independence, to writing about Hindu revolutionaries. As in *Indian War*, he argued that the purpose of *Hindu Pad Padashahi* was not to provide a "detailed history" but rather "to bring out the salient principles and ideals that animated it."[11] Savarkar also developed in it a new concept that is at the centre of his analysis of Maratha history: "Hindu spirit" (he also used "Pan-Hindu spirit").[12] He had introduced the idea of the spirit in *Indian War* and *Essentials of Hindutva*, but in this later text the Hindu spirit was shown as central to this process. Further, it was in the moment of recognising what Savarkar called "the *essence* of Maratha history" that the writer of history and the maker of history came together, signalling an ontological integrity of historian and historical subject.

On the theme of ontological integrity, Judith Butler's conceptualisation of the "desiring subject" – albeit used in a different context – is hermeneutically useful.[13] Savarkar had, as noted earlier, argued that it was necessary to search for the desires and motives of chief actors. But

[10] Savarkar, *Hindu Pad Padashahi*, xiv.

[11] Ibid., ix.

[12] For Savarkar, "Hindu spirit" and "Pan-Hindu spirit" were synonymous, and he used them interchangeably in the text. For purposes of clarity, I have opted to use "Hindu spirit," unless it is in a direct quote, in which case I defer to Savarkar's usage of "Pan-Hindu spirit."

[13] Butler, *Subjects of Desire*.

he pointed out that to recognise these desires was insufficient: what was required was for historians to write about those desires as part of a history in full. This formulation was both Savarkar's explanation of his own desire for Hindutva and of those desiring subjects of his histories for whom he claimed Hindutva. The desiring subjects in Savarkar's histories all shared characteristics of masculinity (bravery, heroism, valour, chivalry) and contrasted with historical figures who Savarkar found effeminate and lacking virility. The more Savarkar wrote about the heroism and bravery of his subjects, the more he himself was identified as heroic and brave. The embodiment of Savarkar as "Veer Savarkar" ("Brave" and "Heroic" Savarkar) is central to understanding the ontological integrity or unity of the historian and his subject. Butler says this longing and purpose is not simply about uncovering the desire of the subject, it is also about interpreting the desire of the author who shares the desires of the desiring subject.[14]

In the second section of Part III I show how Savarkar further complicated this conceptualisation of ontological integrity by writing about the "self" as the writer of history and the maker of history – Savarkar as historian on Savarkar as historical subject. After completing *Hindu Pad Padashahi*, Savarkar produced multiple texts that functioned as both autobiographies and biographies of Savarkar. He had already established a pattern of writing about himself as a revolutionary subject in third person narratives in a series of short essays and newsletters while in London, and he now resumed this practice.[15] He also wrote first person narratives consistent with the genre of autobiographical writings of the time, most noticeably those by Mazzini that Savarkar had read and translated in 1906. But Savarkar was not simply reproducing Mazzini's project; he was using his work to establish continuities between his writings about the Marathas in *Hindu Pad Padashahi* and himself in his autobiographical writings. By turning to the Mazzinian methods of history writing he had taken up in *Indian War*, Savarkar now read against the grain of the established historiography to write about revolutionary heroes in Maratha history.

---

[14] Ibid., 50, 158.

[15] Savarkar, *"Deshbhakta Savarkar ka patra,"* September 27, 1909, *Savarkar Samagra*, vol. 1, 609; and *Samagra Savarkar*, vol. 1, 116–17.

Similarly, he read against the grain of colonial sources and classifications about himself to construct a Maratha revolutionary hero-subject that embodied the idea of "Veer Savarkar." Both genres of writing reflected Savarkar's larger concern with writing "Hindu history." The point was to place a key idea from *Essentials of Hindutva* at the centre: "Hindutva embraces all the departments of thought and activity of the whole Being of our Hindu race."[16] The goal was ontological integrity. Only when the historian was himself the heroic Hindu who embodied Hindutva would there be a true understanding of the meaning of Hindutva as a condition of Being.

## 2. Hindutva Without Politics

The years immediately after Savarkar was transferred from the Cellular Jail were a time of great productivity. He was again able to write without restrictions – as long as he did not discuss politics and lived and travelled within Ratnagiri District; under specific circumstances he could seek permission from the district magistrate to travel outside the district.

However, once Savarkar began publishing his work government officials soon began to believe he was violating the conditions of his release: his writings appeared to be political.[17] He was permitted to deliver lectures in Ratnagiri District on the understanding that he refrain from all political topics. Newspapers started covering his speeches and before long, in 1924, the district magistrate said Savarkar's speeches could be classified as "almost incitements to violence" masked under "social reform propaganda."[18] This official had questioned Savarkar on multiple occasions about his activities and the two had reached an impasse on distinguishing social topics from political ones. Savarkar maintained that all his writings and speeches focused on what he called the "social field." The district magistrate appeared frustrated by

[16] Savarkar, *Essentials of Hindutva*, 4.

[17] MSA, HD Spec File 60-D-(g)-1929, "H.D. (Poll) Note," December 8, 1928, S-39-42. (Author's initials are not legible.)

[18] MSA, HD Spec File 60-I-1933, Letter from Mr. Wilson, CID Office, Poona, to A. Montgomerie, Sec. to Government, HD, November 27, 1924, S-203. (The first name/initials of the author are not legible.)

Savarkar's distinctions, not having sufficient evidence to punish him. He argued: "If accused of making a political speech he will no doubt explain that he was merely urging the youth of the country to be self-sacrificing and rash in the cause of social reform."[19]

By the late 1920s the frequency of Savarkar's speeches increased, as did the government's surveillance of his public appearances. In 1927 an official report stated that "During the past twelve months Savarkar's speeches have been chiefly on the subject of Hindu Sanghatan and un-touchability. They have been close to the border line and have created a certain amount of ill-feeling among Muslims."[20] Officials continued to accuse Savarkar of making arguments for social reform of "untouch-ables" or the idea of constructing a *sanghatan* (organisation) for Hindu solidarity as political acts, to which Savarkar kept responding that his work was "non-political." The correspondence between Savarkar and British officials on this topic is extensive. His case was that his arguments for temple entry by "untouchables" and shared dining with "untouch-ables" were not political. Nor, he said, were his speeches on creating an organisation to promote a unified Hindu identity anything but a desire in the interests of Hindu culture and Hindu civilisation, as was his work with "untouchables" to create a unified Hindu identity. Savarkar's speeches repeated his central arguments in *Essentials of Hindutva*, even as he maintained that they were part of the social and cultural field. For the purpose of communicating with the government, Savarkar's argument was that Hinduva was non-political.

Government scrutiny of Savarkar's activities continued till May 10, 1937, when the restrictions on his travel and political activity were lifted as part of his "unconditional release."[21] Colonial officials may not have realised the significance of the date May 10th, but it was important for Savarkar: it was the date of Mangal Panday's revolt in 1857. For the first time since his arrest in London in 1910, Savarkar was able to travel, publish, and participate in politics without seeking permission. In 1939 Savarkar organised annual celebrations throughout

---

[19] Ibid. Also see, Banerjee, "The Abiding Binary," for a history on the dis-tinctions between the social and political in the writing of South Asian history.

[20] MSA, HD Spec File 60-I-1933, Letter from Mr. Wilson, CID Office, Poona, to J. Monteach, Sec. to Government, HD, January 6, 1927, S-329.

[21] "Mr. V.D. Savarkar Released," *The Times of India*, May 11, 1937.

Maharashtra on May 10th as "War of Independence Day."[22] By 1942 the date was also known as "Anti-Pakistan Day."[23] Savarkar continued to give lectures on Hindutva and the government continued maintaining that he was in danger of violating the terms of his release. The main consequence for Savarkar was that though the initial restrictions were only meant for five years, they lasted for over thirteen. Officials persisted in their view that as soon as all the restrictions were lifted, Savarkar would resume his seditious political activity: "Savarkar has not kept to the letter of the condition not to take part in politics."[24] He remained "anti-British" but now is also called "bitterly anti-Muslim."[25] The same official said Savarkar was no longer interested in bombs, assassinations, and armed revolt but posed a threat to Hindu–Muslim relations. Officials discussed the idea of extending Savarkar's restrictions, as it would be impossible to rearrest him once he was released due to public pressure.[26]

The government also suspected some of Savarkar's writings in newspapers having been published under pseudonyms.[27] In other instances, they thought Savarkar was publishing his own writings under his brothers' names. It was becoming apparent to them that Savarkar's writings could not be properly monitored. Needless to say, this also makes it difficult to properly interpret Savarkar in this period, it being unclear what and how much he authored using other names. He was apparently writing many private letters and posting them; when

[22] "Tribute to the Heroes and Martyrs who Fought Out & the Great Indian Revolutionary War of 1857," in Bhide, ed., *Veer Savarkar's "Whirl-wind Propaganda,"* 546–9.

[23] NMML, V.D. Savarkar Papers, Reel 25, Circular Issued by V.D. Savarkar to all Hindusabha Branches titled "Observe the 10th of May as the Anti-Pakistan Day and the Independence Day," April 27, 1942.

[24] MSA, HD Spec File-D-(g)-1929, "Note by A.S." (no date given) S-16. (Full name or official designation of the author is not provided in the document.)

[25] Ibid., S-16-17.

[26] MSA, HD Spec File 60-D-(g)-1929, "H.D. (Special) Note, August 13, 1928, S-14. (The author's initials are not legible.)

[27] MSA, HD Spec File 60-D-(g)-1929, "H.D. (Special) Report," S-264. (Name of author and date not given. The author's initials are not legible.)

confiscated and read, the topics were "seemingly harmless" but officials felt Savarkar was sending secret messages in them that were indecipherable: "He has never really obeyed the conditions of his release in a way meant by Government. Savarkar has been conducting correspondence for the last 12 months in a Code of his own and . . . the D.M. [district magistrate] has not been able to decipher the messages."[28]

Savarkar not only produced new work, he was able to bypass colonial surveillance; it seems officials were often oblivious even of Savarkar's publications in newspapers that included his name as author. This was the case with his weekly column in the *Kesari* for six months in 1926, when he published autobiographical essays about his incarceration in the Cellular Jail in the Andamans. Savarkar also completed some of his most influential writings in this period, including dramas, poetry, commentaries, and history.[29] After the publication of *Essentials of Hindutva*, *Hindu Pad Padashahi* was Savarkar's most significant work on Hindutva to appear in print – apparently without the knowledge of colonial officials, including those monitoring his mail in the post office.

## 3. Rethinking Maratha Historiography

In the "Author's Foreword" of *Hindu Pad Padashahi*, Savarkar celebrated the work of scholars responsible for establishing an emergent historiography of the Marathas based on vast official sources, state documents, correspondence, and contemporary narratives.[30] He classified the scholarship as a "new light on the history of the Hindu Empire of

[28] MSA, HD Spec File 60-D-(g)-1929, "H.D. (Special) Report," December 16, 1932, S-283-84. (Name of author not given. The author's initials are not legible.)

[29] For example, *Marathi Basheche Shuddhikaran* (1926), *Usshap* (1927), and *Uttarkriya* (1933).

[30] There is no consistency in the literature on the spelling of "Hindu Pad Padashahi" in Marathi, Hindi, or English. *Padshahi* and *padashahi* are both used by different authors. *Padpadashahi*, *padpadashahi*, *patpadshahi*, and *pat padshahi* also appear in texts. I have primarily relied on Savarkar's spelling used in the title of his book. For direct quotes, I have kept the spelling found in the original text or source.

Maharashtra."[31] This body of work was a necessary corrective to histories that reflected what he called "the distorted and dim glasses of foreign scholarship."[32] In many ways the book begins with a critique of scholarship similar to the one in *Indian War*, where he argued that he wanted to show "the light of research."[33] Elsewhere he says, "I threw the electric search-light of the Hindu national point of view on the then extensive but chaotic mass of details about the history of the Marathas."[34] In this new book "the national spirit [is] imbued with Hindutwa," which is of course part of his larger concept of the Hindu spirit. In other words, *Hindu Pad Padashahi* was a text about the "Hindu War of Independence" (and "Hindu War of Liberation") that combined writing strategies and conceptual categories from *Indian War* with interpretations of Hindutva from *Essentials of Hindutva*.

For this new work Savarkar relied on an established historiography with a solid foundation. He specifically celebrated Vishwanath Kashinath Rajwade (1863–1926) as the leading scholar who had produced a revisionist history by turning to extensive materials not considered by other writers.[35] Savarkar was not only aware of Rajwade's twenty-two volumes of documents of Maratha history that were published as *Marathyanchya Itihasachi Sadhanen* (1898–1922), he also cited some of them in *Essentials of Hindutva* and *Hindu Pad Padashahi*.[36] Rajwade had travelled throughout India with the purpose of identifying, documenting, annotating, and reproducing sources as part of his commitment to Maratha history. His Collected Works span thirteen volumes, including writings on the philosophy of history, commentaries on religious texts, analyses of poetry, and discussions of contemporary Marathi politics and culture.[37] As Prachi Deshpande has pointed out, "Rajwade towered over the Marathi literary-cultural sphere in the late

---

[31] Savarkar, *Hindu Pad Padashahi*, vii.

[32] Ibid.

[33] Savarkar, *Indian War*, vii.

[34] Savarkar, *Six Glorious Epochs*, 410.

[35] Savarkar, *Hindu Pad Padashahi*, vii.

[36] For a review of Rajwade's work, see *Indian Historical Records Commission. Proceedings of Meetings, vol. VI, January 1924* (Calcutta: GOI Central Publication Branch, 1924), 66.

[37] Deshpande, *Creative Pasts*, 105.

nineteenth and early twentieth centuries."[38] For Savarkar, Rajwade served an important role in providing an intellectual opening for further work on the Marathas not possible earlier.

Savarkar lamented that despite the important new research on the Marathas, it was not accessible to "non-Maratha scholars" or the "Indian public" as all of it was in Marathi, with the exception of M.G. Ranade's *The Rise of the Maratha Power* (1900).[39] He considered Ranade's book an important contribution in English, but stated that its focus was on an earlier period of Maratha history than his own in *Hindu Pad Padashahi*.[40] On the issue of Maratha historiography he says: "Histories of Marathas were in languages other than Marathi [and] have been mostly written by our age-old enemies like the Muslims, the Portuguese, the English and others with horrid perversion of facts, and unfortunately our Hindu writers from other Indian States have echoed them mostly through ignorance."[41] The consequence of not having a robust historiography in English was that there was a lack of understanding about Maratha history and its central role in the making of Indian history at a national level. The need was for a history of the Marathas in English for "Non-Maratha readers."[42] This was precisely the point Savarkar had expressed to Sardesai. To this end, "Therefore, our chief aim in writing this critical work[,] which is primarily addressed to the public outside Maharashtra, has been to ascertain and appraise the value of the Maratha movement in terms of Hindu history."[43]

When assessing the historiography of the Marathas in English, Savarkar did not include the influential writings of Jadunath Sarkar – not even his *Shivaji and His Times* (1919). Nor did he discuss the work of historians from England or Europe. Jadunath Sarkar, for his part, was not impressed with Savarkar's book or his argument that the Marathas wanted to establish Hindu Pad Padashahi – a Hindu empire. In fact Sarkar made his displeasure known to Sardesai in several letters written

<hr>

[38] Ibid.

[39] Savarkar, *Hindu Pad Padashahi*, vii.

[40] Ibid., ix.

[41] Savarkar, *Six Glorious Epochs*, 406.

[42] Savarkar, *Hindu Pad Padashahi*, viii, 40.

[43] Ibid., ix.

in the 1930s, especially because Sardesai seemed to him to embrace some of the arguments of Savarkar and Rajwade. On August 17, 1933 Sarkar wrote to Sardesai: "Are you prepared to go to the absurdity of Rajwade and be responsible for the opinion that about a dozen men (at least three) tried to establish Hindu Pat Padshahi during the ten years that Jai Singh served Aurangzeb? This would make your book ridiculous."[44] It was not the first time that Sarkar had criticised Rajwade. In fact, after their first meeting in 1908 both had developed a rather healthy antagonism for one another. Rajwade had questioned Sarkar's decision to write history in English instead of Bengali; Rajwade had chosen Marathi as his language and had shunned English.[45] Apparently Rajwade had a dislike for Indian scholars writing in English, and his questioning Sarkar had created an immediate rupture.[46] Even after Rajwade's death, Sarkar did not relent in his attacks against Rajwade. The letters to Sardesai in the 1930s were mild in comparison to the lengthy 1927 obituary titled "The Historian Rajwade," penned by Sarkar in *The Modern Review*, which concludes:

> And hence he lived and died a collector and could not contribute a single history worthy of the name . . . and he was denied the historian's supreme achievement of visualising the *truth* of the past, though he gained the applause of a certain class of narrow provincial (or rather caste) chauvinists, with whom past history is only the bondmaid of current politics of the stump orator brand. But, rest perturbed spirit! Rest. Others will reap where you merely sowed.[47]

Given Sarkar's public writings on Rajwade and what he said to Sardesai in their private letters, the latter was aware of Sarkar's animus. His reply to Sarkar on August 28, 1933 was firm, and he appeared to echo some of Savarkar's arguments from the "Author's Foreword" in *Hindu Pad Padashahi*:

> My main object is to communicate to non-Marathi India what the Maratha mind has been thinking . . . I wish to convey the main idea that

[44] Letter from Jadunath Sarkar to G.S. Sardesai, August 17, 1933, in Gupta, ed., *Life and Letters of Sir Jadunath Sarkar*, 171.

[45] Chakrabarty, *The Calling of History*, 59.

[46] Ibid.

[47] Sarkar, "The Historian Rajwade," 187. Emphasis in the original.

there was a general craving throughout the country for religious toleration & full personal liberty of conscience, of which Aurangzeb in particular deprived the nation so wantonly . . . & there was a general desire for Hindu Empire for India. But apart from this, I wish to impart to all foreign readers what many writers & scholars in Maharashtra have said . . . I can say that some scholars have asserted that there was a general craving for a Hindu Empire.[48]

In 1933 Sardesai had advanced the argument for Hindu Pad Padashahi in his collection of lectures published as *The Main Currents of Maratha History*. His "Preface" to the book was written on December 1, 1933, so Sarkar may not have known the full contents of the text, although Sarkar is thanked for his assistance with the lectures.[49] In fact, in a lecture called "Shivaji's Conception of a Hindu Empire," he cited Sarkar's own translation of a letter written by Shivaji to the emperor Aurangzeb as evidence of Shivaji's interest in "capturing the imperial seat of Delhi" for the purpose of founding a Hindu empire.[50] Sardesai turned to other letters by Shivaji in his lectures as further evidence of this point: "[The letters] contain sentiments which eminently establish Shivaji's object of the *Hindu-pad-Padshahi*."[51] Yet later in the lecture, when discussing the Peshwa, Sardesai conceded that the Hindu Pad Padashahi was more an aspiration that was not fulfilled: "thus it has to be admitted that the *Hindu-pad-Padshahi* which the Peshwas attempted to establish, was more a name than an actually accomplished fact."[52]

The correspondence between Sarkar and Sardesai was extensive; it spanned six decades (1907–52).[53] Savarkar is only mentioned a few times in the letters, mainly by Sarkar, who remained irritated by Sardesai's willingness to accept the argument that the Marathas had sought to establish a Hindu empire. For Sarkar there was no evidence in the historical record to substantiate such a claim. In a letter dated October 20, 1936 Sarkar reiterated his critique to Sardesai by identifying the work of Savarkar and Rajwade as "chauvinistic brag . . . about the purely

---

[48] Letter from G.S. Sardesai to Jadunath Sarkar, August 28, 1933, in Gupta, ed., *Life and Letters of Sir Jadunath Sarkar*, 303.

[49] Sardesai, *Main Currents*, iv.

[50] Ibid., 72.

[51] Ibid.

[52] Ibid., 99.

[53] Gupta, ed., *Life and Letters of Sir Jadunath Sarkar*, viii.

imaginary Hindu Pat Padshahi."[54] On March 18, 1937 he wrote to Sardesai: "I wonder that a cool-headed man like you do not see how Maratha chauvinists like Rajwade and Savarkar make themselves ridiculous by making such absurd boasts about Hindu Pat Padshahi, paramountcy &c."[55] In 1940 Sarkar made another plea on this point: "It is pure moonshine to suggest that Baji Rao and Jai S. planned to co-operate in founding a Hindu Pat Padshahi. We make ourselves ridiculous when we read the ideas and thoughts of 20th century English-educated nationalists into the lives of sectarian or clannish champions of the 17th and 18th centuries."[56] Although he did not mention Savarkar by name, Sarkar's last letter appeared to be a criticism of Savarkar, who in 1940 was president of the Akhil Bharatiya Hindu Mahasabha. In the same year Sarkar also published *House of Shivaji*, in which he reproduced his obituary of Rajwade, who had been dead more than fourteen years. The claim of a Hindu empire clearly had an impact on Maratha historiography: it continued to concern Sarkar, who by this point was considered one of India's best historians.[57] Although Sarkar's criticism of Rajwade and Savarkar centred on their conceptualisation of Hindu Pad Padashahi, there were differences between Rajwade and Savarkar that were not discussed, the most evident being Savarkar's decision to write in English. In addition, Savarkar considered *bakhar*s necessary and reliable sources for his conceptualisation of a history in full, while Rajwade was ambivalent about their veracity and considered them untrustworthy.[58] On this point Sarkar would have been in general agreement with Rajwade.

Sardesai eventually wrote his own history of the Marathas in three volumes in English, titled *New History of the Marathas*, which was published in the late 1940s. Despite Sarkar's many efforts and criticisms, in his writings Sardesai maintained that the Marathas wanted to establish

[54] Ibid., Letter from Jadunath Sarkar to G.S. Sardesai, October 20, 1936, 196.

[55] Ibid., Letter from Jadunath Sarkar to G.S. Sardesai, March 18, 1937, 200.

[56] Ibid., Letter from Jadunath Sarkar to G.S. Sardesai, May 8, 1940, 217.

[57] He received numerous international awards and honours, including a knighthood in 1929. He was given the American Historical Association's Honorary Foreign Membership for distinguished scholarship in 1952.

[58] Deshpande, *Creative Pasts*, 109.

a Hindu empire, a Hindu Pad Padashahi.[59] In volume II of the *New History of the Marathas* he says, "The dream of Hindupad Padshahi was not territorial ambition but mainly limited to the religious field."[60] Sarkar had argued there was no evidence for any such assertion, and yet Sardesai once again cited his work in a footnote as evidence to substantiate his claim – "This is well explained by Sir Jadunath."[61]

Sardesai only mentioned Savarkar once in his correspondence with Sarkar. This was in a passing reference to the Savarkar brothers regularly asking for contributions in newspapers as a form of "beggary."[62] He did not include a discussion of his meeting with Savarkar. Nor is there a reference to Savarkar encouraging Sardesai to write a history of the Marathas in English. Instead, Sardesai says he realised that works in Marathi had a limited circulation and remained largely unknown outside the Marathi literary public. He cited Rajwade's prolific writings as examples of work mainly known only to scholars fluent in Marathi.[63] He pointed to his own volumes on the *Marathi Riyasat* as also having limited circulation, and for the same reason. In consonance with Savarkar's turn to writing a history of the Marathas in English for the purpose of a national Indian audience, Sardesai sought a readership outside Maharashtra, that being the reason for his *New History of the Marathas*, which he said showed the "results of the latest recent research" on the Marathas within "the first attempt to present a fresh and full treatment of Maratha history in English."[64] Savarkar remarked that Sardesai had finally written a "detailed history" of the Marathas in English nearly fifteen years after their meeting.[65]

He did not directly engage with either Sarkar or Sardesai in *Hindu Pad Padashahi*, but in his later writings he reflected on the importance

[59] Sardesai mentions Hindu empire in vol. 1 but returns to the theme of Hindu Pad Padashahi in vols 2 and 3. See Sardesai, *New History of the Marathas,* vol. III, 225, 271.

[60] Sardesai, *New History of the Marathas,* vol. II, 35.

[61] Ibid., 35, fn. 1.

[62] Letter from G.S. Sardesai to Jadunath Sarkar, March 24, 1938, in Gupta, ed., *Life and Letters of Sir Jadunath Sarkar,* 317–18.

[63] Sardesai, *New History of the Marathas,* vol. I, 3.

[64] Ibid., 4.

[65] Savarkar, *Six Glorious Epochs,* 408.

of their work while distinguishing his own method from theirs.[66] "Jadunath Sarkar who wrote in English and Riyasatkar Sardesai who wrote in Marathi had already written books collecting [*sic*] all the available research-work, most laboriously done by several research scholars and assimilating and interpreting it in the best way they could. It is therefore to avoid needless repetition that I did not attempt to write a detailed history of the Marathas."[67] Savarkar says his book was incomplete because as a prisoner he did not have access to sources: "I could not think of writing such a big volume without the aid of reference books!"[68] At another level he repeated a claim articulated in *Indian War*: that is, a detailed history was not necessarily a full history. The fact that Savarkar did not write a detailed history based on primary sources or references did not negate or minimise the fulness of his history – and here one needs to comprehend the meaning he attributed to the word "full." A history in his conceptualisation could only approximate fulness if it included the "essence" of history; that essence, he believed, had been obfuscated by historians of the Marathas. The search for what he called the "extensive but chaotic mass of details" had often prevented them seeing what was essential in history – the principles of history.[69] Jadunath Sarkar was in his view an instance of a historian limited in his approach. Sarkar's shortcomings in this respect did not have anything to do with the quality or quantity of his sources; in fact, Savarkar saw Sarkar as a rigorous researcher. Rather the problem for Savarkar was with Sarkar's interpretation of the history of the Marathas as "self-centred, self-seeking, marauding, bellicose and mediocre."[70] What was missing in all of Sarkar's evidence and rigour was any discussion of the essentials of history. His research provided thick detail without considering the centrality within it of Hindutva. Moreover, Sarkar had also publicly attacked Savarkar and Rajwade as

---

[66] This point requires clarification. The first edition of *Hindu Pad Padashahi* does not include references found in later editions of the text. For example, the second edition includes footnotes to Sardesai's *Marathi Riyasat*.

[67] Savarkar, *Six Glorious Epochs*, 410.

[68] Ibid.

[69] Ibid.

[70] Ibid., 411.

caste chauvinists and linked their arguments about Hindu Pad Padashahi to their identities as Chitpavan Brahmins. This was a point that Savarkar did not respond to in his writings.

Savarkar situated his *Hindu Pad Padashahi* within existing debates on the history of the Marathas in the early decades of the twentieth century. Sarkar had identified parallels between Savarkar's interpretations and Rajwade's writings, and Sardesai shared Savarkar's concern on the need to write in English about the Hindu empire; both were critical of "foreign scholarship" about the Marathas and the need to reclaim and disseminate their own history via English.

Savarkar's *Hindu Pad Padashahi* was, however, generally overlooked or dismissed as part of the emergent debate on Maratha historiography in this period. One exception was a review published in 1926 by L.D. Barnett, Professor of Sanskrit at University College London (1906–17) and the School of Oriental Studies (1917–48).[71] His comments on the book were critical, as he declared that some of the findings were "dubious," "quite unacceptable," and not in the "spirit" of science: "*Hindu Pad Padashahi* . . . claims to be a 'critical review' of the part played by the Marathas in Indian history, but in reality is often highly *tendenziös* in its handling of facts and painting of characters, attributing them ideals of which we may suspect that *L'esser loro v'è in sola credenza.*"[72] Barnett's may have been the only English-language review of the text in a scholarly journal (albeit with Italian terms and phrases), but I include his comments because perhaps unwittingly he correctly identified Savarkar's arguments. What he considered a shortcoming was in fact the whole point and actual purpose of the text. Savarkar chose not to write in an analytical or scientific mode, and his purpose was to impute the "ideals" of Hindutva to his historical subjects. Barnett was also accurate in his assessment that the book was not written in a scientific spirit – Savarkar had in fact stated that his purpose was to examine the Hindu spirit. If this work fell outside what Barnett considered scholarly, it was precisely because Savarkar required his readers to simply accept his interpretation that the actions and thoughts his historical subjects were guided by was an abstract "belief." What he did not specify was that it was a belief in Hindutva.

[71] Meaning that the ideals appeared only to be beliefs. Barnett, "Indica," 756–8.

[72] Ibid.

*Hindu Pad Padashahi*'s reception was likely attributed to, first, Savarkar's conceptualisation of Hindutva, and second, to his critiques of "detailed history" and the absence in his book of normative contemporary methods of historical research. These were by choice as well as the peculiar circumstances of his writing as a political prisoner. Dipesh Chakrabarty's typology of history writing in the first half of the twentieth century provides an important binary between what he calls the "cloistered life of the discipline" (the academic domain) and the "public life of history" (the popular domain).[73] He points out that figures like Sarkar and Sardesai conducted their research and writing *before* historical research was taught in the Indian academy. In other words, the two primarily functioned in the popular domain but influenced the intellectual and institutional formation of the academic domain. The two domains were "enmeshed" in the development of history as a form of knowledge in colonial India.[74] Savarkar's *Hindu Pad Padashahi* may be classified within the popular domain of Maratha history, but for scholars it existed uneasily on the margins of that domain because Savarkar was very clear about the purpose of his book: "*Hindu Patpadshahi* . . . surveys the Hindu War of Independence, carried on by the Marathas from the seventeenth century, from the Hindu national standpoint."[75] Sarkar expressed his concerns about Savarkar explicitly (and privately), while Sardesai did not include any mention of Savarkar in his work even when he appeared to agree with him. These responses to Savarkar's work within the broader discussion of Maratha historiography persist, especially as he interpreted the history of Marathas through his alternative approach centred in Hindutva.

## 4. Pan-Hindu Unity

Savarkar explained that *Hindu Pad Padashahi* was a work of Hindu history written to "transcend the limits of a provincial movement" and had "*Pan-Hindu* importance and treatment."[76] His interpretation of a history of the Marathas was meant to encourage a readership

[73] Chakrabarty, *The Calling of History*, 8–12.
[74] Ibid., 13.
[75] Savarkar, *Six Glorious Epochs*, 411.
[76] Savarkar, *Hindu Pad Padashahi*, ix.

outside Maharashtra (and a Marathi public) that would imagine itself as part of a shared history with the Marathas as Hindus. He chose to write in English, but he could have written the book in Sanskrit or Hindi, in consonance with his arguments about Sanskrit in *Essentials of Hindutva* or his call for Hindi as the national language of India. Publishing in English allowed Savarkar to seek out a national audience for his Pan-Hindu ideas in a way that would not have been possible in Marathi. By the time he wrote *Hindu Pad Padashahi* he already had experience of publishing books in Marathi and English and was aware of the potential of his ideas to spread nationally (and internationally) via English. *Hindu Pad Padashahi* was published in Madras, and it is unlikely that it would have had a wide audience there if he had chosen to write it in Hindi or Marathi, while its reception in Sanskrit would have been nominal. Savarkar's first two books, on Hindutva, were written in English for a national Indian readership: he wanted them read by Hindus across the country and the world.

His work was also a clarion call to fellow Maharashtrians to view themselves and their history as part of Hindu history by adopting "a Pan-Hindu standpoint."[77] While he developed the idea of "Pan-Hindu" in *Hindu Pad Padashahi*, he introduced it in his discussion of the seventeenth-century poet Bhushan Tripathi in *Essentials of Hindutva*, noting that Bhushan was a "Hindu of Hindus" who produced lyrics that highlighted the "national and pan-Hindu" elements of history.[78] Savarkar was concerned about the growth of what he called the "Great Combinations of the day" that involved struggles and conflicts to establish power in the early decades of the twentieth century.[79] He specifically identified pan-Islamism in Asia, the League of Nations and pan-Slavism in Europe, and the pan-Ethiopic movement in Africa and America.[80] These inspired him to argue the necessity of a future pan-Hindu movement even as he sought through writing history to show past pan-Hindu unity.

In February 1925, a few months after Savarkar had finished *Hindu Pad Padashahi*, he was involved in an acrimonious public exchange with Shaukat Ali, one of the leaders of the pan-Islamic Khilafat move-

---

[77] Ibid.
[78] Savarkar, *Essentials of Hindutva*, 46.
[79] Ibid., 125.
[80] Ibid., 125–6.

ment (1919–24) to restore the power and legitimacy of the Ottoman caliph. This argument appears to have been a follow-up to an earlier contentious discussion about Hindu–Muslim unity that took place in November 1924.[81] On May 19, 1925 Shaukat Ali penned an article titled "Through Indian Eyes" in *The Bombay Chronicle* in which he appeared to compliment Savarkar: "my brave brother Vinayak Savarkar . . . has wrongly suffered and is suffering to-day for the love of the country."[82] This was a remarkable admission, given the context of the exchange between Savarkar and Shaukat Ali that appeared in a number of newspapers in India at the time. *The Times of India*, for example, not only covered this discussion between the two figures on the legitimacy of the Khilafat movement, but also repeated Ali's reference to Savarkar as "my brave brother."[83]

The interaction between Ali and Savarkar provides an important context for the emergence of Savarkar's general critique of "Pan-isms," but also his conceptualisation of a pan-Hindu solidarity or unity in this period. What appeared as Shaukat Ali's peace offering was also publicly read as controversial. Newspaper writers were aware of this dynamic as well, and Shaukat Ali's statement was repeated in several articles. Savarkar's formulation "Pan-Hindu" centred on the idea of a different type of brotherhood – what he called "Hindu brethren" and the "co-religionist brotherhood" of Hindus. In *Hindu Pad Padashahi* Savarkar actually addressed this point, although it is not regarding Shaukat Ali specifically but a general comment about unity with Muslims: "[E]ven if the Muhammadans stretched out a hand of peace, it would have been an act of condescension and not friendship, and the Hindus could not have honourably grasped it with that fervour and sincerity and confidence which a sense of equality alone breeds."[84] Needless to say, Shaukat Ali's gesture in calling Savarkar his brother was not welcomed.

This points to Savarkar's discussion of Muslims and some conceptual

[81] Savarkar recounted the dialogue with Ali in his Collected Works. See *"Savarkar aur Maulana Shaukat Ali ke bich vichara yuddha," Savarkar Samagra*, vol. 7, 316–24.

[82] Shaukat Ali, "Through Indian Eyes," *The Bombay Chronicle*, May 19, 1925.

[83] "Through Indian Eyes. Non-violence," *The Times of India*, May 23, 1925.

[84] Savarkar, *Hindu Pad Padashahi*, xiii.

tension in his writings about them. As in *Indian War*, he includes a section addressed to "our Muhammadan readers" to offer his perspective on the responsibility of the historian writing a Hindu history: "The duty of a historian is primarily to depict as far as possible the feelings, motives, emotions and actions of the actors themselves whose deeds he aims to relate."[85] He added that a historian must interpret "faithfully" and without "prejudices" and "fear."[86] He explained that in writing Hindu history the point was not to reproduce past conflicts between Hindus and Muslims in the present. Rather, the purpose of such history should be to understand the "root cause" that led to conflict and bloodshed. The goal should be to interpret the unification of society through violence: "The process of consolidation into larger social units have [*sic*], under the stern law of nature, to get forged into that large existence on the anvil of war through struggle and sacrifice."[87] The Hindu case for "Pan-Hindu" unity, as demonstrated by the Marathas, could only be formed through violence, or what Savarkar refers to as the "deadly struggle with the Muhammadan powers."[88] Hindu history showed that these Hindus fought for the principles of "Dev" and "Desh" as a struggle against Muslims. (Later in the book, Savarkar included the terms *swadharma* and *swadesh* into his analyses, as in *Indian War*.) Hindu and Muslim unity in this context was not possible: "There could not be an honourable unity between a slave and his master."[89] Worth noting here is that Savarkar identifies the Hindu as a slave – a Persian definition of "Hindu" that he had rejected in *Essentials of Hindutva*. The slave–master conceptualisation in *Hindu Pad Padashahi* underscores the existential conflict between Hindus and Muslims but also serves as an explanation for the need for Hindus (as slaves) to unify in the struggle to defeat Muslims (as masters) through violence, cruelty, and vengeance.

Despite this explanation of everlasting hatred as Hindu–Muslim conflict, Savarkar also used the formulation "our Muhammadan countrymen" in *Hindu Pad Padashahi*.[90] In *Essentials of Hindutva* he

[85] Ibid., x.
[86] Ibid.
[87] Ibid., xii.
[88] Ibid.
[89] Ibid., xiii.
[90] Ibid., xi–xii.

had provided many references to "our history" as specifically meaning "Hindu history." His articulation now of Muslims as "our countrymen" opens a number of questions. Is Savarkar's use of "our" here the same as in his discussion of "our Hindu race" or "our Hindu brethren"? What does he mean by "our" in this context, given that he sometimes identifies Muslims as "foreigners"? There is no clear answer, except that Savarkar did not consider it a paradox in relation to his other writings; the phrase remains unresolved in this particular text since, at the same time, his explanation of the existential conflict between Hindus and Muslims is a struggle between slaves and masters.

Why did Savarkar incorporate *padashahi* – a Persian term for statecraft – into his Hindu history? At one level, Savarkar was critical of Persian and Arabic vocabulary in "Indian" languages, i.e. the languages of Hindus. His resolve was to cleanse these languages of their Muslim influence while also arguing for Hindi as a national language. He acknowledged that not everyone who spoke Persian was necessarily Muslim, especially as he had discussed Zoroastrian texts written in Persian or Middle Persian. Rather, his complaint was with what he called "Muhammadanized Persian."[91] (It is not clear if he made similar distinctions regarding Arabic texts written by non-Muslims.) At another level, Savarkar incorporated *padashahi* to discuss the last great Hindu empire. The root of *padashahi* or *padshah* (the translations of the book into Marathi and Hindi use both spellings) is the Persian term *shah*, which is translated as "king."[92] *Padashah* is also considered synonymous and interchangeable with *badshah* (king, monarch, sovereign). The *padashahi* (or *badshahi*) is then kingly, royal, sovereign, and imperial, with the extra prefix *pad* (or *pat*) meaning "throne," "high office," or "good position" to underscore the elevated status of the Hindu king in his *padashahi*.

Savarkar was not the first to use *padashahi* in his writings on the Marathas: Rajwade had earlier claimed that the Marathas had established a Hindu Pad Padashahi. He had also provided a trenchant critique of the influence of Persian on the Marathi language.[93] Whether Savarkar

---

[91] Savarkar, *Essentials of Hindutva*, 62.

[92] In this section, I have benefited from the following: Platts, *A Dictionary of Urdu, Classical Hindi, and English*; Steingass, *A Comprehensive Persian–English Dictionary*; Fallon, *A New English–Hindustani Dictionary*.

[93] Deshpande, *Creative Pasts*, 149.

was directly influenced by Rajwade on this point is less relevant than that he was a proponent of purifying Marathi as part of a *bhasha shuddhi* (language purification) movement that he articulated in the 1920s and 1930s in his writings and speeches.[94] It was, he felt, necessary to eradicate foreign words from all languages spoken by Hindus.[95] His reference to *padashahi* does however have an earlier context, namely the *Sabhasad Bakhar* (c. 1694), a biographical account of Shivaji written by Krishnaji Anant Sabhasad, which has references to *padshah*, *padashahi*, *badshah*, and *badshahi*.[96] Surendranath Sen's English translation of the *Sabhasad Bakhar* (1920) also incorporates both terms.[97] The primary discussions of *badshah* (and its cognates) in the *Sabhasad Bakhar* are in reference to the Mughal emperor in Delhi, but other *badshahs* with *badshahis* in parts of India are mentioned; some are referred to as *badshah* in one part of the text and *padshah* in another. Sen explains that he opted to keep all Persian words in the original without providing a Marathi or English translation – including of *badshah*.[98] He translated a key passage of relevance to Hindu Pad Padashahi – this being a comment made by the "Badshah Zadi" (princess) to the "Badshah"

[94] "Bhasha Shuddi" was a common theme in Savarkar's speeches in the 1920s and 1930s. See Bhide, ed., *Veer Savarkar's "Whirl-wind Propaganda,"* 483. Also, see Thube, "V.D. Savarkar's Language Purification Project," on Savarkar's 1926 publication *Marathi Bhasheche Shuddhikaran*.

[95] Savarkar also advocated a movement for correcting and reforming the writing of language in his text called *Lipi sudharana andolana*, in *Samagra Savarkar,* vol. 10. He argued that the Nagari script should become the "National Script of Hindudom," replacing all regional scripts. Also see Savarkar, "Presidential Address, Akhil Bharatiya Hindu Mahasabha, Calcutta, 1939," in *Hindu Rashtra Darshan*, 84–7; NMML, V.D. Savarkar Papers, Reel 25, Letter from N.V. Damle, to R.L. Wadhua, Sec. Shri Hindu Navjawan Sabha, March 22, 1942, written on behalf V.D. Savarkar on the topic of the Devanagari script; and Reel 28, Press Statement by V.D. Savarkar, June 6, 1944.

[96] Pathan, ed., *Sabhasada Bakhar*. See the following select pages for comparative purposes: *padshah* (22, 34); *padshahi* (29, 31); *badshah* (31); *badshahi* (33).

[97] See Krishnaji Ananta, *Siva Chhatrapati*.

[98] Ibid., x. It is worth noting that Jadunath Sarkar is thanked for "revising" the entire manuscript of the *bakhar*, while G.S. Sardesai is also acknowledged for his library assistance. Yet it was Sarkar who was opposed to the idea of the Hindu Pad Padashahi advocated by Rajwade and Savarkar.

of Bijapur upon learning that Shivaji had killed Afzal Khan: "It seems that Khuda (God) has taken away the Badshahi from the Mohamedans, and conferred it on the Marathas."[99] I quote this to point out that in the original Marathi text "Badshah Zadi" and "Badshah" are listed as "Padshah Jadi" and "Padshah," respectively.[100] These are equivalent terms in Persian and Marathi used interchangeably in the text as well as its translation. By contrast, Jagannath Lakshuman Mankar's earlier English translation of the *Sabhasad Bakhar* (1884) had modified or omitted these Persian terms.[101] His translation of the passage of the "Padshah Jadi" runs: "[The queen-regent] cried out 'Alla, Khuda' . . . and said 'Alla has destroyed the Adilshahi kingdom and given it over to Shivaji. The rule of the Musulmans is now over and that of the Hindoos restored."[102] The Padshah Jadi is translated as "queen-regent," and the Padashahi is identified as "the Adilshahi kingdom." While Savarkar advocated eliminating all Persian vocabulary from Marathi, Hindi, and the other vernaculars, it seems incongruous that in his own writing on Hindu history he placed *padashahi* at the centre.[103] This seems specially so as Mankar's translation had provided an example of moving away from Persian classifications of statecraft. My point here is that Savarkar's Hindu history, even as it reflects the struggle of Hindus against Muslims to forge a pan-Hindu unity, continues an old and unresolved tension at the level of language-use.

Savarkar's concept of "Pan-Hindu" should not be interpreted only as a response to the "Pan-isms" identified in *Essentials of Hindutva*. Mazzini's ideas of Italian unification in the Risorgimento were central to his interpretations of unity throughout. Although Mazzini is not extensively cited or discussed in *Hindu Pad Padashahi*, his key arguments do appear selectively. This happens not only in Savarkar's conceptualisation of "Pan-Hindu," but also in discussing the Maratha turn to guerrilla warfare – which was the theme of an essay that Savarkar translated from Mazzini's writings in 1906.

---

[99] Ibid., 27.

[100] Pathan, ed., *Sabhasada Bakhar*, 15–16.

[101] See Mankar, *The Life and Exploits of Shivaji*.

[102] Ibid., 21.

[103] A similar point can be made about Savarkar's use of the Persian term "peshwa" in his writings.

Throughout *Hindu Pad Padashahi* Savarkar also turns to other concepts that exemplify the idea of unity and unification among Marathas (and by extension Hindus), such as "Hindu Commonwealth," "United States of India," "Maratha Confederacy," and "Maratha Mandal." The phrase "Hindu Commonwealth" was used by nineteenth-century Orientalists to describe the idea of a greater Hindu community in India, and Savarkar had incorporated it in *Essentials of Hindutva*.[104] The "United States of India" not only had parallels to the Italian articulation of Stati Uniti d'Italia – here Savarkar's familiarity with histories of Italian unification is evident – it was also the title of the Ghadar Party's monthly newspaper called *The United States of India*, first published in July 1923 in San Francisco.[105] However, by turning to "Maratha Confederacy" Savarkar was consistent in using an existing category within Maratha historiography commonly employed by nineteenth-century Maharashtrian and English writers to describe Maratha consolidation. Similarly, "Maratha Mandal" (community of Marathas) is used in his book, this being a concept popularised by Rajaramshastri Bhagvat (1851–1908) to reconceptualise a Maratha identity that contested caste hierarchies.[106] Savarkar did not cite Bhagvat, but rethinking the Mandal was certainly of interest to him, as it was to others who promoted the importance of "Maratha Mandal."

This plurality of terms and concepts that were part of a public debate reflects an intellectual conjuncture and an epistemic reckoning that was taking place at the turn of the century about staking a claim for interpreting Maratha pasts. To articulate and celebrate solidarity – however defined – was also central in these arguments. Within the contemporary historiography there was general agreement about Shivaji's military role (and Ramdas' intellectual contributions) in promoting and establishing Maratha unification. However, the meaning of that unity was debated from a number of perspectives. Savarkar was not alone in identifying the role of figures like Shivaji and Ramdas to build unity among Marathas: it was a common theme

104 Savarkar, *Essentials of Hindutva*, 106, 114.
105 See *The United States of India: A Monthly Review of Political, Economic, Social and Intellectual Independence of India*, 1, 1 (1923), which was published by the Pacific Coast Hindustani Association.
106 Deshpande, *Creative Pasts*, 130.

in the literature. For example, M.G. Ranade in *The Rise of the Maratha Power* had quoted the seventeenth-century writing of Ramdas on this point: "Unite all who are Marathas together and propagate the duty or dharma of a great rashtra or united nation."[107] A similar point was put forward by Jadunath Sarkar in *House of Shivaji*: "Before [Shivaji's] rise, the Maratha race was scattered through many foreign kingdoms and lived as servants and subjects and not as their own masters. Shivaji united them into one people by giving them a national State with a national king of their own. This was true 'Hindavi Swaraj'."[108] Sarkar's conceptualisation of the existence of a "Maratha race" that preceded Shivaji's ascendancy is important, especially considering the juxtaposition of some Marathas as masters and others as servants (or subjects). What Shivaji was able to end was the distinction between master and servant. Sarkar points out that Shivaji had "Hindu servants" whom he identified as Brahmins and non-Brahmins, but both reached "the highest civil and military offices."[109] In fact Sarkar adds: "all [castes] found recognition from him."[110] Shivaji's resistance to Aurangzeb was "Hindavi Swarajya" – a form of self-rule, autonomy, and Maratha solidarity that set aside class, caste, race, religion, and office.

G.S. Sardesai says "Hindavi Swarajya" was a phrase used by Shivaji in a letter written to Dadaji Naras Prabhu in 1645, to convey his goal of "a Hindu religious autonomy for the whole country."[111] Shivaji's "main object," he says, "was to win religious freedom and not territory. He certainly would have been foremost to defend the Hindu religion all over India."[112] Well before Sardesai, this point was made by Rajwade in his argument for "Maharashtra Dharma" (the religion of Maharashtra). Rajwade argued that at the centre of Maratha statecraft was the idea of establishing a regional dharma, especially through the Shivaji and Ramdas nexus. Since Maharashtra Dharma had continuity for an extended period of time, it was possible to interpret its meaning by understanding the combination "Deva, Dharma, and the protection

---

[107] Ranade, *The Rise of Maratha Power*, 53.
[108] Sarkar, *House of Shivaji*, 82.
[109] Ibid., 81–2.
[110] Ibid.
[111] Sardesai, *New History of the Marathas*, vol. 1, 267.
[112] Ibid.

of cows and Brahmins."[113] It also meant considering the *place* of "Hindu dharma" in other parts of the country. On this point Prachi Deshpande has offered useful interpretation of Rajwade's argument as a formula: "Maharashtra Dharma (Hinduism in Maharashtra) = Hinduism in India + establishment of righteous rule + protection of cows and Brahmins + freedom + unity + leadership."[114]

Savarkar's entry into this historiography did not explicitly reflect knowledge of or familiarity with the Rajwade formula. But based on the terms used by Savarkar, he rethought Rajwade's conceptualisation and the centrality of Maharashtra Dharma. A key distinction is that Rajwade used the term "Hindu Dharma" in the Marathi text rather than its English translation "Hinduism." In other words, following the logic of the formula, Hindu Dharma was only a discrete component among other components whose sum equalled "Maharashtra Dharma." Savarkar acknowledged that he was influenced by Rajwade's writings, specifically the claim of Hindu Pad Padashahi, but in his book he did not provide further analysis of Rajwade's writings. What he did was adopt select concepts and incorporate them into his own work. Maharashtra Dharma is mentioned a few times in *Hindu Pad Padashahi*, but the priority for Savarkar was to move away from the regional construction of dharma as attached to the land of the Marathas towards a national formulation that had "Hindu Dharma" as its centre. By subsuming Maharashtra Dharma within the larger category of Hindu Dharma, Savarkar made the Maratha case the exemplum of his "Pan-Hindu" argument:

> This word, "Hindavi Swaraj" coming from the pen of Shivaji himself, reveals, as nothing else could have done, the very soul of the great movement that stirred the life and activities of Maharashtra for a hundred years and more. Even in its inception the Maratha rising was neither a parochial nor a personal movement altogether. It was essentially a Hindu movement in the defence of Hindu Dharma for the overthrow of the alien Muhammadan domination, for the establishment of an independent, powerful Hindu Empire.[115]

[113] Rajwade, *Itihasacharya V.K. Rajwade,* vol. 1, 32. Also see Deshpande, *Creative Pasts,* 132.

[114] Deshpande, *Creative Pasts,* 132.

[115] Savarkar, *Hindu Pad Padashahi,* 6.

This specific phrasing, "Hindavi Swarajya" (or Swaraj: both spellings are used), as central to understanding not only Maratha history but also Hindu history was not accidental: by the 1920s the intended audience for the book was likely familiar with Gandhi's *Hind Swaraj* and its ideas. Savarkar never stated whether his discussion of Hindavi Swaraj was a response to Gandhi's *Hind Swaraj* or simply an engagement with an existing conceptual framework within Maratha historiography. But what is evident is that he, along with other writers of Maratha history, had noted Shivaji's seventeenth-century contribution to the conceptual history of Hindavi Swaraj *before* Gandhi's articulation of Hind Swaraj. The similarities are difficult to ignore. All readers familiar with Savarkar and Gandhi would have likely compared the two works that provided a further engagement with the meaning of freedom – *swaraj*. Savarkar began his chapter called "Hindavi Swaraj" with a moment of violence: "The youth rose in rebellion."[116] The contrast with Gandhi's non-violent interpretation of Hind Swaraj could hardly be more pointed: Savarkar does not need to be specific on this matter.

In *Hindu Pad Padashahi* he simply incorporated the category "Hindu Dharma," rather than Hinduism, but did not include his analysis or critique from *Essentials of Hindutva*. However, *Hindu Pad Padashahi* appeared to take up the challenge that Savarkar had raised in thinking of "Hindu Dharma" as conceptually useful for all Hindus: "Thus there would be no loss either in clearness, or in conciseness but on the other hand a gain both in precision and unambiguity which by removing the cause of suspicion in our minor communities and resentment in the major would once more unite us all Hindus under our ancient banner representing a common race and a common civilisation."[117] As a heuristic "Hindu Dharma" allowed Hindus the opportunity to form a solidarity as Hindus on the grounds of commonality – of race, of civilisation, of Hindutva – without the problems associated with "Hinduism." The task was to write *Hindu Pad Padashahi* to illustrate a history of the Marathas that exemplified Hindu Dharma as part of a pan-Hindu movement for unification – as articulated in the book, this was actually congruent with a history in full.

[116] Ibid.

[117] Savarkar, *Essentials of Hindutva*, 95.

# 5. Rethinking the Eighteenth Century

The problem of conceptualising and promoting "Pan-Hindu" unity was an implicit admission that Hindus were actually not united. There was fragmentation, disunity, and civil war. However, Savarkar was not deterred: he perceived examples in the past in which Hindus had colonised or recolonised the territory between the "Indus River and the Seas" to establish a unified Hindusthan. He turned frequently to the example of Ramchandra for colonisation, and Vikramaditya for recolonisation, to promote what was possible in India – as he had argued in *Essentials of Hindutva*. The Maratha confederacy of the eighteenth century marked a far more recent conjunctural shift in which Hindus finally re-established sovereignty and overcame Muslim domination. Already by the 1920s Savarkar had started to reframe this period by placing Hindu subjects at the centre of this history. By returning to the concept of the "people" that he discussed in *Indian War* he illustrated the coming together of divergent castes and communities as part of the unification of Hindu identity. A related theme apparent in contemporary Maratha historiography was the union of Brahmins and non-Brahmins in this period – implying their disunity earlier. Savarkar acutely noted that the emergence of the Brahmins as Peshwas meant that some critics referred to the moment as "the Brahmin Padashahi."[118] For them this was not a period of Hindu solidarity or unity, but a consolidation of power by Brahmins in the guise of Peshwas to re-establish a caste hierarchy within Hindu society.

The purpose of Savarkar's revisionist history of the eighteenth century was, all the same, very different from the works of later scholars who examined the structures of social and economic formation within Indian society. Recent scholarship has shown that the rise of the Maratha movement of the eighteenth century involved members of peasant society, herdsmen, nomads, and tribals who rose to positions of power and social status within the Maratha army. These solidarities and alliances are not defined as a form of Hindu unity. It has been pointed out that between 1780 and 1806 the Marathas dominated large parts of North India, including Delhi and Agra, as part of a larger Maratha

---

[118] Savarkar, *Hindu Pad Padashahi*, 107.

confederacy.[119] Yet this argument about the Marathas is only a small constituent in a broad rethinking about the eighteenth century, where intermediate social groups between state and agrarian society were in the process of growing and consolidating power. Savarkar was not concerned with writing social and economic histories of this variety, even if he was interested in the political movements of the Sikhs and Jats as part of a dynamic history of the period, and the "social inclusiveness" of the Marathas to incorporate various peasant castes.[120] Rather, for Savarkar, the point was that Maratha history of the eighteenth century, as of the history of the Sikhs and Jats, offered an alternative to the narrative of fragmentation and disunity – except this was for him the disunity of Hindus. From his perspective the consolidation of power was along the lines of religion, not economy. In *Essentials of Hindutva* Savarkar had critiqued colonial governmentality in using the census to divide Hindus. Now in *Hindu Pad Padashahi* he was showing an instance of Hindu unity.

North India in the eighteenth century has attracted a great deal of historiographical attention from very divergent perspectives. The fact that Savarkar's *Hindu Pad Padashahi* provided a perspective on the eighteenth century was unexpected, especially as Savarkar only considered the centrality of Maratha history as Hindu history. More important, the eighteenth century comes through in Savarkar's writings as a period of Hindu unity when it had in fact long been considered a century of Hindu decline.

Savarkar relied in his new work on themes he had articulated in *Indian War*. First, he introduced "Hindu spirit" as a category, building upon and incorporating his earlier ideas of "the revolutionary spirit" and "the spirit of patriotism." He also returned to the principles of revolution he had drawn from Mazzini – the "universally accepted principles" for interpreting all revolutions – to conceptualise his Hindu revolution.[121] *Swaraj* and *swadharma* as well as Ramdas as Hindusthan's Mazzini were the other earlier concepts redeployed.[122] Ramdas appears in the new work to enunciate afresh the central principle of

[119] Bayly, *Rulers, Townsmen and Bazaars*, 20.

[120] Ibid.

[121] Savarkar, *Indian War*, 10.

[122] Savarkar, *Mazzini Charitra*, 30; and Savarkar, *Joseph Mazzini*, 29.

revolution: "Die for your Dharma, kill the enemies for your Dharma while you are dying; in this way fight and kill, and take back your kingdom!"[123] Ramdas in fact now seems to have greater meaning for Savarkar than Mazzini since the ideas of Ramdas had influenced the direction of Maratha statecraft. Mazzini's influence is present in the text, but implicit in comparison to the more explicit references to Ramdas.

Second, the master–slave binary plays a much more significant role in writing about Hindu subordination *vis-à-vis* Muslims than it did in his account of British domination of Indians in the mid-nineteenth century. The Hindu slave functioned in an autonomous sphere that could never be crushed by the Muslim master. The Hindu–Muslim unity that Savarkar celebrated in his articulation of the 1857 revolutionary war was now replaced by "Pan-Hindu" unity against Muslims. In both books the victories are short-lived. In 1857 the Mughal emperor was restored to his throne, only to be deposed and arrested. For the Marathas the reign of the Peshwas – the Hindu Pad Padashahi – came to an end with British military victories in the mid-eighteenth century.

Third, in *Hindu Pad Padashahi* Savarkar provides a progression from one chapter to the next, with one Hindu after another functioning like a "hero" – masculine, brave, valorous, and a martyr. He identifies only specific historical actors in Maratha history because he wants to avoid "volumes of detailed and dry criticism."[124] In consonance with "a history in full," his repetitiveness is purposive in that every identifiable action or thought reflects the motive or desire of Hindu subjects guided by the principles of revolution.

Savarkar's text includes a commentary on his motive for writing the book. This is an important shift: that is, Savarkar first wrote about the motives of his historical subjects and then connected them to *himself* as the author. His motive in this is to "appraise and appreciate the value of modern history of Maharashtra from a Pan-Hindu point of view."[125] This is a way to "fit" *this* history into the "comprehensive whole" that is Hindu History – or "the History of the Hindu nation."[126] Ontological

---

[123] Savarkar, *Indian War*, 10.

[124] Savarkar, *Hindu Pad Padashahi*, 24.

[125] Ibid., 221.

[126] Ibid.

integrity is made clear by showing how the motives of Hindu subjects in *Hindu Pad Padashahi* are also his authorial motive as a Hindu subject.

*Hindu Pad Padashahi* starts with the birth of Shivaji Bhonsle in 1627 and ends with the "fall of the Marathas" in 1818. The chapters are generally organised around the reigns of Maratha rulers and include discussions of select military leaders, religious men, chieftains, and minor figures. Maratha women are mentioned only a few times as warriors in their own right, or as pious women who sacrificed themselves as "satis" after the deaths of their husbands on the battlefield. Mathurabai Angre is the sole exception, being described as a figure with a commitment to the principles of Hindutva: "[L]adies like Mathurabai Angre – that distinguished woman whose correspondence with Brahmendra Swami reveals the depth of her patriotic eagerness to see the Hindu land freed from the hands of the foreigners . . . "[127] Savarkar also cites Angre's letter to the same figure in *Essentials of Hindutva* to illustrate that several people were using "Hindu" as a category of analysis in this period.

The key arguments about the Marathas, especially the Chhatrapatis and Peshwas, that Savarkar had developed in *Hindu Pad Padashahi* had been outlined in *Essentials of Hindutva*. His analyses of the main Maratha rulers is inconsistent and incomplete inasmuch as he provides no clear line of succession from one ruler to the next. The names of Maratha rulers are often abbreviated, making it challenging for anyone not familiar with Maratha history to follow the narrative coherently. This is surprising, given that the book was intended for non-Maratha readers.

Savarkar does not even always distinguish between the Maratha king (Chhatrapati) and his prime minister (Peshwa) when discussing who exercised control. This was an important distinction, given that the Peshwas were subordinates in the service of the Maratha kings, until they became the *de facto* leaders of the Marathas. Savarkar simply assumes familiarity with these aspects of Maratha history. For example, the figure of Shahu appears at the start of a chapter (no. 11) without any introduction or context; only later is the reader informed that Shahu was the Chhatrapati, but without explanation of his relationship to his predecessors.

---

[127] Ibid., 50–1.

(He was the son of Sambhaji, not the previous Chhatrapati Rajaram.) Savarkar does not even care to identify the period of Peshwa reign (1713–1818) despite the fact that the focus of his book is Maratha history *after* Shivaji. The book is chronological in the sense that it argues for a beginning and an end of Maratha history, but it is not chronologically organised *per se*.

Savarkar argued that he wanted to examine the establishment of the Hindu Pad Padashahi of the Peshwas. (This was Jadunath Sarkar's objection to the arguments presented by Savarkar and Rajwade.) Yet the discussion of the Peshwas is incomplete. Not all the Peshwas are mentioned, nor are some figures who functioned as leaders between the reigns of Peshwas. Finally, the end of the Maratha empire is not really satisfactorily discussed.

Savarkar is not consistent in his use of dates and calendars. He includes the birth dates of only two figures and dates of death for only six rulers. Other dates are mentioned infrequently, usually around military battles such as when the Marathas took Baroda in 1732 or Gujarat was lost to the "Moslem Empire" in 1735. Some dates include month and day, but the year is not given, or there is a reference to dates in a vernacular calendar, such as "8th of Kartika 1772." In other instances the dates for the reign of a specific ruler are not included. So, overall, this history seems often unclear or obfuscated.

The conditions in which Savarkar wrote help to explain these obvious problems. He says he did not have access to sources; later editions of the book do however include some references to texts that he relied on to write his narrative. What appear as inconsistencies or a lack of adherence to a normative historical methodology of the time may also have been strategic: Savarkar followed his earlier writing method by focusing on key men whose thoughts and actions reflected the principles of revolution. His focus was essentially on moments in battles, wars, conquests, victories, and losses that showed the motives and desires of Marathas as Hindus. Ultimately, this is the priority in all his writings.

In *Hindu Pad Padashahi* he provides an argument for two temporalities by which to understand Hindu history. The first centres around Prithviraj Chauhan, a twelfth-century king who was defeated by Muslim armies from Afghanistan led by Muhammad Ghuri. Prithviraj's reign ended in 1192 CE. The attacks continued for a number of years, eventually leading to the establishment of the Delhi Sultanate in 1206. By the early-nineteenth century Prithviraj Chauhan was frequently remembered as the "last Hindu emperor."[128] The fact that James Tod in *Annals and Antiquities of Rajasthan* (1829–32) repeated this classification helped solidify Prithviraj's reputation, specially as the heroic Hindu who fought against foreigners and inspired India's nationalists in their struggle for independence. In Hindu history Prithviraj was an obvious choice for the martyr seeking Hindu unity to repel Muslims.[129] In this sense Savarkar's themes in *Hindu Pad Padashahi* were consistent with a growing contemporary literature. For him Prithviraj was also an inspirational ruler who represented Hindu sovereignty *before* Muslim dominance, when Hindus were masters of their own territory. Savarkar did not tire of repeating that Hindus had been subjugated for over 700 years: "Since the days of Prithviraj" as well as "Since the fall of Prithviraj" – these phrases function like leitmotifs in his work.[130] The point he belaboured was that, as evident from the rise of the Marathas, seven centuries had not destroyed Hindus. He obliquely establishes a Hindu rulership genealogy when saying that the Maratha empire was the last Hindu empire and a Maratha the last Hindu emperor, not Prithviraj. This was an important lineage: it was necessary to celebrate Prithviraj when celebrating the Maratha achievement of Hindu Pad Padashahi as an alternative Hindu history.

A second temporality established by Savarkar served to function as a hypothetical time period. He argued that it would be sufficient for Hindu Pad Padashahi to last for only a single day. That is to say, even a day of Hindu sovereignty was an important accomplishment in signalling that Hindus had refused to succumb to the power of Muslims for 700 years: "Such a day, even in its short span of life, focuses in its rising splendour the activities and achievements, the rejoicings and sufferings, the trials and tribulations, of centuries of national existence."[131] The brevity of that sovereignty was less important than the fact that Hindus had maintained the idea of Hindu sovereignty in the form of Hindu Pad Padashahi: "For that day proved beyond cavil or

---

[128] See Talbot, *The Last Hindu Emperor.*
[129] Ibid., 249.
[130] Savarkar, *Hindu Pad Padashahi*, 104, 133.
[131] Ibid., 105.

criticism that seven centuries of Moslem persecution and power had failed to crush the Hindu spirit or its vital faculty of rejuvenation."[132] That moment of recognition of Hindus in the past – and thus pointing to a possibility in the present – was confirmation of the survival and persistence of the "Hindu spirit." The eighteenth century marked a rupture in this history of Hindu subjugation – this was the essence of Hindu history. It was also confirmation of Savarkar's larger objective of promoting the idea of ontological integrity – linking the historical subject of the text with himself as its writer.

What Hindu history may have considered its own methodological hybridity was rejected as inappropriate for modern historical writing. Savarkar had, as earlier noted, explained in *Essentials of Hindutva* that he relied on "Oriental research," epics, letters, and conjecture; and Jadunath Sarkar's criticism of Savarkar's book confirmed this by pointing out that the author had not relied exclusively on "facts" and evidence. Savarkar was also open to the tradition of writing found in *bakhar*s. A critique of what has been called the "new Hindu history" in post-colonial India posits that Hindu history does not follow the protocols of historical practice.[133] "Disciplinary history" – despite its own critique of form and the call to an "end of history writing" – still defines normative approaches in the discipline.[134] These protocols include "the separation of the divine and the mundane," "verification," and "contextualization."[135] For Savarkar, of course, the whole point of Hindu history was the converse – to *not* be constrained by the normative methods of the time (or time itself). The need from his perspective was to be historical without always adhering to the disciplinary methods of professional history. History had been functional and purposive when written by colonials to justify colonialism; it had been similarly utilised by other communities; why had Hindus failed to claim it for their own ends?

This was a form of strategic essentialism adopted by Savarkar as central to his interpretation of history. What has not been considered is whether Savarkar's Hindu history, which relied on *bakhar*s, contributed to the formation of a neo-*bakhar* tradition of writing about Hindu

---

[132] Ibid.

[133] Pandey, *Routine Violence*, 91.

[134] Ibid.

[135] Ibid.

pasts – as against Maratha pasts – for the twentieth century. This was not the analytical history of practitioners or professionals who interpreted history as a science or discipline. To truly probe and understand the essence of the meaning that was conveyed by Hindutva, it was necessary to trace the desires, motives, principles, and spirits of valorous past Hindus.

## 6. The Hindu Spirit

The "Hindu spirit" was a new conceptualisation in *Hindu Pad Padashahi* not used as such in Savarkar's earlier books. In *Indian War* he had discussed "the spirits of the dead" that inspired revolution. He had also used "spirit of revolution" and "spirit of patriotism." In *Essentials of Hindutva* the idea of "spirits" was not fully developed and he only mentioned this selectively. Regarding the Maratha Peshwas, he states: "generations after [Shivaji] were animated by the same noble spirit of patriotism."[136] This comment was in reference to the spirit that protected Hindu Dharma: "[Bajirao's] indomitable spirit rose triumphant over all obstacles." Savarkar returned to the idea of the "spirit of revolution" – but also the "spirit of liberation" – in *Hindu Pad Padashahi*, but these are aspects, components, and essences of the Hindu spirit. Every major Hindu subject discussed by Savarkar is identified as having *this* spirit, of which, as noted earlier, he had said: "Seven centuries of Moslem persecution and power had failed to crush the Hindu spirit."[137]

A characteristic of this spirit was that it travelled across time, and from one Hindu body to another. This transition happened in the masculine body of the Hindu male and not in the effeminate body or the effete body that lacked virility. Women are not wholly absent as heroines, but they are few and far between. While Savarkar frequently identifies men as masculine or effeminate, he does not use such categories when writing about women; the women he discusses as revolutionary or patriotic all possess the characteristics of what he identified as masculinity. It is possible to suggest that Savarkar provided an opening for thinking about the masculine woman imbued with the Hindu spirit, though this is not something that he developed in his work. His main point was that for centuries "all virility and even hope was

---

[136] Savarkar, *Hindu Pad Padashahi*, 20.
[137] Ibid., 105.

squeezed out of [India]" with the domination of Muslims and other foreign powers.[138] In this context it is useful to think with Dipesh Chakrabarty's argument about the agency of spirits in the writing of history.[139] For Chakrabarty, historians have typically shunned writing about spirits as agents in history or taken seriously the claims of historical subjects who explained that their actions were guided or directed by spirits. Chakrabarty's critique centres on the debates on peasant rebellions in colonial India in which peasants explain their actions as guided by spirits. Chakrabarty adds: "I take gods and spirits to be existentially coeval with the human and think from the assumption that the question of being human involves the question of being with gods and spirits."[140] Savarkar provides a parallel in that he also asks his readers to consider the role of spirits in the making of history – not the history of subaltern resistance to structures of power in colonial India, but a spirit or *the* Hindu spirit as the centre of a Hindu history guiding Hindus to a higher destiny out of subordination.

In another way, G.P. Deshpande argued that Savarkar's work indicated a commitment to *Geist* – the Hegelian concept of a collective spirit: "And obviously Hindutva for him is that *Geist*."[141] He clarified that Savarkar never cited or discussed Hegel, but "the German philosopher was forever present in his method."[142] For Deshpande Hegel was the European philosopher who had the greatest impact on the formation of Marathi intellectuals, including Rajwade, who specifically acknowledged Hegel's influence on his thinking.[143] Perhaps this was the link with Savarkar. Judith Butler's conceptualisation of the desiring subject as central to interpreting ontological integrity also traces the idea back to Hegel's notion of "desire" in *Phenomenology of the Spirit*.[144] Deshpande did not provide further analysis on his important claim, and I include this discussion here to underscore the difficulty of writing about Savarkar's thought within a genealogy of ideas. The fact that Savarkar did not mention Hegel in his discussion of spirits

---

[138] Ibid., 251.

[139] Chakrabarty, *Provincializing Europe*, 12–16.

[140] Ibid., 16.

[141] Deshpande, *The World of Ideas in Modern Marathi*, 95.

[142] Ibid.

[143] Deshpande, "Rajwade's *Weltanschauung* and German Thought."

[144] Butler, *The Subjects of Desire*.

as part of his idea of a history in full is worth noting, as are the many omissions of other authors with whom he is often linked.

There may be parallels between Savarkar's conceptualisation of the Hindu spirit and Hegel's *Geist*, given that the whole notion of a motivating spirit running through peoples and civilisations was very much in the air; and there remains the possibility that Savarkar read Hegel, or possibly incorporated his ideas given their proliferation in western India at the time as part of the *zeitgeist*. It is equally possible that Savarkar and Hegel followed an altogether different genealogy connected to shared ideas deriving from shared texts that were read in different centuries.

In recent years Hegel has received a great deal of attention by scholars seeking to reinterpret his thought in relation to subsequent historical developments. Susan Buck-Morss has provided the most significant intervention for placing the importance of the Haitian Revolution at the centre of Hegel's thought, even though Hegel completely silenced it in his writings and thereby relegated it to the realm of what might be called his "unthought." Buck-Morss asks: "If it is indisputable that Hegel knew about Haiti, as did indeed the entire European public, why is there not more explicit discussion in his texts?"[145] In contrast, scholars examining Hegel's writings on India observe that nearly every text written by Hegel includes an engagement with Indian thought. Over the course of Hegel's career the philosopher wrote approximately 80,000 words on and about India.[146] While Hegel was explicit in his engagement with Indian philosophy, the significance of this thought on Hegel's writings requires further investigation. I am less clear whether Savarkar needed Hegel's ideas to conceptualise his Hindu spirit (or Hindutva). Savarkar was well versed in Indian philosophy, from which he could build a conceptual grammar to shape his thought on spirits; in which case the argument is less about Hegel's *Geist*, as suggested by G.P. Deshpande, and more about the possibility of Savarkar having read similar (or the same) texts that informed Hegelian conceptualisations of spirit.[147] There is also the fact that Savarkar relied on Mazzini's discussion of spirits, which were likely part of another

---

[145] Buck-Morss, *Hegel, Haiti, and Universal History*, 17.

[146] Rathore and Mohapatra, *Hegel's India*, 4.

[147] See Herling, *The German Gita*.

genealogy that traced their links to Hegel – and possibly back to India again and to the texts that Hegel read.

The word "Hindutva" only appears once in *Hindu Pad Padashahi*, while all the essentials of Hindutva are integrated within the text itself, especially in the thoughts and actions of his Hindu subjects.[148] The fact that it was written in English, immediately after the publication of *Essentials of Hindutva*, leaves open the question which specific definition (or definitions) of "spirit" in Marathi, Hindi, or Sanskrit Savarkar was considering when writing the book, especially as there are many terms related to or definable as "spirit" or "Supreme Spirit" in these languages. In Savarkar's official collected works, *Samagra Savarakar Vanmaya*, the original *Hindu Pad Padashahi* appears in English, and not as a Marathi translation.[149] The translations of Savarkar's *Essentials of Hindutva* and *Indian War* into Marathi and Hindi add further complexity, as it appears that several translators interpreted Savarkar's use of "spirit" differently and without any consistency. This is no surprise, given the complexity of the word in multiple languages, including English.

On this point Chandranath Basu's conceptualisation of Hindutva – generally understood as a compound of "Hindu" and the Sanskrit suffix "-*tva*" – is worth remembering. Savarkar's writings on Hindutva perhaps reflect a different construction of the word. While the primary definitions of *tattva* (and its cognate *tattvam*) are essence and principle, other definitions of the terms in Sanskrit include Supreme Spirit, Supreme Being, and Supreme Soul. These alternative meanings provide additional possibilities for interpreting Savarkar's "Hindu spirit." The most compelling, of course, is the idea that it was just an abbreviated version of Hindu *tattva*, or Hindutva. Every reference to spirit – revolutionary, liberation, patriotic, or otherwise – is then Hindutva itself.

## 7. A History of Spirits

Savarkar's analyses of his historical subjects is minimal. The descriptions are even shorter than the ones he presented in *Indian War*. Since he felt Shivaji and Ramdas were already known to non-Maratha

---

[148] Savarkar, *Hindu Pad Padashahi*, 53.

[149] Savarkar, *Hindu Pad Padashahi*, in *Samagra Savarkar Vanmaya*, vol. 6.

readers, he limited his discussion of the two, arguing that Shivaji's major accomplishment was to liberate "Hindu people" and "Hindu land" from "the hated alien bondage."[150] The principle of Hindavi Swarajya inspired the people to take up arms in this Hindu war of independence or the war of liberation – Savarkar uses both. Shivaji's "duty was clear," given that he was immersed in the epic traditions of the Mahabharata and Ramayana.[151] This guided Shivaji's spirits and inspired him to think of himself as having the potential to "rescue the Hindu world."[152] Savarkar adds, "his spirits [fed] on the glories of our Hindu race, on the memories of Shri Krishna and Shri Rama, of Arjun and Bhima, of Abhimanyu and Harishchandra."[153] Maratha warfare under Shivaji injected Maharashtra Dharma as "a new force" to revive "the dying spirit of the national life of the Hindu race."[154] The act of reviving this spirit became an "ideal" that "inspired" the Maratha leaders of the "War of Hindu Liberation."[155] A return to violence in the Maratha strategies and tactics of warfare liberated Hindus from centuries of losses. As in Mazzini's writings on Italian revolutionaries, Savarkar found that Hindu revolutionaries had succeeded by guerrilla warfare – known as *ganimi kava*. Shivaji's alternative methods against Muslim enemies marked a shift from those of hundreds of Hindu martyrs who had fallen in vain, and thus inspired Hindus from "the banks of the Indus in the north and the seas in the south."[156] This had also been the geography of Hindusthan in *Essentials of Hindutva*; now it signalled Shivaji's absorption in the essentials of Hindutva.

Shivaji's victory was due to Ramdas, a Brahmin intellectual identified as the Maratha warrior's "spiritual and political guide." He is one of the most important figures in Savarkar's interpretation of Maratha history, cited by him in several texts, compared to Mazzini in *Indian War*, and now called a prophet in *Hindu Pad Padashahi*.[157] Once Shivaji succeeded in establishing an independent Hindu kingdom,

---

[150] Savarkar, *Hindu Pad Padashahi*, 11.

[151] Ibid., 5.

[152] Ibid., 4.

[153] Ibid.

[154] Ibid., 3.

[155] Ibid.

[156] Ibid., 4.

[157] Ibid., 10.

he had attributed his victory to Ramdas, and Ramdas had replied: "Shivaji was not the state, the state was Dharma."[158] The other detail Savarkar mentions about Ramdas is the year of his death: 1681. The "real greatness of Shivaji and Ramdas" was henceforth that "heroes and martyrs" were inspired by their example.[159] Their contributions to Maratha history alerted "the general reader of Indian or Hindu history" and served to reveal that later Maratha movements had been largely ignored in the literature.[160] He adds: "The death of Shivaji was the mere beginning of Maratha history."[161] And Ramdas' death was an early part of this history, not its final act, for his spirit motivated and inspired Hindu unity against Muslims.

When Savarkar criticised Jadunath Sarkar as a historian, it was on this specific point of the importance of noble ideals. Sarkar, he says, was not interested in the Hindu spirit, nor in the *essence* of Maratha history – the *tattva* of Maratha history. Historians such as Sarkar, immersed in details and facts, were blind to the thoughts and actions of Hindus. This critique was in consonance with Savarkar's discussion of Mangal Panday in *Indian War*:

> We shall observe how the consciousness of this noble ideal animated their efforts from generation to generation, gave to their distant and widely scattered activities a unity of aim and kinship of interests, made them feel that their cause was the cause of their Dharma – and their Desh – a mission worthy of the efforts of their saints and soldiers alike – carried the Marathas in triumph from step to step to the gates of Delhi, to the banks of the Indus in the north and the seas in the south.[162]

When discussing Shivaji's son Sambhaji, who succeeded his father as Chhatrapati, Savarkar declares him "brave but incapable," yet still managing to embody the Hindu spirit.[163] He lost territory, his forts were destroyed, his treasury was raided, and he himself was captured by Aurangzeb's men who demanded that he convert to Islam; he refused even under brutal torture and was eventually beheaded. This made him

[158] Ibid.
[159] Ibid., 12.
[160] Ibid.
[161] Ibid., 13.
[162] Ibid., 3–4.
[163] Ibid., 14.

"the Maratha lion" who achieved a "martyrdom" that contributed to Shivaji's "moral and spiritual gains."[164] He adds, "Sambhaji, by this one act of supreme self-sacrifice, represented the spirit of Maharashtra Dharma – of the great Hindu Revival."[165] His failure, loss, capture, and death were of secondary importance, as were the details of his life; what mattered to Savarkar was his recognition of the spirit of Maharashtra Dharma as the Hindu spirit which later inspired others in the Hindu War of Independence.

The Marathas came together to seek vengeance by uniting around the leadership of Rajaram, Shivaji's second son, who pledged to defend "Hindu [Dharma] and Hindu Rajya" based on the teachings of Ramdas.[166] Rajaram united the entire population against the "Muhammadan foe," a reminder to the reader that "the patriotic spirit . . . animated the chief actors in this period."[167] Savarkar listed them: "Rajaram, Nilo [M]oreshwar, Prahlad Niraji, Ramachandra Pant, Sankarji Malhar, Parashuram Trimbak, Santaji Ghorpade, Dhanaji Jadhav, Khanderao Dabhade, Nimbalkar, Nemaji Parsoji, Brahmins, Marathas, Prabhus, princes and peasants." Others inserted into the discussion here are described simply as "Maratha Nobles" or identified by name: Khando Ballal, Nagoji Raje, and Shirka.[168] These heroes adopted a number of war strategies, including guerrilla warfare, to fight the Mughals. Their military campaigns were not successful: "In the days of Rajaram, when Aurangzeb overran all the Deccan and the Marathas were no longer able to conduct an organised concentrated state, each began to fight against the common foe as best as he could."[169] No other information is provided about Rajaram, not even his death is mentioned. Nor is there a discussion of the succession conflict after Rajaram in which Tarabai, the elder queen, held power for nearly a decade on behalf of her infant son Shivaji II.[170] Tarabai's decision was disputed; many considered

[164] Ibid., 16.

[165] Ibid., 15.

[166] Ibid., 16.

[167] Ibid., 18.

[168] Ibid., 19.

[169] Ibid., 43.

[170] It is important to note that Savarkar included an excerpt from correspondence between Tarabai and the Peshwa in *Essentials of Hindutva*, but she is omitted from *Hindu Pad Padashahi*.

Sambhaji's son Shahu the legitimate successor despite his being held captive by the Mughals for a number of years. These weaknesses and shortcomings within the Maratha confederacy were no different from those prevalent among *all* Hindus. Savarkar's message to readers was that the significance of this history was beyond both Shivaji's victories and his successors' losses. What was important was that even after Shivaji's death his successors were inspired by the same spirit as the first Chhatrapati: "Thus not only the generation of Shivaji, but the generations after him also were animated by the same noble spirit of patriotism, the consciousness of continuing the same sacred mission of winning back the political independence of the Hindu Race and defending the Hindu Dharma from the attacks of an alien and barbarous foe."[171] The release of Shahu was an important moment: for Savarkar it marked the decline of Aurangzeb, as his armies were exhausted after decades of battles with the Marathas. Shahu was responsible for appointing Balaji Vishwanath as the new Peshwa, thereby starting a hereditary lineage of Brahmins of the Bhat family in this position.[172] The ultimate purpose of writing the book was to show the contributions of these Peshwas as the force for "Pan-Hindu" unity in the form of Hindu Pad Padashahi. Savarkar does not point out the fact that the new Peshwas were Chitpavan Brahmins – like himself.

*Hindu Pad Padashahi* was written as a progression within Savarkar's emergent writings on Hindutva. There were important conceptual continuities from earlier texts, with new ideas introduced to clarify the meaning of Hindutva. This history – as contributing to his conceptualisation of a history in full – was necessarily mimetic. The point was again to repeat key thoughts and actions to demonstrate the longevity of the Hindu spirit. And yet again individuals were omitted from or marginalised in the text if Savarkar believed they did not possess the ideal spirit, motive, principle, or inspiration; such figures were condemned as lacking masculinity and manhood. His discussion of each Peshwa reflects this pattern.

Savarkar explains that under the Peshwas "Pan-Hindu" unity meant the coming together of nobles, land collectors, groups, castes, clans, and

---

[171] Savarkar, *Hindu Pad Padashahi*, 20.
[172] See Gordon, *The Marathas*.

communities (all Hindus) in the war of independence to fight against Muslim enemies (Mughals, Siddis, Moslem Empire, Pathans). This unification was contingent on the annihilation of "Moslem supremacy and strength."[173] His narrative of every Peshwa centres around a series of battles against enemies – usually Muslims, though the Portuguese are also mentioned. Each Peshwa sought to establish a unified movement in war, not always successfully. Bajirao was successful because "The Marathas had grown into a power so strong and so organised as to be able to stand on their feet and defend their land and their Faith against all odds."[174] The same explanation for solidarity and military success is repeated to describe the motives of other Peshwas as well, but articulated as "Hindu Dharma and Hindu Desh."[175] Maratha victories are described as full of vengeance: that is, the cruelty and violence were a direct consequence of the cruelty experienced by Hindus for centuries. He narrates multiple revenge stories around Hindu temples "trampled," "razed," "pulled down," "ruined," and "levelled." The Peshwas helped "liberate" temples, or the land where temples stood before they were destroyed. Yet even in their acts of vengeance Hindus under the Peshwas were ethical in their treatment of Muslims: bazaars were not raided, mosques were not torn down, women were not molested, Muslims were not forced to convert. This is in line with the claim in *Indian War* that Indians – both Hindus and Muslims in that text – were ethical in their acts of violence. Yet these practices had not stopped Hindus losing battles: machinations, intrigues, and conflicts among Marathas themselves, or with other individuals, groups, and communities, had prevented not only "Pan-Hindu" unity but also military victories.

The message of *Hindu Pad Padashahi* was intended to convey significant implications for the rest of India: Hindu unity was only possible in acts against all Muslims. Savarkar's chapter titled "On to the Indus" discusses the Peshwa conquest and reclamation of the Indus river for Hindus: "The Hindus reached Attock. For the first time since the dismal day when Prithviraj fell, a triumphant Hindu flag waved

---

[173] Savarkar, *Hindu Pad Padashahi*, 27.
[174] Ibid., 25.
[175] Ibid., 38.

proudly on the sacred river of the Vedas. The Hindu horse of victory drank the waters of the Indus, gazing fearlessly at himself as reflected in his [*sic*] crystal tides."[176]

The Marathas demonstrated what was possible for all Hindus in India. The only acceptable alternative for Savarkar regarding Muslims which did not necessarily involve violence was their reconversion to "Hinduism" through the purification ceremony of Shuddhi. He lamented the Peshwas' lack of foresight in reclaiming Hindus lost to Islam. Vikramaditya had shown the possibility of reassimilating such Hindus who may have been influenced or coerced by "foreign invaders" in India: "[H]ow regrettable is it that the Hindus, in spite of the Hindu rule that could conquer and crush Moslem thrones and crowns could not convert or even reclaim a few hundred Moslems back *to* Hinduism."[177]

## 8.  The End of Maratha History?

Savarkar ended *Hindu Pad Padashahi* – as he ended *Indian War* – with failure: "The Marathas lost and with them fell the last great Hindu Empire – the last great *Indian* Empire."[178] While providing an important shift from writing about the *Indian* war of independence to the *Hindu* war of independence, *Hindu Pad Padashahi* served to reinscribe or reassert that "Hindu" and "Indian" were really synonymous. The Marathas fought a Hindu war of independence for Hindu liberation from Muslims, but they also fought to liberate the very idea of India from Muslims who had staked their claim to India. This was an important discursive shift in Savarkar's writings. The great pity for him was that the Marathas could not sustain their Hindu empire: antagonistic tendencies within Maratha governance split the leadership between those whom he classified as "selfish" and "denational" and others who made "patriotic sacrifices" for the nation.[179] The consequence was a fractured Maratha empire that simply could not defend itself against the power of the English.

[176] Ibid., 89.
[177] Ibid., 272. Emphasis in original.
[178] Ibid., 287. Emphasis in original.
[179] Ibid., 229, 285.

Savarkar added that Hindus should nevertheless not lament England's victory over the Marathas; England should be admired for its great "skill" in dominating the world "over oceans and seas, over continents and countries."[180] England had created a "magnificent World-Empire" that was unique in offering a hopeful future for the Hindu empire. Strikingly, the message given in *Hindu Pad Padashahi* is not so much about learning from the failure to fight future revolutions, but to turn to the message of Jesus Christ and follow the steps of Mary after Christ's death: "Here then in the year 1818 lies the grave of the last and one of the most glorious of our Hindu Empires. Watch it. Hope, with frankincense and offerings even as Mary did, in loving solicitude."[181] This is an unexpected ending in the book – though it does not come as a total surprise given that Savarkar also concluded *Indian War* with a Biblical reference. As already noted, in his autobiographical writings Savarkar not only said he had read the Bible and Christian devotional literature in prison, but also that his interests in the New Testament and Old Testament dated back to a trip to France:

> In France, I had read the New Testament with close attention. I used to read it daily and meditate upon the text . . . The life of Jesus Christ suggested itself to me, at this juncture, as a proper theme to weave into a song. The setting for it was furnished [to] me by the history of the Jews which I had studied with interest and appreciation when I was reading the Old Testament, especially in relation with the bitter struggle of their nation and its heroes for emancipation from the thralldom into which it had passed in its unfortunate history. Their helplessness and anguish and their efforts to set the race free had struck a sympathetic chord in my heart at the time.[182]

However, it appears that Savarkar was not satisfied with the final sentence in the original 1925 edition of *Hindu Pad Padashahi*, as a new concluding sentence was added in a later edition of the book. It states, *"For who knows when the Resurrection comes!!"*[183] Presumably

<hr>

[180] Ibid., 287.

[181] Ibid.

[182] Savarkar, *My Transportation for Life*, in *Selected Works of Veer Savarkar*, vol. 2, 26; *Majhi Janmathep*, in *Samagra Savarkar Vanmaya*, vol. 1, 282.

[183] Savarkar, *Hindu-Pad-Padashahi* (1942), 288. The new sentence was added in the second edition of the text. Italics in the original.

the purpose of this addition was to suggest that the Hindu dead will be resurrected to create a future Hindu empire. What is not clear is whether the Hindus were also waiting for Jesus Christ's second coming. The idea might sound random or out of place, were it not that Savarkar's brother Ganesh D. Savarkar claimed that Christ was actually a Hindu in a book he authored titled *Jesus, the Christ was a Hindu*.[184]

In the conclusion of his book Savarkar reiterated the purpose of *Hindu Pad Padashahi* along the terms developed in *Indian War* and *Essentials of Hindutva* to define Hindutva as a history in full: "Ours has never been the intention of recounting and examining all the details of the Maratha movement, but only to bring out those which would enable us better to ascertain the leading motive, the underlying principle that inspired and informed it and ascertain, in that light, its real place in the history of our Hindu people."[185] This restatement of "the leading motive" as "the underlying principle" is consistent with all of Savarkar's writings. For readers unfamiliar with his earlier books or essays, Savarkar repeated his interpretation of Hindutva in his writings. All his historical subjects shared thoughts and actions across time (and sometimes space). For Savarkar, mimesis was the point. After completing *Hindu Pad Padashahi*, he embarked on a lengthy project of becoming the subject of his own history as a brave and heroic Hindu; he now described his desires and motives inspired by Hindutva – and the Hindu spirit – as the maker of history and the writer of history.

---

[184] Savarkar, *Jesus, the Christ was a Hindu*. The original Marathi edition of the book was posthumously published after Ganesh D. Savarkar's death in 1945, but I have not been able to locate this edition.
[185] Savarkar, *Hindu Pad Padashahi*, 284.

# MODE 2: AUTOBIOGRAPHY AS
# HINDU HISTORY

My life-story itself became an extensive chapter in the war
of liberation against the English . . . Naturally whatever might
be said about these nation-wide political activities during this
period, from the point of view of Hindutwa, has already appeared
in the written part of my Autobiography.[186]
**Vinayak Damodar Savarkar**

## 1. Introduction

There has been an ongoing discussion in recent decades about whether
Savarkar was *veer*, a Sanskrit word that means "heroic" and "brave," but
which can also be translated as "hero" and "warrior." Savarkar's supporters and disciples insist that his contributions to the nation make
him worthy of the title "Veer Savarkar." They argue that every moment of his life illustrates that he was *veer* in his actions and thoughts:
contesting colonial power; writing histories under surveillance and
the censor; the daring escape from British custody in Marseilles; the
hard labour of prison work in the Cellular Jail; the personal sacrifices
for the nation; the ability to fight for Hindus as a political prisoner.
The examples are many.

Savarkar's detractors and critics argue that he was not *veer*. They cite
letters written by Savarkar to British government officials while serving
two life sentences in the Andamans as evidence of his lack of bravery.
Whereas some argue that Savarkar wrote petitions to have his sentence
reduced and be transferred to another prison in India, others say Savarkar was not "requesting" or "petitioning," he was begging for mercy.
Passages from Savarkar's letters are reproduced in the media to demonstrate that he used the words "beg" and "mercy": "the undersigned
most humbly begs that he should be given a last chance to submit his
case,"[187] and "if the government in their manifold beneficence and

---

[186] Savarkar, *Six Glorious Epochs of Indian History*, 467.

[187] MSA, Home Spec, File 60-D-(b)-1919, Petition from V.D. Savarkar to
Chief Commissioner of Andamans, Cellular Jail, March 30, 1920.

mercy release me, I for one cannot but be the staunchest advocate of constitutional progress and loyalty to the English government."[188] Savarkar's critics explain that such statements simply cannot be the words of a brave or heroic man; no one who is *veer* begs his oppressors or asks for mercy, irrespective of the circumstances, let alone declaring loyalty to the English government. Other nationalists, such as Bhagat Singh and M.K. Gandhi for instance, are referenced as contrasts. Nor does it matter that as a lawyer Savarkar may have been following the formalities of letter writing or using the contemporary vocabulary of the time. Or the fact that he was ill and wanted to be near his family after having spent more than a decade in the Cellular Jail. In 1919, before submitting his 1920 petition to government that is often cited, he wrote a letter to his younger brother saying his health had deteriorated to the point that he was no longer certain he would survive.[189] This is dismissed as an excuse; his word choice, in this view, is evidence of the fact that he was not *veer*.

In the midst of these discussions the point often overlooked is that there was a discursive process through which Savarkar became "Veer Savarkar." I am often asked when he acquired the title.[190] There is no easy answer. The earliest published reference that I have found thus far is the 1924 Marathi biography titled *Swatantraveer Vinayakrao Savarkar* by Sadashiv Rajaram Ranade.[191] Of course, the prefix *swatantra* (independent) is added to *veer* in this context, but within the text Savarkar is never identified as *swatantraveer*. In fact, *veer* is only used as an honorific once in the book, when he is called "Veer Barrister Savarkar."[192] It is also important to remember that Savarkar was

---

[188] Petition from V.D. Savarkar to Chief Commissioner of Andamans, Cellular Jail (date not included), Home Department Proceedings, 1914. The date for this petition is listed as November 14, 1913 in the Cellular Jail History Ticket for Vinayak Damodar Savarkar (No. 32778), MSA, Home (Special) File 60-D-(f)-1923, S-37.

[189] Letter from V.D. Savarkar to N.D. Savarkar, September 21, 1919, in Savarkar, *Letters from Andamans*, in Savarkar, *Selected Works of Veer Savarkar*, vol. 3, 469.

[190] I thank Ajay Skaria for asking this question and prompting me to think about the emergence of Savarkar as "Veer Savarkar" in the twentieth century.

[191] Ranade, *Swatantraveer Vinayakrao Savarkar*.

[192] Ibid., 44. The only other times that Savarkar is identified as *veer* in the

finally released from prison in 1924 and allowed to live in Ratnagiri under an agreement with the government. In other words, Ranade's identification of Savarkar as *veer* (or *swatantraveer*) happened after he left prison. However, it is likely that individuals were already using *veer* (and its analogues) to describe Savarkar and his activities before Ranade. For example, it is possible to trace descriptions of Savarkar as a "hero" and Savarkar's use of "hero" in his English-language writings in the 1900s and 1910s. ("Brave" and "bravery" were also frequently incorporated into the writings.) But Savarkar was not the only figure to be described in this way. During the Nasik Murder Trial in 1910, in which Savarkar was convicted, multiple articles in newspapers reported that the public identified dozens of individuals accused in the case as heroes. *The Times of India* noted that prosecutors in the case lamented this point in court by stating, "They have thereby made popular heroes of political criminals."[193] Heroes in India were legion at this time, and Savarkar was certainly important among them. As one commentator acknowledged, in Bengal alone there was "an orgy of hero worship" after Savarkar's release from the Andamans and his "glowing tributes to the heroes of the pre-war assassinations."[194]

Savarkar celebrated heroes in his own writings, especially in *Indian War*, a point noted during the Nasik trial, when he was described in court as delivering speeches on "the heroes of the Mutiny."[195] In *Indian War* and *Hindu Pad Padashahi* the hero was present throughout in the guise of the revolutionary, while exhibiting in addition the essential principle of Hindu history. The most important hero in all of Savarkar's writings appears in the "Glossary" to *Indian War*, namely Ramchandra, described as "the greatest Hindu hero and king – the hero of the Ramayana."[196] When *Essentials of Hindutva* was translated into Marathi and Hindi, hero/heroic and brave/bravery were generally translated as *veer* (or as part of a word in which *veer* is the root, such

---

text is in reference to him being a heroic child (*balveer*) and a patriot (*deshveer*), 11, 15, respectively.

[193] "A Case for Action," *The Times of India*, July 25, 1910.

[194] "The Tiger's Claws," *The Times of India*, May 21, 1924.

[195] "Nasik Conspiracy. Savarkar's London Speeches," *The Times of India*, September 29, 1910.

[196] Savarkar, *Indian War*, 450.

as *veerata*). When his Marathi writings were translated into English, *veer* became hero.

The concept of *veer* and its cognates was not unique to Savarkar's writings. Bravery, valour, honour, and chivalry were all characteristics central to the discussion of individuals described as *veer* in the *bakhars*. Savarkar himself cited the *Sabhasad Bakhar*, where terms like *veer*, *veerata*, and *veerveeron* are regularly used.[197] English-language translations of the *Sabhasad Bakhar* show these concepts as hero, heroic, and heroism.

In an essay titled *"Veer Chapekar ani Ranade"* Savarkar provided the clearest articulation of the uses of *veer* in his work.[198] He says that when he read a number of works about Damodar, Balkrishna, and Vasudev Chapekar – the Chapekar brothers – and Mahadev Vinayak Ranade, he became saddened by the abusive terms (e.g. *deshdrohi*, or traitors) used to describe them in newspapers following their arrests and executions.[199] In response he started describing them as "*veer*" to provide a counter-message.[200] Savarkar argued that there was a problem with language itself, as he felt limited by the existing vocabulary to describe their characteristics; he continued to search for words more appropriate and precise. Meanwhile *veer* became a term he started using with great frequency. In this essay he also reminds readers that he had actually incorporated *veer* much earlier in his work, especially in his translation of Mazzini's writings into Marathi. He says there was a different challenge in translating Mazzini's concept of "national martyr."[201] His difficulty was to find an appropriate Marathi equivalent for "martyr" – in North India *shahid* was regularly used but he refused to incorporate a word from the Arabic language into his writings. Here

[197] For example, Savarkar, *Essentials of Hindutva*, 49–50.

[198] Savarkar, *"Veer Chapekar ani Ranade,"* in *Samagra Savarkar Vanmaya*, vol. 1, 139-42.

[199] Ibid., 140. Damodar and Balkrishna Chapekar had assassinated Charles Walter Rand, assistant collector of Pune and chair of the Special Plague Committee in 1897. Vasudev Chapekar and Ranade were responsible for killing witnesses who had testified in the trial against Damodar and Balkrishna. All four individuals were found guilty and hanged.

[200] Ibid., 141.

[201] Ibid.

Savarkar forgets or elides the fact that he had used *shahid* in *Indian War*, including when describing "Shahid Mangal Panday."[202] He now says he had initially settled on "*deshveer*" as his translation for martyr: a compound of *desh* (land; nation) with *veer*. But he adds, "There is no comprehensive equivalent for the word 'martyr', as a result, I have experimented with dharmaveer, deshveer, and swatantraveer."[203]

In his English-language writings Savarkar used analogues of *veer*, but the word itself was absent. *Veer* appeared to be reserved for his Marathi works, and hero/heroic and brave/bravery (and sometimes martyr) for his texts in English. What is most worth noting in this essay is Savarkar's assertion that he was experimenting with the term *swatantraveer* to describe martyrs in revolutionary wars as early as 1907, when translating Mazzini. The fact that Sadashiv Rajaram Ranade used the same term to describe Savarkar in his biography complicates the context in which *veer* was popularised not only to describe the subjects of Savarkar's writings but also Savarkar himself. The irony, of course, is that while Savarkar had used *swatantraveer* to classify individuals who had died in a revolutionary war, Ranade modified the term to describe Savarkar in relation to his release from prison – literally as the independent hero.

*Swatantraveer* continued to be used as a title for Savarkar for the rest of his life, but at some point authors started employing *veer* in their English-language works when writing about him. This was likely the moment that "Veer Savarkar" was born as a concept in several Indian languages. By the mid-1920s figures like Shaukat Ali publicly identified Savarkar as brave. Savarkar also pointed out that G.S. Sardesai had called him brave in this period. A discourse of heroism and bravery was emerging around him, especially after he became president of the Akhil Bharatiya Hindu Mahasabha in 1937 – the year when government restrictions were lifted, allowing him to travel and participate in politics. By the late 1930s it appears that the process was complete: he was now formally "Veer Savarkar." In 1938 Bhai Parmanand referred

---

[202] Savarkar, *Indian War*, 85–9.

[203] Savarkar, "*Veer Chapekar ani Ranade*," 141. Savarkar explained that he only found an appropriate term for "martyr" in a conversation with his brother in the Cellular Jail in the Andamans: *hutatma*.

to Savarkar as "Vir Savarkar" in the preface to an edition of *Essentials of Hindutva*. By the 1940s books in a number of languages identified Savarkar as *veer*, including a Tamil biography called *Vira Savarkar* (1940). An organisation called the "Veer Savarkar Satkar Mandal" planned religious and political events.[204] The Hindu Rashtra Dal organised a "Veer Savarkar Week" to celebrate Savarkar's birthday in 1944.[205] Dhananjay Keer published Savarkar's most comprehensive biography in the twentieth century with the title *Veer Savarkar*.[206] His obituary in *The Times* (London), published on February 28, 1966, included this: "Veer Savarkar, as he was called (Veer means hero)."[207] In fact, most of Savarkar's official works published by the current copyright holders of his writings list Veer Savarkar (or Swatantraveer Savarkar) as the author before his full name. The incorporation of the title has been discursively normalised to the extent that many even assume that Veer rather than Vinayak was V.D. Savarkar's first name.

From the above it is clear that for Savarkar the discursive strategies for writing about historical subjects became central to how he described himself. The Hindu spirit was no longer a category used exclusively for understanding Hindus in the past, as in *Hindu Pad Padashahi*; it was also now present within the contemporary figure of Savarkar as "the maker of history." Savarkar's life-story was a topic of great interest throughout India, starting in the 1920s. Ranade's *Swatantraveer Vinayakrao Savarkar* was the earliest Marathi biography to be published, and others appeared in Telugu, Gujarati, Hindi, Urdu, Tamil, and English. Many of these were banned by the government – his biography was considered too dangerous. Yet the most prolific writer of Savarkar's life-story was Savarkar himself, as he published multiple autobiographical texts in the 1920s and 1930s. Being monitored by government officials who regularly objected to these works, his autobiographical projects remained unfinished.

In the period Savarkar was writing his autobiographical texts, the genre of the "life-story" was in the process of being transformed in India.

[204] "Dasara in Bombay," *The Times of India*, October 7, 1943.

[205] "Veer Savarkar Week," *The Times of India*, May 23, 1944.

[206] The original title of the book was *Savarkar and His Times* (1950), but it was changed to *Veer Savarkar* in 1966, when the book was republished.

[207] "Obituary: Mr. V.D. Savarkar: Hindu Nationalist," *The Times* (London), February 28, 1966.

Scholars have pointed out that the emergence of the modern form of the life-story, as biography or autobiography, occurred in India only in the late-nineteenth century.[208] These modern texts built upon earlier hagiographical traditions and religious biographical genres, such as the *carita* (or *caritra*), which incorporated both legend and history in narrating life-stories.[209] At times these accounts maintained the form and style of the early *carita*s, with authors often using the term *carita* in the title. As a literary form, the emergence of the autobiography (*atmacarita*) was a new phenomenon in which the idea of *carita* was rethought to include the discussion of the self (*atma*).[210] Sudipta Kaviraj argues that the *carita* was a "conventional biographical genre" primarily focused on individuals with "religious merit" or "military conquerors."[211] The genre highlighted the exemplary and extraordinary lives of individuals to provide an inspiration for "moral behaviour" and "meritorious conduct." Kaviraj adds that these conventional biographies were distinctive, since there was "a necessary separation between the protagonist and narrator."[212] The emergence of the autobiography, however, led to the collapse of this division: the protagonist and the narrator became one in this literary form.

The narration of the self as a subject in the form of autobiography emerged at the historical conjuncture when intellectuals were also arguing for the political and religious self in the form of *swaraj*, *swadesh*, and *swadharma* in the anti-colonial struggle. Mazzini's collected writings were an important example for Savarkar, combining as they did Mazzini's autobiography with his other writings on Italian independence. While these parallel trajectories are often not examined together, the conceptualising of the "self" in the "self-story" of the autobiography on the one hand, and on the other theorising "self-rule" in political tracts were intimately connected. By the time Savarkar started writing about the personal self, he had already published arguments about *swaraj*, *swadesh*, and *swadharma* in *Indian War* and *Hindu Pad Padashahi*.

My purpose in this section is to examine Savarkar's writing strategies

---

[208] Arnold and Blackburn, eds, *Telling Lives in India*, 8.

[209] Ibid., 7.

[210] Kaviraj, *The Invention of Private Life*, 307.

[211] Ibid.

[212] Ibid.

for his own life-story. These autobiographical texts are central to understanding Savarkar's conceptualisation of Hindu history since they provide a continuity linking Savarkar to his historical subjects as brave, masculine, revolutionary heroes. These writings complete Savarkar's intention of an ontological integrity with his Hindu subjects. In a letter written to S.R. Rana in 1950 Savarkar pleads with him to provide his "recollections" of revolutionaries from their time together in London.[213] He explains that he is collecting writings from "different leaders and actors."[214] He says he wants to complete his autobiography before he dies and considers Rana "amongst the prominent workers in that heroic period" of revolutionary activity.[215] It was possible for him to write more freely now that he was no longer under surveillance by the government censor. Once he received Rana's response, the ultimate goal was for him "to write the full history of that period."[216] As Savarkar sometimes used "full history" as a shorthand for "a history in full," this was affirmation that his autobiographical texts were central to his work around the formulation of Hindutva.

# 2. Writing the Impossible Autobiography

Savarkar finished writing *Hindu Pad Padashahi* in February 1925, and it was published in December that year. In the interim he embarked on a project to narrate his life-story. On July 7, 1925 his first autobiographical essay was published in the Marathi-language newspaper *Kesari*, founded by Tilak and edited at the time by N.C. Kelkar.[217]

[213] Letter to S.R. Rana from V.D. Savarkar, March 22, 1950, in Savarkar, *Historic Statements*, 194–5.

[214] Ibid., 196.

[215] Ibid.

[216] Ibid.

[217] MSA, HD Spec File 60-D-III-1927, Memorandum from Assistant Secretary to the Government of Bombay, HD Pol, to the Oriental Translator to Government, December 8, 1926, S-9. (Author's name is not legible in the letter.) Attached to the Memorandum are the translations of forty-seven of Savarkar's autobiographical essays published in *Kesari* that were later collated and published as *Majhi Janmathep*.

Savarkar continued to write for *Kesari* for six months without interruption, until the British authorities learned of these essays. In all, forty-seven essays were published, primarily focusing on Savarkar's period of incarceration in the Cellular Jail in the Andamans. He also included discussions of his time in other prisons. Officials in the Home Department (Special) – the intelligence unit of the Home Department – realised that surveillance of Savarkar's publications by the government had lapsed as the authorities had no idea of Savarkar's essays despite the fact that he was supposed to be closely monitored. In a letter to S.M.S. Moulvi, Oriental Translator to the Government of Bombay, an official wrote: "I am desired to say that, in view of the nature of the whole series of these articles, they should have been brought to the notice of Government as and when they were published and that the failure on the part of your office to do so is disappointing."[218] He demanded an immediate inquiry into the situation, eventually leading to the translation of all of Savarkar's published essays into English to ensure he was not engaged in political activity.

By the end of December 1925 Savarkar's column in *Kesari* had stopped. However, in an essay published on November 27, 1925, Savarkar had revealed that he was in the process of writing a second series of essays that would be published in a new book.[219] Local officials were concerned that he was not only avoiding government monitors again as he had announced writing plans, but that his book would potentially violate his conditions of release. In February 1927 Savarkar started publishing a new series of autobiographical essays for a Marathi weekly called *Shraddhanand*, a newspaper edited and published by his brother Narayan D. Savarkar.[220] He wrote only seven essays for *Shraddhanand* but then compiled all his autobiographical essays into a

[218] MSA, HD Spec File 60-D-III-1927, Confidential Letter from H.D. (Special), to S.M.S. Moulvi, Oriental Translator for the Government of Bombay, February 1, 1927, S-107. (Author's signature not legible in the letter.)

[219] MSA, HD Spec File 60-D-III-1927, Confidential Letter to Mr. Butler, Personal Assistant to the D.I.G.P., CID, Poona, February 1, 1927, S-109. (Author's signature not legible in the letter.)

[220] There is some confusion regarding Savarkar's first publication in *Shraddhanand*. S.T. Godbole states that the first essay was published in January 1927 in his "Preface" to the 2007 edition of *My Transportation for Life*; British government reports state it was February 1927. MSA, HD Spec File 60-D-III-1927,

single volume published in May 1927 under the title *Majhi Janmathep*. The English translation of this work was published two years later: *My Transportation for Life* (1929).

The book was read carefully by government officials in the Home Department. In August 1927 they produced a report detailing the book's structure and contents. It was noted that the volume not only consisted of Savarkar's writings from *Kesari* and *Shraddhanand* but also included unpublished essays.[221] The report said Savarkar had been cautious in *Majhi Janmathep*: "It may be observed that Savarkar has been careful to shield himself – as he did when he published the first part serially."[222] He had alerted his readers to the fact that the book contained his "thoughts" and "sentiments," but wanted "his narrative to be read from merely an historic point of view."[223] He had also explained that his "present position" prevented him from publishing material that might be considered problematic by the government: "[Savarkar] asks his readers not to draw any definite conclusion as regards his life in the Andamans until the whole story in a well-connected form is placed before them."[224] What concerned officials was Savarkar's declaration that he planned to publish a second edition of the book in which he would "let himself go."

This report was an acknowledgement that Savarkar was censoring his work to ensure it could be published under the terms of his release from prison. Without these restrictions, he would have had a lot more to say. Select pages from the book were identified as "objectionable passages." Most of these centred on Savarkar's descriptions of the activities of the Abhinav Bharat Society in London and Savarkar's admission that

---

Confidential Letter to Mr. Butler, February 11, 1927. (Author's signature not legible in the letter.)

[221] MSA, HD Spec File 60-D-III-1927, "Report, H.D. (Special)," S-111. This report has been initialled by three different officials on three separate dates: June 21, 1927, June 22, 1927, and July 25, 1927. The initials are not legible on S-143.

[222] MSA, HD Spec File 60-D-III-1927, "H.D. (Special) Note," S-197. Initialled by the same three officials on S-143, on August 22, 1927 and August 23, 1927.

[223] Ibid., S-197.

[224] Ibid., S-198.

he participated in a revolutionary movement. His connections to the revolts in 1857 were also considered objectionable, especially the emphasis on how the "spirit of a national awakening" had inspired him. Given the aftermath of the First World War, many of the objections centred on Savarkar's sympathy for Germany in its conflicts with the British. Despite bringing attention to specific passages and pages, the reporting officials concluded that, overall, the text was not worthy of further consideration and the government did not need to take action.

Since Savarkar had already published most of the essays in *Majhi Janmathep* in the two newspapers, his narratives of the years in the Andamans were familiar to many. In line with his argument for writing *Hindu Pad Padashahi* in English a few years earlier, the English translation of the autobiographical work now expanded his readership beyond the Marathi public. Possibly for this reason, the book and its translations were soon banned as a security threat.[225] For the British the problem was that Savarkar's life-story was intended to be read as inspiration by the entire nation, not only by those fluent in Marathi. His narratives about his prison years demonstrated that his life paralleled the lives of the historical subjects in his other books. They provided a context to heroism and bravery that was at the centre of Hindu history. Savarkar as the writer of history had converged with Savarkar the maker of history in the eyes of the British as well. In an early essay titled "Thane Prison" Savarkar explains that he was imprisoned in Thane after his trial in Bombay while waiting to be transported to the Andamans to begin his sentence of two life terms. One night, there was a knock on the door of his cell. A warder asked to speak to Savarkar. He revealed that Savarkar's younger brother Narayan was also being held in the prison; the warder wanted Savarkar to know that he admired him. Savarkar says this warder first celebrated his reputation for bravery and then said "*Tumhi veer ahata*" (You are *veer*).[226] This statement in the English translation in *My Transportation for Life* appears as "You are a hero."[227] The interaction records one of the earliest published

[225] NMML, V.D. Savarkar Papers, Reel 30, "Savarkar's Book on Andamans: Why is it Still Banned?" (No publishing information given.)

[226] Savarkar, *Majhi Janmathep*, in idem, *Samagra Savarkar Vanmaya*, vol. 1, 285.

[227] Savarkar, *My Transportation for Life*, in *Selected Works of Veer Savarkar*,

references by Savarkar identifying himself as *veer*. His autobiographical essays also include references to others who had called him *veer*. While Savarkar did not call himself *veer*, his autobiographical essays include references to others who did.

Implicit in these essays is the idea that Savarkar was already widely identified as *veer*. This point was discussed further by Savarkar when describing his interactions with the main warder in the Thane prison. Sometimes this main warder taunted Savarkar by telling him that he had been duped by powerful men who were free whereas Savarkar was going to suffer in the Andamans. The warder ridiculed him to the point that, Savarkar states, "It became impossible for me, at times, to save myself from this harsh man's cruel badinage."[228] One day the warder called several other warders to witness the humiliation: he performed a "jig and dance" while "flourishing his stick" and punished Savarkar as if he were a caged tiger in a circus.[229] While everyone laughed, the warder mocked him with "*dekho hamara veer*" (behold, our hero).[230] Savarkar's point was to show how popularly he was known as a hero. The ridicule heaped on him by use of the word *veer* was affirmation that the discourse of his *veerata* existed.

His years in the Cellular Jail appear as a period of "suffering" and "exile." He acknowledged that there were many political prisoners across the world who suffered similarly. Prison life everywhere was meant to make individuals suffer: it was the whole point of prison. However, the horrible experiences of prisoners in the Andamans were also specific to its location as a place where malaria and disease were widespread, and because of the particular officials and warders administering the Cellular Jail. Savarkar's personal anguish is interspersed with his narrations of the misery of other prisoners. The violence of

---

vol. 2, 30. The official Hindi translation is "*Aap veer hain*," in *Savarkar Samagra*, vol. 2, 48.

[228] Savarkar, *My Transportation for Life*, in *Selected Works of Veer Savarkar*, vol. 2, 36.

[229] Ibid.

[230] Savarkar, *Majhi Janmathep*, in idem, *Samagra Savarkar Vanmaya*, vol. 1, 289. The translation is from Savarkar, *My Transportation for Life*, in *Selected Works of Veer Savarkar*, vol. 2, 36.

a jailer called Mr Barrie is described at great length. Savarkar says he may have initially fared better than others because Barrie was aware of Savarkar's activities and writings. But soon Savarkar's letters and petitions to government landed him in trouble with Barrie. In fact the focus of many of Savarkar's early essays is Barrie, "The man who ruled the prison with an iron hand; who made the prisoners tremble in their shoes."[231] Questioning Barrie's authority led to severe punishments, including torture, solitary confinement, and prisoners having to toil on an oil-press known as the *kolu*. Savarkar was not spared.

In fact he suffered at all levels during his Andamans incarceration. Savarkar identifies various violent warders as "Mohammadans" and "Pathans" whose contempt for Hindu prisoners was clear throughout his stay in the Cellular Jail.[232] If Barrie represented the British government, the warders symbolised Hindu oppression at the hands of Muslims. Muslim prisoners were given special perquisites only because they were Muslim, especially by the Muslim warders. In contrast, Hindus were greatly persecuted: "the Pathans, as a rule, were bigoted Mohammadans, and were especially notorious for their fanatical hatred of the Hindus."[233] And "A large portion of political prisoners in that jail being Hindus, and I being among them, these warders were regarded by us [as] the greatest terror of our lives."[234] The Cellular Jail is in his narrative a battlefield for conflict between Hindus and Muslims. In an early essay he had clarified that he refused special treatment because he maintained solidarity with other Hindu prisoners. He turned his prison experience into a daily battle against the structures of power for the liberation of Hindus. He appointed himself leader of the prisoners and stressed that it was necessary to fight on the battlefield:

My power and intelligence would have been as n[a]ught, if I had feared and trembled in the hour of my trial, like Arjuna on the battlefield of Kurukshetra. I did not fail in my duty – in my Dharma . . . I exhorted

---

[231] Savarkar, *My Transportation for Life*, in *Selected Works of Veer Savarkar*, vol. 2, 124; *Majhi Janmathep*, in idem, *Samagra Savarkar Vanmaya*, vol. 1, 360.

[232] Savarkar, *My Transportation for Life*, in *Selected Works of Veer Savarkar*, vol. 2, 92.

[233] Ibid., 92–3.

[234] Ibid., 92.

my allies to face danger as their duty had called upon them to do; and I passed through the fiery ordeal which I had insisted that others should pass through. That is fearlessness, that is patience and fortitude . . . A Napoleon dies as exile at St Helena on a foreign soil on a bed of thorns. Does it take away aught from his past triumphs and victories, from his intrinsic greatness? A Laxmibai of Jhansi falls at the second or third stroke of battle! An unknown soldier dies at the first shot. Is her or his valour the less praiseworthy for such a defeat and death? If I had lived free exposing others to the cannon shot, exposing them to win the battle, but not to see the victory, I would not be worth the name of a leader. I chose to be in their ranks and suffer the fate that they had suffered.[235]

Savarkar's formulation is important in marking a transition from him as the victim of Barrie and the warders, to choosing to suffer in solidarity with Hindus as their leader on a battlefield. His incarceration in the Cellular Jail is interpreted as part of his duty as a Hindu – as his Hindu dharma.

Savarkar included multiple references to the Bhagavad Gita throughout these writings. In these essays, perhaps more than in any other work, he provided small clues about the place of the Gita in his everyday life, while also including brief discussions of the text. He first speaks of the Gita while discussing a visit to the jail from his wife and her brother: during the meeting he discussed the prospect of the British allowing his wife to move to the Andaman Islands after a few years, following a policy of reuniting and resettling prisoners with their families. The prison superintendent had abruptly ended the meeting, and, turning to Savarkar, his brother-in-law urged him to repeat a mantra from the Gita every morning. "Looking at him wistfully, I promised to carry out his behest," says Savarkar.[236] Prior to boarding the ship that took him to the island prison, his last personal possessions were confiscated: a pair of eyeglasses and a copy of the Gita: "I was a conspirator; the rule was that a convict of that type lost all his property to the State. My trunks, clothing and books had already been taken in possession and sold by public auction. That my . . . [G]ita and my spectacles, the last things I had with me, should also be taken away from me grieved even my fellow prisoners."[237] In select passages

---

[235] Ibid., 137.
[236] Ibid., 22.
[237] Ibid., 38.

he included references to the Gita's central themes of *swadharma* and dharma and encouraged readers to examine a chapter of the Gita: "Look at the eleventh chapter of the Bhagwat Gita, and remark the manifestation in it of the Divine Spirit as cosmic force, embracing in its sweep both the One and the Manifold".[238] The prison officials eventually returned his copy of the Gita to him.

The fragmentary nature of Savarkar's discussion of the Gita is consistent with his approach to that text in other works; that is, his discussions are brief and appear for random reasons. He assumes familiarity with the text's key ideas. There are two passages providing clues about the Gita which go beyond Savarkar's usual discussions even in his major writings:

> Everyone who presumes to think of his own country, to dabble in politics, and to aspire to political leadership, must . . . possess full and deep knowledge of subjects like politics, economics and constitutional history. To be wanting in such knowledge is to spell yourself inefficient and unfit for responsible self-government, or for high administrative offices in it. As in religion so in politics, *action with knowledge* is the key to salvation . . . When you have plenty of time before you [in prison], a number of years to be passed in enforced idleness, you must add knowledge to service and vision to self-sacrifice. Heroism, to do or die, is not enough. It must be illuminated by deep learning[,] ripening into wisdom. I exhorted them [political prisoners] finally to cast off gloom and despondency, and apply themselves to knowledge[,] which was their proper work there.[239]

He continues:

> We know how in their exile, the Pandavas used to be down-pressed, how they would pity and condemn themselves. They were tortured by their minds for what they had brought upon themselves; despair and melancholy overcast their souls, and they forgot their own valour and greatness. Then Dhaumya and other sages narrated to them stories of Nala and Rama to put courage in their hearts and teach them to defy misfortune and cruelties of fate. And these stories from the past put a new hope in their hearts. Similarly, stirring acts of former heroes in history . . . or discourses

[238] Ibid., 261. Chapter 11 is perhaps one of the most prominent and recognised parts of the Bhagavad Gita. It includes a dialogue in which Krishna reveals to Arjuna that he is the Supreme Deity.

[239] Ibid., 161. Emphasis added.

on the immortality of the soul from the Upanishads and the Bhagawat [G]ita would provide a tonic to the shattered hearts of our political prisoners. That would imbue them with the spirit of defiance.[240]

In the first passage Savarkar evokes the central principles of *karma yoga* (discipline of action) found in the Gita, though without referencing it. This is characteristic not only of his silence on the Gita explicitly, but in general of his silence on the sources that influenced his work. What can be interpreted from this passage? Savarkar was building upon the dialogue between Krishna and Arjuna in the Gita, in which Krishna states that Arjuna, and indeed all men, should follow their own duty (*swadharma*) without being attached to desires, pleasures, or accomplishments. An individual's actions should not be for personal fulfilment, but in the service of God (Krishna). Through everyday actions, in consonance with *swadharma*, an individual acquired true knowledge of Krishna. However, Savarkar reconsidered this general message of the Gita for political purposes. He urged his fellow prisoners to expand the religious context of *karma yoga* into the realm of politics: it was the duty of every prisoner interested in the nation to acquire knowledge of history, politics, and economics, as well as of Krishna for the greater final end of *swaraj*. The idea of "action with knowledge" was necessary for national as much as personal salvation.

The example of the Pandavas in the second passage aims similarly to uplift and motivate fellow prisoners. The forced exile of the Pandavas corresponds with the tortured, daily lives of political prisoners. In other parts of the memoir Savarkar wrote of individuals who, finding prison life unbearable, had committed suicide, which had motivated him to take up his role as teacher and leader in the Cellular Jail. Suicides were evidence of forgetting earlier figures who had overcome their suffering through perseverance and strength. Knowledge of the past would provide a "spirit of defiance."[241]

With prisoners dying of natural causes, exhaustion, torture, illness, and suicide, death became a theme in many of Savarkar's essays. People like Barrie and the Muslim warders had broken the spirit of revolutionaries; this was unacceptable: "Not only did I make up my

---

[240] Ibid., 152–3.
[241] Ibid., 153.

mind to die bravely, but I persuaded all my friends and disciples in that pall that it was their duty, in virtue of the pledge they had taken, to die like heroes. I thus saved many a lonely and wretched human being in that place from the verge of suicide."[242] When fellow prisoners shared their desire to die with Savarkar, he says he narrated celebratory and heroic histories from *Indian War* of bravery in death, especially the example of Rani Laxmibai, a "great hero" and a brave warrior who achieved martyrdom. At the same time, Savarkar instructed fellow prisoners – "Do not die like a woman."[243] But these statements were not contradictory because Laxmibai herself had not died like a woman. Her death represented an ideal, whereas men who declared their intention to commit suicide, or who stopped eating as a form of slow death, were dying like women.

Yet within Savarkar's taxonomy it was possible for fellow prisoners to choose the type of death they wanted. He not only reminded his fellow prisoners that figures like Madan Lal Dhingra had died like heroes, he recounted narratives from Hindu history; in one conversation with a suicidal prisoner on a hunger strike he provided an argument made by the sixteenth-century hero Rana Pratap:

> One was not right in giving up his precious life without exacting full price for it. If one resolved to die, he must die fighting. Patriotic service meant heroism and extorting cent per cent for the sacrifice made, and not the death of a man by hunger and lonely in a cell like a rat. If one killed himself in the name of his country in this fashion, one was harming and not helping the cause of his country.[244]

At other times he restated Ramdas' argument that "if you must die, die fighting like a hero. Kill your enemy and then take leave of this world."[245]

The autobiographical essays reveal several thematic continuities with his earlier writings, especially his interest in tracing the motives and desires of actors in the making of Hindu history. He discussed his own role as a leader of fellow Hindus throughout his writings: he

[242] Ibid., 145.
[243] Ibid., 244.
[244] Ibid., 379.
[245] Ibid., 244.

encouraged prisoners to read books in the Cellular Jail library as a way to understand Hindu history.

Savarkar's readings while in the Andamans allowed him to reconsider the Hindu–Muslim conflict by providing an alternative to violence and vengeance against Muslims. In fact, based on his essays he went one step further than the Marathas, seeking to embrace Muslim prisoners by reconverting them to the Hindu fold. Whereas the Marathas in *Hindu Pad Padashahi* are shown to have simply abandoned Hindus who had been forced to convert to Islam, Savarkar says he promoted a Shuddhi programme of purification borrowed from the Arya Samaj as a way to welcome back individuals he called his co-religionist brothers.[246] This has clear echoes of the narratives of Vikramaditya discussed in *Essentials of Hindutva*, where Vikramaditya "re-assimilated" those Hindus who had strayed from their dharma.

For Savarkar, many of his fellow inmates were revolutionaries who had participated in the ongoing Indian war of independence. The fact that the Cellular Jail was originally constructed to imprison the 1857 revolutionaries allowed Savarkar to make this claim. The Cellular Jail embodied those who had posed a threat to the British empire.[247] In a letter requesting amnesty for all political prisoners, he reaffirmed all the characteristics that were central to his Hindu histories. Whether officials who read this letter were aware of his subtext is not clear, but his purpose in citing the letter in his autobiographical essays was to alert his followers of this ultimate goal of writing a history in full that connected revolutionary heroes of the past with contemporary political prisoners in the Cellular Jail: "People will remember again the martyrs, the soldiers and the heroes who fought bravely for the liberation of our country; and the agitation is bound to awaken in their hearts a feeling of deep sympathy for their sufferings, to make them realise the sincerity of their motives, and to inspire them to fight continually till victory comes to the cause near their hearts."[248] The language used to

---

[246] Ibid., 265–312.

[247] See Anderson, *The Indian Uprising of 1857–58*. Technically – although unlikely – when Savarkar arrived in the Andamans in 1911, there may have been prisoners in the Cellular Jail who had been convicted for crimes in 1857, but this is not discussed by Savarkar.

[248] Savarkar, *My Transportation for Life*, in *Selected Works of Veer Savarkar*, vol. 2, 386.

describe his fellow prisoners is nearly identical to that in the descriptions within *Indian War* and *Hindu Pad Padashahi*. The revolutionary spirit of his historical subjects was now embodied by the prisoners, including himself.

He ended his essays as he began them, by articulating that other people considered him *veer*. But he was not simply any hero: he was now identified with the greatest hero in Hindu history. He explained that people compared his fourteen years of incarceration with Ramchandra's fourteen years of exile from Ayodhya in the Ramayana: "All the inmates of the prison, my fellow-countrymen, prisoners and officers . . . said with one voice, 'Savarkar you have been an exile from your country like Rama . . . You have passed through similar trials'."[249] But of course there was an important distinction between him and Ramchandra: that is, Ramchandra killed the demon Ravana, whereas his own demon was still alive.[250] However, there was still time for him to slay the demon and equal Ramchandra, and when he left the Andaman Islands and arrived in India "the whole country . . . hailed me as [*veer*] and patted me on the back."[251] Savarkar did not shy away from writing about himself as an equal to Arjuna or Ramchandra – the epic Hindu heroes *extraordinaire*.

After completing the writings on his years in prison, Savarkar published autobiographical essays in a new Marathi weekly newspaper edited by Narayan D. Savarkar titled *Hutatma Shraddhanand*.[252] Officials

[249] Ibid., 542.

[250] Ibid.

[251] Ibid., 543. (In the English translation, Savarkar is called a hero.) In the Marathi text, he is identified as *veer* in this sentence. Savarkar, *Majhi Janmathep*, in idem, *Samagra Savarkar Vanmaya*, vol. 1, 696.

[252] MSA, HD Spec File 60-D-III-1927, "H.D. (Special) Report," S-201. (The initials of the officials are not legible. Two dates are provided on the report: November 12 and 18, 1931.) As Savarkar had noted in "*Veer Chapekar ani Ranade*," he was dissatisfied with the existing translations of "martyr" into vernacular languages. However, he also wrote that after a series of conversations with his brother Ganesh D. Savarkar, he thought that *hutatma* was the best translation of martyr. The meaning of "martyr Shraddhanand" in the title of the publication was linked to the figure Swami Shraddhanand, a leader of the Arya Samaj who was involved in *shuddhi* and Hindu reform. Shraddhanand was assassinated by Abdul Rashid in 1926. Also, NMML, Hindu Mahasabha Papers, File C-26, Statement by V.D. Savarkar, January 8, 1940.

responded quickly and argued that the only reason Narayan Savarkar started the new publication was to provide a venue for his brother to publish essays about his life-story.[253] Narayan Savarkar was also editor of *Shraddhanand* before it was forced to shut down under the Press Ordinance. Savarkar's autobiographical essays in *Hutatma Shraddhanand* quickly drew the attention of government: his narration contained "objectionable passages" that potentially violated the conditions of his release.[254] These were no longer essays about Savarkar's prison years as they focused instead on his childhood. One official commented, "Savarkar is probably trying to give vent to some more of his feelings which he suppressed on the last occasion."[255] This figure recommended that Savarkar be required to submit all his essays to government for review and approval prior to publication. A translator was assigned all of Savarkar's writings that had appeared in *Hutatma Shraddhanand*: their translation into English would ensure he was not violating government guidelines. However, the official speculated that Savarkar could have already completed his autobiography, in which case the government needed more information before it was published.[256]

The first issue of *Hutatma Shraddhanand* appeared on July 12, 1931 and included a section called, "An Autobiography of the Hero of Independence, Barrister Savarkar."[257] (In later issues the title was sometimes abbreviated to "An Autobiography of Barrister Savarkar.") However, it appears that Narayan Savarkar, in his capacity as editor, had penned the first essay, in which he explained that the purpose of the section was to introduce key selections from Savarkar's autobiography; Savarkar himself was in the process of completing "an unfinished portion" of the

[253] MSA, HD Spec File 60-D-III-1927, "H.D. (Special) Report," S-201.
[254] Ibid.
[255] Ibid., S-202
[256] Ibid., S-202-203.
[257] MSA, H.D. (Special), File 60-D-III-1927, *Hutatma Shraddhanand*, October 25, 1931, H.D. (Special) Report, S-199; "Translation of an article headed 'Barrister Savarkar's Autobiography' (Article No. 1 of the series)," *Hutatma Shraddhanand*, July 12, 1931, S-207. "Barrister Savarkar's Autobiography" was written by Narayan D. Savarkar, the editor of the newspaper. This information was revealed in a later document stating that the introduction to Savarkar's essays in the first issue was written by his younger brother. See H.D. (Special) Report, November 12, 1931, S-273 of the same file.

book and "bringing it up-to-date."[258] Narayan Savarkar made it clear that these essays were originally written by Savarkar in 1908 in London, where he had drafted his autobiography with the title "My Reminiscences."[259] He added that Savarkar had "nearly completed the first part of [the] book" and "sent it to us in India."[260] Savarkar had apparently smuggled out a part of the book while in the Andamans, in which he discussed his conviction and sentencing. This is somewhat surprising, since Savarkar himself had regularly emphasised his limited access to paper and pen in the Cellular Jail: this is the first reference to other writings that he may have completed during his incarceration. Narayan Savarkar says the fragmentary pages he had received meant that the texts his brother sent him required editorial additions and changes:

> Those parts which we received from time to time were preserved through many difficulties by us and a number of our patriotic sympathisers with as much devotion as is bestowed on preserving a sacred religious book. In spite of this many omissions and much confusion did take place in those loose papers. Making a firm resolve not to allow those important papers to rot in the same discorded state hereafter, we made up our mind to publish at least as much a portion of this attractive book as can be published in these circumstances.[261]

*Hutatma Shraddhanand* had an important role in publishing his brother's autobiography; Narayan Savarkar says the autobiographies of revolutionaries are important in offering the arguments of such people in their own words. While Savarkar had stated that he was not ready to publish his autobiography in the late-1920s due to government surveillance, it appears that the circumstances had changed. Narayan Savarkar noted that the British had allowed the publication of a number of autobiographies at this point, including works by Barin Ghosh, Ullakar Dutt, Upendranath Bannerjee, Hemachandra Das, Raja Mahendrapratap, and Bhai Parmanand.[262] The first published work identifying his brother as a revolutionary was a government report – the

[258] MSA, H.D. (Special), File 60-D-III-1927, *Hutatma Shraddhanand*, July 12, 1931, S-207.
[259] Ibid., S-207-209.
[260] Ibid., S-209.
[261] Ibid., S-209-211.
[262] Ibid., S-213.

Rowlatt Report, in which the "lives and acts of revolutionaries" were fully documented. Moreover, he pointed out, Savarkar was already well known in Europe as the "Prince of Indian Revolutionaries."[263] Thus the time was right to publish these autobiographical essays in *Hutatma Shraddhanand*.

The government disagreed, rejecting Narayan Savarkar's claim that the essays were written in London in 1908. One official wrote: "It seems most likely that the instalments of the autobiography which are now being published are actually being written by him at the present. The statements made . . . are apparently a camouflage to protect him in case Government object to any objectionable matter published in the course of the autobiography."[264] He noted that Savarkar's essays on his childhood were likely to "incite his readers to follow in the wake of his revolutionary ideas."[265]

The essays are in fact full of descriptions of Savarkar as a precocious child who was not only aware of the anti-colonial politics of the late-nineteenth century, but who was also, even as an adolescent, a prolific writer, an avid reader, and a political activist fighting against Muslim oppression. In other words, Savarkar describes himself as endowed with the Hindu spirit in the brave and heroic actions of his early life. The government was convinced that the newspaper's primary purpose was to promote Savarkar's "revolutionary ideas to the Indian public." Plans were set to not only "recall" all the published papers, but also demand that all future writings be read, censored, and expunged if necessary.[266] On January 2, 1932 *Hutatma Shraddhanand* shut down, six months after it had started.

The publication of Savarkar's autobiography remained incomplete, though officials were sceptical that it had ceased. Savarkar was interviewed by the district magistrate of Ratnagiri, W. Gilligan, on January 11, 1932 about his writings, when he stated he had nothing to do with the publication of the essays in *Hutatma Shraddhanand*: his brother Narayan as the editor was solely responsible.[267] He reasserted that the

---

[263] Ibid.

[264] MSA, HD Spec File 60-D-III-1927, "H.D. (Special) Report," November 12, 1931, S-274. (Signatures and initials not legible.)

[265] Ibid., S-275.

[266] Ibid.

[267] MSA, HD Spec File 60-D-III-1927, Letter from W. Gilligan, District

autobiographical essays were written before the restrictions imposed by the government, a point already rejected by officials.[268]

> *Savarkar*: I remember the last warning you gave me. As regards the "Huta-tma Shraddhanand," I state that it closed down about 3 weeks ago. I am willing to show my papers at any time you call on me to do so, that means the files of the Shraddhanand articles. I went to see the articles to which you refer . . . I had nothing to do with the publication of those articles. The very openings of those articles, there the Editor has explained all about their origin. Those articles the Editor received many years ago as he himself admitted, and part was written in the Andamans with all my books a part fell into his hands. According to my condition, I am not writing any political articles at all. If I happen to write anything even bordering on politics, I shall surely consult the District Magistrate before I print.

> *DM*: Will you therefore arrange for the cessation of articles being printed, which you state were written by you many years beforehand, because such explanation might even be given for an article from you today?

> *Savarkar*: I shall try my best to persuade the Editor not to print the articles any longer in the said paper even if it be restarted.

> *DM*: Or in any other paper?

> *Savarkar*: How can I be responsible?

> *DM*: Won't I make you responsible?

> *Savarkar*: I wish to continue . . . [the original document is torn here] . . . Manuscript which are not in my possession . . . I will be helpless, but nevertheless, I will try my best to stop publication in any paper what-soever, is all I have to say. One word more, if I ever find . . . if unable to stop the publication, I shall consult the District Magistrate and inform him of the facts.

> *DM*: Before or after publication?

> *Savarkar*: Of course, beforehand – if I could.

At this point officialdom was suspicious that Savarkar was publishing texts under the names of his brothers, or using pseudonyms.[269] His

---

Magistrate, Ratnagiri, to Secretary to the Government of Bombay, HD Pol, January 22, 1932, S-277.

[268] MSA, HD Spec File 60-D-III-1927, "Savarkar File, V.D. Savarkar, Ratnagiri, is called by the District Magistrate, January 11, 1932," S-279-280.

[269] MSA, HD Spec File 60-D-III-1927, Confidential Memorandum, from

writings were more difficult to monitor than the government had anticipated: they considered him the possible author of all writings attributed to his brothers. In their view Savarkar was trying to promote his revolutionary ideas at all costs, including publishing narrations of his life-story as a revolutionary under various pen names. What the government did not inititally consider was Savarkar's argument that he was an extraordinary Hindu too, and therefore that others were interested in publishing work on his life. But soon enough the commissioner of police found himself investigating a pseudonymous biography, *Life of Barrister Savarkar* (1926) by Chitra Gupta, for connections with Savarkar's writings. Savarkar's essays were often published under "The Autobiography of Barrister Savarkar." There appeared to the official to be many similarities besides the title, but the inquiry did not establish any links. In the end, the commissioner concluded, "It has no connection with the autobiography appearing in the 'Hutatma Shraddhanand'."[270] This assessment was actually incorrect.

## 3. Biography as Autobiography

Savarkar was clearly interested in completing his autobiography. Officials were aware that he had a lot more to say about himself than in what had been published in the 1920s and 1930s, but government restrictions prevented him from proceeding. Even his childhood as represented in *Hutatma Shraddhanand* had been considered dangerous and with the potential to incite violence; his account of later events was bound to be worse since he tended to focus on himself as the heroic figure who had contested power throughout his life, especially against

the Acting Secretary to the Government of Bombay, HD, March 7, 1932, S-283. (Names are not included in the document.)

[270] MSA, HD Spec File 60-D-III-1927, Note from the Deputy Commissioner of Police, Bombay, S.B., to Deputy Director, I.B., New Delhi, February 12, 1932, S-283. Another investigation was opened in 1934, but without any resolution at the time. See MSA, HD Spec File 60-D-V-1934, Note written by Deputy Inspector General of Police, CID, Bombay Presidency. This note is included in a report from the Secretary to Government, HD Spec, Bombay, November 9, 1934, S-321-322.

British rule. Each narrative was also meant as inspirational. Individuals close to Savarkar had already committed acts of violence in India and Britain; others might follow suit. His discussions of Muslim persecutions of Hindus were also viewed as having the potential to provoke violence. In short, the very subject of Savarkar's life was dangerous.

The fact that multiple accounts of his life were already circulating in India in several vernacular languages was thus a security threat. Biographies about Savarkar were available in the 1920s. Ranade's publication of *Swatantraveer Vinayakrao Savarkar* (1924) was probably the first biography of many. Chitra Gupta's *Life of Barrister Savarkar* was the first English-language biography; it was published by B.G. Paul & Company – the Madras-based publisher who had done *Hindu Pad Padashahi*. The impact of *Life of Barrister Savarkar* was immediate. The government banned the book, even as it was either translated into vernacular languages or used in combination with Savarkar's autobiographical essays for biographies of him in Telugu, Bengali, Marathi, Tamil, Urdu, and Gujarati.[271]

This was naturally seen as seditious underground writing because the

[271] A number of biographies on Savarkar were published after *Life of Barrister Savarkar*. I have not been able to identify the full publication information for all the texts on account of the wide range of sources consulted, but I provide this list in chronological order for illustrative purposes (I have maintained the spellings found in the sources without the diacritical marks): Mudiganti Jaggamna Sastri, *Vinayak Savarkaru jiva tamu* (Cocanada, 1927), Telugu; Raghunath Ganesh Bhope, *Svantraya Vir Savarkar Yanche Charitra* (1928), Marathi; Ra. Srinivasavaratan, *Paristtar Cavarkkar carittiram* (Cennai: Sri Parata Piracuralayam, [1929], Tamil; Pandit Satya Dev Siddhant, *Janbaz Savarkar, ya Marhattah inqilab pasand* (Lahore: Sant Ram Publisher, 1930), Urdu; Shantilal K. Trivedi, *Savarkar* (Bombay: Usma Printery, 1932), Gujarati/Marathi?; Raghunath Ganesh Bhope, *Barrister Vinayakrava Savarkara* (Poona, 1937), Marathi; Jagananda Bajpai, *Vir Savarkar* (1939), Bengali; S.N. Naracimmaraju, *Antaman cirai virar V.D. Cavarkkar carittiram* (Celam: Raju Piras, 1940), Tamil; S. Krishnamurthi Ayyar, *Vira Savarkar* (c. 1941), Tamil. With regard to Shantilal K. Trivedi's *Savarkar*, officials investigated this text for its links to Savarkar's writings, and it was determined that it was a translation of *Life of Barrister Savarkar*. However, the officials did not specify the language into which Trivedi had translated it. See MSA, HD Spec File 60-D-III-1927, H.D. (Special) Correspondence, S-287-293.

government had in essence proscribed all of Savarkar's published books in English and Marathi, as well as translations of them into vernacular languages. The subject of Savarkar's life had been declared seditious, as had been his corpus of writings. In other words, the power of his texts was at the centre of all official discussions. Savarkar's work and life had shaded entirely into each other and colonial subjects throughout India would see the borderlines had blurred. Savarkar's life-story had come to symbolise and represent his ideas on Hindu history.

*Life of Barrister Savarkar* was highly influential, leading many to inquire about the identity of its pseudonymous author Chitra Gupta, especially as the book included personal and intimate details about Savarkar's life, including aspects of his childhood that were known only to Savarkar and his family. In addition, the text includes many direct quotes that appear to have been written or spoken by Savarkar himself, thereby raising questions regarding Chitra Gupta's uncommonly close relationship to Savarkar. But the selection of the pseudonym appears to have a historical context too. It was popularly known that Chitragupta was the chief scribe of Yama, the god of death, responsible for not only maintaining a written record of all human actions, but also providing judgments on those actions.[272] As early as the 1760s, Raghunath Yadav used the pen name Chitragupta when he wrote biographical narratives and historical chronicles about Shivaji.[273] His work was known as the *Chitragupta Bakhar*.[274] By the twentieth century there were others who had adopted the name Chitragupta to hide their identities while writing in India, but it is naturally difficult to ascertain how many authors actually used it. It is not known whether in using the name the anonymous author was evoking Raghunath Yadav, Yama's scribe, or someone else altogether. But there is a secret meaning inscribed within the name itself that is important to note. The name "Chitra Gupta" is the combination of two words: *chitra* (portrait or picture) and *gupta* (hidden): literally, the hidden portrait, or the hidden picture. Perhaps the popularity of the pseudonym over two centuries was directly linked

[272] Among the community of religious scribes known as Kayasthas, Chitragupta was worshipped as a deity. See Kaliprasad, *The Kayastha Ethnology*.

[273] Krishnaji Ananta, *Siva Chhatrapati*, 251.

[274] Kulkarni, ed., *Bakhar of Panipat Original and Complete written in 1761 by Raghunath Yadav 'Chitragupt'*.

to the meaning of *chitragupta* – something that the author would have known. Readers have assumed that the title page of the book lists author and title: Chitra Gupta, *Life of Barrister Savarkar*. What has not been considered is the alternative: that is, "Chitra Gupta" as an aspect of the title itself, *The Hidden Portrait: Life of Barrister Savarkar*.

The "Publisher's Preface" of *Life of Barrister Savarkar* does not reveal direct information about the author, although it includes a discussion about the sources used when writing the book. The author of the preface, whose name is not given, states, "the publishers have ventured to bring out this short sketch, chiefly based on the reminiscences of many a contemporary of Mr. Savarkar, the recorded trials, and the Rowlatt Report."[275] The author explains that the book has a "narrator" but then also says: "[We] have jotted down whatever scraps of information we could gather in more or less connected form and brought them out in this booklet."[276] There appears to be some slippage in articulating whether the text is authored by one individual or is a collaborative project. On the other hand the "Publisher's Preface" makes clear that there was a discussion with Savarkar when bringing out his autobiography prior to publishing *Life of Barrister Savarkar*. The author says Savarkar was concerned about the timing of its appearance, given the government restrictions on his writings: "As Mr. Savarkar does not think it wise to write an autobiographical sketch in the trying circumstances . . . we thought it better not to wait any longer for fuller information."[277] The preface notes that Savarkar was publishing essays of his experiences in the Andamans in *Kesari* at the time. B.G. Paul & Company, of course, had a prior relationship with Savarkar with the publication of *Hindu Pad Padashahi*, but the preface also indicates that they had published editions of *Essentials of Hindutva* and *The Echo from the Andamans* – Savarkar's letters to his brother from the Cellular Jail.[278] The public is asked to

---

[275] "Publisher's Preface," Gupta, *Life of Barrister Savarkar* (1926), v.

[276] Ibid.

[277] Ibid.

[278] There is no consistent title of Savarkar's published letters to his brother. While *The Echo from the Andamans* is given in the preface, the following are other titles: *An Echo from Andamans* (1924); *Echoes from Andaman* (1984); *Letters from Andamans* (2007).

read *Life of Barrister Savarkar* along with Savarkar's other books to understand his ideas and interpretations. I mention these links between Savarkar and the publisher to emphasise that *Life of Barrister Savarkar* was published with Savarkar's approval. In addition, B.G. Paul & Company planned to bring out Savarkar's complete autobiography as "a sequel" to the book.[279]

The "Publisher's Preface" also provides an important clue worth considering: a lengthy two-page statement from N.C. Kelkar, described as "the well-known Maratha leader," is quoted within the preface.[280] This description of Kelkar was modest to say the least: he was a lawyer, a major intellectual, and a prolific writer of histories, novels, plays, and dramas. He was also very close to Tilak – in fact, he wrote a biography of Tilak and published the court proceedings of the 1908 "Tilak Trial." He served as editor of *Kesari* and *Mahratta* and became president of the Akhil Bharatiya Hindu Mahasabha.[281] The statement begins with Kelkar noting that he had never met Savarkar and only knew him by reputation, until he came into "personal contact with him before his release."[282] This was an indication that Kelkar had met Savarkar before he wrote this statement, presumably prior to Savarkar's release from prison in Ratnagiri or Pune. Kelkar made clear that he admired Savarkar's "heroic spirit" but differed from his political views, which he associated with revolutionaries from Ireland and Italy. Kelkar also wrote about his discussions with Gopal Krishna Gokhale and Dadabhai Naoroji on Savarkar's ideas, while also briefly mentioning Savarkar's interpretations of the First World War and the League of Nations. He concluded by pointing out that Savarkar's escape from British custody in Marseilles, and the subsequent legal case against the British by the French government, brought international attention to India's problems. Kelkar's short statement does not reveal any new

[279] Gupta, *Life of Barrister Savarkar* (1926), viii.

[280] Ibid., v–vii.

[281] K.N. Watve, "Sri Narasimha Chintaman 'Alias' Tatyasaheb Kelkar," *Annals of the Bhandarkar Oriental Research Institute*, 28, 1–2 (1947), 156–8; "Mr. N.C. Kelkar, Long Leave Because of Health," *The Times of India*, December 28, 1927. Also, D.V. Gokhale, ed., *The Contempt of Court Case against Mr. N.C. Kelkar, editor, the 'Kesari'* ([Poona: D.V. Gokhale], 1924).

[282] Gupta, *Life of Barrister Savarkar* (1926), v.

information about Savarkar, with the exception of the fact that he met Savarkar prior to writing it. This is an important point in the present context because Kelkar's statement in the "Publisher's Preface" to *Life of Barrister Savarkar* is actually an English translation of his original Marathi "Preface" to Ranade's *Swatantraveer Vinayakrao Savarkar*.

At first the inclusion of Kelkar's "Preface" in *Life of Barrister Savarkar* appears a curious choice, especially since there is no discussion of Ranade's book elsewhere in the text. However, when I compared *Swatantraveer Vinayakrao Savarkar* with *Life of Barrister Savarkar*, what became immediately clear were the extensive overlaps and intimate connections between the two. Many sentences and full paragraphs are translated from one text to the other. There are select passages in English that are found in both books. (See Table 1) Savarkar's poem "*Sagaras*" (Oh, Ocean) is repeated in both books, along with his "*Majhi Mrtyu Patra*" (My Will and Testament). The texts are chronologically organised and cover the same time period in Savarkar's life: from his childhood to his conviction and transportation for life in the Andamans. The descriptions of specific events and details are identical, as are parts of select chapters. Some short paragraphs in one text are summaries of long paragraphs in the other. As with the tradition of *bakhar*s, it appears that parts of *Swatantraveer Vinayakrao Savarkar* were directly incorporated into *Life of Barrister Savarkar*. The example worth considering here is the *Chitragupta Bakhar*, in which Raghunath Yadav – as Chitragupta – fully integrated and copied most of the life-story of Shivaji from the *Sabhasad Bakhar* into the body of his text.[283]

The production of *Life of Barrister Savarkar* involved considerable processes of translation and editing: some Marathi descriptions were abbreviated and rewritten in English, while others were omitted. For example, a brief description of the importance of Karl Marx's *Capital* for Communists and Socialists appears as part of a discussion of Jean Longuet in *Swatantraveer Vinayakrao Savarkar*, but is not included in *Life of Barrister Savarkar*.[284] Most errors in the English language passages were corrected when they were published in *Life of Barrister Savarkar*.

On the other hand, these works are not identical. There are different emphases in each book, along with the inclusion of different

---

[283] Deshpande, *Creative Pasts*, 31.

[284] Ranade, *Swatantraveer Vinayakrao Savarkar*, 75.

## Table 1: A Comparison of Passages
### (with page numbers)

| Ranade's *Swatantraveer Vinayakrao Savarkar* | Chitra Gupta's *Life of Barrister Savarkar* |
| --- | --- |
| "He is bound to be a great *demeyogue*". (29) | ". . . the youth was likely to turn out one of the most dangerous demagogues in India." (21) |
| "He was an ill *tongned* messenger of extremism from the very start." (32) | ". . . he had ever been an ill-tongued messenger of extremism." (26) |
| "He is at *The* most twenty-two, but he is already an accomplished orator of an enviable rank." (35) | ". . . though he could have hardly been 22, he had already developed into an accomplished orator of an enviable rank." (19) |
| [*Valantine Chirole*] "He was one of the most brilliant advocates of a later rebellion." (41) | "Valentine Chirol, one of the most brilliant of modern Indian revolutionists." (2) |
| "No! No! not unanimously!" (45) | ". . . no! no! not unanimously." (61) |
| "Youth and intelligence were stamped upon his face."(45) | "Youth and intelligence seem stamped upon his face. (47) |
| "*Genvine* British Blow" and "a Straight Indian Lathi" (47) | "Genuine British Blow" and "Straight Indian Lathi" (64) |
| "Their political catechism…" (49) | ". . . their political catechism . . . " (68) |
| "Sir I am sorry I cannot keep you here, you must quit this room! The police are after me . . . " (50) | ". . . the keeper of that boarding house returned, apologized and informed Mr. Savarkar that he could not board him there any longer as the detectives had already posted themselves . . . " (69) |
| "It is a mockery to talk of constitutional agitation where there is no constitution at all. But it a greater mockery—even a crime—to talk of revolution when there is a constitution, that allows the fullest development of a nation." (51) | ". . . it is mockery to talk of constitutional agitation where no constitution exists at all. But it would be worse than mockery, even a crime, to talk of revolution and freest development of a nation." (72) |

Table 1 (*Contd.*)

| Ranade's *Swatantraveer Vinayakrao Savarkar* | Chitra Gupta's *Life of Barrister Savarkar* |
| --- | --- |
| "She is an Indian princess." (53) | "She is an Indian princess!" (75) |
| "This is the flag of Indian Independence. Behold it is *boon*! It is already sanctified by the blood of the martyred Indian youths! I call upon you, gentlemen! To rise and salute this flag of new India of Indian Independence." (53) | "... this is the flag of Indian independence. Behold, it is born! It is already sanctified by the blood of martyred Indian youths. I call upon you gentlemen to rise and salute this flag of India – of Indian independence." (75) |
| "Thou art a general! Thou must not go to the trenches." (56) | "You are a general and must not rush to the firing line with the rank." (77) |
| "*Upto* this time *yon* have seen how I tried my best to work much. Now let me see if I can also suffer much!" (57) | "*Uptil* now I have worked to the utmost of my capacity, now I will suffer to its utmost." (83) |
| "Now or never!" (67) | "Now or never!" (106–7) |
| "Shri Swatantra Laxmi Ki Jai!" (79) | "Swatantrya Laxmi-Ki-Jai" (53) "Hail thee, Goddess of Independence!" (53, 116) |
| "Ab Kaidi Hai! Pakdo, Maro!" (79) | "Pakdo, Maro! Ab Kaidi Hai!" (116) |
| "I am prepared to face ungrudgingly the *extrem penall* of your laws in the belief that it is through suffering and sacrifice alone that our beloved motherland can march on to an assured, if not a speedy, triumph!" (80) | "I am prepared to face ungrudgingly the extreme penalty of your laws in the belief that our Motherland can march on an assured if not a speedy triumph." (117) |

*Note*: The italicised terms here are spelling errors in the original text. For purposes of comparison of the passages, I have not corrected these errors.

poems: "*Desi Phataka*" and "*Sri Sivarayanci Aarti*" in *Swatantraveer Vinayakrao Savarkar*; "Consolation" and "First Instalment" in *Life of Barrister Savarkar*.[285] The structures of the texts are distinct as well. Whereas *Life of Barrister Savarkar* is organised into chapters written in

[285] Both texts include additional poems or stanzas of poems written by Savarkar without including the titles.

a narrative form, *Swatantraveer Vinayakrao Savarkar* has small sections separated from one another within short chapters. Ranade included Kelkar's preface and wrote an introduction. *Life of Barrister Savarkar* has a "Publisher's Preface" along with appendices that appear to be written by Savarkar's comrades and additional source material from the trial – these materials are not included in *Swatantraveer Vinayakrao Savarkar*. The main distinction, of course, is that the books are written in different languages. *Swatantraveer Vinayakrao Savarkar* is a Marathi text with select passages in English, while *Life of Barrister Savarkar* is in English.

The fact that *Swatantraveer Vinayakrao Savarkar* was published two years before *Life of Barrister Savarkar* provides a new context for thinking about the significance of Ranade (and Kelkar) in the writing and production of *Life of Barrister Savarkar*, especially as scholars have not considered the links between these two works. Ranade's introduction to *Swatantraveer Vinayakrao Savarkar* provides important clues. He explains that he admired Savarkar's life-story and enjoyed listening to his poetry. He decided he wanted to get as much information about Savarkar's life as needed to write a *carita* for the people of Maharashtra, but also wanted to promote Savarkar's poetry by publishing it in a book.[286] However, getting access to information was not an easy task. In 1924 Savarkar came to Ranade's village, Makhjan in Ratnagiri District, though it appears that the two had met earlier too.[287] However, Ranade explains that Savarkar did not assist him in getting information. Instead, Ranade revealed his sources as Ganesh Savarkar, Narayan Savarkar, and Ramachandra Triambak Chiplunkar – Savarkar's father-in-law.[288] In addition, Vishwanath Vinayak Kelkar, one of Savarkar's distant relatives, had arrived in Makhjan to meet him, and this Kelkar was not only a member of the Hindu Mahasabha and a prominent lawyer and editor

---

[286] Ranade, *Swatantraveer Vinayakrao Savarkar*, 7.

[287] Ibid.

[288] Ibid., 8. Ranade lists the following in the text: "Shri Ganeshpant, Dr. Narayanrao, Shri Bhausaheb Chiplunkar." Ganesh Savarkar was frequently referred to as Ganeshpant in published works, while Savarkar's father-in-law was also known as Bhasaheb or Bhaurao Chiplunkar. Narayan Savarkar was a dentist and thus referred to as "doctor".

based in Nagpur, he was also the publisher of *Essentials of Hindutva* and *An Echo from Andamans*. Kelkar was also close to Keshav Baliram Hedgewar and M.S. Golwalkar and helped to found the Rashtriya Swayamsevak Sangh in 1925.[289] Ranade, in other words, had access to Savarkar's confidants when writing his book. His statement that Savarkar did not help him may have been strategic, given that Savarkar had been recently released from prison and forbidden all political activity, including the writing of a text that might be perceived by officials as an autobiography in the guise of a biography.

Ranade says he travelled with Savarkar to Nasik in 1924. While the length of time the two spent together is not clear, it is evident that Savarkar's biography was discussed. At one point Ranade notes that during the journey they met an elderly man who provided Ranade with narratives about Savarkar's early life.[290] The full details of this trip are not included in the text, nor the name of the elderly man. However, the government had authorised Savarkar's petition to travel outside the boundaries of Ratnagiri District because of the infestation of plague-carrying rats near his home.[291] He was permitted to reside in Nasik for three months, which was extended on account of the ongoing plague crisis in Ratnagiri. Newspapers reported the government's decision to allow Savarkar to travel.[292] On July 3, 1924 Savarkar and his family – as well as Ranade – arrived in Nasik to a large crowd. A procession that stretched approximately for a mile had formed.[293] N.C. Kelkar was also present in Nasik and presided over the "Savarkar Purse Fund Committee" which was raising money for Savarkar.[294] He organised a number of lectures for Savarkar in Nasik and neighbouring towns and villages – including in Bhagur, Savarkar's

---

[289] See Sinha, *Dr. Keshav Baliram Hedgewar*.

[290] Ranade, *Swatantraveer Vinayakrao Savarkar*, 13.

[291] MSA, HD Spec File 60-I-1933, Petition from V.D. Savarkar, to Governor of Bombay, May 27, 1924, S-7-8; Letter from Dy Secretary to the Government of Bombay, HD, to Vinayak Damodar Savarkar, June 14, 1924, S-15.

[292] "Mr. Vinayak Savarkar," *The Bombay Chronicle*, July 2, 1924.

[293] "Savarkar in Nasik. An Enthusiastic Reception," *The Bombay Chronicle*, July 5, 1924.

[294] "Purse to Barrister Savarkar," *Mahratta*, July 20, 1924; "A Nasik Presentation. Barrister Honoured," *The Times of India*, September 1, 1924.

birthplace. Savarkar was a popular figure in the locality and thousands of individuals are reported to have attended his lectures. Government officials were, as always, concerned with Savarkar's activities, especially as it was noted in one report that he was "in close touch with his old-time associates."[295] This was the context in which Ranade completed *Swatantraveer Vinayakrao Savarkar* in August 1924; it also opens up a new perspective for interpreting *Life of Barrister Savarkar*.[296]

There has been some speculation by scholars that, because *Life of Barrister Savarkar* was published in Madras, C. Rajagopalachari was the author Chitra Gupta.[297] However, no evidence is cited to substantiate this claim.[298] In fact archivists and scholars who have worked closely with Rajagopalachari's Collected Works have pointed out that there is no source that actually links Rajagopalachari to the text.[299] Others have suggested that it could have been V.V.S. Aiyar, one of Savarkar's comrades who was associated with India House in London. Again, Aiyar's connections to Madras are cited as the reason he is mentioned in this discussion, although Aiyar died in 1925 – a year before publication of the book. The fact that Savarkar had already published *Hindu Pad Padashahi* with B.G. Paul & Company seems to have been

[295] MSA, HD Spec File 60-I-1933, "Home Department Note," October 28, 1924, S-137-138. Initials of author unclear.

[296] The exact date of publication is not given, but Ranade lists the date of introduction as August 15, 1924. Ranade, *Swatantraveer Vinayakrao Savarkar*, 8.

[297] Srivastava, *The Epic Sweep of V.D. Savarkar*, ii; Jaffrelot, *Hindu Nationalism*, 377; and Pincince, "On the Verge of Hindutva," 23, fn. 7.

[298] This is not to suggest that Savarkar and Rajagopalachari did not have interactions or communications with each other. NMML, V.D. Savarkar Papers, Reel 30, Letter from V.D. Savarkar, to Chandra Gupta Vedalankarji, January 10, 1941. Savarkar noted that Rajagopalachari was going to assist him by circulating 5000 copies of the Hindi translation of his presidential address to the Akhil Bharat Hindu Mahasabha. Also, Reel 28, Press Statement on Raja Gopalachariaji by V.D. Savarkar, August 24, 1944.

[299] To further understand the links between Rajagopalachari and *Life of Barrister Savarkar*, I contacted Deepa Bhatnagar, an editor of the *Selected Works of C. Rajagopalachari*, and the former Head of Research and Publications at the NMML Archives in New Delhi. In a personal communication, Bhatnagar stated that she had not come across any document in her research related to Rajagopalachari that could substantiate that he authored the book on Savarkar. Special thanks to Aditya Balasubramanian for his input on this issue.

bypassed as the obvious explanation for the publication of *Life of Barrister Savarkar* with the same publisher. The identity of Chitra Gupta remained a mystery for many decades.

The second edition of *Life of Barrister Savarkar* (1987) published by Balarao Savarkar – the copyright holder of Savarkar's writings at the time – and printed by the Veer Savarkar Prakashan reveals that Savarkar was actually the author of the book and had used the pen-name Chitra Gupta.[300] This little-known fact about the authorship has not been discussed in analyses of Savarkar's political thought, nor has this been considered a text that contributes to his oeuvre. It is important to note that Savarkar did not officially claim to be the author of *Life of Barrister Savarkar* during his lifetime, and as he died in 1966 it is unclear if he had even authorised posthumous disclosure of this information. However, the identity of Savarkar as the author is discussed by Ravindra Vaman Ramdas, the author of the new preface to the 1987 edition. He asserts that "Chitragupta was none other than Veer Savarkar," and says it will "remain a mystery" why Savarkar never disclosed his identity.[301] This revelation also has consequences for interpreting the authorship of *Swatantraveer Vinayakrao Savarkar*, given the overlap between the two texts.

As Balarao Savarkar published this specific edition of the book, it is necessary to consider the context of his relationship to Savarkar.[302] Balarao was Savarkar's personal secretary for a number of years before his death. They also had a close intellectual relationship: Balarao was responsible for assisting him with his later writings, including completing Savarkar's references and footnotes. Harindra Srivastava reveals that Balarao also served as Savarkar's confidant in a period of personal crisis when Savarkar contemplated suicide.[303] Srivastava says he interviewed Balarao, who explained that he convinced Savarkar it was necessary

---

[300] Chitragupta, *Life of Barrister Savarkar* (1987). This is an argument that I first discussed in Chaturvedi, "A Revolutionary's Biography." The issue has now been taken up in the media with publications like *Organiser* and *Caravan* further adding critiques about the veracity of the claims about Savarkar as the author of the book.

[301] Chitragupta, *Life of Barrister Savarkar* (1987), ii.

[302] In Chaturvedi, "A Revolutionary's Biography," 126, I incorrectly identified Balarao Savarkar as Savarkar's brother.

[303] Srivastava, *The Epic Sweep*, 113.

for him to live in order to continue the struggle to create a Hindu nation. Later, Balarao was entrusted with maintaining and promoting Savarkar's writings after his death, based on Savarkar's specific instructions. As a result, Balarao was responsible for the publication of several of Savarkar's texts – not to mention his own writings. His decision to publish a second edition of *Life of Barrister Savarkar* was linked to one Professor S.G. Malshe, who had apparently shared a rare first edition of the book with him in the mid-1980s. It is important to note that Balarao was a major figure in the Hindu Mahasabha in his own right: he was an officer for a number of years, then served as its president for five years. Before his death Balarao had collated and edited four volumes of Savarkar's personal writings and memoirs.

Following the second edition of *Life of Barrister Savarkar*, all subsequent official editions of the book published by the current copyright holders have reproduced the statement that Savarkar was indeed its author. Himani Savarkar, copyright holder of Savarkar's writings till her death in 2015, was responsible for publishing and translating Savarkar's works, including later editions of the book that appeared with modified titles, marking a shift from Barrister Savarkar to Veer Savarkar: *The Life of Swatantra Veer Savarkar* and *The Life of Veer Savarkar*. The official electronic library of the Bharatiya Janata Party maintains a digital copy of *Life of Barrister Savarkar* which is a reproduction of Balarao Savarkar's edition, and it includes the statement that Savarkar was the author of the book.[304] However, the publishers of Savarkar's writings *before* Himani Savarkar also listed *Life of Barrister Savarkar* as part of Savarkar's oeuvre as early as 1927.[305] In 1933 Savarkar published a play called *Uttarkreya* in which an advertisement was printed with the heading "Savarkar's literature should be in every library!"[306] The advertisement was devoted to Chitra Gupta's *Life of Barrister Savarkar*, although a small listing for *Majhi Janmathep* was

[304] Chitragupta, *Life of Barrister Savarkar*, Bharatiya Janata Party e-Library, http://library.bjp.org/jspui/handle/123456789/290 (accessed August 11, 2021).

[305] The earliest advertisement for *Life of Barrister Savarkar* as part of *Savarkar Vanmaya* that I have found was printed on the back cover of Savarkar's play *Usshap*, published in 1927. MSA, HD Spec File 60-D-IV-1927, S-210.

[306] MSA, HD Spec File 60-D-V-1934, Advertisement for *Life of Barrister Savarkar* by Chitragupta, in Vinayak Damodar Savarkar, *Uttarkreya* (Ratnagiri:

also included at the bottom. In 1989 an advertisement for "Books by Savarkar" sold at Balarao Savarkar's Veer Savarkar Prakashan listed *Life of Barrister Savarkar* along with his other major writings.[307] The point is that the individuals and institutions responsible for publishing Savarkar's writings posthumously have publicly acknowledged and maintained that Savarkar was indeed the author.

Several editions of *Life of Barrister Savarkar* have been reproduced based on the edition published by Balarao Savarkar. Yet in all these books there is no discussion of Indra Prakash's 1939 updated and revised version of *Life of Barrister Savarkar*. This 1939 edition was published when Savarkar was president of the Akhil Bharatiya Hindu Mahasabha. Prakash had an important administrative role in the Hindu Mahasabha for some decades. He wrote a number of official key works, including *A Review of the History & World of the Hindu Mahasabha and Hindu Sanghatan Movement* (1938), which included an introduction by Savarkar and a foreword by Bhai Parmanand. As Savarkar and Prakash had collaborated on a number of texts, there is no way that Prakash could have written and published the revised edition of *Life of Barrister Savarkar* without Savarkar's permission.[308] In fact, when Prakash published a Hindi translation of *Essentials of Hindutva* without Savarkar's knowledge, he received a stern letter from Savarkar saying he as author was unhappy with the transgression. Savarkar said he would forgo all royalties, but he demanded fifty copies, and for all future translations and reprints he expected a hundred copies so that he could circulate them as propaganda.[309]

---

Balvant Press [1933]), S-2. The file also includes another published advertisement for the book as part of *Savarkar Vanmaya* on pages S-112-114.

[307] Advertisement for Veer Savarkar Prakashan, in *Savarkar Commemoration Volume* (Bombay: Savarkar Darshan Pratishthan, 1989), x. (The page number is listed as "x", but the advertisement is located between pages 136 and 137.)

[308] NMML, Hindu Mahasabha Papers, File C-26, Letter from V.D. Savarkar, to Indra Prakash, Secretary, Hindu Mahasabha, New Delhi, July 20, 1940, regarding *The History of the Hindu Mahasabha* and *Essentials of Hindutva* (Hindi and English). Also, Letter from J.D. Malekar, to Indra Prakash, August 1, 1940, regarding *Life of Barrister Savarkar* and other books.

[309] NMML, Hindu Mahasabha Papers, File C-26, Letter from V.D. Savarkar, to Indra Prakash, Secretary, Akhil Bharatiya Hindu Mahasabha, June 27, 1940.

Prakash began the book by stating, "There is something very fascinating in the life story of Barrister Savarkar."[310] His main purpose was to "bring up-to-date" Chitra Gupta's biography by adding five chapters to the original text. Prakash also pointed out that he was not able to write the chapters in the "poetic language" of the original author: "I could not do full justice to the hero."[311] Prakash's book also includes a foreword by Parmanand which begins with the question, "What is Swatantra Veer Savarkar?"[312] Perhaps this was an error: Parmanand's focus was actually to answer "Who is Swatantra Veer Savarkar?" He provided a brief biography of Savarkar's life but also discussed his personal interactions with Savarkar – from their time together in London to their period of incarceration in the Cellular Jail. It was also a celebration of Savarkar and his family: "The whole family of Veer Savarkar is one of heroes – unparalleled in the history of the world."[313]

Prakash did not reveal the identity of Chitra Gupta, but he appears to have relied heavily on Savarkar's published autobiographical writings to complete the five new chapters in the book, which include discussions of Savarkar's incarceration in the Cellular Jail. Within the text Savarkar is only identified as Barrister Savarkar or Mr Savarkar, until the last chapter of the book, which is called "Veer Savarkar as Hindu Rashtrapati."[314] But there is a discursive shift as Savarkar is identified as "Veer Savarkar" for the first time in the text: "His party agreed to cooperate on certain conditions one of which was that the Ministry be permitted to release Veer Savarkar from Ratnagiri."[315] For the remaining pages of the book, Savarkar is mostly referred to as "Veer Savarkar." In the conclusion, Prakash argues that "in the annals of Hindu History" Savarkar's name will "stand as a beacon light to call forth all that is best in Hindu patriotism."[316] Savarkar wanted

---

[310] Prakash, [Preface], in Gupta, *Life of Barrister Savarkar* (1939), page not given.

[311] Ibid.

[312] Bhai Parmanand, "Foreword," in Gupta, *Life of Barrister Savarkar* (1939), i.

[313] Ibid.

[314] The only exceptions are photographs that have been inserted throughout the book which all identify Savarkar as "Veer Savarkar."

[315] Gupta, *Life of Barrister Savarkar* (1939), 248.

[316] Ibid., 258.

to make "a happy, prosperous, free Hindu India" that would have a "proper and rightful place" among all the nations of the world.[317] The book concludes: "That is Veer Savarkar's ideal for which he has lived and suffered and which he will achieve."[318] In the end, the point is to underscore that Savarkar, as Veer Savarkar, lived and suffered for the Hindu Nation, the Hindu Rashtra. Ultimately, it is this idea that was central to identifying Savarkar as *veer*, an identity that Savarkar sanctioned.

## 4. A Hidden Life

While scholars have debated the identity of Chitra Gupta, there has been little engagement with *Life of Barrister Savarkar*. Nor have scholars considered Savarkar's relationship with and interpretations of the text. The entire debate around the authorship of *Life of Barrister Savarkar* needs to be rethought, especially as Savarkar's autobiographical writings actually provide answers to a conundrum that has persisted for nearly a century. It is only then that we can get close to a fuller understanding of Savarkar's strategy for writing his own life-story. To begin this process requires a close reading of selections from his autobiographical texts together with *Life of Barrister Savarkar* and *Swatantraveer Vinayakrao Savarkar*.

On October 25, 1931 Savarkar published an essay on his childhood in *Hutatma Shraddhanand*.[319] It was provocative: Savarkar explained that as a child he had a "political ambition" influenced by "revolution."[320] He says "I used to hate keenly the religious atrocities of the Musalmans and the political atrocities of the British."[321] In response to these political atrocities he and some school friends used to walk around with canes and pretend they were wielding swords in a field of plants with yellow flowers and thorny leaves. They would seek out

---

[317] Ibid., 259.

[318] Ibid.

[319] MSA, HD Spec File 60-D-III-1927, *Hutatma Shraddhanand*, October 25, 1931, S-245. (Translation of the article was completed by the Oriental Translator – name not provided.)

[320] Ibid.

[321] Ibid.

and destroy these specific plants with their canes because they were "*vilayati*" (foreign): "While making a wholesale massacre of that 'Vilayat' we could enjoy the satisfaction of massacring even the Vilay-atwallas just as intensely as the 'mutineers' massacring Englishmen in the revolutionary war of eighteen fifty-seven."[322] In other words, the spirit of revolution was already an inspiration for Savarkar as a child; he shows a continuity linking himself as a revolutionary subject to the historical subjects of *Indian War*.

Savarkar also narrated an incident reflecting his desire for vengeance against what he considered religious atrocities by Muslims. He had read newspaper accounts of Hindu–Muslim riots in Bombay and Pune in 1894–5.[323] He was concerned that Hindus were not appropriately retaliating against Muslims. As a result he decided to take action with a group of friends in his home town, Bhagur:

> I gathered together my young friends and decided to make a reprisal for this national insult at Bhagur, and what can be a better way to doing so than to march upon the only deserted mosque outside the village gate? Done. That batch of boys – nay heroes! – aged below twelve or thirteen proceeded one evening to storm the mosque stealthily according to the mode of guerrilla warfare. There was of course no one in the mosque! Could not the enemy possibly have fled away being afraid of our immense army of 10 or 12 heroes? We damaged the mosque to our hearts' content and, fully conscious that we were copying the ABC of the invasions of Shiva Chhatrapati we executed as early as possible the very last brave deed of the Shivaji cult, that of flying promptly from the battlefield![324]

In this description Savarkar identifies himself with the Hindu spirit of *Hindu Pad Padashahi*. His actions and thoughts reflect his desire to protect Hindu dharma. This essay is remarkable in that Savarkar seamlessly establishes connections to the subjects of his major historical writings. The latter narrative about attacking the mosque is also remarkable for a different reason – the same description and details appear in *Swatantraveer Vinayakrao Savarkar* and *Life of Barrister*

[322] Ibid.
[323] Ibid., S-245-247.
[324] Ibid., S-247.

*Savarkar.*[325] The considerable overlap between these two books makes it unsurprising that both reproduce the same narrative of Savarkar's life. An important question to consider is: how did Ranade come to know about this specific moment in Savarkar's life-story? It is not a detail that appeared in the press. Nor is this narrative a part of Savarkar's writings from Britain that were published in India. It is possible that Savarkar himself revealed these details to either Ranade or Kelkar, or they were revealed by one of Savarkar's brothers. Narayan Savarkar pointed out in *Hutatma Shraddhanand* that Savarkar had sent him autobiographical essays in 1908: perhaps these essays were shared with Ranade, who then incorporated them into the book.

The key point is that Savarkar claimed *this* narrative as part of his autobiographical essay in *Hutatma Shraddhanand,* irrespective of the fact that it was published in two biographies. The narrative was eventually published as part of his autobiographical essays in *Samagra Savarkar Vanmaya* in 1963.[326] Further, there are other essays that Savarkar included in his autobiography that were first published in *Swatantraveer Vinayakrao Savarkar* and *Life of Barrister Savarkar.* Some aspects of his autobiography were in *Life of Barrister Savarkar* but were missing in *Swatantraveer Vinayakrao Savarkar* (and vice-versa). What is immediately apparent are the similarities in the narratives of both books that are also found in the autobiographical writings, starting with a description of Savarkar's father Damodarpant Savarkar, and his two brothers Ganesh and Narayan. Both works discuss Damodarpant's introduction of select texts to Vinayak, including the epics and *bakhars.* Stories of Shivaji are mentioned in both, in similar places. Other family members are not included at this point in the books, but a discussion of Savarkar's mother and her premature death is also found later in the first chapters of both. There are also details that are included in one text but not the other. For example, in an essay in

---

[325] Ranade, *Swatantraveer Vinayakrao Savarkar,* 11; Gupta, *Life of Barrister Savarkar* (1926), 4–5.

[326] The narrative about the attack on the mosque from *Hutatma Shraddhananad* appears in the autobiographical essays of *Samagra Savarkar Vanmaya,* vol. 1, 120–1; *Savarkar Samagra vol. 1,* 152–3. Nearly the entire book follows a similar pattern for narratives across these texts.

*Hutatma Shraddhanand* Savarkar, when discussing his mother's death, provided details about turning to the goddess Laxmi for support. He specifically mentioned that he "never missed our mother" after her death.[327] *Life of Barrister Savarkar* includes the same description, with the goddess Durga replacing the goddess Laxmi, and the statement that he "never missed . . . mother."[328] In *Swatantraveer Vinayakrao Savarkar* the discussion of his mother's death is abbreviated and does not include the same number of details.

A close reading of Savarkar's autobiographical essays with these two texts illustrates many other overlaps. Both books reproduce large passages from other works as they appear within quotation marks (citations are not provided). For example, both books include excerpts of Savarkar's essays that he wrote for newspapers in Maharashtra while living in London. Parts of an essay titled "Sir Curzon Wyllie Killed," originally written by Savarkar in London on July 30, 1909, is reproduced in *Swatantraveer Vinayakrao Savarkar*, and then translated and incorporated into *Life of Barrister Savarkar*.[329] The full version of the essay was published in *Samagra Savarkar Vanmaya* as part of Savarkar's writings from London. Some of these passages are easily identifiable as Savarkar's writings, while others are more difficult to identify given issues of translation and multiple publications. The fact that the books are written in two languages also accounts for differences in emphases,

[327] MSA, HD Spec File 60-D-III-1927, "My Mother," *Hutatma Shraddhanand*, September 27, 1931, S-239.

[328] Gupta, *Life of Barrister Savarkar* (1926), 7. Savarkar published additional essays on the mother goddess in *Hutatma Shraddhanand* and Laxmi as the goddess of independence in *Savarkar Samagra*, vol. 1, 296–7, and *Samagra Savarkar*, vol. 1, 86–7. But Savarkar makes references to both Durga and Laxmi in his writings.

[329] For example, the description of the meeting of Indians in London following Madan Lal Dhingra's assassination of Curzon Wyllie (and its aftermath) illustrates the links between Savarkar's writings from London in *Samagra Savarkar Vanmaya*, vol. 4 (pages 126–9), Ranade's *Swatantraveer Vinayakrao Savarkar* (pages 44–50), and Gupta's *Life of Barrister Savarkar* (1926: pages 60–5). In other places in the texts, the overlap and repetition of words, terms, phrases, and complete sentences and paragraphs is evident between the latter three texts.

descriptions, and vocabulary. This point is most evident in the selection of Savarkar's poetry in the books.

There are many continuities across these texts, but Savarkar's critique of the interpretations and findings of the government's Sedition Committee (1918), headed by S.A.T. Rowlatt, is perhaps the most significant.[330] The resolution authorising the committee stated that its purpose was to "investigate and report on the nature and extent of the criminal conspiracies connected to the revolutionary movement in India."[331] As revolutionaries were guilty of sedition in their conduct and speech, the committee's goal was to advise the government about future legislation in response to the rise in revolutionary activity. Savarkar explained that he first read the Sedition Committee Report in 1924 when he was living in Ratnagiri.[332] He wrote an essay titled "Rowlatt Report" that was eventually published as part of his autobiographical essays in his Collected Works.[333] It is clear that members of the public had access to the report shortly after it was published, so it would not have been unusual for Savarkar to have read it.[334] His criticism centred on the fact that the report was inaccurate and revealed the limits of British surveillance practices, especially as in it he was a major subject

[330] *Sedition Committee Report, 1918* (Calcutta: Superintendent Government Printing, 1919).

[331] Resolution, Government of India, Home Department, Delhi, December 10, 1917, in *Sedition Committee Report*. (Page number not given.)

[332] Savarkar, *Inside the Enemy Camp*, 63; Savarkar, *Shatruchya Shibirata*, 128.

[333] Savarkar, *Inside the Enemy Camp*, 61; Savarkar, *Shatruchya Shibirata*, 124–6.

[334] M.K. Gandhi, for example, wrote a commentary responding to the findings of the committee regarding revolutionary activity in India, as was noted in *The Times* at the time. He argued that there was a fundamental misunderstanding by the committee that Indians were violent. As the committee was established to investigate the propensity of violence by revolutionaries in India and the UK, it was bound to conclude the centrality of violence by political actors. For Gandhi, what was missing in the report was a perspective that not all Indians advocated revolutionary violence. In other words, if the committee had focused on *ahimsa*, the conclusions would have revealed that Indians were actually non-violent.

of inquiry. Savarkar itemised the errors regarding dates and locations of meetings, chronology of events, and influences on his intellectual formation: "[I]t will be clear that many activities of Indian revolutionaries were not known to the C.I.D. Many details have been wrongly reported . . . But the information about them in the Rowlatt report is sketchy, incomplete, false or twisted."[335] He argues that the reason the British government had poor information about Indian revolutionaries was that the revolutionaries were able to evade government due to their own counter-surveillance, organisational skills, or autonomy.

The Rowlatt Committee Report was significant in providing one of the first biographical writings of revolutionaries in modern Indian history.[336] Since it was read publicly at an important historical period of anti-colonialism in India it also helped establish and promote the category of the political prisoner.[337] This was certainly the case for Savarkar, as his biographical details and revolutionary activities were discussed for the period between 1905 and 1914. All the other major figures of the time similarly had their capsule biographies included in this single government source. In many ways the report became the primary document for basic information about revolutionaries throughout India and was subsequently used to write biographies in the twentieth century.[338]

Savarkar remained ambivalent about the report as an official source. At one level he was genuinely impressed with the rigour and expansive network of British surveillance that produced such a volume. When read critically, he felt such reports could also be valuable for information often lost from memory: "In my active life, I had forgotten many details, but the British kept records of my activities. Their tenacity is

---

[335] Savarkar, *Inside the Enemy Camp*, 63; Savarkar, *Shatruchya Shibirata*, 129–30.

[336] See Ghosh, *Gentlemanly Terrorists*, 35–50.

[337] Ibid.

[338] Also see, BL, APAC, India HD Pol Proceedings, B Series, IOR. Pos.8966, "Maharatta Brahmin Extremists and Irreconcilables," in Central Provinces Police, CID, Special Publication of 1909, No. I, Report on Extremism and Extremists in Nagpur.

[339] Savarkar, *Inside the Enemy Camp*, 58; Savarkar, *Shatruchya Shibirata*, 118.

worth praising. Some of the details were published in Government reports. These are now useful for writing my autobiography."[339] This is an important revelation: he could revert to his strategies of reading against the grain to write his own life-story. His autobiographical project was in one respect a critique of colonial sources, but it was also unique in relying on these sources for material.

All the same, the number of factual errors pointed out by Savarkar meant the report was politically dangerous: if the details of his life were inaccurate, they were likely so for other revolutionaries: "Therefore the history of our revolutionary movement should not be based purely on these reports."[340] Errors in the report would be reproduced by some writers and could be codified within some histories: "It is clear how innocent writers can make such mistakes. And once they do, the mistakes become permanent."[341] In an essay called "The Story of Agamya Guru" he provided a discussion of Agamya Guru, an individual mentioned in the Sedition Committee Report as having directly influenced his politics.[342] He says he met Agamya Guru at a big function in Poona in 1906. They had a brief conversation in which Savarkar asked his advice about students interested in political activity. The Guru did not provide a response that satisfied Savarkar, especially as he asked him to organise students to collect money: "My contact with the Guru was very short. I would not have mentioned his name in my autobiography, but the Rowlatt Report . . . had made a mountain of a mole[hill]."[343] And "I have already explained how wrong it is to think that my political activities began after my meeting with Agamya Guru."[344] In fact he says the only reason Agamya Guru was

[340] Savarkar, *Inside the Enemy Camp*, 64; Savarkar, *Shatruchya Shibirata*, 130.

[341] Ibid. On this point, Savarkar appears to anticipate arguments that Ranajit Guha presented in relation to primary, secondary, and tertiary discourses. See Guha, "Prose of Counter-Insurgency."

[342] Savarkar, *Inside the Enemy Camp*, 62; Savarkar, *Shatruchya Shibirata*, 126–9.

[343] Savarkar, *Inside the Enemy Camp*, 62–3; Savarkar, *Shatruchya Shibirata*, 126.

[344] Savarkar, *Inside the Enemy Camp*, 61; Savarkar, *Shatruchya Shibirata*, 124.

included in his autobiography was the erroneous view in the Sedition Committee Report.[345] A discussion of Agamya Guru also appears in an abbreviated form in *Swatantraveer Vinayakrao Savarkar* and *Life of Barrister Savarkar*.[346] The *Life of Barrister Savarkar* says —

> [Mr. Savarkar] interviewed Agamya Guru – the Swami . . . After an informal talk for a while the swami made some ordinary and common place remarks on organisation and the interview ended. This was all that happened between Mr Savarkar and the Swami and this incident would have been forgotten as trivial but for its funny sequence. The Police seem to have marked it all and reported to their higher officers and they to theirs: till years afterwards one day Mr Savarkar was much amused to read in the Rowlatt report a passage which seriously stated that he owed his first political inspiration to Swami Agamya Guru . . . It is at times such ill-informed reports and statements that commissions sit solemnly pondering over and generally base their serious conclusions upon.[347]

While the "Publisher's Preface" to *Life of Barrister Savarkar* says the Sedition Committee Report was used to write the book, it does not explain how the author would have known Savarkar's response to the description of Agamya Guru in the report itself. (The description that Savarkar was amused by the claim that Agamya Guru introduced him to politics is also found in *Swatantraveer Vinayakrao Savarkar*.) Savarkar went on to provide a longer critique of Agamya Guru as part of his autobiography more than two decades after *Life of Barrister Savarkar*.

My purpose of providing multiple examples from Savarkar's writings that were integral to *Life of Barrister Savarkar* and *Swatantraveer Vinayakrao Savarkar* is to underscore Savarkar's involvement with both texts. In the end, nearly every narrative found in these works also appears in Savarkar's autobiographical writings, often with greater detail and information. In fact, given the involvement of Ganesh and Narayan Savarkar, Bhaurao Chiplunkar, V.V. Kelkar, and N.C. Kelkar, it would have been impossible for Ranade to publish *Swatantraveer*

<hr>

[345] *Sedition Committee Report*, 5–6.

[346] Ranade, *Swatantraveer Vinayakrao Savarkar*, 34–5; Gupta, *Life of Barrister Savarkar* (1926), 30–1.

[347] Gupta, *Life of Barrister Savarkar* (1926), 31.

*Vinayakrao Savarkar* without Savarkar's approval, authorisation, or sanction – whether implicitly or explicitly. The same can be said about *Life of Barrister Savarkar*, especially as the publisher B.G. Paul & Company secured Savarkar's approval to publish the book – as noted in the preface. At one level, it may seem unnecessary to provide these details, given the discussion of the book's authorship in the official publication of the second edition by Balarao Savarkar for Veer Savarkar Prakashan. But my argument is that it is crucial to consider Savarkar's role and involvement in these various projects in order to understand his contribution to the account of himself as an idealised revolutionary subject in the making of Hindu history. It is also necessary to explore the multiple methods of circulating Savarkar's ideas and writings within a colonial context that influenced the reception of Savarkar's life and work in the twentieth century. This is especially important because there remains an epistemic refusal by some scholars to consider Savarkar's contribution to his own biography.

Given that Savarkar's writings form the foundation for *Life of Barrister Savarkar* and *Swatantraveer Vinayakrao Savarkar*, the question that remains open for debate is whether Savarkar himself selected (and/or edited) his own texts for inclusion in *Life of Barrister Savarkar*, or whether there was an intermediary who collaborated in the process of creating an authorised edited collection and translation of Savarkar's writings (including selections of his poetry) that was then marketed as a biography.[348] Ranade's introduction to *Swatantraveer Vinayakrao Savarkar* explains that his purpose was to make accessible Savarkar's poetry, writings, and life-story to the people of Maharashtra. In consonance with Savarkar's other books, the text needed to be published in English so that Savarkar's life-story could be read nationally. Narayan Savarkar pointed out that he had possession of his brother's publications and drafts of his autobiography, which is clear from the many direct quotes from them in *Life of Barrister Savarkar*. It is also clear that Savarkar either wrote new material or narrated the information included in the book after his release from the Andamans, especially as figures

[348] "Just Out! Order At Once. Life of Barrister Savarkar by Chitragupta," Advertisement, *Bombay Chronicle*, March 19, 1927. The advertisement also mentions the involvement of "a close friend," but no other information is given.

like Kelkar had met Savarkar prior to writing their own work about him. The spelling errors in *Swatantraveer Vinayakrao Savarkar* were corrected in *Life of Barrister Savarkar*. Savarkar's signature epigraphs appeared at the start of every chapter but were not present in Ranade's book. The fact that the narratives from *Life of Barrister Savarkar* and *Swatantraveer Vinayakrao Savarkar* were included in Savarkar's autobiographical writings makes it clear that these were basically autobiographical narratives of Savarkar's larger project to tell the story of his life.

The fact that Savarkar was unable to publish his autobiography due to restrictions imposed by the government is the primary factor that helps to explain the unusual publication history of these texts. An unintended consequence of these publications is that they appear to follow methodological practices used by the authors of *bakhar*s, in which research shows authors typically consulting individuals who had specific knowledge, dependable sources, and personal experience of events to write their narratives.[349] At times the information was conveyed orally, but in other instances written texts were consulted. We recall in this context that in 1909 Savarkar had promoted the idea of speaking to witnesses and participants of 1857 for writing histories. In a *bakhar* the author sometimes relied on older narratives to construct a new narrative. Some *bakhar* authors fully incorporated an entire *bakhar* when writing a new *bakhar*, especially when writing the life-story of Shivaji. In the process shorter *bakhar*s served as the foundation for writing longer *bakhar*s with new materials and con-temporary interpretations. Not surprisingly, each version of the *bakhar* was scrutinised, as interpretations of the new version were contested and the authenticity of the author challenged.

The process at work with Savarkar's life is similar. Published and unpublished writings and oral narratives provided the material for Ranade (and Kelkar) in *Swatantraveer Vinayakrao Savarkar*. Parts of the text were incorporated, sometimes verbatim, into *Life of Barrister Savarkar*, which also included additional material by Savarkar and new sources in the appendices. There was a reliance on sources and narratives from the earlier book, but *Life of Barrister Savarkar* was in

---

[349] Deshpande, *Creative Pasts*, 28–39.

English with translations of Marathi texts included. Indra Prakash then copied seven chapters of *Life of Barrister Savarkar* and added five new chapters of material based on additional writings by Savarkar. The fact that *Life of Barrister Savarkar* was revised and translated into multiple languages further adds to the conclusion that it functioned as a modern *bakhar* for those interested in Savarkar's life-story.[350]

The most important work that relied on the narratives in *Life of Barrister Savarkar* was Dhananjay Keer's *Savarkar and His Times* (1950). Keer produced the best-known and most widely read biography of Savarkar in English. In 1966 he published a revised edition of the book with a new title: *Veer Savarkar*. This added seven chapters to the original edition. As with the practice of writing *bakhars*, Keer not only incorporated narratives (and poems) that appear in *Life of Barrister Savarkar*, he also says the book was written in consultation with Savarkar: "The valuable new information and new facts I could get through research and through a plethora of material which was kindly made available to me by Savarkar himself and through his kind interviews, were inserted at their proper places in historical sequence."[351] Keer's book was the last biography of Savarkar in which Savarkar himself was actively involved.

In sum, it can be said with considerable certainty that until 1966, when he passed away, Savarkar either authored or was substantially involved in every biography and narrative centred on his life.

## 5. The Plural Identities of the Hero

It is important to consider the plurality of identities included in *Life of Barrister Savarkar*, the text that helped to define the meaning of *veer* in relation to Savarkar. The book also serves as a reminder that

---

[350] Karandikar's *Savarkar Charitra Kathan* appears to expand the idea of a critical edition of Savarkar's writings in the guise of a biography by incorporating many sources, including Savarkar's essays, letters, and poems, as well as newspaper articles and official reports to construct a more robust text covering the exact period in *Life of Barrister Savarkar* and *Swatantraveer Vinayakrao Savarkar*.

[351] Keer, *Veer Savarkar*, vii.

the categories used to describe Savarkar were already part of public debates. The Sedition Committee Report, for example, said Chitpavan Brahmins in Maharashtra were participants in revolutionary activities against the British government in India and Britain. Its lengthy analysis of Savarkar showed his Brahminism as connected to his revolutionary politics. For government, these links helped to explain the nature of criminal activity at the time. For Savarkar, they helped to reveal aspects of his bravery. *Life of Barrister Savarkar* provided a corrective to the government's classifications of Savarkar. The plural identities of Savarkar in it serve as antonyms to the official record – a point that Savarkar repeated in his autobiographical writings. Savarkar embodies a plurality of identities that allow him to be formally identified as the ultimate hero of Hindu history. "Veer Savarkar" was now the authorised identity of Savarkar as the writer of history *and* the maker of history.

## The Chitpavan Brahmin

*Life of Barrister Savarkar* begins with a brief genealogy, a characteristic often found in *caritas*. But despite the fact that Savarkar's father Damodarpant is named in the book's first sentence, it is not the typical genealogy that specifically focuses on the patrilineal origins of Savarkar's family. Rather, it is a modern political genealogy connecting Savarkar, who is identified as "the distinguished patriot," to "an unbroken succession" of "Maratha Brahmin" men known as Chitpavans.[352] Chitpavan Brahmins are also described as "the vanguard of the Indian forces in the struggle for Indian freedom."[353]

> The first Peshwa Balaji Vishwanath was a [C]hitpavan. Bajirao, who was one of the foremost generals India ever produced, was a [C]hitpavan; the hero of Panipat was a [C]hitpavan[.] Nana Fadnavis the great Indian Statesman, Nana Saheb, who rose in the national rising of 1857, Vasodeo Balwant, who revolted against the British Government and aimed to achieve Indian Independence, the Chapekar brothers and Ranade who were hanged as murderers for killing the British officers responsible for the

[352] Gupta, *Life of Barrister Savarkar* (1926), 1.
[353] Ibid.

Plague administration in Poona, were all [C]hitpavans. Shrijut Gokhale, Justice Ranade and the Great Tilak . . . were [C]hitpavans.[354]

his genealogy provides a direct link between Savarkar and the Peshwas discussed in *Hindu Pad Padashahi*, along with the revolutionary leaders in *Indian War*. The caste of the Chitpavan Brahmin was not only central to the development of Savarkar as a revolutionary, but also all the major figures Savarkar had discussed: "No wonder then that destiny should have chosen this particular caste to bring forth and nestle the child which was to be . . . one of the most brilliant modern Indian revolutionists."[355] In other words, *Life of Barrister Savarkar* begins with the birth of Savarkar as the modern political subject whose identity as a Chitpavan Brahmin is intertwined with being a "patriot," a "man," a "son," a "brother," a "Maratha," an "Indian," "an anti-imperialist," and a "revolutionary" – all in the first paragraph. It is assumed that the readers will understand the ontological links between Savarkar as a Chitpavan Brahmin and his political subjectivity. The only other reference to Savarkar's caste is discussed in an episode when an Arab vowed to forcibly convert Savarkar to Islam by "thrusting a piece of fried fish into his Brahmanic mouth."[356] This was "the approved method" used by Muslim boys to target Brahmins. While Savarkar's identity as a Chitpavan Brahmin frames the entire life-story in *Life of Barrister Savarkar*, no further explanation is given about Savarkar's Brahminism. Nor is there any further discussion about caste in the book.

## *The Maratha*

In addition to locating Savarkar in the Chitpavan Brahmin genealogy in *Life of Barrister Savarkar*, he was also identified as a Maratha.[357] "A Maratha" was his pen name in *Essentials of Hindutva* and the two identities could not be disentangled here: all Chitpavan Brahmins were

---

[354] Ibid., 1–2.

[355] Ibid., 2.

[356] Ibid., 5.

[357] The book is full of references to Savarkar and other Chitpavan Brahmins as Marathas: "Maratha Brahmin" (1); "[M]aratha nationalists" (3); "Maratha patriot" (19); "Maratha leader" (113).

Marathas. It is clear in the text that this interpretation of "Maratha" is from the perspective of a Chitpavan Brahmin man. The distinction implies alternative ways of being a Maratha: examples are given of Marathas who were not Chitpavan Brahmin men; these individuals were clearly not the "vanguard," but they were important Marathas nonetheless. The contributions of Maratha women are also celebrated: they had "sailed the waters of Bombay," and "commanded flotillas" over the past two centuries,[358] contrasting with the "unmanly" status of contemporary men.[359] Shivaji is of course the exemplary Maratha male who, though not a Brahmin, provided major contributions to the making of "the Maratha."

*Life of Barrister Savarkar* suggests in addition that Savarkar's Maratha identity is based not only on his caste (Chitpavan Brahmin) and masculinity, but also on a shared territory (Maharashtra), a shared language and literature (Marathi), and a shared history. However, there is no explicit description or genealogy of the "Maratha," in comparison to the "Chitpavan Brahmin." Rather, there are examples of everyday practices that constituted his Maratha identity, especially during his formative childhood. His "patriotic and poetical inclinations" are attributed to his father, who introduced him to the oral and literary traditions of the Marathi language.[360] At a young age Savarkar was immersed in the world of Marathi poetry, ballads, songs, and histories. By the time he was ten, he was already producing Marathi poetry, following in a long line of established Marathi poets such as Moropant and Vaman. He had also learned about Maratha figures like Shivaji, Pratap, and Bhau by reading *bakhars* his "mental food."[361] These *bakhars* made him familiar with "the exploits of the Marathas in their Imperial days." He learned about Shivaji's war tactics, including guerrilla warfare. He was also interested in visiting important historical locations in Maharashtra with fellow Maratha students, because "history was his special pursuit" – it provided examples of Maratha heroes.[362] Savarkar, as a member of the Maratha "vanguard," took it

[358] Ibid., 34.
[359] Ibid.
[360] Ibid., 2.
[361] Ibid., 3.
[362] Ibid., 18.

upon himself to serve on the frontline in not only educating Maratha men but also leading them by example:

> He and his comrades . . . undertook trips to the old castles associated with heroic deeds of their forefathers. In one such trip they visited Sinhgad, immortally associated with Tanaji's name, and there they restated their faith and standing in reverence to the heroic memory of the dead warrior, reaffirmed their determination and prayed that they might be given strength to die doing their duty by their race and their people and their motherland even as faithfully as Tanaji had done.[363]

Savarkar is also shown as influenced by contemporary intellectuals writing in Marathi newspapers: Bal Gangadhar Tilak, Shivram Mahadeo Paranjape, and Chiplunkar. His goal like theirs was to influence the "minds of Indian youth" to effect political change.[364] Reading newspaper accounts of suffering Marathas in places like Bombay, Poona, and Yeola created an emotional response in the young Savarkar, who vowed vengeance against the enemy and took to "Marathi eloquence and revolutionary literature."[365] Maratha patriotism in public life was thriving due to the efforts of a number of great men, including Savarkar. In addition to delivering public lectures throughout Maharashtra, Savarkar introduced the Maharashtrian festivals of Shivaji and Ganpati into his village, Bhagur. Throughout *Life of Barrister Savarkar*, Savarkar is described as contributing to Marathi literary culture as a poet, journalist, polemicist, and historian. Excerpts from Marathi poems by him illustrate his influence. For example, a moment in England when Savarkar was overcome with emotions about "home" led him to produce a poem now on the "lips of all Maharashtra":

> Take me Oh[,] ocean!
> Take me back to those my native shores!
> I long, I pine for those native shores!
> Take me Oh[,] ocean to those my native shores![366]

[363] Ibid., 21–2.
[364] Ibid., 2.
[365] Ibid., 20.
[366] Ibid., 70.

## *The Son / The Man*

Vinayak was the middle son of Damodarpant Savarkar. Ganesh was the eldest, Narayan the youngest. The "Savarkar Brothers," as the three were known, had a sister; her name is not given. Nor are the names of his mother, who died when Vinayak was ten, or of his wife. In fact, the names of the women in Savarkar's personal life are not mentioned in *Life of Barrister Savarkar* and they are only identified by their relationship to him: that is, "sister," "sister-in-law," "wife," and "mother." The only woman named in the text is Madame Bhikaiji Cama, a member of his political organisation in London and Paris, and a public figure in Europe. The names of Savarkar's father and brothers are introduced in the context of the political genealogy of Chitpavan Brahmin men; no women are included in the genealogy. Cama, as a woman and Zoroastrian, could not belong to Savarkar's political genealogy. In other words, in addition to Savarkar's Brahminism, what also frames the life-story in *Life of Barrister Savarkar* is masculinity. In fact, the epigraph to the chapter entitled "Childhood and Early Youth" is an excerpt from "Oh, Hush Thee, My Baby" by Sir Walter Scott, which describes how the life of a baby will be transformed when he awakes from his sleep into "manhood."[367] Becoming a "man" is not without conflict and struggle. Scott is further quoted: "For strife comes with manhood and waking with day." It was essential for Savarkar to understand his own awakening into manhood as central to the life-story. And, the first lessons in becoming a man meant understanding the importance of being the son of Damodarpant Savarkar.

Savarkar is described as a dutiful son who sat at his father's feet listening to poetry, songs, and epic stories. The Mahabharata, the Ramayana, and the "old Bhakars" helped form his identity as a patriot. But he also enjoyed the stories of Agamemnon and Achilles, and the Marathi poetry of Vaman, Moropant, and Tukaram. By the age of ten he was publishing his own poetry in newspapers, reflecting his father's literary influences and marking his birth as a writer. Damodar recognised his son's precocity and interest in revolutionary politics and "discouraged" him from writing ballads, poetry, or articles that might be considered seditious. He guided him towards "lighter" and "gayer" topics more suited to a child: "Child, thou art still too

---

[367] Ibid., 1.

young . . . When thou comest to manhood thou will be more able to fashion ways and means to render thy mission fruitful."[368] But even as an adolescent Savarkar opted to continue his political work in secrecy as part of an underground political movement in western India. Unfortunately, Damodarpant was unable to witness Savarkar's accomplishments: he died during the plague epidemic in the early 1890s. Despite being now orphaned, Savarkar could not "desist from or forget his political mission."[369]

Before his father's death he had already found a surrogate mother: the goddess Durga. He shared with her his hopes and dreams; to her he confided his secrets and anxieties; he spent hours taking care of her; he wrote poems for her. In response, she provided "miraculous help."

> Durga had grown into a living and loving and as real a mother as any incorporated human being could be . . . At her feet he would sit for hours and hours, at times so completely lost in communion as to lose all outward consciousness. To her he would relate to [as] a mother . . . invoke her assistance in his dreamy schemes of waging terrible wars for the liberation of his land and his race.[370]

In this way Savarkar continued a dutiful son despite the absence of biological parents: "Vinayak especially never missed his mother."[371] This was in part because his father made Savarkar and his siblings "forget that they had ever lost a mother."

As the son of Durga, Savarkar was linked to the heroic Shivaji: "[Savarkar] exhorted Her to bless the cause of Indian Independence even as She blessed it in the days of Shivaji."[372] Durga's great powers are associated with the political power of dutiful sons. But Savarkar had noted a problem: his mother was in "bondage" and needed to be "liberated." Durga was not simply his mother, she was also "Mother India." Her survival was the survival of India. It was the duty of the son to help his mother, which meant helping India:

> [Savarkar] solemnly stood up and took the vow of dedicating his life and if need be his death to the mission of liberating India from the fetters that

[368] Ibid., 12.
[369] Ibid., 15.
[370] Ibid., 7.
[371] Ibid.
[372] Ibid., 10.

held Her in bondage. He would carry forth the torch of his fiery resolve and set the youth of India aflame! He would organise a secret society, arm and equip his countrymen and fight out the grand struggle and if need be to die sword in hand in Her cause.[373]

This moment of recognising the plight of the mother marked an important shift for Savarkar. As her son he was committed to fighting for "Mother India" despite the persistence of those who refused to accept Durga, or her bondage as real. He acknowledged that many benighted individuals might consider his arguments "childish," "cynical," or "delusional." But what mattered to him was that Durga accepted him as her son: "[She] stood there he thought, smiling, parental, witnessing his high resolve."[374] She guided him to travel to England so that he could fulfil his potential as a man and a revolutionary: "She wants her sons to go to foreign lands for a while, that they may learn what the world is like, what the strength of their foes and what the weaknesses of themselves. She wants them to grow strong and manly and daring . . . and learn how to organise a Revolution."[375] It is worth noting that the first sentence of *Life of Barrister Savarkar* begins by identifying Savarkar's father while its last sentence centres on the mother. At the end of *Life of Barrister Savarkar*, Savarkar is described as citing a song celebrating the role of the mother as responsible for not only the "birth" of her children, but also for providing food and nourishment. As Mother India she represents her children politically: "Oh Mother . . . rout the forces of Evil . . . [and] plant the golden Banner of Righteousness and Independence on the triumphant Tops of the Himalayas."[376] Children are forever "indebted" to the mother for her "service."

## *The Hindu*

By the time Savarkar completed *Life of Barrister Savarkar*, *Essentials of Hindutva* had already been in circulation for four years. His definition of a Hindu was part of public debate. There are, of course, traces of

[373] Ibid.
[374] Ibid.
[375] Ibid., 35.
[376] Ibid., 118.

his interpretation of a Hindu found in the text, especially his arguments about civilisation and culture. Further, the framing of Savarkar's identity, as the "Chitpavan Brahmin," the "son," and "man" are central to his understanding of "the Hindu." In *Life of Barrister Savarkar*, the period between 1893 and 1895 is characterised as "fanaticism" because of communal violence between Hindus and Muslims. As a child of that time Savarkar is identified as an avid reader of newspapers that informed him of "tales of Moslem outrages of the usual inhuman type" against Hindus.[377] This "fired the blood of young Vinayak. He could not rest without wreaking some vengeance on the Moslem for the outrages they had inflicted on his co-religionists in Bombay and other places in India."[378] Vengeance, as in Savarkar's other writings, binds Hindus as the real and imagined community. The confirmation of being a Hindu lies not simply in the recognition of the plight of other Hindus, but in acts of violence against their Muslim oppressors. Despite his childhood uncertainties about fulfilling this desire for violence, he did not stop inventing "mock fights" between Hindus and Muslims in which Hindus always won their battles against the "Aliens." Savarkar's identity as a Hindu was now complete.

## *The Revolutionary*

While Savarkar has plural identities in the text, "the revolutionary" is central among them. In the preface to the second edition of *Life of Barrister Savarkar*, Ravindra Vaman Ramdas argued that the author had a specific purpose in writing the book: celebrating Savarkar as *the* revolutionary: "The Life [of Barrister Savarkar] deals with the formative years of work of the Revolutionary on European soil."[379] It starts with a discussion of Savarkar as "one of the most brilliant Indian revolutionists," and the early chapters emphasise his childhood as guided by revolutionary principles.[380] His father "[was] anxious as to the dangerous turn that his young son's life was likely to take if allowed long to feed

---

[377] Ibid., 4.

[378] Ibid.

[379] Ravindra Vaman Ramdas, "Preface," in Chitragupta, *Life of Barrister Savarkar* (1987). (Page number not listed.)

[380] Gupta, *Life of Barrister Savarkar* (1926), 2.

itself on such revolutionary thoughts unchecked."[381] By the age of fourteen Savarkar had taken a vow to commit his life to political agitation against British rule. He soon began a propaganda campaign to inspire other youth and was himself inspired by the Chapekar brothers – who had assassinated the British official W.C. Rand in 1897. After the Chapekars were arrested and executed, the young Savarkar produced a "fiery ballad," further exemplifying his "revolutionary thoughts."[382] In 1900 he founded a secret society called Mitra Mela, described in *Life of Barrister Savarkar* as a "revolutionary organisation" set up for "Instruction, Insurrection, and Action."[383] Its primary objective was to achieve "Political Independence of India," even by "armed rebellion." Under Savarkar's leadership, the Mitra Mela was very active, organising the Shivaji and Ganpati festivals, delivering public lectures on "revolutionary doctrines," and running study groups to discuss history. It served as a "real national university" to "train patriots to think [and] act," whose purpose in learning history was "not only to admire the heroes that died for their country in the past, but also to act themselves as patriotically and die as heroically even in the present."[384] What is striking about *Life of Barrister Savarkar* is that nearly every page of the slim text has a reference to Savarkar as a revolutionary.

In 1901, as a student at Fergusson College in Pune, Savarkar was able to spread his political message throughout Maharashtra. Over the four years he was a college student he was "ceaselessly circulating his revolutionary tenets" and had read "almost all revolutionary history".[385] His immersion in the study of world history by reading all the volumes of the "Story of the Nations" attracted him to Mazzini, Shivaji, Garibaldi, and Ramdas. He began to compose "revolutionary songs" while also delivering lectures on the "stages of revolutionary evolution" by discussing the history of the Italian revolution.[386] His purpose was to "sow the seeds of revolution in Maharashtra."[387]

[381] Ibid., 13.
[382] Ibid., 11–12.
[383] Ibid., 16.
[384] Ibid., 17.
[385] Ibid., 18.
[386] Ibid., 20, 27.
[387] Ibid., 20.

His supporters came to be known as the "Savarkar Camp." They would meet on Sunday evenings at an abandoned temple to craft a plan to "arm the nation for the War of Independence."[388] To become members of "Savarkar's Camp" students had to take a vow to "sacrifice in the sacred cause of Indian Independence." Savarkar's supporters "all dressed alike, lived frugally, studied hard, passed their examinations regularly, used swadeshi, took manly exercises[,] and discussed nothing but the political questions [of how] nations in the world shook off their fetters of bondage . . ."[389]

By 1905 Savarkar was on a lecturing campaign in Maharashtra, often delivering up to four lectures a day in front of thousands of people. He conceived the idea of boycotting foreign-made cloth and is shown as the first person in India to organise the burning of such cloth in large bonfires across Maharashtra. *Life of Barrister Savarkar* suggests Savarkar was the founder of the Swadeshi movement – which later took hold in Bengal.

Later in the year Savarkar graduated from Fergusson College with a Bachelor of Arts, and was now committed to spreading revolution beyond Maharashtra, in all the neighbouring provinces. In this period he brought a number of secret organisations together to form the Abhinav Bharat Society. This organisation had a lasting impact in India and Europe, but Savarkar wanted to emphasise its origins as part of his political activity. He composed revolutionary songs and ballads to convey his message to the masses. The government banned his compositions because of their seditious content, but because of the oral culture of Maharashtra "the ballads lived and thrived . . . [they] can still be heard recited in towns and hamlets amidst admiring circles of the Maratha people."[390]

In 1906 Savarkar moved to England to study law at Gray's Inn. But his real purpose was to "scatter the seeds of Indian revolution."[391] More generally, he argued it was essential for Indians to travel to Europe to further their education: "We must go to England, France and Russia and learn how to organise a Revolution, [and] win back our

[388] Ibid.
[389] Ibid., 21.
[390] Ibid., 27.
[391] Ibid., 29.

Freedom."[392] He saw it was necessary to contact fellow Indian students so that they could be "initiated and trained to revolutionary thought and action."[393] He was interested in meeting revolutionaries in Russian secret organisations to learn their tactics for overthrowing the Russian czarist regime. Upon arriving in London he moved into India House, which was headed by Shyamji Krishnavarma, a leading voice of anti-imperialism in Britain. Savarkar is described as assuming the leadership of all Indian revolutionaries in Britain, many of whom resided in India House. Here he converted Krishnavarma to revolutionary politics as well. He delivered speeches on the history of revolutionary wars in Italy, France, and the United States. As his influence grew, he was soon organising revolutionaries from different parts of the world for a global revolution against British imperialism. Although this plan did not come to fruition, his leadership role is shown as comparable to that of Garibaldi and Lenin; his life is compared to that of Mazzini, Lajos Kossuth (the Hungarian revolutionary leader), and Peter Kropotkin (the Russian anarcho-communist). No explanatory discussion is provided for these choices.

Singlehandedly he transforms the political landscape in Britain, while influencing every intellectual who interacted with him – even those who opposed his revolutionary politics. He is depicted as prophetic in anticipating the development of revolutionary politics in India and beyond. Indians across the globe adopted his ideas and were translating them into revolutionary acts, big and small. This was also possible due to Savarkar's ability to smuggle weapons into India, publish newspaper articles, establish collaborations with political groups in Europe, deliver speeches on Indian revolutionary movements, and publish revolutionary pamphlets.

Savarkar's activities, along with those of his collaborators, are shown as reaching an important conjuncture when Madan Lal Dhingra assassinates Curzon Wyllie and Savarkar publicly defended him for his ethical act of revolutionary violence against an official who persecuted Indians for their desire to defend "Mother India."

His support to Dhingra increased government efforts to control his activities, and Krishnavarma's India House was eventually shut down.

[392] Ibid., 35.
[393] Ibid., 29.

Most individuals fled Britain to Paris to escape prosecution. Savarkar also arrived in Paris but was mistaken in returning to London, being arrested in 1910. His fellow revolutionaries were apparently "demoralised" by this unjust act. The British government decided it would not try Savarkar in London; it shipped Savarkar back to India for a criminal trial. Savarkar is described as drawing inspiration from the story of an unnamed Russian revolutionary who escaped from a prison in czarist Russia. The last chapter of the text discusses Savarkar's escape from British custody in Marseilles, France, and his eventual recapture. Savarkar was by this time recognised as a political prisoner and revolutionary throughout the world.

*Life of Barrister Savarkar* ends with how Savarkar continued promoting the revolutionary principles of the Abhinav Bharat Society to other prisoners while on trial. He "refused to recognise the authority of British Courts in India."[394] He said: "I am prepared to face ungrudgingly the extreme penalty of your laws, in the belief that it is through sufferings and sacrifice alone that our beloved Motherland can march on to an assured . . . triumph!"[395] His power to convert individuals to a "revolutionary mentality" continued despite his conviction to two life-terms in the Cellular Jail.

## 6. Conclusion

Savarkar wanted to remain hidden as an author of his texts, but he also wanted the subject and the name "Savarkar" to be public. Prior to his arrest in 1910 he was an established public intellectual. In addition to authoring books, his journalistic writings were published in India, Britain, and the US. His political activities were discussed in newspapers around the world. Even before the publication of *Life of Barrister Savarkar*, his life was the subject of public debate. The fact that he was in British custody meant it was impossible for him to be present in public, yet Savarkar's texts found their way into print, especially in the 1920s. His body of work was now traversing India, even as the government restricted his movements.

[394] Ibid., 117.
[395] Ibid.

Savarkar's writing strategies had a lasting impact. He presented himself as a heroic subject in the very terms he had discussed historical heroes. He was no longer only a writer of Hindu history; he was also the maker of Hindu history. The Hindu spirit had travelled across time and was embodied by Savarkar in his thought and actions. The government remained opposed to his autobiography and biography even decades after the publication of *Life of Barrister Savarkar*. For example, on April 4, 1941 the Madras High Court rejected S. Krishnamurthi Ayyar's petition to have his Tamil-language biography *Vira Savarkar* removed from a list of proscribed works under the Press (Emergency Powers) Act of 1931.[396] The Crown Prosecutor C.J. Leach argued that the publication of Savarkar's life-story was likely to "encourage the commission of murder" or "incite" other acts of violence.[397] The judges agreed with the government's assessment.[398] A similar decision was reached in the Bombay High Court in 1943 regarding S.L. Karandikar's *Savarkar Charitra Kathan*. The court upheld the government's proscription of the book on the grounds that "the book contained matter which expressed admiration of persons who had been convicted and tended to incite the commission of offences."[399] It was irrelevant that Savarkar had been released from British custody after having served as a political prisoner in 1937. Nor did it matter that Savarkar as president of the Akhil Bharatiya Hindu Mahasabha (1937–44) was already a public figure whose name and activities regularly appeared in the regional, national, and international press.

Savarkar had used pseudonyms for three of his four texts, but officials were able to ascertain his authorship in each case. In these texts Savarkar

[396] A.I.R. (29) 1942 Madras 690, Special Bench, Leach, C.J., Mockett and Krishnaswami Ayyangar, in regards S. Krishnamurthi Ayyar, Petitioner, April 4, 1941, in *The All India Reporter, 1942: Madras Section* (Nagpur: D.V. Chitaley, 1942), 690–1.

[387] Ibid.

[398] For a case on *Life of Barrister Savarkar* in the Bombay High Court, see "Security Order Set Aside. High Court Decision," *The Times of India*, October 13, 1944.

[399] "Poona Press's Appeal," *The Times of India*, December 17, 1943. In 1946 the government allowed Karandikar's book to be published. See "Bombay Training in Police," *The Times of India*, May 2, 1946.

appears to put on what Derrida calls a "community of masks."[400] The pseudonyms, or masks, provided Savarkar with a "yield of protection" and a type of "surplus value" that allowed him to put his own name forward in public without actually revealing his proper identity. For Derrida the pseudonym contributes to the "ruse of life" of the author – a trick for advancing the author's life and work. On the other hand the surplus value of the pseudonym diminishes when the author is unmasked; this consequence is also a possibility for the "proper name" of the author who opts to hide his or her identity.

Savarkar's case suggests otherwise. The revelation of Savarkar as "A Maratha" and "An Indian Nationalist" only elevated his status among many readers. In fact Savarkar came to embody both "Maratha" and "Indian Nationalist" throughout his political career, especially in narrative accounts of his life and work. At another level, remaining hidden protected Savarkar, providing him the mask necessary to put forward his life and work in *Life of Barrister Savarkar*. He gained enormous "surplus value" in the twentieth century by advancing his corpus, his life-story, and his "proper name."[401] Chitra Gupta's interpretation of the life of Savarkar became central to all later narrative accounts; it also influenced or inspired individuals across the political spectrum through the twentieth century.

The great irony is that some incidents narrated in *Life of Barrister Savarkar* show Savarkar as obscure. In one incident, Savarkar waits to be interviewed by a newspaper journalist in London. The journalist walks into a waiting room where Savarkar is sitting, turns to a maid, and asks, "But where is Mr. Savarkar?" The maid points to Savarkar: "There he is: That is Mr. Savarkar." The journalist is still not convinced and refuses to believe her. He then asks Savarkar if he is "really Savarkar." Savarkar replies, "Yes!"[402]

There is another moment in the book when Savarkar is described as attending a large public meeting in London after Madan Lal Dhingra's assassination of Curzon Wyllie. Savarkar is the sole dissenting voice at the meeting when Dhingra is denounced. Savarkar shouts his objection several times before he is heard. His opposition to the verdict

[400] Derrida, *The Ear of the Other*, 7.
[401] Ibid.
[402] Gupta, *Life of Barrister Savarkar* (1926), 47.

angers the crowd, with many asking, "Where is he! Who is he! What is his name?" Savarkar replies, "It is me and here [I] am; my name is Savarkar."[403]

*Life of Barrister Savarkar* is not the life of a religious leader or military officer, as often found in conventional biographies of the time, yet the text appears to be influenced by earlier traditions of genealogies and hagiographies. It is not a complete portrait, focusing only on the period between 1883, the year Savarkar was born, and 1911, when he was convicted. This portrait was revised and expanded by Indra Prakash to account for Savarkar's life between 1911 and 1939, but it too remained an incomplete picture.

The unmasking of Savarkar has made it difficult to identify the genre of *Life of Barrister Savarkar*: it is both a biography and an autobiography, without necessarily being committed to either form or structure. Savarkar evoked both genres as narrator and protagonist while keeping his identity hidden. Ironically, there is a discussion in an appendix about the need for a "worthy biographer" to write a "life-sketch" of Savarkar, perhaps suggesting that *Life of Barrister Savarkar* was either incomplete or insufficient as a biography, or both. It was also noted in an appendix to *Life of Barrister Savarkar* that future biographies would have to provide "the fuller history of his life."[404] This was an important provocation. Savarkar's conceptualisation of Hindutva as a history in full was articulated as a strategy for writing about his thoughts and actions. Veer Savarkar was now a subject of Hindu history for posterity.

403 Ibid., 61.
404 Ibid., 126.

# PART IV

# The Impossible History

To Hinduise your activities by buying all Hindu literature,
Veer Savarkar's books, Hindu-Patriots' Photographs,
Hindu-badges-flags, legitimate weapons & Hindu-made
articles useful in daily life.
**Advertisement for *Hindu-Bhandar* (Bombay), 1941,
taken from Bhide, ed., *Veer Savarkar's
"Whirl-wind Propaganda"***

*Left to Right:* Vinayak Damodar Savarkar, Narayan Damodar Savarkar, and Ganesh Damodar Savarkar, photographed by Narayan Vinayak Virkar (c. 1920s–1930s).
*Photo credit:* This image was previously published in Kirti Phadtare Pandey, "The Other Savarkar," *The Quint*, March 16, 2021.

# 1. Introduction

Nathuram Godse, who killed M.K. Gandhi by shooting him three times on January 30, 1948, made a special request to the court after his arrest. In order to prepare his official statement, Godse wanted to read Vinayak Damodar Savarkar's presidential addresses delivered at the annual Akhil Bharatiya Hindu Mahasabha meetings from 1937 to 1942.[1] On December 30, 1937 Savarkar was elected president of the Akhil Bharatiya Hindu Mahasabha and delivered his first presidential address in Ahmedabad.[2] During his tenure as president his speeches included discussions of the key arguments of *Essentials of Hindutva*, while also providing analyses of major events affecting Hindus in the context of Indian nationalism in the 1930s and 1940s. They were accessible interpretations of the text meant for a mass audience. To put it differently, Savarkar's conceptual writings on Hindutva were being put on view in juxtaposition with the praxis of Hindu nationalist politics.

Godse's request to read Savarkar's addresses appeared to be consistent with the last statement he made in court on May 5, 1949 in the "Answer to Charge Sheet."[3] He stated: "[A]bove all I have studied very closely whatever Veer Savarkar and Gandhiji had written and spoken, as to my mind these two ideologies have contributed more to the moulding of the thought and action of the Indian people during the last thirty years or so, than any other single factor has done."[4] His assassination of Gandhi would therefore seem the apotheosis of translating Savarkar's thought into action. But Godse, who completed a short book called *May It Please Your Honour* – in which he offered what he saw as a full explanation for murdering Gandhi – denied inspiration

---

[1] "Arms From Kirkee Arsenal Men: Approver's Evidence," *The Times of India*, July 28, 1948. I owe special thanks to Neeti Nair for this reference. The speeches were later published in a volume titled *Hindu Rashtra Darshan* in 1949.

[2] Bhide, ed., *Veer Savarkar's "Whirl-wind Propaganda,"* v; "Presidential Address, 19th Session of the Akhil Bharatiya Hindu Mahasabha, Ahmedabad, 1937," in Savarkar, *Hindu Rashtra Darshan*, 5–27.

[3] Godse, *May It Please Your Honour* (1977), 15.

[4] Ibid.

from Savarkar.[5] He argued in it that Savarkar did not influence him: "I deny categorically what the Prosecution has so falsely maintained that I was guided in my action by Veer Savarkar."[6] Savarkar was tried as one of the nine conspirators in Gandhi's death but eventually acquitted due to insufficient evidence. Godse was found guilty and executed.

For over seven decades, scholars have debated Savarkar's role in the assassination.[7] Godse did see himself as Savarkar's disciple – on this the historical record removes the possibility of doubt, thereby connecting the two for posterity. And Savarkar's association with, or link to, Gandhi's murderer was not a surprise for officials. In 1936 G.K. Joshi, the district magistrate of Ratnagiri, submitted a report to the government in which he explained that it was possible to imagine that Savarkar *could* kill Gandhi: "In the India of 1937–38, I wonder what [Savarkar] will say about Mr Gandhi and Mr Gandhi about him. Sitting in an armchair, it is easy to visualise Savarkar with a revolver in hand following someone for his blood. But it is far more difficult to do what one visualises."[8] Joshi's report was filed while Savarkar's movements were restricted to Ratnagiri. In other words, twelve years before Gandhi's assassination, an official perception was already circulating about the plausibility of Savarkar's role in a future murder of the Mahatma. Perhaps this was to be expected: government officials were well aware of Savarkar's connection with other assassinations. His first major appearance in the Indian and British press began, as we have seen, with his public defence of Madan Lal Dhingra in July 1909. In December 1909 a handgun sent by Savarkar from London to India was used in the assassination of A.M.T. Jackson, the district magistrate of Nasik. Savarkar was eventually arrested and convicted for his role

[5] Also, NMML, Akhil Bharat Hindu Mahasabha Papers, File C-88, Letter from Nathuram Godse, to All the Friends, November 15, 1949.

[6] Godse, *May It Please Your Honour* (1977), 10.

[7] Gandhi, *"Let's Kill Gandhi!"*; Ghosh, *Gandhi Murder Trial*; Khosla, *The Murder of the Mahatma*; Malgonkar, *The Men Who Killed Gandhi*; Nandy, "Final Encounter"; Noorani, *Savarkar and Hindutva*.

[8] MSA, HD Spec File Number 60-D (g), part I (1936), Report from G.K. Joshi, District Magistrate, Ratnagiri, to the Secretary to Government, HD Pol, Bombay, November 1, 1936. Emphasis added.

in the Nasik case. He was viewed as the inspiration of the murderers; he was never the individual who pulled the trigger.

Gandhi's death marked an important turning point in Savarkar's political career. In many ways it marked the end of his public life despite the official judgment that there was insufficient evidence to convict him. With the exception of a small number of dedicated followers, he was now largely viewed as *the* enemy because his political opponents continued to associate him with the murder. Godse's final writings explain that he felt estranged by Savarkar's decision to recognise Congress as leading the "National Government of Hindusthan" while also being "loyal" to the "Free Indian State."[9] For Godse, any acknowledgement of India in this context necessarily meant an acceptance of Partition. Godse had also been made unhappy by Savarkar reprimanding him: "[W]hen Veer Savarkar read the report of [our] demonstration, instead of appreciating our move, he called me and blamed me privately for such anarchical tactics."[10] Godse claimed he had decided that he would no longer consult Savarkar or confide in him about any of his plans.

Observers had forgotten that Savarkar and Gandhi had first disagreed about the centrality of violence during their public meeting in London in 1909. Both appeared to have conceptualised their ideas as counter-arguments, without formally addressing each other. Neither wanted to cede the political vocabulary that shaped their thoughts on concepts like *swaraj*, civilisation, Hindu, and violence. Nor were Gandhi and Savarkar interested in letting the other provide the normative interpretations of texts such as the Bhagavad Gita and the Ramayana. This was an epistemic battle for the dominance of ideas with a violent end. Dialogue on this was no longer an option after Gandhi's death, although Gandhi's arguments for non-violence continued to haunt the direction of Savarkar's thought. Savarkar could hardly have not been aware that the essentials of Hindutva he had articulated in the 1920s and promoted as president of the Akhil Bharatiya Hindu Mahasabha were largely ignored in independent India. This notwithstanding, for Savarkar the fact that in 1947 "Hindusthan" was divided into two

[9] Godse, *May It Please Your Honour* (1977), 20.
[10] Ibid., 19.

nation-states – India and Pakistan – did not mean that Hindus needed to abandon Hindutva. Instead, the post-colonial moment following Partition was precisely when Hindus needed to unite.[11] Hindutva was now marginalised, but he considered this a temporary phenomenon.

In Part IV, I discuss that Savarkar was not deterred by contemporary politics; his resolution was to return to writing Hindu history. In 1963 he completed his last major work, titled *Bharatiya Ithihastil Saha Soneri Pane* (hereafter *Saha Soneri Pane*) – literally, the six golden pages (or leaves) of Indian history. His book provided a long history of Hindus dating back to antiquity and illustrating that Hindus had experienced crises in the past. One purpose in his writing the book was to show that Hindutva was not fleeting: it spanned several millennia over which Hindus had remained resilient in working towards creating and protecting a Hindu nation despite major obstacles. This was Savarkar's final volume on Hindutva – and history.

For those who had followed Savarkar's writings and speeches, the central arguments in *Saha Soneri Pane* were very familiar. In *Essentials of Hindutva* Savarkar had forcefully expressed the importance of writing about "every page in our history."[12] Now, his new book's title indicated he would examine six of those pages. However, the English translation of the book is titled *Six Glorious Epochs of Indian History* (1971; hereafter *Six Glorious Epochs*). This was again an echo from the past: Savarkar had also mentioned the importance of writing about "the most glorious epoch of our history" in *Essentials of Hindutva*.[13] The fact that Savarkar wrote this history in Marathi was a departure from his other major writings on Hindutva. It also signalled a retreat from writing in English for a national audience attempted in *Essentials of Hindutva* and *Hindu Pad Padashahi*. The book's circulation, at first limited to the Marathi-speaking public, was overcome with its posthumous publication in an English translation. Savarkar had approved the translation before his death but been unable to complete the citations and references, according to Balarao Savarkar. This task S.T. Godbole finished in his capacity as translator.[14]

[11] Savarkar, "Protest Against the Vivisection of Hindusthan," 167.

[12] Savarkar, *Essentials of Hindutva*, 75.

[13] Ibid., 18.

[14] For Part IV, I have consulted multiple editions of this text: *Saha Soneri*

*Saha Soneri Pane* remains the least known of Savarkar's writings on Hindutva.[15] The reason for this is a general perception that it reiterates Savarkar's earlier arguments about Hindu history, even as the combination of Gandhi's assassination by Godse and India's adoption of a constitution guaranteeing secularism and equality of citizenship regardless of religion made Savarkar's work look irrelevant. I argue here that *Saha Soneri Pane* is in fact Savarkar's most comprehensive work and provides his final interpretation of the essentials of Hindutva.

In narrating this long history it is evident even from its title that Savarkar did not wish to go back to the founding of Hindutva. He would focus only on "glorious epochs" and "golden pages" of history as shortcuts to accessing the Hindu hero. A Hindu history was necessarily temporally limited, but in this work Savarkar suggests it was limited in other ways as well. We will see here that the power of the Hindu spirit which inspired Savarkar's early conceptualisations was now being reconsidered. He argues now that the thoughts and actions of Hindu heroes had historically failed to live up to their full potential – a point that would later lead to a number of individuals burning the book in protest at Savarkar's criticism of Shivaji.[16] The tone of the new book also reflects Savarkar's awareness of the methodological limits of *his* history writing in a period in which the Hindu nation had failed to come to fruition. The intention of writing a history in full had been to approximate Hindutva (and Being) through language and text, but the project had to be left incomplete. It had become clear to Savarkar

---

*Pane* in *Samagra Savarkar*, vol. 3 (1993); *Chhah Svarnim Prstha* in *Savarkar Samagra*, vol. 6 (2003); and *Six Glorious Epochs*. For purposes of direct quotations, I have largely relied on the Godbole translation approved by Savarkar: *Six Glorious Epochs*. For select footnotes, I have provided the page numbers of citations from *Six Glorious Epochs* and *Saha Soneri Pane*. I also discuss some of the problems of translation of concepts related to these texts.

[15] For example, Panikkar, "General President's Address," 9, describes *Six Glorious Epochs* as Savarkar's "relatively less known work." I include Panikkar's comment here to note that he was one of the first scholars to analyse *Six Glorious Epochs* in multiple essays in the 1990s and 2000s. One of the most astute summaries of the book was J. Patrocinio de Souza, "A Committed Hindu," *The Times of India*, October 10, 1971.

[16] Suryawanshi, "Militant Youth Wing Burns Savarkar Book."

that at least at this point Hindutva was an impossible history. What this history showed him was that Hindus had not only existed in a state of war in the past, but that they also needed to embrace permanent war as part of their future. Only then could another page of Hindu history be written.

## 2.  Bharat as India

*Saha Soneri Pane* was Savarkar's only major work published after Indian independence and the first written without the monitoring of colonial officials and censors. All of Savarkar's writings that had been banned by the British government had become available in India. The restrictions on his life story had also been lifted. In titling his history *Bharatiya Ithihastil Saha Soneri Pane* Savarkar was not moving away from writing Hindu history towards "Indian history," even if the English translation of his title contains that phrase. Rather, for Savarkar "Bharatiya Itihastil" or Indian history *was* Hindu history.[17] In any case this was not the first time that Savarkar had used the term "Bharat" as the geographical name for India: Bharatkhanda and Bharatvarsha were terms he had used as heuristics in *Essentials of Hindutva*. Moreover, his earlier references to Bharat were not necessarily geographical equivalents of "India" – the post-colonial nation-state which was now the Republic of India. Nor was Savarkar alone in translating India as Bharat in this period. In the debates of the Constituent Assembly of India in 1949 there were discussions about selecting a synonym or equivalent of "India" in an Indian language. H.V. Kamath, a member of the Constituent Assembly, argued that India as Republic deserved a new name:

> The prominent suggestions have been Bharat, Hindustan, Hind and Bharatbhumi or Bharatvarsh and names of that kind. Now, those who argue for Bharat or Bharatvarsh or Bharatbhumi, take their stand on the fact that this is the most ancient name of this land. Historians and philologists have delved deep into this matter of the name of this country, especially the origin of this name Bharat.[18]

[17] See Savarkar, "A Message to Hindus in Gujerat," in Bhide, ed., *Veer Savarkar's "Whirl-wind Propaganda,"* 259–60.

[18] Comments by H.V. Kamath, Member, Constituent Assembly of India,

Kamath formally recommended "Bharat." But he was quite specifically concerned over the aesthetics of the language to be used in the constitution to explain that "India" was the English-language equivalent of "Bharat." He proposed "Bharat, or, in the English language India."[19] He wanted to borrow the terminology from the 1937 Irish constitution, which states "The name of the State is Eire, or, in the English language, Ireland." However, Kamath's proposal was rejected. Instead, after further debate members of the Constituent Assembly agreed that the first sentence of the *Constitution of India* should state, "India, that is Bharat, shall be a Union of States."[20]

In comparison to his earlier writings, Savarkar's use of Bharat in his book was extensive, but he did not abandon Hindusthan; he used it in conjunction with Bharat throughout. In fact, at public gatherings he regularly asked Hindus to take a vow stating "Hindusthan, this Bharat Bhoomi from the Indus to the Seas is our Fatherland and Holy Land."[21]

Bharat as defined in the *Constitution of India* was not the same geographically as the Bharat of Savarkar's writings. This did not seem a contradiction to Savarkar, especially as he considered the partition of Hindusthan (and the creation of Pakistan) to be temporary. What did Savarkar mean in the context of these changed circumstances? On July 3, 1947 Savarkar delivered a speech titled "Protest Against the Vivisection of Hindusthan" in which he pointed out that it was necessary for Hindus to reassess "all things past and present" – by which he meant Hindu history.[22] It was important to show that historically Hindus had faced crises even more devastating than those of recent years. The power of Muslims in Hindusthan had substantially declined over the past millennium, to the extent that it had been reduced to the idea of Pakistan: "My message to Hindudom even on this Black Day in our

---

New Delhi, September 18, 1949, in *Constituent Assembly of India Debates (Proceedings)*, vol. IX, loksabhaph.nic.in/writereaddata/cadebatefiles/C18091949.html (accessed March 2, 2021).

   [19] Ibid.

   [20] Ibid.

   [21] Savarkar, "Protest Against the Vivisection of Hindusthan," 203.

   [22] Ibid., 201.

History is to assure it once more, 'Despair not! – a glorious future awaits the Hindus – if only they do not betray themselves!!"[23] For him the point was what Hindu history had illustrated – the "amazing capacity for resurrection, of renaissance[,] of rejuvenation" of the "Hindu Nation."[24] He cited examples from *Essentials of Hindutva* and *Hindu Pad Padashahi* to demonstrate that Hindus were capable of establishing power. This speech is also important because it provides a preview of key arguments that Savarkar developed in *Saha Soneri Pane*.

Savarkar delivered many speeches in which he addressed contemporary concerns, while also summarising key arguments about Hindutva. The fact that some of the speeches were published in pamphlets and newspapers, or at least summarised in some dailies, allowed Savarkar's ideas to circulate widely. In addition, thousands of copies of his presidential addresses were printed and circulated free of cost after the annual Hindu Mahasabha conferences.[25] Even for those who had not read Savarkar's writings, his ideas were accessible as part of political debate. In many ways, the speeches provided some of the most important insights into Savarkar's thought. By the time *Saha Soneri Pane* was published, Savarkar had revised, expanded, and clarified key ideas and concepts that he had first introduced in his early writings on Hindutva. This is important to note as Savarkar did not fully explain some of the nuances of his arguments in this last book: "As such the compilation and interpretation from the Hindu standpoint of the history of the period has been fully done in my writings and speeches made on every occasion during these fifty or sixty years."[26] It appears that he assumed readers would know the trajectory of his interpretations culminating in *Saha Soneri Pane*.

[23] Ibid.

[24] Ibid.

[25] NMML, V.D. Savarkar Papers, Reel 25, Letter from V.D. Savarkar, to Har Ram Shath, Maurawan, March 12, 1942; Reel 30, Letter from V.D. Savarkar, to Chandra Gupta Vedalankarji, January 10, 1941; Letter from V.D. Savarkar, Jwala Prasad Shrivastav, President, Oudh Provincial Hindusabha, January 10, 1941. Also, see Western Language Collections, Hoover Institution Library and Archives, Stanford University, S.P. India, Publications of the Akhil Bharat Hindu Mahasabha.

[26] Savarkar, *Six Glorious Epochs*, 469–70; Savarkar, *Saha Soneri Pane*, 408.

It is worth further considering Savarkar's turn to Bharat/Bharatiya (or India/Indian) as categories of analysis in his book. In *Indian War* he had privileged "Indian" when writing of a unified revolutionary struggle by Hindus and Muslims. Then in *Hindu Pad Padashahi* he had shifted his focus to Hindu subjects in the making of wars of independence. Now, Savarkar's use of Bharatiya and Indian reflected the *zeitgeist* of nationalist debates about nomenclature, but he did not by this indicate a return to his earlier articulation of "Indian" as conveying the idea of Hindu–Muslim unity. He stated in his 1938 presidential address in Nagpur: "India must be a Hindu land, reserved for the Hindus."[27] He acknowledged the need to address the *place* of minorities in India as well, but argued that there would necessarily be a "differential" approach to each religious community. It should be remembered that Savarkar did not classify Jains, Buddhists, and Sikhs as minorities in India: he interpreted their religious doctrines as acknowledging that India was their fatherland and holy land. Thereby, within his taxonomy they were Hindus. He further explained that Zoroastrians (Parsis) were most "akin" to Hindus in terms of "race, religion, language, and culture."[28] He believed "They have gratefully been loyal to India and have made her their only home."[29] The question of loyalty to India and seeing it as a homeland were important to Savarkar, especially in his discussion of Jews, Christians, and Muslims. Jews being numerically insignificant in India, in them he saw no political or cultural conflict with Hindus. Moreover, Jews were already well integrated with Hindus, and since Christians were "linguistically and culturally" aligned with Hindus, they could also be "assimilated" into Hindu India. He viewed Christians as a "civil" minority that did not have "extra-territorial political designs against India."[30] All the same, there was a residual ambivalence in Savarkar's view of Christians because he felt it was important for Hindus to "reconvert" Christians as part of a Shuddhi movement.[31]

[27] Savarkar, "Presidential Address, 20th Session of the Akhil Bharatiya Hindu Mahasabha, Nagpur, 1938," in Savarkar, *Hindu Rashtra Darshan*, 57.

[28] Ibid., 56.

[29] Ibid.

[30] Ibid.

[31] Ibid.

The focus of Savarkar's concern regarding minorities centred on Muslims. At one level he believed that Hindus had promoted the ideal of a "Human State" open to "all mankind."[32] He says: "If all India with one-fifth of the human race could be united irrespective of religious, racial and cultural diversities, merging them all into a homogeneous whole, it would be but a gigantic stride taken by mankind towards the realisation of that human political ideal."[33] The idea of homogeneity was a reference to creating a unified Hindu identity within a Hindu Nation. He saw Zoroastrians, Jews, and Christians as either already assimilated with Hindus, or with the potential to be assimilated by choice – or via conversion in the case of Christians. Over time, all minorities would become part of a homogeneous Hindu whole. Only Muslims were historically unwilling to work towards creating this idealised Human State in India; they were incapable of assimilation. He had first introduced his understanding of the "Human State" in *Essentials of Hindutva* as a global project of humanism.[34] Now he pointed out that nationalism (and nationalists) were necessarily partial in their approach to conceptualising "nation" as an ideal. The creation of a Human State was therefore impossible. In the late 1930s Savarkar appeared to be returning to his original conceptualisation, albeit with a modification, to argue that Hindus wanted to create a Human State in India. In other words, to be Human was to be Hindu in India.[35] To contest the Hindu ideal, or to reject India as a territorial unity, also meant the negation of participation in a Human State.

This was an important development in Savarkar's thought. He pointed out that "Indian Nationality" was a "new concept" that converged with the unified territory of India. It was a public recognition that "India" was the Hindusthan of Savarkar's *Essentials of Hindutva*.[36] Savarkar confirmed this point when he alerted his audience of this discursive shift:

The Hindus for one found nothing revolting even in that assumption to their deepest religious or cultural or racial sentiments. Because their

[32] Ibid., 41.

[33] Ibid.

[34] Savarkar, *Essentials of Hindutva*, 72.

[35] NMML, V.D. Savarkar Papers, Reel 30, Message from V.D. Savarkar, May 15, 1941.

[36] See Ahmed Asif, *The Loss of Hindustan*.

national being had already been identified with that territorial unit, India, which to them was not only a land of sojourn but a home, their Father-land, their Motherland, their Holyland and all in one! Indian Patriotism to them was but a synonym of Hindu Patriotism. If Hindusthan was called India but continued to be a Hindusthan, it made no difference in essentials.[37]

The essentials of Hindutva, that is.

Savarkar explained that Muslims refused to assimilate with Hindus in India because of their advocacy of a "theological concept of [the] state."[38] Muslims divided land into two categories: "Muslim Land" and "Enemy Land." All land controlled by Muslims was considered Muslim land (Dar-ul-Islam); territory inhabited by non-Muslims or ruled by non-Muslims was the land of the enemy (Dar-ul-Harb). In the latter case, Muslims were not meant to remain loyal to the land of the enemy. Instead their goal was to convert non-Muslims to Islam and establish Muslim power: "You will then see that the whole Moslem history and their daily actions are framed on the design I have outlined above. Consequently, a territorial patriotism is a word unknown to the Moslem . . . unless in connection with a Moslem territory."[39]

Savarkar's interpretations of Muslims had shifted from his earlier writings. In *Essentials of Hindutva* he had suggested that some Shia Muslims, such as the Borahs and the Khojahs, still had the option to reassimilate with Hindus. He had also provided the option of recon-version for Muslims in *Majhi Janmathep*. These ideas were no longer part of Savarkar's interpretations of Muslims – in part because most Muslims had rejected Savarkar's idea of performing a Shuddhi cer-emony to "assimilate" with Hindus. Savarkar concluded that Muslims would not join Hindus in creating an Indian nationality: "They never looked upon our [*sic*] Hindusthan as their country, nation . . . it is to them already an alien land, and enemy land – a 'Dar-ul-Harb' and not a 'Dar-ul-Islam'!"[40]

Throughout his 1938 presidential address Savarkar was adamant about his idea of the Hindu Nation as India: "[W]e Hindus are a Nation

---

[37] Savarkar, "Presidential Address, Nagpur, 1938," in Savarkar, *Hindu Rashtra Darshan*, 42.

[38] Ibid., 49.

[39] Ibid.

[40] Ibid., 50.

by ourselves. Because religious, racial, cultural and historical affinities bind us intimately into a homogeneous nation and added to it we are . . . a territorial unity as well."[41] This was an important corrective to his argument in his 1937 presidential address to the Akhil Bharatiya Hindu Mahasabha in Ahmedabad, in which he had stated, "India cannot be assumed today to be a unitarian and homogeneous nation, but on the contrary there are two nations in the main: the Hindus and the Moslems, in India."[42] These were "two antagonistic nations living side by side in India."[43] He maintained that his initial purpose was to argue for the creation of an idealised Indian state: "Let all citizens of that Indian state be treated according to their individual worth irrespective of their religious or racial percentage in the general population."[44] His point was that distinctions of religion and race should not be recognised by the Indian state; rather, all decisions should be determined by the majority without any accommodations made for minorities. His purpose in saying this was to argue for equality within the Indian state, in which Hindus as a nation resided as equals with all minorities. Hindus would provide protection to the religion, culture, and language of minorities, but any aggression by minorities against Hindus would not be tolerated in the new state. He recognised that his interpretation was not acceptable to most Muslims as he promoted the idea that, ultimately, the Indian state would be formed out of the Hindu nation (or Hindusthan).

Savarkar's claim that Hindus and Muslims formed two nations became a topic of public debate immediately after his 1937 presidential address, leading many to state that Savarkar was the first to advocate the two-nation theory in India. He was interviewed a number of times to clarify his argument. He said his purpose was not to accept the idea of creating two states: he insisted that he had only advocated a single Indian state. He clarified that he had frequently discussed the simultaneous existence of a plurality of nations within a single territory. Now, to outline the existence of two nations in India, he stated:

<hr>

[41] Ibid., 52.

[42] Savarkar, "Presidential Address, 19th Session of the Akhil Bharatiya Hindu Mahasabha, Ahmedabad, 1937," in Savarkar, *Hindu Rashtra Darshan*, 24.

[43] Ibid.

[44] Ibid., 18.

Islam is a theocratic nation based on the Koran right from its inception. This nation never had geographical boundaries. Wherever the Mussulmans went, they went as a nation. They also came to Hindusthan as a nation. As per the principle of Mussalmans, the earth is divided into two nations: Dar-ul-Islam and Dar-ul-Harb. As per their religious command, their campaign on Hindusthan was as a separate nation. They conquered the Hindu Nation as an enemy nation, not as One Nation. The Hindu Nation arose again and having defeated the Mussulmans at various places, saved the whole of Hindusthan to establish Hindu Pad Padashahi also as a separate Hindu Nation opposed to Muslim nations . . . Mussalmans never gave up their principle of theocratic or scriptural nationalism and the feeling of being a nation separate from the Hindu Nation.[45]

For Savarkar the idea of the nation did not necessarily correspond with the formation of a state *per se*. Savarkar had discussed the founding of the Hindu nation under the leadership of Ramchandra in *Essentials of Hindutva*, and articulated the idea of the Maratha nation as part of the Hindu nation in *Hindu Pad Padashahi*. He also explained that many *rashtras* existed at the same time within Hindusthan without negating the centrality of the Hindu nation. All the same, Savarkar's statement that two antagonistic nations existed in India became a catchphrase to the extent that it continues to be cited into the twenty-first century as evidence that he was responsible for its articulation.

Ayesha Jalal has pointed out that in the 1880s Syed Ahmad Khan had discussed the idea of "two nations" in which he urged Muslims to separate themselves from the Indian National Congress.[46] She adds that Syed Ahmad Khan's statements were made in the background of late-nineteenth-century intellectual debates in North India, and should thus be viewed as distinct from twentieth-century articulations of the two-nation theory.[47] In this perspective, Muhammad Ali Jinnah had proposed that Muslims were a nation as a way of avoiding "the

---

[45] Savarkar was interviewed by journalists on August 15, 1943 and August 23, 1943 to clarify his statements about "two nations." The excerpt cited here is from an interview published in *Aadesh*, a Marathi weekly, on August 28, 1943. As I was unable to locate the original interview, I have relied on an official translation made available on savarkar.org/en/encyc/2017/5/29/Q-A6.html (accessed March 2, 2021).

[46] Jalal, *The Sole Spokesman*, 52, fn. 30.

[47] Ibid.

logic of numbers" that had rendered Muslims "a perpetual minority within a united India."[48] These debates had existed for nearly half a century and were powerful in harnessing support because the size of the nation did not matter *per se* – nations existed in all sizes. What mattered was that Muslims saw themselves as a nation. In 1940 Jinnah, in his presidential address to the All India Muslim League, proposed an interpretation of the "two-nation theory," arguing that Islam and Hinduism were "different and distinct social orders."[49] It was impossible that Hindus and Muslims could form a "common nationality," and, more important, there was a possibility that the formation of one Indian nation would eventually lead to its own destruction:

> The Hindus and Muslims belong to two different religious philosophies, social customs, and literatures. They neither intermarry nor interdine together and, indeed, they belong to two different civilisations which are based mainly on conflicting ideas and conceptions. Their aspect on life and of life are different. It is quite clear that Hindus and Mussalmans derive their inspiration from different sources of history. They have different epics, different heroes, and different episodes . . . To yoke together two such nations under a single state, one as a numerical minority and the other as a majority, must lead to growing discontent and final destruction of any fabric that may be so built for the government of such a state.[50]

Jinnah's interpretation of the "two-nation theory" differed from Savarkar's formulation in arguing for the creation of a sovereign Muslim state – as against a single Indian state.[51] Jinnah also wanted a formal treaty between Pakistan and Hindustan to reconcile differences between the two nations (and states). In the midst of great public debate on the idea of India containing two antagonistic nations, Savarkar's clarification of his interpretation of two nations and the idea of the creation of a *singular* Indian state was often overlooked.[52]

There were, of course, exceptions, and Savarkar had some notable critics. B.R. Ambedkar argued against Savarkar's interpretations in *Essentials*

[48] Ibid., 52.

[49] Jinnah, "Presidential Address at the All India Muslim League, Lahore Session, March 1940," 13.

[50] Ibid.

[51] Afghan, "Big Question Before Indian Muslims," 396.

[52] Savarkar, "It is Absurd to Talk of the Two Majorities in India," August 12, 1941, in Bhide, ed., *Veer Savarkar's "Whirl-wind Propaganda,"* 456–61.

*of Hindutva* of defining Hindus as a nation, especially the idea of classifying all "Depressed Classes" as Hindus.[53] But he also explained that Savarkar's idea of two nations in India – a Hindu nation and a Muslim nation – did not mean that Savarkar called for a partition of territory. On the contrary, Ambedkar correctly pointed out, Savarkar's priority was to maintain geographic unity. In fact Ambedkar noted that Savarkar's ambition was not for a Hindu nation to coexist with a Muslim nation within India; instead, he wanted Hindus to establish "an empire over Muslims" for the purpose of creating "an imperial race" of Hindus.[54] In other words, the resurrection of the Hindu empire noted in *Hindu Pad Padashahi* was part of Savarkar's imperial ambition via the formation of an Indian state. This was a point that Ambedkar fully understood.[55]

What is evident is that there was no agreement about the interpretation of the idea of "two nations" in relation to the formation of one or more states. Ambedkar's interpretation of Savarkar's argument was likely its most significant summary, but it did not have a popular reception, given that Savarkar continues to be named as the most vocal advocate of the two-nation theory. Perhaps a distinction worth considering is that Savarkar's articulation of two antagonistic nations centred around a united Indian state, while Jinnah's promoted a dual-state solution. For Savarkar this distinction was important in not only arguing for the establishment of the Hindu nation as an Indian state, but also for writing a Hindu history as an Indian history in *Saha Soneri Pane*. This was an important shift in his oeuvre. The themes discussed in *Saha Soneri Pane* show a continuity with Savarkar's earlier writings, but important concepts and themes are also developed that reflect the context of nationalist debates in which Savarkar participated as president of the Akhil Bharatiya Hindu Mahasabha.

In case there remained anyone who had misunderstood his discussion of two antagonistic nations, Savarkar in his presidential address

---

[53] Ambedkar, *Pakistan or The Partition of India*, 120–35.

[54] Ibid., 134.

[55] In consonance with Ambedkar's argument, it is helpful to consider an interpretation by Jyotirmaya Sharma, who has suggested that Savarkar's use of two nations in his 1937 presidential address was likely closer to his use of race as a category in his writings, rather than an articulation of the need for two separate states. Sharma, *Hindutva*, 168.

of 1938 further clarified his argument in favour of a one-Indian-state solution. The strength of Hindu numbers meant that any conflict with Muslims would be met with vengeance: "[I]f we Hindus grow stronger in time these Moslem friends of the league type will have to play the part of German-Jews."[56] What did Savarkar mean by this? In early November 1938 Jews were subjected to anti-semitic violence when Joseph Goebbels initiated a campaign to attack institutions of the Jewish community.[57] On November 9, 1938, a month before Savarkar's presidential address, the Nazis in Germany had carried out a series of anti-Jewish actions in which approximately a hundred Jews were killed, thousands of businesses looted, and hundreds of synagogues destroyed. Nearly 30,000 Jewish men were herded off to concentration camps. The event came to be known as *Kristallnacht* (night of broken glass) and marked an important date in the persecution of Jews in Nazi Germany, with the implementation of anti-Jewish legislation.[58] *The Times of India* carried a report: "Disgust is felt by ordinary educated people outside Germany for virulent anti-Semitism. How is it possible that these things can happen almost in the middle of the 20th century in Western Europe?"[59] Did Savarkar want to assure his audience that Hindus in the Indian state had a plan for Muslims inspired by the Nazi persecution of Jews in Germany? Whatever his intent, his address was certainly read as a message and celebrated at the Akhil Bharatiya Hindu Mahasabha meeting in Ahmedabad in 1939, where the closing speaker Bhai Parmanand recommended that Savarkar "make [the presidential address] your Mein Kampf." Parmanand then turned to the audience and said: "Make Savarkar your Fuehrer. And in no time your nation [will] rise to the pinnacles of glory."[60]

Savarkar did not expatiate on a "solution" of the Nazi variety. His position was that Hindus did not need to worry about the two-nation

[56] Savarkar, "Presidential Address, Nagpur, 1938," in Savarkar, *Hindu Rashtra Darshan*, 53. Also, see Savarkar, "India's Foreign Policy," November 3, 1938, in Bhide, ed., *Veer Savarkar's "Whirl-wind Propaganda,"* 50–3.

[57] Evans, *The Third Reich in Power 1933–1939*, 580.

[58] Ibid., 580–610.

[59] "A Letter From Berlin: The Nazi Campaign Against the Jews," *The Times of India*, December 8, 1938.

[60] Bhai Parmanand, "Heralding the New Dawn," *The Hindu Outlook*, January 11, 1939.

theory in a unified India. He simply repeated his arguments about Hindutva every time he spoke publicly about the creation of a new Indian state. In his presidential address in Bhagalpur in 1941 he said the purpose was to create a "mental revolution" to "awaken the Hindu spirit."[61] Needless to say, this is in continuity with a major theme in *Hindu Pad Padashahi* that was now part of his political discourse to rally Hindus around the creation of the Indian state; it was also a theme at the centre of *Saha Soneri Pane.*

## 3. *Itihaas*, Research, Translation

*Saha Soneri Pane*, as Savarkar's final book of *itihaas* and Hindutva, shows a continuity of themes and concepts with his earlier writings on history as well as his speeches in the 1930s and 1940s. His focus on brave heroes identified as *veer* exists throughout, as does his interest in wars of revolution dating back to antiquity. In fact, it provides Savarkar an opportunity to develop and expand ideas and interpretations that he had originally discussed in *Essentials of Hindutva*. Returning to writing Hindu history in Marathi was important as well, marking a reversal of his earlier claims in *Essentials of Hindutva* and *Hindu Pad Padashahi* of the need to write in English to establish pan-Hindu unity beyond the Marathi public. *Saha Soneri Pane* is a history of India before the 1947 Partition. Inscribed in the text is the idea of a unified India – of Bharat, of Hindusthan – that can be resurrected, an argument Savarkar made as president of the Akhil Bharatiya Hindu Mahasabha. He also authorised and approved the English translation of the book, posthumously published as *Six Glorious Epochs of Indian History* in 1971. Not surprisingly, the English translation had wider circulation nationally and globally than the Marathi original.

Savarkar had by now spent his entire career developing the idea that "Hindutva is a history in full" in English, with "*itihaas*" as its equivalent in Marathi and Hindi translations. *Saha Soneri Pane* maintains key aspects of his interpretation of *itihaas* but shows significant modifications because of the clear influence of contemporary historiographical debates on research. Savarkar explains that historical writing

---

[61] Savarkar, "Presidential Address, 23rd Session of the Akhil Bharatiya Hindu Mahasabha, Bhagalpur, 1941," in Savarkar, *Hindu Rashtra Darshan*, 179.

needs to be based on multiple sources of evidence to produce robust interpretations that can be proven: "The main criterion of history is that the dates and places and descriptions of events referred to therein must necessarily bear the stamp of authenticity, and they should be corroborated as far as possible by foreign as well as indigenous evidence."[62] This represents a change from his earlier argument in *Essentials of Hindutva* advocating conjecture. In the first sentence of *Saha Soneri Pane* he says that according to "today's research" the birth of the nation dates back five thousand to ten thousand years.[63] Temporally, this was an important distinction: he wanted to underscore that his purpose was to write about the golden pages of history in historical time that could be measured – not mythological time, Puranic time, or even the time before time. Puranic texts were "ancient mythologies" that supported "ancient history," but the time they spoke of was not measurable as historical time. Savarkar clarified that he was not abandoning the Puranas.[64] Nor was he supporting his earlier claim that the Puranas should be interpreted as true unless there was research-based evidence to suggest otherwise. His point now, in this specific book, was to formally indicate his departure from conjecture as a means to interpret the past.

Savarkar also now engaged with Oriental Studies and contemporary historical research to substantiate his interpretations. Select authors and books are discussed in the main text of *Saha Soneri Pane* and *Six Glorious Epochs*. For example, Vincent A. Smith's *The Early History of India* (1904) and K.P. Jayaswal's *Hindu Polity* (1924) are cited throughout the latter.[65] Savarkar points out that Jayaswal was a member of the Abhinav Bharat Society in London alongside him (Savarkar).[66] He was, moreover, a "world famous Orientalist."[67] Smith was a member of the Indian Civil Service in the late-nineteenth century, a prolific Orientalist, and a member of St John's College, Oxford, in the early-twentieth

[62] Savarkar, *Six Glorious Epochs*, 2; Savarkar, *Saha Soneri Pane*, 1.

[63] Savarkar, *Six Glorious Epochs*, 1; Savarkar, *Saha Soneri Pane*, 1.

[64] Ibid.

[65] Smith, *Early History of India*; Jayaswal, *Hindu Polity*.

[66] BL, APAC, India HD Pol Proceedings, B Series, IOR.POS.8963, Weekly Report of the Director of Criminal Intelligence, Simla, September 25, 1909.

[67] Savarkar, *Six Glorious Epochs*, 7; Savarkar, *Saha Soneri Pane*, 6.

century. In his 1924 edition of *The Early History of India* he made clear his disagreements with many of the interpretations of Jayaswal and other Indian scholars. He added extensive new footnotes in response to Jayaswal's writings.[68] Given that Savarkar included many quotes from Smith's writings in the book, it is evident that he was familiar with Smith's critiques of Jayaswal. I mention these two scholars not only because Savarkar cited both and identified Jayaswal and Smith as exemplary, but also because their interpretations allowed Savarkar to validate that he was engaging with both "Indian and Western Orientalists" to substantiate his own claims. (It should be noted that in this context, the classification of Indian in "Indian Orientalist" meant "Hindu.") Other scholars and authors Savarkar identifies in the book provided alternative interpretations that are also discussed: these being "Muslim writers," "Greek writers," and "Chinese travellers."

Savarkar appeared to situate his writings in historiographical debates and provided critiques of sources of his earlier work as a development in his writing on *itihaas*. This was an attempt to rethink the writing of Hindu history by turning to the methodological innovations of disciplinary history. Yet Savarkar was not in fact consistent in this approach in *Saha Soneri Pane*: he violated the basic protocols of what he had identified as "today's research." (In *Six Glorious Epochs*, Godbole translated "today's research" as "modern historical research."[69]) Savarkar had long been concerned about biased, partial, and distorted histories; he had pointed out these in multiple texts, including *Indian War* and *Hindu Pad Padashahi*. In *Saha Soneri Pane* he articulated these distortions as the "perverted sense of virtue" adopted by historians.[70] What did this mean? Ultimately, if an interpretation of the past did not prioritise the Hindu subject as defined by Savarkar, it was dismissed in scathing terms: "And such a country like India . . . is derided by some half-crazy jealous historians, foreign as well as Indian,

[68] The fourth edition of Smith, *The Early History of India* (1924) includes nineteen new references responding to K.P. Jayaswal's *Hindu Polity*. This edition is cited by S.T. Godbole.

[69] Savarkar, *Six Glorious Epochs*, 1.

[70] Ibid., 167; Savarkar, *Saha Soneri Pane*, 147. Savarkar used the term *sadagunavikriti* throughout the text, which was translated as "perverted conception of virtues" by Godbole.

or by some Hindu-haters like Dr [B.R.] Ambedkar or by some quite ignorant writers."[71] This tension exists throughout the book as Savarkar advocates the writing of Hindu history within the parameters of what he considers contemporary research – while also being committed to his idea of a history in full.

Savarkar cites Ambedkar only a few times in the book, and specifically objects to one of Ambedkar's statements: "Indian history from the beginning is a history of a slavish people, sunk deep into foreign bondage and constantly trampled under foreign heels."[72] He says Ambedkar provided "vulgar" and "hateful" comments about Hindus that were antithetical to his, Savarkar's, interpretations.[73] It is clear that, having espoused the need to use modern historical research, Savarkar has pushed himself into a methodological corner. This becomes clear because, when evaluating multiple texts as a way to write *itihaas*, Savarkar accepts the interpretations of Western Orientalists or English historians when it suits his objectives, even as he dismisses those he finds critical of Hindu history. The fact that Ambedkar had converted to Buddhism in 1956, along with several hundred thousand "untouchables," as a way to reject Hinduism, likely had an impact on Savarkar. As noted earlier, during the late 1920s and the 1930s Savarkar had embarked on an anti-caste programme demanding both temple entry and normalised interdining with "untouchables" in Ratnagiri District. Ambedkar's denunciation of Hinduism contradicted Savarkar's pan-Hindu unity programme which sought to widen the frame of Hindu dharma. In 1929 W. Gilligan, the district magistrate of Ratnagiri, had noted in a confidential report that Savarkar's agenda could create conflict and interfere with the work of Ambedkar in the region.[74] Savarkar had travelled throughout Ratnagiri District delivering lectures on the problems of the caste system, while also demanding the removal of restrictions against "untouchables." Based on the reports of the press and government officials, it seems these events had been attended by hundreds and sometimes thousands. Little is known about how Savarkar's

[71] Savarkar, *Six Glorious Epochs*, 281; Savarkar, *Saha Soneri Pane*, 249.

[72] Ibid.

[73] Ibid.

[74] MSA, HD Spec File 60-D(g)-(3)-1930, Confidential Letter by W. Gilligan, District Magistrate, Ratnagiri, June 22, 1929, S-27.

messages were actually interpreted, but Gilligan offered a partial answer when saying "The Brahmins dislike him on account of his interests in the Mahar classes."[75] Brahmins had raised the strongest objections, asserting that Savarkar's demands for "untouchable" rights were damaging to the sentiments of orthodox Hindus. Savarkar's argument that he was working towards a unified Hindu identity naturally had little influence over the powerful upper castes.

Members of the Sanatan Dharma – the Sanatanis – were especially vocal in their opposition to Savarkar.[76] Upper-caste Hindu protesters confronted him at many events, demanding that he stop his work with "untouchables." The government received letters of protest demanding that Savarkar not be allowed to present his ideas on temple entry and interdining in Ratnagiri.[77] In a petition to the governor of Bombay, the *inamdar* of Malwan Anant Dattatraya Sabhale argued that Savarkar was delivering "immoral and irreligious preachings" that "hurt the feelings of Sanatani Hindus."[78] For Sabhale the government's role in allowing Savarkar to speak about untouchability was a violation of what he called the "Government's neutrality in religious matters as guaranteed by . . . the Queen's Proclamation of 1858."[79] Another individual, Ramchandra Mahadev Soni, organised a petition on parallel grounds claiming that Savarkar was "wounding the feelings of orthodox Hindus" by promoting activities that are "opposed to the tenets of the Sanathan Hindu religion."[80] He pleaded that the government needed to "protect the people" from Savarkar's ideas by removing him from Ratnagiri altogether. The result was that Sanatanis organised boycotts of these

[75] Ibid.

[76] MSA, HD Spec File 60-D-(g)-pt. II-1937, Extract from the Weekly Confidential Report of the District Magistrate, Sholapur, June 30, 1937, S-75.

[77] Ibid., Summary of a Letter from V.V. Davare, President of the Maharashtra Varnashram Swaraj Sangh to V.D. Savarkar, in Extract from the Bombay Presidency Weekly Letter, No. 26, July 3, 1937, S-91-2.

[78] MSA, HD Spec File 60-D-(g)-1929, Petition from Anant Dattatraya Sabhale, Inamdar of Malwan, District Ratnagiri, to Governor of Bombay, January 14, 1934, S-305.

[79] Ibid.

[80] Ibid., Petition from Ramchandra Mahadev Soni, Someshwar, District Ratnagiri, to Governor of Bombay, January 15, 1931, S-197.

events, which were also marked by numerous incidents of violence that included the hurling of rocks and *chappals* at Savarkar's supporters.[81] (Official reports are not specific about Savarkar as the intended target.) Local officials interrogated Savarkar, fearing that he may have instigated the attacks. His house was searched for arms and seditious materials. When he was interviewed about his activities in May 1934 by Sardar Muhammad, the district magistrate, Savarkar stated: "I have been conducting the removal of untouchability movement in such an open and definite fashion that hundreds of lectures [were] delivered by me and which had been regularly reported to Government."[82] As Savarkar was not allowed to participate in political activities at the time, he had been given permission to work on social reform; he had taken the opportunity to put forward his arguments from *Essentials of Hindutva* and *Hindu Pad Padashahi* for pan-Hindu unity.

After Savarkar's election to the presidency of the Akhil Bharatiya Hindu Mahasabha in 1937 his agenda had expanded to harness support among what Ambedkar had called the "Depressed Classes" for his programme to spread the essentials of Hindutva. Whereas Savarkar had provided an extensive discussion of Hindu blood in *Essentials of Hindutva* – to try moving away from the casteist argument that some Hindu bodies were polluted at birth – Ambedkar had successfully created a mass movement in which "untouchables" had left the Hindu fold *en masse*. The direction of Ambedkar's trenchant critiques of Brahminism led him towards what he saw as the more egalitarian ethos of Buddhism.[83] Ambedkar had argued for a number of years that Buddhism had provided the main resistance to Brahminism. The most significant religious battle that defined the history of India was the "mortal conflict" between Buddhism and Brahminism, and in this lay the roots of resistance by "untouchables" against oppression and discrimination.[84]

[81] There are many reports of these protests against Savarkar's speeches in the Weekly Confidential Reports of the District Magistrates of Ratnagiri and Sholapur. See MSA, HD Spec File 60-D-(g)-pt. II-1937, S-75, S-173, S-187-191, S-195.

[82] MSA, HD Spec File 60-D-(g)-1929, Statement of V.D. Savarkar, Ratnagiri, May 7, 1934, S-317.

[83] See Ambedkar, *Annihilation of Caste*.

[84] Ambedkar, "The Triumph of Brahminism," 267.

What Savarkar did not discuss – though perhaps it was implicit in his book – was that Ambedkar was also involved in a revisionist history project to rewrite the history of India starting in antiquity.[85] In many ways it was a parallel project to Savarkar's Hindu history, except that Ambedkar rejected the centrality of Aryans – and Hindus – in the making of history. He began by revising the narrative of the successful invasion of India by Aryan tribes and offering an alternative: "The political history of India begins with the rise of a non-Aryan people called Nagas, who were a powerful people, whom the Aryans were unable to conquer, and whom the Aryans were compelled to recognise as their equals."[86] For Ambedkar the Nagas were essential because of their role in resisting the Aryans and their religion, culture, and social system of Brahminism, which was responsible for oppressing India's population, including the "untouchables." The Nagas had made India "great" and "glorious," and not – as Savarkar had argued – the Aryans who had dominated the existing narratives of India's ancient history.[87] Ambedkar argued that the Nagas not only remained autonomous in the period of Aryan expansion, but they proved to be the descendants of the greatest Buddhist ruler of India, Ashoka. While Buddhism reigned supreme for nearly 140 years, Ambedkar noted that its decline witnessed campaigns of persecution and the oppression of its followers by those who adopted Brahminism. Ambedkar's project remained incomplete due to his death on December 6, 1956, but its ambition and scope served as a counter-narrative to Savarkar's.

But to revert to Savarkar's new historical method, and to why he did not adhere to his own argument about the need for evidence to substantiate historical claims: this difficulty is discussed in *Six Glorious Epochs* by S.T. Godbole. Savarkar's translator says he himself inserted "basic references" as "proof" of Savarkar's statements because of Savarkar's age and health – which had made it difficult for Savarkar even to write the book. Identifying and inserting all the references had therefore been beyond Savarkar at this stage of his life.[88] Godbole

[85] The discussion in this paragraph builds on my argument in Chaturvedi, "Histories of Politics after Political History."

[86] Ibid.

[87] Ibid.

[88] Godbole, "A Word in Confidence," in Savarkar, *Six Glorious Epochs*. (The page number is not included in the original text.)

explains that the citations he inserted on behalf of Savarkar should nonetheless be considered as consistent with Savarkar's arguments, not least because Savarkar had approved the translation: "[E]very chapter went to the illustrious author who honoured me by going through it very carefully and when I had the good fortune to meet him personally . . . he obliged me by saying that he was satisfied with the translation and appreciated the hard labour it entailed."[89] What Godbole did not discuss is whether Savarkar had provided him the names of the texts he had used to write the book, nor whether he had approved the citations and bibliography compiled by Godbole. Nor is there any indication whether Balarao Savarkar, as the publisher of *Six Glorious Epochs* and Savarkar's personal secretary, was consulted in this process. In the end, all we can say is that Godbole compiled a bibliography with over two hundred texts – mostly in English and a select number in Marathi – that represented the most significant books, journal articles, and primary sources on India from the nineteenth and twentieth century. These included works by Romila Thapar, Thomas R. Metcalf, Percival Spear, R.C. Majumdar, Dhananjay Keer, Jawaharlal Nehru, G.S. Ghurye, and Surendranath Sen.[90] Whether the citations provide a guide to what Savarkar actually read remains unclear.

Another complication with interpreting Savarkar's ideas in his last book centres on Godbole's translation of "*saha soneri pane*" (six golden pages) as "six glorious epochs." Savarkar had used the phrases "pages of history" and "epochs of history" in his writings, but that is as far as an explanation goes for this specific translation. Since one of Savarkar's main goals was to discuss Hindutva's temporality, it may have made sense to use "epochs of history," rather than conceptualising "*saha soneri pane*" as units of time. Also, Orientalist scholars of astronomy had provided analyses of "epoch" to understand Hindu history's temporality dating back millions of years. For example, Thomas Maurice in *The History of Hindostan* (1795) defined "epoch" to clarify its use for readers who may have been confused by his interpretation: "By astronomers the word EPOCHA is used to denote that particular point of the orbit of a planet, wherein that planet is, at some known moment

---

<sup>89</sup> Ibid.
<sup>90</sup> Savarkar, *Six Glorious Epochs*, 559–66.

of mean time, in a given meridian."[91] John Bentley provided extensive calculations of astronomical tables to identify epochs in Hindu history in *A Historical View of Hindu Astronomy* (1825). Based on his estimates, Bentley also linked units of time to date figures from the Ramayana and the Mahabharata to argue that there was an "Epoch of Rama" and an "Epoch of Yudhishthira."[92] Many other epochs were identified in Bentley's writings, as well as in the writings of others who contributed to the field of Hindu astronomy.

By the end of the nineteenth century Romesh Chunder Dutt provided an alternative interpretation in *A History of Civilisation in Ancient India* (1893), arguing that there were five epochs of Hindu history in a period of thirty centuries.[93] Dutt's use of "epoch" diverged from earlier nineteenth-century writings as he interpreted the measure of time linked with "great historical events" associated with a civilisation.[94] He says, "[T]he history of Ancient India divides itself into several distinct and long periods or epochs. Each of these periods has a distinct literature, and each has a civilisation peculiar to it, which modified itself into the civilisation of the next period under the operation of great political and social causes."[95] Dutt's notion of epochs in Hindu history centred on the major literature of that period, which he saw as creating a specific Hindu civilisational characteristic of that epoch. He classified each in the following terms: First Epoch/*Vedic Period* (2000 BC–1400 BC ); Second Epoch/*Epic Period* (1400 BC–1000 BC); Third Epoch/*Philosophical Period* (1000 BC–242 BC); Fourth Epoch/ *Buddhist Period* (242 BC–500 AD); Fifth Epoch/*Puranik Period* (500 AD–1194 AD).[96] These interpretations of epochs stopped at the end of the twelfth century to mark the fall of Hindu kings in Delhi, Ajmer, Benares, and Kannauj by Shahabuddin Ghori.[97] The implication was that the epochs of Hindu history ceased at this point.

Dutt's arguments about early India were consistent with those of

<hr>

91 Maurice, *The History of Hindostan*, 140.

92 Bentley, *A Historical View of the Hindu Astronomy*, xxix–xxx.

93 Dutt, *A History of Civilization in Ancient India*.

94 Ibid., 4.

95 Ibid., 5.

96 Ibid., 5–21.

97 Ibid., 21.

other writers in the first half of the twentieth century – and not only those who were interested in prioritising Hindu history. For example, in 1930 Jawaharlal Nehru explained that there were "great periods in the life of nations" in which ordinary people were not only "committed to a great cause," but created history that was "epoch-making."[98] In *The Discovery of India* (1946) he argued that periods of history were characterised by "bursts of creative effort in the fields of thought and action, in literature and drama, in sculpture and architecture."[99] These epochs were disrupted by "disharmony and conflict" within India as well as "intrusions from outside."[100] Like Dutt, Nehru dated the end of the most dynamic period of Indian history as around the eleventh century CE: "The last great period of such activity in a variety of directions was the classical epoch which began in the fourth century after Christ. By about 1000 AD or earlier, signs of inner decay in India are very evident."[101] Where Nehru differed from Dutt was on the point that it was possible to meet the challenges of the conflicts with the creation of new ideas in India. For Nehru, in this period the "coming of new races with different background" functioned like a "new driving force" that provided new possibilities, even if there were also new problems.[102] While Nehru did not propose a formal list or ordering of epochs, the point is that like several contemporary writers he was interested in linking epochs to the greatness of Indian culture and civilisation.

Savarkar expanded the interpretation of temporalities by arguing that Hindu history was made up of hundreds of "golden pages," or what Godbole translated as "hundreds of glorious epochs."[103] In consonance with Dutt and Nehru, Savarkar explained that each glorious epoch was defined by specific characteristics classified as a part of Hindu civilisation, such as "poetic exuberance, music, prowess, affluence, the height of philosophy and depth of theology."[104] Within the hundreds of epochs of Hindu history he identified six that were extraordinary.

[98] Nehru, "A Birthday Letter for Indira Priyadarshini on her Thirteenth Birthday," October 26, 1930, in idem, *Glimpses of World History*, 2.

[99] Nehru, *The Discovery of India*, 85.

[100] Ibid.

[101] Ibid.

[102] Ibid.

[103] Savarkar, *Six Glorious Epochs*, 2; Savarkar, *Saha Soneri Pane*, 2.

[104] Ibid.

While Dutt's five epochs covered a period of just over 3000 years (2000 BCE–1194 CE), Savarkar's six glorious epochs lasted approximately 2500 years (4th-6th century BCE–20th century CE). Based on Savarkar's claim that there were hundreds of epochs in Hindu history, his larger conceptualisation of time was closer to the millions of years discussed by astronomers. Savarkar did not provide an exact starting point for his first glorious epoch, except to say that Indian history began with the "Buddhist period."[105] This was a shift from *Essentials of Hindutva*, in which he had put forward the idea that Hindutva was formed over a period of forty centuries.

Savarkar was clear that his purpose was to continue his project of Hindu history as Indian history. But in order for him to make any claim about temporality, especially what he called *deshkaal* (the time of the nation), he needed to verify and confirm all measurements of time based on "foreign" and "indigenous" sources. For Savarkar there was agreement in the literature that the Buddhist period marked what he called "the starting point of our history."[106] This also meant that temporalities that could not be substantiated with evidence and cor-roborated by multiple scholars (Indian and Western) should not be classified as Indian history *per se*. Yet Savarkar proposed that future methodological innovations might lead to the discovery of new evidence for interpreting the beginning of Indian history, such that the "Puranic period" could one day be considered historical.[107]

Savarkar maintained that each *soneri pane* (glorious epoch) was defined by the culture or civilisation of any given period (similar to the ideas put forward by Dutt and Nehru), but he added an important characteristic that distinguished his interpretation. His "Glorious Epochs" (as distinct from "glorious epochs") were specifically identified as periods in which Hindus were victorious in wars of independence against foreigners:

[B]y Glorious Epoch I mean the one [epoch] from the history of that war-like generation and the brave leaders and successful warriors who inspire and lead it on to a war of liberation in order to free their nation from the shackles of foreign domination, whenever it has the misfortune to fall

[105] Ibid.
[106] Ibid.
[107] Ibid.

prey to such a powerful fatal aggression and to grovel abjectly under it, and who ultimately drive away the enemy making it an absolutely free and sovereign nation.[108]

This definition of "Glorious Epoch" was paradoxical, given that *Indian War* and *Hindu Pad Padashahi* had, as described by Savarkar, ended in failure. Yet he reclaimed the histories in both texts as central to his discussion of "Glorious Epochs." He also incorporated the main themes from these texts, along with *Essentials of Hindutva*, to provide a continuous Hindu history dating back to antiquity. Each "Glorious Epoch" exemplified the principle of revolution in which the Hindu spirit inspired and motivated brave heroes to rise up against foreign invaders who had crossed the Indus river to enter Hindusthan. Savarkar's goal, as noted, was to exemplify the mimetic nature of Hindu history: this was his method for substantiating the persistence of the principle of history as a manifestation of Hindutva.

It seems clear that Savarkar had at this time simply pushed his interpretation back to the fourth century BCE to place Hindu wars of independence at the centre of each "Glorious Epoch." His turn to modern historical research meant that he was confronted with the limitation of sources and evidence with which to write Hindu history. In the middle of the book he once again reflects on the purpose of his text – the objective was not to write a detailed history: this being a re-current explanation through his oeuvre. Detailed history was a genre of writing not compatible with Hindu history.

Perhaps to pre-empt criticism, Savarkar says that "The present book . . . is not really a history of India but a critical treatise."[109] In *Saha Soneri Pane* he uses the term *samiksana*, which can be defined as close investigation or search. What remains unclear is if Savarkar's conceptualisation of *samiksana* or critical treatise was a return to an earlier form of writing, such as *Essentials of Hindutva*, in which he had brought together multiple sources – in which case it could be seen as an extension of the earlier text. Alternatively, the treatise was a genre of writing and analysis that had now inspired Savarkar. This point was never unpacked or discussed in the text. Needless to say, there remains an

---

[108] Savarkar, *Six Glorious Epochs*, 2–3.
[109] Savarkar, *Six Glorious Epochs*, 217; Savarkar, *Saha Soneri Pane*, 192.

epistemic tension throughout the book: Savarkar regularly returns to conjecture as method, even as he criticises Hindus for their failure to truly establish a Hindusthan exemplifying the heights of Hindu civilisation that he had posited. This is also the point raised by J. Patrocinio de Souza in one of the few English-language reviews of *Six Glorious Epochs* that appeared in *The Times of India*: Savarkar, he says, did not write "an authentic history of India" but put together "a curious mélange of fact and fiction, reality and fantasy."[110] Savarkar's modification of his methodology resembles more a rhetorical argument for turning to "today's research" in meaning to bring contemporary approaches to writing Hindu history, while in fact selecting sources that suit his argument about Hindutva and Hindu history.

## 4. Silencing Hindu Pasts

Apart from arguing that the writing of history in colonial India had silenced Hindu pasts, Savarkar saw the system of education established by the British in India as having "perverted Indian history" in schools and colleges.[111] Textbooks not only ignored major Hindu heroes, but centuries of Hindu history were simply missing from the curriculum. The result was that Hindu students had been deceived and misinformed about their own history for generations. Savarkar was particularly concerned at English writers of Indian history having narrated the history of Hindus as a story of "foreign aggression" and "national defeats."[112] The circulation of these English-language texts meant that this narrative became globally dominant: "Absurd and malicious statements implying that India as a nation has always been under some foreign rule or the other that Indian history is an unbroken chain of defeat after defeat of the Hindus, have been used like currency and are accepted by our people without affront or remonstrance or even a formal protest."[113] Hindus with a Western education had repeated

---

[110] de Souza, "A Committed Hindu," *The Times of India*, October 10, 1971, 8.

[111] Savarkar, *Six Glorious Epochs*, 4; Savarkar, *Saha Soneri Pane*, 4.

[112] Ibid.

[113] Ibid.

the arguments of the English historians. Savarkar, as earlier noted, had raised a similar critique in *Indian War*, where he had called some of these Indian historians "sycophants."[114] English historians had ignored the principles of history because it was not in their interest to "admit the truth."[115] By contrast his purpose was to counter the interpretations of the English historians and their Indian counterparts "for the sake of historical truth."[116] In consonance with his earlier work, Savarkar now again argued that he wrote against the grain of the dominant narrative, which in this case meant writing a revisionist history negating the idea that Hindu history was a history of defeats at the hands of foreigners; in fact to write a history of Hindu victories was a "national duty."[117] And "I have decided here to describe the historical achievements of those generations and of their representative leaders who vanquished the aggressors from time to time and liberated their country."[118]

In his Presidential Address to the Akhil Bharatiya Hindu Mahasabha in 1938 Savarkar provided a discussion of the impact of the writings of Thomas B. Macaulay on education in India.[119] Western education as promoted by Macaulay was a "de-nationalising scheme" meant to "undermine the very concept of a Hindu nation amongst the rising generation of Hindu youths."[120] He did not mention the famous 1835 "Macaulay's Minute" by name in his address.[121] Instead, to illustrate his point he opted to analyse a letter written by Macaulay.[122] The ultimate goal of Western education, he says, was to target Hindus to not only become Westernised but also to adopt Christianity as a method of destroying the Hindu nation: "[T]he first generations

[114] Savarkar, *Indian War*, 5.

[115] Ibid.

[116] Savarkar, *Six Glorious Epochs*, 4; Savarkar, *Saha Soneri Pane*, 4.

[117] Ibid.

[118] Ibid.

[119] Savarkar, "Presidential Address, 20th Session of the Akhil Bharatiya Hindu Mahasabha, Nagpur, 1938," in Savarkar, *Hindu Rashtra Darshan*, 37.

[120] Ibid.

[121] "Minute by the Hon'ble T.B. Macaulay, dated the 2nd February 1835," in H. Sharp, *Selections from Educational Records*, Part 1, Bureau of Education, India (Calcutta: Superintendent Government Printing, 1920), 107–17. (Hereafter, "Macaulay's Minute.")

[122] Savarkar explained that in one of Thomas B. Macaulay's letters to his son-in-law, he argued that Western education would eventually lead Hindus to

of the Hindu youths who took to Western education . . . were on the whole cut off from their old moorings of Hinduness, of Hindutva. They knew nothing of Hindu history, Hindu religion, Hindu culture and all that they knew of Hindutva were only its weak points."[123] The formalisation of Western education had created a cadre of men who were taught to copy the social and cultural life of their English counterparts. These "English-educated Hindus" would eventually "cease to be Hindus."[124] Savarkar says: "Fed on the Western literature and history and cut off from any contact with Hindu thoughts and Hindu policy, they naturally came to the easy conclusion that if they imitated the West, and especially England in every detail of individual and collective life they and their country would be benefited and saved."[125] Savarkar articulated his ambivalence to the colonial discourse put forward by Macaulay, especially the argument for the need to "form a class of persons Indian in blood and colour, but English in tastes, opinions, in morals and in intellect."[126] As a Hindu educated in the English language, he himself was resistant to what has been called "colonial mimicry."[127] His essence as a historian had been to see through the colonial strategy and not abandon Hindutva.

<hr>

convert to Christianity. However, this appears to be an error on Savarkar's part, given that Macaulay did not have any children (or a son-in-law). It is possible that Savarkar was referring to his sister Hannah Trevelyan's son-in-law (or son), especially as Macaulay was very close to Hannah and her family. On the other hand, the details of the letter cited by Savarkar in his 1938 Presidential Address are similar to a letter sent by Macaulay to his father Zachary Macaulay from Calcutta on October 12, 1836, in which he wrote the following: "The effect of this education on the Hindoos is prodigious. No Hindoo who has received an English education ever remains sincerely attached to his religion . . . some embrace Christianity. It is my firm belief that, if our plans of education are followed up, there will not be a single idolater among the respectable classes in Bengal thirty years hence." This letter is reprinted in Trevelyan, *The Life and Letters of Lord Macaulay*, vol. 1, 398–9. Special thanks to Ashok Hegde for discussing the details of Thomas B. Macaulay's biography.

[123] Savarkar, "Presidential Address, 20th Session of the Akhil Bharatiya Hindu Mahasabha, Nagpur, 1938," in Savarkar, *Hindu Rashtra Darshan*, 37.

[124] Ibid., 38–9.

[125] Ibid., 38.

[126] "Macaulay's Minute," in Sharp, *Selections from Educational Records*, 116.

[127] See Bhabha, "Of Mimicry and Man."

Savarkar appears prescient on this point of the impact of an education policy on colonial subjects following "Macaulay's Minute." The discipline of English, it has been shown most acutely in our own time, was linked to the imperial mission of educating and "civilising" Indian society.[128] English literary education was vital in establishing administrative and political control and therefore "irrevocably alter[ed]" after "Macaulay's Minute," as the passing of the English Education Act (1835) mandated the study of English literature for Indians.[129] This insight into the structures of disciplinary knowledge formation is in a way anticipated by Savarkar. He was not strictly speaking of history as a discipline in his critiques, but he does provide a parallel argument when arguing that an epistemic rupture had occurred as a direct consequence of the imposition of Western education on Indians. Its negative impact, in his interpretation, had been on the writing of Hindu history. The first few generations of Hindu men after Macaulay were "carried off their feet" as they "fell in love with everything Western."[130] Savarkar explained that he himself had escaped this variety of cultural hegemony, ignoring even the influence of Mazzini on his own thought and work by seeing it as somehow separate from Western education (or thought). Savarkar did not discuss whether writing *Saha Soneri Pane* in Marathi was a form of epistemic resistance to Western education. However, he did make clear that his book was written to contradict a historiography dominated by English historians promoting the idea that Hindu history was only a history of subjugation and defeat by foreign invaders.

## 5. Foreigners and Hindus in Ancient History

Savarkar used the terms *paraka* and *parakiya* to identify all "invaders" into Hindusthan; he also incorporated *mlenccha* to specifically identify Muslims as foreigners, outsiders, and demons in this text.[131] He says

---

[128] See Viswanathan, *Masks of Conquest.*

[129] Ibid., 45.

[130] Savarkar, "Presidential Address, 20th Session of the Akhil Bharatiya Hindu Mahasabha, Nagpur, 1938," in Savarkar, *Hindu Rashtra Darshan*, 38.

[131] Savarkar, *Six Glorious Epochs*, 9; Savarkar, *Saha Soneri Pane*, 8. Savarkar used *parakiya* on the first page of *Saha Soneri Pane* and it is found throughout

he did not consider Greeks *mlenccha* – only Muslims.[132] The Sanskrit root *para* means Other or "different," but it can also be defined as distant, removed, or remote. As a result, in Sanskrit *parakiya* is used to describe those belonging to another domain, or a stranger who is hostile. In Marathi *paraka* (and *parakiya*) can mean Other, foreign, or strange. I include the etymology of the terms used by Savarkar to indicate the range of meanings of "foreign" in *Six Glorious Epochs* that might otherwise be missed. "Foreign" did not simply signify Otherness or strangeness to Savarkar, he believed that inscribed within the term was a sense of hostility. Beyond that, he added another specific characteristic to his meaning of *paraka*: non-Hindu. This is an important distinction throughout the book: some individuals he sees as remaining *paraka* (and *parakiya*) despite centuries of their ancestors living in Hindusthan – namely Muslims; while others are simply assimilated as Hindus into society over centuries or millennia. *Mlenccha*, in constrast, is treated as synonymous with Muslims throughout the text. Needless to say, this means that all Muslims forever belonged to a Muslim nation and never to Hindusthan (or India). The only alternative for Muslims was to abandon Islam and become Hindu in order to shed their foreign identity.

Savarkar's text is organised to emphasise the differences between foreign invaders in "ancient history" (*prachin*) and "modern history" (*arvachin*).[133] Ancient history is defined as the period from 600 BCE to 700 CE – the first four Glorious Epochs – in which all foreigners were defeated and assimilated within Hindu society. Modern history was made up of the Fifth and Sixth Glorious Epochs for the years 700–1947 CE. This was a period of conflict with Muslims and Christians who wanted to annihilate Hindus and Hindusthan. Hindus had been sometimes victorious in their wars to regain power in the modern period, but the war of independence had continued into the present because Hindus had not succeeded in establishing complete dominance.

Savarkar's binary classification of Indian history into ancient and

---

the entire work, as is *mlenccha*. It appears that in Godbole's translation, *paraka* and *parakiya* are translated as foreigner or invader throughout.

[132] See Ahmed Asif, *Loss of Hindustan*, 10.

[133] Savarkar, *Six Glorious Epochs*, 128–9; Savarkar, *Saha Soneri Pane*, 109–10.

modern history marked a shift in the existing periodisation. Romila Thapar has argued that historians of India have largely continued James Mill's tripartite taxonomy of Indian history in his *History of British India* (1817).[134] Mill had divided Indian history into three periods – Hindu, Muslim, and British – that were later identified as Ancient, Medieval, and Modern, respectively.[135] Thapar states, "The periodisation . . . which is generally accepted by most historians of India and by most universities teaching Indian history, is basically the same as that of Mill, since the Ancient period usually ends with the establishment of Muslim dynasties and the Medieval period with the acquisition of political power by the East India Company."[136] In a related argument proposed by Harbans Mukhia, the medieval period is often conflated with "Muslim India" on account of the religion of the new rulers.[137] A "static view of Islam" in this view prevents seeing the differentiations and changes in Indian Islam over a thousand years. It also presumed that no forces other than Islam and Muslim rule shaped social, cultural, political, economic processes in India over the so-called Muslim Period.

[134] Thapar, *Ancient Indian Social History*, 4–5.

[135] The debates on the periodisation of Indian and South Asian history have now grown beyond the tripartite categories. For example, C.A. Bayly proposed the importance of temporal border-crossing in the writing of South Asian history of the eighteenth and nineteenth century, rather than studying what he called "periods of history . . . in self-contained compartments." Bayly, *Rulers, Townsmen, Bazaars*, viii. Also, see Travers, "The Eighteenth Century in Indian History," and Alavi, ed., *The Eighteenth Century in India*. What has also emerged in parallel with some of these debates on the eighteenth century is the conceptualisation of "Early Modern India" and "Early Modern South Asia" to describe the period between 1500 and 1800 CE, but also as a critique of the earlier idea of dividing the historiography into Ancient, Medieval, and Modern. Sanjay Subrahmanyam's writings on Early Modern histories have been significant in helping shape a new temporal parameter in the historiography. See Subrahmanyam, *From Tagus to the Ganges* and Subrahmanyam, *Mughals and Franks*. For a further critique of the debates on periodisation of the "medieval" and "early modern" in South Asian history, see Ali, "The Idea of the Medieval."

[136] Thapar, *Ancient Indian Social History*, 23, n. 6.

[137] Mukhia, "Medieval Indian History and the Communal Approach," 22.

Savarkar's idea of modern history begins with the arrival of Muslims in India, but its primary focus is on what he called the Hindu–Muslim Epic War. This begins much earlier than in the periodisation used by Dutt and Nehru, who marked the eleventh century as a turning point in Indian history by linking it to the raids of Mahmud of Ghazni and the establishment of the Ghaznavid dynasty in India. Savarkar also moved away from the classifications used by Mill and later historians by eliminating "Medieval India" as a category of Indian history. He continued to use the terms "Muslim historians" and "Muslim histories" in his text, viewing the latter as works produced by foreign historians about India. For him the key was that modern history represented a new series of wars – first with Muslims and later with Christians – that differed from those in ancient history. But he believes that modern history also started with a new Glorious Epoch in which Hindus were ultimately, and once again, the victors.

In Savarkar's conceptualisation of "foreign invaders," his own earlier argument that Hindusthan was formed as a direct consequence of Hindu conquest and the colonisation of land in the subcontinent is overlooked. We recall here that in *Essentials of Hindutva* the formation of Hindus *as* Hindus is about domination and subjugation: Hindus were the colonisers over those who were not Hindus; the latter *became* Hindus through conquest, violence, assimilation, and cultural imperialism. Savarkar was at this point clearly not concerned with the early history he had discussed in *Essentials of Hindutva*; rather, he began the First Glorious Epoch by discussing Alexander the Great: "Alexander's attack on India is the first well-known foreign invasion during the ancient period of Indian history. It took place in 326 bc."[138] The fact that Alexander's conquests were well documented meant that he had achieved world notoriety. Because he was victorious against the Persian and Babylonian empires, he assumed he would be victorious in India as well. His was the initial attack, unprovoked and unjustified. In all epochs, this was the pattern – foreign invaders were the first to violate Hindusthan and Hindu civilisation.

Savarkar's main critique of historiographical representations of Alexander centred on the idea of his supposed greatness: "Alexander was a conqueror! But he was not a world-conqueror! Conqueror of

---

[138] Savarkar, *Six Glorious Epochs*, 5.

India he never was!!"[139] He was referred to as "Alexander the Great" because he was assumed to have expanded the Greek empire all the way to India. But it was in India that Alexander and the Greeks had been stopped. For Savarkar this was an important omission in European histories, specifically by those that celebrated the Greeks – but especially the subject of Alexander – as central to understanding Western civilisation. Alexander had been brought to "tears" because he could not "defeat India completely."[140] He was likely "disturbed" at the prospect of territorial loss by the heroic Indian rebels who were fighting a war of independence against the Greeks. This was an aspect absent in histories written by Europeans, and Indians had incorporated the same interpretations in their histories without considering an alternative reading – and this was a consequence of Indians having received an English education. Savarkar's solution is clear:

> This perversion of history and the misunderstanding it has created in the minds of our people should no more be tolerated hereafter. We may not mind the other traditional anecdotes about Alexander, but those at least which are connected with Indian [Bharatiya] history and which extol Alexander disproportionately to the derogation of the Indian people, must be deleted from our school text-books and from our literature.[141]

At one level this implies the vital importance of history in the creation of a hegemonic discourse, shaping character through teaching history, and inculcating nationalism through carefully selective history; at another level it advocates the erasure of ideas, interpretations, and histories that might influence susceptible Hindus to accept specific arguments about a past that celebrates foreigners. In fact Savarkar's whole point is the need to write history in exclusive celebration of Hindu achievement and to the exclusion of Muslim, Christian, and other "foreign" achievement, to set aside any work that negates or overlooks Hindu subjectivity in resisting foreign invasions. The invaders and foreigners had been sufficiently celebrated by their own historians; the need of the hour was a competitive history to contradict those narratives. The underlying assumption is that every history ever written is in

[139] Ibid., 58.
[140] Ibid.
[141] Ibid., 57.

the service of a community, a nation, a group interest of some variety or other. Savarkar's book marked an important discursive moment in which Hindus were no longer the failures in or losers of history. To write Hindu history was to ensure highlighting Hindu victories at all costs, including removing interpretations of the past and turning to conjecture when necessary.

Perhaps all of this seems a belabouring of what has long been obvious, a reiteration of what permeates Savarkar's oeuvre. But Savarkar had not formally articulated such a strategy as clearly and forcefully in his earlier work. He had now produced a text chronologically organised into Glorious Epochs, and within each epoch his interpretations deviated conspicuously from his own objective of writing Indian history based on evidence.

As in *Indian War* and *Hindu Pad Padashahi*, Savarkar inserts dialogue spoken by historical actors and articulates what he imagines as their emotions at the time – Alexander was in tears; Alexander was disappointed.[142] Savarkar has now assumed the role of omniscient narrator of all Indian history; he has achieved ontological integrity with his historical subjects – the warriors, the *veer*, the heroes, the brave, the Hindus. His narration is ultimately *their* narration based on the significance of the Hindu spirit that had travelled from Hindu hero to Hindu hero and from ancient history to modern history.

What the story of Alexander's invasion illustrated to him was the ability of Indians to respond with a "warlike spirit" for "Indian independence" in the First Glorious Epoch.[143] The key characteristics of resistance to the Greeks are here nearly identical to the discussions in *Indian War* and *Hindu Pad Padashahi*; they also share parallels with Savarkar's own activities in his autobiographical writings.

The question of what Savarkar considered relevant in his history is clear: each Glorious Epoch is identified with a foreign invader and Hindu heroes who fought for independence. Everyday forms of Hindu resistance are celebrated against the Greeks in the First Glorious Epoch, as are two Hindu heroes: Chandragupta Maurya and Chanakya (Kautilya). Brief biographical accounts of both are offered with the

142 Ibid., 58.
143 Ibid., 70.

caveat that these are entangled in legends, myths, and anecdotes. Savarkar says he only wants to present aspects that are historically accurate and verifiable — by which he means material likely cited or presented in multiple sources. But though he recommends that interested readers should consider Radha Kumud Mookerji's *Chandragupta Maurya and His Times* (1943) as an important source, we also find that this does not limit Savarkar's use of what he himself calls anecdotes to make assertions about figures like Chandragupta and Chanakya.[144] For Savarkar the key was to understand that Chandragupta was a royal prince who became the emperor and fought off the Greeks with the assistance of master strategist and scholar Chanakya (very possibly the author of the *Arthashastra*). In Savarkar's account the two hatched a plan to bring down the Greeks in India while also quelling the internal rivalries of indigenous rulers seeking power. Chanakya's heroism consists in enunciating the principles of a warlike spirit and armed strength in every aspect of life to build a unified empire. Savarkar does not provide any analysis of Chanakya's arguments in the *Arthashastra*; his descriptions resemble his discussions of Ramdas in relation to Shivaji in *Hindu Pad Padashahi*. The significance of Chandragupta lies in "the singular victory" that pushed the Greeks back to the Indian frontiers.[145] Chanakya's theory of warfare had restored Hindu sovereignty, while Chandragupta as emperor had signed treaties with the Greek emperor Seleucos to create a period of "political and international friendship."[146] There had been a happy ending: Chandragupta married Seleucos' daughter and the remaining Greeks in India became assimilated as Hindus. This marked the "First Glorious Epoch of Hindu Victories over the Aggressor."[147]

The first four Glorious Epochs largely follow a similiar pattern. Foreign invaders enter India with expectations of conquest, colonisation, and annihilation: the Bactrian Greeks in the Second Glorious Epoch; the Sakas and the Kushanas in the Third; and the Huns in the Fourth. A valiant Hindu hero emerges in each epoch, harnesses the support of fellow Hindus, and fights off the foreigners: these heroes are Pushyamitra, Vikramaditya, and Yashodharma, respectively. They exemplify the Hin-

[144] See Mookerji, *Chandragupta Maurya and His Times*.
[145] Savarkar, *Six Glorious Epochs*, 43.
[146] Ibid., 56.
[147] Ibid., 59.

du spirit, and each Glorious Epoch is organised around their accomplishments. The thousands of Hindu warriors who fight alongside them are also important in Savarkar's narrative: each individual has refused to cede any part of Hindusthan without a fight. Foreigners who lose the war are assimilated into Hindusthan as Hindus. For example, the Sakas initially "hated the Vedic religion," but were inspired after their defeat by the "fighting spirit" of Hindu civilisation.[148] These Sakas not only learned Sanskrit and *sanskriti*, most also converted to the Vedic religion.[149] A similar narrative is provided for the Huns after their defeat; they "took over willingly to Indian religions and languages and customs and within a generation or two merged so completely with the Hindus that they could never recollect their Hunnish extraction."[150]

However, one major problem plagued India's ancient history and threatened all Glorious Epochs: Buddhism. Throughout Savarkar's seminal writings, especially in *Essentials of Hindutva*, he shows ambivalence about the Buddha and Buddhism: his saying that Indian history begins in the Buddhist period is merely his view of chronology and not intended as compliment. In some ways the Buddha is obviously what Chanakya was not: the Buddha's non-violence was responsible for the long-term subjugation of Hindus by foreign invaders. The real antagonist in Savarkar's work is thus logically Ashoka (r. BCE 268–232) – grandson of Chandragupta Maurya – who propagated a "*dhamma*" that emphasised non-violence and compassion.[151] This is an expansion of Savarkar's earlier critique of Ashoka in *Essentials of Hindutva*. Here, the "Ashokan epoch" does not meet "the criterion" or "scope" of a Glorious Epoch.[152] As a result, "we cannot do anything more than bypass him with only a slight reference." What was Ashoka's mistake? Ashoka's abandonment of a theory of warfare after his victory in the Kalinga war had made India vulnerable to foreign attack.[153] Ashoka was "anti-national": at a time when he could have consolidated his power, his turn to Buddhism weakened India. Buddhist monks

[148] Ibid., 97.
[149] Ibid., 97–8.
[150] Ibid., 123.
[151] See Lahiri, *Ashoka in Ancient India*.
[152] Savarkar, *Six Glorious Epochs*, 61.
[153] Hardiman, *Gandhi in His Time and Ours*, 175.

encouraged by Ashoka spread the news that India had abandoned a theory of warfare in favour of non-violence. For Savarkar this encouraged new imperial ventures into India, starting with the Kushanas, the Sakas, and the Huns, culminating in the invasions by Muslims and Christians. Savarkar asks rhetorically: "Were the non-violent Buddhists violent? Is [Buddhism] extreme kindness or extreme cruelty?"[154]

Violence, once again, appears central in Savarkar's understanding of what it means to be a Hindu. Now he raises the conceptual stakes, so to speak, by arguing that both bloodshed and vengeance are parts of Nature. Ashoka's non-violence was antithetical to being a Hindu and thus ultimately also unnatural in the sense of being against Nature. Ashoka's descendants perpetuated the problem by not protecting the integrity of India's empire, as they had no theory of warfare. Savarkar specifically laments the failure of the emperor Brihadrath Maurya, who he says practised Buddhism to India's cost. A military general named Pushyamitra assassinated Brihadrath and "The Buddhistic Mauryan Empire met its doom that day!"[155] This advocacy of violence against proponents of non-violence is voiced with great clarity: "It is for the sake of free development of human virtues that the principle of non-violence, which emasculates human beings with the curse of weakness, should be at times killed by cruel violence."[156] For Savarkar, cruel violence is sometimes the best option: Brihadrath was not simply assassinated, he was beheaded: "Pushyamitra had to cut off the head of Brihadrath Maurya . . . simply as a national duty."[157] The coupling of assassination with beheading is found frequently in Savarkar's descriptions of Hindu perpetrators of violence because he sees them as having been unjustly and "brutally murdered" by foreign invaders. Hindus in general used more ethical forms of violence when killing.[158] A straightforward assassination can be a moral act: "Chandragupta and Chanakya had to assassinate, as an unavoidable national duty, Samrat Mahapadma Nanda."[159] Pushyamitra's heroism lies in abandoning the principle of non-violence, resuming warfare against "foreign invaders,"

[154] Savarkar, *Six Glorious Epochs*, 122.

[155] Ibid., 78.

[156] Ibid., 351.

[157] Ibid.

[158] Ibid., 168.

[159] Ibid.

and defending Hindu territory. Buddhism continued, but Hindus had regained dominance, enabling the arrival of more Glorious Epochs.

Savarkar ends his period of ancient history with a discussion of a *devaduta*, meaning "messenger of the gods" in Marathi.[160] In *Six Glorious Epochs* the word is translated as angel – "Let us for a moment imagine that a certain Angel who has been observing the affairs of this Earth . . . and has once again come down on the Himalayan peaks and is surveying the Indian scene."[161] Not unlike Walter Benjamin's conceptualisation of the "Angel of History" in his "Theses on the Philosophy of History," this *devaduta* also looks at the past, though what he observes is very different.[162] Benjamin's angel sees a catastrophe in which piles of wreckage are growing upon his feet, as a storm is blowing from Paradise with great violence. He points out that the angel would like to "awaken the dead" and "make whole what has been smashed."[163] Benjamin concludes: "The storm irresistibly propels him into the future to which his back is turned, while the pile of debris before him grows skyward. The storm is what we call progress."[164] Savarkar's *devaduta* would like to speak to the dead to ask if "foreign invaders" remain in Hindusthan; the *devaduta* does not know exactly what has happened – he is not omniscient and asks: "In one part of India there were some kingdoms and communities of Sakas and the Kushanas. Is there any one of them to be found here now?"[165] The *devaduta* learns that none are left: neither Greeks nor Huns nor any others. The *devaduta* is "awe-stricken."[166] He asks: "Well, tell me at least if there [are] any . . . of those Hindus who fought bravely with all these foreign aggressors and ruled over India?"[167] The answer he hears repeatedly from three hundred million Indians is, "Yes, I am that Hindu!" The *devaduta* learns that only Hindus now live in the territory and have laid the foundations for the "Hindu nation and the Hindu State."[168]

[160] Savarkar, *Saha Soneri Pane*, 107.

[161] Savarkar, *Six Glorious Epochs*, 125.

[162] See Benjamin, "Theses on the Philosophy of History."

[163] Ibid., 257.

[164] Ibid., 258.

[165] Savarkar, *Six Glorious Epochs*, 126.

[166] Ibid.

[167] Ibid.

[168] Ibid.

What may be called the *itihaaschi devaduta* (Angel of Hindu History?) knows of the violence perpetrated by "foreign aggressors," but he also knows of the violence with which Hindus can counter-attack and resist. Unlike Benjamin's "Angel of History," who saw horrors in the past that served as guides for conceptualising a different future, Savarkar's *devaduta* laments no storm of progress.[169] What he sees in the past is that Hindu history is always a history in which Hindus annihilate foreign aggressors and then assimilate survivors as Hindus. The story of ancient Indian history is the story of Hindu victory.

## 6. The Great War in Modern History

Savarkar's discussion of the Fifth Glorious Epoch is the single largest part of *Saha Soneri Pane*. It occupies approximately two-thirds of the entire text. Its primary focus is what Savarkar called the *mahayuddha* (great war) or the "Epic Hindu Muslim War."[170] This 1200-year war defined the "modern age of Hindu history."[171] Savarkar acknowledges the existence of a robust historiography about Muslims in India as well as the writings of "age-old enemies like the Muslims, the Portuguese, the English."[172] He himself relies heavily on the writings of Govindrao Sakharam Sardesai, Vishwanath Kashinath Rajwade, Jadunath Sarkar, and M.G. Ranade are mentioned in the text, especially for the Maratha period in the Fifth Glorious Epoch, of which a full history had never been written: "What we intend to do here is to examine thoroughly and from the Hindu standpoint this epic struggle and the period covered by it as searchingly, as faithfully and as fearlessly as it ought to have been done – but unfortunately has not so far been done."[173] His standard caveat reappears: "[I]t should be clear that a detailed account of the continuous, long-drawn, fierce and gigantic Hindu–Muslim struggle is not intended here."[174]

[169] See Eagleton, *Walter Benjamin*.

[170] Savarkar, *Six Glorious Epochs*, 128–9; Savarkar, *Saha Soneri Pane*, 110.

[171] Savarkar, *Six Glorious Epochs*, 129.

[172] Ibid., 406.

[173] Ibid., 128.

[174] Ibid.

The Fifth Glorious Epoch is not organised chronologically; Savarkar says readers interested in both chronology and details of this historical period have the benefit of a vast extant literature. From his point of view, to study the invasions of Muslims did not require specificity, qualification, or differentiation because of the homogeneity of the perpetrators: they were all Muslims.

Why was this important? Savarkar points out that not all wars were the same; wars against foreign invaders in ancient history were fought against those who had aspirations for "political ascendancy" rather than "religious enmity."[175] Religion was not an issue in the early wars because the invaders practised religions that he considered "more or less like the offshoots of Hindu [dharma] itself."[176] In fact, Savarkar argues that many of the millions who came as invaders decided to settle in India and assimilate into Hindu society. This was only possible because these early conflicts were about politics, not religion. The major shift occurred with the emergence and spread of Buddhism, which promoted "extreme non-violence, kindness, love, [and] truth."[177] The Hindu polity became susceptible to new invasions, especially after Ashoka; and though Pushyamitra may have been successful in limiting the influence of Buddhism in statecraft, its ideas remained popular. The destruction and annihilation of the Hindu polity only became apparent when "Islam invaded Hindu [dharma]" and many Hindus still lacked a war strategy: "Why were they [the Hindus] afraid? Why did they feel it to be against their Hindu religion itself to launch such armed counter-offensive[s] against the Muslims?"[178] Savarkar blames Hindus squarely for accepting Buddhism rather than eradicating it from India. Muslims, who aspired to both religious and political power, now dominated battlefields against the Hindus. Not only were Hindus defeated, but millions were converted to Islam. Moreover, Muslims were impervious to assimilation by Hindus.

The problem facing Hindus was exacerbated by the arrival of "Christian nations" in the sixteenth century, such as the Portuguese, Dutch,

---

[175] Ibid., 256.
[176] Ibid., 258.
[177] Ibid., 256–7.
[178] Ibid.

French, and British, who had their own objective of religious and political conquest along the pattern set by Muslims. The resolution in this period of the *mahayuddha* differed from those in the earlier Glorious Epochs. Since the entire Hindu population did not convert to Islam, Savarkar argues that Hindu resistance was thriving; moreover, select Hindus regularly rebelled against Muslims by turning to violence and vengeance. These were the widespread Hindu heroes who made the Fifth Glorious Epoch possible.

Savarkar's priority was clearly not to write a history of Muslims in India, let alone an Indian history of Muslims: the latter was in fact an epistemic impossibility in Savarkar's conceptualisation since he had removed the period of Indian history often identified as "Muslim history." What then did Savarkar have to say about most Muslims? He states: "All the . . . Muslim States right from the Arabs to the Mongols invaded India one after another and carried on for seven or eight centuries continuously the bitterest, bloodiest and cruelest wars and at last when the regime of Allauddin practically the whole of India passed under the Muslim sway round about the year AD 1310, the Muslim ambition seemed almost fulfilled!"[179] His point was that regardless of whether these were Turks, Mongols, Mughals, Arabs, Pathans, or Abyssinians, they had all arrived in India as foreign Muslim invaders, raiders, aggressors, and dominators. There was a similarity to every invasion: Hindu territories were looted, Hindu temples destroyed, Hindu women and men raped, Hindu children kidnapped, and millions of Hindus converted to Islam. In instances of Muslim aggressors settling down to establish rule, Savarkar's focus is on what he sees as internal attacks against Hindu kingdoms. The Fifth Glorious Epoch is thus not centrally about the victimisation of Hindus: it centrally demonstrates that, despite more than a thousand years of Muslim invasions, Hindus still emerged victorious, most specially because of the rise of the Hindu Pad Padashahi by the Marathas.

To understand Savarkar's narration of these invasions, it is helpful to consider his view of Mahmud of Ghazni in the eleventh century. Savarkar refers to Mahmud throughout the book as symbolic of all

---

[179] Ibid., 327.

Muslim invaders. Mahmud, he says, was not the first Muslim to attack India – that was Mohammad Bin Kasim in 711 CE – but Mahmud was considered the first to cross the Indus and violate the geographic sanctity of Hindusthan. Mahmud had taken a vow to "wipe out the Kafir Hindus from India" and his series of attacks marked the start of this process.[180] One territory after the next was raided, temples destroyed, women abducted, men killed, gold and jewellery looted: Thaneshwar, Mathura, Kannauj, and Gwalior were all defeated. With every Muslim invasion, there was Hindu resistance. Mahmud's invasion of the Somnath temple in Saurashtra in 1026 had a major impact for centuries: it had put fear into King Bheem of Saurashtra, who is described as having shamefully fled the territory with his army.[181] For Savarkar there were always Hindus like Bheem illustrating the cowardice that heroic Hindus had to overcome: this was a development of a theme that Savarkar had raised in *Indian War*. Such Hindus had arrived in their tens of thousands; they were not trained soldiers but yet fought with honour and bravery. Fifty thousand of them were killed and the Somnath temple was lost to Mahmud in that "holy battle."[182] Each individual Hindu had had the option of converting to Islam to save himself from death, but had chosen martyrdom. Mahmud had gone on to launch at least fifteen major invasions of India before his death in 1030.[183]

Savarkar says his specific narratives are corroborated by "Muslim historians," especially with regard to the number of Hindus who died in the major battle at Somnath.[184] He implies here that Hindu historians had first noted the number of deaths. Why is this important? For Savarkar, this is sufficient evidence authenticating his historical interpretation: he could show he had relied on two bodies of work, Hindu and "foreign." He could simultaneously cast doubt on the anti-Hindu bias in other histories: "while narrating this invasion of Mahmud on Somnath, not only the foreign historians but many Hindu historians, ungrateful as they too are, have mocked at the simple faith of the

[180] Ibid., 148.
[181] Ibid., 151.
[182] Ibid., 150–4.
[183] Ibid., 154.
[184] Ibid., 151.

priesthood and other Hindu population of the place, and have not uttered a single word in praise of those Hindu warriors."[185] Savarkar's priority was to elevate the fifty thousand Hindus whom he believed had died in battle – the Hindu heroes exemplifying the Hindu spirit.

To remember these heroic Hindus Savarkar includes a poem in the middle of his discussion of the battle at Somnath. The short poem is an eulogy to Horatius, the Roman hero who had died protecting a temple to the gods. Here, in the context of the desecration of a Hindu temple, it works as analogy. The title of the poem is not given, and its author is described only as "an English poet."[186] Ironically, Savarkar here reproduces the first stanza of "Horatius" by his *bête noire* Thomas B. Macaulay, whose *Lays of Ancient Rome* (1842) was a collection of poems famous in its day.[187] Savarkar's criticism of Macaulay's argument about Western education for Indians had not stopped him incorporating a part of the poem into the body of his text. Macaulay's literary skills capturing the sentiments of a classic Roman heroic figure are thus relied on to interpret the heroic Hindus of Somnath. To be fair, "ironic" is not the only possible interpretation here of Savarkar's reliance on Macaulay. His turn to poetry in this context was consistent with his broader argument about aesthetics and style in *Six Glorious Epochs*. He says he has moved away from simply narrating a "prosaic account of bare facts," even if "bare records" of historical events are the "basis for history."[188] "Without such a blending of history and poetry descriptions of such events can never be living . . . Simple dry prose will never be able to sustain it."[189] His writings occupied a liminal space – what he called a "border-land" between "pure history" and "pure poetry."[190] In the act of writing or narrating the past, Savarkar says "history becomes poetry." Also, "Such occasions and events can never be effectively described without resorting to mythological and romantic metaphors and grand poetic style. But human nature demands that

[185] Ibid., 152.
[186] Ibid.
[187] Macaulay, *Lays of Ancient Rome*.
[188] Savarkar, *Six Glorious Epochs*, 403.
[189] Ibid.
[190] Ibid.

everything that is stupendous and splendid and exciting, must be expressed in a highly emotional and ornate style."[191]

Savarkar regularly cited poetry in his oeuvre, and he was of course a major composer of poems in Marathi such as "Gomantak" and "Kamala," for which he had received acclaim.[192] Several of his poems were also reproduced in *Swatantraveer Vinayakrao Savarkar* and *Life of Barrister Savarkar*. As discussed in Part II, Savarkar used the literature of Hindi, Braj Bhasha, and Marathi to substantiate his claims about the uses of "Hindu" in works dating back to the thirteenth century, including a range of poems. The influence on him of English literary texts is also clear: Shakespeare's *Romeo and Juliet* appears in *Essentials of Hindutva*. Literary epigraphs often head his chapters: in *Hindu Pad Padashahi* he regularly begins with quotes from Ramdas and Prabhakar and cites poems by Thomas Moore, Charles Wolfe, Robert Burns, and Terence J. MacSwiney. Moore appears to have been a favourite – his poetry is cited in *Life of Barrister Savarkar*, which also has epigraphs from Sir Walter Scott and Ralph Waldo Emerson. The point is that Savarkar was familiar with poetry from the Western literary canon that conveyed ideas and sentiments useful for interpreting Hindutva. The argument that has been made on the influence of English literature as a discipline in colonial India is borne out quite clearly by Savarkar. More important than that, perhaps, is the fact that his father had introduced him to the poetry of Vaman, Moropant, and Tukaram, and to Alexander Pope's interpretation of Homer's *Iliad*.[193] In other words, Savarkar's incorporation of Macaulay's poem to serve the purpose of his context was in character with his idea of an elevated and suitable prose style for the writing of history: the exception here is mainly that the poem is not used as an epigraph.

Savarkar's trenchant critique of Macaulay's argument about Western education does naturally raise the question of how he viewed his own subjectivity in this context, given that he not only read (and cited) the Bible, but was influenced by Thomas à Kempis' *The Imitation of*

[191] Ibid.

[192] Savarkar's poetry is published in *Savarkar Samagra*, vol. 10. Also, see Joshi, *Glimpses of Veer Savarkar's Poetry*.

[193] See Gupta, *Life of Barrister Savarkar*.

*Christ.*[194] Savarkar's answer to this would have been that while he was interested in the allusive range made available by Western education, the more important point was that he was impervious to the epistemic influences of Western education in terms of language, literature, and religion – because he properly understood the importance of Hindu civilisation.

## 7. Hindu Civility and the Bhagavad Gita

In *Essentials of Hindutva* Savarkar had identified civilisation as an essential of Hindutva best expressed by the word *sanskriti*. His focus on establishing the commonalities among Hindus in terms of culture, history, heroes, art, law, rituals, and so on came with the caveat that his was not an "exhaustive" interpretation, but that any individual who identified himself as a Hindu must claim Hindu civilisation as his own.[195] Savarkar's argument about civilisation is not articulated beyond this point, and in *Saha Soneri Pane* he turns to the phrase "Hindu *sabhyata*" – translated as "Hindu civility" by Godbole – as a characteristic of Hindu *sanskriti*.[196] What does Savarkar mean by this phrase?

He explains that there was an exemplary code of conduct prescribed within Hindu civilisation that needed to be at the centre of all social and political interactions. This meant that Hindus needed to protect their civilisation at all costs by exhibiting bravery, valour, and heroism. This represented an expansion of Savarkar's arguments about *veer* and *veerata* in his early writings. Since he was primarily interested in periods of warfare, he argues that any understanding of civility must also take into account the virtuous, ethical, and necessary uses of violence. In fact, he suggests that any interpretation of civility that ignores the centrality of violence is antithetical to Hindu civility – and by extension to Hindu civilisation.

This distinction that he makes between Hindu civility and Hindu civilisation is made more difficult to interpret by the fact that he often

---

[194] Savarkar, *My Transportation for Life*, 260.
[195] Savarkar, *Essentials of Hindutva*, 87.
[196] Savarkar, *Saha Soneri Pane*, 195.

uses the terms interchangeably. To clarify: *sabhyata* can be defined as cultivated, politeness, or educated manners. However, I do not think this is how Savarkar is using the term. Instead, he appears to define the term as culture, civilisation, and civilised state.[197] Savarkar's inclusion of Hindu *sabhyata* is further complicated by the fact that in his other writings he typically translates *sanskriti* rather than *sabhyata* as civilisation. In other instances, *sanskriti* is defined as culture; in some places it is both civilisation and culture. I delineate these distinctions here not to suggest contradictions in Savarkar's writings, but rather to point to some of the difficulties in interpreting his thought based on the terms that he uses across his many texts.

The overlap (or distinction) between culture and civilisation is certainly not specific to Savarkar's writings, or to works on *sabhyata* and *sanskriti*. The global history of civility (and its cognates) is complex and entangled in specific historical processes (and languages). For example, the starting point for Norbert Elias' *The Civilizing Process* is a discussion of the complex conceptual histories of the German uses of *Kultur* and *Zivilisation*.[198] He points out that the English, French, and German interpretations of both terms are contingent within each society and language, but they also change over time. This point is further articulated in a comparative study of the concept of civility in thirteen languages in Europe and Asia, in which it is argued that the concept's "semantic networks" function differently in different languages and cultures across time.[199] In other words, and not surprisingly, the meanings of culture and civilisation are not fixed and were often overlapping. The challenge, of course, is to study the specific uses of each term within a given context in time that allows for a greater understanding of the historical meanings of each term.

Savarkar's conception of Hindu civility contributed to robust public debates in the twentieth century on defining and interpreting the concept of civility in colonial and post-colonial India.[200] Among intellectuals in India there were divergent ideas of how to define Hindu

[197] This is consistent with Mohinder Singh's argument that in the late-nineteenth to early-twentieth-century period, *sabhyata* was a translation of civilisation in Hindi. Singh, "Negotiating a Civilizational Figure in Hindi," 188.

[198] See Elias, *The Civilizing Process*.

[199] Pernau and Jordheim, eds, *Civilizing Emotions*, 3.

[200] See Bhattacharya, *Talking Back*.

civilisation, Indian civilisation, and civilisation more generally. In part, these were anti-colonial responses to writings that had declared Indians lacked civilisation. There were also nationalists' claims to a civilisation (and antiquity) as part of their nationalism. As a consequence there was no agreement about the modes of behaviour that exemplified civility. Savarkar was not interested in contemporary interpretations of civility within India, especially interpretations that conflated civility with non-violence, peace, and passive resistance. He also appeared to reject normative arguments about civility and civilisation emerging out of colonial writings that privileged the developmental process of Western civilisation, while simultaneously asserting that civilisation in India remained at a primitive stage of human society. As one of the many thinkers who sought to stake a claim within the intellectual debate, Savarkar provided an interpretation of civility that distinguished itself from all others by arguing that violence was a characteristic of civility. In other words, for Savarkar his interpretation was a trenchant critique of normative analyses of civility while promoting an alternative discourse of Hindu civility.

By the time Savarkar wrote *Saha Soneri Pane*, Gandhian principles of non-violence continued to have a popular reception in independent India, even after – and partly perhaps because of – Gandhi's violent death. Savarkar was, quite obviously, fundamentally opposed to Gandhi's political discourses on non-violence, and therefore to the celebration of his ideas in the second half of the twentieth century. On December 18, 1921 Gandhi had published an article titled "Civility" in *Navajivan*, explaining key arguments around the concept.[201] He begins with a critique of the nature of politics in the early-twentieth century: "[C]ivility, good manners and humility – these virtues are at such a discount these days that they seem to have no place at all in the building of our character."[202] Civility was really an expression of what Gandhi called "the spirit of non-violence"; in contrast, "incivility and insolence" were indicative of "the spirit of violence."[203] Why was this an important distinction? Gandhi proposed that all politics of non-cooperation needed to adhere to the principles of civility;

[201] Gandhi, "Civility," 287–90.
[202] Ibid., 287.
[203] Ibid., 288.

incivility had to be avoided at all costs, for it was really synonymous with "brutishness." This not only meant being courteous towards the government and its supporters, but also showing manners, respect, and politeness in all interactions. The purpose was to exhibit a "spirit of love" as an effective means in the pursuit of political interactions. Gandhi concluded by arguing that civility should not only be considered a "virtue," but each individual should try to "cultivate it" as part of individual and national culture.[204]

This essay shared many of the themes in *Hind Swaraj*. Although Gandhi never named the individual or individuals who inspired his figure of the revolutionary, he was clear in his later writing that the purpose of *Hind Swaraj* was very specific: "[it] was written in answer to the revolutionary's arguments and methods."[205] The book was his reply to contemporary revolutionary thought that was circulating globally. I suggest that Gandhi's essay on civility is not merely an extension of his reply to an unnamed revolutionary, it is an intervention in the public debate on civility in India. When this essay was published, Savarkar was imprisoned in the Cellular Jail, and it preceded any of Savarkar's interventions on civility and civilisation. Given Gandhi's own explanation of his rationale for writing *Hind Swaraj*, scholars have tended to accept that Gandhi was replying to revolutionary thought.[206] What is typically not discussed is the other side of the argument – the likelihood that Savarkar was responding to Gandhian conceptions of civilisation and civility.

To further interpret the meaning of Hindu civility, Savarkar turned to an analysis of the Bhagavad Gita. In writing about the *mahayuddha* between Hindus and Muslims, he argued that many Hindus had either forgotten or distorted the central message of the Bhagavad Gita: *karma yoga*, or the discipline of action.[207] This reflected a larger existential problem for Hindu civilisation, especially if Hindus did not properly comprehend the right strategies for fighting the "injustice" perpetrated by Muslims in India. We have seen Savarkar use passages from the Bhagavad Gita in his histories of warfare as early as *Indian*

---

[204] Ibid., 290.

[205] Ibid., 286.

[206] Parel, "Editor's Introduction," *Hind Swaraj*, xxvii–xxviii.

[207] Savarkar, *Six Glorious Epochs*, 168.

*War*; in *Saha Soneri Pane* his engagement with the Bhagavad Gita is greater than in his other writings.

He says now that the Bhagavad Gita should not be considered *the* singular or monolithic text for the creation of the Hindu nation. In a speech in Pune on July 7, 1937 he says the Bhagavad Gita is a seminal work that needs to be read alongside diverse literary texts within the Hindu tradition.[208] Savarkar's claim for textual pluralism was a direct response to contemporary arguments that Hindus needed to elevate the Gita to the status of the Bible in Christianity or the Koran in Islam as a way to strengthen the foundation of Hindu *dharma* in the making of modern India.

Savarkar was also aware of other contemporary public debates around the Gita and its central concepts. There was general disagreement over whether the Gita's message of disciplined action was to be taken allegorically or literally.[209] At the centre of this debate was the question of whether the Gita promoted non-violence or advocated new forms of violence within a colonial context. For example, Tilak in his *Bhagavadgita Rahasya* had explained that it was the duty of individuals to take up arms and fight against exploitation and oppression based on the principle of *karma yoga*. Gandhi by contrast was the main proponent of *ahimsa*, his view being that it was incorrect to interpret the Gita as inciting violence; "fighting" or warfare described in the Gita was in his interpretation an allegory. As Gandhi noted in relation to his interactions with Savarkar in London, the two had disagreed about the fundamental message of the Gita. Gandhi discussed this point further in "Discourses on the 'Gita'." He says: "[T]he physical battle [in the Gita] is only an occasion for describing the battle-field of the human body. In this view the names mentioned [e.g. Krishna and Arjuna] are not of persons but of qualities which they represent. What is described is the conflict within the human body between opposing moral tendencies imagined as distinct figures."[210] The Gita was not advocating, promoting, or encouraging violence; it represented the ultimate internal struggle in all humans that was resolved by a moral commitment to non-violence.

---

[208] V.D. Savarkar, *"Ek hi dharma-pustaka nahin, yeh achchha hai!"* Pune, July 7, 1937, *Savarkar Samagra*, vol. 7, 313–14.

[209] See Sawhney, *The Modernity of Sanskrit*.

[210] Gandhi, "Discourses on the 'Gita'," 76.

For Savarkar, who identified key periods in the past when the idea of non-violence became a dominant – and therefore disastrous – discourse in India with Buddhism, and who provided his contrary resolution to this historical problem, the proponents of non-violence, i.e. those who accepted Gandhi's view of the Gita, could not be more wrong. And without correctly understanding the Gita, Savarkar feared that the condition of Hindus would further deteriorate: "But at this time of the Hindu–Muslim war the Hindu nation forgot even the Bhagawat Geeta . . . Why [Hindus] even twisted the message of the Geeta itself."[211] He referred to Chapter VII of the Gita as a way to discuss the importance of the three characteristics – *satvika*, *rajas*, and *tamas* – necessary for all Hindus to fight Muslims (and later Christians) in India.[212] The combination of these characteristics provided a "three-edged weapon" necessary for all Hindu warriors to win victory over injustice on the battlefield. Researching and writing history had the power to reveal when the Gita had been forgotten in periods of India's past, but also showed when individuals turned to this text to challenge the power of invaders and create a "social revolution."[213]

Savarkar also argues that Hindus maintained an ethical code in their wars. Battles were fought between enemies based on agreed guidelines derived from Hindu texts. *Dharmayuddha* – literally, righteous or legitimate warfare – was a principle adopted by the warring clans of the Gita, but it was also a principle found in religious texts to discuss battles between gods as well as in general:

> [T]he ethics of war . . . demanded that a charioteer must fight with another charioteer only, the sword should meet another sword alone, that the armed warrior ought not to fight with an unarmed one, till he has been armed equally, that a fallen senseless warrior was never to be attacked till he had regained consciousness . . . No single charioteer was to be attacked by many charioteers; the submissive or surrendering warrior was to be given his life. Such considerations for justice and injustice were to be actually shown on the battle-field. This ethics of war was preached because it was honoured by both the contending parties.[214]

[211] Savarkar, *Six Glorious Epochs*, 168; Savarkar, *Saha Soneri Pane*, 148.

[212] Savarkar, *Six Glorious Epochs*, 167–8; Savarkar, *Saha Soneri Pane*, 147–8.

[213] Savarkar, *Six Glorious Epochs*, 168; Savarkar, *Saha Soneri Pane*, 148.

[214] Savarkar, *Six Glorious Epochs*, 237, 255–6; Savarkar, *Saha Soneri Pane*, 209, 226.

Even after the arrival of Muslims in India, Hindus either promoted "extreme non-violence" or maintained the principles of *dharmayuddha*. Taking advantage of Hindu ideas of fair play, Muslims were able to dominate India. Once it was known to Hindus that Muslims were not willing to accept *dharmayuddha* or any other Hindu principle, Hindus should in Savarkar's view have resorted to the alternative war strategy found in the Gita. The act of killing is at the centre of the dialogue between Krishna and Arjuna; however, not all forms of violence – and by extension killing – were considered legitimate: not all was fair in war. However, there were exceptions to *dharmayuddha*. Even Krishna had argued that it was necessary to abandon a code of ethics with an enemy who was unjust or unethical.[215] Savarkar says, "The Pandawas themselves had violated, at the instance of Lord Krishna, many of these chivalrous rules of war!"[216]

No longer could wars be fought with a common understanding of the rules of engagement based on *dharmayuddha*. Wars fought against invaders had of necessarity to be unjust: "Were a serpent (an inveterate national enemy) to come with a view to bite the motherland, he should be smashed into pieces with a surprise attack, deceit or cunning or in any other way possible."[217] These principles are understood by true heroes who have absorbed Hindu civility; they are the individuals who turn to the Gita when others forget its message. Tactics and methods that had been labelled unjust and cruel could in wars against invading Muslims and Christians be both ethical and central to Hindu civility.

While Savarkar had provided a typology of cruelty in *Indian War*, his primary focus in *Saha Soneri Pane* was on the progression of cruelty from one Glorious Epoch to the next. Since Hindus were never the first violaters of the ethics of warfare for him, they were justified in taking up acts of "super-savage cruelty" or "excessive cruelty" in response to the cruelties inflicted on them: this was in consonance with the acts of the gods in the epics.[218] It has been argued that not all

[215] NMML, V.D. Savarkar Papers, Reel 25, Letter from Vinayak Damodar Savarkar, to Nathuram Shukla, Secretary, Mahakoshal Provincial Hindusabha, February 25, 1942.

[216] Savarkar, *Six Glorious Epochs*, 237; Savarkar, *Saha Soneri Pane*, 209.

[217] Savarkar, *Six Glorious Epochs*, 268.

[218] The term used by Savarkar is *savai kraurya*. Savarkar, *Six Glorious Epochs*, 255–6; Savarkar, *Saha Soneri Pane*, 225.

forms of what is normatively understood as "violence" was necessarily interpreted as violence in ancient India: "In contexts where injuring or killing another can be established as necessary, meaningful, or even beneficial, it should not be considered violence at all."[219] Needless to say, if there are divergent interpretations of what constitutes violence, it adds complexity to interpreting the word. To put it differently, some actions considered ethical could never be interpreted as violent. These legitimate and ethical activities were later classified as violent based on new interpretive norms in India. Savarkar's writings are full of references to specific acts of violence that are reinterpreted as ethical when viewed from his framework of a history in full. He used "cruelty" to underscore that Hindus were victims of unethical violence. Hindus who sought vengeance inflicted "excessive cruelty" – Hindu cruelty – that was both legitimate and ethical.

This typology of cruelty persists from his earlier work into the Glorious Epochs as part of his interpretive framework of Hindu history; he now asserts in addition that the cruelty of one epoch was surpassed by the cruelty of the next epoch. Alexander the Great had a "cruel military code" that was used to "cruelly crush down the states which had opposed him."[220] In the Second and Third Glorious Epochs, the Sakas were "crueller" and more "bloodthirsty" than the Greeks, but the Kushans were "crueller" than the Sakas.[221] In the fourth the Huns are "fiercer and far more cruel than their predecessors."[222] By the Fifth Glorious Epoch Mahmud of Ghazni is "a hundred times more fanatical and far crueller than his father," who was crueller than his forerunners.[223] Allauddin Khilji of the thirteenth century is described as having "surpassed every other Sultan before him in cruelty in the persecution of the Hindus."[224] Within this progression of cruelty what remains unclear, or perhaps unfulfilled, is an assessment of the nature of cruelty in relation to his own work on 1857. Were the British, by this logic of the progression of cruelty, crueller than earlier "foreign invaders"? Or were they less cruel because Christians were inherently less

[219] Singh, *Political Violence in Ancient India*, 8–9.
[220] Savarkar, *Six Glorious Epochs*, 27.
[221] Ibid., 99.
[222] Ibid., 112.
[223] Ibid., 148.
[224] Ibid., 293.

cruel than Muslims? This is not fully addressed, but overall Savarkar argues that the nature of cruelty in the first four Glorious Epochs was independent of religion. In the Fifth and Sixth Glorious Epochs, the ultimate goal for Islam and Christianity was to "destroy most cruelly the Hindu religion" despite their respective claims about their own religions being about peace and love.[225] In their own histories, violence and cruelty perpetrated against Hindus had been justified as moral and righteous – and necessary for humanity. Savarkar had discussed General James George Smith Neill in *Indian War*, who had classified all Indians as inhuman; killing Indians had been justified in the cause of Humanity. There could thus be only one response to such justifications: "super-savage cruelty" against the enemies of Hindusthan. He repeated what he had said in his earlier work: "[G]ods and god-like emperors, too, considered it the holiest duty to show super-savage cruelty to beat down the cruelty of the Rakshasas [demons], to be arch-devils against the devils."[226]

To illustrate his argument Savarkar discusses the case of Narsinh, an incarnation of the deity Vishnu who appeared in the form of half-lion and half-man to save a devotee named Prahlad.[227] From a very early age, Prahlad had committed himself to the passionate worship of Vishnu, much to the consternation and anger of Prahlad's father, the king Hiranyakashipu. The father demanded that his son stop his devotion to Vishnu, but Prahlad refused to obey him. The king inflicted numerous punishments through which he intended to kill his son, but the non-violent Prahlad refused to resist, being protected from harm by Vishnu. Hiranyakashipu had received, much earlier, a boon from Brahma that protected him from being killed by human or animal or god. Hiranyakashipu could not be killed during the day or night, on soil or in the air, or by any weapon, leaving the king to believe he was invincible. One day, as Hiranyakashipu attempted to kill his son, Vishnu appeared as neither fully human nor animal, and he arrived at dusk – between day and the night – and slew Hiranyakashipu with his lion's claws. What appealed to Savarkar about this narrative

[225] Ibid., 169.

[226] Ibid., 255.

[227] For recent renderings of this narrative, see Doniger, *The Hindus*, 492–3; Devji, "Bhakt Prahlad."

was that Narsinh did not simply murder the king, he demonstrated "merciless valour" by "tearing open the entrails of Hiranyakashipu."[228] It was a form of super-savage cruelty against a "reckless tyrant" who had terrorised Prahlad. Equally important was the message that Prahlad's non-violence was of no use in his conflict with his father. (It is worth noting here that Prahlad was celebrated by Gandhi as an exemplary devotee of God and an ideal *satyagrahi*.[229]) The only remedy against Hiranyakashipu's violence was "cruel violence" which was "truly righteous" and "truly religious."[230] Such cruelty was a necessary feature not only of Hindu civility, but also for the development of "human culture." He considered Narsinh's example of killing a "noble principle" and an act of "human kindness" as it provided an example for improving the condition for Hindus.[231] Sometimes this meant perpetrating super-savage cruelty against other Hindus; other times it was against Muslims.

## 8. The Problem of Hindu Chivalry

If at the centre of Savarkar's understanding of Hindu civility was the necessity of violence, Hindu chivalry was its antithesis in promoting politeness, courtesy, consideration, and non-violence. In Savarkar's view this was a fundamental flaw within Hindu civilisation. He uses the phrase *Hindunche shatrustridaksinya* to discuss the treatment of women in the *mahayuddha* between Hindus and Muslims.[232] While *Hindunche* is a cognate of Hindu in this context, the second term is a compound of *shatru* (enemy), *stri* (female or woman), and *daksinya* – defined as politeness, civility, and courtesy in Sanskrit, and chivalry and consideration in Marathi. I mention these definitions to indicate the range of meanings of *shatrustridaksinya* that Savarkar may have implied in his discussion of women. However, the translation of

---

[228] Savarkar, *Six Glorious Epochs*, 351.

[229] Gandhi's writings are full of references to Prahlad. See, for example, Gandhi, "Johannesburg Letter."

[230] Savarkar, *Six Glorious Epochs*, 351.

[231] Ibid.

[232] Savarkar, *Saha Soneri Pane*, 157.

this phrase is "Hindu chivalry towards enemy women" in *Six Glorious Epochs*.[233] Savarkar explains that Hindu chivalry represents the ethical treatment of Muslim women by Hindu men. Yet, in consonance with his argument about violence as central to Hindu civility, he views *Hindunche shatrustridaksinya* as a problem brought on by non-violence. Muslim men had exhibited no chivalry in their treatment of Hindu women. In fact, Muslim women had participated in subjugating Hindu women for Muslim men: they had encouraged Muslim men towards the "kidnappings" and "atrocities" of Hindu women.[234] For Savarkar, this process lasted nearly a millennium, during which millions of Hindu women were forced to convert to Islam and then reproduce the same pattern of oppression against Hindus.

The narrative about Hindu women was important in Savarkar's discussion of the Fifth Glorious Epoch: it provided a counter to the treatment of Muslim women by Hindu men, who remained chivalrous and non-violent, especially by refusing to participate in sexual violence: "The Muslim women never feared retribution or punishment at the hands of any Hindu for their heinous crime . . . If the Hindus [won in battle] and a Hindu power was established in that particular place the Muslim-men alone, if at all, suffered the consequential indignities[,] but the Muslim women – never!"[235]

Whereas Muslim men are represented in Savarkar's writings as a homogeneous group that was masculine and sexualised for its willingness to use violence, Hindus were divided into two categories: the *"veer* Hindu" and the "effeminate Hindu." A similar explanation in *Indian War* has been noted already. Given the range of texts Savarkar consulted for writing the book, it certainly appears that he was familiar with British colonial writings on the recruitment of "martial races" into the British Indian Army to quell rebellions. However, Savarkar's interpretation inverted the idea of a martial race of Indians by arguing that such men were not heroic. In fact, because they did not participate in the war of independence – and in fact fought against the principles of *swaraj* and *swadharma* – they were effeminate. Once again, he had

---

[233] Savarkar, *Six Glorious Epochs*, 178; Savarkar, *Saha Soneri Pane*, 157.

[234] Savarkar, *Six Glorious Epochs*, 178–9; Savarkar, *Saha Soneri Pane*, 157–8.

[235] Savarkar, *Six Glorious Epochs*, 178; Savarkar, *Saha Soneri Pane*, 157.

provided an antonym to a colonial category for the purpose of reading against the grain. Ultimately, for Savarkar the persistence of nonviolence was a signal to all Muslims that the idea of Hindu chivalry was a sign of "cowardice" rather than "strength and bravery."[236] As a consequence Hindus had a perverted conception of virtues and were emasculated by opting for chivalry over civility in the *mahayuddha*. If only Hindus had emulated the kidnappings, sexual violence, and forced reconversions of Muslim women, there would have been a remarkable outcome for Hindus, according to Savarkar:

Suppose, if from the earliest Muslim invasion of India, the Hindus also, whenever they were victors on the battlefields, had decided to pay the Muslim fair sex in the same coin or punished them in some other ways, i.e., by conversion even with force, and then absorbed them into their fold? [*sic*] Then with this horrible apprehension at their heart they would have desisted from their evil designs against any Hindu lady. If they had taken such a fright in the first two or three centuries, millions and millions of luckless Hindu ladies would have been saved all their indignities, loss of their own religion, rapes, ravages and other unimaginable persecutions. Our woman-world would not have suffered such a tremendous numerical loss, which means their future progeny would not have been lost permanently to Hindu [dharma] and the Muslim population could not have thrived so audaciously. Without any increase in their women-folk the Muslim population would have dwindled into a negligible minority.[237]

Did this mean that all forms of violence – including sexual violence – were central features of Hindu civility? This is not a question that Savarkar directly addresses in his writings, but he does repeat his argument that seeking vengeance for atrocities against Hindu women involves attacking Muslim women:

Let the Sultans and their peers take a pledge that in the event of a Hindu victory our molestation and detestable lot shall be avenged on the Muslim women. Once they are haunted with this dreadful apprehension that the Muslim women too, stand in the same predicament in the case of the

---

[236] Savarkar, *Six Glorious Epochs*, 178; Savarkar, *Saha Soneri Pane*, 157.
[237] Savarkar, *Six Glorious Epochs*, 180–1; Savarkar, *Saha Soneri Pane*, 159.

Hindus win, the future Muslim conquerors will never dare to think of such molestation of Hindu women.[238]

Not all Hindu women reflected passive femininity. Savarkar had mentioned the valour of Maratha women in *Hindu Pad Padashahi* and now emphasises that Hindu women actively prevented capture of their own bodies, sometimes by choosing suicide. At other times they burned themselves – individually or collectively – as an act of "valour" and "prestige" for saving "one's own self and one's own religion." This reflected a "warlike spirit" in Hindu women.[239] He says, "[W]ives, mothers, daughters, hundreds of them, with babies at their breasts, used to leap into the burning pyres."[240] Women could be Hindu martyrs – in fact for non-warriors martyrdom was possible only if they were women. Moreover, the choice made by such women to kill themselves was central to the continuity of the Hindu nation: "That is the only reason why the Hindu nation could still remain alive!!"[241]

In *Majhi Janmathep* Savarkar had argued against suicide for fellow prisoners in the Cellular Jail as he considered it a womanly form of death. Instead, he had offered the example of the Rani of Jhansi who died a heroic warrior. He had encouraged suicidal men to follow the Rani's example. In *Indian War*, the Rani has another heroic dimension: she prevents the capture of her body out of fear of sexual violence. When severely wounded on the battlefield, she asks her servant Ramchandra Rao Deshmukh to cremate her body immediately after her death for fear that English soldiers will "defile even her dead body."[242] Ramchandra Rao saves his Rani's body from what Savarkar calls the "touch of slavery."[243] He also thereby prevents acts of "imperial necrophilia."[244] Savarkar offers other such examples. The sixteenth-century figure of Rani Durgawati is described as having "bravely defended the cause

238 Savarkar, *Six Glorious Epochs*, 179; Savarkar, *Saha Soneri Pane*, 158.

239 Savarkar, *Six Glorious Epochs*, 135; Savarkar, *Saha Soneri Pane*, 116.

240 Savarkar, *Six Glorious Epochs*, 30; Savarkar, *Saha Soneri Pane*, 25.

241 Savarkar, *Six Glorious Epochs*, 290; Savarkar, *Saha Soneri Pane*, 257.

242 Savarkar, *Indian War*, 400.

243 Ibid.

244 I borrow this phrase from Shohat, "Post-Third-Worldist Culture," 200. But, of course, I use it in a different context.

of Hinduism" against Akbar. [245] She refused to compromise with the Mughal emperor, and when it became clear that she might be captured she opted to kill herself. Like the Rani of Jhansi, she instructed her attendant to burn her corpse to ensure that no Muslim could touch it.[246] Megha Kumar has argued that Savarkar not only "essentialised" all Muslim women as collaborators of sexual violence against Hindu women, he also rendered them the "symbols of honour" of Hindu men.[247] In this perspective, women in Savarkar's writings are largely identified as or limited to the classifications of "booty" or the "property" of victorious men.[248] Kumar adds: "Savarkar made clear his beliefs and message that women are symbols of honour of the family, the community and the nation and that they should choose death rather than let the masculine actors of the 'other' community defile them or worse, convert them."[249]

In a related aspect pertaining to women, Savarkar says Hindus neglected to recognise the Hindu woman who had been converted to Islam by force. It never occurred to Hindus – men as well as women – that these Muslim women should be converted back into the Hindu fold. He asks rhetorically: "But if the Hindus could not rescue thousands of their own women who were being abducted, polluted, and forced into Islamic religion, in their very presence, through centuries, why should the Muslims not ridicule the Hindu chivalrous idea?"[250] In other words, if Hindus had viewed Muslim women not as enemies by adhering to *Hindunche stridaksinya* (rather than *shatrustridaksinya*) this period of Hindu history would have had a very different outcome. Hindu chivalry had failed these women. What was worse, Savarkar says over thirty million Hindus had been forced to convert to Islam, whereas Hindus had never attempted to reconvert any Muslim: "Neither those Maratha warriors, nor their commanders, nor the Sardars and Chieftains, nor the Shankaracharyas, nay not even the Peshwa at Poona, nor the Chhatrapatis of Satara and Kolhapur – alas! Not a

---

[245] Savarkar, *Six Glorious Epochs*, 381; Savarkar, *Saha Soneri Pane*, 339.
[246] Ibid.
[247] Kumar, "History and Gender in Savarkar's Nationalist Writings," 44–5.
[248] Ibid., 46.
[249] Ibid., 45.
[250] Savarkar, *Six Glorious Epochs*, 181; Savarkar, *Saha Soneri Pane*, 160.

single Hindu soul ever dreamt of this simple way of reconversion of those ill-starred Hindus."[251]

To explain this situation Savarkar returned to a discussion of blood that he had raised in *Essentials of Hindutva* – but by this time it seems he had moved away from his earlier interpretation that all humans had the same blood – polluted blood. He argues now that Hindus who had converted to Islam still possessed blood that was purely Hindu despite the fact that they had abandoned Hindudom.[252] Even if, by converting, these individuals had changed their religion and nationality to become Muslims, Savarkar says that biologically and by nature – they technically retained the purity of Hindu blood. These new converts could still have been rescued or saved by Hindus – had they only properly understood Hindu civility. In essence, Hindus could, by force if necessary, always reconvert those Muslims whose blood remained Hindu blood. Of course the time for such reconversion was limited: once Hindus who had converted to Islam started intermarrying with other Muslims – especially with those who did not possess Hindu blood – the opportunity for reconversion was lost.

Savarkar did not trace this back to his decision to reconvert prisoners in the Cellular Jail through Shuddhi ceremonies. He simply points out that Hindus themselves had raised the greatest obstacles against their own success in the Fifth Glorious Epoch: "Because of their morbid ban on reconversion no effective remedy could be found against the drain of its life-blood. Very like the invalid patient meekly bearing the death-pangs of an incurable disease the then Hindus endured this blood-draining deadly disease."[253] Savarkar says that the caste system advocated *shuddhibandi* – i.e. a ban on purifying individuals who had left the Hindu dharma and converted to another religion. As against this position, his view was that Hindus had created a series of *bandi*s (bans) for the protection of other Hindus without understanding that the consequence was the shackling of all Hindus: *lotibandi* (ban on sharing drinking water); *rotibandi* (ban on sharing food); *betibandi* (ban on inter-caste marriages); *sparshbandi* (untouchability); and *sindhubandi*

---

[251] Savarkar, *Six Glorious Epochs*, 232; Savarkar, *Saha Soneri Pane*, 204–5.

[252] Savarkar, *Six Glorious Epochs*, 190; Savarkar, *Saha Soneri Pane*, 168.

[253] Savarkar, *Six Glorious Epochs*, 240; Savarkar, *Saha Soneri Pane*, 212.

(ban on travelling on the seas).[254] The whole purpose of founding the caste system, in his view, had been to establish unity among Hindus in specific contexts in ancient history, but many doctrinaire aspects of Hinduism were ossifications of tradition that had caused harm to society in modern history during the epic war:

> Although we can gratefully cite many other things regarding the caste-system which brought about the cohesiveness of the diversified Hindu society and had lasting effects on it, it would be equally ungrateful on our part if we desist from criticising with sufficient severity the unlimited harm done by the caste-system and the irrational and obstinate pride that Hindus took in it, when the Muslims began to knock on their doors.[255]

Savarkar's critique of the interpretations of caste was a significant intervention in explaining the Hindu refusal to see some Muslims as Hindus. This was certainly an unexpected analysis within a text where violence and super-savage cruelty were put forward as normative responses to foreign invasions by Muslims. Perhaps the greatest disappointment for Savarkar had been the signal failure of the Marathas to reconvert Muslims back into the Hindu fold, especially following military and political battles in which they had been successful. Maratha battalions and companies had remained "supremely unconcerned about the two or three hundred thousand of their miserable Hindu brethren in Muslim bondage."[256] It has been pointed out that Savarkar specifically criticised Shivaji for promoting "a perverse notion of virtue in respecting the chastity of Muslim women."[257] Given that Shivaji was a popular hero celebrated for his role in challenging the Mughals, this was controversial. Savarkar's argument in *Hindu Pad Padashahi*, in which he narrated Shivaji's main accomplishments as heroic, was now a matter he seems to have reconsidered. He says many waited in vain for the soldiers to "recognise" them as Hindus, but this never happened, with the result that they "resigned themselves helplessly to Muslim bondage and rotted till death or bringing forth Muslim

---

[254] Savarkar, *Six Glorious Epochs*, 157; Savarkar, *Saha Soneri Pane*, 137.

[255] Savarkar, *Six Glorious Epochs*, 160; Savarkar, *Saha Soneri Pane*, 139.

[256] Savarkar, *Six Glorious Epochs*, 232–3; Savarkar, *Saha Soneri Pane*, 204–5.

[257] Agrawal, "Surat, Savarkar and Draupadi," 35.

offsprings."[258] Even those Muslims who retained pure Hindu blood lost all hope from their blood brethren, the Hindus, once they began producing children; now their conversion to Islam was complete and could not be undone. For Savarkar this was another instance of Hindus not really understanding the principles of Hindu civility. The struggle to resolve the meaning of Hindu civility and the treatment of women in this epic war of the Fifth Glorious Epoch had clearly created a new rupture in Savarkar's understanding of Hindu history. [259]

Savarkar identifies many Muslims who invaded or settled in India in the Fifth Glorious Epoch – his list is long: Mohammad Ghori, Kutubuddin, Jalalludin Khilji, Gyasuddin Tughlak, Tamurlang, Shikander Lodi, Ibrahim Lodi, Babur, and Tipu Sultan are only select names discussed from the eleventh to the eighteenth centuries. By the sixteenth century the French, English, Dutch, and Portuguese had also entered India. While the frequency of these foreign invasions had consumed other historical narratives, Savarkar's ambition was to present the making of a Glorious Epoch by Hindus, for Hindus. This was reiterated as the argument of the establishment of the Hindu Pad Padashahi by the Peshwas in the eighteenth century. Savarkar's purpose was not to repeat what he had already presented in his history of the Marathas, because the problems of Hindu chivalry that he had now identified posed a major problem in interpreting the essence of Hindutva as a history in full. It appears that Savarkar was at this point caught in the middle – so to speak – of having on the one hand to explain the rise and demise of Hindus whose actions and thoughts reflected the Hindu spirit, and on the other hand to condemn Hindus – including brave

[258] Savarkar, *Six Glorious Epochs*, 233; Savarkar, *Saha Soneri Pane*, 205.

[259] In *Indian War*, Savarkar had already introduced his concerns about the treatment of enemy women by Indians. He pointed out that Nana Saheb sought to protect English women from a massacre: "Nana Sahib did not show the treacherous enemy who ruined individuals, the nation, and religion even a hundredth part of the severity and cruelty, which, in similar conditions and under similar provocations, England herself has shown to India." Upon learning that his men had captured and hidden some English women, he immediately intervened to rescue them and punished the soldiers. The women were kept safely during the battle in what Savarkar described as an "excessive humanity." Savarkar, *Indian War*, 192–3.

heroes – who had not lived up to the principles of history and Hindu civility, especially in relation to their treatment of women. Looking at *Saha Soneri Pane* alone, it would seem that despite there being many Hindu heroes, no "true" Hindu Hero had thus far existed in history with the exception of Arjuna in the Bhagavad Gita and Ramchandra in the Ramayana. (It should be remembered that Savarkar had compared himself to Arjuna and Ramchandra in *Majhi Janmathep*.)

Despite Savarkar's assertion that his purpose was to write a modern history based on evidence, and despite his mentioning his reliance on scholarly texts, in his last work he returns to conjecture as a method for interpreting Hindu history via the epics, much as he had done in *Essentials of Hindutva*. Hindu history was unravelling in his hands as he wrote the most comprehensive book of his career: in this work it becomes most evident that Hindutva was *the impossible history*. His initial idea of tracing the desires and motives of historical actors to a source that had sustained his earlier books appeared as a part of the first four Glorious Epochs. But that ambition remained unfulfilled in the Fifth Glorious Epoch: here, the thoughts and actions of Hindus appear to have disappointed Savarkar. Nonetheless, the purpose of addressing the paradox of Hindu civility remained essential in his effort to raise awareness among Hindus in the twentieth century.

## 9. The Incomplete Epoch?

Savarkar's description of the Sixth Glorious Epoch is short, and his book ends abruptly. Despite the fact that Savarkar calls this chapter "India Freed From British Domination," he does not devote much space to discuss the epoch in which he himself lived. Savarkar states that he is ill, and he has already said everything he wanted to say:

> Now I don't think it necessary for me to add even a single word to the published work of mine running to about seven to eight thousand printed pages in the form of books or otherwise, leaving aside hundreds of my speeches, interviews, articles and the written work that is now lost beyond recovery and now at this age – the eightieth year of my life – when I am confined to bed I have not the physical strength left in me to go on repeating it once again![260]

[260] Savarkar, *Six Glorious Epochs*, 470; Savarkar, *Saha Soneri Pane*, 412.

However, to readers unclear about his approach to history by this point, he provides a reminder: "In this chapter on the Sixth Glorious Epoch of Hindu victories it is not at all necessary to give a detailed account of how . . . the Hindu nation could make itself independent."[261] His only purpose in writing the chapter is to consider "salient points" in the war of independence that all historians had "purposely overlooked" in their writings – their detailed histories.[262] His goal to place Hindutva at the centre of the history is reiterated one final time: "I have done that for the most part in my other books, as far as it was necessary to do so."[263]

In this chapter Savarkar provides analyses of his own writings as central to interpreting the process of how Hindus fought in wars of independence against the British. In his own assessment, he was *the* writer of history – Hindu history. He outlines key moments in this Sixth Glorious Epoch that were important for Hindus but does not discuss them. Instead, he refers us back to his other texts and recommends that all Hindus read them. When discussing Maratha resistance to the British in the Anglo-Maratha Wars, he states: "In my book, *Hindu Pad Padashahi* I have sufficiently discussed from the standpoint of the Hindu nation. The curious readers should do well to read it."[264] For the rebellions of 1857, he refers us to *Indian War*. He also mentions his book on the history of the Sikhs that was lost in transit and never found. In the middle of his discussion on the centrality of his works of history, he says his autobiography is important to understand the Sixth Glorious Epoch: he is *the* maker of Hindu history. After his release from the Andamans, he was in "intimate contact with millions of the avowed believers in Hindutva."[265] He was the transformative figure who had knowledge of all the main historical actors of the late-nineteenth and twentieth century involved in the freedom movement. He lists the names of a large number of major figures and says the absence of names of others should not make them seem marginal. He includes a description of Gandhi: "I happened to be closely acquainted

<hr>

261 Savarkar, *Six Glorious Epochs*, 455; Savarkar, *Saha Soneri Pane*, 399.
262 Ibid.
263 Savarkar, *Six Glorious Epochs*, 455–6; Savarkar, *Saha Soneri Pane*, 399.
264 Savarkar, *Six Glorious Epochs*, 456; Savarkar, *Saha Soneri Pane*, 400.
265 Savarkar, *Six Glorious Epochs*, 469; Savarkar, *Saha Soneri Pane*, 411.

in a friendly way when he had come to England where he was then known simply as Barrister Gandhi and thereafter throughout our lives we came together and many times in conflict – in the political arena in India."[266] Needless to say, while this seems a curious remembrance at the end of Savarkar's last work of history, it is perhaps a gesture of respect towards the individual with whom he had debated the nature of violence in the Ramayana and Bhagavad Gita in London, and with whom he had vehemently disagreed at every step.

Unlike *Indian War* and *Hindu Pad Padashahi*, *Saha Soneri Pane* does not end in failure. For Savarkar, the ending of the Sixth Glorious Epoch remains full of optimism. He points out that the British as "foreign aggressors" have left India for good: "Thus disappeared the mighty English empire! And when it did disappear, it did so, so very suddenly and speedily, so very completely."[267] While a new sovereignty was established in India, Savarkar offers his supporters hope for a future, despite the Partition of 1947. Hindusthan may have been divided into two nation-states, but he reminds his readers that this is a temporary situation. Hindus had fought for nearly a thousand years to reach this point. For Savarkar, Hindus needed to maintain a strategy that would inspire and motivate Hindus for "the greater glory of Hindutva."[268] Only then would Bharat be theirs. Once Hindus controlled India, the task of re-establishing Hindu unity over lost territories would follow. Hindus had been fighting a permanent war for millennia and what distinguished them since antiquity was the fact that they "did not refrain from avenging the spilling of Hindu blood by shedding enemy blood" – including the blood of Hindus.[269] Since the Hindu became a Hindu in the act of violence in the past, this would continue in the future – guided by the Hindu spirit. This is how the next page of Hindu history would be written.

---

[266] Savarkar, *Six Glorious Epochs*, 468; Savarkar, *Saha Soneri Pane*, 410.
[267] Savarkar, *Six Glorious Epochs*, 475; Savarkar, *Saha Soneri Pane*, 416.
[268] Savarkar, *Six Glorious Epochs*, 474; Savarkar, *Saha Soneri Pane*, 415.
[269] Savarkar, *Six Glorious Epochs*, 472; Savarkar, *Saha Soneri Pane*, 414.

# Conclusion

Suspects in Mahatma Gandhi Assassination Trial (May 27, 1948).
*Left to Right: Back row:* V.D. Savarkar and Dr Dattatrey Parchure;
*Front row:* Nathuram Godse, Narayan Apte, Vishnu Karkare;
*Middle row:* Madan Lal Pahwa, Gopal Godse. Shankar Kistayya and
Digamber Badge are obscured and not shown in this image.
*Photo credit:* Bettmann Archive via Getty Images.

At some point in the early 1960s Savarkar penned an essay entitled "How Hindu organisers should read and write their national history."[1] It was eventually printed in *Savarkar Samagra*, but its original date of publication is not given. Savarkar explained that he had for a number of years intended to write the essay, but decades of prioritising social and political work had prevented it. He lamented that, since he was nearing the end of his life, many of his intellectual objectives and goals remained incomplete. This essay was an exception. It was intended for Hindu organisers – politicians, journalists, intellectuals – whom Savarkar believed would carry his thoughts and methods forward after his death.

There is little new in the essay. It largely summarises the main ideas from his writings and speeches. He explains that Hindus live in the midst of a war to protect the Hindu Nation, and "One of our main tools in this struggle is *itihaas*."[2] In India's permanent war, Savarkar's primary focus for Hindu organisers centres on history, by which he means of course Hindu history, covering the Vedic period to the present.[3] Even without repeating "Hindutva is a history in full," Savarkar restates and reframes his original argument for a future generation. The essay provides a guide for the formation of an intelligentsia to continue his ideas. He adds that Hindu history is only possible with a twofold approach combining warfare with knowledge formation.[4] His extensive writings need one final supplement – a guide, a manual, a plan for conveying that Hindutva *is* history. This essay is roughly that plan.

Savarkar here offers reflections on the importance of "truth" in the writing of history.[5] The conceptualisation of truth, he says, is entangled with Hindutva, and his truth lives in language, rituals, and traditions. But it also lives in memories, in the land, in temples, and in books.[6]

[1] Savarkar, "*Hindu sanghatankarta swarashtra ka itihaas kisa taraha likhen aur parhen,*" *Savarkar Samagra*, vol. 5, 443–52.

[2] Ibid., 443. I have not translated *itihaas* as history in this sentence. Special thanks to Yogeshwar Chaturvedi for discussing the multiple meanings of this sentence in the original.

[3] Ibid., 443–4.

[4] Ibid., 445.

[5] Ibid., 446–7.

[6] Ibid., 449.

The truth of Hindutva is everywhere. To write it means turning to the epics and mythologies, while providing accurate reports of the past. History needs to be divided temporally to account for foreign invasions and Hindu victories; and it is necessary to situate Hindu history in a comparative framework with the histories of other nations.[7] This will create a space to discuss the Hindu colonisation of other countries in the world, and a context for Hindus to understand the strength and superiority of *itihaas* as made by Hindus.[8] Every Hindu organiser is instructed and encouraged not only to have a solid foundation in Hindu history based on Savarkar's interpretations, but also to write and publish new books based on this knowledge.[9] He says it is important to publish short books that are aesthetically appealing. He says the life-stories of key Hindu figures have to be understood alongside key texts such as the *Arthashastra*.[10] Savarkar also wants books for young Hindus that examine the impact of the Hindu Empire and Greater India. He demands that every individual in a Hindu organisation read all such volumes – his idea is to create a new generation of intellectuals modelled on himself. Savarkar's essay prescribes a method for "Hindu hegemony" for future generations. In the 1930s he had once argued the need to protect "Hindu hegemony," but he had not fully explained what he meant by this formulation.[11] Nor had he explained the process for achieving Hindu hegemony. This essay perhaps comes closest to such an explanation.

However, Savarkar was largely a marginalised figure when he wrote the essay for future Hindu organisers, much as he was when he authored

[7] Ibid.

[8] NMML, V.D. Savarkar Papers, Reel 30, Statement by V.D. Savarkar, "Hindu Assam in Danger," July 8, 1941, addresses on the ongoing processes of colonisation. Also Akhil Bharat Hindu Mahasabha Papers, File C-153, Letter from General Secretary to P.R. Puri, August 18, 1947, regarding the establishment of Hindu Sabhas in East Africa. This file also contains similar letters for the creation of Hindu Sabhas globally: Fiji, Kenya, South Africa.

[9] Savarkar, "*Hindu sanghatankarta swarashtra ka itihaas kisa taraha likhen aur parhen,*" 444–5.

[10] Ibid., 445.

[11] NMML, V.D. Savarkar Papers, Reel 23, Letter from V.D. Savarkar to C.P. Ram Swami, Prime Minister, Travancore State, September 19, 1938.

*Sara Soneri Pane.* His essay signals that his plan is fragile: there was great uncertainty whether Hindutva would thrive in the future, given his own status. His desire for Hindu solidarity was an implicit acknowledgement that Hindus were not yet united. Creating an intellectual vanguard to educate the masses based on Savarkar's writings and ideas – while also creating new knowledge based on Savarkar's methodology – meant that the resurrection of Hindusthan was possible once Hindus were united.

In writing *Hindutva and Violence* I have argued that Savarkar's interpretation of history needs to be taken seriously as part of his formulation, "Hindutva is not a word but a history." Hindutva cannot be conceptualised without history. He, more than anyone before or since, established a formal unity of the two terms. For Savarkar, it was possible to approximate Hindutva, to make it knowable, because of history.

Yet Savarkar's prolific writing career did not resolve his struggle to define Hindutva. In fact, to the best of my knowledge, he did not explicitly articulate the meaning of the word, except to say it is a history in full. It seems to me that Hindutva remained a conceptual entity that Savarkar linked to Being. He provided interpretations of historical actors that exhibited the motives and desires of a source that was inspired by a Hindu spirit. Whether this was a manifestation of Being (or Being itself) was never explained. The act of writing a Hindu history was Hindutva; so too was the act of making Hindu history. The convergence of being the writer *and* the maker of history set Savarkar apart from others. By sharing his plan with Hindu organisers, Savarkar provided a template to be followed. That template was Savarkar.

The historian Sumit Sarkar voices the view of contemporary disciplinary history when he argues that the diversity of political and methodological approaches in the Humanities and Social Sciences – the Cambridge School, Marxists, Subalternists, feminists, post-modernists, anti-modernists – would all find Savarkar's arguments about the homogeneous classification of Hindus and Muslims "unacceptable."[12] Such scholars also reject Savarkar's interpretations of geography and

---

[12] Sarkar, *Beyond Nationalist Frames*, 254. Sarkar also places the writings of M.S. Golwalkar in this context.

temporality, along with the idea that Muslims as a community ruled over Hindus as a community for centuries in medieval India. In Sarkar's view, "It needs to be emphasised that today, for state-of-the-art historical understanding anywhere in the world where South Asia is being studied, the assumptions of Savarkar . . . would appear to be so absurd as hardly worth refutation or debate."[13] However, Sarkar's argument was made nearly two decades ago, and there is now a greater sense that the most important thinker of Hindutva in the twentieth century can no longer be ignored. As argued by G.P. Deshpande, the political left in India must engage with Savarkar's ideas in order to contest, challenge, and resist the new hegemonic forms of institutional and cultural power in India that are motivated and inspired by the principles of Hindutva.[14]

It is worth noting that the epistemic refusal to engage with Savarkar is largely a post-colonial phenomenon. I suspect it has a lot to do with M.K. Gandhi's murder and its legacies, but also the visceral response to many of his ideas about Hindus, Muslims, and Christians that were presented in a polemical and combative style not considered scholarly in the formal sense. The spectre of the horrors of Partition violence certainly resonated as well.

At the same time, there were those who fundamentally disagreed with Savarkar's interpretations but celebrated him. Here I am thinking of Manabendra Nath Roy, the Indian revolutionary and political theorist who founded the Mexican Communist Party and was a delegate to the Second World Congress of the Communist International.[15] M.N. Roy was close to many Bolsheviks, including Lenin. He was an international revolutionary who travelled the globe, including as a member of Stalin's Comintern Delegation to China. Roy spent years in prison convicted of sedition by the colonial government. He eventually left the Communist Party to pursue his interest in radical humanism. Immediately after Savarkar's formal release from all government restrictions in May 1937, Savarkar travelled across Maharashtra to attend the many celebrations organised by the newly formed Savarkar Reception Committee. On June 27, 1937 Roy was one of the main speakers at a

[13] Ibid.
[14] See Deshpande, *World of Ideas in Modern Marathi.*
[15] See Manjapra, *M.N. Roy.*

function in Bombay and he publicly celebrated Savarkar.[16] Roy stated that he admired Savarkar and identified him as a major influence in his political life. Savarkar was a "source of inspiration" who had motivated him to not only "fight for freedom" but also to join "the struggles of the oppressed people in the world."[17] In Roy's memoirs, Savarkar is described as having "exerted a big influence on [Roy's] mind."[18] Roy says that he and Savarkar were in solidarity in the "fight for independence," even if they disagreed on "political issues" related to the conflicts between Hindus and Muslims.[19] Savarkar's retort was that Roy focused too much on inequality based on economic structures, while he emphasised the need to abolish untouchability. Savarkar also added that the goal of equality for all Hindus was compatible with the progress towards Socialism that Roy championed.

In 1938 Roy had an appointment with Savarkar in Bombay. The writer and filmmaker J.G.H. Wadia spoke to Roy on the day of the meeting, describing Roy in the following terms: "Roy was very anxious to meet Veer Savarkar . . . Of course, intellectually both were poles apart."[20] He added that Roy was "immaculately dressed in a long flowing dhoti in Bengali style, a kurta and a shawl and a cap." Roy apparently stated, "I am going to pay my respects to Veer Savarkar and I thought I should do it in the fittest manner possible. I am sure the old man will be pleased to see me dressed as a full-fledged Indian rather than a Westernised revolutionary."[21]

[16] "Bombay's Homage To 'Soldier of Liberty': Savarkar Assures that He Won't Lag Behind in Freedom's Fight," *Bombay Chronicle*, June 28, 1937. Also, MSA, HD Spec, File 60-D-(g)-pt. II-1937, Report on V.D. Savarkar, Bombay, June 28, 1937, S-69.

[17] Ibid.

[18] V.B. Karnik explained that he wrote the "Epilogue" of M.N. Roy's memoir based on the autobiographical fragments written by Roy. Karnik, "Epilogue," 567. V.B. Gogate also provides a similar description of Savarkar's influence after having read his biography as a child. Centre for South Asian Studies Archive, University of Cambridge, V.B. Gogate Collection, Interview of V.B. Gogate, April 24, 1970, 1.

[19] "Bombay's Homage To 'Soldier of Liberty'," *Bombay Chronicle*, June 28, 1937.

[20] Wadia, *M.N. Roy*, 32.

[21] Ibid.

My purpose in discussing these interactions is to underscore that there have been varying responses to Savarkar and his ideas that are sometimes lost or overlooked by scholars.[22] Roy's public celebration of Savarkar likely caused official consternation in the formation of new political solidarity. In the mid-1920s some colonial officials were convinced that Savarkar was going to align with the Communist Party, or at least have a major influence on the Youth League.[23] The primary concern was that Savarkar was ready to collaborate with Communists on revolutionary tactics. However, one official rejected this argument: "I doubt if he will ever be a down-right Communist – he would cease to be a Chitpavan!"[24] It is of course also important to point out here that M.N. Roy's important work, *Historical Role of Islam*, was first published in December 1937. And though Savarkar is not directly mentioned in the text, Roy's statement that "No civilised people in the world is so ignorant of Islamic history and contemptuous of the Mohammedan religion as the Hindus" can be read as a reply to their public disagreement about Hindus and Muslims.[25]

Partha Chatterjee has shown that the idea of turning to Puranic history or mythic history as elements in the construction of a national history had been practised in Bengal in the nineteenth century. This was part of what Chatterjee calls a "modern historiographic practice" to reclaim the past, including the classical past as central to the idea of the modern Indian nation and nationalism.[26] The conceptualisation

[22] Bhagat Singh is another figure to consider in this context. He was influenced by Savarkar's biography and required recruits to the Hindusthan Socialist Republican Association to read Chitra Gupta's *Life of Barrister Savarkar*. See Chaturvedi, "A Revolutionary's Biography." In addition, in Bhagat Singh's prison writings he directly quotes passages from Savarkar's *Hindu Pad Padashahi*, including one about Ramdas' advice about getting "killed while killing to conquer . . . in the cause of Righteousness." See Lal, ed., *Bhagat Singh*, 79.

[23] MSA, HD Spec File 60-D-(g)-1929, "Note by A.S.," Home (Spl.), August 20, 1928, S-18-21.

[24] MSA, HD Spec File 60-D-(g)-1929, Report signed "Secy, H.M. H.E.," S-43-44. No date or other information is provided.

[25] This sentence is not included in the first edition of the book, but it appears in the second edition published in March 1938. Roy, *The Historic Role of Islam*, 4.

[26] Chatterjee, *The Nation and Its Fragments*, 77–84.

of Hindutva as history was part of this process. He argued that following the basic protocols of history writing were not his priority: "Yet mere[ly] to list out the correct dates and years of historical events, to note the deaths and births of certain individuals, or to keep a record of battles fought or the occurrence of famines and floods cannot be called history, although such a bare record of these various events is the basis of history."[27] Yet Savarkar was engaged with contemporary debates, and histories of the present informed and shaped his writings. He navigated his work between genres; he had an interest in writing both biographies and autobiographies without necessarily being committed to either. Mazzini's ideas were important influences in Savarkar's histories, and there was a clear commitment to comparative histories in unusual and unexpected ways – sometimes to celebrate Hindu history, at other times to establish parallels or contrasts with Nazis, Zionists, Fascists, Anarchists, revolutionaries, communists, and so on. There is little doubt that Savarkar's work often reflects and responds to the *zeitgeist* of contemporary historical debates and global politics. Savarkar's interpretive techniques often appear as antecedents or analogues of a number of contemporary fields and debates. Some seem prescient – from his use of antonyms as discursive displacements of colonial categories of analyses, to promoting oral history as a method that had the potential to provide counter-narratives of colonial interpretations. Reading against the grain, as he so often does, was in his day a novel strategy to disrupt normative interpretations. His critiques of colonial governmentality reflect an unusually sharp intelligence ferreting out the reality beneath the rhetoric, especially when he argues that the colonial census is responsible for the construction of a proliferation of categories of castes and tribes to the detriment of the ruled – even if his focus is largely on the category that he prioritised: Hindu. His readings of colonial surveillance records and commission reports are critical of colonial epistemology based on information that was inaccurate or simply false. He warns against using official documents to write critical biographies or histories that ignore the alternative perspectives of Indian revolutionaries. In regularly turning to poetry, drama, and literature – in English, Marathi, and Hindi – to

---

[27] Savarkar, *Six Glorious Epochs*, 403.

substantiate or complement his arguments about history, Savarkar is in surprising ways interdisciplinary. At the same time, Western education in the English language does not stop him criticising many aspects of Western thought. He shows perspicacity in arguing that all Indians do not necessarily or blindly mimic their English counterparts. Using English to create a national consciousness is consistent with his approach of creating a pan-Hindu identity – all the while arguing for Hindi as a national language.

Savarkar's argument that the formation of Hindus *qua* Hindus was a process linked to colonialism and violence is central to any understanding of the meaning of Hindutva. Hindus were the perpetrators of violence who conquered *and* assimilated non-Hindus as Hindus in a process that can be described as dominance with hegemony. Savarkar considered this violence legitimate. Yet while he maintained that he "abhorred all violence" when perpetrated by a dominant force or entity, he believed it was justifiable for victims to seek vengeance against an oppressor.[28] Hindus were in a permanent war – as victims of the past – in which violence was necessary to negate unjust violence. The mere existence of a Muslim or a Christian in India meant that the "foreign invader" was still present. The only resolution lay in the *veer* seeking vengeance – in what Etienne Balibar has called the "infinite circularity" of violence that has no end.[29]

The survival of Hindutva as an idea requires the unceasing repetition of *this* history: Hindutva may very well become hollowed out without it. All critiques of Savarkar's history are necessarily meant to annihilate the epistemic conceptualisation of Hindutva. I am uncertain whether we are in a "state of emergency" – or that we will be in a "real state of emergency" as articulated by Walter Benjamin. But what is clear to me is that Hindutva cannot be ignored.[30] And that being so, nor can Savarkar's ideas about history. If Hindutva is of Being, then the very idea of the "Hindu," as constructed by Savarkar, is at stake. To understand the fundamental thought that "Hindutva is not a word but a history" marks the continuation of this struggle.

[28] Letter from V.D. Savarkar to N.D. Savarkar, July 6, 1920, *Letters from the Andamans, Selected Works of Veer Savarkar*, vol. 3, 477.

[29] Balibar, *Violence and Civility*, 17.

[30] Benjamin, "Theses on the Philosophy of History," 257.

# Coda

Perhaps there is only one way to end this book: to return to its intellectual starting point. What initially started as a curiosity about the origins of my name many years ago developed into a longer-term preoccupation with Savarkar's writings – well beyond what I had expected. I began this book with an autobiographical framing, but this is not an autobiography – although when reading Marshall Berman I feel he best captures my sentiments when he says, "This is far from a confessional book. Still, as I carried it for years inside me, I felt that in some sense it was the story of my life."[1] This coda explains how it all began.

During the spring of 1969 Virbati Chaturvedi – my grandmother, who I called Bai – took me to a Dr Dattatrey Sadashiv Parchure for a physical examination. Apparently, as an infant I had been quite ill and Bai had given up on the standard remedies prescribed by my paediatrician. She had convinced my parents that a consultation with Dr Parchure might reveal alternative therapies for my illness since he specialised in Ayurvedic medicine and had acquired a prominent reputation as a local healer in the central Indian city of Gwalior. After a brief examination, so I am told, Dr Parchure, when filling out a prescription for some medication, queried my grandmother about my name. Bai replied that the family had not given me an official first name, but that I had an informal household name. Dr Parchure asked if it would be possible for him to give me the name Vinayak, and my grandmother accepted the doctor's request.

Unfortunately, Bai passed away before I could speak to her about her interaction with Dr Parchure. In a recent conversation my mother stated that Bai was initially resistant to the idea of giving me any official name, Vinayak or otherwise, and had only agreed out of respect for Dr Parchure. It is far from uncommon in India for families to wait several years before giving formal names to children: some argue this has to do with wanting to give a name that matches the child's personality;

---

[1] Berman, "Acknowledgements," *All That is Solid Melts into Air*. (The page does not have a number.)

others say these are the cultural practices of a society that has high infant-mortality rates. In my case I suspect that Bai was worried by the latter, especially as I was regularly ill.

Throughout my childhood, aunts and uncles often recounted the story of my name and I had grown accustomed to the idea that it had a somewhat unusual origin. Relatives also reminded me that Vinayak was another name for Ganesh, the auspicious elephant deity celebrated as the remover of obstacles.[2] It was a common name among some communities in western and southern India, but certainly not within my clan in North India. I had long accepted that Dr Parchure, as a Maharashtrian Deshastha Brahmin, had probably favoured the popular Ganesh and felt the need to give the name Vinayak to sick children who needed many obstacles removed: after all, it had been an age-old practice to name children after Hindu deities.

The story of my name could have ended here, and I often wish it had. But those who are more familiar with the complexities of studying oral narratives will know that "hidden transcripts" and silences often have a history of their own: this was especially true in the uncovering of the secret origins of my name. At some point in the mid-1980s one of my aunts revealed a piece of information about Dr Parchure's past that had never been voiced to me before, even though it was clear that the entire family was aware of its significance: Dr Parchure had been arrested and convicted as a conspirator in the 1948 murder of M.K. Gandhi.

From that day I began to wonder if Dr Parchure's desire to name male children Vinayak had anything to do with his involvement in Gandhi's murder. I remember quickly searching through my books for any information about the murder and the trial. I was looking for a clue that would satisfy my curiosity, when I came across a copy of a book I had kept from my first undergraduate course in modern Indian history – *Freedom at Midnight* by Larry Collins and Dominique Lapierre. I recalled that somewhere within the text were the names of the men tried for killing Gandhi: Nathuram Vinayak Godse, Gopal Vinayak Godse, Vinayak Damodar Savarkar, Narayan Apte, Vishnu Karkare, Digamber Badge, Madan Lal Pahwa, Shankar Kistayya, and Dattatrey S. Parchure. As I read over the names of the accused, I began to see how the story of my name may have had less to do with the god

---

[2] For an etymology of the name Vinayak, see Narain, "Ganeśa," 21–5.

Ganesh and more to do with a legacy of the Mahatma's murder. At the same time, I felt that my suspicion may have been unfounded: after all, Savarkar was the only one with the name Vinayak, and the Godse brothers had inherited their father's first name following a practice common in western India. Additional conversations with my parents and relatives about the links between Parchure, the accused, and the naming issue left me dissatisfied and with no additional information. However, for reasons that continue to evade me, I decided against further investigation of this story.

In April 2001 I returned to Gwalior after a long interval. I cannot remember how my aunt Uma Chaturvedi and I began speaking of Dr Parchure one afternoon, but it must have had something to do with recounting stories about Bai. My aunt, as a secular and lifelong supporter of the Congress Party, had regularly been critical of the Hindu nationalist Bharatiya Janata Party (BJP), and for her the conspirators to Gandhi's assassination were some of the early trouble-makers in a lineage leading to today's right-wing Indian leadership. She argued that Dr Parchure's politics was fundamentally problematic, if not completely corrupt, especially as he had supplied the automatic pistol used by Nathuram Godse to kill Gandhi. As much as I had chosen to avoid the subject of my name, I now felt that it was impossible to do so. I wanted to meet Dr Parchure; I wanted to ask him about the significance of naming; I wanted to know why the name Vinayak was so important; I wanted to know who was Vinayak.

Unfortunately, I had waited too long. Dr Parchure was dead. In fact he had passed away in 1985, a couple of years before I first discovered his links to Gandhi's murder. My aunt suggested I speak to one of his two sons who still lived in Gwalior.

I contacted Upendra Dattatrey Parchure. He had trained as an Ayurvedic doctor, like the senior Dr Parchure, and continued to practice in his father's office. I wanted to retrace Bai's steps and return to the location where the story of my name began. This seemed like the obvious place to start. Initially, I was apprehensive about how to introduce myself and explain why I was interested in speaking about Dr Parchure. There were important problems to be considered prior to the meeting: some intellectual, some political, some ethical, and some personal. An interview to secure oral testimony about the past is generally a difficult, complex process in itself, but in this case the nature of the problem was linked to my desire to come to terms with my own subjectivity: that is, not only the subjectivity of an oral historian, but also because I was somehow the passive subject of some historical and ideological processes intertwined with the life-story of Dr Parchure.

My first meeting with Upendra Parchure was brief, barely lasting ten minutes. I introduced myself as someone whom his father had named Vinayak; I narrated how my grandmother had consulted his father when I was ill; I explained that I was hoping to have a conversation about his father. I also made it clear that I was researching modern Indian history and was interested in writing about the intellectual development of Hindu nationalism.

The doctor's first question was whether my parents had decided to keep the name Vinayak or replace it with another. I assured him that my grandmother had promised his father back in 1969 that the family would not change the name, and that my formal first name was Vinayak. He was obviously pleased, but now wanted to know my surname. Those who are familiar with the legacies of India's multicultural politics will know that family names often reveal a great deal about one's background: caste, language, region, and even class. I was aware that my Chaturvedi kinship affiliation would identify me as an educated, middle-class, local, Hindi-speaking Brahmin, but I was also acutely cognisant of the fact that, in this situation, my position of social privilege would be welcomed by Upendra Parchure, who came from a similar – though Maharashtrian – background. After a few additional questions about my father and grandfather to establish a patriarchal genealogy, the doctor asked if it would be possible for us to meet in his home where we could speak privately and at length; he stated that the kinds of things I wanted to know were best discussed outside the purview of his patients and staff. We agreed to meet the following week.

From the start of the second meeting I realised that Upendra Parchure was uncertain about the nature of the interview. He repeated his questions from our first meeting and wanted to know what I intended to do with the information about his father. I stated that I was interested in knowing more about his father for two primary reasons: first, I had long wondered about the origins of my name; and, second, I wanted to write about his father's political activities in the locality as part of a research study on Hindu nationalist intellectuals. Apparently satisfied with my explanation, Upendra Parchure pursued an in-depth conversation about his father's public and private life for the next three hours. It began with a narrative of some major events about the senior Dr Parchure's life.

Upendra Parchure wanted me to know that, more than anything else, his father, who was born in 1902, was a strong man, a strong nationalist, and a strong Hindu. He described his father with awe and pointed out that he was a big, powerful man with broad shoulders, thick thighs, and large arms.[3] His physical strength and martial prowess were also illustrated by the fact that he was a skilled wrestler, winning the Gwalior State title in his late teens. Although specific details of Dr Parchure's training were not discussed, what can be inferred is that the process of becoming a local or regional wrestling champion would have involved years of regimented and disciplined training with a guru and a cohort throughout childhood.[4] The Indian wrestler is typically dedicated to a distinct ideology that is centred on somatic principles and requires the acceptance of an ethos of wrestling as a way of life.[5] Initially, I was unclear why Upendra Parchure emphasised his father's masculinity, until later in the conversation it occurred to me that this was a consistent theme in how Dr Parchure was remembered in his personal and public life. This point was further clarified when Upendra Parchure celebrated the values and ethics his father learned while training as a wrestler, linking them to the development of his politics as a nationalist. It is not clear whether Dr Parchure intended to make this connection himself, or if this is how his son remembers him. However, recent scholarship suggests that central to Hindu nationalism from the 1920s has been the need to set political agendas which rely on power, masculinity, and strength, both discursively and institutionally.[6] Dr Parchure's political career may have had a beginning during his teens in ideologies of "wrestling nationalism," but according to his son the application of some of these strategies later in life translated into brutal forms of violence, at home and in the public

[3] For a further physical description of Dr Parchure, see Malgonkar, *The Men Who Killed Gandhi*, 135.

[4] See Alter, *The Wrestler's Body*.

[5] Ibid., 1.

[6] See Basu, *et als.*, *Khaki Shorts*. Also, "Hindus Should Improve Their Physique and Should Become Militant," *The Hindu Outlook*, January 11, 1939.

sphere.[7] At another level, as I was soon to discover, the assertion of masculinity was also at the centre of naming male children Vinayak.

According to Upendra Parchure, his father founded the Gwalior Branch of the Hindu Sabha, an organisation first established in 1915 to defend and protect Hindu interests.[8] The idea of creating the national-level Akhil Bharatiya Hindu Mahasabha, however, emerged out of a regional collective known as the Punjab Hindu Sabha, which originally had incorporated a broad range of ideas of high-caste Hindu thinkers on the themes of nationalism and patriotism.[9] By the 1920s the Hindu Mahasabha had transformed its image into that of a "hard-line" organisation marginalising the moderate Hindu leadership from within. This marked an important conjuncture in nationalist politics of the early-twentieth century, when the development of Hindu nationalism was firmly established and incorporated the idea of creating a powerful and militant Hinduism that was both anti-British and anti-Muslim.[10] For Upendra Parchure, his father ranked among a group of elite Hindu nationalists in India during this period; he argued that Dr Parchure had established himself as president of the local branch of the organisation for the purpose of promoting an independent Hindu nation. He had led a grassroots movement, travelling to villages and small towns in Central India – between Gwalior, Bhind, Sheopur, and Guna – with the aim of "injecting a pure Hindu spirit" and creating a pan-Hindu *jati*, including both high and low castes.

It occurred to me during the conversation that the ideas expressed about Dr Parchure's politics appeared consistent with those articulated by Vinayak Damodar Savarkar. And, it came as little surprise when Upendra Parchure described his father as a "true Savarkarite" who had

---

[7] Alter, *The Wrestler's Body*, 261–3.

[8] Upendra Parchure stated that the Hindu Sabha in Gwalior was founded in 1935; however, Hindu Mahasabha documents show it started on June 19, 1938. See "Extracts from the Diary of Br. V.D. Savarkar, President Hindu Mahasabha: Gwalior," in Bhide, ed., *Veer Savarkar's "Whirl-wind Propaganda,"* 497–9. Also, *Akhil Bharat Hindu Mahasabha 50th Golden Jubilee Session at Gwalior Held on 15th–17th May, 1966* (New Delhi: Akhil Bharat Hindu Mahasabha, [1969]).

[9] Jaffrelot, *The Hindu Nationalist Movement*, 17–25; Corbridge and Harriss, *Reinventing India*, 182–3.

[10] See Pandey, "Which of Us are Hindus?"

for many years followed his icon's writings on revolutionary politics, Hindutva, and anti-colonial nationalism. I felt that the mystery of my name had finally been solved: Dr Parchure was evoking Savarkar when naming male children. I wanted to know more about the naming issue, but Upendra Parchure continued on more important themes: his father's place within an emergent Hindu nationalism and his connections with Savarkar, Nathuram Godse, and Gandhi's murder. I remained silent and listened.

Dr Parchure had trained as a medical student and received his M.B.B.S. from Grant Medical College in Bombay during the 1920s. According to Upendra Parchure, his father continued to practice medicine in Bombay till 1935, when he was dismissed for insubordination from the Jamsetjee Jeejeebhoy Hospital. And by 1937, disillusioned with the methods of Western medicine, he began a study of Ayurvedic medicine, specialising in paediatrics – called Kaumarabhirtya.[11] The narrative of Dr Parchure's professional life appeared rather fragmented, and little else was discussed about the significance of the events around his firing, or why Ayurveda acquired such an important role. However, it may be worth saying something about the relationship between the medical profession and nationalism as a way to further contextualise the development of Dr Parchure's politics in the mid-1930s.[12]

The decades of the late-nineteenth century were marked by the "return of Hindu science," especially in reviving the fields of "indigenous" medicine, specifically Ayurveda.[13] It has been argued that this revivalist movement in medicine was predominantly a corollary to the emergence of Hindu nationalism in the 1890s.[14] At one level, Ayurveda represented a type of authentic indigenous response to colonial intervention in medicine, especially in a period when state policies to control epidemic diseases, like the bubonic plague, were popularly considered coercive and draconian. Ayurvedic medicine was viewed as a legitimate replacement of the Western system, which had come to dominate with British colonial expansion in India. However, at another level Ayurveda also provided a complementary direction to the development of Western medicine that could rely on, even

---

[11] Mukhopadhyaya, *History of Indian Medicine*, 3.
[12] See Jeffery, "Doctors and Congress."
[13] Arnold, *Science, Technology and Medicine*, 169–70.
[14] Ibid., 176.

boast, Indian contributions to the making of modern science.[15] Indian nationalists like Tilak and Gandhi had engaged in public debates on the importance of the medical profession in India, though neither wholeheartedly accepted the claim of the revivalists who sought to replace Western medical practices with Ayurveda.[16] Tilak had called for a "judicious combination" of the two systems of medicine, while Gandhi remained altogether troubled with all fields of medicine. He condemned European medicine, arguing that "the English have certainly effectively used the medical profession for holding us . . . [and] for political gain," and "to study European medicine is to deepen our slavery."[17] However, there were doctors trained in Western medicine who were inspired by the Ayurvedic revivalism and sought to professionalise and modernise this system of knowledge by publishing textbooks and opening colleges, hospitals, and clinics, while also participating in the freedom movement.[18] It has been suggested that the presence of these doctors in formal nationalist politics acquired prominence after 1920, especially in the inter-war period.[19] According to Upendra Parchure, his father's decision to take up Ayurveda after abandoning Western medicine occurred at this time, when medical politics became increasingly significant in public debates throughout India. Dr Parchure's decision to study Ayurvedic medicine was in consonance with the practices of other doctors throughout India, most of whom were also inspired by the ideology of Hindu revivalism, a key component of the emergent Hindu nationalism.

Dr Parchure met Savarkar for the first time when Savarkar travelled to Gwalior on June 17, 1938.[20] According to Upendra Parchure the meeting

---

[15] Ibid., 169–70, 176–7.

[16] Arnold, *Colonizing the Body*, 321, n.100.

[17] Gandhi, *Hind Swaraj*, 62–4.

[18] Leslie, "The Ambiguities of Medical Revivalism," 363.

[19] Jeffery, "Doctors and Congress," 166. For a discussion of revolutionary activities in Gwalior in this period, see "The Gwalior Conspiracies," in *Sedition Committee Report*, 1918, 8.

[20] For Dr Parchure's role in Gwalior State, see NMML, V.D. Savarkar Papers, Reel 25, Letter from N.V. Damle, Secretary, Hindu Mahasabha, President's Office, to Trilokinath Bhargav, General Secretary Madhya Bharat Hindu Sabha, February 9, 1942. Also, NMML, Akhil Bharat Hindu Mahasabha Papers, File P-68, "Hindu Sabha in Gwalior State Papers" (1945).

was an important moment for his father, who, by this point, considered himself a disciple of Savarkar. Dr Parchure, like many other Indian nationalists, had followed Savarkar's illustrious political career. Although Upendra Parchure emphasised his father's dedication to Savarkar's principles, there was very little discussion about the specific details of these ideas. He may have believed that the intellectual connections with Savarkar were too obvious to discuss with me, or simply chose not to explain them. However, for me this point marked an important transition in the interview. Upendra Parchure had thus far celebrated his father's accomplishments, but now the nature and tone of the conversation changed as it moved towards the topic of violence.

In 1939 Dr Parchure formed a paramilitary-style organisation in Gwalior known as the Hindu Rashtra Sena (literally, Hindu National Army), which boasted a cadre of three thousand volunteers.[21] The development of this organisation probably had something to do with the meeting with Savarkar in the same year, but according to Upendra Parchure his father specifically had grown tired of what he believed to be Muslim persecution of Hindus in Hyderabad State, and felt that a local riposte was necessary. In fact the Hindu Mahasabha had under Savarkar's leadership been agitating against the Nizam of Hyderabad in southern India between October 1938 and July 1939 to secure demands for Hindus, arguing that a Muslim ruler was suppressing their "civil liberties" and "culture."[22] Dr Parchure, as President of the Hindu Rashtra Sena, subsequently began organising Hindu attacks on Muslim localities.[23] In the process, he acquired the notoriety of being "the most controversial political figure in Gwalior."[24]

Nathuram Godse was a frequent visitor to the Parchure family

---

[21] Malgonkar, *The Men Who Killed Gandhi*, 136.

[22] Godse, *May It Please Your Honour* (1977), 23, 93, 100; Bhide, ed., *Veer Savarkar's "Whirl-wind Propaganda,"* 57–88, 101–14, 180–1.

[23] Gopal Godse, "Events and Accused," in Godse, *May It Please Your Honour* (1977), xv. M.K. Gandhi is reported to have received a telegram from "some Muslims in the Gwalior State" that stated, "The Hindus attacked our village and beat us, destroying our houses and crops and the State authorities take no notice in spite of requests." The date of the telegram is not given, but the incident appears to correspond with the activities of the Hindu Rashtra Sena. Full details are given in *RCI*, pt II, vol. IV, 72.

[24] Malgonkar, *The Men Who Killed Gandhi*, 135.

home in Gwalior. These may have been long-standing ties, but during the interview I was unable to establish the origins of Dr Parchure's relationship with Godse. However, a brief examination of Godse's activities reveals important parallels relevant to the discussion here. Sometime during the early 1930s, Godse joined the Pune branch of the Hindu Mahasabha and the Rashtriya Swayamsevak Sangh (RSS).[25] It has been suggested that for Godse – and the argument can be expanded to include Dr Parchure – participation in these organisations represented a "Hindu search for self-esteem" and "political potency" through the use of power and violence.[26] Godse abandoned the RSS after some years, claiming that it lacked proper levels of militancy, and co-founded the Hindu Rashtra Dal – an organisation whose name and objectives closely matched Dr Parchure's Hindu Rashtra Sena.[27] In 1942 Savarkar had promoted the idea of establishing the Dal as a secret volunteer organisation among a small group of disciples in the Pune Hindu Mahasabha, disciples who, like Godse, held similar opinions of the RSS.[28] Savarkar required volunteers to take an oath of loyalty to him and perform underground activities that could not be sanctioned by the Mahasabha.[29] The group's primary objective was to propagate "Savarkarism" as a way to "protect Hindudom and render help to every Hindu institution in their attempt to oppose encroachment on their rights and religion."[30] Training camps were set up throughout western and central India, advocating villagers to take up arms, teaching individuals "Indian games, physical exercises, [and] shooting exercises."[31] In addition, the intention was to spread Savarkar's ideas by holding weekly meetings where his writings, speeches, and literature would be discussed.[32]

[25] Godse, *May It Please Your Honour* (1977), 15–16; Nandy, "Final Encounter," 81.

[26] Nandy, "Final Encounter," 81.

[27] Godse, *May It Please Your Honour* (1977), 18, 37. Also, NMML, Akhil Bharat Hindu Mahasabha Papers, File C-62, "Hindu Rashtra Dal and Its Main Objectives" (1944–5).

[28] *RCI*, pt II, vol. IV, 66–7.

[29] Ibid., 67.

[30] Ibid.

[31] Ibid.; *RCI*, pt I, vol. III, 263.

[32] NMML, Akhil Bharat Hindu Mahasabha Papers, File C-62, Letter from

Dr Parchure and Nathuram Godse are said to have met on several occasions to discuss the activities of the Hindu Mahasabha.[33] In fact it has been argued that Dr Parchure, while on a political lecture tour in Pune, approached Godse with the aim of merging the Sena and the Dal. The deliberations failed, but both agreed to proceed with their separate yet intimately connected projects. Further links between Dr Parchure's Hindu Rashtra Sena and the Dal remain unclear, especially relating to the exact nature of the collaboration between Dr Parchure, Savarkar, and Godse.

I asked Upendra Parchure if his father had kept any personal letters, diaries, or writings about the activities of this period – anything pertinent to his interactions with Godse and Savarkar. He explained that Dr Parchure did not believe in holding evidence that might incriminate him, and, more importantly, the government had confiscated all the documents in their house when his father was arrested in 1948. However, it can still be suggested that important intellectual and personal ties were forged in this period. An individual by the name of Panna Lal Chaube told government officials that Dr Parchure and Nathuram Godse were travelling companions who had arrived in Alwar, in Rajasthan, around October 1947 for the specific purpose of acquiring a handgun from comrades in the local Hindu Mahasabha.[34] Chaube claimed to have met Dr Parchure and Godse, and to have discussed the plan to murder Gandhi with them. According to Chaube, Dr Parchure argued that "it was not in the interest of the country that the Mahatma should live and that Godse alone could assassinate Gandhi."[35] The two left Alwar dissatisfied with the quality of pistols offered to them.

On December 2, 1947 Dr Parchure returned to Pune as the main speaker at a Hindu Mahasabha meeting at the Tilak Samarak Mandir, where Godse and Savarkar were likely present.[36] An official report of Dr Parchure's speech provides an insight into his position:

---

A.S. Bhide to Pandit Chandragupta Vedalankar, Secretary, All-India Hindu Mahasabha (no date).

[33] The discussion of the interaction between Dr Parchure and Nathuram Godse is given in Malgonkar, *The Men Who Killed Gandhi*, 135–6.

[34] Evidence of Panna Lal Chaube, Witness Number 47, *RCI*, pt I, vol. II, 239–41.

[35] Ibid., 239.

[36] *RCI*, pt I, vol. III, 265.

He was described as a second Savarkar and that so great was his influence that on every mosque in Gwalior flew the Bhagwa flag. In his speech Dr Parchure, after referring to the state of affairs in Gwalior, advocated the use of force to achieve whatever they wanted. He also said that Gwalior Army was full of Muslims who were in a majority and that the State was increasing the Muslim elements . . . The trend of speech was anti-Congress and extremely anti-Muslim. He criticised Pandit Nehru's policy as regards Kashmir and pointed out the quiescence of Hindus in the face of Mohammedan aggressiveness. In the end he made a significant remark, the importance of which was perhaps not then appreciated, that *Gandhiji and Nehru would surely reap the fruits of their sins in a short time.*[37]

Dr Parchure appears to have achieved a prominent status within the inner circle of the organisation by this point, especially as he was now being compared with Savarkar. His anti-Muslim and anti-Congress positions were consistent with those advocated by Savarkar and the Hindu Mahasabha, even though Savarkar had by then resigned from the presidency of the organisation. Dr Parchure's other intellectual and political connections with the Mahasabha, Sena, and Dal are not as apparent in this period. Nevertheless, Dr Parchure acquired an enormous public profile when he was convicted for helping Nathuram Godse to arrange for the handgun that was used to assassinate Gandhi.

Upendra Parchure shifted the discussion away from his father's public life at this point in the conversation and began talking about some personal details. The separation between the public and private spheres has been a topic of much debate in the scholarship, especially about how to think about Indian politics within this framework. At the time, the debates had little to offer as I was faced with the dilemma of interpreting private details within the context of Dr Parchure's public life as president of the Gwalior Hindu Sabha and Hindu Rashtra Sena. And, as my questions never even broached the subject of Dr Parchure's private life, I was surprised when Upendra Parchure openly narrated an incident about family abuse.

Dr Parchure spent three-fourths of the income from his medical practice to fund his two organisations. One day, Upendra Parchure's

---

[37] Ibid., 265. Italics in original.

mother Sushilabai needed money to purchase items for the family.[38] Dr Parchure was apparently unavailable, so his wife decided to take a few rupees from his organisational fund. Upon discovering that Sushilabai had taken the money, Dr Parchure proceeded to beat his wife till she was unconscious. Upendra Parchure stated: "It is only by the grace of god that my mother did not die that day."

This was the only time his mother was mentioned in the conversation, but it was clear that this was not an isolated incident. The conversation appeared to have triggered a son's memory about his parents' conflictual relationship which had often resulted in violence against his mother. I wondered why Upendra Parchure wanted to ensure his father's abuse was included in the narrative of Dr Parchure's politics. Two parallel narrative lines strike me as plausible explanations. First, Upendra Parchure wanted to establish a continuity between his father's activities in the public sphere and his violence at home. This was his way of celebrating his father's commitment to Hindutva, even if it meant discussing violence against his mother.[39] Second, the discussion of attacks against innocent Muslims and his mother was one way to prevent the construction of a hagiographical account of his father's life, especially as he knew I was conducting an interview for the purpose of writing about Dr Parchure.

Hindu nationalists in western India had already developed discourses on the themes of domesticity, the home, and family life by the end of the nineteenth century.[40] Inscribed within these debates was a view that the "domestic sphere" was central for the preservation of Hindu spiritual values, and a necessary space for "respectable women" to serve their duty as "devoted wives" and "enlightened mothers" in the making of the nation.[41] It has been suggested that these processes were corollaries to the re-emergence of Maharashtrian Brahmins in the nineteenth century, when forms of Brahmanic Hinduism became important determinants for social behaviour, especially on the

---

[38] Inamdar, *The Story of the Red Fort Trial*, 1, 47, for a brief discussion about Sushilabai Parchure.

[39] I owe special thanks to Tanika Sarkar for this insight.

[40] See O'Hanlon, *A Comparison Between Women and Men*; Sarkar, *Hindu Wife, Hindu Nation*.

[41] O'Hanlon, *A Comparison Between Women and Men*, 51.

"woman's question."[42] Tilak and other conservatives writing in the 1880s argued against the education of Hindu women on the grounds that reading was likely to encourage "immorality" and "insubordination," and thereby challenge Hindu traditions and religion.[43] Savarkar later contributed to these debates in an essay entitled "The Profit-Loss of a Woman's Beauty," arguing that nation, children, and home were the main duties for Hindu women.[44] Although Savarkar was not against formal education for women, he felt they should be trained in areas suited to their "temperament": that is, women primarily needed to be educated as mothers to create a new generation of patriots for the betterment of the nation.[45] For example, in a speech given in 1937 he encouraged women "to be mothers of fine, healthy progeny," while the "kitchen and children were the main duties of women."[46] Women who digressed from their duty in the domestic sphere, as prescribed by Savarkar, were "morally guilty of a breach of trust."[47] Public debates on the topic of female improprieties that violated emergent Hindu norms within the domestic sphere often concluded with harsh resolutions, such as advocating the use of violence against "weak" and "wicked" women.[48] Were Sushilabai's actions of taking a few rupees from Dr Parchure's organisational fund an immoral act and a transgression from her duty as a devoted wife? Upendra Parchure's account did not offer an answer.

The conversation next turned to Gandhi's murder. The leadership of the Hindu Mahasabha and its affiliates had declared the partition of India and the creation of Pakistan a failure. It had been condemned by Savarkar, for example, on the grounds that the "vivisection of the Motherland" was an insult to all Hindus, and the idea of Pakistan was a threat to the making of a Hindu nation in the aftermath of

[42] Ibid., 10.

[43] Ibid., 16.

[44] Savarkar, *"Lalna-lavanny ki labh-hani,"* in *Savarkar Samagra*, vol. 4, 501–13.

[45] Keer, *Veer Savarkar*, 210, 213–14.

[46] Ibid., 230.

[47] Ibid., 214.

[48] O'Hanlon, *A Comparison Between Women and Men*, 36–8.

British rule.[49] For Savarkar's followers, like Godse and Dr Parchure, Gandhi and the Indian National Congress were to blame for the turn in political developments leading up to the Partition in 1947, a period in which it was argued that the rights of Hindus were not being protected. Godse echoed Savarkar's claims:

> I stoutly maintain that Gandhiji . . . has failed in his duty which was incumbent upon him to carry out, as the Father of the Nation. He has proved to be the Father of Pakistan. It was for this reason alone that I as a dutiful son of Mother India thought it my duty to put an end to the life of the so-called Father of the Nation who had played a very prominent part in bringing about vivisection of the country – Our Motherland.[50]

According to Upendra Parchure, Nathuram Godse and Narayan Apte travelled from Delhi to Gwalior by train on January 28, 1948.[51] They arrived at the Parchure family home for the purpose of securing a gun which was to be used to assassinate Gandhi. Godse was unhappy about the gun he already had in his possession because it was not an automatic and frequently locked without firing. Upendra Parchure remembers his father showing a pistol to Godse; he says he even saw Godse firing it outside. The pistol was said to have originated in Europe and only came to Gwalior when one Mr Deshmukh, a military officer in the Gwalior State Army, acquired it while on a training exercise in Germany.[52] The connection between Dr Parchure and Deshmukh remains unclear in this narrative. Upendra Parchure's only other comment about Godse was that he was someone who was shy and afraid in the presence of women. Although this point has been made by scholars studying Godse's life, it is unclear why the comment

[49] See Savarkar, "Protest Against the Vivisection of Hindusthan."

[50] Godse, *May It Please Your Honour* (1977), 110.

[51] For the official narrative of events relevant to Gandhi's assassination, see *RCI*, pt I, vol. I. Also see Inamdar, *The Story of the Red Fort Trial*; Malgonkar, *The Men Who Killed Gandhi*; Ghosh, *Gandhi Murder Trial*.

[52] Malgonkar suggests that the gun was manufactured in Italy in 1934 and was in the possession of an officer in Mussolini's army. An officer in the 4th Gwalior State Infantry, fighting in Abyssinia, had acquired the gun when his Italian counterpart surrendered. Malgonkar, *The Men Who Killed Gandhi*, 137.

was inserted at this point in the conversation, except as a way to high-light some apparent tension or paradox within Godse's personality.[53] On January 29th Godse and Apte left Gwalior for Delhi, and on the following evening Godse walked up to Mahatma Gandhi and fired three rounds from the automatic pistol into his body.[54]

Dr Parchure reportedly celebrated Gandhi's death by distributing sweets in Gwalior.[55] On February 3rd Dr Parchure was detained by the police and then formally arrested for conspiracy to commit murder two weeks later.[56] He confessed to his role in Gandhi's murder on February 18th while being interrogated by R.B. Atal, the First Class Magistrate of Gwalior.[57] Later he retracted his confession, arguing that it was "untrue" and forcibly extracted.[58] Dr Parchure and five others were found guilty of the conspiracy to murder Gandhi and sentenced to transportation for life.[59] It was determined that Godse and Apte were the primary perpetrators. They were ordered to be executed. Savarkar was acquitted of all charges with no direct evidence linking him to the murder. Digamber Badge became the official approver in the case and was released after the trial. Dr Parchure filed an appeal in the Punjab High Court, arguing that he had no role in the conspiracy, even though he had met Godse and Apte prior to the murder.[60] He stated that the two had arrived in Gwalior to recruit volunteers from the Hindu Rashtra Sena for some demonstrations in Delhi. Apte and Godse corroborated Dr Parchure's testimony during the trial, and Godse argued that the automatic pistol used to kill Gandhi was purchased through an arms dealer in a Delhi refugee camp.[61] The

[53] See Nandy, "Final Encounter."

[54] In January 2021 the Akhil Bharatiya Hindu Mahasabha opened a library and archives called the Godse Gyan Shala in Gwalior to celebrate the life and work of Nathuram Godse. See "Hindu Mahasabha Opens Nathuram Godse Library in MP," *Scroll.in*, January 11, 2021.

[55] Ghosh, *The Gandhi Murder Trial*, 100.

[56] *RCI*, pt I, vol. I, 57.

[57] Ghosh, *Gandhi Murder Trial*, 115.

[58] Ibid., 119.

[59] *RCI*, pt I, vol. I, 60.

[60] For a full discussion on Dr Parchure's case and subsequent appeal, see the reflections on the trial by his lawyer in Inamdar, *The Story of the Red Fort Trial*.

[61] Godse, *May It Please Your Honour* (1977), 7, 13–14.

High Court accepted Dr Parchure's claim that coercion was used to extract his initial confession, and that there was enough doubt about the exact nature of his interactions with Godse and Apte to warrant a complete acquittal.[62] According to Upendra Parchure his father was banned from Gwalior for two years following his release from prison, but he finally returned in 1952 on condition that he would no longer participate in public politics.[63] He re-established his medical practice and continued to live in Gwalior till his death in 1985.

Upendra Parchure did not mention that there was a controversy about his father's involvement in Gandhi's murder. Officially, Dr Parchure was acquitted of all charges, but within the family he has continued to be celebrated as one of the conspirators. Dr Parchure's original confession described how he had instructed an individual by the name of Dandavate to purchase a gun from one Jagdishprasad Goel.[64] Dandavate returned to Dr Parchure's house with a 9 mm Beretta automatic and about ten rounds of ammunition. Nathuram Godse tested the weapon in Dr Parchure's yard and agreed to purchase it for Rs 300.

Upendra Parchure's narrative of events generally appears to be consistent with his father's original confession, except that there is no discussion of Dandavate and Goel, while there is the addition of the military officer Deshmukh – who was not mentioned by Dr Parchure. The senior Parchure's exact role remains unresolved today, but it is popularly accepted that he assisted Godse with the purchase of the gun. "The Official Mahatma Gandhi eArchive & Reference Library" even has a brief history of the murder weapon titled "The Gun: a 9 mm Beretta Automatic" and states that Dr Parchure had organised Godse's acquisition of the weapon.[65] In an interview, Gopal Godse claimed that Dr Parchure did help his brother but was not part of the inner circle that plotted Gandhi's murder: "Nathuram managed to

---

[62] See Inamdar, *The Story of the Red Fort Trial.*

[63] Inamdar suggests that Dr Parchure's period of absence was set at six months through an "order of Externment from the Gwalior division of the state of Madhya Bharat." Inamdar, *The Story of the Red Fort Trial,* 220.

[64] See *RCI,* pt I, vol. I.

[65] "Dr Dattatraya Sadashiv Parchure" and "The Gun" at http://www.mahatma.org.in/conspirators (accessed September 7, 2001).

get an automatic pistol from Dr Dattatrey Parchure from Gwalior, though he was not a part of the conspiracy, and was later released by the High Court."[66]

Upendra Parchure finally turned to the question of naming children. He believed his father had probably named "dozens upon dozens of children Vinayak," if not "hundreds upon hundreds." He personally knew seven Vinayaks presently living in Gwalior who had acquired the name as patients in his father's clinic; I happened to be number eight. Upendra Parchure was very clear that his father's desire to name boys Vinayak was in honour of Savarkar. Dr Parchure had spent his adult life promoting the ideologies of his guru, initially through the Hindu Mahasabha and the Hindu Rashtra Sena, and then, later in his life, when forced out of public politics, he had adopted alternative strategies to promote Savarkarism. Upendra Parchure argued that I should feel very proud to have been named after such a strong and powerful nationalist who had spent his entire life fighting for Hindu rights. He said, "the spirit of Savarkar now lives through you."

Since that moment in the interview, I began questioning why my family decided to keep the name Vinayak, especially as they knew Dr Parchure's background. Were they aware of his hidden agenda that was directly tied to Savarkar? I have repeatedly asked my parents about this over the years, but the answers fail to explain the intricate details that interest me. My mother states that I was named after Ganesh, the decision was not political, and she was unaware that Dr Parchure had an agenda. She reminds me that Bai was not interested in giving me any name; I was too ill. In one conversation she stated that Dr Parchure told Bai my health would improve, and because it did the family decided to keep the name. My father repeats my mother's explanation but reminds me that he was not even in Gwalior when I was named. I find it difficult to probe my parents any further about my name, not least because they have grown frustrated with my questions. I certainly get a sense that my illness was very serious, my recovery a tremendous relief for a family that had already lost one child to an illness, and Dr Parchure was being thanked for his medical advice and honoured by naming

[66] "The Men Who Killed Gandhi," *Asian Age Online* (August 18, 2001), http://www.hclinfinet.com/2001/AUG/WEEK3/7/AOSCS2frame.jsp (accessed September 8, 2001).

me Vinayak. Needless to say, Savarkar does not emerge anywhere in their narratives.

Dr Parchure's strategy of naming children as a way to promote Savarkarism initially appeared rather innocuous, especially for someone who had achieved national-level notoriety for his public politics. It is not clear when Dr Parchure began giving the name Vinayak, but it may be suggested that the process began after Savarkar's death in 1966. However, it is important to note that Dr Parchure was not the first to take up the idea of using the name Vinayak for political purposes. In fact, he may have been following a pattern set by other disciples of Savarkar, namely Nathuram Godse and the conspirators who plotted Gandhi's murder. In the months leading up to the assassination, these individuals regularly used a half-dozen or so aliases when travelling, mostly centring on the name Vinayak in honour of Savarkar.[67] Dr Parchure, who in 1947 was described as a "second Savarkar," would have been well versed in his guru's writings, especially *Essentials of Hindutva*.

I would suggest that Dr Parchure's desire to give names was a return to the basic principles outlined by Savarkar in *Essentials of Hindutva*, especially considering that the first section of the book begins with the title "What is in a name?" and that the others following include "Name older still," "Other names," and "How Names are Given."[68] In *Essentials of Hindutva* there appears no specific prescription of naming individuals; instead, the focus is on the importance of naming a society and a nation. Savarkar, of course, was focusing on these issues as a way to identify the etymology of Hindu and Hindusthan, and to establish a genealogy of names connecting Hindus and Hindusthan with India and Indians. However, an examination of Savarkar's argument for "what is in a name" provides a clue to Dr Parchure's tactics:

> For, things do matter more than their names, especially when you have to choose one only of the two, or when the association between them is either new or simple. The very fact that a thing is indicated by a dozen names in

[67] Nandy, "Final Encounter," 96–7, n. 36. For example, Nathuram Godse used the aliases Vinayakrao and N. Vinayak Rao. *RCI*, pt I, vol. I, 59, 78. Also see Malgonkar, *The Men Who Killed Gandhi*, 115; Ghosh, *Gandhi Murder Trial*, 90.

[68] Savarkar, *Hindutva* (2003), 1–16. It is worth noting that these section titles were added after the publication of the first edition of the book.

a dozen human tongues disarms the suspicion that there is an invariable connection or natural concomitance between sound and the meaning it conveys. Yet, as the association of the word with the thing it signifies grows stronger and lasts long, so does the channel which connects the two states of consciousness then to allow an easy flow of thoughts from one to the other, till at last it seems almost impossible to separate them. And when in addition to this a number of secondary thoughts or feelings that are generally roused by the thing get mystically entwined with the word that signifies it, the name seems to matter as much as the thing itself.[69]

Upon reading this passage I was reminded of Upendra Parchure's vivid declaration that "the spirit of Savarkar" was now living through me, and by extension through the dozens or hundreds of other Vinayaks. It certainly may be argued that Dr Parchure held the belief that inscribed within the name Vinayak was a signifying system tied to Savarkar and the principles of Hindutva. Those versed in semiotics would suggest that Dr Parchure was aware of the power of the name-sign, and by naming children he had hoped to evoke a mental image of Savarkar as an icon in everyday life.[70] Indeed, the name Vinayak has become more popular in India over the past generation than in previous ones; at the same time, it would be incorrect to assume that all the links go back to Savarkar. My own parents say they had no clue about Dr Parchure's interest in naming boys, and I wonder if other parents and their sons named Vinayak also have remained oblivious of this possibility over the years, and believe that the origins of the name are only tied to Ganesh. But here too there is a "hidden transcript" with a history intertwined with the ideological development of Hindu nationalism.

It may be worth saying something more about the long-term significance of Ganesh, as every conversation about the name Vinayak usually begins with it. The worship of Ganesh in western India began as early as the sixth or seventh century, although it was primarily limited to Maharashtrian Brahmins.[71] By the eighteenth century Ganesh had been popularised in temples and festivals around Pune through the

---

[69] Savarkar, *Essentials of Hindutva* (1923), 1–2.

[70] See Makolkin, *Name, Hero, Icon.*

[71] Courtright, "The Ganesh Festival in Maharashtra," 76–7.

patronage of the Peshwas, but there was a significant decline with the subsidence of Peshwa power after 1818 and the arrival of the British in the area.[72] In the 1890s Ganesh's popularity had a resurgence under the leadership of Tilak, who began mobilising large numbers of Hindus from upper and lower castes around an annual Ganesh festival.[73] Tilak was concerned with harnessing mass support against colonial rule, while simultaneously using the symbol of Ganesh to articulate a political agenda linking Hindu revivalism with Indian nationalism. His was considered an "extremist" form of nationalism for its celebration of Maharashtrian "martial prowess."[74] Its militantly anti-Muslim character is not in doubt.[75] In fact, it has been argued that Tilak's invention of a Ganesh tradition was primarily in response to, and corresponded with, the annual Muslim festival of Muhharam. This point is generally obscured in today's popular memory of the Ganesh festival's origins, especially as it has achieved national appeal throughout India, moving beyond local and regional centres in Maharashtra. Tilak's role is also important in this discussion for another reason: namely, that Dr Parchure, Savarkar, and the others in the Hindu Mahasabha and its affiliated organisations were heavily influenced by Tilak's nationalist politics.[76]

The fact that over the years neither my parents nor I were cognisant of Dr Parchure's naming practice is irrelevant for the politics of Hindutva. It may be argued that for Dr Parchure the celebration of Vinayak as Ganesh, or as Savarkar, was equally powerful, because inscribed in both were the legacies and inspirations of Hindu nationalism. I have scores of Ganesh idols and images at home – gifts I have received from friends and family, each of whom stated that they purchased an idol because of my name. I often wonder how many other Vinayaks are out there who share a similar story, but part of me simply does not want to meet a Vinayak who actually embodies the myriad characteristics that would make Dr Parchure proud. For Savarkar and his contemporary

---

[72] Courtright, *Ganeśa*, 226.

[73] See Cashman, "The Political Recruitment of God Ganapati."

[74] Bayly, *Origins of Nationality in South Asia*, 108–9.

[75] Hansen, *Wages of Violence*, 29–30.

[76] Gopal Godse, "Events and Accused," in Godse, *May It Please Your Honour*, xii.

disciples, the creation of a Hindu nation was a long, multi-generational process that could not be achieved in their lifetime. Savarkar was keenly aware of the risks and limitations of his political strategies, but advocated that his followers promote the ideals of a Hindu nation, even in minute ways, for the benefit of future generations:

> The seed of the banyan tree is so trivial as to be smaller than the mustard seed. But it holds within itself the rich promise of a luxuriant expanse. If we are to live with honour and dignity as a Hindu Nation . . . that nation must emerge under the Hindu flag. This my dream shall come true – if not in this generation, at least in the next. If it remains an empty dream, I shall prove a fool. If it comes true, I shall prove a prophet.[77]

Savarkar's principles are very much alive today, and the new generation of Hindu nationalists have been openly working towards the goal of creating a Hindu Rashtra by following Savarkar's prescription: "The nation that has no consciousness of its past has no future. Equally true it is that a nation must develop its capacity not only for claiming a past but also for knowing how to use it for the furtherance of its future."[78]

In India there are many who have been inspired by the writings and activities of Savarkar and his disciples. And one does not need to look very hard to find these individuals and groups, especially as their public presence cannot be avoided in everyday life. The discursive project of Hindutva, led by the BJP and its subsidiaries, for example, promotes the changing of names in consonance with Savarkar's ideals. In November 1995 the Maharashtrian state government led by the Shiv Sena (Shivaji's Army) changed the official name of Bombay to Mumbai.[79] The Shiv Sena as a nativist organisation had been demanding the vernacularisation of the city's name since its founding in 1966 but could only change it once it had secured the patronage of the BJP government at the centre. The process was extended to replacing the names of streets, buildings, railway stations, neighbourhoods, and anything

---

[77] Savarkar, "This My Legacy," in Raje, ed., *Savarkar*, 3. It is worth noting that Savarkar's reference to the mustard seed in this context is a rethinking of the "parable of the mustard seed" from the Bible found in Gospels of Matthew (13:31–2), Mark (4:30–2), and Luke (13:18–19).

[78] Savarkar, "Author's Introduction," *Indian War*, vii.

[79] Hansen, *Wages of Violence*, 1.

deemed necessary to rid the city of its Portuguese and British titles, and as a way to reinscribe a Hindu identity in the city. Institutionally, the project has played an important role in targeting Muslims, Christians, and other minorities: reincarnations of the Hindu Rashtra Sena and the Hindu Rashtra Dal frequently make their presence felt.

I asked Upendra Parchure about his views on the direction of today's Hindu nationalism. To my surprise he was dissatisfied with the current leadership and their national programme. He argued that today's politicians were corrupt, and consequently they did not live up to the ideals of creating a Hindu Rashtra as articulated by Savarkar, his father, and the others involved in the Gandhi murder case. Upendra Parchure reiterated that the assassination was necessary for the betterment of the nation, to ensure that India could develop into a strong, powerful homeland for Hindus. For Upendra Parchure I was part of the future generation his father and Savarkar had hoped would serve as the messengers of Hindutva. As Vinayak I could embody the characteristics of power, strength, and masculinity inscribed in my name, and participate in the making of a Hindu Nation. As I stated at the outset, I wish the story of my name had ended many years ago and did not require such a long, unsettling journey.

I thanked Upendra Parchure for his time and sharing memories of his father's life-story. My last request, however, was to see a photograph of Dr Parchure, whose image was the only one conspicuously missing among the numerous photographs of the group arrested in Gandhi's murder. Upendra Parchure said he only had two photographs of his father in his house. I was taken into his bedroom where they were hanging: the first was a picture of Dr Parchure as a young wrestler, flexing his chest and arms; the second showed Dr Parchure with his wife, probably taken shortly after their wedding. As I was leaving, Upendra Parchure asked if I had noticed the third photograph in the room that had been carefully positioned above the door. I imagined that this was a reference to a picture of Ganesh, who is often placed in such a location as an auspicious symbol for all those who pass through the doorway. Instead, it was a large image of the assassin Nathuram Godse, who was being celebrated as an incarnation of Vinayak and the remover of obstacles.

# Bibliography

## Archival Sources

*Asia, Pacific and Africa Collections, British Library, London*
Bombay Home Department Proceedings
Bombay Judicial Department Proceedings
European Manuscripts
India Home Department (Political) Proceedings
India Port Blair Proceedings
Information Department Records
Political and Secret Department Records
Political (Confidential) Proceedings
Public and Judicial Department Records
Record Department Papers

*Centre for South Asian Studies Archive,
University of Cambridge*

V.B. Gogate Collection
G.V. Ketkar Collection

*Hoover Institution Library and Archives,
Stanford University*

Western Language Collections, S.P. India, Publications of the Akhil Bharat
 Hindu Mahasabha

*Maharashtra State Archives, Mumbai*

Home Department (Political) Files
Home Department (Special) Files

*Nehru Memorial Museum and Library, New Delhi*

Akhil Bharat Hindu Mahasabha Papers
V.D. Savarkar Papers

## Newspapers and Newsmagazines

*The Academy* (London)
*Amrita Bazar Patrika* (Calcutta)
*The Athenaeum* (London)
*Bombay Chronicle* (Bombay)
*The Guardian* (Manchester)
*Herald of the Revolt* (London)
*Hindu Outlook* (New Delhi)
*The Indian Sociologist* (London and Paris)
*Kesari* (Pune)
*The Leader* (Allahabad)
*Mahratta* (Pune)
*The Times* (London)
*The Times of India* (Bombay)
*The Tribune* (Lahore)

## Official Published Sources

*Akhil Bharat Hindu Mahasabha 50$^{th}$ Golden Jubilee Session at Gwalior Held on 15$^{th}$–17$^{th}$ May, 1966* (New Delhi: Akhil Bharat Hindu Mahasabha, [1969]).

*All India Reporter, 1942: Madras Section* (Nagpur: D.V. Chitaley, 1942).

*Constituent Assembly of India Debates (Proceedings)*, vol. IX, loksabhaph.nic.in/writereaddata/cadebatefiles/C18091949.html (accessed March 2, 2021).

*Indian Historical Records Commission. Proceedings of Meetings, vol. VI, January 1924* (Calcutta: Government of India Central Publication Branch, 1924).

*Indian Law Reports*, Bombay Series, vol. XXXV, 1911.

Khan, Mirza Mehdy, *Report on the Census Operations, Part I, in Census of India, 1891, vol. XXIII. His Highness the Nizam's Dominions* (Bombay: Jehangir B. Marzban & Co., 1893).

*Legal Proceedings in the Case of Tilak v. Chirol and Another, Before Mr. Justice Darling and a Special Jury, January 29$^{th}$ 1919–February 21$^{st}$ 1919, 2 vols* (London: Published for the Government of Bombay, by H. Milford, Oxford University Press, 1920).

Old Bailey Proceedings Online, Trial of Madan Lal Dhingra, July 19, 1909 (Reference Number t19090719-55), www.oldbaileyonline.org, version 8.0 (accessed February 16, 2019).

*Report of the Commission of Inquiry into Conspiracy to Murder Mahatma Gandhi by J.L. Kapur* [New Delhi: Ministry of Home Affairs, Government of India, 1970].

*Report on the Administration of Andaman and Nicobar Islands and the Penal Settlement of Port Blair for 1904–05* (Calcutta: Office of the Superintendent of Government Printing, India, 1906).

*Report on Native Papers Published in the Bombay Presidency* (1890–1920).

*Savarkar Arbitration. Counter-Case Presented on Behalf of the Government of His Britannic Majesty to the Tribunal Constituted Under the Agreement Signed in London on the 25th day of October, 1910, between the Government of His Brittanic Majesty and the Government of the French Republic* (London: The Foreign Office, 1911).

*Sedition Committee Report, 1918* (Calcutta: Superintendent Government Printing, 1919).

Sharp, H., *Selections from Educational Records,* pt 1, Bureau of Education, India (Calcutta: Superintendent Government Printing, 1920).

## Published Writings of Vinayak Damodar Savarkar

A Maratha, *Essentials of Hindutva* (Nagpur: V.V. Kelkar, 1923).

A Maratha, *Hinduism* (Nagpur: V.V. Kelkar, 1923).

An Indian Nationalist, *The Indian War of Independence of 1857* ([n.p.], 1909).

An Indian Nationalist, *Indien im Aufruhr* (Berlin: Hans Kurzeja, 1940).

Bhide, A.S., ed., *Veer Savarkar's "Whirl-wind Propaganda," (Statements, Messages & Extracts from the President's Diary of His Propagandistic Tours, Interviews from December 1937 to October 1941)* (Bombay: A.S. Bhide, 1941).

Joshi, G.M., and S.S. Savarkar, eds, *Historic Statements by V.D. Savarkar* (Bombay: Popular Prakashan, 1967).

Joshi, G.M. and S.S. Savarkar, eds, *Historic Statements (Prophetic Warnings): Statements, Telegrams & Letters, 1941 to 1965* (Bombay: Veer Savarkar Prakashan, 1992).

Parkash, Satya, ed., *Hindu Rashtravad: Being an Exposition of the Ideology & Immediate Programme of Hindu Rashtra as Outlined by (Swatantrayaveer) V.D. Savarkar* (Rohtak: Dr Satya Parkash, 1945).

Savarkar, Veer, *Inside the Enemy Camp*, trans. V.S. Godbole ([n.p.], [n.d.]).

Savarkar, Veer, *Inside the Enemy Camp*, trans. V.S. Godbole, https://savarkar.org/en/pdfs/inside_._enemy_camp.v001.pdf (accessed August 16, 2021).

Savarkar, Vinayak Damodar, *An Echo from Andamans: Letters Written by Br. Savarkar to His Brother Dr. Savarkar* (Nagpur: V.V. Kelkar, 1924).

Savarkar, Vinayak Damodar, *Hindu Pad Padashahi, or A Review of the Hindu Empire of Maharashtra* (Madras: B.G. Paul & Company, 1925).

Savarkar, Vinayak Damodar, *Indian War of Independence*, 2 pts (Calcutta: R. Bhattacharya, 1930).

Savarkar, Vinayak Damodar, *Hindutva* (New Delhi: Central Hindu Yuvak Sabha, 1938).

Savarkar, Vinayak Damodar, *Hindu Sanghatan, Its Ideology and Immediate Programme* (Bombay: N.V. Damle, 1940).

Savarkar, Vinayak Damodar, "India's Foreign Policy," in A.S. Bhide, ed., *Veer Savarkar's "Whirl-wind Propaganda"* (Bombay: A.S. Bhide, 1941), 50–3.

Savarkar, Vinayak Damodar, "A Statement on the Jewish International Question," in A.S. Bhide, ed., *Veer Savarkar's "Whirl-wind Propaganda"* (Bombay: A.S. Bhide, 1941), 70–2.

Savarkar, Vinayak Damodar, "Celebrate the Hindu Nation Day," in A.S. Bhide, ed., *Veer Savarkar's "Whirl-wind Propaganda"* (Bombay: A.S. Bhide, 1941), 130–3.

Savarkar, Vinayak Damodar, "A Message To Hindus in Gujerat," in A.S. Bhide, ed., *Veer Savarkar's "Whirl-wind Propaganda"* (Bombay: A.S. Bhide, 1941), 259–60.

Savarkar, Vinayak Damodar, "Hindu Sabhas, Watch Out: The Coming Census & Your Duty," in A.S. Bhide, ed., *Veer Savarkar's "Whirl-wind Propaganda"* (Bombay: A.S. Bhide, 1941), 266–76.

Savarkar, Vinayak Damodar, "The Census Week," in A.S. Bhide, ed., *Veer Savarkar's "Whirl-wind Propaganda"* (Bombay: A.S. Bhide, 1941), 293–6.

Savarkar, Vinayak Damodar, "The Census & The Pan-Hindu Fold," in A.S. Bhide, ed., *Veer Savarkar's "Whirl-wind Propaganda"* (Bombay: A.S. Bhide, 1941), 311–15.

Savarkar, Vinayak Damodar, "It is Absurd to Talk of the Two Majorities in India," in A.S. Bhide, ed., *Veer Savarkar's "Whirl-wind Propaganda"* (Bombay: A.S. Bhide, 1941), 456–61.

Savarkar, Vinayak Damodar, "Extracts from the Diary of Br. V.D. Savarkar, President Hindu Mahasabha: Gwalior," in A.S. Bhide, ed., *Veer Savarkar's "Whirl-wind Propaganda"* (Bombay: A.S. Bhide, 1941), 497–9.

Savarkar, Vinayak Damodar, *Hindu-Pad-Padashahi, or A Review of the Hindu Empire of Maharashtra* (Poona: Manohar Mahadeo Kelkar, 1942).

Savarkar, Vinayak Damodar, *The Volcano, or The First War of Indian Independence 1857–1859* (Kuala Lumpur: Jayamani S. Subrahmanyam, 1945).

Savarkar, Vinayak Damodar, *The Indian War of Independence (National Rising of 1857)* (Bombay: [n.p.], 1946).

Savarkar, Vinayak Damodar, *The Indian War of Independence: Authorized Abridged Edition* (Bombay: Dhawale-Popular, 1947).

Savarkar, Vinayak Damodar, *Who is a Hindu?* (Poona: S.P. Gokhale, 1949).

Savarkar, Vinayak Damodar, *Hindu Rashtra Darshan: A Collection of the Presi-

*dential Speeches Delivered from the Hindu Mahasabha Platform* (Bombay: L.G. Khare, 1949).

Savarkar, Vinayak Damodar, *Majhi Janmathep*, in *Samagra Savarkar Vanmaya*, vol. 1 (Poona: Maharashtra Prantik Hindusabha, 1963).

Savarkar, Vinayak Damodar, "*Veer Chapekar ani Ranade*," in *Samagra Savarkar Vanmaya*, vol. 1 (Poona: Maharashtra Prantik Hindusabha, 1963), 139–42.

Savarkar, Vinayak Damodar, "Oh Martyrs," in *Samagra Savarkar Vanmaya*, vol. 5 (Poona: Maharashtra Prantik Hindusabha, 1963), 443–6.

Savarkar, Vinayak Damodar, in "Independent Jewish State," *Samagra Savarkar Vanmaya*, vol. 6 (Poona: Maharashtra Prantik Hindusabha, 1964), 558–9.

Savarkar, Vinayak Damodar, *Samagra Savarkar Vanmaya*, 9 vols (Poona: Maharashtra Prantik Hindusabha, 1963–5).

Savarkar, Vinayak Damodar, *Saha Soneri Pane* (Bombay: Majestic Book Stall, 1968).

Savarkar, Vinayak Damodar, *The Indian War of Independence, 1857* (New Delhi: Rajdhani Granthagar, 1970).

Savarkar, Vinayak Damodar, *Hindu-Pad-Padashahi, or A Review of the Hindu Empire of Maharashtra* (New Delhi: Bharati Sahitya Sadan, 1971).

Savarkar, Vinayak Damodar, *Six Glorious Epochs of Indian History*, ed. and trans. S.T. Godbole (Bombay: Bal Savarkar, 1971).

Savarkar, Vinayak Damodar, *Echoes from Andaman* (Bombay: Veer Savarkar Prakashan, 1984).

Savarkar, Vinayak Damodar, *The Indian War of Independence, 1857* (New Delhi: Rajdhani Granthagar, 1986).

Savarkar, Vinayak Damodar, "This My Legacy," in Sudhakar Raje, ed., *Savarkar: Commemoration Volume* (Bombay: Savarkar Darshan Pratishthan 1989).

Savarkar, Vinayak Damodar, "Protest Against the Vivisection of Hindusthan," in G.M. Joshi and S.S. Savarkar, eds, *Historic Statements (Prophetic Warnings): Statements, Telegrams & Letters, 1941 to 1965* (Bombay: Veer Savarkar Prakashan, 1992), 167–9.

Savarkar, Vinayak Damodar, *Samagra Savarkar*, 10 vols (Mumbai: Veer Savarkar Prakashan, 1993).

Savarkar, Vinayak Damodar, *Shatruchya Shibirata*, in *Samagra Savarkar*, vol. 1 (Mumbai: Veer Savarkar Prakashan, 1993).

Savarkar, Vinayak Damodar, "*Deshbhakta Savarkarche patra*," in *Samagra Savarkar*, vol. 1 (Mumbai: Veer Savarkar Prakashan, 1993), 115–16.

Savarkar, Vinayak Damodar, *Saha Soneri Pane*, in *Samagra Savarkar*, vol. 3 (Mumbai: Veer Savarkar Prakashan, 1993).

Savarkar, Vinayak Damodar, *Joseph Mazzini,* in *Samagra Savarkar,* vol. 8 (Mumbai: Veer Savarkar Prakashan, 1993).

Savarkar, Vinayak Damodar, *Savarkar Samagra,* 10 vols (New Delhi: Prabhat Prakashan, 2000–3).

Savarkar, Vinayak Damodar, "*Veer Chapekar aur Ranade,*" in *Savarkar Samagra,* vol. 1 (New Delhi: Prabhat Prakashan, 2000), 171–4.

Savarkar, Vinayak Damodar, "*Deshbhakta Savarkar ka patra,*" in *Savarkar Samagra,* vol. 1 (New Delhi: Prabhat Prakashan, 2000), 609.

Savarkar, Vinayak Damodar, "*Vijayadashami,*" in *Savarkar Samagra,* vol. 1 (New Delhi: Prabhat Prakashan, 2000), 609–12.

Savarkar, Vinayak Damodar, "*Lalna-lavanny ki labh-hani,*" in *Savarkar Samagra,* vol. 4 (New Delhi: Prabhat Prakashan, 2000), 501–13.

Savarkar, Vinayak Damodar, "*1857 ka swatantra sangrama,*" in *Savarkar Samagra,* vol. 5 (New Delhi: Prabhat Prakashan, 2000).

Savarkar, Vinayak Damodar, "*Hindu sanghatankarta swarashtra ka itihaas kisa taraha likhen aur parhen,*" in *Savarkar Samagra,* vol. 5 (New Delhi: Prabhat Prakashan, 2000), 443–52.

Savarkar, Vinayak Damodar, *Chhah Svarnim Prstha,* in *Savarkar Samagra,* vol. 6 (New Delhi: Prabhat Prakashan, 2003).

Savarkar, Vinayak Damodar, "*Ek hi dharma-pustaka nahin, yeh achchha hai!*" in *Savarkar Samagra,* vol. 7 (New Delhi: Prabhat Prakashan, 2003), 313–14.

Savarkar, Vinayak Damodar, "*Savarkar aur Maulana Shaukat Ali ke bich vichara yuddha,*" in *Savarkar Samagra,* vol. 7 (New Delhi: Prabhat Prakashan, 2003), 316–24.

Savarkar, Vinayak Damodar, *Mazzini Charitra,* in *Savarkar Samagra,* vol. 8 (New Delhi: Prabhat Prakashan, 2003).

Savarkar, Vinayak Damodar, *Hindutva: Who is a Hindu?* (New Delhi: Hindi Sahitya Sadan, 2003).

Savarkar, Vinayak Damodar, *The Maratha Movement (Hindu Pad Padashahi), Or A Review of the Hindu Empire of Maharashtra* (New Delhi: Hindi Sahitya Sadan, 2003).

Savarkar, Vinayak Damodar, *My Transportation for Life,* in *Selected Works of Veer Savarkar,* vol. 2 (Chandigarh: Abhishek Publications, 2007).

Savarkar, Vinayak Damodar, *Selected Works of Veer Savarkar,* 4 vols (Chandigarh: Abhishek Publications, 2007).

### Published Sources

Afghan, Yusuf, "Big Question Before Indian Muslims: To Wind Up League or Continue," Annex to No. 253, F.25 (Part II)-GG/265, dated December 7, 1947, in Z.H. Zaidi, ed., *Quaid-i-Azam Mohammad Ali Jinnah*

*Papers,* First Series, vol. 6 (Islamabad: Quaid-i-Azam Papers Project, 2001), 395–7.

Aggleton, Sabrina "The Crystallization of the Impossible: Derrida and Merleau-Ponty at the Threshold of Phenomenology," in Zeynep Direk and Leonard Lawlor, eds, *A Companion to Derrida* (Chichester: John Wiley & Sons, 2014), 269–86.

Agrawal, Purshottam, "Surat, Savarkar and Draupadi: Legitimising Rape as a Political Weapon," in Tanika Sarkar and Urvashi Butalia, eds, *Women and Right-Wing Movements: Indian Experiences* (London: Zed Books, 1995), 29–57.

Ahmed Asif, Manan, *The Loss of Hindustan: The Invention of India* (Cambridge: Harvard University Press, 2020).

Alavi, Seema, ed., *The Eighteenth Century in India* (Delhi: Oxford University Press, 2002).

Aldred, Guy A., "To the English Proletariat! Appeal of the Savarkar Release Committee," *The Indian Sociologist,* 6, 8 (1910).

Aldred, Guy A., "The Savarkar Infamy," *The Freewoman: A Weekly Humanist Review,* 2, 32 (1912), 113–14.

Aldred, Guy A., "Savarkar Arrested," *The Word,* 11, 7 (1950), 65.

Aldred, Guy A., ed., *Rex v. Aldred: London Trial, 1909, Indian Sedition Glasgow Sedition Trial, 1921* (Glasgow: Strickland Press, 1948).

Ali, Daud, "The Idea of the Medieval in the Writing of South Asian History: Contexts, Methods and Politics," *Social History,* 39, 3 (2014), 382–407.

Alter, Joseph S., *The Wrestler's Body: Identity and Ideology in North India* (Berkeley: University of California Press, 1992).

Ambedkar, B.R., *Pakistan or The Partition of India* (Bombay: Thacker & Co., 1946).

Ambedkar, B.R., "From Millions to Fractions," in Valerian Rodrigues, ed., *The Essential Writings of B.R. Ambedkar* (Delhi: Oxford University Press, 2002), 332–50.

Ambedkar, B.R., "Statement Concerning the Safeguards for the Protection of the Interests of the Depressed Classes as a Minority in the Bombay Presidency and the Changes in the Composition of and the Guarantees from the Bombay Legislative Council Necessary to Ensure the Same under Provincial Autonomy" (May 29, 1928), in Hari Narke, ed., *Dr. Babasaheb Ambedkar Writings and Speeches, vol. 2* (New Delhi: Dr. Ambedkar Foundation, 2014), 429–58.

Ambedkar, B.R., "The Triumph of Brahminism," in Hari Narke, ed., *Dr Babasaheb Ambedkar Writings and Speeches,* vol. 3 (New Delhi: Dr Ambedkar Foundation, 2014), 266–331.

Ambedkar, B.R., *Annihilation of Caste: The Annotated Critical Edition*, ed. S. Anand (London: Verso, 2016).

Amin, Shahid, "Gandhi as Mahatma: Gorakhpur District, Eastern UP, 1921–2," in Ranajit Guha, ed., *Subaltern Studies II: Writings on South Asian History and Society* (Delhi: Oxford University Press, 1983), 1–57.

Anand, Vidya Sagar, *Savarkar* (London: C.A. Woolf, 1967).

Anderson, Benedict, *Imagined Communities: Reflections on the Origins and Spread of Nationalism*, revised edition (London: Verso, 2006).

Anderson, Clare, *The Indian Uprising of 1857–58: Prisons, Prisoners and Rebellion* (London: Anthem Press, 2007).

Anderson, J.D., "Stress and Pitch in Indian Languages," *The Journal of the Royal Asiatic Society of Great Britain and Ireland* (1913), 867–74.

Anderson, Perry, "The Antinomies of Antonio Gramsci," *New Left Review*, series 1, no. 100 (1976), 5–78.

Anderson, Perry, *A Zone of Engagement* (London: Verso, 1992).

Anderson, Perry, *Spectrum: From Right to Left in the World of Ideas* (London: Verso, 2005).

Arnold, David, *Colonizing the Body: State Medicine and Epidemic Disease in Nineteenth-Century India* (Berkeley: University of California Press, 1993).

Arnold, David, "Gramsci and Peasant Subalternity in India," in Vinayak Chaturvedi, ed., *Mapping Subaltern Studies and the Postcolonial* (London: Verso, 2000), 24–49.

Arnold, David, *Science, Technology and Medicine in Colonial India: The New Cambridge History of India*, III.5 (Cambridge: Cambridge University Press, 2000).

Arnold, David, "Death and the Modern Empire: The 1918–19 Influenza Epidemic in India," *Transactions of the Royal Historical Society*, 29 (2019), 181–200.

Arnold, David, and Stuart Blackburn, eds, *Telling Lives in India: Biography, Autobiography, and Life History* (Ranikhet: Permanent Black, 2004).

Bakhle, Janaki, "Country First? Vinayak Damodar Savarkar and the Writing of *Essentials of Hindutva*," *Public Culture*, 22, 1 (2010), 149–86.

Bakhle, Janaki, "Savarkar (1883–1966), Sedition and Surveillance: The Rule of Law in a Colonial Situation," *Social History*, 35, 1 (2010), 51–75.

Bakhle, Janaki, "Putting Global Intellectual History in Its Place," in Samuel Moyn and Andrew Sartori, eds, *Global Intellectual History* (New York: Columbia University Press, 2013), 228–53.

Balibar, Étienne, *Violence and Civility: On the Limits of Political Philosophy* (New York: Columbia University Press, 2015).

Ball, Charles, *The History of the Indian Mutiny: Giving a Detailed Account of the Sepoy Insurrection in India; and a Concise History of the Great Military Events Which Have Tended to Consolidate British Empire in Hindostan*, vol. 1 (London: The London Printing and Publishing Company, 1812).

Banerjea, Surendranath, *A Nation in the Making: Being the Reminiscences of Fifty Years of Public Life* (London: Oxford University Press, 1925).

Banerjea, Surendranath, "Joseph Mazzini," in *Speeches and Writings of Hon. Surendranath Banerjea* (Madras: G.A. Natesan & Co., [1925]).

Banerjee, Gooroodass, *Essentials of Hinduism* (Madras: G.A. Natesan, [1919]).

Banerjee, Prathama, "Chanakya/Kautilya: History, Philosophy, Theater and the Twentieth-century Political," *History of the Present: A Journal of Critical History*, 2, 1 (2012), 24–51.

Banerjee, Prathama, "The Abiding Binary: The Social and the Political in Modern India," in S. Legg and D. Heath, eds, *South Asian Governmentalities: Michel Foucault and the Question of Postcolonial Orderings* (Cambridge: Cambridge University Press, 2018), 81–105.

Banerji, K.K., "Review: *Hindu-Pad-Padashahi*," *The Indian Historical Quarterly*, vol. 2 (1926), 432.

Barnett, L.D., "Indica," *The Journal of the Royal Asiatic Society of Great Britain and Ireland*, no. 4 (1926), 756–8.

Barua, Ankur, "Vedantic Variations in the Presence of Europe: Establishing the Hindu Dharma in Late Nineteenth Century Bengal," *International Journal of Dharma Studies*, 5, 1 (2017), https://doi.org/10.1186/s40613-017-0050-3.

Basu, Chandranath, *Hindutva: Hindur Prakita Itihas* (Calcutta: Medical Library, 1892).

Basu, Manisha, *The Rhetoric of Hindu India: Language and Urban Nationalism* (Cambridge: Cambridge University Press, 2017).

Basu, Tapan, Pradip Datta, Sumit Sarkar, Tanika Sarkar, and Sambuddha Sen, *Khaki Shorts Saffron Flags: A Critique of the Hindu Right* (New Delhi: Orient Blackswan, 1993).

Bayly, C.A., *Rulers, Townsmen and Bazaars: North Indian Society in the Age of British Expansion, 1770–1870* (Cambridge: Cambridge University Press, 1983).

Bayly, C.A., *Origins of Nationality in South Asia: Patriotism and Ethical Governance in the Making of Modern India* (Delhi: Oxford University Press, 1998).

Bayly, C.A., "Liberalism at Large: Mazzini and Nineteenth-Century Indian Thought," in C.A. Bayly and Eugenio F. Biagini, eds, *Giuseppe Mazzini*

430  BIBLIOGRAPHY

*and the Globalization of Democratic Nationalism, 1830–1920* (Oxford: Oxford University Press, 2008), 355–74.

Bayly, C.A., "India, the Bhagavad Gita and the World," *Modern Intellectual History*, 7, 2 (2010), 275–95.

Bayly, C.A., *Recovering Liberties: Indian Thought in the Age of Liberalism and Empire* (Cambridge: Cambridge University Press, 2012).

Bayly, C.A., and Eugenio F. Biagini, eds, *Giuseppe Mazzini and the Globalization of Democratic Nationalism, 1830–1920* (Oxford: Oxford University Press, 2008).

Bayly, Susan, *Caste, Society, and Politics in India from the Eighteenth Century to the Modern Age* (Cambridge: Cambridge University Press, 1999).

Bayly, Susan, "Imaging 'Greater India': French and Indian Visions of Colonialism in the Indic Mode," *Modern Asian Studies*, 38, 3 (2004), 703–44.

Benjamin, Walter, "Theses on the Philosophy of History," in Hannah Arendt, ed., *Illuminations: Essays and Reflections* (New York: Schocken Books, 1968), 253–64.

Bentley, John, *A Historical View of the Hindu Astronomy from the Earliest Dawn of that Science in India to the Present Time* (London: Smith, Elder, & Co., 1825).

Berman, Marshall, *All That is Solid Melts into Air: The Experience of Modernity* (New York: Penguin Books, 1988).

Bhabha, Homi, "Of Mimicry and Man: The Ambivalence of Colonial Discourse," *October*, no. 28 (1984), 125–33.

Bhatt, Chetan, *Hindu Nationalism: Origins, Ideologies and Modern Myths* (New York: Berg, 2001).

Bhattacharya, Sabyasachi, *Talking Back: The Idea of Civilization in the Indian Nationalist Discourse* (Delhi: Oxford University Press, 2011).

Blunt, Alison, *Domicile and Diaspora: Anglo-Indian Women and the Spatial Politics of Home* (Oxford: Blackwell Publishing, 2005).

Bose, A.C., *Indian Revolutionaries Abroad: 1905–1927, Select Documents* (New Delhi: Northern Book Centre, 2002).

Boyesen, Hjalmar Hjorth, *The Story of Norway* (London: G.P. Putnam and Sons, 1894).

"A Brahman," *The Thoughts on India* (Benares: Arya Press, 1881).

Brown, D. Mackenzie, "The Philosophy of Bal Gangadhar Tilak: Karma vs. Jnana in the Gita Rahasya," *Journal of Asian Studies*, 17, 2 (1958), 197–206.

Brückenhaus, Daniel, *Policing Transnational Protest: Liberal Imperialism and Surveillance of Anticolonialists in Europe, 1905–1945* (Oxford: Oxford University Press, 2017).

Buck-Morss, Susan, *Hegel, Haiti, and Universal History* (Pittsburgh: University of Pittsburgh Press, 2009).

Burbank, Jane, and Frederick Cooper, *Empires in World History: Power and the Politics of Difference* (Princeton: Princeton University Press, 2010).

Butler, Judith, *Subjects of Desire: Hegelian Reflections in Twentieth-Century France* (New York: Columbia University Press, 1999).

Cashman, Richard, "The Political Recruitment of God Ganapati," *Indian Economic and Social History Review*, 7, 3 (1970), 347–73.

Casolari, Marzia, "Hindutva's Foreign Tie-Up in the 1930s: Archival Evidence," *Economic and Political Weekly*, 35, 4 (2000), 218–28.

Chakrabarty, Dipesh, *Provincializing Europe: Postcolonial Thought and Historical Difference* (Princeton: Princeton University Press, 2000).

Chakrabarty, Dipesh, *The Calling of History: Jadunath Sarkar and the Empire of Truth* (Chicago: University of Chicago Press, 2015).

Chatterjee, Partha, *The Nation and Its Fragments: Colonial and Postcolonial Histories* (Princeton: Princeton University Press, 1993).

Chatterjee, Partha, *The Politics of the Governed: Reflections on Popular Politics in Most of the World* (New York: Columbia University Press, 2006).

Chatterjee, Partha, and Anjan Ghosh, eds, *History and the Present* (Ranikhet: Permanent Black, 2002).

Chatterjee, Sudhakar, "Binayak Damodar Savarkar," in Ermine A. Brown, ed., *Eminent Indians* (Calcutta: Shanti Mitra, 1946), 101–9.

Chattopadhyaya, B.D., *The Concept of Bharatavarsha* (Ranikhet: Permanent Black, 2017).

Chaturvedi, Vinayak, *Peasant Pasts: History and Memory in Western India* (Berkeley: University of California Press, 2007).

Chaturvedi, Vinayak, "Rethinking Knowledge with Action: V.D. Savarkar, the Bhagavad Gita, and Histories of Warfare," *Modern Intellectual History*, 7, 2 (2010), 417–35.

Chaturvedi, Vinayak, "Histories of Politics after Political History: Reflections from South Asian Historiography," *Perspectives on History*, 49, 5 (2011), 28–30.

Chaturvedi, Vinayak, "A Revolutionary's Biography: The Case of V.D. Savarkar," *Postcolonial Studies*, 16, 2 (2013), 124–39.

Chirol, Valentine, *Indian Unrest* (London: Macmillan and Co., 1910).

Chitragupta, *Life of Barrister Savarkar* (Bombay: Veer Savarkar Prakashan, 1987).

Cole, Juan, *Napoleon's Egypt: Invading the Middle East* (New York: Palgrave MacMillan, 2007).

Copland, Ian, "Crucibles of Hindutva? V.D. Savarkar, the Hindu Mahasabha, and the Indian Princely States," *South Asia: Journal of South Asian Studies*, 25, 3 (2002), 211–34.

Corbridge, Stuart, and John Harriss, *Reinventing India: Liberalization, Hindu Nationalism and Popular Democracy* (Cambridge: Polity Press, 2000).

Courtright, Paul B., *Ganeśa: Lord of Obstacles, Lord of Beginnings* (New York: Oxford University Press, 1985).

Courtright, Paul B., "The Ganesh Festival in Maharashtra: Some Observations," in Eleanor Zelliot and Maxine Berntsen, eds, *The Experience of Hinduism: Essays on Religion in Maharashtra* (Albany: SUNY Press, 1988), 76–93.

Crome, Andre, *Christian Zionism and English National Identity, 1600–1850* (Gewerbestrasse: Palgrave Macmillan, 2018).

Das Gupta, R.K., "Mazzini and Indian Nationalism," *East and West*, 7, 1 (1956), 67–70.

De Donno, Fabrizio, "The Gandhian Mazzini: Democratic Nationalism, Self-Rule, and Non-violence," in C.A. Bayly and Eugenio F. Biagini, eds, *Giuseppe Mazzini and the Globalization of Democratic Nationalism, 1830–1920* (Oxford: Oxford University Press, 2008), 375–98.

de Saussure, Ferdinand, *Course in General Linguistics* (New York: Philosophical Library [1959]).

Derrida, Jacques, *The Ear of the Other: Otobiography, Transference, Translation* (Lincoln: University of Nebraska Press, 1988).

Derrida, Jacques, *Heidegger: The Question of Being & History*, trans. Geoffrey Bennington (Chicago: University of Chicago Press, 2016).

Deshpande, C.D., "A Note on Maratha Cartography," *The Indian Archive*, 7, 2 (1953), 87–94.

Deshpande, G.P., "Rajwade's *Weltanschauung* and German Thought," *Economic and Political Weekly*, 27, 43/44 (1992), 2361–3.

Deshpande, G.P., *The World of Ideas in Modern Marathi* (New Delhi: Tulika Books, 2009).

Deshpande, Madhav M., trans., *The Meaning of Nouns: Semantic Theory in Classical and Medieval India* (n.p.: Springer Science+Business Media Dordecht, 1992).

Deshpande, Prachi, *Creative Pasts: Historical Memory and Identity in Western India, 1700–1960* (New York: Columbia University Press, 2007).

Devare, Aparna, *History & the Making of Modern Hindu Self* (New Delhi: Routledge, 2011).

Devji, Faisal, "Bhakt Prahlad," *Public Culture*, 33, 2 (2021), 33.

Dirks, N.B., *Castes of Mind: Colonialism and the Making of Modern India* (Princeton: Princeton University Press, 2001).

Doniger, Wendy, *The Hindus: An Alternative History* (New York: Penguin Books, 2009).

Doniger, Wendy, and Brian K. Smith, trans., *The Laws of Manu* (London: Penguin Books, 1991).

Dutt, Romesh Chunder, *A History of Civilization in Ancient India Based on Sanscrit Literature* (London: Kegan Paul, Trench, Trübner & Co., 1893).

Eagleton, Terry, *Walter Benjamin: Or, Towards a Revolutionary Criticism* (London: Verso, 2009).

Eck, Diana L., *India: A Sacred Geography* (New York, 2012).

Edney, Matthew H., *Mapping an Empire: The Geographical Construction of British India, 1765–1843* (Chicago: University of Chicago Press, 1999).

Elias, Norbert, *The Civilizing Process: Sociogenetic and Psychogenetic Investigations*, trans. Edmund Jephcott (Oxford: Blackwell Publishing, 2000).

Evans, Richard J., *The Third Reich in Power 1933–1939* (New York: Penguin Press, 2005).

Fallon, S.W., *A New English–Hindustani Dictionary, with Illustrations from English Literature and Colloquial English translated into Hindustani*, assisted by Lala Faqir Chand (Banaras: E.J. Lazarus and Co., 1883).

Fasana, Enrico, "*Deshbhakta*: The Leaders of the Italian Independence Movement in the Eyes of Marathi Nationalists," in N.K. Wagle, ed., *Writers, Editors, Reformers: Social and Political Transformations of Maharashtra 1830–1930* (New Delhi: Manohar, 1999), 42–63.

Fazl-I-Ali, Maulawi, *A Dictionary of the Persian and English Languages, Designed for the Use of Military and Civil Officers and Schools* (Byculla: Education Society's Press, 1885).

Fischer-Tiné, Harald, "Mass-Mediated Panic in the British Empire? Shyamji Krishnavarma's 'Scientific Terrorism' and the 'London Outrage', 1909," in Harald Fischer-Tiné, ed., *Anxieties, Fear and Panic in Colonial Settings: Empires on the Verge of a Nervous Breakdown* (Cham: Palgrave Macmillan, 2016), 99–134.

Flora, Giuseppe, "The Changing Perception of Mazzini within the Indian National Movement," *Indian Historical Review*, 19, 1–2 (1992–3), 52–68.

Gandhi, Mohandas K., *Indian Home Rule [or Hind Swaraj]* in Anthony Parel, ed., *Hind Swaraj and Other Writings* (Cambridge: Cambridge University Press, 1997), 1–125.

Gandhi, Mohandas K., "Joseph Mazzini: A Remarkable Career," in *The Collected Works of Mahatma Gandhi, volume 4 (23 May, 1904–4 November, 1905)* (New Delhi: Publications Divsion, Ministry of Information and Broadcasting, 2000), 366–7.

Gandhi, Mohandas K., "Curzon Wyllie's Assassination," in *The Collected Works of Mahatma Gandhi, volume 9 (23 July, 1908–4 August, 1909)* (New Delhi: Publications Division, Ministry of Information and Broadcasting, 2000), 427–9.

Gandhi, Mohandas K., "Vijaya Dashami," in *The Collected Works of Mahatma Gandhi, volume 10 (5 August, 1909–9 April, 1910)* (New Delhi: Publications Division, Ministry of Information and Broadcasting, 2000), 189–90.

Gandhi, Mohandas K., "Civility," in *The Collected Works of Mahatma Gandhi, volume 25 (27 October, 1921–22 January, 1922)* (New Delhi: Publications Division, Ministry of Information and Broadcasting, 2000), 287–90.

Gandhi, Mohandas K., "At It Again," in *The Collected Works of Mahatma Gandhi, volume 31 (22 March, 1925–15 June, 1925)* (New Delhi: Publications Division, Ministry of Information and Broadcasting, 2000), 285–9.

Gandhi, Mohandas K., "Discourses on the 'Gita'," in *The Collected Works of Mahatma Gandhi, volume 37 (11 November, 1926–1 January, 1927)* (New Delhi: Publications Division, Ministry of Information and Broadcasting, 2000), 75–354.

Gandhi, Mohandas K., "Joseph Mazzini: A Remarkable Career," in *The Collected Works of Mahatma Gandhi*, vol. 5 (New Delhi: Publications Division, Ministry of Information and Broadcasting, 2000), 27–8.

Gandhi, Tushar A., *"Let's Kill Gandhi!": A Chronicle of His Last Days, the Conspiracy, Murder, Investigation and Trial* (New Delhi: Rupa Publications, 2007).

Ghosh, Durba, *Gentlemanly Terrorists: Political Violence and the Colonial State in India, 1919–1947* (Cambridge: Cambridge University Press, 2017).

Ghosh, Tapan, *Gandhi Murder Trial* (London: Asia Publishing House, 1973).

Godbole, S.T., "Savarkar's Approach to History," in Sudhakar Raje, ed., *Savarkar: Commemoration Volume* (Bombay: Savarkar Darshan Pratishthan 1989), 192–7.

Godbole, V.S., *Rationalism of Veer Savarkar* (Thane: Itihas Patrika Prakashan, 2004).

Godse, Nathuram, *May It Please Your Honour* (Pune: Vitasta Prakashan, 1977).

Godse, Nathuram, *May It Please Your Honour* (Delhi: Surya Prakashan, 1989).

Gogate, Prasad P., and B. Arunachalam, "Area Maps in Maratha Cartography: A Study in Native Maps of Western India," *Imago Mundi*, vol. 50 (1998), 126–40.

Gokulji, Radhamohan, *Mahatma Mazzini* (Nagpur: Pranvir Pustakamala Office, 1922).

Gordon, Stewart, *The Marathas 1600–1818* (Cambridge: Cambridge University Press, 1993).

Griffith, Gwilym O., *Mazzini: Prophet of Modern Europe* (New York: Howard Fertig, 1970).

Grover, Verinder, *Vinayak Damodar Savarkar: A Biography of His Vision and Ideals* (New Delhi: Deep & Deep, 1998).

Guha, Ranajit, *Elementary Aspects of Peasant Insurgency in Colonial India* (Delhi: Oxford University Press, 1983).

Guha, Ranajit, "The Prose of Counter-Insurgency," in Ranajit Guha, ed., *Subaltern Studies II: Writings on South Asian History and Society* (Delhi: Oxford University Press, 1983), 1–42.

Guha, Ranajit, *Dominance Without Hegemony: History and Power in Colonial India* (Cambridge: Harvard University Press, 1997).

Guha, Sumit, "Speaking Historically: The Changing Voices of Historical Narration in Western India," *American Historical Review*, 109, 4 (2004), 1084–2004.

Guha, Sumit, *Beyond Caste: Identity and Power in South Asian, Past and Present* (Leiden: Brill, 2013).

Gupta, Chitra, *Life of Barrister Savarkar* (Madras: B.G. Paul & Co. Publishers, 1926).

Gupta, Chitra, *Life of Barrister Savarkar*, revised and expanded by Indra Prakash (New Delhi: The Hindu Mission Pustak Bhandar, 1939).

Gupta, Hari Ram, ed., *Sir Jadunath Sarkar Commemoration, vol. 1: Life and Letters of Sir Jadunath Sarkar* (Hoshiarpur: The Department of History, Panjab University, 1957).

Hakala, Walter N., *Negotiating Languages: Urdu, Hindi, and the Definition of Modern South Asia* (New York: Columbia University Press, 2016).

Halsey, Le Roy J., *Life Pictures from the Bible, or Illustrations of Scripture Character* (Philadelphia: Presbyterian Board of Publication, 1860).

Hansen, Thomas Blom, *Wages of Violence: Naming and Identity in Postcolonial Bombay* (Princeton: Princeton University Press, 2001).

Hardiman, David, *Gandhi in His Time and Ours: The Global Legacy of His Ideas* (New York: Columbia University Press, 2003).

Hawley, John Stratton, "Naming Hinduism," *The Wilson Quarterly*, 15, 3 (1991), 20–34.

Heidegger, Martin, *Being and Time*, John Macquarrie and Edward Robinson, trans. (New York: HarperCollins, 2008).

Heredia, Rudolf C., "Gandhi's Hinduism and Savarkar's Hindutva," *Economic and Political Weekly*, 44, 29 (2009), 62–7.

Herling, Bradley L., *The German Gita: Hermeneutics and Discipline in the Early German Reception of Indian Thought* (New York: Routledge, 2006).

Inamdar, P.L., *The Story of the Red Fort Trial 1948–49* (Bombay: Popular, 1979).

Islam, Shamsul, *Savarkar, Myths and Facts* (Delhi: Media House, 2004).

Jaffrelot, Christophe, *The Hindu Nationalist Movement and Indian Politics: 1925 to the 1990s* (New York: Columbia University Press, 1996).

Jaffrelot, Christophe, *Hindu Nationalism: A Reader* (Princeton: Princeton University Press, 2009).

Jalal, Ayesha, *The Sole Spokesman: Jinnah, the Muslim League and the Demand for Pakistan* (Cambridge: Cambridge University Press, 1994).

Jayaswal, K.P., *Hindu Polity: A Constitutional History of India in Hindu Times* (Calcutta: Butterworth & Co., 1924).

Jeffery, Roger, "Doctors and Congress: The Role of Medical Men and Medical Politics in Indian Nationalism," in Mike Shepperdson and Colin Simmons, eds, *The Indian National Congress and the Political Economy of India 1885–1985* (Aldershot: Avebury, 1988), 160–73.

Jinnah, Muhammad Ali, "Presidential Address at the All India Muslim League, Lahore Session, March 1940," in *India's Problem of Her Future Constitution* (Bombay: M.H. Saiyid, 1940), 1–15.

Joglekar, Jaywant D., *Veer Savarkar: Father of Hindu Nationalism* ([n.p.], [2006]).

Johnson, Francis, *Dictionary, Persian, Arabic, and English* (London: W.H. Allen and Company, 1852).

Jones, William, "A Discourse on the Institution of a Society," *Asiatick Researches or Transactions of the Society Instituted in Bengal, for Inquiring into the History and Antiquities, the Arts, Sciences, and Literature, of Asia*, vol. 1 (Calcutta: Manuel Cantopher, 1788), ix–xvi.

Josh, Bhagwan, "V.D. Savarkar's *The Indian War of Independence*: The First Nationalist Reconstruction of the Revolt of 1857," in Crispin Bates, ed., *Mutiny at the Margins: New Perspectives on the Indian Uprising of 1857, vol. 6* (New Delhi: Sage Publications, 2014), 29–41.

Joshi, D.B., *Glimpses of Veer Savarkar's Poetry* (Bombay: Veer Savarkar Prakashan, 1992).

Joshi, G.M., "The Story of this History," in Vinayak Damodar Savarkar, *The Indian War of Independence, 1857* (Bombay: Phoenix Publications, 1947), ix–xx.

Joshi, G.M., and Bal Savarkar, "The Story of this History," Vinayak Damodar

Savarkar, *The Indian War of Independence, 1857* (New Delhi: Rajdhani Granthagar, 1986), xiii–xxiv.

Kaliprasad, Munshi, *The Kayastha Ethnology; Being an Inquiry into the Origin of the Chitraguptavansi and Chandrasenavansi Kayasthas* (Lucknow: American Methodist Mission Press, 1877).

Kapur, Sudarshan, "Gandhi and Hindutva: Two Conflicting Visions of Swaraj," in Anthony Parel, ed., *Gandhi, Freedom, and Self-Rule* (New Delhi: Vistaar Publications, 2002), 119–37.

Karandikar, S.L., *Savarkar Charitra Kathan* (Pune: Modern Book Depot Prakashan, 1947).

Karandikar, S.L., *Ase Hote Vira Savarkara!* (Pune: Sitabai Karandikar, 1966).

*Karl Marx and Frederick Engels Collected Works*, Volume 1 (Moscow: Progress Publishers, 1975).

Karnik, V.B., "Epilogue," in *M.N. Roy's Memoirs* (Bombay: Allied Publishers, 1964), 565–604.

Kaviraj, Sudipta, *The Invention of Private Life: Literature and Ideas* (New York: Columbia University Press, 2004).

Keer, Dhananjay, *Savarkar and His Times* (Bombay: A.V. Keer, 1950).

Keer, Dhananjay, *Veer Savarkar* (Bombay: Popular Prakashan, 1966).

Keer, Dhananjay, *Mahatma Gandhi: Political Saint and Unarmed Prophet* (Bombay: Popular Prakashan, 1973).

Khosla, G.D., *The Murder of the Mahatma and Other Cases from a Judge's Notebook* (Bombay: Jaico Publishing, 1968).

King, Hamilton, *Letters and Recollections of Mazzini* (London: Longmans, Green and Co., 1912).

Krishan, Shri, "Discourses on Modernity: Gandhi and Savarkar," *Studies in History*, 29, 1 (2013), 61–85.

Krishnaji Ananta, Sabhasad, *Siva Chhatrapati: Being a Translation of Sabhasad Bakar with Extracts from Chitnis and Sivadigvijaya, with Notes*, trans. Surendranath Sen (Calcutta: University of Calcutta, 1920).

Krishnavarma, Shyamji, trans., "A Sanskrit Ode Addressed to the Congress of Orientalists at Berlin," *The Journal of the Royal Asiatic Society of Great Britain and Ireland*, New Series, 13, 4 (1881), 573–6.

Kulkarni, Uday S., ed. and trans., *Bakhar of Panipat Original and Complete Written in 1761 by Raghunath Yadav 'Chitragupt'* (Pune: Mula Mutha Publishers, 2014).

Kumar, Aishwary, *Radical Equality: Ambedkar, Gandhi, and the Risk of Democracy* (Stanford: Stanford University Press, 2015).

Kumar, Megha, "History and Gender in Savarkar's Nationalist Writings," *Social Scientist*, 34, 11/12 (2006), 33–50.

Lahiri, Nayanjot, *Ashoka in Ancient India* (Cambridge: Harvard University Press, 2015).

Lal, Chaman, ed., *Bhagat Singh, The Jail Notebook and Other Writings* (New Delhi: LeftWord Books, 2007).

Laursen, Ole Birk, "Anarchist Anti-Imperialism: Guy Aldred and the Indian Revolutionary Movement, 1909–14," *The Journal of Imperial and Commonwealth History*, 46, 2 (2018), 286–303.

Leslie, Charles, "The Ambiguities of Medical Revivalism in Modern India," in Charles Leslie, ed., *Asian Medical Systems: A Comparative Study* (Berkeley: University of California Press, 1976), 356–67.

Longuet, Jean, *Mémoire présenté àla Cour d'Arbitrage de La Haye au nom de M. Vinayak Damodar Savarkar par Me J. Longuet* (Paris: [n.p.], 1911).

Lopriano, Antonio, *Ancient Egyptian: A Linguistic Introduction* (Cambridge: Cambridge University Press, 1995).

Macaulay, Thomas, B., *Lays of Ancient Rome* (London: Longman, Brown, Green, and Longmans, 1843, third edition).

Maclean, Kama, *A Revolutionary History of Interwar India: Violence, Image, Voice and Text* (New York: Oxford University Press, 2015).

Majumdar, R.C., *Penal Settlement in Andamans* (New Delhi: Ministry of Education and Social Welfare, Government of India, 1975).

Makolkin, Anna, *Name, Hero, Icon: Semiotics of Nationalism through Heroic Biography* (Berlin: De Gruyter Mouton, 1992).

Malgonkar, Manohar, *The Men Who Killed Gandhi* (Madras: Macmillan India Press, 1978).

Mamdani, Mahmood, *When Victims Become Killers: Colonialism, Nativism, and the Genocide in Rwanda* (Princeton: Princeton University Press, 2002).

Manjapra, Kris, *M.N. Roy: Marxism and Colonial Cosmopolitanism* (New Delhi: Routledge, 2010).

Mankar, Jagannath Lakshuman, *The Life and Exploits of Shivaji. Translated into English from an Unpublished Marathi Manuscript* (Alibag: Hitsagar Press, 1884).

Markovits, Claude, "Turning Mazzini on His Head: Gandhi's Polemics against Savarkar in Hind Swaraj," in Tiziana Leucci, Claude Markovits, and Marie Fourcade, eds, *India and Italy: Intellectual, Political and Artistic Encounters* (Paris: Éditions de L'École des hautes études en sciences sociales, 2018).

Marx, Karl, and Frederick Engels, *The First Indian War of Independence 1857–1859* (Moscow: Progress Publishers, 1959).

Marx, Karl, "Theses on Feuerbach," *Marx/Engels Internet Archive*: marxists. org (accessed May 11, 2020).

Maurice, Thomas, *The History of Hindostan; Its Arts, and Its Sciences, as Connected with the History of the Other Great Empires of Asia, During the Most Ancient Periods of the World*, vol. 1 (London: W. Bulmer and Co., 1795).

Mazzini, Giuseppe, *The Duties of Man* (London: Chapman & Hall, 1862).

Mazzini, Giuseppe, *Life and Writings of Mazzini*, 6 vols (London: Smith, Elder, and Co., 1891).

McGregor, R.S., *The Oxford Hindi–English Dictionary* (Oxford: Oxford University Press, 1993).

Menon, Priyanka, "Between Bodies and Borders: The Place of the Natural in the Thought of M.K. Gandhi and V.D. Savarkar," *Modern Asian Studies*, 55, 1 (2021), 116–51.

Mill, James, *History of the British Empire, vol. 1* (London: Baldwin, Cradock, and Joy, 1817).

Minor, Robert, ed., *Modern Indian Interpreters of the Bhagavad Gita* (Delhi: Sri Satguru Publications, 1991).

Misra, Amelendu, "Savarkar and the Discourse of Islam in Pre-Independent India," *Journal of Asian History*, 33, 2 (1999), 142–84.

Misra, Amelendu, *Identity and Religion: Foundations of Anti-Islamism in India* (New Delhi: Sage Publications, 2004).

Monier-Williams, Monier, *Hinduism* (London: Society for Promoting Christian Knowledge, 1877).

Mookerji, Radha Kumud, *The Fundamental Unity of India* (London: Longmans, Green & Co., 1914).

Mookerji, Radha Kumud, *Chandragupta Maurya and His Times: Sir William Meyer Lectures, 1940–41* (Madras: G.S. Press, 1943).

Mukerji, U.N., *A Dying Race* (Calcutta: Mukerjee & Bose, 1909).

Mukhia, Harbans, "Medieval Indian History and the Communal Approach," in Romila Thapar, Harbans Mukhia, and Bipan Chandra, *Communalism and the Writing of Indian History* (Delhi: People's Publishing House, 1969), 24–38.

Mukhopadhyaya, Girindranath, *History of Indian Medicine: From the Earliest Ages to the Present Time, vol. 1* (New Delhi, 1974).

Nair, Neeti, *Changing Homelands: Hindu Politics and the Partition of India* (Cambridge: Harvard University Press, 2011).

Nandy, Ashis, "Final Encounter: The Politics of the Assassination of Gandhi," in idem, *At the Edge of Psychology* (Delhi: Oxford University Press, 1980), 70–98.

Nandy, Ashis, "A Disowned Father of the Nation in India: Vinayak Damodar Savarkar and the Demonic and the Seductive in Indian Nationalism," *Inter-Asia Cultural Studies*, 15, 1 (2012), 91–112.

Narain, A.K., "Ganeśa: A Protohistory of the Idea and the Icon," in Robert L. Brown, ed., *Ganesh: Studies of an Asian God* (Albany: SUNY Press, 1991), 19–48.

Narke, Hari, ed., *Dr. Babasaheb Ambedkar Writings and Speeches*, vol. 2 (New Delhi: Dr Ambedkar Foundation, 2014).

Nehru, Jawaharlal, *Glimpses of World History* (New York: The John Day Company, 1942).

Nehru, Jawaharlal, *The Discovery of India* (New York: The John Day Company, 1946).

Noorani, A.G., *Savarkar and Hindutva: The Godse Connection* (New Delhi: LeftWord Books, 2004).

Noorani, A.G., "Savarkar's Mercy Petition," *Frontline*, 22, 7 (2005), https://frontline.thehindu.com/the-nation/article30204154.ece (accessed March 15, 2021).

O'Hanlon, Rosalind, *A Comparison between Women and Men: Tarabai Shinde and the Critique of Gender Relations in Colonial India* (Delhi: Oxford University Press, 1994).

O'Hanlon, Rosalind, "Contested Conjunctures: Brahman Communities and 'Early Modernity' in India," in *The American Historical Review*, 118, 3 (2013), 765–87.

Olivelle, Patrick, trans., *The Law Code of Manu* (Oxford: Oxford University Press).

Ollett, Andrew, *Language of the Snakes: Prakrit, Sanskrit, and the Language Order of Premodern India* (Berkeley: University of California Press, 2017).

Orne Jewett, Sarah, *The Normans—Told Chiefly in Relation to Their Conquest of England* (New York: G.P. Putnam's Sons, 1898).

Owen, Nicholas J., *The British Left and India: Metropolitan and Anti-Imperialism, 1885–1947* (Oxford: Oxford University Press, 2007).

Pal, Bipin Chandra, *Memories of My Life and Times* (Calcutta: Upendra Chandra Bhattacharyya, 1932).

Palshikar, Sanjay, "Virtue, Vice and the Origins of Militant Nationalist Thought in Western India," in V.R. Mehta and Thomas Pantham, eds, *Political Ideas in Modern India: Thematic Explorations*, vol. X, pt 7 (New Delhi: Sage Publications, 2006), 26–45.

Pandey, Gyanendra, "Which of Us are Hindus?" in idem, ed., *Hindus and Others – The Question of Identity in India Today* (New Delhi: Viking, 1993), 238–72.

Pandey, Gyanendra, *Routine Violence: Nations, Fragments, Histories* (Stanford: Stanford University Press, 2006).

Panikkar, K.N., "General President's Address: Culture as a Site of Struggle," *Proceedings of the Indian History Congress*, 69 (2008), 1–18.

Pantham, Thomas, "Religious Diversity and National Unity: The Gandhian and Hindutva Visions," in V.R. Mehta and Thomas Pantham, eds, *Political Ideas in Modern India: Thematic Explorations*, vol. X, pt 7 (New Delhi: Sage Publications, 2006), 221–37.

Parel, Anthony, "Editor's Introduction," in M.K. Gandhi, *"Hind Swaraj" and Other Writings* (Cambridge: Cambridge University Press, 1997), xiii–lxii.

Paranjape, Makarand R., "Hindutva before Savarkar: Chandranath Basu's Contribution," in *DNA*, April 22, 2017, www.dnaindia.com (accessed November 11, 2019).

Parmanand, Bhai, "Foreword," in V.D. Savarkar, *Hindutva* (New Delhi: Central Hindu Yuvak Sabha, 1938).

Pathan, Y.M., ed., *Krishnaji Ananta Sabhasada Virachit Sri Sivaprabhunche Charitra, Sabhasada Bakhar* (Aurangabad: Samartha Prakashan, 1974).

Pennington, Brian K., *Was Hinduism Invented? Britons, Indians, and the Colonial Construction of Religion* (New York: Oxford University Press, 2005).

Pernau, Margrit, and Helge Jordheim, eds, *Civilizing Emotions: Concepts in Nineteenth Century Asia and Europe* (Oxford: Oxford University Press, 2015).

Phadke, Narayan Laxman, *Ajneya mimansa* ([Pune]: Balvant Ganesh Dabholkar, [n.d.]).

Pincince, John R., "V.D. Savarkar and *The Indian War of Independence*: Contrasting Perspectives of an Emergent Composite State," in Crispin Bates, ed., *Mutiny at the Margins: New Perspectives on the Indian Uprising of 1857, vol. 6* (New Delhi: Sage Publications, 2014), 42–60.

Pinney, Christopher, "The Tiger's Nature, but Not the Tiger: Bal Gangadhar Tilak as Mohandas Karamchand Gandhi's Counter-Guru," *Public Culture*, 23, 2 (2011), 395–416.

Pinnock, William, *Comprehensive Grammar of Modern Geography and History* (London: Holdsworth & Ball, 1834).

Platts, John T., *A Dictionary of Urdu, Classical Hindi, and English* (London: W.H. Allen & Co., 1884).

Popplewell, Richard J., *Intelligence and Imperial Defence: British Intelligence and the Defence of the Indian Empire 1904–1924* (London: Frank Cass, 1995).

Prakash, Indra, *A Review of the History & World of the Hindu Mahasabha and Hindu Sanghatan Movement* (New Delhi: Akhil Bharatiya Hindu Mahasabha, 1938).

Prasad, Durga, *An English Translation of the Satyarth Prakash of Swami Dayananda Saraswati, Being a Guide to Vedic Hermeneutics* (Lahore: Virjanand Press, 1908).

Purandare, Vaibhav, *Savarkar: The True Story of the Father of Hindutva* (New Delhi: Juggernaut Books, 2019).

Raghavan, T.C.A., "Origins and Development of Hindu Mahasabha Ideology: The Call of V.D. Savarkar and Bhai Parmanand," *Economic and Political Weekly*, 18, 15 (1983), 595–600.

Ragni, Stefano, "From 'The Duties of Man to Dharma': The Political Ideology of Mazzini in the Teachings of Sri Aurobindo and Mahatma Gandhi," in Lorenzo Angeloni and Maria Elettra Verrone, eds, *There's Something in the Air: 70 Life Stories from Italy and India* (New Delhi: Juggernaut Books, 2018), 63–72.

Rai, Lajpat, *The Arya Samaj: An Account of its Origin, Doctrines, and Activities, with a Biographical Sketch of the Founder* (Bombay: Longmans, Green and Company, 1915).

Rai, Lajpat, *Giuseppe Mazzini*, in B.R. Nanda, ed., *The Collected Works of Lala Lajpat Rai, vol. 1* (New Delhi: Manohar, 2003), 283–310.

Raje, Sudhakar, ed., *Savarkar: Commemoration Volume* (Bombay: Savarkar Darshan Pratishthan, 1989).

Rajwade, Vishwanath Kashinath, *Itihasacharya V.K. Rajwade, Samagra Sahitya, vol. 1*, ed. Murlidhar B. Shah (Dhule: Itihasacharya V.K. Rajwade Samsodhan Mandal, 1995).

Ramakrishna, Yasavanta Date, *Maharashtra Sabdakosa* (Pune: Maharashtra Kosamandala, 1932–50).

Ramaswamy, Sumathi, *The Goddess and the Nation: Mapping Mother India* (Durham, 2010).

Ranade, M.G., *The Rise of Maratha Power* (Bombay: Punalekar & Co, 1900).

Ranade, Sadashiv Rajaram, *Swatantraveer Vinayakrao Savarkar: Hyancem sanksipta charitra* (Mumbai: Lokmanya Chapakhana, 1924).

Rao, Vassant, V., "Govind Sakharam Sardesai," in S.P. Sen, ed., *Historians and Historiography in Modern India* (Calcutta: Institute of Historical Studies, 1973), 222–34.

Rathore, Aakash Singh, and Rimina Mohapatra, *Hegel's India: A Reinterpretation, with Texts* (Delhi: Oxford University Press, 2017).

Ray, Rajat Kanta, "Moderates, Extremists, and Revolutionaries: Bengal, 1900–1908," in R. Sisson and S. Wolpert, eds, *Congress and Indian Nationalism: The Pre-Independence Phase* (Delhi: Oxford University Press, 1988), 62–89.

Richards, Robert J., *Darwin and the Emergence of Evolutionary Theories of Mind and Behavior* (Chicago: University of Chicago Press, 1987).

Richardson, John, *A Dictionary, Persian, Arabic, and English* (Oxford: Clarendon Press, 1777).

Richardson, John, *A Dictionary, Persian, Arabic, and English* (London: William Bulmer and Company, 1806).

Richman, Paula, ed., *Many Ramayanas: The Diversity of a Narrative Tradition in South Asia* (Berkeley: University of California Press, 1991).

Risley, H.H., *The Tribes and Castes of Bengal: Ethnographic Glossary*, vol. 1 (Calcutta: Bengal Secretariat Press, 1892).

Roy, M.N., *The Historic Role of Islam: An Essay on Islamic Culture* (Bombay: Vora & Co. Publishers, 1938).

Roy, M.N., *M.N. Roy's Memoirs* (Bombay: Allied Publishers, 1964).

Sampath, Vikram, *Savarkar: Echoes from a Forgotten Past 1883–1924* (Gurgaon: Penguin Random House India, 2019).

Sampath, Vikram, *Savarkar: A Contested Legacy, 1924–1966* (Gurgaon: Penguin Random House India, 2021).

Sardesai, G.S., *Main Currents: The Main Currents of Maratha History* (Bombay: Keshav Bhikaji Dhavle, 1933).

Sardesai, G.S., *New History of the Marathas, volume I: Shivaji & His Line, 1600–1707* (Bombay: Phoenix Publications, 1946).

Sardesai, G.S., *New History of the Marathas, volume II: The Expansion of the Maratha Power 1707–1772* (Bombay: Phoenix Publications, 1948).

Sardesai, G.S., *New History of the Marathas, volume III: Sunset Over Maharashtra 1772–1848* (Bombay: Phoenix Publications, 1948).

Sarkar, Jadunath, "The Historian Rajwade," *The Modern Review*, 41, 2 (1927), 184–7.

Sarkar, Jadunath, *House of Shivaji (Studies and Documents on Maratha History: Royal Period)* (New Delhi: Orient Longman, 1979).

Sarkar, Sumit, *Swadeshi Movement in Bengal, 1903–1908* (Bombay: People's Publishing House, 1973).

Sarkar, Sumit, *Beyond Nationalist Frames: Relocating Postmodernism, Hindutva, History* (Ranikhet: Permanent Black, 2002).

Sarkar, Tanika, *Hindu Wife, Hindu Nation: Community, Religion, and Cultural Nationalism* (Ranikhet: Permanent Black, 2001).

Savarkar, Bal, "Life Sketch of Veer Vinayak Damodar Savarkar," in Vinayak Damodar Savarkar, *The Maratha Movement (Hindu Pad Padashahi), Or A Review of the Hindu Empire of Maharashtra* (New Delhi: Hindi Sahitya Sadan, 2003).

Savarkar, Ganesh Damodar, *Jesus, the Christ was a Hindu*, trans. P.V. Vartak (Rohtak: Indian Foundation for Vedic Science, 2003).

Sawhney, Simona, *The Modernity of Sanskrit* (Minneapolis: University of Minnesota Press, 2009).

Scott, James C., *Weapons of the Weak: Everyday Forms of Peasant Resistance* (New Haven: Yale University Press, 1985).

Scott, James C., *The Art of Not Being Governed: An Anarchist History of Upland Southeast Asia* (New Haven, 2010).

Schwartzberg, Joseph E., "South Asian Cartography: Geographical Mapping," in J.B. Harley and David Woodward, eds, *The History of Cartography*, vol. 2, book 1 (Chicago: University of Chicago Press, 1992), 388–493.

Sen, Amiya P., "A Hindu Conservative Negotiates Modernity. Chandranath Basu (1894–1910) and Reflections on the Self and Culture in Colonial Bengal," in Rafael Klöber and Manju Ludwig, eds, *HerStory – Historical Scholarship between South Asia and Europe: Festschrift in Honour of Gita Dharampal-Frick* (Berlin: CrossAsia eBooks, 2018), 175–88.

Sen, Satadru, "Contexts, Representation and the Colonized Convict: Maulana Thanesari in the Andaman Islands," *Crime, History & Societies*, 8, 2 (2004), 2–21.

Seth, Sanjay, *Subject Lessons: The Western Education of Colonial India* (Durham: Duke University Press, 2007).

Shamasastry, R., "Chanakya's Land and Revenue Policy," *Indian Antiquary: A Journal of Oriental Research*, vol. 35 (1905), 5–10.

Shamasastry, R., "The *Arthasastra* of Chanakya, Books I–IV," *Mysore Review* (1907).

Shamasastry, R., trans., *Kautilya's Arthasastra* (Bangalore: The Government Press, 1915).

Sharma, Jyotirmaya, "History as Revenge and Retaliation: Rereading Savarkar's 'The War of Independence of 1857'," *Economic and Political Weekly*, 42, 19 (2007), 1717–19.

Sharma, Jyotirmaya, *Hindutva: Exploring the Idea of Hindu Nationalism* (Noida: HarperCollins Publishers, 2015).

Shohat, Ella, "Post-Third-Worldist Culture: Gender, Nation, and the Cinema," in M. Jacqui Alexander and Chandra Talpade Mohanty, eds, *Feminist Genealogies, Colonial Legacies, Democratic Futures* (New York: Routledge, 1997).

Silvestri, Michael, "The Bomb, Bhadralok, Bhagavad Gita, and Dan Breen: Terrorism in Bengal and Its Relation to the European Experience," *Terrorism and Political Violence*, 21, 1 (2009), 1–27.

Singh, Mohinder, "Negotiating a Civilizational Figure in Hindi," in Margrit Pernau and Helge Jordheim, eds, *Civilizing Emotions: Concepts in Nineteenth Century Asia and Europe* (Oxford: Oxford University Press, 2015), 187–206.

Singh, Upinder, *A History of Ancient and Early Medieval India: From the Stone Age to the 12th Century* (Delhi: Pearson Longman, 2008).

Singh, Upinder, *Political Violence in Ancient India* (Cambridge: Harvard University Press, 2017).

Sinha, Mrinalini, *Colonial Masculinity: The 'Manly Englishman' and the 'Effeminate Bengali' in the Late Nineteenth Century* (Manchester: Manchester University Press, 1995).

Sinha, Rakesh, *Dr. Keshav Baliram Hedgewar* (New Delhi: Publications Division, Ministry of Information and Broadcasting, GOI, 2015).

Skaria, Ajay, "The Strange Violence of *Satyagraha*: Gandhi, *Itihaas*, and History," in Manu Bhagavan, ed., *Heterotopias: Nationalism and the Possibility of History in South Asia* (Delhi: Oxford University Press, 2010), 142–85.

Smith, Denis Mack, *Mazzini* (New Haven: Yale University Press, 1994).

Smith, Vincent A., *The Early History of India: From 600 B.C. to the Muhammadan Conquest Including the Invasion of Alexander the Great* (Oxford: Clarendon Press, 1904).

Smith, Vincent A., *The Early History of India: From 600 B.C. to the Muhammadan Conquest Including the Invasion of Alexander the Great* (Oxford: Oxford University Press, 1924, fourth edition).

Srivastava, Gita, *Mazzini and His Impact on the Indian National Movement* (Allahabad: Chugh Publications, 1982).

Srivastava, Gita, "Historical Biographies of Italian Nationalist Leaders in Indian Literature During the Freedom Movement of India," *Rassegna storica del Risorgimento*, 83, 3 (1996), 323–38.

Srivastava, Harindra, *Five Stormy Years: Savarkar in London June 1906–June 1911* (New Delhi: Allied Publishers, 1983).

Srivastava, Harindra, *The Epic Sweep of V.D. Savarkar: An Analytical Study of the Epic Sweep in the Life and Literature of Vinayak Damodar Savarkar* (New Delhi: Savarkar Punruththan Sansthan, 1993).

Steingass, Francis, *A Comprehensive Persian–English Dictionary, Including the Arabic Words and Phrases to be Met with in Persian Literature* (London: Routledge & K. Paul, 1892).

Subrahmanyam, Sanjay, *From Tagus to the Ganges: Explorations in Connected History* (Delhi: Oxford University Press, 2012).

Subrahmanyam, Sanjay, *Mughals and Franks: Explorations in Connected History* (Delhi: Oxford University Press, 2012).

Subrahmanyam, Sanjay, V. Narayana Rao, and David Shulman, *Textures of Time: Writing History in South India, 1600–1800* (Ranikhet: Permanent Black, 2001).

Suhrud, Tridip, "Gandhi's Key Writings," in Judith M. Brown and Anthony Parel, eds, *The Cambridge Companion to Gandhi* (Cambridge: Cambridge University Press, 2011), 69–92.

Suryawanshi, Sudhir, "Militant Youth Wing Burns Savarkar Book," *DNA*, October 26, 2013, dnaindia.com/Mumbai/report-militant-youth-wing-burns-savarkar-book-1908947 (accessed March 2, 2021).

Talbot, Cynthia, *The Last Hindu Emperor: Prithviraj Chauhan and the Indian Past, 1200–2000* (Cambridge: Cambridge University Press, 2017).

Taneja, Nalini, "The Myth of Early Savarkar: His 'Nationalist' 1857 Book," in Sitaram Yechury, ed., *The Great Revolt: A Left Appraisal* (New Delhi: Tulika, 2008), 224–35.

Thapar, Romila, *Ancient Indian Social History: Some Interpretations* (New Delhi: Orient Longman Ltd, 1978).

Thapar, Romila, "Imagined Religious Communities? Ancient History and the Modern Search for a Hindu Identity," *Modern Asian Studies*, 23, 2 (1989), 209–31.

Thapar, Romila, "The Theory of Aryan Race in India: History and Politics," *Social Scientist*, 24, 1–3 (1996), 3–29.

Thapar, Romila, Harbans Mukhia, and Bipan Chandra, *Communalism and the Writing of Indian History* (Delhi: People's Publishing House, 1969).

Thube, Surajkumar, "V.D. Savarkar's Language Purification Project was a Precursor to Creating a 'Hindu Language'," *Scroll.in*, August 31, 2020, https://scroll.in/article/971696/vd-savarkars-language-purification-project-was-a-precursor-to-creating-a-hindu-language (accessed July 23, 2021).

Tilak, Bal Gangadhar, *Srimad Bhagavadgita Rahasya or Karma-Yoga-Sastra, 2 vols*, trans. Bhalchandra Sitaram Sukthankar (Delhi: Low Price Publications, 2002).

Trautmann, Thomas R., *The Aryan Debate* (Delhi: Oxford University Press, 2005).

Travers, Robert, "The Eighteenth Century in Indian History: A Review Essay," *Eighteenth-Century Studies*, 40, 3 (2007), 492–508.

Trehan, Jyoti, *Veer Savarkar: Thought and Action of Vinayak Damodar Savarkar* (New Delhi: Deep & Deep Publications, 1991).

Trevelyan, G. Otto, *The Life and Letters of Lord Macaulay, vol. 1* (New York: Harper & Brothers Publishers, 1876).

Trivedi, Poonam, and Dennis Bartholomeusz, eds, *India's Shakespeare: Translation, Interpretation and Performance* (Newark: University of Delaware Press, 2005).

Truschke, Audrey, *The Language of History: Sanskrit Narratives of Indo-Muslim Rule* (New York: Columbia University Press, 2021).

van Buitenen, J.A.B., trans., *The Bhagavadgita in the Mahabharata* (Chicago: University of Chicago Press, 1981).

Visana, Vikram, "Savarkar before Hindutva: Sovereignty, Republicanism, and

Populism in India, c. 1900-1920," *Modern Intellectual History*, 18, 4 (2021), 1106–29.

Viswanathan, Gauri, *Masks of Conquest: Literary Study and British Rule in India* (New York: Columbia University Press, 1989).

Wadia, J.B.H., *M.N. Roy – The Man: An Incomplete Royana* (Bombay: Popular Prakashan, 1983).

Wagner, Kim A., *The Skull of Alum Bheg: The Life and Death of a Rebel of 1857* (New York: Oxford University Press, 2017).

Watve, K.N., "Sri Narasimha Chintaman 'Alias' Tatyasaheb Kelkar," *Annals of the Bhandarkar Oriental Research Institute*, 28, 1–2 (1947), 156–8.

Winichakul, Thongchai, *Siam Mapped: A History of the Geo-Body of a Nation* (Honolulu: University of Hawaii Press, 1997).

Wolf, Siegfried O., "Vinayak Damodar Savarkar's 'Strategic Agnosticism': A Compilation of His Socio-Political Philosophy," *Heidelberg Papers in South Asian and Comparative Politics*, Working Paper Number 51 (2010), 1–27.

Yajnik, Indulal K., *Shyamaji Krishnavarma: Life and Times of an Indian Revolutionary* (Bombay: Lakshmi Publications, 1950).

Zavos, John, *The Emergence of Hindu Nationalism in India* (Delhi: Oxford University Press, 2000).

## Unpublished Manuscripts

O'Brien, Erin Kellie, "Active Awakening: *Swaraj* in Gandhi's *Hind Swaraj* and in Savarkar's *The Indian War of Independence*," unpublished M.A. thesis, University of Calgary, 2006.

Pincince, John, "On the Verge of Hindutva: V.D. Savarkar, Revolutionary, Convict, Ideologue, c. 1905–1924," unpublished Ph.D. thesis, University of Hawaii, 2007.

Sanadhya, Varun, "V.D. Savarkar and the Impossibility of Hindutva: A Rereading of Schmitt on the National Myth," unpublished M.A. thesis, Illinois State University, 2014.

Savarkar, Vinayak Damodar, "Preface," *Mazzini Charitra*, Pranshu Prakash, trans., 2018.

# Index